THE CORE AND THE CANON

A National Debate

edited by

L. Robert Stevens
G. L. Seligmann, Julian Long

University of North Texas Press

Printed in the United States of America

10 9 8 7 6 5 4 3 2 1

The paper in this book meets the minimum requirements of the
American National Standard for Permanence of Paper for Printed
Library materials, z39.48-1984.

Library of Congress Cataloging-in-Publication Data

The Core and the canon : a national debate / edited by L. Robert
Stevens . . . [et al.].
p.   cm.
Includes bibliographical references.
ISBN 0-929398-49-1
1. Selected papers from conferences held at the University of
North Texas. 2. Education, Humanistic—United States—Curricula—
Congresses. 3. Education, Higher—United States—Curricular—
Congresses. 4. Education, Higher—United States—Aim and objec-
tives—Congresses.   I. Stevens, Lewell Robert.
LC1023.C67   1993
378.1'99'0973—dc20   92–33431
                                                             CIP

CONTENTS

3) COHERENCE IN THE LIBERAL ARTS

4) GREAT BOOKS: ELITIST OR ESSENTIAL

5) INTERFACES: LIBERAL ARTS IN A PLURALIST SOCIETY

6) INTERFACES: LIBERAL ARTS IN A PLURALIST CURRICULUM

7) CONTENTS OF THE CORE

8) PLEASURES OF THE INTELLECT

9) CURRICULA AND SOCIAL CHANGE

11) PEDAGOGY: OPPORTUNITIES IN THE CLASSROOM

FOREWORD

The Classic Learning Core at the University of North Texas is a distinguished curriculum for integrating the humanities requirements into a coherent sequence. This curriculum has enjoyed grant support from both the Fund for the Improvement of Post Secondary Education and the National Endowment for the Humanities. In 1988 and 1989 the Classic Learning Core and the College of Arts and Sciences at UNT sponsored national conferences on the core and the curriculum. The articles which appear in this book are—with one exception—printed from among the papers presented at those conferences. The one exception is that of Jocelyn Chadwick-Joshua, who originally read her paper at a meeting of the American Association for the Advancement of Core Curriculum.

The lead article by Jerry Martin was delivered at the 1989 conference, just after the "Fifty Hours" report from NEH had begun to generate a broad national discussion of these themes. The editors are grateful to him for allowing us to use it. His article is particularly helpful in constructing a phenomenology of the positions which contemporaries have taken relative to the curriculum. Special gratitude to Georgia Caraway who saw this book through the press. Her faithfulness to the project has enriched it significantly.

1

THE CANON, PRO AND CON

THE CORE CURRICULUM AND THE CANON: THE STRUGGLE AND THE DEBATE

Jerry L. Martin
Assistant Chairman for Programs and Policy
National Endowment for the Humanities

It is a pleasure to be here. You have no idea how heartwarming it is to see so many faculty from so many institutions dedicated to the effort to provide students with a strong liberal education. I would also like to express Lynne Cheney's regrets that circumstances made it impossible for her to be with you this evening. Working on *50 Hours* made her more aware than ever how difficult it is to design and to implement a strong general education curriculum, how few the rewards are in terms of salary and status in many institutions, and how few faculty devote the kind of energy and thoughtfulness to this task that you all do. One day, as we were struggling to fit everything we wanted into the 50 hour timeframe, Lynne said, "You know, this is really difficult—imagine what it would be like if we had faculty, departments, deans, students, alumni, and legislators to worry about!" Well, you all do have all those things to worry about—not to mention the everpresent fiscal constraints.

Nevertheless, even in designing a curriculum on paper, we faced many of the same problems you all do. And, as you do, we had to make some compromises. At an early stage we laid out everything we wanted to see in a curriculum, including adequate time for majors, minors, capstone courses—the works—and it added up to about 180 hours. Finally, we decided to accept the discipline—as you all must—of working within a realistic number of credit hours. Fifty hours is realistic, and so we worked within that limit.

Then the tradeoffs began. We would have preferred that the Cultures and Civilizations sequence, which forms the heart of our curriculum, be more extensive. It is the most synoptic and integrative of the courses, and it forms the skeleton of the program, a framework to which students can relate what they learn in other courses. But how could we ask for more than eighteen hours for just the humanities part of the core? So we lay the foundation for the study of civilizations on various continents in the course on the "Origins of Civilization," proceed to two semesters of Western civilization, one of American civilization, and two semesters of the study of two different civilizations not covered in the Western or American courses.

In each course one faces almost impossible tradeoffs: how to combine a reasonable degree of comprehensiveness without sacrificing vital depth, how to provide sufficient historical background and yet concentrate on the careful reading of texts. Of course, we realized that there are many other choices—other ways of balancing these tradeoffs—that can be made, and some are described in the report. Remember that this curriculum is not offered as the one true model, but merely as a concrete suggestion, a way of focusing and stimulating discussion. We hope that you will find ways to adapt it, or improve it, or replace it with something that better suits your own situation.

One of the most difficult questions we faced was how to study cultures other than the West. We found the problems of a single comprehensive World History to be staggering intellectually and pedagogically. In some sense history needs to be a story, and it is not clear if there *is* a single coherent story line you can give to the world as a whole. William McNeill does about as well as anyone, but much of the story becomes the rise and expansion of the West, and its impact on other cultures. We felt it was important to study each civilization on its own terms, not merely as an adjunct to global movements. Similarly, although there are some interesting experiments in the direction of comparative courses, we found that they face a number of special problems. They tend to be non-historical, slicing across cultures rather than following a coherent historical narrative. They assume cross-cultural categories—that you can talk about "religion" or "feudalism" across cultures in a reasonably unproblematic way. They require students to dip into diverse cultures—to look at kinship or legal systems or whatever—without prior study of the culture. In many ways, comparative courses are more suited for students with the background seniors have than for freshmen.

Every course posed its own problems. We were tempted to require students to pair their foreign language courses with a course on the civilization expressed in that language. But in practice such a requirement would deter students from studying East Asian Civilization unless they were willing to take Chinese or Japanese. In the natural sciences, against the advice of some but not all scientists we consulted, we argued against making liberal arts students take the same introductory course that majors take; but, against the advice of some but not all non-scientists we consulted, we argue for its being a lab course.

I will not mention all the issues we faced, though I hope we will have an opportunity to discuss other issues informally today and tomorrow. I just want to let you know that we have been through the exercise; we have been through it with a lot of people who often gave us contradictory advice; and we know some of the intellectual and pedagogical challenges you all face. And, after fifteen years in a philosophy department, I know the problems posed by limited funding, staffing, and interdepartmental politics as well. To overcome these intellectual, pedagogical, and institutional problems is what I call the "struggle" for a core curriculum. The National Endowment for the Humanities is in this struggle with you.

But in addition to the *struggle* for a core curriculum, there is also a *debate* over curriculum and the canon. How the debate affects the struggle is a subject I want to return to. But first let me take off my NEH hat for a moment and outline the way one philosopher sees the debate. (On NEH policy, I can speak for the agency. When it comes to epistemology, I'm on my own.)

There are at least five views or groupings of views that one can discern in the debate. I will be painting with a broad brush as I characterize these views; we can clarify critical details during the discussion.

The first view, which I will call the Old Canon view, is that there is a fixed canon, a body of Great Books that varies little if at all over time. The canon varies little because the works meet standards of excellence that are valid and hence themselves vary little if at all over time. At this point the first view subdivides into two subviews. The True Old Canon view holds that the standards of excellence that determine the canon are really standards of truth, that the reason we should read Plato and Dante is that they are premier bearers of the truth. I won't say who the True Old Canon people are—far be it from me to be naming names— but you know who you are. I have never quite understood why many True Old Canoneers also advocate the study of authors like Hume and Nietzsche, whom they usually regard as bearers of error. Inconsistency or not, it certainly makes their courses more interesting.

The other Old Canon View—the Best Old Canon view—holds that the kind of excellence that distinguishes works in the canon is not that they are necessarily bearers of the truth—they couldn't be, since the Great Works contradict each other—but that they address the most fundamental questions of human existence and that they do so in the most thoughtful, insightful, multi-dimensional, beautiful, provocative, incisive, arresting, moving, etc., etc., etc., way. Since it is palpably true that the Great Books do precisely this—a fact to which we can all attest from our own experience—there is much to be said for the Best Old Canon view.

The third view—which I will call the Expanded Canon view—is that there is not—or at least should not be—a fixed canon. On this view, many works that are thoughtful, insightful, multi-dimensional, etc., have been overlooked—overlooked, in some cases, not just incidentally, but systematically. The works of large categories of people—especially women, minorities, and non-Western authors— have hitherto been neglected. According to this view, such authors as Frederick Douglass and Kate Chopin, Fukuzawa and Achebe, should be included in the curriculum. This is a view that Best Old Canon folks have trouble resisting, since it opens up the canon by appeal to their own criteria. The sticking point for Best Old Canoneers is, in the limited time available in any course, whom do you drop to make room for these additions? Suppose it is an American Civilization course and you want to add Douglass and Chopin. Whom do you drop? My candidate is Henry Wadsworth Longfellow, but after him, who? Walt Whitman? Emerson? Twain? Faulkner? It gets hard. These are difficult decisions, but you can see room for constructive discussion and compromise. Designing a course is not simply a matter of listing the ten greatest writers of all time. It is often a matter of selecting for different periods, genres, styles; why not look for other diversities as well—so long as each work is still quite excellent?

There is also a variant on the Expanded Canon view, which calls not only for an expanded list but expanded standards as well, and hence I call this the Expanded Standards view. On this view, not only has the canon been too exclusive, the standards themselves have been too exclusive. It is one thing to admire works that are thoughtful, insightful, multi-dimensional, etc., but—at least in practice, particularly in the hands of the New Critics—application of these standards has often led to a preference for a very narrow kind of particularly dense poetic expression—supposedly the highest of the high literature. For a time, epics were considered rambling works saved only by having some good poems embedded in them; novels sometimes fared better but suffered from ephemera like character and plot. Expanded Standards folks say, "Let's rethink our criteria and how we apply them, still looking for excellence but being more open to its many varieties; we may find new riches of meaning and insight in—who knows where?—the tales of Native Americans? the oratory of black preachers? the letters of pioneer women? corporate memos? We won't know until we've looked." An Expanded Canon person should be open to this view, to questioning and rethinking standards; otherwise standards become mere dogmatic fixtures. However, to open the question is not to predetermine the answer. One might reevaluate one's standards and conclude that they need only minor revision and that Native American tales, preachers' oratory, pioneer letters, and corporate memos—or even Kate Chopin and Frederick Douglass—interesting and worth reading in certain respects—are still not good enough to displace Whitman and Faulkner. But, again room is open for a constructive discussion; and, in the tradeoffs that make up the curriculum, there may be reason to include works whose virtues shine only when somewhat revised criteria are applied.

The Best Old Canon people, and the Expanded Canon and Expanded Standards folks, all hold views that can make a constructive and important contribution to the struggle for a substantial and vibrant core curriculum. It is not clear that the same can be said for the fifth view, the No Standards view. (It should be called the "No Standards But . . ." view, but I didn't allow the other views to add subclauses to their titles, so I'll be consistent here. We will get to the "But" in a moment.)

No Standards views come in many shapes and sizes, but a generic No Standards view consists of something like the following: Expanding the canon is not enough. The whole idea of a canon—the idea that some works are excellent, and others are not—is based on a discredited epistemology. There are no standards of excellence. There is no such thing as *the* human condition for such works to be thoughtful and penetrating *about*. Consequently, there are no standards of thoughtfulness and insight. There is no reason to prefer multi-dimensional works to unidimensional or non-dimensional works. In fact, there are no meanings, no texts, no reality, no *things*—apart from interpretation. (This is the "But . . . .") The one and only reason for preferring some works to others is that some works fit the norms of one's group, norms which ultimately reflect the interests of the group. And the crucial determinants of one's interests are often taken to be class, race, and gender. Consequently, the task of the critic and teacher of literature becomes one of debunking the "great works" that supposedly reflect the interests of a hitherto dominant class, race, and gender. Or, as one No Standards theorist puts it, the role of the professor of literature should be to unmask "non-socialist works" and to produce works "conducive to the victory of socialism." Now I am not a socialist, and perhaps if I were this view of how to study literature would sound more appealing. But I'm not sure I would feel any better if someone wanted to limit literature courses to works "conducive to the victory of capitalism." Sounds pretty dreary.

There is something else that bothers me about the No Standards view. In many of its expressions, it seems awfully certain of itself. Of course, every theory presents itself as the best, and holds that the others are all wrong. But there is something different here—an odd belief that, even though the issues of realism and relativism, objectivity and subjectivity, etc., have been around for a couple of thousand years, somehow here in the latter part of the twentieth century, in the intellectual centers of France and the United States, we suddenly woke up, the scales fell from our eyes, and we saw the awesome and final truth that there is no truth. It is as if this is not a position to be discussed, a voice in a debate, a new version of an ancient view that has had its ups and downs throughout history—no, it is presented as an advent, an epiphany, the end of modernity, the end of philosophy, perhaps the end of history.

I find this attitude both strange and disturbing. It is strange because the arguments for relativism are so old, and have so often been answered. From the Sophists and the Academic Skeptics, to Montaigne's problem of the criterion, Descartes' evil genius, Hume's doubts about induction and Nelson Goodman's new riddle of induction, the Egocentric Predicament and Bertrand Russell's doubts about the past, philosophers have debated various arguments for scepticism or relativism. To my mind, the anti-sceptics, anti-relativists have the better of the argument, but that is not the point here. It is not strange that someone might agree with the Sophists, Montaigne, Hume, or Nietzsche, rather than with their critics. What is strange, and dogmatic in a rather peculiar way, is that someone would regard their reaching a sceptical or relativistic conclusion as an ephocal, history-ending event, as though they had just won the epistemological war to end all wars.

I find this sense of finality doubly disturbing because the arguments presented for the No Standards view sometimes seem facile and even fallacious. Not just fallacious-in-general, but prone to one particular fallacy, the Fallacy of False Dichotomies. This fallacy occurs when an argument proceeds as if there are only two alternatives but in fact there are others. Refuting one (often extreme) alternative, the argument concludes that the other (often extreme) alternative must be correct.

For example, No Standards theorists sometimes assume that *either* there is an eternal, unchanging list of great works *or* there is no distinction at all between great works and others. Refuting the idea of an eternal unchanging list, they promptly conclude that there is no distinction at all. This inference is based on a false dichotomy; as we have seen, there are reasonable positions one may hold that lie between these two alternatives.

No Standards theorists sometimes assume that *either* it must be possible to achieve a totally impersonal, timeless, transcendent objectivity—in effect, to "step outside" one's belief system and judge it in some transcendent way—*or* there is no such thing as objectivity or even degrees of objectivity or even a distinction between objectivity and, say, bias or prejudice. But there is a wide range of epistemological views, many of which try to do justice to both subjectivity and objectivity. The No Standards theorist presents us with a false dichotomy—in effect, either you agree with Descartes or you must accept relativism.

It is sometimes assumed that *either* ideas are eternally valid *or* they have a history. But ideas can both have a history and be valid according to some objective standards. In this case, the dichotomy is false because the alternatives are not mutually exclusive. They could both be true.

It is sometimes assumed that *either* meanings are formal and transparent *or* they are contextual and created by the reader. But meanings can be both formal and contextual in different respects; and meanings can be contextual without being created by the reader. All the possible combinations and complexities that may be required by an adequate philosophy of language are swept to one side.

It is sometimes assumed that *either* human nature is an eternal, immutable, fixed essence *or* it is nothing but a nexus of such contingencies as race, gender, and class. But it seems quite possible that human nature is a product of both a fixed nature and circumstances, that it is both adaptable and bounded. Moreover, even if human nature were a nexus of contingencies, why should the contingencies be limited to these three traits?

8

While we should not be persuaded by arguments based on false dichotomies, we should keep in mind that the issues raised by relativism are important ones and deserve careful attention. The sceptical tradition is one of the most powerful in Western thought (and, in a very different form, in Eastern thought as well); and much of Western thought, sceptical or anti-sceptical, cannot be understood without feeling the force of arguments developed by this tradition. I would not object for a moment to teaching works in this tradition, and neither would any defender of the canon I know. I have in fact taught them and will do so again, because it is important for students to participate in this and the other great debates of Western—and of Eastern—thought. Participating in these debates is the only way they will be empowered to shape their own views on this and other questions.

But what is profoundly troubling is the idea that the curriculum should be driven by the *assumption* that the No Standards view is correct; that students should be taught only "pro-socialist" or "pro-(put in any ism you want)" views; that students be taught that there are no standards of objectivity or of justice to strive for; that they be taught that there is no *difference* between objectivity and bias, evidence and propaganda, reason and manipulation; that they be told that they are only what their race, gender, and class make them.

When students enter our classrooms, they put their lives in our hands in ways we often do not realize. Especially for those in late adolescence, our power over them is tremendous. We are not mere men and women. For good or ill, we may be heroes or heroines, superegos, substitute parents, role models, gurus, tyrants, images of their hopes or their fears. For many we offer new vistas—ideas, questions, a look into corners of the universe or of the psyche they could not have dreamed of—and, with expanded vistas, often they discover new directions, new identities, new freedoms. It is more power than we could have wished. We would rather just teach a course, discuss a book, grade a paper. But it is a power we as professors have whether we want it or not. And it brings with it a terrible responsibility, for us as individual professors and as faculty of colleges, to fashion an education, in our own classroom and beyond, that will give students the resources of intellect and imagination that will enable them to create a world for themselves. It is not, at least, a lonely task. It is a task that brings us together, in some ways in common cause, in some ways in deep disagreement.

But I have put it wrong—discussing the deep and important differences we may have with each other *is* our common cause. Indeed, that is what the humanities are all about. And that is why I would like to thank you for allowing a once and future philosopher to join the discussion.

THE WESTERN TRADITION: FOUNTAINHEAD OF PREJUDICE OR PERENNIAL WISDOM?

Ernest Marshall
East Carolina University

In the present debate over curriculum reform in higher education, much heated discussion concerns the so-called "Western tradition" of writings, ideas, and ways of thinking, and poses the question: does making the Western tradition the bedrock of higher education serve to transcend barriers of gender, class, race, and ethnicity, or rather, to perpetuate them?

In this paper I argue that it primarily accomplishes the latter. My thesis is that a core curriculum based upon the Western tradition is more divisive in its effect than unifying, and that one which involves some balance or blend of traditions could do more to convey a uniform set of criteria for cultural perception and appreciation. In developing my argument I shall discuss what I take to be some of the flaws and confusions in Allan Bloom's *The Closing of the American Mind* and "The Politics of Curriculum Building" by Sidney Hook. According to Bloom, a loss or corruption of the Western tradition has occurred in education, which has in turn resulted in the triumph of relativism. I argue that this relativism is rather primarily the result of cultural forces other than intellectual ones, and indeed in so far as the factors are intellectual, they lie squarely within the Western tradition itself. According to Hook's position, rejection of the classics of the Western tradition in favor of such as "Third World" literature reinforces cultural prejudice and political bias, and undermines habits of rational and objective thought. I argue that his quarrel is not with including works other than the Western classics in basic liberal arts curricula, but with certain ways of teaching them (by methods of "indoctrination"), and that, if properly approached, these non-Western works are just as effective in conveying "human" values and concerns.

In addressing the question of whether teaching "the Western tradition" divides and alienates, or unifies and edifies, I must distinguish this question from three others with which it is commonly confused. First of all, what is the worth of the Western tradition as compared with non-Western traditions? Is the art, literature, philosophy, and so forth, of the former superior to the latter? Secondly, is the Western tradition more pedagogically viable than the non-Western tradition?

To begin with the last question, two dimensions of "the Western tradition" must be distinguished. First of all, it is Western rather than Eastern, and thus includes, for example, the *Republic* of Plato but not the *Analects* of Confucius; or more specifically, it is a tradition originating with the ancient Greeks and Romans and developed by the Medieval and Modern Europeans. It is thus a tradition that historically, culturally, and geographically, excludes most of the countries of the world. Secondly, for the most part at least, it is the tradition of only part of the total society, namely, the culture of the middle and upper classes, and thus excludes, for example, the folk culture of all classes.[1] For brevity's sake in what follows I shall refer to the former dimension of the Western tradition as the Euroamerican tradition, and to the latter, as the Elite tradition.

Those who defend the hegemony of the Western tradition in education are generally more willing to incorporate works outside of the Euroamerican tradition than works outside of the Elite tradition. For example, in his essay, "The Politics of Curriculum Building," Sidney Hook finds it acceptable that the proposed Humanities Core Curriculum at Boston University includes the *Analects* of Confucius, the *Tao Te Ching* of Lao Tzu, the *Bhagavad Gita*, and the *Qour' an*, whereas he strongly criticizes curriculum changes at Stanford for what he refers to as their orientation toward race, sex, and class. He cites the Boston University case as an example of how "great works by women and people of color could easily have been incorporated not because of the sex and color of the authors but because of the inherent qualities of their works."[2]

Because of the importance of Hook's statement to his stance on the issues and supporting argument it deserves discussion at this point. *Prima facie* Hook's claim is beyond reproach. Yet I think it concerns two distinct questions, each of which requires a yes-and-no answer. Certainly works should not be studied just because they were authored by, for example, women or blacks. This is surely the other side of the same bad coin of sexism and racism, or if you will, this is "reverse-bigotry." However, being female or black has cultural implications. We in the United States have a certain degree of cultural identity in virtue of our common national language, common laws, common political ideals and institutions, and so forth. Yet we are of diverse ethnic backgrounds and social class origins.[3] We are thus nurtured by different "works" (literary *and* oral traditions, and so forth); and due to this diversity of origins, the works in question are expressive of experiences, ideas, and evaluations that are different in important ways.

Also as Hook asserts, works should be chosen and appraised according to their inherent qualities. But if it is true, as I have just suggested, that the experiential, conceptual, and normative content of works outside the Western tradition is appreciably different, the question of inherent worth or quality becomes more complex. In the last analysis, we may need to include within basic humanities curricula the best of novels, plays, poems, and philosophical essays, and so forth, of women, blacks, and others representing non-Western traditions, along with the best of the Western tradition, much as we now feel obligated to

11

expose students to the best novels, *and* plays, *and* poems, *and* philosophical essays. That is to say, we need not give up standards to acknowledge the existence of types or genres, or to make revisions among them. A poem is not necessarily better or worse as to its inherent qualities than a novel, nor again as to a lyric versus narrative poem, or a realist versus romantic novel, and so forth. Likewise a "black novel" need not be better or worse than novels in the Western tradition, yet "black novels" can themselves be better and worse in virtue of their inherent qualities.[4] What is thus needed of humanist scholars is for us to identify and analyze for appreciation the best, "the classics," if you will, of each genre, rather than to defend the ramparts of some elitist and ethnically-exclusive tradition.

Ever since the appearance of Allan Bloom's *The Closing of the American Mind*, such considerations as these raise the specter of relativism. Bloom claims that the chief "virtue" of our society and educational system is an openness to every fad and opinion tantamount to a close-minedness to reason and truth.[5] But Bloom's defense of this thesis indicates that he has not come to terms with important changes that have occurred both in educational institutions and intellectual history. First of all, there are the deep and seemingly permanent changes that have taken place within American education. As David Brock has said:

> The traditional role of the university was to educate an elite for leadership, not to teach people to do things. The promise and pressures of democracy have changed that. But Bloom does not believe in inevitability.[6]

Secondly, Bloom's adamancy about universal standards and objective truth lends itself to a "closedness" of mind comparable to that which relativism encourages. William Greider has gone so far as to compare Bloom with Jerry Falwell and "other right-wing televangelists" and accuse him of "peddling fundamentalism for high-brows."[7] I would agree to the extent that Bloom's summary of Western intellectual history has little to say about such philosophical revolutions as those inspired by Freud, Marx, and quantum physics. After the unsettling insights that they made available to us about ourselves, our social order, and our universe, surely we are less certain about the truths we can know, and even about the very nature of truth. It will simply not do to maintain, as Bloom would seem to have it, that Plato has the last word on matters of truth, beauty, and goodness, and that existentialism, or the "relativism" of Nietzsche and Heidegger, is Plato's only gainsayer.[8]

These criticisms of Bloom notwithstanding, he seems to be correct in claiming that relativism has become rampant in academia and our society at large. Aside from the fact that "relativism," or the view that truth is equivalent to whatever an individual happens to believe, is logically and psychologically incoherent, it is utterly dogmatic or close-minded.[9] Rather than being the opposite of viewpoints that equate truth with the pronouncements of such authorities as Church or State, it is an atomistic version of the same. The dogmatic authority of individuals simply replaces that of institutions. The absence of reason is the same, and the possibility of wisdom perhaps even less.

Hence Bloom's enthusiastic reception in many quarters is as it should be regarding this point. But understanding how relativism won the field, became the "official epistemology," so to speak, is quite another matter. Regarding this question it should first of all be noted that insofar as our philosophical malaise is itself philosophical, the main source is the Western tradition itself. That is to say, relativistic theories, or at least views that call objectivist and universalist theories into question, are as old and as "Western" as the debates of ancient Greek philosophy. Being an eminent Plato scholar, Bloom rather naturally views the classical Greek tradition through Platonic spectacles, with the resulting distortion of vision that sees the tradition of the Sophists as only a foil to the wisdom of their advisory Plato, and sees Aristotle as one who mostly mimics his teacher's conclusions. But different philosophical traditions originate here that sharply challenge Plato's (and Bloom's) standpoint.[10] To offer one example among others, in the chapter on the attraction of young people to rock music, the case against their music in the name of the Western tradition is purely Platonic.[11] Rock music, we are told, appeals to our "lower nature" ("Rock music has one appeal only, a barbaric appeal, to sexual desire"), it corrupts the soul ("ruins the imagination of young people"), and it affects the listener by way of "imitation," i.e., one becomes as the music one listens to. Aristotle, on the other hand, would give a very different analysis. In his *Poetics* he claims that the purpose or final cause of tragedy is to purge the soul of emotion (pity and fear), and thus to have a morally beneficial effect.[12] This catharsis theory of art is the ancestor of Freud's, the proverbial intellectual godfather of today's "liberal" sexual attitudes.

However, even more important than my point that the Western philosophical tradition is not as monolithic as Bloom makes it appear, the source of today's relativism is mostly other than Bloom claims. Again in Platonic fashion, Bloom sees the causes as intellectual, moral, and political. If Bloom were a more even-handed classics scholar, and drew equally upon Aristotle for his inspiration and arguments, he would give more attention to "material causes," and perhaps perceive that the chief source of today's relativism is a socio-economic system that belies both the ethical imperatives of social existence and the ontological givens of the human condition.

I think that there are probably three major components of our present socio-economic system contributing to the prevalence of relativistic attitudes. First, the capitalist system produces and distributes goods and services for profit rather than according to need. Second, the orientation of that system (insofar as it is not simply profit-oriented) is to individual consumer wants to the exclusion of social needs. Finally, there is our heedless use of technology. As this viewpoint on the analysis and critique of our society is hardly news, I shall not develop it here except as is necessary to address issues of what a core humanities curriculum ought to comprise. The first of the above three points is common to the Marxist critique of society, from Marx and Engels forward; the second point is pursued, for example, by Herbert Marcuse and others of the "Frankfurt school" of social criticism; and among the outstanding defenders of the final point is Hans Jonas, as in his recent book, *The Imperative of Responsibility: In Search of an Ethics for the Technological Age*.[13]

By undermining the ethical imperatives of social existence and the ontological givens of the human condition, this socio-economic system promulgates relativism. That is to say, it denies "the absolutes," if you will, of ethics and ontology. Regarding ethics, our socio-economic system engenders the view that the ends of human action are "given," or beyond dispute, and the means don't morally matter: in short, materialism (i.e., material means and the gratifications they can purchase are the only things valuable as ends in themselves) and expediency. The corporate-profits and individual-consumer capitalist system reduces the question of ends to that of material goals (a high-paying job, an expensive car, and so forth); and our illusion of technological omnipotence trivializes decisions about appropriate means. In contrast to this, I take it as a given of ethics that there are a plurality of legitimate human ends which must be pursued only in conscientious ways. In short, many are our human needs, but few are the paths to be taken to them.[14]

The givens of "human ontology," or the limits imposed by our humanity, are also controverted by our high-tech, profit-and-consumer-oriented capitalist system. Engendered is the illusion that everything is obtainable, that "everything has its price." Such illusion not only wishes away moral obstacles, such as scrupulousness as to means, but presumes that technology and an ever-expanding economy will gratify every human desire. Capitalist enterprise offers get-rich-quick schemes, advertising prompts dreams of a happy, hassle-free existence, modern medicine promises the indefinite prolongation of health and even life, and so forth. The doctrine thus propagated is that of human infinitude, or the denial of the "absolutes" of the human condition, such as those of want, work, estrangement, aging, and death. Here I must add the disclaimer that I cannot provide a definitive list of these "absolutes" of the human condition. My claim is only that there are such, and I should think it a central part of the task of a study of works included in a humanities curriculum to attempt to discover what they are.[15]

Therefore I propose that the record of and reflection on the human encounter with these ethical and ontological "absolutes" can provide the basis for a core humanities curriculum and in such a way as to accommodate both Bloom's concerns and the relevance and richness of other than the Western tradition. My view is admirably expressed by William M. Shea:

> The classics carry universal meanings in shocking particularity, and perhaps this very particularity militates against a canon of them. Higher education needs, not a debate over the canon, but a debate over what it means to be human. ... The classics, in fact, live today because the question ["What does it mean to be human?"] lives and is not definitely answered.[16]

I would also propose a blend or balance of works from both the Western and non-Western traditions, maintaining that the best way to transcend barriers is to view the range and variety of the human family—with its differences of gender, race, class, and so forth—but with attention to our common confrontation with life's moral dilemmas, our foibles and frailties, and other human givens.[17] Thus, for example, the "feminist" novel, *Tell Me a Riddle*, by Tillie Olsen,[18] explores growing old and dying, albeit from a woman's perspective, and the "Third World" novel, *Things Fall Apart*, by Chinua Achebe, examines cultural change and the struggle for identity.[19] What are the unsung classics—from both the Western and non-Western traditions—and what are their human themes? Answering this question and creating a curriculum that includes the best of these from various traditions is an important part of today's task in teaching the humanities.

Finally, teaching works from different traditions is not inherently divisive; however, teaching a single cultural tradition *is*—be it Western, Eastern, Third World, Feminist, or what have you. Knowledge of the Western tradition is important to membership in a liberal society, but knowledge of non-Western traditions is just as important to membership in a global society. On the other hand, works of any tradition become divisive if taught in a dogmatic and doctrinal manner. Thus, as Sidney Hook asserts, "indoctrination," or "a process of teaching through which acceptance of belief is induced by non-rational or irrational means, or both," is to be avoided.[20] As Hook says, this means that commitment to political causes is not to corrupt objective scholarship and teaching, and requires the study of politically offensive works (such as *Mein Kampf* or *Das Kapital*, depending upon one's political bent) and dissenting views in addition to ones considered "politically correct." Furthermore, a "canon" or standardized lists of "great books" may itself be a potential for indoctrination, but as Hook points out, it is the way in which they are studied rather than the works themselves that is crucial.[21]

Therefore there is no reason why rational, objective, and non-indoctrinating methods of teaching and scholarly discussion are not equally employable in a humanities curriculum framed to achieve a balance of works from different traditions.[22]

NOTES

1. A very interesting example of how folk traditions function to crystallize and communicate experience and values in a manner complementary to the Elite tradition appears in Karen Baldwin, "Practice and Remembrance in the Folk Medical Traditions of North Carolinians," in *Herbal and Magical Medicine: Traditional Healing Today*, (Durham: Duke University Press, 1992). It should also be said (as her article points out) that folk traditions are to be found at every socio-economic stratum of a culture, yet they have in common media and methods alternative to the literary texts of the Elite tradition.

2. Sidney Hook, "The Politics of Curriculum Building," *American Philosophical Society Proceedings*, vol. 62, 708.

3. Throughout this paper I in effect assume that women have a non-Western group membership, in virtue of their exclusion from the Elite dimension of Western culture (in contrast to white men). In this way I intend to disclaim taking any position on the controversial issue of gender difference, hotly debated both inside and outside of Feminist philosophy.

4. The point is obscured by the two-fold value judgment latent in the concept of the Western tradition. Even if one adopts a cosmopolitan viewpoint embracing non-Euroamerican traditions, the class identification of the Elite tradition often remains to be overcome.

5. Allan Bloom, *The Closing of the American Mind* (New York: Simon & Schuster, 1987). The claim is a made throughout the book, beginning with the Introduction. It should be noted that much the same claim also has been argued by thinkers of "radical left" persuasion. See, for example, *A Critique of Pure Tolerance* (Boston: Beacon Press, 1965), featuring articles by Herbert Marcuse and Robert Paul Wolff.

6. David Brock, "A Powerful Indictment of Relativism," *Insight*, May 11, 1987, 12.

7. William Greider, "Bloom and Doom," *Rolling Stone*, October 8, 1987, 40.

8. The potent influence of Plato on Bloom is evident throughout the book. Indeed, the book's theme is similar to that of other Platonists whose writings have influenced Bloom. See, for example, *Natural Right and History*, by Leo Strauss (Chicago: University of Chicago Press, 1953.) In Parts Two and Three, Bloom discusses Nietzsche and Heidegger as his principle examples of modern philosophical nihilists.

9. Bloom defines the term "relativism" a bit differently, but I believe, incorrectly. He conceives it in terms of abandoning the concept or objective of truth altogether: "The point is not to correct the mistakes and really be right; rather it is not to think you are right at all" (26). "Nihilism" is a better term for this standpoint.

10. An interesting alternative reading of the history of Western philosophy (that treats Plato as something of a retrograde development in the history of thought) is Bertrand Russell's *A History of Western Philosophy*.

11. Bloom, ibid., Part One, "Music," 68 ff.

12. The main source for this theory in Aristotle's writings is his *Poetics*, Chapters 6, 13, and 14.

13. Hans Jonas, *The Imperative of Responsibility: In Search of an Ethics for the Technological Age*, (Chicago: University of Chicago Press, 1984).

14. It would suffice to make my main claim here to contend only that the question of ultimate ends (what makes something good as an end in itself) can never be settled (a point that was established by G. E. Moore early in this century), rather than beg the question as to whether they are one or many. I am, however, committing myself here to a deontological viewpoint: morally right actions are not just those that maximize the good.

15. An interesting view on this question, and one that I am perhaps not prepared to fully adopt, is that one's sex, race, age, culture, and economic class are themselves among these "absolutes," explored by Robert Paul Wolff in "There's Nobody Here But Us Persons," in *Women and Philosophy: Toward a Theory of Liberation*, edited by Carol Gould and Marx Wartofsky (New York: G. P. Putnam's Sons, 1976).

16. William M. Shea, "John Dewey and the Crisis of the Canon," *The American Journal of Education*, May 1989, 308.

17. Indeed, non-Western literature may presently be a richer source of confrontation with "human problems." As Gay Wilentz says in an unpublished paper entitled "The 'Passing' of Allan Bloom's Mind": ". . . it is precisely in international, ethnic, women's, and other expansive studies, that concern for values as well as cultural conflicts is being presented. In studying the conflict in South Africa, my students learn a lot about values— and we certainly do not have a value-relative stance toward white-minority rule there."

18. Tillie Olsen, *Tell Me a Riddle* (New York: Dell Publishing Co., Inc., 1956).

19. Chinua Achebe, *Things Fall Apart* (New York: Fawcett Crest Books, 1959).

20. Hook, ibid., 713.

21. This point is neglected by William J. Bennett, when he reasons that: "Because colleges and universities believed they no longer could or should assert the primacy of one fact or *one book* over another, all knowledge came to be seen as relative in importance" [emphasis mine]. "To Reclaim a Legacy: A Report on the Humanities in Higher Education." (Washington, D.C.: National Endowment for the Humanities, 1984).

22. Mary Alice Morgan argues in "Politicizing the Humanities Course" (*Humanities in the South: Newsletter of the Southern Humanities Council* Number 69, Spring 1989) that we teachers ought to bring these very debates about the content and purpose of a core humanities curriculum (such as this conference concerns) into the classroom, so that they can be debated there in an open and rational way. This both extends and nicely complements Hook's view.

FINDING A CURRICULUM FOR THE LIBERAL ARTS FACULTY

Roger Johnson, Jr.
Lewis Clark State College

If a curriculum does not take into account that its beneficiaries are students, then the whole discussion of content misses the point. Arguments about the canon—whether there should be one and, if so, what should go into it—seem sometimes, indeed, to miss the point. A verbal footnote can be cast into discussion of canon, "Well, it goes without saying that students are important!" The footnote is, I believe, inadequate cover. Moreover it is obscured by more vague and enticing notions: "Contemporary culture is important, and what I do is really important."

Traditional great books do constitute much of the curriculum in the humanities program that I helped bring into being at the University of Southern Mississippi. Given a certain amount of freedom in defining a curriculum, my colleagues and I managed to include the Bible, the *Aeneid*, the *Papyrus of Ani*, the *Origin of Species*. Perhaps less obvious in the consideration of curricula and their coherence is that content—the curricular stuff—of our program is one element that is student-centered.

The problem of finding a curriculum for the faculty has therefore actually been one of finding a curriculum for students. Thus the definition or discovery of a curriculum smacked somewhat of utility. We aimed to help students toward three goals: knowing important matters, writing well and clearly, and thinking independently. Our problem turned to defining what was important. Since the program was student-centered, we meant what was or seemed to be important for students—not necessarily important either for faculty members or for satisfaction of agenda extrinsic to learning.

It should come as no surprise that our student-centered undergraduate humanities curriculum generally lacked survey courses with their built-in biases to "cover the material" and to discourage reflection and thoughtful reaction, what I would call real learning. The content of a survey course should probably be the sweep of history, a thorny topic that ought, if it is to be treated honestly, to include questions of causality, influence, genre, and progress—none of which can usually be addressed. Of the undergraduate students I have known during twenty years of teaching, I do recollect a few who were made enthusiasts during a survey. Without exception they were actually "converted" by one or two texts that happened to occur within the course, not by the pseudo-historical pretensions of the chronologically organized syllabus. Scorn is easy, but scorning survey courses unfortunately did not not solve the immediate questions of how many works to include in a course, how to organize them, and which parts to read if they were not to be read as a whole.

The answers are, however, not hard to find. A course ought to include as many works as the student can profit from efficiently. If a wide-ranging class includes Goethe's *Faust*, and if after three weeks of exposure the students find no more aspects of the work to be grasped, then it is time to move on. If, on the other hand, students are still digging and learning, it is folly to switch off, to curtail thought in order to cover something or other on the extrinsic agenda. We all recognize that an advanced seminar in *Faust* can easily last a year, at the end of which time one has the feeling of just having learned enough to begin. Undergraduates probably could not profit from a year on *Faust*. They have neither the cultural background, the reading skills, nor the maturity to continue working that particular mine profitably. But we should not assume that they cannot work it at all, that their profit lies in regurgitating key lines we have selected from Part I and cliches that begin as meaningless and finish as the stuff of examinations.

The assumption about substance which underlies these views is that substantiality of a work in an undergraduate humanities course is the degree to which the work has a meaningful educational effect on the student.

Just as we can have reasonable expectations of faculty members, we can have reasonable expectations of content. A work in the curriculum should accomplish some of the following:

1. It should have cultural resonance. It should reflect a culture or at least comment on one. Of course many works help define a culture, making it more understandable to those in it and accessible to those outside it. Such are the works of Naguib Mahfouz (*Midaq Alley*, *Miramar*) or of his less famous countryman Yusuf Idris. Many works allow students to gain perspective on their own heritage, viewing it from inside or outside. Such are the works of Cicero or Thomas Jefferson.

2. The work should contain ideas, concepts, and values; it should not be trivial as regards intrinsic thought. Moreover, its significant ideas and concepts should be useful in a broad educational sense. I add the latter qualification not in order to censure ideas but to recognize that there is reason to exclude, for example, antisemitic tracts and even *Mein Kampf* from the curriculum of great works. (If *Mein Kampf* is to be read as part of a project to understand Nazism or politics, there is, of course, reason for it to be read. But its ideas and values are not as broadly applicable as I want for my classes or for curricula upon which I have an influence.)

3. The work should be attractive to students. Not pandering, the work needs sufficient esthetic qualities so that one does not need to apologize for it. I would thus avoid a work which I enjoyed tremendously, George Eliot's *Daniel Deronda*, and

include instead her *Middlemarch*. I would not promote Puccini's *Turandot* at the expense of his *Tosca*.

4. The work should have historical significance for a culture with which the student is becoming acquainted. Here I would include the contemporary, but carefully. My colleagues and I have simply not had the confidence to say that a given work will have a major effect. Sometimes we think so, but generally we reserve contemporary texts for other sorts of courses. I note that sociological theory (part of our curriculum) operates with refreshing notions of what is contemporary and what has passed to the realm of "classics." The turning point seems to be between eight and twenty years ago.

5. The work has to be accessible. There are translations so bad that one can barely glimpse the work or the world it implies. For some works, there must be notes in addition to a helpful hand from scholar/teachers. Imagine the *Divine Comedy* raw. I have discovered to my disappointment that the *Pyramid Text* as recorded in the Pyramid of Unas, is practically inaccessible, despite its apparent historical importance and the interest it holds for those who hear it is the oldest extant religious text in the world.

6. The work needs to be pertinent, in some way, to the student's life, and this pertinence has to be of a sort that can eventually be perceived by the student. The pertinence can be engineered on occasion, as when we introduced students to modern opera and discussed its relationship to other forms of modern music and to the history of opera before taking students to Gian Carlo Menotti's *Consul*.

I am not embarrassed to tell you that our curriculum has turned out to be fairly traditional. There are works we can see as valuable but inaccessible at the present time. Some works meet all of our expectations, but we have no one to teach them, given our commitment to the strictures of scholarly teaching. Yet, there is still plenty to do. Why construct a curriculum with this work and not another? There is, of course, no absolute and universal answer; but I propose a response that I assure you is not flippant: Why not? If a work meets the educational needs of students and can be taught honestly, there is no need to exclude it. If, on the other hand, it lacks cultural resonance, exhibits no ideas, fails esthetically, lacks historical import, is neither accessible nor pertinent—then it is time to search again.

RHETORIC AS LIBERAL EDUCATION

Robert Hariman

Drake University

Perhaps it is fitting that the one session on rhetoric at this convention was scheduled to meet in the Miss America Room.[1] Like the beauty pagent, the practice of rhetoric can be critiqued as a celebration of the cosmetic that subjugates the very people it seems to celebrate. To continue the analogy, they both involve gratuitous competition regarding transitory appearances achieved by much luck and a little art, warp our values as they entertain us, and while manipulating others ultimately injure the performers themselves.

This was exactly Plato's critique of rhetoric,[2] and his caricature remains very much our conventional wisdom: As mere stylistics, rhetoric manipulates diverse appearances; as crass advertising, it manipulates individual persons; as cruel propaganda, it manipulates whole polities—surely, none of these practices should be a part of a liberal arts education. There is an unhappy irony here, however, for as long as Plato's legacy of lambasting rhetoric continues to dominate the academy, we are less likely to nurture the high quality public discourse that might overcome base rhetorics. And Plato's legacy is with us still, not least of all at the National Endowment for the Humanities. Note, for example, how the proposed Fifty-Hours Curriculum, though it provides many welcome recommendations, ignores the rhetorical tradition, and note also how the agency's commentary on liberal education continues to rely upon the host of assumptions contained in Plato's dichtomy between (valid) logic or dialectic and (perverse) rhetoric.[3]

This ignorance and denigration of the rhetorical tradition is peculiar, if only, in that it prevents us from understanding our own origins. Advocates of liberal education dedicate a good part of their work to helping students understand the precursors of modern intellectual culture. Yet how few among those now celebrating the liberal-arts ideal give credit to the Sophists who discovered it, to Isocrates who articulated it, to Cicero who theorized it, to Quintilian who institutionalized it, and to Augustine, Petrarch, Erasmus, and many others who continued to recover, expand, and bring it forward into their world?

To put the point more directly, our inattention to the history of our ideals of rational discourse, civility, civic virtue, and so on, is at once a cause and a telling sign of the incoherence in our conceptions, and as Bruce Kimball has argued, once we come to understand how the history of liberal education has included in a significant sense the history of rhetorical studies, we can better understand and implement our commitment to that education.[4] Furthermore, not only do our ideals not come in the main from Plato, they come from a contest involving Plato and philosophy on one side and rhetoricians on the other, and in that contest, Plato and his colleagues were far more the foes than the friends of those skills and values crucial for modern conceptions of liberal arts education.[5] In fact, it is hard to see much of Plato's elitist, highly transcendental, and deeply anti-political philosophy in many of the recent calls for core curricula, general-education courses, and other programs for invigorating public education for democracy.[6] Notwithstanding such willful ignorance, the rhetorical tradition is the wellspring of our culture of public discourse and of the liberal education meant to nurture that culture. Our idea that there can be two or more sides to a question comes from Pythagorean *dissoi logoi*, or two-sided argument. Our seemingly modern recognition that someone else's account of something might reflect a different (and equally valid) experience stems from his maxim that "man is the measure of all things." The insistence that we need proof, that each of us is obligated to bring our reasons and evidence into a realm of shared appearance, rests on the Sophists' insight that any truth must be validated in some presentation for particular people if we are to have critical thinking and personal freedom.

In short, the ideals at the heart of liberal-arts education—arguing in public, learning from others, supporting our claims, standing by our words, and criticizing our own deeds, and so forth[7]—come from a set of people and texts seldom included in the curricula of liberal education. Consequently, the rationale for liberal education appears to be made of whole cloth, and rhetorical studies themselves become defined as at most a marginal counter-tradition within the modern academy.[8] I doubt, however, that we have faced one consequence of this condition, which at current practices of liberal education are in danger of becoming as trivial or perverse as degenerate practices of rhetoric. In response to this danger, I offer two theses: First, and most generally, remarks on liberal education need to be remarks on rhetoric. Specific rhetorical practices constitute the subject and end of that education, complicated rhetorical norms guide its conduct, and the tradition of rhetorical studies provides a context for reflection upon its application in a changing world. Liberal education must become more manifestly a practice for inculcating communicative competencies, analyzing and motivating political action, and understanding social experience.

The second, and more daring thesis, is that liberal education, to become authentic and effective for our times, must return to its roots in rhetoric. Furthermore, this return should involve more than adding *De Oratore* to the canon. Though we need to recover the texts defining rhetoric as a tradition of erudition in order to explain the purpose of liberal education, we also need to restructure the practice of liberal education according to rhetorical principles. I am not going to argue on behalf of these claims, however, as that would avoid the emphasis upon application that rightly is the emphasis of a conference on pedagogy. Instead, this essay will illustrate how I have used one introductory course in rhetorical studies to introduce students to the liberal arts ideal. Although I will discuss only my own example, I hope the reader can consider how similar measures could be developed for other introductory classes across the human sciences.

The rest of this paper will discuss a course I offer at Drake University, entitled Rhetoric as a Liberal Art. I developed the course when I realized that my students had no idea why they should pursue a liberal arts education. Even students thoroughly engaged in the liberal arts curriculum reported that they felt defenseless when challenged by students in other, more "professional" programs to defend their studies. Nor did I feel the situation was helped when other educators responded by arguing that study in the liberal arts would improve the students' mobility in a changing economy, or that one day their personal happiness would depend upon it. (Are we really to believe that one should study the Civil War because there might be openings for Confederate generals in twenty years, and do we really want to consign the humanities to filling up the Golden Years?) As the students' inarticulateness also seemed to account for their befuddlement regarding course selection and their middling motivation in the classroom when taking required courses, it seemed to me that the stakes were high. My own experience offered a helpful perspective on this problem, moreover, as new students in rhetorical studies usually are unaware of the rationale for their own tradition of inquiry, and ever after they have to contend with questions of the legitimacy of that tradition. Consequently, I designed a course to solve both problems at once: Rhetoric as a Liberal Art begins with the premise that rhetorical studies and liberal arts education have the same origin (the Sophists) and intertwined histories, and that both traditions can be understood most sensitively and applied most effectively only through engagement with the problems, habits of thought, and insights of the other.

The Syllabus

These themes are suggested by two quotations serving as epigraphs on the course syllabus. The first, from James Boyd White, states, "to put it in a single word, I would say that our subject is rhetoric, if by that is meant the study of the ways in which character and community—and motive, value, reason, social structure, everything, in short, that makes a culture—are defined and made real in performances of language."[9] The second, from Bruce Kimball asserts that "The history of liberal education is the story of a debate between orators and philosophers."[10] These themes serve as the principles of design for the course: We begin with the Sophists, reading some of their fragments to introduce the foundational questions about language, education, and polity that they struggled with, as well as basic hermeneutical issues pertaining to the translation and interpretation of texts, the uses of history, and the like. We move to the "second generation" reconstruction of their problematic by both Isocrates and Plato, which represent contrasting formulations of the liberal arts ideal.

This dialectic then is developed further through first Aristotle, and then, Cicero, as subsequent attempts to either manage or promote rhetorical studies. This unit on the classical debates is concluded by reading Hannah Arendt on the public-private distinction, in order to develop that topic (which is crucial for the course) while demonstrating a model appropriation of classical texts by a modern thinker. The first half of the course then is completed by turning to the reprise of the foundational debates in the Renaissance, where Eramus and Machiavelli are both compared and read back into their classical sources, while Bacon is counter-poised to modern assumptions about truth-telling, sincerity, and the like.

The second half of the course reveals the subtext of the course, which could be called "Sophists Old and New." Beginning with representatives of the several versions of the "linguistic turn" taken early in the twentieth century, including both Wittgenstein and Kenneth Burke, this half of the course illustrates how the re-discovery of communication can direct inquiry and evaluation of contempo-rary social processes. Furthermore, in this half of the course there is increasing emphasis upon the practical criticism of specific discourses: we read a wide range of speeches and other documents, as well as commentaries on popular music, advertising, and television. The course concludes by returning to specific discus-sions of the relationship between, first, contemporary education and popular culture, and second, the modern university and the liberal arts ideal. Throughout the course, the students are encouraged to consider both how principles of education involve assumptions about practices of communication, and how the study of communication can equip one to understand and act politically in contemporary culture. The overarching argument of the course is that there is a particular conception of the role of rhetorical study in the liberal-arts education, which was articulated best by Isocrates and Cicero, that it is one which I think that students have an obligation to understand if they want to see themselves as liberally educated persons, and that mastering it today requires attention to a wide range of contemporary thinkers who can contribute to the criticism of contempo-rary discourse. Thus, a course that begins with Protagoras can end with the problematic of postmodernism, integrate classical texts and contemporary cul-tural theorists, and in doing so provide students with both a rationale and an introduction to requisite skills for becoming a liberally educated person.

The Exercises

The syllabus is only half the story, however. What I regard as the secret of the success of this course are the exercises that I have designed to accompany the

24

readings. The course alternates between days when I lecture in response to a text read in common and days when I put the students into small groups of about five people each, which are lead by a student who has taken the course before. (These student assistants receive neither academic credit nor money for their work.) The first exercises are modeled on exercises in the classical handbooks on rhetoric; as the course develops, I increasingly emphasize the analysis of contemporary discourse as a means for cultural criticism. Let me describe two exercises and suggest how they serve as an agency for inculcating a commitment to the liberal arts ideal.

The first exercise, which follows discussion of the Sophists, consists of the classical *suasoriae et controversiae*. The students are asked to argue a question, which reads: "Someone has paid a fisherman in advance for his catch. When a bag of gold is netted, the fisherman claims that it is his, for he was not paid to catch gold but fish. The other claims that the fisherman was paid for the contents of the net, not just the expected contents. Who should receive the gold?" Obviously this case is contrived for a particular purpose to allow the students to exercise the faculties of critical thought which liberal educators regard as crucial to producing good arguments. When the students first look at this exercise they are stumped; then they stumble forward and become enthralled. They argue back and forth, become passionate and exasperated, and generally begin to encounter the thrill and the norms of public debate. Yet it is very much an exercise from another time and place.

As the session continues, the students work through a few more like the first, then all of a sudden they encounter this one "A married woman contracts to be impregnated with another man's sperm and to sell the baby to him for $10,000. When the baby is born, she decides to keep it. The father and his wife sue to obtain sole parental rights to the child. Who should have the child?" This looks very much like a school exercise, doesn't it? It looks equally contrived, but of course it is the famous Baby M case. It is a case in our own day, involving real people, and of obvious moral and legal and political significance within the students' own world. And several more like it follow.

By now, the students are starting to catch on. At the end of the session, I ask them several questions. First, who was the most competent in your group? They will all pick somebody. Then I will ask how did each of you feel when you were not competent? Invariably they say the same thing: they felt ashamed. Then we recall how the classical authors claimed you should feel ashamed if you are not competent as a communicator, and we can begin to appreciated what they are saying about the relationship between speech and human community.

The next question which I ask them is what did you need to know in order to be competent? And again, they always say two things. First, they say that, in order to go through these exercises, they had to know something about the different parts of their culture. In other words, if they were to argue well and form good judgments on a broad range of topics—all the topics, that is to say, of public affairs—they had to have copious minds. This is exactly the intelligence that Isocrates was trying to impart to his students, and it is the best rationale available for our requirements that students study a broad range of courses. Second, they also say that they need technical skill as communicators. They needed to know the difference between a good and a bad syllogism. They needed to know what to do when they heard this kind of argument versus that kind of argument. They needed to know what to do when another student was making fun of them. They needed to have a sense, not just of logic, but of strategy. In other words, they needed to learn rhetoric, and now they could understand why the liberal arts degree requires core courses in basic skills of communication.

By this time, we have established a basic dialectic internal and intrinsic to the liberal arts education between cultural competency and communicative competency. Moreover, we have situated these "educational" norms within a thoroughly political context, as both of these standards are understood to serve the larger end of preparing citizens for active participation in public affairs. And we have begun to raise questions about rhetorical dimension of effective communication. In addition, this educational framework fosters deeper appreciation of the classical rhetoricians—, of why Gorgias would be disposed to claim that technical competency in communication could suffice for other types of knowledge, or why Cicero could denigrate technical philosophy in respect to a program of study directed to nurture copiousness.

The rest of the exercises elaborate these ideas while representing the issues of the other units of the course. For example, an exercise on forensic ethics begins with something called the truth game. Any student in a group can ask any question of any other student in the group, and all agree either to give truthful answers or to check out of the game. As soon as you check out, you lose. The longer you can hold on, the more you win. It is a very dangerous game, and the students play it assiduously. Often the questioners quickly become more embarrassed than the answerers, and soon the students start to see the ways in which all of our world is zoned into realms of what can be said and what cannot be said, zones of the speakable and the unspeakable. Then we see just what Socrates meant by "truth"—how we can push back that line from the speakable (public, visible) into what was unspeakable (private, hidden). We get some sense of how it can be truly therapeutic, truly beautiful, truly noble to see someone who insists on telling the truth, who reveals the *unnecessary* shamefulness in the audience. On the other hand, the students also learn quickly that there is another value that we set against truth, the value of discretion. At some point, everyone checks out, and everyone says that sometime we should honor values other than telling the truth. At that point, we have to moderate Plato's criticism of rhetoric. Once we establish that we cannot or will not live by truth alone, then there is good reason to learn the arts of concealment (and, incidentally, good reason to read Bacon on the subject), and also an impetus to developing rhetorical studies as a mode of reflection upon social practice. This general understanding then is tested and refined further through additional problems in the exercise, which ask the students to lie on behalf of a CEO, tell a false story in order to be elected to public office, and the like. As the students shift from a categorical attitude (prohibiting all lies) to a more relative standard and more subtle discriminations (allowing some distortion), they have the opportunity both to experience the difficulties of public life, and also come to appreciate the manner in which honesty, precision, and other such values of speaking and thinking are genuine achievements.

I hope these few examples can suffice to suggest how the tradition of rhetoric offers the means to both define and motivate important elements in the liberal arts education. If the course in Rhetoric as a Liberal Art succeeds fully, it provides the student with a historically defined rationale for the liberal arts education, an introduction to a human science, and a genuine connection between theory and practice. If our goal is to produce the articulate citizen, we must recognize that the challenge facing the professor is not in inculcating the values of a higher order, but in bringing students to discover the means in their own time for communicating in a manner advantageous to both speaker and audience.

NOTES

1. The Core and the Canon: A National Debate, sponsored by the National Endowment for the Humanities, University of North Texas, October 26–28, 1989.

2. For summary and criticism of the Platonic account, see Brian Vickers, *In Defense of Rhetoric* (Oxford: Clarendon Press, 1988), 83–147.

3. A typical example came during the conference keynote address by Gerald Martin, a professor of philosophy and now associate director of the NEH. After a speech warning cogently against false dichotomies, Martin concluded by urging (without a hint of irony) that his audience hold the crucial line between (good) logic and (bad) rhetoric. Although Martin went out of his way the following day to profess his interest in the rhetorical tradition as a promising source for liberal education, his every other mention of rhetoric cautioned against its capacity to mislead. This Platonic habit has become so basic to academic and western cultures that even when we try, it is hard for us to meet rhetoric on its own terms.

4. Bruce A. Kimball, *Orators and Philosophers: A History of the Idea of Liberal Education* (New York: Teachers College Press, 1986). For additional discussion, see my review of the book in *Rhetorica* 6 (1988): 199–204.

5. See also Samuel Ijsseling, *Rhetoric and Philosophy in Conflict* (The Hague: Martinus Nijhoff, 1976), Vickers, Kimball.

6. The major exception, of course, is Allan Bloom, *The Closing of the American Mind: How Higher Education Has Failed Democracy and Impoverished the Souls of Today's Students* (New York: Simon and Schuster, 1987).

7. See Wendall Berry, *Standing by Words*, (San Francisco: North Point Press, 1983).

8. See Robert Hariman, "Status, Marginality, and Rhetorical Theory," *Quarterly Journal of Speech*, 72, (1986), 38–54; John S. Nelson, "Political Theory as Political Rhetoric," *What Should Political Theory Be Now?* Nelson, ed. (Albany: State University of New York Press, 1983), 159–240. Also see Michael C. Leff, "Modern Sophistic and the Unity of Rhetoric," John S. Nelson, Allan Megill, and Donald N. McCloskey, *The Rhetoric of the Human Sciences: Language and Argument in Scholarship and Public Affairs* (Madison: University of Wisconsin Press, 1987), 19–37; Dilap Parameshwar Gaonkar, "Rhetoric and Its Double: Reflections on the Rhetorical Turn in the Human Sciences," *The Rhetorical Turn: Invention and Persuasion in the Conduct of Inquiry*, Herbert W. Simons, ed. (Chicago: University of Chicago Press, 1990).

9. James Boyd White, *When Words Lose Their Meaning: Constitutions and Reconstitutions of Language, Character, and Community* (Chicago: University of Chicago Press, 1984), x–xi.

10. Kimball, *Orators and Philosophers*, 2.

2

THE LIBERAL ARTS
HISTORY AND DEVELOPMENT

THE MUSES AS PEDAGOGUES OF THE LIBERAL ARTS

Dennis Quinn
University of Kansas

Before I begin, I have two points to make. First, the pedagogical theory that I present is not new. Its foundations are in classical antiquity, notably in Plato's *Republic*; Aristotle later endorsed it in the *Politics*. Its briefest enunciation occurs in the *Laws*, where Plato's spokesman says, "Shall we begin with the acknowledgement that education is first given through Apollo and the Muses?" (*Laws* 654A). I take Plato to mean here that the Muses furnish the principle which not only begins education but permeates and sustains it in all stages. This musical approach was actually implemented by the Greeks and others in Western culture (and no doubt in others as well), but I have no intention of arguing that historical point here or even that the theory is Plato's. What I wish to do is to describe the theory and defend it as a principle of integrating the teaching of liberal arts.

A second prolegomenous note is that I have actually employed the theory I shall advocate. It was the animating principle of the Integrated Humanities Program, a four-semester Great Books course which I directed and in which I taught at the University of Kansas from 1966 until 1982. This program was highly successful in attracting and retaining large numbers of underclass students, most of whom felt it to be the most valuable part of their college education. This program was strongly influenced by the Great Books idea promoted by Mr. Adler. Our approach to Great Books, however, differed precisely in the emphasis placed on the muses, instead of the dialectical approach dominant in the Chicago, Columbia, and St. John's programs. I repeat the title of the Kansas experiment: The Integrated Humanities Program. It was our intention to give students an introduction to various humanistic disciplines, but there is no reason that the whole of the liberal arts and sciences cannot be similarly integrated.

What do I mean by education by the Muses? Or to use a more convenient term, Musical (capital M) education? We all know the deities that the Greeks called Muses—the nine daughters of Zeus, begotten upon Mnemosyne, goddess of memory. They are the inspirers of various kinds of poetry (tragic, comic, lyric, religious, and epic) and of dance, history, and astronomy. Education begins with the Muses because children begin their learning with things Musical. We first teach children stories and songs, to which, along with dancing, children are naturally drawn. This is not an advanced education, but rather one that is elementary. The word "elementary" unfortunately has taken a pejorative connotation, as if it involves something contemptible and childish, as in Sherlock Holmes' condescending "Elementary," when Watson expresses amazement at the detective's deductions. The word means just the opposite of its derogatory sense of trivial; for what is elemental is essential, primary, constitutive, concerning principles—as air, earth, fire, and water were the ancient elements.

Nor is the elementary merely what is easy. An element is something simple, in the sense that it is indivisible, without parts. That is the etymological meaning of *simple—semel ply*, not folded over, as opposed to the complex. The word *simple* has suffered the same fate as "elementary" in acquiring a connotation of triviality. Sherlock Holmes, again, says that his abstruse cases are "ridiculously" or "childishly simple." Although simple things may appear to be obvious, they are not easy precisely because they cannot be broken down into parts, subjected to analysis. The soul is an example, or the point in geometry, or love, or God. Things elementary are, in fact supremely mysterious—easy to recognize, but hard to describe. Milton said that poetry is simple, and so it is, despite the efforts of critics and scholars to render it complex. All of the Muses and their products are simple, and they address what is the simple—the real, human sorrow, the good, the true, and the beautiful.

The Muses are integrative because they deal with things as wholes that are greater than the sum of their parts. The simplest love lyrics (and the simpler the lyric the better) always tell us something about the whole of love. Thus, education by the Muses begins with the assumption that the whole should be learned before the parts, whereas contemporary education under the influence of the analytical sciences (I almost said analyrical sciences), gives us the parts first and pretty much expects us to make a whole out of them for ourselves.

Apollo and the Muses educate beginners, amateurs, those who seek understanding for the love of it, rather than for the prospect of gain, as is so common among the career oriented. At the university we call the beginners freshmen, who are capable of hearing the song of the Muses because they present life fresh, as if experienced for the first time. In philosophy Socrates is the great beginner, the perennial freshman, who never lost his amateur status and who insisted that philosophy is nothing more than what the word means literally, the love of wisdom. The sophomore, the sophisticate, and the Sophists have in common the claim of possessing wisdom.

At the beginning of any art or science is a principle. The word "principle" itself means "first," and it is related to the word "fresh." Hence in Latin the book of Genesis begins, *in principio*. Once again, however, we recall that principles are not first only as the first in a sequence is first. The letter "A" for example is not the principle of the alphabet, but only the first letter. The number one, on the other hand, is the principle of number because all numbers contain one. This is why the Greeks said that one is not a number at all. To speak philosophically, principles are *per se nota*, known by themselves or self-evident, fundamental because they are not based on any more elementary truth. Like all simple things, principles are obvious but profoundly mysterious. One learns them by experience—not by one particular kind of experience, but by all experience. In the study of logic as an art, we learn the principle of non-contradiction, but those who have never observed the existential bearing of this principle in life, will never learn it in logic. The

32

principle of ethics is that the good must be done. Great poets take this as given, teaching it without asserting it explicitly. The principle of philosophy, as Plato and Aristotle affirm is the passion of wonder, the fundamental passion that the Muses arouse.

What excites the passion of wonder is the confrontation of mystery, the dominant domain of the Muses. Mystery is in the very root of their name, the Greek *mu*. The same syllable occurs in the Greek *mythos*, which means "story." Perhaps the root goes back to the closed-lipped sound that calls for silence—as in "mum's the word." Hence the word *mute* comes from the same root as music, myth, Muse, and mystery. Our posture before the great mysteries of ordinary experience is one of suspended and silent attention or musing, not of active inquiry. This is precisely the attitude begotten by wonder. Mystery may best be understood by contrasting it to the problematic. Songs, stories, pictures do not deal with problems for which there are definitive solutions, but rather with what Gerard Manley Hopkins called "incomprehensible certainties," truths obvious but dark. One great lover of definitive solutions (including the 7 percent variety) is Sherlock Holmes, again. The cry of that admirable sleuth (himself an object of wonder) is, "Give me problems!" and his dismissive question, "What is the mystery in all this?"

The Muses address the beginner not only in their presentation of elementary things, but also in their mode of presentation. They do not address the intellect primarily; they do not descant in dialectic. They are not rhetoricians who aim to persuade. They do not pretend to "prove" anything. We have become accustomed to ideological novels, but the Muse deserts even Tolstoi when he begins to preach.

Our initial response to anything musical is simple delight, which naturally arises when we see or hear something well represented or imitated. We look at the horses on the Parthenon frieze and exclaim, "Yes, those are horses! That is how they are!" Now that realization does require an act of intellectual judgment, but it is not a high level of abstraction; it involves only the ability to see similarities and to see particular objects as good in relation to ourselves. The Muses ask very little of us really in the way of thought. They often say no more than "Behold!" as when they speak through Gerard Manley Hopkins: "Look at the stars! look, look up at the skies!/O look at all the fire-folk sitting in the air!" (70–71). Kipling has a poem with a refrain that puts the matter very well:

> For to admire and for to see
> And for to behold this world so wide.
> It never done no good for me,
> But I can't drop it if I tried. (455–56)

That is the "evening song" of a Cockney soldier. The word "admire," by the way, means to look upon with praising wonder.

Much of what the Muses do is simply to cultivate and awaken attention to the world—what Wordsworth called "passionate regard" and Hopkins called an "ecstasy of interest." It is deplorable that college students cannot write and read and work mathematics and speak well; but it is worse when they are blind and deaf, insensible to the "world so wide." Contemporary students often find it difficult to follow a train of reasoning, but the cause of that deficiency is not insufficient training in logic but rather the failure to use their senses, for, as Aristotle teaches, all knowledge begins in the senses.

The Muses, I should add, are not responsible for the direct training of the senses. That part of education, which should precede that of the Muses, is gymnastic, training in the immediate or naked contact with sensible reality. This essential aspect of education, so important to the ancients, is sadly neglected today because of the exaggerated emphasis on competitive sports. Among the Muses, Terpsychore, the goddess of the dance, combines gymnastic and musical education, however. In the Integrated Humanities Program, we taught students the waltz; it was immensely popular.

As the daughters of Mnemosyne, the Muses particularly address the memory and the closely related faculty of imagination. After the external senses, it is these senses that must be educated. Clearly, the works of the Muses have a natural affinity for the memory. The first thing to do with a poem or a song is simply to learn it by heart. Modern educationists have made a bugbear of memorization, but it is a necessary, healthful, and even pleasant activity, especially where the material is pleasing. It is good to know poetry and songs by heart because they conform the soul to harmony and eloquence by their own power. If it is objected that we should never memorize something we do not understand, I only reply that poetry is never fully understood, but that once it is in the memory it is possible for an experience to occur which will illuminate its meaning. Moreover, poetry known by heart also makes experience possible. Those who know Robert Burns' "My love is like a red, red rose" are more likely to recognize the experience of love when the occasion arises. In the Integrated Humanities Program all students memorized ten standard English poems each semester. They learned them orally and in small groups from older students who already knew the poems. This was one of our most popular experiments. One notorious defect of the modern fragmented curriculum is that students have no common knowledge. A group of American college students asked to sing a song or talk about one book, often can not do so because they have no song or book in common.

I have spoken so much of poetry and music that it may be thought that those are the only subjects to be taught under the Muses, but there are also Muses of History and Astronomy. Musical astronomy is simply what used to be called observational astronomy, although in the Integrated Humanities we simply called it star-gazing. Some twenty years ago the University of Kansas taught an extremely popular course in observational astronomy. When the Professor who taught it retired, it was replaced by astrophysics. This happens widely, and it is paradigmatic of the fatal tendency to dispense with the elementary and plunge at once into the advanced, which because it is always more specialized, divides, separates, and fragments. Astronomy is a noble science, and educated people should have some knowledge of it, but before they begin to learn about curved space, they should know about curves; before Einstein, Euclid; before black holes, the pole star. Before a student touches a telescope, he should know the visible sky as he knows his own neighborhood; and, for that matter, he should know his own neighborhood before Tibet.

Clio, the Muse of history, derives her name from a verb that means "praise." In the first sentence of *Persian Wars*, Herodotus says the purpose of history is to honor and preserve the deeds of great men. The histories of Herodotus, whose nine books are traditionally named after the Muses, are often scorned as inferior to those of Thucydides, but the author of the *Peloponnesian Wars* was a scientific historian, and if history is a science at all (which I doubt), it should not be studied before poetic history. Herodotus, regarded by antiquity as the Father of History, is a great storyteller. From him we learn that history is made by humans, not by impersonal "forces"; we learn to praise and honor those who deserve, rather than to belittle; we learn that greatness itself does not consist of mere power or wealth.

I cannot consider here how every subject can be taught poetically; I only repeat my general rule, that one must always start at the beginning. Biology should start in the field, not in the lab; mathematics should begin with the numbering of things; economics with the ordering of the household and hence with the *Oeconomicus* of Xenophon. As for advanced study, I believe with Mr. Adler that it belongs in post-graduate, professional, and specialized vocational training.

I spoke earlier of the power of the Muses to inspire wonder, the principle of philosophy, and I want to end on that note. The motto of the Integrated Humanities Program (devised by a student) was *Nascantur in admiratione*, "Let them be born in wonder." A true schooling in the liberal arts should be like the birth of the human spirit, an entry into a new world that excites interest because it is seen in the light of wonder. The passion of wonder itself arises from a consciousness of our ignorance before the mystery of being, and from that passion begins the lifelong pursuit of wisdom.

Perhaps the greatest fictional antagonist of wonder is the eminent Victorian pedagogue in Dickens' *Hard Times*, George Gradgrind—the ultimate antithesis of the Muses, "With a rule and a pair of scales, and the multiplication table always in his pocket . . . ready to weigh and measure any parcel of human nature and tell you exactly what it comes to" (Ch. 2, 2). Gradgrind's own wretched children suffered under their father's tutelage. (How he would have adored our new electronic educators!)

No little Gradgrind had ever learned the silly jingle, Twinkle, twinkle, little star; how I wonder what you are! No little Gradgrind had ever known wonder on the subject, each little Gradgrind having at five years old dissected the Great Bear like a Professor Owen, and driven

Charles' Wain like a locomotive engine driver. No little Gradgrind had ever associated a cow in a field with that famous cow with the crumpled horn . . . , or with that still more famous cow who swallowed Tom Thumb; it had never heard of those celebrities, and had only been introduced to a cow as a gramnivorous, ruminating quadruped with several stomachs. (Ch. 3, 8)

To my regret I find that, in general, new college students (especially the most academically able of them) are pretty much what Gradgrind had in mind as star pupils. Although ignorant of nearly everything, they think they know everything, or if they do not can get it from some reference book or computer. Late adolescent Prufrocks, they have never heard the Muse's song and never wondered what the whole thing is about. Fortunately, it is not too late for them, but if they find the university to be only another Gradgrind academy, their future is likely to be the Wasteland, a universe where, as in the university that takes its name from the universe, all semblance of unity has disappeared.

LITERATURE CITED

Dickens, Charles. *Hard Times*. London: J. M. Dent, 1966.
Hopkins, Gerard Manley. *Poems of Gerard Manley Hopkins*. Ed. W. H. Gardner, New York: Oxford University Press, 1952.
Kipling, Rudyard. *Rudyard Kipling's Verse*. New York: Doubleday, 1940.
Plato. *The Dialogues of Plato*. Tr. Benjamin Jowett. New York: Random House, 1937.

FREDERICK RUDOLPH'S *AMERICAN COLLEGE AND UNIVERSITY: A HISTORY*—ITS PLACE IN THE CANON OF HISTORICAL SCHOLARSHIP ON AMERICAN COLLEGES AND UNIVERSITIES

David S. Webster
Oklahoma State University

Almost thirty years ago, Frederick Rudolph published *The American College and University: A History*. It is an important and widely celebrated book which remained in print, either in hardcover or paperback or both, from 1962 until 1985 and sold about 55,000 copies; very few scholarly works sell nearly so well. The book has been widely and almost always favorably reviewed. Among the many publications which praised it were major historical journals like the *American Historical Review* (Barker 1963) and the *Mississippi Valley Historical Review* (Jackson 1963); educational journals like the *Teachers College Record* (Harrison and Shoben, Jr. 1962) and the young *History of Education Quarterly* (Madsden 1963); what were then often called "highbrow" magazines for the cultivated general reader such as *Harper's* (Pickrel 1962) and the *Saturday Review* (Walton 1962); and dozens of newspapers, including the *New York Times* (Horn 1962), the *Hartford Courant* (Weaver 1962) and the *Providence Sunday Journal* (McLoughlin, Jr. 1962). Among the numerous reviewers who praised it were such well-known scholars as Bernard Bailyn (1962), now a University Professor at Harvard; David Tyack (1967), now Professor of Education and History at Stanford; and Theodore Sizer (1963), now Professor and Chairman of the Department of Education at Brown. Not only was *American College and University* praised shortly after it was published, but it has had an exceptionally long scholarly life. From 1980 through August, 1988—that is, from eighteen to twenty-six years after it was published—it was cited 79 times in the *Social Sciences Citation Index*. That was almost twice as many as the 43 citations given during the same period to the only other general history of American higher education published during the last 30 years (Brubacher and Rudy 1958), even though by 1980 that book had been published in revised and expanded editions in both 1968 and 1976.

SCHOLARLY VIRTUES

As one would expect of a book so long in print, so widely praised in a variety of publications, and so frequently cited, *American College and University* has many virtues. For one, it uses an enormous number of disparate sources, many of them long forgotten, difficult to obtain, of mainly local interest, and of indifferent quality, and weaves them into a history of American colleges and universities that is useful, even today, to both the scholar and the general reader. For another, although Rudolph wrote, in his Preface, that he had "not attempted a definitive history" of American higher education and was conscious "of the need for compression, even of omission" (vii), he produced, all things considered, an exceptionally comprehensive book. In almost 500 pages of text it covers some 300 years of the history of American colleges and universities, from the founding of Harvard in 1636 to events well into the twentieth century. It discusses hundreds of colleges and universities and is based on hundreds of sources, including more than 150 histories of individual institutions. Although Rudolph pays particularly close attention to the role of students in shaping the history of American colleges and universities, he also discusses the development of university governance and the role of the faculty. While he pays much more attention to campus life than to institutions' relations with the wider society, he considers the effect that major events such as the Revolutionary War and the Civil War had on colleges and universities and does not ignore the role that such organizations as the College Entrance Examination Board and the leading philanthropic organizations played in the history of higher education. Perhaps the book's most important break with previous histories of American higher education is the great importance it attributes to students and student life in the history of American colleges and universities. As one observer (Peterson 1964) has commented: Rudolph's most significant methodological departure is his attempt to capture the "total environment" of the college as experienced by the student, giving the rise of football almost as much space as the rise of the elective system (239). Rudolph strongly believes that students have been far more important in the history not only of their own campuses but also of higher education in general than others have recognized. In an essay published a few years after *American College and University* (Rudolph 1966), he developed this position at length. "College students," he wrote, "constitute the most neglected, least understood element of the American academic community" (47). Rudolph believes that the American historical tradition acknowledges the rise and fall of presidents, professors, courses of study, and endowments. As for students, however, they flow rather aimlessly in and out of our picture of the past. . . . This [portrayal of them] is both unfair and inaccurate, for unquestionably the most creative and imaginative force in the shaping of the American college and university has been the students (Rudolph 1966, 47). In *American College and University*, Rudolph endeavors to give students their due. The rise of intercollegiate football, students' participation in extra-curricular activities such as literary societies, and student life and hi-jinx in dormitories, dining halls, fraternities, and chapel are all carefully described. So vividly does

Rudolph depict campus life that *American College and University* remains the most useful comprehensive history of American students' college life ever published, despite the recent publication of a book devoted to that subject (Horowitz 1987). He is especially skillful at capturing student activities at rural colleges with spacious campuses and an abundance of "college life" in the traditional sense of that term. *American College and University* depicts campus life at schools like Williams and Princeton so much more successfully than life at urban commuter schools that one may speculate that Rudolph finds schools with attractive campuses and an abundance of traditional "college life" irresistibly attractive. That would be consistent with his having chosen, as an undergraduate, to attend Williams, one of America's most beautiful colleges located in one of its most beautiful college towns, and why he chose to go for his M.S. (1949) and Ph.D. (1953) in history to Yale, which, despite its less than bucolic environs in recent decades, is certainly a school with an abundance of "college life." It would also be consistent with Rudolph's returning to Williams in 1951 and serving on its faculty for more than thirty years until he retired in 1982. Such a fascination with traditional college life would also be consistent with his having chosen to write his dissertation and first book on mid-nineteenth-century Williams, with his remaining in Williamstown, where Williams is located, since he retired from the Williams faculty, and with his having taken the time to write, for popular magazines and alumni newsletters, pieces on college sports and games (Rudolph 1959a; 1959b) and on campus heroes (Rudolph 1962b). Another virtue of *American College and University* is Rudolph's exceptionally lively and appealing prose style. The book's early reviewers comment, one after another, on how entertaining the book is. Indeed, there are few works of scholarship so consistently enjoyable to read and few scholars who can make material like relations between church and state in the colonial college or the arguments the contenders presented in the Dartmouth College Case so vital, so alive. *American College and University* is so consistently entertaining that even Rudolph himself could not match it in his other book that covers much the same territory (Rudolph 1977), which is much heavier going. Finally there is, of course, the exceptionally useful bibliographical essay that Rudolph wrote instead of providing a conventional bibliography. In this widely praised essay, "Historiography of Higher Education in the United States," Rudolph laments that professional historians have paid relatively little attention to the history of higher education. They therefore left it largely in the hands of nostalgic alumni, whose historical efforts Rudolph considers "often saccharine and pietistic" (499), and of professional educators, who had little interest in studying the past for its own sake and "for whom educational history became a source of inspiration and a guide to action" (499). Rudolph goes on to discuss very knowledgeably which topics, like faculty-student relations and the history of teaching, had seldom been tackled by historians, and which topics, such as the founding of American colleges and universities before the Civil War, had been treated in books that were, however, long out-of-date. There is scarcely a topic in the history of American higher education that Rudolph considers covered by one or more good, recent books.

SCHOLARLY LIMITATIONS

Rudolph's *American College and University,* then, is a book with many virtues, but one that is not without limits. One of them is the very un-even coverage that Rudolph gives to the some 325 years between when Harvard was founded and when he wrote the book. Having recently published a book on Williams College in the mid-nineteenth century (Rudolph 1956), Rudolph pays far more attention to the nineteenth century than to earlier or later periods. He polishes off the 150 year history of colonial colleges in some forty pages, then devotes more than 300 pages to nineteenth-century colleges and universities which were, to be sure, far more numerous and sometimes far larger and more complex than their colonial counterparts. (Rudolph has argued, in a personal communication to the author, that the large amount of space he devoted to the nineteenth century was justified because that century was when most four-year American colleges were founded, established their identities, and decided whether to remain colleges or to try to become universities.) *American College and University*, published in 1962, pays little attention to the years after World War I and virtually no attention to anything after 1940. According to its index, Rudolph discusses or mentions nineteenth-century college and university presidents Francis Wayland in nineteen places in his book; Mark Hopkins in fifteen places; and Daniel Coit Gilman, Eliphalet Nott, and Philip Lindsley in nine places each. By contrast, he discusses such important twentieth-century university presidents as Nicholas Murray Butler in four places, Abbott Lawrence Lowell in two places, and Robert M. Hutchins once. He devotes a full page to the activities of the Lyceum of Natural History at Williams College in the nineteenth century (227–28), while including not even a word on the effects of the Cold War or the launching of sputnik on American higher education. While Rudolph has published an article in the *American Historical Review* about the life of the American Liberty League, 1934–1940 (Rudolph 1950) and a number of pieces about contemporary American higher education, most of what he has written is about pre-twentieth-century American higher education, and he said in a recent phone conversation that as an historian he feels more comfortable dealing with the past than with the present. Another limitation of the book is that Rudolph pays so much attention to the students, the curriculum, and the extra-curriculum that other subjects—especially those involving administrators and faculty, rather than students—are sometimes slighted. He pays scant attention, for example, to such matters as academic freedom, faculty tenure, faculty research, and the development of the academic disciplines. Rudolph also concentrates almost entirely on liberal arts colleges and on universities. He has little to say about engineering schools and very little to say about community colleges, teachers colleges, Catholic colleges and universities, black colleges, and almost all specialized schools such as military academies and schools concentrating on theology, music, or art. (Concerning the types of institutions to which he paid little attention, Rudolph, in a personal communication to the author, has written: "The book was clearly intended to be about 4-yr. colleges. The omission of the separate professional schools that often did not require a B.A. for admission and of 2-yr. junior and community colleges was not accidental nor dictated by bias. Nor was it easy in 1962 to figure out at what time the black colleges and Catholic colleges could be considered to have become true 4-yr. colleges rather than extended high schools.") Also, Rudolph has perhaps relied too heavily, particularly for the first 250 or so years about which he writes, on institutional histories—that is, histories of individual colleges and universities—to the relative neglect of every other kind of source. Brubacher and Rudy, by contrast, use such histories sparingly in all three editions of *Higher Education in Transition*, and in the first edition they disparage these sources' usefulness:

> Histories of individual colleges and universities abound but few are helpful in constructing the larger picture of higher education in the United States. Too many local histories have been written to arouse nostalgic memories among alumni of ivied walls, student pranks, professorial idiosyncracies, and athletic victories. Too few histories intimately expound the educational policies which illuminate the aims, curriculum, and methods of instruction of the institution on which the historian's affection is lavished. (1958, vii)

Rudolph obviously thinks otherwise about institutional histories; in the first ten pages of chapter three, "The College Movement," he refers thirty-nine times to them and only eight times to any other sources; of these eight references, five are to the same book (Tewksbury 1969). One reason Rudolph relies so heavily on institutional histories is the paucity of material about the history of American higher education in major history journals. He writes, in his bibliographical essay, that " . . . probably no more than half a dozen articles on the history of higher education have appeared in the leading professional historical journals—the *American Historical Review* . . . and the *Mississippi Valley Historical Review*" (515). And, of course, there was much less material available in history of education journals, too. When *American College and University* was published in 1962, *History of Education Quarterly* was only one year old, and the *History of Higher Education Annual* would not be founded for another nineteen years. That Rudolph relied, as extensively as he did, upon institutional histories is unfortunate. For, having relied so heavily upon them, while he is able to present occasional statistics about an individual campus—for example, what, in a particular year, its enrollment was or its faculty members were paid—there are remarkably few statistics anywhere in this book that show the extent or prevalence, over many institutions or for the nation as a whole, of important characteristics of American colleges and universities. It is nearly impossible to find, anywhere in this densely-packed five-hundred page book, information on what proportion of American youth, in a given year, were enrolled in college, what proportion of those who entered graduated, and what proportion of adults were college graduates. Rudolph seems, in general, to have little use for statistics in writing history; he has complained, concerning the historical writing of professional educators, that "statistics frequently serve as a substitute for analysis" (501). Another limitation of this book is that throughout it Rudolph may give too much credit to the innovators, to those who tried new ways, and too little credit to those who, no matter how effectively they led their campuses, did not break sharply with tradition. He writes, for example: The creators in American educational history—Thomas Jefferson, Francis Wayland, Andrew D. White, Charles W. Eliot, Daniel Coit Gilman, William Rainey Harper—were not defenders, and the memorable inheritors—John Leverett, Jeremiah Day, Mark Hopkins—were privileged to establish their reputations in an age less caught up in change [than when Rudolph wrote] (492). Elsewhere, he praises four reformers—"noble dreamers," he calls them (124)—Jacob Abbott of Amherst, James Marsh of the University of Vermont, George Ticknor of Harvard, and especially Philip Lindsley of the University of Nashville, now called Vanderbilt. He applauds them even though their reforms were "modest" (124) and despite the fact that each was, in the end, "a prophet without honor" (124) because "the fulfillment of his larger plans awaited another generation" (124). Throughout, Rudolph may give too much credit to the leaders of those institutions, like Harvard and Chicago, that were often in the vanguard of change, and too little credit to the leaders of institutions like Princeton and Yale, which, though seldom among the innovators, did succeed, decade after decade since at least the late nineteenth century, in giving their students a first-rate education by the standards of the day. Also, while Rudolph's book is, in general, an exceptionally entertaining work of scholarship, he seems constitutionally incapable of resisting a charming anecdote, even (especially?) when the behavior it describes is strange and sheds little light on the topic he is discussing. As he read through the institutional histories he collected, he seems to have selected a disproportionate number of bizarre anecdotes concerning unusual behavior for inclusion in his history. In considering early nineteenth-century American colleges, for example, he includes a page-long list of colleges whose buildings burned down (45–46). In discussing the "collegiate way," he includes a list of students, professors, and presidents at various schools who were stabbed, stoned, or killed (97). Concerning tutors, he mentions the Harvard tutor whose students one year presented him a gift of "a suitably engraved silver chamber pot" (162). Discussing the role of the nineteenth-century college faculty in disciplining students, he cannot resist mentioning the professor at South Carolina College who . . . in pursuit of a student with a stolen turkey . . . stumbled and fell on a pile of bricks, got up, rubbed his shins, and was heard to exclaim, "Mein Gott!! All dis for two tousand dollars" (106). Nor can he resist including, though it reveals little about the early American professoriate, the story of one Charles Kraitser, a nineteenth-century "Hungarian wanderer," who after being fired from the University of Virginia lamented:

> The Board of Visitors . . . were gentleman whom it was hard to please. They had kicked [his precedessor] out because he had whipped his wife, and they have kicked me out because I have been whipped by my wife. What did they really want? (157)

On his use of anecdotes, Rudolph has written to the author as follows: "It is curious that these bizarre anecdotes should get a new lease on life in your essay, but even more curious that you should quote them without context or without acknowledging the informed use to which they were put. The burning buildings lead into a consideration of the chancy, ephemeral, hard-pressed nature of the colleges. The stabbings, killings, rebellions lead into a consideration of the meanings of residential life. The Kraitser quotation which raises a question of what the Board of Visitors really wanted leads into a consideration of the kind of professor the colleges indeed did want. The anecdotes may be objectionable but not as pointless as they are made to appear here. My use of anecdotes was based on the degree to which a particular anecdote could soundly and properly be allowed to speak for a widespread condition or development, etc."

RECENT VIEWS OF THE PRE-CIVIL WAR AMERICAN COLLEGE

Finally, much has been published since 1962 about the history of American higher education. Based on this scholarship, the early history of American colleges seems to have been quite different, in some respects, from what it appeared to be when Rudolph wrote. To make this point is not to demean Rudolph, who did an excellent job of synthesizing the material that was available to him. Nowhere is this more evident than in the reconsideration of pre-Civil War American colleges that has been under way since at least the early 1970s. A number of careful historians have described the development of these colleges in ways strikingly different from the way Rudolph has presented it in this book. According to them, the "traditional" view of the pre-Civil War American college can be traced back to a very influential book by two distinguished historians (Hofstadter and Metzger 1955). In it, Hofstadter, who wrote the portion of the book dealing with the years up to 1860, depicted the early nineteenth-century American college as a backward, dreary place, of little value to its students or to American society. In a section called "The Great Retrogression," he wrote:

> During the last three or four decades of the eighteenth century the American colleges had achieved a notable degree of freedom, vitality, and public usefulness and seemed to have their feet firmly on the path to further progress. The opening decades of the nineteenth century, however, brought a great retrogression in the state of American collegiate education. . . . While advances had been made in curricula and teaching methods from about 1730 to about 1800, the succeeding forty years, despite much educational unrest and considerable experimentation, could show only modest improvements in the best institutions, to be weighed against the inadequate and unprogressive system of collegiate education that was being fixed upon the country at large. (1955, 209)

Hofstadter's view of the early nineteenth-century American college, according to several recent historians of that subject, was far too gloomy. See, for example, Axtell (1971). Some of them have argued that such colleges were not nearly so dismal, their curricula not nearly so moribund and out of touch with society as Hofstadter had thought. Nevertheless, Hofstadter's view prevailed for at least ten or fifteen years after the publication of *Development of Academic Freedom in the United States* in 1955. Among the historians he influenced was Rudolph, who in *American College and University* presented what one historian (Potts 1977, 28) has called "the standard account" of the early nineteenth-century American college. In the last twenty years, this account has been sharply challenged by a number of historians, two of the most prominent of whom are David Potts and James McLachlan. Here are five areas in which these historians have taken issue with Rudolph's portrayal of the pre-Civil War American college.

1. Rudolph writes that as many as seven hundred colleges opened and failed before the Civil War (47; 219). Here he follows Tewksbury's *Founding of American Colleges and Universities Before the Civil War*. But Tewksbury's

method of arriving at his figures has recently been attacked (Naylor 1973). Among other dubious procedures, Tewksbury considered every institution that had been granted an official charter by its state to confer degrees in the liberal arts a "college." Thus he counted as colleges many "paper colleges," which, although chartered, never opened. When he found that "colleges" such as these did not exist by the time of the Civil War, he concluded that they had opened and then failed. He greatly overestimated the number of colleges that had opened and therefore the number that had failed.

2. Rudolph thinks that the most important cause of the proliferation of colleges in pre-Civil War America was rivalry among religious denominations (55 and elsewhere). But Potts, citing his own previous work and also the work of eight others, argues that, "Studies of sixteen Baptist colleges, fifteen northeastern colleges, early Catholic colleges, nonreformer observations of higher education, and major education societies find little or no evidence of narrow sectarian zeal or denominational proselytizing" (1977, 31). Similar arguments are made by Naylor (1973, 266–70) and McLachlan (1978).

3. Rudolph thinks that colleges, during the early nineteenth century, were attended largely by the sons of the affluent. Discussing the years of Andrew Jackson's presidency, he writes "that the colleges were peculiarly vulnerable to the 'rich-man's college' epithet there can be no doubt" (206). Potts, though, citing his own previous work and also that of two other historians, thinks otherwise: "Work on the social origins of students and on college costs produces no signs of aristocratic dominance or tendencies." (1977, 30) For a lengthy discussion of the modest financial backgrounds from which antebellum students in New England often came, see Allmendinger, Jr. (1973, especially 7–43). For an observation similar to the one by Potts quoted above, see McLachlan (1978, 296).

4. Rudolph thinks that during the early nineteenth century, college enrollments declined. He writes as follows, "Statistics showed that in New England the number of students in colleges was declining both actually and proportionately to the population, and if such a thing was happening in New England, God save the United States from what was happening elsewhere!" (218) Potts, on the other hand, has argued (1981, 89) that "to the degree that enrollment data indicates anything about public favor or disfavor toward colleges, it suggests a slow but steady increase in popularity from 1800 to 1860." Elsewhere, Potts summarizes some of the evidence that American college enrollments increased from 1800 to 1860, as follows:

> Current studies are beginning to generate data that suggest antebel-
> lum college enrollments comprised a steadily increasing proportion of
> the college-age group in the general population. . . . [The] annual growth

rate for enrollments in higher education from 1800 to 1860 is estimated to exceed that for either the second half of the nineteenth century or the first half of the twentieth. . . . . A new study limited to New England colleges found that even in this region the numbers of early nineteenth-century college graduates expanded at a faster rate than that found in the growth of the region's total population. (1977, 40)

Rudolph has commented, in a personal communication to the author, that Potts' extremely cautiously worded observations—"current studies are beginning to generate data that suggest. . . . "—scarcely constitute a strong refutation of Rudolph's position. However, Church and Sedlak (1976, 38), McLachlan (1978, 295–96), and Burke (1982, 53–89) also present evidence that college enrollments in early nineteenth-century America were not declining.

5. Rudolph presents the pre-Civil War college curriculum as a tightly prescribed, classical course of study (124, 156, and 198); one which was "almost immovable" (135); and which condemned the students who studied it to "thousands of days of boredom" (135). Potts, on the other hand, citing his own previous work and that of two other historians, argues that:

> Despite their major commitment of resources to maintaining low direct student costs, antebellum colleges also managed to develop curricula characterized by steady growth in breadth and diversity. The academic programs of these colleges—including preparatory departments, partial and parallel courses, and a basic bachelor-of-arts curriculum that contained a wide range of courses in addition to those usually labeled classical—were designed to attract widespread attendance and support. (1977, 38)

CONCLUSION

Since 1962, when Rudolph published *American College and University*, much useful scholarship about American colleges and universities has been done. This scholarship has included, in recent years, critiques of Potts', McLachlan's, and other recent historians' reassessment of early nineteenth-century American colleges (Kimball 1986; Blackburn and Conrad 1986). Rudolph himself, in *Curriculum: A History of the American Undergraduate Course of Study Since 1636* (1977), included a bibliography almost nine pages alone of scholarship, much of it historical scholarship, on higher education that had been published in 1960 and later. It would not be true now to say about American higher education, as Rudolph said about the field of education in his Preface to *American College and University*, that: "For some time now the general reader and the professional historian have had greater access to the history of almost any skirmish of the Civil War than they have had to the history of education in the United States" (vii). There are many reasons why it is time for another general history of American higher education. These include the facts that Rudolph's history is now almost thirty years old; that in it he pays little attention to the years after World War I and almost no attention to anything after 1940; that recent historians, using an abundance of material not available to Rudolph, have reached very different conclusions from his about the nature of pre-Civil War American colleges; and that the most recent edition of Brubacher and Rudy's *Higher Education in Transition* is thirteen years old. Other reasons include the fact that the only book which attempts to treat most of the period that Rudolph treats so sketchily (Henry 1975), which covers the years 1930–1970, has very little to say about individual college campuses. Indeed, it is, in a sense, almost a mirror-image of *American College and University*. Rudolph's book, relying as heavily as it does on institutional histories, is often more enlightening about developments on individual campuses than it is about how colleges and universities interacted with the wider society. Henry's book, on the other hand, focuses almost exclusively on how colleges and universities, as a group, responded to important events in American history—the Depression, World War II, the G.I. Bill, the launching of sputnik, and so on—and has virtually nothing to say about individual colleges and universities. In its index, for example, Harvard is mentioned once; the University of California, MIT, Princeton, Stanford, and Yale are not mentioned. In short, it is time—in fact, past time—for a new general history of American colleges and universities.

WORKS CITED

Allmendinger, Jr., David F. *Paupers and Scholars: The Transformation of Student Life in Nineteenth-Century New England.* New York: St. Martin's Press, 1975.

Axtell, James. "The Death of the Liberal Arts College." *History of Education Quarterly* 11, no. 4 (Winter 1971): 339–52.

Bailyn, Bernard. Review of *The American College and University*, by Frederick Rudolph. *Williams Alumni Review* (July 1962).

Barker, Charles A. Review of *The American College and University*, by Frederick Rudolph. *American Historical Review* 68, no. 2 (Jan. 1963): 472–73.

Blackburn, Robert T. and Clifton F. Conrad. "The New Revisionists and the History of U.S. Higher Education." *Higher Education* 15 (1986): 211–30.

Brubacher, John S. and Willis Rudy. *Higher Education in Transition: An American History, 1636–1956.* New York: Harper and Brothers, 1958.

Burke, Colin B. *American Collegiate Populations: A Test of the Traditional View.* New York: New York University Press, 1982.

Church, Robert L. and Michael W. Sedlak. *Education in the United States: An Interpretive History.* New York: Free Press, 1976.

Harrison, Josephine and Edward Joseph Shoben, Jr. Review of *The American College and University*, by Frederick Rudolph. *Teachers College Record* 64, no. 2 (Nov. 1962): 180–82.

Henry, David D. *Challenges Past, Challenges Present: An Analysis of American Higher Education Since 1930*. San Francisco: Jossey-Bass, 1975.

Hofstadter, Richard and Walter P. Metzger. *The Development of Academic Freedom in the United States*. New York: Columbia University Press, 1955.

Horn, Francis H. "It Takes More than Ivy to Make a College." *New York Times Book Review* (August 26, 1962): 7.

Horowitz, Helen Lefkowitz. *Campus Life: Undergraduate Cultures from the End of the Eighteenth Century to the Present*. New York: Alfred A. Knopf, 1987.

Jackson, Frederick H. Review of *The American College and University*, by Frederick Rudolph. *Mississippi Valley Historical Review* 50, no. 1 (June 1963): 153–54.

Kimball, Bruce A. "Writing the History of Universities: A New Approach?" *Minerva* 24, nos. 2-3 (Summer-Autumn 1986): 375–89.

McLachlan, James. "The American College in the Nineteenth Century: Toward a Reappraisal." *Teachers College Record* 80, no. 2 (Dec. 1978): 287–306.

McLoughlin, Jr., W. G. "A Sound and Lively History of Our Colleges." *Providence Sunday Journal* (November 4, 1962): S-19.

Madsen, David. Review of *The American College and University* by Frederick Rudolph. *History of Education Quarterly* 3, no. 3 (Sept. 1963): 173–76.

Naylor, Natalie A. "The Ante-Bellum College Movement: A Reappraisal of Tewksbury's Founding of American Colleges and Universities." *History of Education Quarterly* 13, no. 3 (Fall 1973): 261–74.

Peterson, George E. *The New England College in the Age of the University*. Amherst, Mass.: Amherst College Press, 1964.

Pickrel, Paul. Review of *The American College and University*, by Frederick Rudolph. *Harper's* (Aug. 1962): 95–96.

Potts, David B. "'College Enthusiasm!' As Public Response, 1800-1860." *Harvard Educational Review* 47, no. 1 (Feb. 1977): 28–42.

_____."Curriculum and Enrollments: Some Thoughts on Assessing the Popularity of Antebellum Colleges." *History of Higher Education Annual* 1 (1981), 88–109.

Rudolph, Frederick. *Curriculum: A History of the American Undergraduate Course of Study Since 1636*. San Francisco: Jossey-Bass, 1977.

_____. *Mark Hopkins and the Log: Williams College, 1836–1872*. New Haven: Yale University Press, 1956.

_____. "Neglect of Students as a Historical Tradition." In *The College and the Student*, edited by Lawrence E. Dennis and Joseph F. Kaufmann, 47–58. Washington, D.C.: American Council on Education, 1966.

_____. *The American College and University: A History*. New York: Alfred A. Knopf, 1962a.

_____. "The American Liberty League, 1934–1940." *American Historical Review* 56, no. 1 (October 1950); 19–33.

_____. "The First College Baseball Game." *Holiday* 25, no. 5 (May 1959a): 191; 197.

_____. "What's Become of the Campus Hero?" *Mademoiselle* (Dec. 1962b): 94–95; 112; 120.

_____. *Williams and Amherst: Baseball and Chess! Muscle and Mind!* Williams Newsletter (Spring 1959b): 5–8.

Sizer, Theodore R. Review of *The American College and University*, by Frederick Rudolph. *New England Quarterly* 36, no. 3 (Sept. 1963): 414–15.

Tewksbury, Donald G. *The Founding of American Colleges and Universities Before the Civil War*. New York: Arno Press, 1969.

Tyack, David. Review of *The American College and University*, by Frederick Rudolph. *Educational Forum*, 31, no. 4 (May 1967): 519–20.

Walton, John. "A Land of Colleges." *Saturday Review* (August 18, 1962): 59.

Weaver, Glenn. "Concerns about Colleges." *Hartford Courant Magazine* (September 30, 1962): 14.

PRESENT AT THE CREATION

Donald K. Pickens
University of North Texas

Editor's Note: Professor Pickens was a founder of the successful Classic Learning Core at the University of North Texas. This program correlates nine liberal arts in a coherent curriculum allowing faculty members to draw on information provided in other courses and other semesters. With significant grants by NEH and by FIPSE, the CLC has been cited as a concrete instance of reforms recently encouraged by the Carnegie Foundation and others.

Where did it begin? I am speaking of the Classic Learning Core at the University of North Texas, and apparently it began in the mind of Thomas R. Preston, Dean of Arts and Sciences. He, in turn, asked John Kincaid to head an exploratory committee to which I and several others were then appointed. Professor Kincaid's low-key manner and comfortable leadership were important to the success of the meetings. In discussing a theme for our vision of an integrated curriculum, I suggested that the secular trinitarian ideology of modernism— Liberty, Equality, and Fraternity—would provide coherence and intellectual substance; but the committee thought it would be more politic to recast these themes for contemporary students. In writing the proposal, John Kincaid suggested Virtue, Civility, and Reason (VCR to friends). These unifying notions have provided coherence to our work ever since.

The grant proposals to NEH and FIPSE were successful. In the next year, before beginning in the classroom, a series of faculty workshops were held. Participating faculty members were volunteers to the program; all discussed and cussed the issues of coherences and values in the curriculum. In that process something happened. A real community, a fraternity of interest emerged in which faculty members gained information and insight. A major result for me was that I gained a deepening admiration for colleagues I had known for years. Now we had time to discuss what was on our minds beyond the pleasant give and take of cocktail parties. Here was a real education. I don't want it to end.

The University of North Texas was "destined" to have such a program as the Classic Learning Core. In my twenty-five year tenure with the university, it has moved in and out of fashion by not moving at all. Such are the trends of higher education. Straws were in the wind, however. For over ten years North Texas has maintained an Honors Program, and two Great Books courses (eighteen hours of credit in history, literature, and philosophy) taught by an interdisciplinary team of faculty. More recently, under Dean Preston's leadership, significant improvements were made in upgrading the academic standards of the College of Arts and

Sciences. Slowly, like the sun burning away morning mists, the university is revealing the treasures of human experience.

A number of decisions were made regarding coherence. We could have opted for a series of interdisciplinary courses, a tried but not always successful route; or we could opt for the less-trod path of closely coordinated multidisciplinary courses. Most of the faculty had taught in Honors or the Great Books Program (both interdisciplinary)—and most of us had mixed emotions about that approach. The multidisciplinary approach was unknown, yet we opted for this difficult way.

Two principal reasons motivated our choice. Prior experience had taught the faculty that advantages gained from interdisciplinary classes were often more apparent than real; and faculty members are creatures of disciplines. We think in disciplinary terms; it is difficult to escape disciplinary contexts.

The second reason was simple. The Classic Learning Core faculty wanted something different. A tightly structured, well-coordinated series of courses, each taught by a specialist using when possible, a common core of important texts was not easy, but it was possible. Whereas a political scientist might see John Locke as one in a chain of political theorists, an historian sees him as the theoretical father of the Declaration of Independence. The views are mutually reinforcing. Moreover, this multidisciplinary approach had another feature to recommend it: it was not as "threatening" to the faculty as interdisciplinary teaching. Not often discussed, this factor is significant. Sharing instructional authority is not easy. All of us enjoy being the resident authority in the classroom.

Other problems remained. Sharing classical texts across disciplines required a sequencing of courses over several years. It also required basic agreement on the fundamental readings. The first, already prescribed by the Arts and Sciences core was fairly easy. Four semesters of English, two of American history, and two of Texas and United States government were naturals. Art appreciation, classical argument and world history fit nicely into our version of a good education and into distribution requirements of the basic core. At the junior and senior levels, courses on ethics, developing societies, history and philosophy of the natural sciences, and history and philosophy of the social sciences fit the CLC vision. The program is crowned by a senior capstone seminar. Latin was the foreign language of choice, with German permitted as a modern language alternative. Other languages are accepted, but we do not yet have resources to coordinate them into the CLC curriculum. Picking the classical texts was more difficult; the faculty finally chose sixty-three texts ranging from ancients to moderns, but the list remains open.

The Classic Learning Core is working well. Student response has exceeded projections; the goal was fifty freshmen in the Fall of 1986; about one hundred enrolled. The goal for Fall 1987 was a hundred, but two hundred enrolled. CLC is not an honors program. Aiming at "typical" college students, the minimum SAT is 850.

Coherence in the Arts and Sciences is possible, but not automatic. It requires planning and coordination. It requires a faculty willing to discuss hard issues and trust their colleagues. They do not have to agree, but they must be willing to accept judgments and interpretations contrary to their own as being plausible. This alone takes time and commitment. Yet, something else is happening, something larger, more profound than the heart-warming story of a "small" school acquiring federal dollars and creating a Classic Learning Core.

The something of which I speak is historicism. My definition of the term has two elements; both, however, turn on the assumption that history surrounds us, melts into our metaphysical bones, that we are part of a particular time, place, and experience that shapes our being and our consciousness; history exists. Our philosophical reaction to that existence is critical. A historian's response is equally critical. J. H. Hexter suggests that historians are either splitters or lumpers (they split the data to illuminate the uniqueness of events, or merge it to illuminate classes). An idea of "progress" can be nicely smuggled into this distinction. Americans are attracted to this orientation since we like to believe that all is new, all is possible.

One expression of this historicism encourages relativism. The chronic legacy of this historicism is fear of alienation and exploitation. In this view, history leaves unsightly warts on the face of the past; the warts indicate that the few, some sort of elite, has gained something at the expense of the many, which is innately unjust. In a culture predicated on democratic-republican rhetoric, this assumption is intolerable, since all are equal, and the desired social policy seeks equality of conditions and results: all values (beliefs, assumptions) are equal (relative). Because no hierarchy of distinction is allowable (for fear of alienation and exploitation), the canon (curriculum) should be opened up. After all, this major-ity-based sociology of knowledge is the most just system for all people; they can pick and choose their values in the freedom of contemporary normlessness in the Wal-Mart of pop culture where trendy cultural Marxism unites with educational marketing to meet students' assumed ultimate need—a good job. Little wonder that history is devalued; it is just some "old guy's" idea about the past. The chronic romanticism and assumed purity of youth's instincts and institutions in their present age does nothing to ease the painful cry of this polemic.

The second form of historicism asserts that since history is all men have, the resources of the past can provide the means of restoring authority and legitimacy to the present, values denied by relativist interpretations. Hegel is right; history is a process of freedom realized through a series of totalities. People can achieve a perspective grounded in the operational authority and cultural legitimacy from this organized past. It is both possible and desirable—warts and all. Since nature is indifferent to human purpose, people can shape the world and recognize the meaning and purpose of this world as their own.

The critical point, however, is that history is not a cosmic game of tennis played without a metaphysical net. History provides that net. In short, history, the story of human beings, has trans-historical merit. It is, after all, all that men have.

What makes the current discussion so culturally sharp today is that this latest trashing of the past is sparked in no small way by over a hundred years of bourgeois bashing. In the tangled origins of modernism, one thing is clear: outrage at the middle class manifested in many ways today in popular culture, music, and fashion. The snotnose rebellion of rock and roll (now just a corporate engine of money-making) is the popular culture aspect of a deeper philosophical development in the last two centuries—the longing for total revolution. As Bernard Yack points out in *The Longing for Total Revolution: Philosophical Sources of Discontent From Rousseau to Marx and Nietzsche* (1986), total revolution against the dehumanizing spirit of modernity is self-contradictory.

The solution is ironical. Humanities can counter the spirit of cultural fragmentation by illustrating the past with treasures of thought and art. Even that high priest of modernism Nietzsche recognized that the historical sense raises men above animals. For animals cannot remember, but humans cannot help but remember. Yet as Bruce J. Smith noted in *Politics and Remembrance* (1985), the traditions of civility, the ideals of public life, have lost their force. This "forgetting" more recently has come to be seen as only a part of a larger crisis of modernity—a crisis of authority. In that context, the Classic Learning Core is an effort to reconnect the past with the present and the future. Smith says, "If there is a teaching in these considerations of political memory [there is that *polis* again], it is not that we should restore the past, but that we must have one." The CLC is based on that assumption, however quaint, however unhip.

The tragedy of the western civilization reading list at Stanford is not just that an elite school is flapping in the current winds of doctrine by which teachers must give attention to issues of race and class, as if they have ignored these elements in the past. The tragedy is the assumption that western civilization does not have a metaphysical center. The echoing cries of exploitation, of alienation are heard once again in the academy. Scholars of good will can argue over the composition of the canon; but the assumption remains that a canon *does* exist.

WORKS CITED

Hexter, John H. *Our Historians*. Cambridge: Harvard University Press, 1979.
Smith, Bruce J. *Politics and Remembrance, Republican Themes In Machiavelli, Burke, and Tocqueville*. Prince, N. J.: Princeton University Press, 1985.
Yack, Bernard. *The Longing For Total Revolution, Philosophic Sources of Social Discontent From Rousseau to Marx and Nietzsche*. Princeton, N. J.: Princeton University Press, 1986.

ELITISM AT THE CORE: DARE WE CALL IT RHETORIC?

James Como
York College, CUNY

Have not most of us heard (and chanted) some variation on the theme, "You aren't a teenager—you don't understand"? The collective noun may, of course, designate any group thought by the speaker to occupy ineffable status; and the claim may vary among "don't," "can't," and "won't," (for the listener's stance) and "understand," "see," and "know" (for the listener's epistemology). The permutations certainly do not mean the same, and each may be true, in a way, under certain circumstances. But as commonly uttered, the theme is usually false: It is the speaker who [does/can/will] not [invite/permit/direct] the listener to [understand/see/know]; the status of the designated group is not, after all ineffable, notwithstanding the sincerity of the speaker, whose actual purpose may be to enact, or to display emotion, rather than to assert objective truth.

This tendency toward communicative skepticism is common both to public and private discourse and has the effect, not only of isolating persons (and thus communities), but of demoting speaker and listener alike to inarticulate, posturing, near-pongoid species: subpersons. What is mistakenly labelled "autonomy" (the "freedom to be you and me," to feel strongly and to exhibit those feelings) necessarily subverts political sovereignty, as implied by E. D. Hirsch's reasonable premise,

> that underlies our national system of education in the first place—that people in a democracy can be entrusted to decide all matters of importance for themselves because they can deliberate and communicate with one another . . . the [ground] for Martin Luther King's [vision] as well as for Thomas Jefferson's. (12)

The implication is inescapable, and whatever we call this belief, it is not an expression of ideology, which is neither my prey nor my premise (Hirsch's neither, in my opinion). After discussing the traditional allusiveness, formal correctness, and eloquence of *The Black Panther* revolutionary newspaper, Hirsch concludes, "to be a conservative in the *means* of communication is the road to effectiveness in modern life, in whatever direction one wishes to be effective" (23).

Discourse is parabolic, at variance with reality; yet it is the world of discourse that we inhabit. The breadth, efficacy and textural richness of that world depend on our ability to make meaning: to manipulate, apprehend and interpret the elements of discourse that constitute the world. In "The Rhetorical Situation," Lloyd Bitzer calls attention to the rhetorical exigency: an incompleteness inherent to circumstances that require a symbolic response if the situation is to be resolved. Incoherence in liberal arts curricula is such an exigency; rhetoric, the oldest academic discipline in the West, remains the best response.

The "situation" as we find it is largely entropic. In the polity proper, we cry out for pluralism, but there is too little understanding of its civic nature (rooted in pragmatism) and too erratic a consensus to attain a genuine pluralism. Individuals are at once credulous ("Elvis lives!") and "substitious" (a term coined by Wayne Booth). Between the polity and the individual hovers higher liberal learning, flaccid when not downright amorphous. Within each of these spheres there is incoherence, and just so is it in the whole. And within each sphere that incoherence derives from *a deterioration of discourse*. The sorry irony is that this decline has accompanied—and partly resulted from—the rise of "rhetoric" as a devil-term and the demise of rhetoric, the first and best rationale for ordered communication, as the hub of education. To paraphrase C. S. Lewis, we have cut out the organ, yet wonder at the loss of its function.

What may we take rhetoric to be? It is a skill, largely verbal, social in application, instrumental, probabilistic, and occasional; as a branch of ethics and of politics, its goal is persuasion and it encompasses theory, method, practice and product. Its art lies in the proper adjustment between speaker, audience, and subject matter. It is ontologically a branch of psychology, a permanent and ineluctable feature of everyone's interior landscape, "the *faculty*," as Aristotle put it, "of observing in the particular case the available means of persuasion." He could easily have begun his great book on the subject with the words "all men by nature love to, and must, rhetorize." In short, rhetoric largely defines the species; to maximize this faculty is to maximize our humanity. It is at our core. To cultivate the faculty—to rehabilitate the organ—rhetoric must be restored to its proper place, the core of higher learning. Then the function will follow: Rhetoric is the antidote to discursive entropy.

Entropy in higher learning has been much documented of late. Notwithstanding Bloom's bad humor and ill will, he and others have set the terms of debate, and hold the field as well. Moral and intellectual relativism, the want of intellectual authority properly exercised (a confusion of *magisterium* with *imperium*), trivial utilitarianism, radical subjectivism, and emotional hedonism have not only brought standards of structure and rigor into disarray, but have worn out the very idea of "standards." Yet the diagnosis is not new. Over a decade ago, in that masterpiece of social criticism *The Culture of Narcissism*, Christopher Lasch wrote:

. . . no aspect of contemporary thought has proved immune to educationalization. The university has boiled all experience down into "courses" of study—a culinary image appropriate to the underlying ideal of enlightened consumption. . . . Doing so, however, compounds its intellectual failures—notwithstanding its claim to prepare students for "life." Not only does higher education destroy students' minds; it leaves them unable to perform the simplest task. (153)

Under such circumstances how can pluralism—*unfragmented* diversity—flourish? Wayne Booth argues that we are a nonpublic (in Dewey's terms) because standards of reasoned discourse have virtually disappeared, and we do not notice. "Every man in this newly levelled egalopolis, is entitled to his own brand of nonsense, and woe to the elitist who demands evidence" (*Now Don't Try* 133). Martin Marty argues similarly. Fragmentation militates against pluralism, which has no chance in the absence of "cohesive sentiment" based upon shareable discourse, including the ability "to argue more intelligently" than we presently do. True pluralism requires a coherently educated public capable of discursive integrity.

A recovery of rhetoric reintroduces the person, and thus accountability, for the prototype of all human communication is direct oral communication. "Personal presence is itself symbolic," according to Carroll C. Arnold, a formidable contemporary rhetorician. It represents the speaker's entire "physical and psychological organization," so that more than signification occurs. "A self that is not an abstraction but has a body supportively authorizes each signification" (65).

The reintroduced self brings with it an organizing ability inherent in rhetorical skill. Richard McKeon calls it *architectonic*: capable of "structuring all principles and products of knowing, doing, and making. If rhetoric is to be used to contribute to the formation of . . . the modern world, it should function . . . in the resolution of new problems and architectonically in the formation of new [genuinely pluralistic] communities" (2). According to McKeon, four traits enable rhetoric to function with such sweep: 1) it is the art of debate; 2) and of invention and disposition; 3) it makes use of all means of persuasion (including the preconceptions of the audience); 4) as an art of selection it is an art of coping with new problems (108–09). "Thus rhetoric covers the vast field of non-formalized thought," as Chaim Perelman argues. "We can thus speak of the 'realm of rhetoric' . . . the once and future queen of the human [arts]" (162).

If liberal learning was once based on this art, and if that learning now suffers entropy, then higher learning ought to be home once again to an architectonic paradigm. Furthermore, the liberal arts *are* the arts of language, opinion, and action and thus "provide the laws of thought and expression, induction and deduction, community and communication" (McKeon, 107). Perhaps this has been put most succinctly by Donald C. Bryant, one of the greatest twentieth-century rhetoricians: "Rhetoric is the organon of the liberal studies, the formulation of the principles through which the educated man . . . attains effectiveness in society. A complete rhetoric is a structure for the wholeness of the effective man, the aim of general education" (32). That sort of education underlies all knowledge, provides the means of communication and bases of community to all people (especially in a democracy conceived of as using reason to come to agreement by discussion), and forms a framework whereby "*all experience* of individual men" may be organized (McKeon, cited in Booth *Knowledge Most Worth Having* 188).

It can be no coincidence that, as rhetoric has declined as a discipline, the meretricious practice of rhetoric has inclined sharply. We do indeed live in a "rhetorical age, if we mean by that . . . an age in which men try to change each other's minds without giving good reasons" (*Now Don't Try* 39). Booth continues:

> I know of no past culture where power was so persistently thought of as power to manipulate men's minds . . . where the truth of propositions was so persistently judged by whether this or that group accepts them . . . where, finally, educational goals and methods were so persistently reduced to the notion of conditioning or of imposing already formed ideas or practices upon infinitely malleable material. (*ibid*)

Thus ought we to welcome the revival of interest in rhetoric that has been underway for some fifteen years. "Not so long ago, rhetoric was disdained in Europe. In the United States, where speech departments were numerous, they were hardly held in esteem by the academic community. Today rhetoric is rehabilitated" (Perelman 162). New societies and learned journals are devoted to rhetoric, neo-rhetorical schools, theory-building, recovery of learning, and—most important—the reintroduction of rhetoric to core curricula of liberal arts schools (as at the University of North Texas and York College, CUNY). Rhetoric not only helps to "furnish" the mind, but to order it as well (the idea of 'topos' is indispensable); it inheres to the critical thinking movement. Without it ethics, psychology, politics, and pedagogy would be disconnected from lives as they are actually lived. It is implicitly agreed that

> to engage with one's fellow men in acts of mutual persuasion is a noble thing when it becomes mutual inquiry. Indeed none of the corruptions found in our rhetorical time would even be possible in a society which had not also laid itself open to the great virtues of moral and intellectual suasion when properly used. (*Now Don't Try* 39)

Perhaps the "great conversation" is required for true pluralism.

Our goal must be to make the best people possible, to maximize their humanity. This we may do by maximizing that faculty which, from Genesis, Aristotle, and St. John the Divine through Dante, McKeon and (I believe) Chomsky, distinguishes us from the animals and makes us persons. Our goal *ought* to be elitist: the training of people capable and willing, not only of giving and of demanding "good reason," but of establishing whole regions of rhetoric, that is, communities. Aristotle was an elitist in a dangerous and undesirable sense, but he surely was no pluralist. Do we really want the "egalopolis" that would result from siding with former Senator Roman Hruska who defended a Supreme Court nominee with the argument that mediocrity deserves representation by one of its own? This is a view—and application—of rhetoric which is old, but not irrelevant; "elitist," but not therefore unfair—rather the opposite, since an educational elitism is best suited to combatting the malignant social variety.

There are other implications, too. The goddess Peitho ("I believe") is the goddess of rhetoric, and she is most often found in the company of Aphrodite herself. Dante, in the *Convivio*, routinely Christianizes the pair, confirming that together they occupy the third of the heavenly spheres. Walker Percy, writing as a semiotician, brings Love and Word down to earth:

> [E]xistentialists have taught us that what man is cannot be grasped by the science of man. The case is rather that man's science is one of the things that man does, a mode of existence. Another mode is speech. Man is not merely a higher organism responding to and controlling his environment. He is . . . that being in the world whose calling it is to find a name for Being, to give testimony to it, and to provide for it a clearing. (158)

Rhetoric, the architectonic faculty, at the core of our calling, and of our polity, thus belongs at the core of our higher learning—and, certainly, the best we can make it. The beliefs we would share ought to be no less than that.

Works Cited

Arnold, Carroll C. "Oral Rhetoric, Rhetoric, and Literature." *Contemporary Rhetoric: A Reader's Coursebook*. Ed. Douglas Ehninger. Glenview, Illinois: Scott, Foresman and Company, 1972, 60–73.

Bryant, Donald C. "Rhetoric: Its Function and Scope." *Contemporary Rhetoric: A Reader's Coursebook*. Ed. Douglas Ehninger. Glenview, Illinois: Scott, Foresman and Company, 1972, 15–38.

Bloom, Allan. *The Closing of the American Mind*. New York: Simon and Schuster, 1987.

Booth, Wayne C. *Critical Understanding: The Powers and Limits of Pluralism*. Chicago: University of Chicago Press, 1979.

_____, ed. *The Knowledge Most Worth Having*. Chicago: University of Chicago Press, 1967.

_____. *Modern Dogma and the Rhetoric of Assent*. Chicago: University of Chicago Press, 1974.

_____. *Now Don't Try to Reason with Me*. Chicago: University of Chicago Press, 1970.

Hirsch, E. D., Jr. *Cultural Literacy*. Boston: Houghton-Mifflin, Company, 1987.

Lasch, Christopher. *The Culture of Narcissim*. New York: W. W. Norton Company, 1987.

Marty, Martin. "A Task for Pluralists: Promote Cohesion." *International Herald Tribune*, 5 April 1988: 5.

McKeon, Richard. *Rhetoric: Essays in Invention and Discovery*, ed. Mark Backman. Woodbridge: Ox Bow Press, 1987.

Percy, Walker. *Lost in the Cosmos: The Last Self-Help Book*. New York: Farrar, Straus and Giroux, 1983.

_____. *The Message in the Bottle*. New York: Farrar, Straus and Giroux, 1975.

SPECIALIZATION AND THE COLLEGE CURRICULUM

Leslie M. Thompson
Texas Woman's University

During the past twenty-five years societal pressures and the information explosion have dramatically altered university curricula. In this era, we have witnessed new courses in witchcraft, cosmetology, genetics, and astrophysics nestled uneasily alongside courses in English, history, and chemistry. Like Athena, who came to birth from Zeus' ear, whole new programs of study have appeared on the university scene. As a result, colleges must now sort out and assess these changes while also adjusting to a continual stream of new courses and programs. Perhaps the most important curricular influence during the past twenty-five years, however, has been the dramatic organizational changes wrought by the increasing specializaton of the university itself. In fact, specialists and specialization not only dictate the curriculum of most universities, but to a large extent the structure of the university as well. These massive changes determine everything in a student's program from the nature of general education requirements to the scope and content of the major and minor. The increasing proliferation of information and of the specialists who burrow through this information gives every indication that these trends will be hard to arrest in the foreseeable future.

One can find much to praise in the offerings of a modern university, but all is not well with most university curricula. We have, according to Hoke L. Smith of Towson State University, atomized the curriculum. Unable, despite our best efforts, to develop an integrated curriculum, we give in to paroxysms of anxiety. Numerous forces, ranging from our attempts to educate massive numbers of people to the changing nature of the educational process itself have contributed to the disintegration of college curricula. I would like to focus, however, upon the major roles that technology, specializaion, and the information explosion are playing in the curricular revolution.

Specialized information threatens to overwhelm university curricula. When carefully scrutinized, in fact, a large number of curricula reflect far more the accretions resulting from faculty interest and specialization than they do coherent, meaningful programs. Accordingly, college curricula become hodgepodges of poorly digested information indiscriminately lodged within courses. Departments frequently respond to this problem by resorting to the add-on theory of curriculum development: adding new courses—often at the expense of electives or general education—in a process that could easily be perpetuated *ad infinitum*. More, however, has not necessarily meant better as this encroachment of specialization into the curriculum has led to an undue emphasis on the major, the diminution of general education requirements, and a stifling of the whole curricular process.

Broad intellectual considerations and not mere specialized, departmental concerns and external pressures should govern curricular changes. Helene Moglen notes that any significant reshaping of the curriculum ". . . is not simply a matter of adding a book here and subtracting a reading there: it is a matter of changing perspectives" (52). Changing perspectives, however, will not be an easy matter. By training and professional experience educational specialists have deep-seated investment in their courses and programs. Each person genuinely believes, moreover, that his or her area of expertise is absolutely crucial to the betterment of humanity and the development of well-rounded citizens. Or, at the very least, these specialties stress their own importance to the graduate's attempt to succeed in a profession.

Specialties and departments did not, however, descend from some divine archetype, nor can universities respond to new knowledge by indefinitely adding new courses to the curriculum. What must take place is a total reconceptualization of many programs of study, an integration into these programs of the basic paradigms on which the profession is built, the inculcation of the basic tenets of practice in that profession, and a coherent, well-developed plan of study which will allow graduates to enter successfully into their professions. Such plans of study must take into account the increasingly interdisciplinary nature of research. These programs must also transcend departmental limitations, thereby enhancing the likelihood of success for their graduates.

Undoubtedly, the information glut has created havoc among university curricula. The growth of specialties and subspecialties has modified the curriculum, the pedagogy, the nature of research, and even the structure of the university. This revolution has spawned new approaches to the sciences and social sciences as well as the arts and humanities. Instead of selecting judiciously from this information, educators have too frequently added courses with abandon. However, we can no longer indulge in the luxury of indefinitely adding courses and expanding majors.

The advances of science and technology and the proliferation of information have also rapidly expanded the number of disciplines and subdisciplines on campuses. In addition, increased curricular specialization has contributed to narrow departmentalization which has become a barrier to the promotion of creativity or to the establishment of relationships between courses or disciplines. Burton R. Clark asserts,

> Today the academic profession stands as a plethora of disciplines, a widening array of subject affiliations, a host of subcultures that speak in

strange tongues. Who can fathom an econometrician in full stride, let alone a biochemist or an ethnomethodologist newly tutored in linguistics and semiotics? (36)

More and more undergraduates now major in narrow specialties, and up to fifty percent of the majors offered by America's colleges and universities are in occupational fields.

Of course, specialization has become necessary in the modern university, and in itself has been an appropriate response to many societal needs and has made significant contributions to science, technology, and society as a whole. Nevertheless, an unthinking response to societal demands, and the creation of highly specialized courses often result in narrowly educated graduates unable to adapt to life in a technological society.

Harland Cleveland asserts,

It is a well known scandal that our whole educational system is geared more to categorizing and analyzing patches of knowledge than to threading them together. Yet the experts obviously don't have the answers, and we are exposed to daily and dramatic demonstrations of experts in the service of expertise rather than in the service of values. (20)

Departments define disciplines and encourage professional growth, but the professionalization and restricting of general education courses, the elimination of most electives for baccalaureate students, the increased number of hours for the major, and the intense specialization of courses within the major combine to produce graduates in many instances unsuited to work in the larger cultural or organizational milieu. Most current world problems do not lend themselves to departmental perspectives, and we have increasing evidence that much specific information imparted to majors does not equip them to deal adequately with such major societal problems as unemployment, inflation, the nuclear arms race, terrorism, poverty, and declining natural resources.

Specialization permeates the curriculum. Social and natural sciences attempt to become more scientific in method and even the humanities and fine arts attempt to arrive at some positivistic, value-free utopia. Literature and history, for example, develop increasingly specialized, arcane fields of study with jargons and methodologies meaningless except to other specialists. Few specialists attempt to transcend the boundaries between disciplines, much less to share with persons outside academia the richness of our culture.

The conditions described above do not lend themselves to some quick fix such as reshuffling the current courses within the curriculum. Rather, we must consider reconceptualizing disciplines, redesigning courses, and altering when necessary the basic premises of the discipline. An overhaul of the major must also take into account the needs for an expanded and revitalized role for general education and the removal of many strictures that now deny students flexibility in the use of electives. Some current degrees, for example, dictate that students must take "required" electives, and majors further expand by requiring courses with extensive prerequisites.

As we revamp curricula, we must also rethink current, reductionistic teaching and testing practices which stress the memorization and regurgitation of unrelated facts. A wise but impractical step would be for universities to combine curricular innovations in some instances with significant organizational and administrative changes. Such a drastic change would have little opportunity for success in light of strong vested interests within departments as well as opposition from accrediting agencies and other groups external to the university. This strategy would, however, correlate with the increasingly interdisciplinary nature of advanced research in many fields, the multifaceted approach needed to address complex scientific, social, religious, and ethical problems, and the multidisciplinary viewpoint needed to help specialists succeed throughout life in their professions.

Obviously, no one approach to revitalizing general education and restructuring majors will suffice. Each university must tackle this difficult problem in light of its own history, its unique mission, and the strengths and limitations of its own faculty and administration. In his defense of poetry, Shelley avows, "We have more moral, political and historical wisdom than we know how to reduce into practice . . ." (134). We have, it also appears, more theories about how to reform general education or revitalize curricula than we are able to implement.

At present, we can benefit from traditional wisdom as well as the spate of reports and studies urging reform in the undergraduate and, to an increasing degree, the graduate curriculum as well. In addition, state governors and higher education boards are now taking more active roles in assessing and changing higher education. Such reports as *Involvement in Learning, Integrity in the College Curriculum: A Report to the Academic Community*, William Bennett's NEH report *To Reclaim A Legacy*, and the so-called Newman Report from the Carnegie Foundation for the Advancement of Teaching attack in various ways the problems of specialization in the curriculum and advance ideas to address this problem. Unwittingly and indirectly these reports underscore Shelley's vision quoted above by stressing the need for bold action.

To rescue the curriculum from the grip of specialists calls for dramatic action. As Frances D. Fergusson wisely notes, "It is our failure of nerve that a college curriculum today takes no stand, but simply reflects the fragmentation of our society" (16). Fergusson further notes that "as we move to effect curricular reform, we all need to be braver, even at the risk of having our ideas misunderstood or, worse disregarded" (17). In making its recommendations, the Newman Report cautions against simplistic solutions. Newman also warns that fear of censure and failure creates a stifling atmosphere and engenders the belief that there is one right answer to each problem. The authors of *Integrity in the College Curriculum* also remind us that no curriculum is a fixed truth. They further claim that bold administrators and responsible teachers must combine efforts to escape the confines of departments in order to engage in interdisciplinary efforts.

Undoubtedly, we will develop more imaginative approaches to the curriculum, but it seems to me that our most pressing need is for faculty and administrators to act upon the knowledge on hand, to address the limitations of specialized knowledge, and to initiate reforms to correct the problems resulting from increasingly specialized curricula. Such initiatives will require political, pedagogical, and moral courage on the part of all participants, for they will confront powerful vested interests. In theory most people support the revision of the curriculum, and a vast majority of faculty and administration at least give lip service to the need for general education and for broadly educated graduates. Most of these same people, however, will also fight to the death in order to keep from having one course removed from their curricula or from making any innovation whatsoever that would require rethinking their field or sacrificing any vestige of their domain. Our problem is both philosophical and theoretical; but more basically, it is pragmatic and requires wise, patient leadership and a well thought out process for change.

Specialization has made possible many great advances in modern science, and the development of strong disciplines has contributed significantly to the growth of students and professors alike. Nevertheless, specialization has also engendered difficulties by producing narrow graduates unable to function effectively in a rapidly changing society. The increasing specialization of knowledge and the accompanying proliferation of information have led many universities merely to expand their curricula rather than to rethink them. It is now time for reassessment. Technical competence in a specialty cannot compensate for human indifference or ignorance about broader social issues. Value-free education which stifles curiosity and fetters the imagination will not suffice in an increasingly interdependent world demanding the full flowering of the human spirit in an ongoing interaction of the emotions with the intellect. In training professionals— whether in the sciences or the liberal arts—we must, as William Blake reminds us, avoid "mind-forg'd manacles."

WORKS CITED

Clark, Burton R. "Listening to the Professoriate." *Change* 17.4 (1985): 36–43.
Cleveland, Harlan. "Educating for the Information Society." *Change* 17.4 (1985): 13–21.
Fergusson, Frances D. "Fostering Community: Liberal Learning and Core Curricula." *National Forum* 65.3 (1985): 13–16.
Moglen, Helene. "Erosion in the Humanities." *Change* 16.7 (1984): 49–54.
Shelley, Percy. *Complete Works*. Eds. Roger Ingpen and Walter Peck. 10 vols. New York: Gordian Press, 1965. Vol. 7.

3

COHERENCE IN THE LIBERAL ARTS

DESIGNING AN INTEGRATED, FOUR-YEAR CORE

William Craft and Thomas F. Flynn
Mount Saint Mary's College

In teaching our students to think, write, and speak with clarity and imagination, we at Mount Saint Mary's endorse the goals of all good liberal education. We share the concern expressed in many reports about the problems in general education. And we particularly applaud the view, expressed in *50 Hours* and elsewhere, that a common set of courses is needed to bring order and coherence to disparate requirements, to help give shape and direction to students' task of learning about themselves and their world, and to foster genuine academic community. Today, we will describe the intellectual and ethical framework within which our own students pursue the goals of liberal education. That framework is a sixty-one hour, four-year sequence of core courses and cocurricular activities that initiates students, regardless of major, into the humanist tradition of inquiry through dialogue, narrative, and experiment. The program initially devotes two years of study in the humanities and sciences to Western Civilization; a third year to our students' American and Christian heritages, with emphasis on the Catholic intellectual tradition, and a final year to the examination of a non-Western culture and to reflection on contemporary moral problems in the larger context of ethical theories and students' experience and background.

Part 1: The Context of the New Core

Recent general education reform at Mount Saint Mary's, as at many schools, began and gained momentum as a local imperative, prompted by the College's need to address its own challenges in self-definition as a liberal arts college with a preponderance of professionally oriented students. Reform was undertaken too at the initiative of a relatively small cadre of faculty, most of them untenured, both in response to student and faculty perceptions of the existing general education program and as part of their vision of a more fully realized academic community of faculty and students. Not only did our evaluation and planning processes commence prior to the release of the national reports but, with one or two exceptions, faculty leaders of the reform were unaware of developments in other schools and in the higher education community. Yet that larger context is an important one, so we turn to it briefly.

All of us gathered at this conference can chant a litany of criticism of general education programs, though we would differ both about their relative legitimacy and their solution. To summarize only a few prevalent themes, we could cite their lack of clear definition, both in purpose and design; their failure to address student needs and to assess their impact on students (or outcomes as they're now called); the absence of strong faculty and institutional commitment to their support.

Perhaps a more helpful approach is to recognize, as does *A New Vitality in General Education*, that an ongoing, somewhat contentious debate about this topic is inevitable due to some inherent tensions:

> between what to teach and how to teach it, between the great classics of the past and contemporary works, between the classroom and students' out-of-class life, between students' individual objectives and the needs of the community, between what students want and what their institutions think they need, and between its means and ends—that is, between its reality of daily assignments and its goal of fostering the desire and capacity to continue learning (5).

Many might concede the assertion of the National Endowment for the Humanities that "some things are more important than others" (*New Vitality* 5) and that too often, as *Humanities in America* states, it "is luck or accident or uninformed intuition that determines what students do and do not learn" (5). But there would be little consensus about what knowledge, if any, should be emphasized, much less required for study, in the curriculum. (We think here particularly about the rich debate in our own discipline of literature concerning the relative merits of canons and the processes of their formation.) There would also be tension between those wishing to emphasize the content of the curriculum and those preferring instead to stress students' need to develop skills, competencies, and facility with various modes of thought. One final tension, particularly relevant for the reform process, would involve differences of approach between those wedded almost exclusively to discipline-based thinking and teaching, for reasons political as well as intellectual, and those more comfortable with and committed to cross-disciplinary exchange. We at Mount Saint Mary's were not immune to these tensions, and later in our paper we'll address the issues that were debated most vigorously during faculty deliberations as well as the principles which shaped our eventual consensus.

About 180 years old, Mount Saint Mary's has always emphasized an extensive general education program. A decade ago, following a two-year review of several alternate curriculum models, the faculty voted overwhelmingly to make only minor changes beyond the addition of a foreign language requirement. The number of departmental requirements was almost doubled while the lists of available courses were somewhat narrowed, but interdisciplinary courses and other forms of cross-departmental cooperation were emphatically rejected as impractical and undesirable. (The total number of credits was increased slightly from forty-eight to fifty-two.)

The recent reform began in 1983. As part of a comprehensive review of the undergraduate experience, faculty and students were surveyed regarding their perceptions of the general education program, and all department chairs were interviewed by a faculty team. Two themes emerged strongly from faculty and students alike. Students praised particular classes and teachers but could discern neither a central purpose nor unifying principles to the curriculum; core courses appeared disconnected and were perceived merely as "a long series of obligations to be fulfilled in no particular order." This perception was particularly troubling at Mount Saint Mary's where half of our students major in pre-professional fields and so gain their understanding of the liberal arts in general education programs or not at all. Faculty perceptions differed only slightly; we agreed our core curriculum lacked rationale and purpose; some of us also decried its lack of integration. Yet there was neither widespread commitment to reform nor consensus as to solutions to the problems. The core, concluded the review somewhat enigmatically, "appears to have great potential, but remains an unfinished symphony."

Part 2: The Planning of the New Core

Developing the new core curriculum at Mount Saint Mary's took four years. It started with the 1983 self-study noted above and ended with the faculty's vote of approval in the spring of 1987. One member abstained; the rest voted for the new core.

In the spring of 1985 our academic vice president asked the Faculty Academic Council to draft a rationale for the Mount's required general education courses and a set of goals against which they could be measured. (The Academic Council is an elected body with divisional representation and a faculty chair.) During the 1985–86 academic year, the full faculty debated, revised, and ultimately approved a rationale statement for a core curriculum "based on the humanist tradition of Western culture" and guided by "a Catholic perspective," yet "conscious of other values and viewpoints within Western and non-Western cultures." The new rationale acknowledged the value of discipline-based thinking, but emphasized liberal education's ultimate goal of personal synthesis and integration of knowledge. Specific objectives were developed in the areas of Knowledge, Values and Attitudes, and Skills; these would be the standards applied to evaluate the existing program and to shape any necessary revisions.

Several related elements of academic planning helped build momentum for a complete revision of the core curriculum. An internal study of student attrition had suggested the formation of a comprehensive freshman year program centered on a common curriculum component. During the 1985–86 academic year, faculty piloted paired humanities courses for freshmen: European literature with Philosophy; American literature with American history. A Freshman Year Committee forwarded to the Faculty Academic Council several models for unifying the freshman year curriculum along with its endorsement for a fully-integrated four-year core curriculum. This was the first time a major reform of general education requirements was envisioned.

The Academic Vice President then directed the Academic Council to evaluate the existing general education courses in light of the newly adopted rationale and goals statement, to review the Freshman Committee's recommendations, and to propose any needed revisions. Over the summer of 1986 that group interpreted this charge as a liberal one—as it was—allowing a thorough examination and restructuring of the all-college courses. That group devised a new core curriculum; the new core was modified by the full Academic Council in consultation with department chairs and then submitted to faculty debate in spring 1987, where it received an overwhelming endorsement.

Part 3: The Purpose and Structure of the New Core

The new core at Mount Saint Mary's is a four-year sequence of twenty courses: fifteen in the humanities, four in the sciences and math, one in non-Western studies. Of the twenty, fourteen must be taken by all students in a designated order, the other six are chosen from among options during the first two years. Ordinarily, students will take four core courses per term (out of five) as freshmen, three per term as sophomores, two as juniors, one as seniors.

The new core is not much bigger than the old set of general education courses (twenty vs seventeen). It differs in having a more openly and clearly articulated purpose and a structure that enables students to achieve it. It also differs in its insistence on making primary texts and data the center of every core course. The aim is to empower our students to see themselves as the heirs and the makers of their culture, a culture that interweaves European, American, Christian, and non-Western visions of human experience. The core's structure is fashioned to foster this insight in two ways: by initiating students into the Western tradition of narration, dialogue, and experiment as means of inquiry; and by ordering courses so as to encourage in students a personal integration of different disciplines and diverse ideas.

In current curriculum wars, as Stanley Fish has noted in *National Forum*, the battle is often drawn between the foundationalists, who look to eternal/universal truths to justify their curriculum, and the historicists, who look to the shifting forces of temporal, human culture (13). At Mount Saint Mary's, we can say that the foundation of our core is history: we make the assumption that human life is lived within political, linguistic, biological, and spiritual realities that both constrain and liberate each person. We assume that it is better to know and act on this "historical foundation" than not. We assume that this history is alive not dead, always open not only to present change but to re-visions of the past. And so our core is not a fixed list of books but an organized inquiry—if you like, a joint expedition.

The first two years are devoted to study of the events, artifacts, and ideas of Western civilization from Homer to Hitler, Plato to NATO. A year-long Freshman Seminar, taught by faculty from all disciplines, seeks to nurture the rhetorical arts of writing and speaking through student exploration of texts about choices to be made in education, work, and social life. The teacher of each fifteen-student section serves as academic advisor to those students. Freshmen also take a year-long course in Western history, paired each term with a contemporaneous course in literature or fine arts. Jointly planned syllabi and assignments by the faculty in each pairing (cluster) help students discover connections between various cultural developments and help them see "history" as an act of mental construction accomplished by themselves as well as their teachers.

In a year-long philosophy sequence, sophomores shift from the narrative mode that dominates the freshman Western clusters to a dialogic and analytical form of inquiry. Called "From Cosmos to Citizen" and "From Self to Society," the two courses in this sequence are historical in the sense that the first uses ancient and medieval texts and the second modern. But the questions that organize these courses—questions of epistemology, of defining human nature, of the distinction between faith and reason—are asked throughout the sequence.

As one of the modern humanities and as the progenitor of the modern sciences, philosophy serves as an intellectual bridge to the required natural science course, usually taken by sophomores. The core course in math equips students with the analytical and conceptual language they will need in both natural and social science requirements. The two social science courses, taken in the first two years, provide a historical perspective by teaching about the development of their discipline even as they introduce methodologies that contrast with those in freshman and sophomore humanities classes. The two required terms of foreign language, usually taken by freshmen, complement the cluster study of Western civilization and underscore how much language shapes one's understanding of experience.

In the junior year, attention is focused more narrowly on students' heritage and experience as Americans and as people formed by faith. In a yearlong, interdisciplinary course in American culture taught by pairs of instructors from History and English, students discover how the interactions of race, ethnicity, religion, class, and gender have modified the Western tradition they explored during their first two years. A year-long theology sequence allows students to build on philosophical methods of inquiry learned as sophomores and to distinguish the particular insights and demands of revealed Christianity, especially as interpreted in the Catholic intellectual tradition.

In the final year, students take two core courses: non-Western culture and ethics. In studying a non-Western society, students are enabled to see the Western tradition as one among several world views of human experience; this course concludes a four-year process of debate about the assumptions on which world views are based and about how such views shape one's personal ethos. The ethics course, taught from a philosophical or theological perspective, encourages students to confront moral questions in relation to ethical theory and personal experience. In identifying such questions as students conclude college and prepare for their careers, the ethics course affirms Philip Sidney's humanist conviction that "the end of all earthly living is virtuous action" (83).

A quick review of this core curriculum will reveal that it involves several sequences: it moves from a narrative mode in the first year, to a dialogic and analytical one in the second, to a combination of them in the last two years; it moves from multidisciplinary teaching in the first two years to interdisciplinary in the junior American Culture course and the senior non-Western requirement; from studying the broader Western tradition in the first two years, to the more particular American and Christian experience in the third, to a stepping beyond all of these in the senior non-Western course. There is also a sustained inquiry into value questions, from the Freshman Seminar through Philosophy through Theology to Ethics. The effect of the whole—we hope—will be to impart a tolerance and respect for diverse points of view, to foster an individual synthesis of such diversity, and to prompt our students to become active makers of a culture that is the product of intellectual dialogue and social change.

Part 4: The Debate Over the New Core
The process of building consensus for a new curriculum, particularly one of the size and scope of Mount Saint Mary's, requires diverse individuals to share common values as well as the perception that curricular change is in the institution's (and preferably their own) best interests. The overwhelming endorsement of the new core was the result of lengthy deliberations, but it is also explained by several shared convictions which formed an almost unspoken consensus of faculty opinion throughout the process: first, that a liberal arts education was central to the College's mission both for its intrinsic worth and its value as the best preparation for life and work after college; second, that a revised and strengthened core curriculum would significantly enhance the quality of undergraduate education and intellectual life on campus; third, that the historical perspective was a conceptually sound and workable unifying principle for the core and that, within this perspective, the diverse human experience resulting from race, class, gender, or ethnicity could be effectively explored; fourth, that the new curriculum should emphasize the reading, discussion, and written analysis of primary texts and that the development of students' critical skills was a responsibility shared by faculty

74

throughout the college; fifth, that uniform competency in writing and mathematics should be determined not by a single test but rather a series of exercises.

While little persuasion was needed to elicit faculty support for these general principles, curricular leaders faced the challenge of addressing the major concerns raised by those opposed to or uncommitted to the proposed curriculum: its increased size (from fifty-two to sixty-one credits); its four-year structure and sequencing of courses; its elimination of most distribution requirements in favor of prescribed courses; its emphasis on cross-disciplinary integration; its definition of departmental core offerings as general education courses not introductions to the majors; and its inclusion of requirements in foreign languages and non-Western studies.

For most faculty the proposed core's coherent purpose and design outweighed any potential disadvantages resulting from its size or scope. When some in preprofessional programs worried that the increase in required core courses would impinge on students' majors, colleagues observed that at a liberal arts college the core curriculum should have at least equivalent importance to any departmental program. Those concerned about the apparent inflexibility of such a structured curriculum were reassured that special sequences would be designed for transfer students and that students would have ample opportunity to pursue a second major or other academic interests. Those decrying the relative lack of student choice in many core areas were reminded that their own departmental programs were comprised almost entirely of prescribed requirements.

Some faculty in the social and natural sciences strongly objected to the core model's emphasis on cross-disciplinary integration and on the broad liberal arts goals of core courses. Initially, courses in the social and natural sciences were paired with the sophomore philosophy sequence to offer contrasting methodologies and perspectives; strong opposition to that plan and a lack of consensus concerning a creative alternative resulted in the traditional configuration of science area requirements, with the experimental design retained as a component of the College Honors Program. Agreement was more easily reached concerning the redefinition of core courses once faculty were convinced that disciplinary integrity would be preserved and that departments could count core courses toward their major requirements. Rather than serving narrowly as introductions to particular majors, core courses would be designed primarily to fulfill core goals in the "knowledge area": they would place each discipline in the broader context of the Western, liberal arts tradition and emphasize method principally in the context of acquainting students with different modes of inquiry. The foreign language and non-Western requirements were seriously challenged only by those interested in reducing the total number of courses and by a few who questioned their relative importance. The former was defended easily as an indispensable

75

element of a liberal education in an increasingly pluralistic society and interdependent world; the latter was viewed by most both as a necessary component of a curriculum with a preponderantly Western emphasis and an important opportunity to challenge our students' parochial cultural biases.

To avoid potentially fragmented and divisive debate on each of the proposal's forty-five recommendations, advocates of the new curriculum adopted the deliberate strategy of depicting it as a unified program not the product of disparate elements. Not only was it difficult, if not impossible, to "tinker" with such an integrated curriculum model through minor amendments, but proponents argued successfully that the new core depended for its intellectual integrity on its interrelated sequences. Few doubted the intrinsic merits of the specific course sequences, but considerable debate ensued concerning the guiding principle of the entire curriculum—"the great god of 'integration,'" according to one disgruntled chairman. The new core was integrated in structure and method; it was a four-year program with identifiable sequences of courses, many of which would be taken simultaneously by all students; core courses were to be taught with sufficient consistency of content, rigor, and pedagogy to establish a common educational experience for students. And as curricular leaders frequently observed, beyond building a spirit of intellectual community—among students, among faculty, and among students *and* faculty—the curriculum was intended to provide individual students with a more coherent liberal education. They would be better able to make connections among courses and disciplines; to recognize historical, thematic, and methodological relationships in their cultural studies; and to develop personal values informed by their critical reflection on the Christian humanist heritage and the Catholic intellectual tradition.

A more integrated curriculum depended at a minimum on enhanced communication within departments among faculty teaching sections of the same course. Yet it also required far more frequent and substantive "conversations" across disciplinary boundaries and, in several instances, extensive collaborative planning (freshman-year courses) and even team-teaching (junior-year courses). In endorsing the principle of integration, the faculty determined that minor personal accommodations could be made without compromising disciplinary integrity or unduly sacrificing individual flexibility. New courses needed to be developed; existing ones, redesigned to center on primary texts or to include coverage of the discipline's historical development; teaching styles, modified to elicit students' response to course materials through active class dialogue, stimulating writing assignments, and collaborative projects. Finally, and perhaps most importantly, the Academic Council—not the individual departments—would approve all core courses and share with the Dean the responsibility of overseeing the entire curriculum.

Final Reflections

A carefully articulated planning process—featuring extensive consultation between curricular leaders and academic administrators, department chairs, and a range of colleagues—was essential to the development of the new curriculum. This strategy built broad support and momentum for substantive change and helped foster an atmosphere in which faculty resolved their differences through candid discussion and gained a sense of genuine ownership of the core project. The cooperative spirit which both produced the new curriculum at Mount Saint Mary's and was one of the unintended benefits of its collaborative planning process has characterized the program's implementation. Once the core had been approved by the President and Board of Trustees, the College committed over $50,000 to support faculty responsible for developing the new freshman-year courses. Almost half of the College's faculty contributed to the design of the successful NEH grant proposal, a project now directed by two of the leaders of the curricular reform movement. Subsequently, in many core courses, extensive collaboration among faculty has become the norm. Each year, for example, faculty in the nationally recognized freshman seminar program choose several common texts and assignments to unify the two-dozen sections of this full-year course and employ collaborative grading of major writing assignments to ensure consistent standards of writing proficiency.

Such cooperation cannot be imposed by administrators or even by faculty leaders. It is possible only through individual dedication, shared commitment, and a spirit of intellectual and professional community.

Works Cited

A New Vitality in General Education: Washington, D.C.: Association of American Colleges, 1988.

Cheney, Lynne V. *50 Hours: A Core Curriculum for College Students*. Washington, D.C.: National Endowment for the Humanities, 1989.

Fish, Stanley. Interview. "Canon Building: The Basic Issues," *National Forum*, 69 (Summer 1989), 13–15.

Sidney, Sir Philip. *A Defence of Poetry. Miscellaneous Prose of Sir Philip Sidney*. Ed. Katherine Duncan-Jones and Jon Van Dorsten. Oxford: Clarendon Press, 1973.

Humanities in America: A Report to the President, the Congress, and the American People. Washington, D.C.: National Endowment for the Humanities, 1988.

COMMERCE AMONG THE ARCHIPELAGOS: RHETORIC OF INQUIRY AS A PRACTICE OF COHERENT EDUCATION

John S. Nelson
The University of Iowa

General education: the words are dull, their images diffuse and undirective. But that is apt, because the goals and strategies of college education remain vague and uninspiring. Scattered in our oceans of mediocrity, there rise some atolls of startling imagination and success. Yet they are few, far between, and largely isolated from one another. Worse, intermittent storms and monotonous tides undo even these islands—clogging their harbors, eroding their beaches, swamping their lowlands, battering their foundations. How could we be surprised, then, to learn again that the realities of general education disappoint us all—teachers, students, parents, and citizens alike?

To be sure, some universities speak instead of *liberal education*, an older but more vital and evocative term even today. Many a small college conceives itself as a "liberal arts" institution, and I myself teach in the widely encompassing college of liberal arts sustained by a state university. Still, we fare little better under that rubric, for similar reasons.

The main trouble is that our practices of general education lack good principles. They lack any rationale strong enough to withstand the corrosive forces of our culture. *General education* itself scarcely coheres as a concept. Mostly it is a curricular sell-out to the territorialism and professionalism that characterize post modern multiversities. Never is it a coherent enterprise in its own right. And no longer, at least in my experience, does it provide sound principles of higher education for citizens to make their way responsibly through cultures at once common and uncommon.

We must do better. And we can, by reinventing the specifically republican and rhetorical principles that began American education. The times and challenges have changed. That is how we became confused about educational purposes and practices. New conditions mandate reconceiving our principles. Yet these continuing changes increase our reason to reinvent republican and rhetorical education. For that tradition provides the kinds of principles we need to meet the educational challenges likely to come, as well as those already at hand.

Whatever Happened to Liberal Education?

The erratic jumble of courses that we call "general education" seldom aspires even to the integrity of bricolage. Catalog justifications typically assert, in a ritual sentence or two, that a general education "by itself prepares students for a broad range of occupations." They say that its courses "provide the necessary foundation for the specialized . . . training that . . . professions require." They include the usual laundry list of fields and skills: "To understand our complicated world," students need introductory courses in "the natural and social sciences, the arts and humanities, the languages and cultures of foreign lands," and possibly a physical-education class or two. "To meet the challenges of the future," they conclude, today's students must learn "to think, speak, write, and act with the critical intelligence" imparted by general-education courses.

Requirements for general education, please remember, are almost always an oddly logrolled collection of courses—splattered across the balkanized curricula of the insular departments that dominate "higher" instruction in America. Perhaps the deans and professors who draft such cliches believe deeply in them. Maybe these professionals even think that our colleges and universities practice such phrases to good effect. But I don't, for the most part. Nor do more than a few of my faculty colleagues. Nor, still more to the point, do students and citizens. Nor should you.

Some educators deserving our respect have a way of describing our plight that is at once illuminating and misleading. Unfortunately, they argue, specifically *liberal* education has lapsed into vacuously *general* education. And they are right to insist on a historical separation of liberal from general education. There really was a kind of "liberal education" substantially distinct from what Americans now call "general education." It was an education for life in the metropolis (if not the cosmopolis). It sought to fit Americans for productive contributions to a civil society of marketplaces diverse in almost every way. And in its most political forms, it strove to equip individuals with the critical information and intelligence to keep them independent of social or governmental indoctrination.

Such talk still echoes around some programs of general education. But most lack detailed commitment to the commercializing, nationalizing, and individual-izing values of authentically liberal education. Instead they herd students through huge lecture classes. These teach, by text and example, all the personal advantages of diffuse professionalism. By comparison to the practices (even more than the values) of liberal education, our current systems of general education must look limp and superficial. Yet they also look decently diverse, and they tend to stay safe from wars over master disciplines.

Before we call for a return to genuinely liberal arts, however, let us notice that it was modern liberalism that eventually gave us general education. Even if we find some version of liberal education worthy as an ideal, we ought to worry about why the versions practiced in America have degenerated into general education. If nothing else, such historical developments may give us educational reasons to doubt the desirability of liberal ideals.

In a nutshell, the evolution of America's various strains of liberalism turned nineteenth-century commitments to tolerance, enlightenment, and technical capability into twentieth-century trends of specialization, superficiality, and trained incapacities to communicate. Earlier liberal education promised to integrate students into a common culture, where each person could act independently yet cooperatively to produce a better world. But our later liberalisms have learned to distrust that ambition as covertly totalitarian. Thus it threatens to integrate students into the common beliefs that define a mass society, and fit them for the common behaviors that feed a spreading bureaucracy. Worse, these later liberalisms come to pursue a common culture in ways that are openly reductive. The resources for independence are the first to go, in the name of greater efficiency in instruction.

Thus we might conclude that recent debates over general education and required curricula lack a theory. In particular, we might think, they lack a theory of liberal education adequate to life and learning late in the twentieth century— let alone in the twenty-first. We fail to discover principles of liberal education in haphazard course lists. We fail to detect liberal learning and debate in insular disciplines. We fail to discern canons of crucial texts persuasive to diverse teachers or attractive to numerous students. And we fail to locate essential elements of cultural literacy in fundamental facts, necessary skills, recurrent issues, prominent positions, popular ideologies, or basic requirements of justification. Even in keeping the company of good books, one of my favorites among the recent calls to better curricula, we fail to cultivate the specifically political intelligence and ethics needed for coming to coherent terms with the diverse disciplines, practices, and principles that configure our lives.[1]

In one way or another, these endeavors incline to collapse from their own cross-purposes and practical contradictions. Or so I would argue, if this were a different occasion, better suited to extended attention to what has gone wrong and why. Of course, there is no reason for you to accept my critical claims until you face good arguments for them. But that matters little for the moment, because my mission now is not to confront you with such criticisms—let alone to defend them.

What Can—and Can't—We Learn from the Critics?

Instead I want to write mostly in a positive vein—to evoke an alternative that arises from experiments in antiquity, Iowa, and elsewhere. By now, though, you are bound to be puzzled about my title; so let me begin by saying a few words about it. Perhaps you recognize already that "Commerce among the Archipelagos" refers to stimulating intellectual trade among the islands of education that we now term "academic disciplines." But what about the subtitle ("Rhetoric of Inquiry as a Practice of Coherent Education")? Whoever typed it onto a program when I first began to formulate these remarks made an interesting mistake, reporting the subtitle to be "Rhetoric of Inquiry as a Practice of Coheren*ce* Education"—rather than "Coheren*t* Education." In reflecting on this mistake, I have since decided that what I should do is explain how the two different claims relate to one another, and how *both* are correct titles for my argument. To do so, though, I need to say a few more words about what is missing from recent practices of liberal education and how we hurt ourselves by proceeding without a plausible theory of general education.

Few educational critics offer a decent account of why we need liberal education now. On this subject, their words are sometimes seething, sometimes soothing, but seldom more than superficial. The easy example, and in some ways the most powerful, is the claim by many a university president that, *of course we need liberal education, because our students are going to change careers several times during their lives.* Neither many presidents nor their students bother to think through what the link might be. It is not as obvious as they assume. Nor do its implications point in the directions presumed by most general-education programs.

Presumably the link to career changes is that general education should equip students to learn on their own a host of new and diverse things. Thus general education must enable students to go beyond the established methods, particular facts, or current theories taught in college. That way, graduates can learn throughout later life what they need to succeed at new careers and other challenges, many unforeseeable today. But how does general education do this? Merely by exposing students to introductory courses in several fields? Also by developing minimum skills of calculation and communication? Or perhaps by teaching skills of criticism and independent thinking? If so, then why do the chief executive officers of businesses nationwide insist that college graduates come to new firms ill-equipped to analyze and communicate and learn effectively? And even if general education were to excel in these particular terms, we would still have to wonder how it could cultivate in students the ability to navigate well among the many shoals and eddies involved in moving among diverse kinds of careers.

Our educational failure is to confront the condition of living among archipelagos. Starkly put, we fail to come to terms with our own *pluralism*. Intellectually, culturally, politically, *we are many* as much or more than we are one. Rather than address our condition, however, educators who worry about the admitted troubles of pluralism try simply to wish it away. They condemn it as weakness of cultural will or as intellectual incoherence. They divert worry to various disasters said to follow from an alleged incompatability of pluralism with the certified foundations of fact or method presumed necessary for independent, critical thinking.[2] Yet as they fret over the dangers of pluralism, they fail to figure out what kinds of critical thinking we need in order to navigate our pluralistic world: a world strikingly diverse—a world of archipelagos.

81

This is the main thing we can learn from recent critics of general education, even when we have to learn it from their failures. Their common lesson is that we must face up to our many specializations and pluralisms, not wish them away.[3] And if we learn this indirectly, though tracing various shortcomings of the criticisms back to their shared source, it remains a valuable lesson. It allows us to see how recent debates about curriculum tend to dress special-interest pleading in confused abstractions about serving "the public interest." Thus the recent debates become stupidly partisan: lacking coherent, encompassing principles for assessing educational needs and resources, the attempt to address them degenerates into warring currricular programs that try to elevate particular insights into imperial principles. Facing up to our intellectual, cultural, political, and other pluralisms is a lesson in humility and tolerance than can help us avoid the vehemence of such off-center debates, which have become a trouble in their own right.

Our times combine civilizational pluralisms with academic specialization and mass education. So far, we have turned this situation into college recipes for the bland dishes and fragmented diets of cafeteria curricula. Too few university professors think much—let alone well—about the challenges of general education under these conditions. Therefore a second valuable lesson from the critics is the urgency of attending thoughtfully to general education. For the most part, of course, university professors have been content to assume that there is no important problem in principle: a smorgasbord is fine, even though the students have to integrate issues and possibilities far beyond the collective ken of their professors. But it is not.

Few existing programs of general education have minimally coherent rationales. And after decades of educational reform, it cannot be surprising to find that the major alternatives remain long on eloquent criticisms but short on workable practices. The truly astonishing thing is that so few of the most cogent critics advance adequate principles to defend their proposals. Some serve a broth of ancient principles for education that simmer in juices of personal prejudice against popular cultures, especially those of younger generations. In these respects, there is much to be said for Allan Bloom's recent indictment of American education;[4] yet it passes off onto the theory of liberal education a number of Bloom's political worries about the cultural fallout of the 1960s in this country. As Bloom is right to recognize, a prominent effect of that period in American history has been to generate a host of cultural and intellectual pluralisms that confound American culture and education still. But we cannot address these adequately by confining ourselves—as does Bloom—to pointing out a few of their problems. Even if we were to agree with Bloom about the problems, we could not merely gesture in their directions, pronounce a plague on all their houses, and then expect their precipitating situations to go away. Public education must face our full diversity and deal with it constructively, not denounce it in principle and then pretend to put it back into the bottle.

Other critics—such as E. D. Hirsch[5]—boil a mixture of high-culture, scientific, and otherwise miscellaneous nuggets of demographic, technocratic, or other putative facts into a watery stew of educational staples. Unfortunately most of the mixtures couldn't even nourish for long the contestants on tv quiz shows. To beef up these "curricula," some critics try to turn them into devices for avoiding philosophical phantoms of nihilism and relativism. These get justified, at least in my hearing, by deploring the occasional student declaration that anybody's values are as good as anybody else's. Yet this is hardly to say that relativism and nihilism are becoming practical dangers within our classrooms. Nor is it to say that the recommended responses can become—or much inform—helpful classroom programs, let alone that they can instruct practical life possibilities and courses of action. Instead such discourse becomes only another way to avoid providing an adequate account of what a good general education must be now, for us late- or post-moderns. None of these kinds of criticisms imply a decent account of what a good liberal education must do these days in order to have much chance of success.

Please don't misunderstand me. I do not say such things because I think that E. D. Hirsch, Allan Bloom, or their colleagues are all wrong. Rather to the contrary, I am dismayed at the extent to which they do not and apparently cannot defend the best aspects of their own views. My argument is that that they cannot specify and defend good courses of public education precisely because they tend to exclude—or at least to forget—rhetoric.

A few of these critics omit or overlook rhetoric as a classical and long-standing tradition of education, even though this contradicts their commitment to a pedagogy informed by classical virtues and ideals. But what is worse—from my standpoints in the humanities and social sciences—is that most of these critics would denigrate or even exclude rhetoric in its more recent forms. They downplay rhetoric as instruction in composition and speech; in fact, the National Endowment for the Humanities' recent model curriculum for *Fifty Hours* of general education does not even mention it. They also condemn current rhetorics as practices of textual interpretation—seeming to fear that they must ignore classic texts, teach radical politics, and distract from the true substance of humanities and hard sciences alike. Finally, they distrust rhetoric as the systematic study of strategy, communication, and audience that we more readily recognize these days under the label of "the social sciences." After all, are the social sciences not the sworn foes and would-be supplanters of humanistic disciplines of inquiry?

They are not; nor are the other worries generally justified.[6] On the contrary, good public education begins by recognizing rhetoric to be among the earliest of the humanities and perhaps the first of the social sciences. Rhetoric was created some twenty-five hundred years ago by the Sophists, specifically to be the first self-conscious practice and systematic study of politics.[7] Thus it offered the first intertwined theory and practice of specifically public education. As a continuing tradition and evolving discipline, moreover, rhetoric still encompasses the concerns which the social sciences properly share with the humanities.

Accordingly my argument is that we now need an updated rhetorical tradition. We need constructive ways to distinguish good rhetoric from bad. And we need insightful ways to talk in detail about the challenges of communication and action in a world of archipelagos.

What Does It Mean to Pursue Public Education?

To have a chance of success at general education, therefore, we have to ask a further question: success at what? On this, fortunately, the debaters agree—at least in general terms. Yet unfortunately they miss the main implications of their own goals. A truly general, fully liberal education is a course of academic study and personal development that enables its graduates to participate wisely, skillfully, and responsibly in a wide range of adult activities—especially activities pertinent to public affairs. Given this agreement to feature the skills and concerns of *public* life, in a sense derived directly from the republicanism of Rome and the Renaissance, I am continually surprised that debates over general and liberal education learn so little from the practices and principles of *republicanism*. In particular, they learn little about what Hannah Arendt, John Dewey, and other recent theorists of politics have identified as the crucial features of what we typically call the public arena, the public thing, that is, the *res publica*.

Here we might do well to summarize Arendt's republicanism in terms she identified as "the human condition."[8] She wrote thus in an attempt to skirt the old debate about "human nature" versus "human nurture." To be sure, there are some general things to say about human capabilities and limits. But Arendt cautioned that human learning must make us careful about what we conceive the limits to be and how we conceive them to function.

Arendt regarded the proper conditions of humanity as perhaps eight in number, though they are highly interconnected and she cared more to relate than to separate them. They are easiest to explain in two sets of four conditions. The first grouping includes natality, plurality, equality, and mortality; and the second four are common sense, glory, speech, and action.

Natality is the human condition that we are all born individually into the world. By virtue of that, however, we have a capacity to surprise—a capacity growing out of the mysterious and deep resource of individuals to do something different. In a word, *natality* means that we as individuals are—or at least can be— *free*. The second condition is *plurality*: we humans are different as individuals. Though it might be misleading in other contexts, here we may take this as tantamount to a celebration of the modern self as a unique actor in human history.

84

In terms of this or any other cultural tradition, Arendt argued that there is a fundamental need to recognize that we are not all one and the same person. The third condition is a kind of *equality*: each human individual enjoys the crucial standing of being a "human." Human equality is a challenge and entitlement to investigate its own meaning. It is not a confident declaration that we always already know its significance; nor is it a mere claim that we are all in the human condition (somehow) together and (somehow) on the same footing. And the fourth condition is that we humans can recognize that we are all mortal. Therefore the condition of *mortality* means not only that our deaths are as inevitable as some taxes; it also means that we have strong reason to share some concerns in structuring our lives to move from the condition of natality to that of mortality, always through plurality and equality.

Arendt argued that participation in public spaces is the best practical fulfillmment of what it means to be genuinely human. Thus she identified the first four conditions because she considered them crucial to understanding participation in public arenas. And their ties to public participation become evident through the other four aspects of the human condition. The fifth condition of humanity is a *common sense* of shared reality: you do not have a world, said Arendt, unless you are in a public. A public is a distinctive texture of stories and speeches and decisions and deeds that bind us together into a real world, where we can act. The sixth condition is the *glory* of high ambitions and great accomplishments, as acknowledged by other humans participating in the same public spaces. Even when individual humans do not themselves achieve or aspire to such glory, they help to make it possible by appreciating and remembering greatness (and perhaps other virtues) in word and deed. Therefore the seventh condition of humanity is our sharing of realities and possibilities through *speech*—the ways we communicate and therefore exist in communities. Speech details our acts and situations—so that they can take specific, constructive shape in the world and so that we can evaluate them, ethically and otherwise. Thus speech enables us to make decisions about what is good and what is bad; it lets us judge events, correcting them in later deeds and connecting them into patterns capable of glory. The last condition of humanity, then, is the *action* enabled by our shared freedom. When we act in a public space, other people who also can act—and who thus can understand the difficulties, complications, and challenges of action—witness what we do. These other potential actors tell stories about our words and deeds, remember them, and judge them; otherwise our putative action would be mere activity and would go largely for nought. Surely we would lack the kinds of conditions relevant to a liberal education.

As many westerners since Aristotle have maintained, these sorts of features explain why *politics as participation in public affairs* is at once the greatest challenge and the permeating, culminating activity of human life and learning at its best. It is not particularly surprising or persuasive that I, as a political theorist, would be attracted to such an argument. For it could be read as one more endorsement of politics as "the master discipline." Yet many another activity can serve us in related ways to explain the need and advantage of "public education." What I recommend for politics is what I would have us do with many of these other activities. Therefore the proposal is to regard politics as *one* of a large set of potentially but partially architectonic approaches to understanding and practicing human affairs.

To feature education for public life in the twenty-first century need not be "architectonic" at all in the old, singular, arrogant, and exhaustive sense. Instead the specifically political contributions to current education in public knowledge and skills should be recognized as one among several needed ways to network our archipelagos of living and learning. This is because our societies now have many publics, not just the one encompassing arena of government earlier envisioned by the likes of Aristotle, Arendt, and Dewey.[9] The challenge is to take advantage of the facility of political learning for linking disparate communities into networks—to work with all our islands of specialization, to help each use its distinctive resources to cultivate communication, trade, and decision with the others. Such politics becomes one of the archipelagos devoted to exploring how all the islands can relate one to another. Rhetorics readily form another networking isle. And pursued with a keen public, rhetorical sensibility, so also can our economics and psychologies and histories and other fields serve public education in this way.[10]

Or, if you accept my characterization of rhetoric as another name for a good (if old) kind of political science (in need of updating), we can make the same point in terms of the sort of politics most self-conscious about its rhetoricity. This is the republican politics (with a lower-case *r*) promoted by the American founders. As Arendt herself argued, the public character of politics makes *speech* the preeminent aspect of full humanity. This is an argument that politics and rhetoric are one, in an important way, and it is a case for pursuing specifically *public* education. As the Romans and the Renaissance Humanists knew in similar terms, adequately strategic studies of speech are the same as decently systematic studies of politics—and both are called rhetoric. The republican argument, therefore, is that most recent arguments about curricular requirements lack a proper appreciation of the roles of rhetoric in inquiry and instruction.

Arendt, Dewey, and others have made helpful inquiries into the crucial features of the public spaces still pertinent to our times. Yet little of this work directly encourages much hope that we can regenerate the classic public or that its brand of education can equip us to live well in a world of archipelagos. In that connection, though, we need to overcome one of the fundamental biases evident in Arendt, Dewey, and many another theorist of public participation. Borrowing

86

a premise from ancient times, such theorists write in terms of *the public*—in the singular. Then they recognize that the diversification of our lives has become thorough and long-standing. Consequently they lament that any remnant of a univocal and all-encompassing public is collapsing into smaller, fragmented arenas. And they bemoan that even these partial publics are washing away under tides of mass society that transform our interactions into rituals of impersonality and mediocrity. Along with many other students of twentieth-century society, these theorists trace how the social, procedural, and technocratic commitments connected with our sciences, bureaucracies, and professions divide "the public" to the point of utter corruption—or dissolve it to the point of complete disappearance. Does this mean that distinctively public education has become outmoded or impossible? It is depressing to acknowledge that Dewey could hold out more hope early in the century than Arendt toward its end. Along with criticisms from Bloom, Booth, and Hirsch, Arendt's prose paints a bleak picture of our prospects for reviving either public politics or public education.[11]

Are republican principles of education relevant to societies that lack a singular public? Can these principles cope with our world of archipelagos? I think so—because the archipelagos are themselves special kinds of publics, because ample commerce can make them better as publics, and because an updated republican and rhetorical education can enable us to accomplish the needed commerce.

Updated republican principles can appreciate that we have been proliferating vital and diverse publics, in the plural, even as we have been dethroning "the public" in the singular. Our archipelagos are manifold, disseminated arenas for people to participate in managing their own lives in concert and effecting their own priorities in practice. As specialized fields of endeavor, they remain too limited to address concerns of "the commonwealth," the more economic version of the classical "public." But that is why commerce among the archipelagos is so crucial: it weaves together our separate spaces of mutual endeavor, so that the network of archipelagos can encompass the overarching issues of the community as a whole.

To be sure, this changes somewhat the classical conception and practice of a singular public. Yet it enables us to achieve a far more hopeful, realistic, and productive politics than defenders of the classical public have been able to project for our times. When we figure out how to communicate within these initially partial publics, and especially how to communicate among them, then we have a real chance to make headway with the problems of general education. Both are tasks of rhetoric, practiced as an updated edition of the classical discipline of political education—because both face our conditions of pluralism by pursuing better, more responsible action by individual human beings in their manifold communities.

How Can the Trivium Keep from Becoming Trivial?

What scholars and students share across their diverse fields is argument, persuasion, expression—in a word, communication. The same goes for what people share across their distinct specialties and other practices of living late in the twentieth century. Yet the study and practice of communication is rhetoric, arguably the most ancient among the scholarly disciplines. Rhetoric concerns who says what to whom, when, where, why—and especially how. Politically it considers who speaks, who listens, and who not. Ethically it explores how intentions or situations matter and how not. Aesthetically it examines what form is content and what not, when substance is style and when not, where medium is message and where not. And epistemically it explains which claims are persuasive, which not, why—and how we might make them better.

Perhaps the most promising attempts to launch plausible theories of liberal education are the various efforts to refit the classical principles of the trivium and quadrivium, suiting them to the new rigors of sailing our late modern seas of research and instruction. At least these reconstruction vessels typically escape their home harbors intact. Yet they still tend to run aground on the manifold reefs and shoals of our diverse archipelagos of learning: the quarrels among fields of inquiry confident of their special virtues and ignorant of their actual limits, competitions, and complements.

Turned on inquiry, rhetoric becomes crucial for connecting the archipelagos of learning which characterize universities late in the twentieth century. Under many names, rhetoric of inquiry has grown in the last decade toward the kinds of understandings needed for improving projects throughout the academy. To replace a priori postulation of a singular method for science, rhetoric of inquiry offers epistemic advice at once practical and critical, immanent and comparative, unified and differentiated. It is unified in saying that there is one thing that we all have in common: the concern with argumentation or persuasion. But that concern differs importantly from one archipelago to the next. Thus we should also recognize that rhetoric of inquiry is comparative: that it encourages commerce across our archipelagos. Rhetoric of inquiry investigates how all fields rely on rhetoric—yet each field configures differently its topics, tropes, stories, evidence, audiences, authorities, and other elements of rhetoric.

In a time of fragmenting fields, furthermore, rhetoric of inquiry provides the principles and devices required for coherent education. It appreciates that specializations enhance teaching and research only when they lead to active trade among diverse fields. It helps students and faculty alike to cross divides, renegotiating boundaries among otherwise insular disciplines. And it encourages commerce among them by inventing ways for each to learn from the others.

Another implication of rhetoric as a discipline at once classical and updated is that instruction in rhetoric is not mainly a training in the use of particular tools or instruments of persuasion. A horrendous feature of many required courses in English composition is a focus on writing skills assumed to have little or no epistemic substance in their own right. Even where rhetoric instructors don't treat their work this way, their colleagues in other disciplines do, and therefore so do most of their students. Reducing rhetoric to a set of skills and tools is tantamount to dismissing rhetoric as mere ornamentation or technique: sheer form and not an ounce of real content. As Plato demonstrated, moreover, this is the first step toward condemning rhetoric as immoral pandering to the most debased tastes of "the public," with the teacher of rhetoric the worst kind of "gun for hire" to coerce and otherwise manipulate "the masses."

In featuring persuasion rather than manipulation, rhetoric rightly regards itself as substantive inquiry, not technical instruction alone. It complements the means/ends reasoning of modern expertise with the performative judging prized in antiquity and needed just as much today. Thus rhetoric of inquiry appreciates how the speaking of politics, the writing of science, and the technical pursuit of any practice must form an integral aspect of its substance and results. To take a rhetorical standpoint is to understand the impossibility of any pure method that would come entirely before the substance starts, directing it neutrally from afar. And a rhetorical standpoint knows also the impossibility of any undistorted communication that would arise only after the discovery is done, conveying noiselessly a message formed fully apart from its transmission. The standpoint of rhetoric appreciates how form is content and vice versa, how medium and message are one, how means and ends lose their separation in performance. Bringing such a rhetorical standpoint to all our archipelagos is the practical, educational mission for rhetoric of inquiry.

How Can the Quadrivium Encompass the Multiversity?

In terms of college curricula, there are at least seven key lessons of substance for us to learn from taking a rhetorical standpoint. One way to summarize them is to show how rhetoric of inquiry updates the trivium—improving our practical sense of the relationships among grammar, logic, and rhetoric. I have taken that road elsewhere; but it might seem a higher, drier, longer way around.[12] Let us instead walk a lower and less spectacular route, but one more direct and developed, explaining how rhetoric of inquiry can help the ancient quadrivium to encompass the post-modern multiversity.

1. Disciplinary Practices

The first substantive teaching from rhetoric is the *coherence* lesson. We need to understand our archipelagos, fields, disciplines, activities, and the like in cultural, as well as academic, terms. We need to understand them as "practices," in something like Alasdair MacIntyre's sense.[13] There we have a coherent set of rules which define internal goods, but those internal goods cannot stand defined fully and completely within the practice alone—as though only economists could evaluate adequately the work of economics. Only in exchange among practices can they be evaluated adequately, for they require serious external scrutiny— effective communication across the archipelagos.[14]

Political scientists have some useful things to say about economics, about what economists are not doing very well. Likewise economists have useful things to say about what political scientists aren't doing very well, could improve, and how. Both have interesting and sometimes valid things to say about what English professors are doing well and not, and why. And vice versa. No more than disciplines can stand alone, do practices endure in isolation from other practices. To understand, criticize, and improve themselves, all practices need commerce with others. Thus the lesson of practices just *is* the lesson of coherence. A curriculum that pursues no connections and comparisons among fields is a balkanized and barren land intellectually.

Moreover the lesson of practices is the lesson of coherence*s*. One part of this lesson is that specializations can achieve distinctive understandings and values. Fields cohere to achieve effective depth, practical meaning, and personal usefulness. A smattering of foreign languages, a dollop of mathematics, a pinch of art, a part of physics, a dash of history, and small amounts of other disconnected ingredients are a recipe for nothing much. Another part of the lesson is that *coherence* is intrinsically a plural noun. Without putting diverse fields into constructive conversation, no discipline advances very far.

The lesson of coherence is a big part of what rhetoric of inquiry can tell us. There is no simple, syllogistical formula that makes all coherence into avoiding the fallacies identified by logicians and statisticians. As rhetoricians have taught, we deal in a world of contraries, far more than a world of contradictories. Contradictions make a practical mess of most of our situations. Black versus non-black is less relevant than black versus white versus gray versus various colors. Likewise our world of archipelagos is not much science versus non-science, as positivists once imagined. Instead it is logic versus rhetoric versus psychology versus history and so forth. Rhetoric shows how a coherent curriculum is a coherence curriculum. Therefore rhetoric of inquiry explores how our disciplines and practices do in fact cohere, converse, and not. Thus public education needs to explore the character of our archipelagos, enabling each of us to live on some of them and move among all of them ever better than before.

2. Intellectual Trade

The second substantive lesson from rhetoric is that a world of archipelagos serves us well only when we conduct ample commerce among them. For specializations to be productive, they must *trade*. This turn toward economic imagery comes courtesy of my colleague and collaborator, Donald McCloskey.[15] We would do well in addition to regard the "trade" rhetorically as "communication," epistemically as "learning," culturally as "interaction," even politically as "negotiation." In any of these languages, the lesson for teachers and researchers is largely the same: if academic specialization is to be productive and defensible, we cannot let each little archipelago go off by itself. That is what we do in the post-modern multiversity when we encourage each to proclaim itself to be its own architectonic science of nearly everything, but then we abandon each to make out as best it can for purposes of consultation. Nor can we let each island define its limited special place in the world, where that special contribution is to be made by keeping the home place pure, unsullied by foreign principles or interests.

We have to wonder as well how much better it can be when we abandon our students to figure out ways to navigate from one island kingdom to another? That has become the philosophy-in-practice of most general education. We know that few students even try, and fewer still succeed. Can we be surprised, when we reward their teachers for staying at home to cultivate only one kind of garden?

We know this best at the level of the curriculum, but it is just as true at the level of research. We do not get good inquiry from economists when they hold themselves aloof from political science and psychology and history and geography and comparative literature.[16] The same holds every other way around. If we are going to solve our main problems of teaching, we might as well at the same time figure out somewhat better things to teach—under the heading of economics or English. Accordingly the second substantive lesson from rhetoric is that these things are related, and we will learn how to improve our curricula and our research when we practice the importance of intellectual trade.

3. Academic Persuasions

The third substantive lesson from rhetoric is that we must focus on *persuasion, reasoning, and argument* in moving among our archipelagos. That, after all, is what these island specialties are: distinctive persuasions. "Your language and examples feature economics, Professor Nelson, so are you of the economic persuasion?" "No, I am more of the political persuasion, thank you, but I enjoy teasing my friends of the other persuasion—and I know that Americans are more comfortable with economic words and images when the time comes to get practical."

This third lesson from rhetoric implies that we must problematize our diverse practices of persuasion, argument, reason. This is to say that we must expressly pluralize them, and recognize how they have been pluralized already. This puts a premium on reflexivity. To pluralize official rationality is to explore many of our

91

actual rationalities; it is to shift from philosophical logic to practical rhetorics. It is to cultivate in teachers and students one of the skills-and-goals dearest to advocates of liberal education: better self-awareness and greater self-criticality.

4. Rhetorical Analysis

A fourth substantive lesson from rhetoric focuses on the typical, even characteristic categories of rhetorical analysis: tropes, topics, ethos, mythos, etc. A general statement of this lesson might be that rhetoric offers many useful ways to carry out the educational project of greater awareness, criticality, and improvement in our work. Focusing on the classical concerns and devices of rhetoric is a good starting point for almost every discipline in the post-modern multiversity. We do not, for instance, know or teach nearly enough about tropes. Thus we do not appreciate how psychologies are held together by distinctive sets of tropes, just as the new criticism and the new historicism in literary studies cohere through other families of tropes.[17]

Here I mean *tropes* not merely in the paleo-Aristotelian sense of poetics, where there are figures only of speech. Instead I have in mind the updated, neo-Aristotelian sense that recognizes *tropes of argument and consciousness*. This holds because rhetoric is not merely elliptical argument or its study, as Aristotle defined *rhetoric*. All arguments must be elliptical, we might say: since we are not gods, we can never give an exhaustive articulation of any argument. This means that we must argue as we must live—from archipelagos—and therefore that we need all the navigation, trade, communication, and commerce we can get among them.

To say that there are no arguments without ellipsis is also to say that the notion of elliptical argument—Aristotle's notion of rhetoric—is odd, misleading, and unhelpful in crucial ways. In Aristotelian traditions and especially in modern philosophies, the connection between completeness of argument and literality of meaning is strong. Yet the human impossibility of complete argument undermines the Aristotelian and particularly the modern opposition between literality and figurality. That is why I would argue that all argument is tropal. But if all argument is tropal, then we must focus on how the different tropes work. In other words, we must attend to their logics, as we might call them, because we will never get to something more basic than tropes.[18]

Focusing on topics—which was more prominently and incontestably Aristotle's approach, to the extent that he tried to deal with different areas of focus or specialization—is helpful as well.[19] And we should let this lead us into creative use of the rhetorical concerns of *ethos* and *mythos*. For the classical rhetorician, ethos is one's standing as a speaker in or before a community: the speaker's credibility with the audience, we might say, in abbreviated terms. But in a broader sense, it is all of *ethics*. Thus the modern sense of *ethos* as inspiriting atmosphere points to the aesthetics, the style of speech and action that we know to make important differences in our lives, even when our modern languages do not easily let us say how.[20] So we talk about *esprit de corps* as crucial to whether a teaching program succeeds or not, but then we forget about it when it comes to rewarding the more easily measurable research business of the post-modern multiversity. So that leads into *mythos*: understanding how we bind together all the tropes, topics, and the like into a set of *stories*, specifically. Alasdair MacIntyre and others have been very much right, I think, to argue that we must focus more on the narratives that we tell to keep our communities together.[21]

5. Interested Audiences

An additional substantive lesson from rhetoric is to focus on *audiences*. This is where to start educationally, and where to go from there. If nothing else, rhetoric says to begin with the students rather than the subject matter. As an educational theory for commerce among the archipelagos, rhetoric of inquiry gives the lie to the academy's standard assumption that a discipline's objectivated knowledge can tell a teacher what the students need to know and how they can come to learn it. Through rhetoric's traditional sense of the dynamics of desire and attention that make and unmake audiences, rhetoric of inquiry can yield a far more effective pedagogy than general-education courses have developed to date.

Furthermore, the rhetorical emphasis on audience turns out to help us attend to the "interests" of students and scholars alike—though in Hannah Arendt's sense, rather than the usual meaning. We Americans typically speak and hear the term only as commercial or even crass "interest." Then everybody is just grinding axes of "self-interest," and there can be no aspiration to any sort of selfless or caring action—short of irrational behavior or the peculiar kind of "altruism" that stems from a self somehow possessed by a preference for the welfare of another. The rhetorical concern with audience is often heard the same way. The rhetorician sells out as a hired gun: tell me your interests and I as expert rhetorician will tell you how to manipulate others to support them. But that is not the classical, rhetorical, *ethical* concern with audience. It starts instead with coordinating the people and worlds needed to comprise an audience, respecting them as they are as well as how they might become. Thus rhetoric attends to *inter-est* as what *is-among* us to share.

And this merges into a concern for motivating students to learn. Over the years, I have heard many a professor say in exasperation that it is the job of students to motivate themselves to find a subject significant; the teacher's job is not to make the material inter-esting but to make it intelligible, useful, and well-ordered. Teachers are not entertainers, these professors insist. And they are right to suggest that teachers should not pander to their student audiences, replacing a course on the structure and function of the presidency with one of jokes about presidents. But they are wrong to shun the responsibility of showing how the subject is significant and exciting. Why expect the audience to listen well to a material that they have little reason to understand as important and pertinent to them. Neglecting to interest the audience is usually disastrous, especially for public education, and teaching informed by rhetoric knows better.

6. Creative Orality

The sixth lesson relates to orality, aurality, memory, and creativity. It borrows in a way from the work by E. D. Hirsch to notice that creativity depends on memory for substance and inspiration. But then it learns further from rhetoric that such creative memory stems especially from conversation, oratory, and other kinds of orality, practiced as extemporaneous speaking and spontaneous listening.

Hirsch is right to insist that we attend more vigorously to our cognitive wherewithal for thinking. As Hirsch understands, the need is not to memorize facts or cultural lore. Instead, as rhetoricians know, it is to cultivate the kinds of speaking and listening—as well as reading and watching—featured by public spaces of appearance. Such publics just are textures of publicly supported memories. A great loss of twentieth-century civilization has been the culture of memorization for oral performance that used to be nurtured in primary and secondary education in America. College students now lack the little vignettes of poetry, drama, myth, and aphorism which school no longer gives them reasons or occasions to acquire but which college professors can still appreciate as the mental material for independent, creative thought. In conversation (or writing), crucial insights rise to the tongue courtesy of some little phrase memorized long ago. Such phrases are contents needed for skillful, critical, creative thinking. They are the stuff of which our most apt and surprising mental connections are made.[22]

Accordingly there is a good case for parts of the Hirsch approach, though it is not exactly the case he makes. No one can provide a simple inventory of sayings or data to teach as an end in themselves. There is no small set of facts and phrases, no crucial apparatus of culture to be read and then recognized on some test. To think creatively, educated people need the kinds of oral and aural memories that spring to our use in practical situations of everyday and professional life. Producing, defending, and developing this kind of position pivots on the sorts of training pursued precisely for public speaking.

This makes the college reduction of rhetoric to writing skills an especially unfortunate trend. The sad fact is that few college teachers in any discipline attend directly and critically to student speaking. Occasionally professors grade students for "discussion," but do even those students receive detailed instruction in how to discuss or speak better? With such a neglect of orality is it any wonder that holders of American PhDs have too little sense of how to address a classroom, where the activity remains largely oral? Orality and aurality remain crucial in our lives, and higher education has responsibilities for appreciating and improving our speaking and our listening.

7. Critical Communicating

Accordingly the last of these substantive lessons from rhetoric involves writing, reading, speaking, listening, computing, and criticizing—the usual litany of "skills" needed for effective, independent action in current societies. If any requirements should be central to college curricula, these rhetorical activities are the ones. And rhetoric of inquiry explains how they are equally central to the skills and findings we cultivate as professional researchers. As we know all too well, however, many a general education fails to instruct students at all decently in these crucial "skills" of communication.

For a variety of rhetorical reasons, we might do better than to call these "skills." The liberal pragmatism of that word is apt enough for republican and rhetorical education, but the instrumentalism is not. Thus Arendt's account of publics emphasizes how they cannot be comprehended or practiced well in terms of ends and means. Together these "skills" comprise a craft; yet a craft blends skill, style, and substance indistinguishably. Perhaps we should call them "talents." The Biblical parable suggests that talents are not natural endowments, though they might sometimes stem from gifts, but are to be developed through personal initiative and industry. And rhetoric is the craft of developing them. As the craft of speech, writing, reading, criticism, and invention, rhetoric is the key to achieving commerce among our scattered academic worlds. In these ways, rhetoric offers the material and the modality needed for better commerce among our intellectual and educational archipelagos.

How to Practice Republican, Rhetorical Education

At this level, we have reason to be appalled that rhetoric is missing from a largely admirable curriculum of *Fifty Hours* proposed by the NEH. Neither in its model curriculum nor in its grant guidelines does the NEH say anything specific about rhetoric as composition and speech. Nor does it include any requirement to cultivate talents for the kinds of performance in speech and writing long considered crucial to the humanities. Nor does it promote the rhetorical resources needed for endeavors in most other domains. In no direct way does the NEH curriculum for general education acknowledge a need for rhetoric as the comparative study of argument across the curriculum.

It is easy to imagine how this might happen, because we are not used to featuring the role of rhetoric in communication, let alone in inquiry. Where can we find recent experience in republican, rhetorical education for college students? If we think of this as practicing general education in a specifically rhetorical way, then a number of experiments from my home institution become available as beginning answers. The University of Iowa has an amazing array of professors who pursue rhetoric of inquiry in separate courses for students beginning and advanced. Moreover it is starting to invent programmatic curricula for making them more coherent.

Iowa now offers several introductory courses which have been restructured on rhetorical terms. This happens because the individual professors associated with the Project on Rhetoric of Inquiry (POROI) are doing this in concert with their research. Thus they offer some introductions to Western Civilization in rhetorized terms, they survey American politics and political theory as rhetorical studies, they introduce micro- and macro-economics as kinds of conversation about economies, and the like. So far, at least, these courses have excelled in effectiveness and popularity. Students particularly appreciate rhetoric of inquiry as a focus on the style and substance of arguments in a field, for it draws them into the ongoing contests of ideas and images.

Many of these courses feature distinctive exercises that reach well beyond the usual assignments for reading, research, and writing. In my case, these begin with intense scrutiny of written argumentation. But they also involve assigning projects of rhetorical analysis, after the class talks in detail about political or scientific rhetoric. Students diagram arguments for trajectories of ethos, logos, pathos, and mythos. They trace the dynamics of argument implicit in using aggregate data, survey research, depth interviews, and participant observation. They write alternate histories in a science-fiction mode, and they formulate new myths in a fantasy mode. They plan campaigns of political advertising, they extrapolate cultures from imaginary characters or vice versa, and they sketch films for addressing various political problems or audiences. Such exercises encompass a variety of simulations: we often forget how the role-playing and drama of most simulations feature specifically rhetorical dynamics of acting and learning. To improve the spoken word, these classes also perform oral exercises in class, and they add oral examinations to their written tests. All these rhetorical activities involve students in communicating with one another and in investigating how we communities are dynamics of communication.

A friend down the road from Drake University, Robert Hariman, suggests that we need "copious minds." As he explains, this means that we need to focus on activities and abilities of communication. But it also means that we must put our educational theories and practices into mutual communication, making them cohere as only rhetoric of inquiry can. This is the theory-in-practice point, the praxis directive, dear to the hearts of Aristotelians and Marxians alike. In post-modern times, though, we lack confident recourse to the simplistic senses of contradiction long dominant in western treatments of practical theory. Consequently we need rhetoric of inquiry to explore the many modes of tension and coherence crucial for keeping our archipelagos distinct, intact, and in communication. In various kinds of courses, we Iowans are deploying rhetoric's resources of argument and persuasion to explore the dimensions and dynamics of coherence in our world of disciplines.

These are good starting points, but we need more. Another pioneered by POROI cultivates the kinds of coherence that arise from faculty members arguing constructively with one another in class. New courses at Iowa feature Rhetoric and Debate by replacing lectures with debates between professors and discussions with several kinds of debates among students. This helps immensely to educate students in "methods of inquiry," without reducing strategies of study to rote procedures.

Still another set of innovations cluster in courses specifically devoted to issues of rhetoric and communication. At Iowa, these are most visible in Rhetoric and Communication Studies, but the key point is how they pop up elsewhere as well. In such courses, students encounter distinctively rhetorical treatments of politics, economics, journalism, business, art, law, and the like. These thematize rhetorical issues by examining the phenomena of other fields as rhetorical occurrences. How does a painting pursue a visual rhetoric? How do pricing, marketing, and accounting proceed as exercises in persuasion? The effort is to appreciate how politics, economics, literature, and even the formal languages of statistics and mathematics can be conceived to study communities and communication. Thus a friend in Mathematics who frequents the Institute for Advanced Study teaches advanced algebra and beginning calculus to Iowa students by immersing them in the discursive history of the community of mathematicians. In similar ways, some Iowa classes learn about practices far from the academy by learning how their practitioners relate to one another rhetorically.

Much the same holds also for seminars in methodology, which a few Iowans now teach as explorations of rhetoric. A more rhetorical topic is hard to imagine, since these courses address how to address various subjects. Such courses consider how modern methods distinguish between substance and method, content and form. Then they pursue rhetoric of inquiry in exploring how that substance and method are dimensions of each other.

Further inventions at Iowa are taking shape as a few experiments, but their success encourages a more systematic pursuit. One idea is to support team-teaching of faculty members in rhetoric and faculty members in the natural and social sciences. Then professors in realms that have conceived themselves to be the most distant from rhetoric can overcome their defense mechanisms against better, more rhetorical instruction. These professors often argue that they should not be asked to teach rhetoric because no one ever taught them any advanced skills in how to speak and write. You can tell, they say, from reading some of their own papers! Thus they protest that no one should want them to inflict their ignorance on the students. Yet an experimental program in the Languages of Learning, as my

97

colleague Frederick Antczak calls it, would provide ways of improving rhetorical and other dimensions of their teaching. And it would yield greater coherence for our curricula through greater sophistication about rhetoric and its relevance to diverse studies.

Another relevant effort newly begun at Iowa is named the PEOPLE Program. PEOPLE is an acronym for Philosophies and Ethics Of Politics, Law, and Economics. It is a three-college program where faculty members interested in social and political theories can interest juniors and seniors with the argumentative resources of several disciplines. The new curriculum depends on faculty coordination of courses across fields, recognizing expressly the dynamics of argumentation shared in otherwise different fields of inquiry.

The Rhetoric and Debate courses might even be moving toward a new curriculum for general education at Iowa. Iowa kept "general-education requirements" (GERs) for the liberal arts throughout the 1960s and 70s; and in the 1980s, it inaugurated a special "core curriculum" called "the Unified Program." For a limited group of students, this covers most courses for the first two years of college. POROI is planning a track of that program to coordinate *all* the courses needed to satisfy the GERs with an emphasis on rhetoric of inquiry as the study of argument across the curriculum. Previous tracks of the Unified Program group students together for the GERs so that they get to know one another well enough to talk vigorously inside and outside class. But their teachers do not, leaving connections among courses entirely up to the students. The POROI innovation would have professors in continual communication with one another—debating in class, creating assignments, teaching in tandem, sharing meals with students, and so on. Exchanges on argument across the curriculum already inform their research, why not practice the implications full-fledged in curricular planning and day-to-day collaboration on particular courses. We suspect that this will become one of the best ways to attain an adequately coherent curriculum for public education, since it favors the kinds of coherence that come from tracing arguments across the rhetorics of varied disciplines. Otherwise general education remains scattered insights pieced together haphazardly by students with little help from their professors. Fifty hours of courses left uncoordinated cannot do students nearly as much good. They need the commerce among the archipelagos provided by rhetorical analysis.

We Iowans have also been contemplating a new curriculum on Discourse, Rhetoric, and Culture, which would grant an interdisciplinary certificate to PhD students. It should do for graduate students what other Iowa innovations do for undergraduates: encouraging commerce among the archipelagos, so that specializations do not overwhelm them. Moreover it would offer a way to propagate this rhetorical approach beyond the University of Iowa, since the graduate students later will become members of faculties at other institutions of higher education.

98

We have learned from years of individual courses for graduate students that such coordinated attention to rhetoric really does help graduate education cohere. And already there are heart-warming tales of Iowa PhDs taking these gains to other places in need of their own rhetorical revolutions. (If nothing else, we rhetorized Iowans imbue students with rhetoric of inquiry as a modest kind of missionary spirit.)

Thus the Project on Rhetoric of Inquiry (POROI) pursues commerce among our academic archipelagos by originating research, curricula, and teaching techniques that accomplish more rhetorical—and therefore more coherent—education. The pattern and details of these endeavors show how rhetoric of inquiry already is starting to serve as a practice of coherent education at my institution. And they suggest how it might do likewise at other schools, colleges, and universities.

Notes

1. See John S. Nelson, "Ironies in Action: Rhetorics and Ethics of Pluralism in the Works of Wayne Booth," *The Critical Theories of Wayne Booth*, Frederick J. Antczak, ed., Norwood, NJ: Ablex, forthcoming.

2. See John S. Nelson, "Political Foundations for Rhetoric of Inquiry," *The Rhetorical Turn*, Herbert W. Simons, ed., Chicago: University of Chicago Press, 1990, 258–89.

3. For such an argument at only one of our many levels of archipelagos, see Judity N. Shyklar, "Facing Up to Intellectual Pluralism," *Political Theory and Social Change*, David Spitz, ed., New York: Atherton Press, 1967, 275–95.

4. See Allan Bloom, *The Closing of the American Mind*, New York: Simon and Schuster, 1987.

5. See E. D. Hirsch, Jr., Joseph F. Kett, and James Trefil: *Cultural Literacy*, Boston: Houghton Mifflin, 1987; *The Dictionary of Cultural Literacy*, Boston: Houghton Mifflin, 1988.

6. See John S. Nelson, Allan Megill, and Donald N. McCloskey, eds., *The Rhetoric of the Human Sciences*, Madison: University of Wisconsin Press, 1987.

7. See John S. Nelson, "Political Theory as Political Rhetoric," *What Should Political Theory Be Now?* Nelson, ed., Albany: State University of New York Press, 1983, 169–240.

8. See Hannah Arendt, *The Human Condition*, Chicago: University of Chicago Press, 1958.

9. See John S. Nelson, "Principles of Liberty: An Argument for Political Rhetorics Rather Than Analytical Philosophies of Freedom," Liberty Fund Conference on the Rhetoric of Liberty, Cosponsored by the Political Economy Research Center and the Project on Rhetoric of Inquiry, Lone Mountain Ranch, Big Sky, MT, 1990.

10. For explanations of how additional disciplines of the humanities and social sciences can contribute to networking the archipelagos of our times, see John S. Nelson, "Discipline and Present: Argument and History in Academic Fields," *Argument and Critical Practices*, Joseph W. Wenzel, ed., Annandale, VA: Speech Communication Association, 1987, 549–55.

11. See Hannah Arendt, *Between Past and Future,* New York, Viking Press, (1963), expanded edition, 1968.

12. See John S. Nelson and Allan Megill, "Rhetoric of Inquiry: Projects and Prospects," *Quarterly Journal of Speech,* 72, 1, February, 1986, 20–37.

13. See Alasdair MacIntyre, *After Virtue,* Notre Dame, IN: University of Notre Dame Press, (1981), second edition, 1984.

14. See John S. Nelson, "Account and Acknowledge or Represent and Control?" *Accounting, Organisation and Society,* forthcoming.

15. See Donald N. McCloskey, *The Rhetoric of Economics,* Madison: University of Wisconsin Press, 1985; *If You're So Smart,* Chicago: University of Chicago Press, 1990.

16. See Arjo Klamer, Donald N. McCloskey, and Robert W. Solow, eds., *The Consequences of Economic Rhetoric,* New York: Cambridge University Press, 1988. Also see John S. Nelson, "Economical Rhetoric: An Outsider Listens to Talk Among the Econ," Ford Foundation and the National Endowment for the Humanities Conference on the Rhetoric of Economics, Wellesley College, Wellesley, MA, 1986.

17. See John S. Nelson, "Models, Statistics, and Other Tropes of Politics," *Argument in Transition,* David Zarefsky, Malcolm O. Sillars, and Jack Rhodes, eds., Annandale, VA: Speech Communication Association, 1983, 213–29.

18. See John S. Nelson, *Tropes of Politics,* Madison: University of Wisconsin Press, forthcoming.

19. See Michael C. Leff: "Topical Invention and Metaphoric Interaction," Southern Speech Communication Journal, 48, Spring, 1983, 214–29; "The Topics of Argumentative Invention in Latin Rhetorical Theory from Cicero to Boethius," *Rhetorica,* 1, 1, Spring, 1983, 23–24.

20. See Donald N. McCloskey and John S. Nelson, "The Rhetoric of Political Economy," *From Political Economy to Economics . . . And Back?* James H. Nichols Jr. and Colin Wright, eds., San Francisco: Institute for Contemporary Studies Press, 1990, 155–74, on 171–74.

21. See Michael Calvin McGee and John S. Nelson, "Narrative Reason in Public Argument," *Journal of Communications,* 35, 4, Autumn, 1985, 139–55.

22. See John S. Nelson, "Polity and Orality: On the Advantages of Talking Theory over Writing It," *A Companion to Rhetoric of Inquiry,* John S. Nelson and Gloria B. Neckerman, eds. New York: Basil Blackwell, forthcoming.

AN INTEGRATED LIBERAL ARTS EXPERIENCE

Michael Carbone and Christopher W. Herrick
Muhlenberg College

"The university now offers no distinctive visage to the young person. He finds a democracy of one discipline. . . . The democracy is really an anarchy, because there are no recognized rules for citizenship and no legitimate title to rule. In short there is no vision, nor is there a set of competing visions of what an educated human being is" (337).

We quote Allan Bloom further, "The question has disappeared . . . There is no organization of the sciences, no tree of knowledge. Out of chaos emerges dispiritedness . . . better to give up on liberal education and get on with a specialty in which there is at least a prescribed curriculum and a prospective career" (337). We begin with a lengthy quotation because no matter where one might side on the idea of coherence in liberal education, Bloom certainly captures the essence of the issue. It is clear that for some time the central feature of liberal education, the influence of the whole has become problematical. Whether undone by the advent of modern science, the breakdown of universals, or the sociopolitical critique of the canon, the result is the same—the absence of a binding agent for coherence. One could argue that the essence of liberal education has remained unchanged, that it is complete unto itself as it has always been, for it reveals the truth of an unchanging human nature. Yet, this assertion alone will not restore what has come under question.

A unified body of knowledge lying at the center of the curriculum becomes difficult to imagine in the modern age. The growth of technical knowledge, competing claims about human nature, the absence of community and the proliferation of positivist modes of research suggest that we may be at an impasse. Real problems do exist: the explosion of knowledge, the proliferation of new forms of study, and the fact that a purely western focus is simply not enough in today's interdependent and culturally diverse world. Too, various views about the relationship between man and nature cannot be ignored. All of this has necessitated a refocus on the canon. And those of us interested in liberal learning are challenged to think of ways—either programmatic or curricular—to help students find coherence in their studies.

It is not within the scope of this paper to unravel the complexities of this theme. Rather we suggest that there are several important aspects to liberal education which if carefully considered, do suggest points at which we may begin to define for our students a kind of coherence. The Dana Program at Muhlenberg

College was planned and is directed to this end. Its themes are:
1) education is a process not an end, and continues beyond schooling;
2) liberal education implies commitment to becoming aware of the human situation and as a result carries certain responsibilities;
3) liberal education should enable us to make meaning of experience;
4) an interdisciplinary focus implies an interconnectedness of knowledge; and,
5) the drawing out and development of intellectual skills through active learning.

The Dana Program is committed to the idea that through various and carefully selected experiences juxtaposed to one another the student can begin to see that education does not end with the diploma. The focus on the necessary connection between work and formal schooling forces the issue of career to become a question to be studied and considered within the context of ideas presented in the more liberally focused classes. The foundation for this examination begins in the Dana seminar component of the program and is worked throughout.

As students begin to explore the interconnectedness of formal education and work (effectively, the world beyond schooling) the traditional focus of liberal learning upon the human question takes on significance. The themes of technology, alienation, human scale, management, the political economy, science, and the human environment provide important openings for students to explore the meaning of the humane in modern times. Students need to call not only on the traditional disciplines, but also on their own interpretations of their experiences in order to begin to explore this question. A kind of central focus emerges.

The idea of responsibility becomes central. What are the responsibilities of a liberally educated individual beyond academe? The debate centers upon paradigms of the meaning of liberal education and the educated person. While Bloom has suggested that no one vision exists, our seminar task is to engage students in a dialogue about a vision that might be necessary in our current historical period. This yields a kind of meta-knowledge which forces students to think about what they are learning, its meaning, and why or why not it might be important to them. Again, while this does not provide a single answer, it does begin to suggest a sort of coherence as students struggle with their own paradigms. Certainly one way to regain some purpose for liberal education beyond "skills" conceptualizations is to restore a discussion of "oughts" to educational aims. For example, what ought to be the responsibility of a liberally educated person in the last quarter of the twentieth century? What sort of education might facilitate the development of such an individual? While some students show initial resistance, they soon find challenge in normative ideas, particularly as they relate those ideas to real world problems. The essence of the liberal education experience may then center on the issue of how we may in a creative and humane manner seek to impose meaning of a fractious world, both in our private and public lives.

Apart from the initial seminar, the Dana Program incorporates four other elements which provide the student an opportunity to explore the meaning of learning as well as the responsibilities of the liberally educated person beyond the classroom. These components are a series of discussions of learning styles based upon a reading of the Myers-Briggs test, a series of four mentorships with faculty members on a research project of mutual interest, two internships, and a final synthesizing paper.

Group discussions of learning styles based on the Myers-Briggs test seek to sensitize students not only to the variety of learning styles, but, more important, to the effect of these styles on the manner in which students interact with their world.

Moreover, the discussions stimulate an awareness of the effect of various styles on group dynamics in ascribing meaning to action, the selection of problems to be solved and methods chosen to address problems. Ultimately, these discussions try to lead students to a more complete understanding of how their own learning style may be responsibly applied to serve not only their own interests, but those of the wider community of which they are a part. Ideally, the mentorship component of the Dana Experience provides an opportunity for students to explore the meaning of the humane in the modern world. First, the mentorship heightens the student's awareness of the responsibilities inherent in the acquisition and application of knowledge. At the same time, students are encouraged to make meaning of the content of knowledge by being aware of the influence of social and economic factors on the nature and content of research. Moreover, the mentorship program provides an opportunity for individual experiences to be shared and evaluated by the entire group of Dana Associates through discussion sessions held periodically throughout the semester. While Dana Associates are pursuing a wide variety of majors ranging from Drama to Physics as preparation for an equally diverse set of careers, we will elaborate on three mentorship experiences in the sciences, humanities, and social sciences as examples of the integration goals of the Dana Program. These three mentorships are illustrative of the manner in which the responsibility, humanity, and recontextualizing of knowledge may infuse the mentoring component.

A number of students in the natural sciences have been engaged in a project to develop a test to identify aluminum levels in blood. Apart from mastering the chemical techniques involved in measuring a predisposition to Altzheimer's disease, each participating student has also learned a significant amount about the potential psychological, familial, and societal costs of the disease through discussion with the faculty mentor.

A second mentoring project explored the ramifications of counterinsurgency strategy. This project, conducted under a member of the philosophy faculty, not only sensitized the student to the wide range of ethical issues posed in the application of a strategy to real world situations, but also provided the student with an opportunity to view firsthand the way in which the tools of a discipline often said to be divorced from practical concerns may make an impact upon the world beyond academe.

A third project in the Social Sciences has involved an assessment of the need for a variety of county services among the citizens of two Pennsylvania counties. Participating students viewed firsthand the practical application of a technique (survey research) which had been discussed in the classroom. Beyond this, however, students had an opportunity to explore the range of problems faced by individuals in the wider community and the manner in which public policy has met or failed to meet the needs of the community.

The next component of the Dana Associates Program at Muhlenberg, the internship, provides another opportunity in which students not only become more aware of the responsibilities of a liberally educated person, but also develop intellectual skills through active learning and make meaning of brute experience.

Coincidentally, the internship is structured in such a way as to hone the skills and orientations to knowledge that allows students to continue their education apart from the formal classroom once they have completed the liberal arts degree program. Through a formal, reflective journal coupled with a major paper (a critical examination of the application of formal knowledge to the work situation), the internship attempts to inculcate an attitude toward work which students may carry forward into future careers. This orientation toward work may, in turn, prevent them from falling prey to the tunnel mentality of the careerist.

The senior paper required of all Dana Associates provides a final synthesizing experience for participants to reflect upon their liberal education in the context of a wider world. In this paper students are encouraged to explore the ethical/moral and personal dilemmas that may be posed by the application of theoretical concepts or techniques of their major field of study to specific instances in the world beyond academe. Through this exercise, the Dana Associate is brought face to face with at least one aspect of the responsibilities of a humanely educated person to humanity in general.

Through the seminar, mentoring, interning, and a final synthesizing paper, the Muhlenberg Dana Program seeks to force students to reflect upon their experiences in light of their ideas about liberal education. No longer should problems or issues present themselves as one-dimensional, but rather we stress that things must be viewed ecologically. In effect our Dana Program strives to recontextualize knowledge from the various disciplines into some sort of liberal learning/world of work focus.

The hard intellectual work which students must do to make their experience within the program meaningful does stress active learning. The program is structured in such a way as to force the student to actively make connections at all kinds of levels. This of course is quite different from the idea that meaning will just emerge from content alone; rather, it suggests that we must do something with content in order to make something of it. It should be noted that this is not existential or even solipsistic in nature, but seems to challenge students to find communal or shared visions so as to create some sense of community. The final senior project becomes the vehicle for articulating these ideas and to draw together the various components of the program.

Clearly, the Dana Program does not restore a universal definition of the canon, or a single vision of human nature. It tries to accomplish a framework to introduce some idea of coherence in a fragmented curriculum. It provides a sort of intellectual scaffolding through which to think about liberal education and captures the career focus of students and renders it problematic.

Can liberal education ever recapture the sort of coherence which Bloom nostalgically writes about—in fact, insists upon? The issues raised earlier are real and not likely to disappear. Our contention is that broadly defined features of liberal education can be used in such a way as to create some sort of coherence for students so that they do not become the dispirited and vulgar careerists which Bloom describes.

WORKS CITED

Bloom, Allan. *The Closing of the American Mind.* New York: Simon and Schuster, 1987.

THE NOAH'S ARK PHENOMENON IN LIBERAL EDUCATION: PICK-A-PAIR
(In Search of Connections in a Liberal Education)

Maurine G. Behrens and Lucy A. O'Connor
Whittier College

Whittier College is an independent, coeducational college located in the Los Angeles area of Southern California. While Whittier offers several advanced degrees, high quality undergraduate education is its primary mission. In this context, the College's major goals are:

(1) to provide an intellectually challenging program of instruction that expands the student's knowledge and competence while developing a love of learning and a delight in the life of the mind; (2) to provide an atmosphere in which students can develop as individuals and within which each member of the community is obligated to engage in a responsible search for standards of value and knowledge of self; an environment which fosters sensitivity to and tolerance of others and offers the student an opportunity to become informed about a world that is international and interdependent; a milieu wherein the social implications of ideas and decisions are considered; and (3) to create a sense of community within the College and to foster an identity with the surrounding community through academic, cultural, social service and athletic programs. (From: Whittier College *Catalog 1988–90*)

One part of a college education is acquiring specific skills and learning about a particular field of study. Specialized knowledge is necessary to prepare for coping in our complex society, and the academic major is a means of achieving this. Equally important for successful living are flexibility and the ability to see problems in broad perspective. Today's college students must be prepared to live in a world where many present careers will have disappeared, and new careers are being created. Specialization can become a handicap if it leads to narrowness of view. Career flexibility is enhanced by learning to see one's specialty within a larger context, and life is enhanced by seeing oneself in relation to others. Good liberal education helps students make connections, take a broader view of problems, and consider the significance and consequences of their place in the social and natural universe.

The goal of the liberal education requirement at Whittier College is to provide a student's academic program outside of his major field with a sense of coherence similar to the major. To this end, our liberal education curriculum aims at achieving the following: 1) awareness of the interrelatedness of the various branches of knowledge, a sense of integration transcending disciplinary boundaries, and ability to make connections between disciplines and perspectives; 2) breadth of learning to complement the concentration in the major; 3) awareness of the necessity to transcend the limitations of one's period and culture; 4) development of the capacity to make intelligent, informed, and responsible choices; 5) participation in an intellectual community that extends beyond the classroom; and 6) recognition of the value of the lifelong pursuit of learning. In order to achieve these aims, we propose a curriculum that provides both structure and choice. The basic structure consists of six principal subject areas: English Composition, Mathematics, Natural Sciences, World Civilizations, Contemporary Society and the Individual, and Fine Arts and Humanities. Within each area, students may choose among several courses. (From: Whittier College Liberal Education Program, May 1981)

The liberal education program requires students to complete a two-course sequence Introduction to College Writing, one course in Mathematics, a two-course sequence in Natural Science, one course in Fine Arts (critical appreciation), one course in Humanities, and two courses in each of the following areas: European and North American Civilizations; Asian, African, and Latin American Civilizations; and Contemporary Society and the Individual. Students also participate in planned writing programs in their major disciplines, and are expected to complete the college writing requirement by submitting a substantial piece of written work for a course in the junior or senior year.

The liberal education courses total 41 semester units, of which any in the student's major discipline may also apply to the major. The major typically requires 30–36 units, and 120 units are needed for graduation. Thus more than one-third of the student's coursework is elective, allowing for self-directed exploration and development in many areas.

Whittier College's liberal education program provides opportunities to acquire breadth and the ability to make connections, as well as substantive knowledge, specific skills, and qualities of mind that each student needs to function as an educated member of the greater community. Most colleges assure breadth by requiring students to take selected courses from various disciplines, but students are left on their own to see how these courses relate to their educational goals or to each other. Whittier College's liberal education program is unusual in that learning about "the connectedness of things" is built into specially designed team-taught or paired courses in three areas: European and North American Civilizations (ENAC); Asian, African, and Latin American Civilizations (AALAC); and Contemporary Society and the Individual (CSI). The team-taught course is an interdisciplinary two-semester sequence that is taught by faculty from two different disciplines—for example, The Western Mind (English and History) or Arabs and Muslims (Sociology and History). The pair consists of two courses from different disciplines which deal with the same theme from different perspectives and in different contexts. These two courses must be taken concurrently. In these courses students are challenged to see things from more than one perspective, to make connections, and to appreciate the interrelatedness of knowledge.

The authors have had considerable experience with two of the more innovative aspects of this liberal education program: the paired courses and the structured writing program in the major discipline. However, the particular aspect dealt with here is the paired course.

PAIRED COURSES

An interesting feature of the liberal education program is the pairing of two courses from different disciplines. Each pair is developed by its instructors to present students with different views of a specified topic within one of the three categories mentioned earlier (ENAC, AALAC, or CSI). Students have joint assignments (which might include reading, lectures, films, essays, field trips, etc.) designed to emphasize the relationships between the disciplines. To assure breadth of perspective, the instructors attend and participate in each other's classes. A broad perspective is further enhanced by the presence in each class of students with differing goals and backgrounds and by keeping class size small enough to allow and encourage discussion.

Paired courses must be taken concurrently to receive liberal education credit. If a student fails one of the courses, units of credit are recorded as earned for the course that was passed. However, the student must successfully complete another appropriate pair to meet the liberal education requirement.

There are several advantages to using pairs of courses to meet the "breadth and connectedness" goals of liberal education. One already mentioned is that students can apply those courses within their major disciplines to the major. This so-called "double dipping" helps students to better understand how their own specialities fit with other frameworks and to see their specialities from other points of view. Another advantage—especially for a small faculty—is that many existing courses, needed for majors, can be easily modified to fit into a pair.

108

Perhaps the most gratifying outcomes for faculty have been the intellectual stimulation and collegiality that have resulted from pairing. Faculty have willingly accepted the extra demands on their time and energies because of the personal and professional benefits. Students also benefit intellectually and socially. Seeing each instructor as a learner in the other's class gives students good models for active, effective learning that have resulted in high levels of interest and better student work. Having both instructors, as well as some of the same students, in both classes seems to promote better understanding and closer relationships with other students and with faculty.

Developing a Pair

New pairs may be motivated by the dean's request for new pairs in a specific category, by the faculty member's desire to do something different (i.e., work with a different person, course, or discipline), and/or by the fact that participation in the Liberal Education program is relevant in tenure and promotion considerations. A new pair ordinarily originates in one of two ways: either the instructor of an unpaired course seeks out the instructor of another appropriate course, or two colleagues whose informal discussion has led to interesting connections between their disciplines mutually decide to develop a pair. In either case, the process that follows is similar.

Usually the initial stage involves discussion of course goals, structure, and content, as well as philosophy of education and approach to students. (Since we have a small faculty who tend to be well acquainted with each other, instructors generally do not enter this stage without some expectation that they will be able to work effectively and cooperatively with the other person.) Usually the first stage is brief—one or two short conversations. Stage two involves sitting down together to determine how the courses can meet the guidelines for pairing and working out ways of putting the courses together. This results in a proposal which the Liberal Education Committee considers and then accepts or rejects. If the pair is accepted, the real work of specifying the mechanisms begins: course requirements, schedules, and assignments, etc., are structured to allow each course to stand alone while also connecting with the other.

After the preliminaries, the pair is offered. In spite of extensive planning, modifications may be needed during the semester, so instructors get feedback from students, monitor carefully, and modify when needed. This ongoing evaluation process is supplemented with formal end-of-term student evaluations of the pair, in addition to evaluations of each course. Students and faculty have tended to agree about the success or failure of a particular pair. Those that work well are usually repeated, with minor modifications if needed. Those that don't work well are either modified extensively or dropped.

Two examples of the authors' current pairs are discussed below. Brief descriptions of their other pairs are appended.

Youth in Fact and Fiction

"Youth in Fact and Fiction" is an example of one pair that is offered in the Contemporary Society and the Individual area of the liberal education program. It connects two sophomore/junior level courses—one is a Psychology course, Psychology of the Adolescent, and the other an English Literature course, The Twentieth Century Novel.

Although ten-year-old human beings have never been able to get to the age of twenty-five without passing through the teens and early twenties, that particular passage is especially significant for the twentieth century. In pre-industrial societies, economic, social, and physical maturity may come more or less at the same time, often marked by appropriate rituals which symbolize the transition from childhood to adulthood. In our society, however, this is not the case, and the prolonged period spent in formal education and preparation for adult life, plus the absence of clearly defined roles and positions into which one naturally grows, have created a period that is often stressful and generally very significant in the development of the life pattern. The study of this period is, moreover, especially interesting for students of the usual undergraduate age, who are trying to make sense out of developments in their own lives and whose thinking is much stimulated by the discovery that similar patterns exist and have existed in other lives.

Psychology and Literature are (in fact) obvious disciplines for pairing; writers must be at least intuitive psychologists in order to create characters, and Freud's description of the Oedipus complex is the most famous, but certainly not the only, instance of psychological theory drawing on literature for illustration, and perhaps inspiration. The pairing is especially relevant for the twentieth century, in which novelists not only draw upon their own perceptions of human nature, but are very likely to have read the systematic formulations upon it that have been produced by psychological theory, and certainly reflect the influence of psychological theory on the general intellectual milieu. (From: Proposal for a CSI Paired Course Offering, 1982)

The pair is currently being offered for the third time, with a different instructor for the literature course, and the modifications of the individual courses required in order to present them as a pair have continued to be fairly minor.

1. The novels selected for study had to be selected with the period, conflicts, and issues of adolescence in mind. For example, Faulkner's *Go Down Moses* was selected rather than *Light in August*, and Lawrence's *Sons and Lovers* was selected instead of *Women in Love*.

2. The text selected for the psychology course needed to present the study and facts of adolescent development in a historical and international context, as well as an American one. It required some searching to find such a text because most Adolescent Psychology texts present material almost entirely on current American youth.

3. The order of presentation of topic areas in the psychology course and the novels in which these issues were important had to be coordinated in so far as possible. This was probably the hardest task. On the one hand, textbooks are often written in such a way that the chapters are meant to be presented in order, and students do not always respond well to being asked to jump around in their text. On the other hand, novels are often best presented in some logical order such as chronological order of publication.

4. The discussions of the novels in the literature class always included consideration of the psychological development, conflicts, and relationships of the adolescent characters with reference to the appropriate discussions of these issues held in the psychology class.

5. In the psychology course the adolescent characters of the novels were used not only as case studies of particular relationships and conflicts, but also as illustrations of adolescence in an earlier time and/or in a different cultural setting.

6. In both courses, common readings of original writings of some of the famous psychologists, such as Freud and Erikson, whose works have influenced thinking in both disciplines, were added. In the future a common novel may be required reading for both courses to help tie non-pair students into the process.

7. The examinations in both courses require the pair students to answer at least one essay question which requires integration of information gleaned from both courses. Examples of such questions might be: "1) a. Discuss the nature of Erikson's 'Identity Crisis'. How does Marcia's 'Identity Statuses' view suggest that adolescents resolve this 'crisis'? b. If you are taking this course as part of the pair, use illustrations of the above, where applicable, taken from the 6 novels you studied. If you *are not* taking the course as part of the pair, use illustrations taken from the text, class discussions, or your own real life experiences." or "2) a. Discuss the roles and relative importance of the family and the peer group in the development of the young person as he/she goes through the adolescent period. How do parenting style, working parents, and communication skills affect this development? b. If you are taking this course as part of the pair, compare and contrast the above for you, as compared with two of the main characters of the 6

novels you studied."

8. The final term project (a 10-page paper in each course) was combined for the students taking the courses as a pair. The first time the pair was offered this was a 20-page paper for the pair students which included both a literary analysis of the novel(s) and a psychological analysis of the adolescent character(s). Later, the regular final term project for the psychology course was changed to an annotated bibliography, so the final common project was also changed. Pair students were now asked to select one adolescent issue in at least two of their novels. They wrote an 8–10 page paper for the literature class which presented a literary analysis of those novels and the relevant characters and their handling of their problem or issue. Accompanying that paper was an annotated bibliography, selected from the professional psychological literature, of current sources of information on that same adolescent issue or problem.

Overall this pair has been quite successful. As far as the adolescent psychology course is concerned, for instance, it has given the pair students some real understanding of what it was like to be their age and gender in earlier generations through the concerns and reactions of the characters in the novels. Parenting would have been autocratic, marriages would have been arranged, children were seen and not heard, disobedient young people were whipped. What was it like to live like that? They get a real sense, again through the eyes of the novel characters, of what it would be like to be their age and gender in other countries and in other cultures. They come to see why some current laws on child labor, education, and women's right were necessary. On the other hand, where the literature course is concerned, it has given the students there a better understanding of why some of the issues and situations presented in the novels were felt to be important enough to write about at that time, why some of the characters in the novels were characterized as behaving and reacting as they did. Students come to understand better the nature and dynamics of the conflicts and situations the novel characters find themselves involved in.

Worlds of Childhood

"Worlds of Childhood" combines two junior/senior level courses—one a Psychology course, Advanced Child Psychology, and the other an Anthropology course, The Child in Other Cultures—as a pair in the Asian, African, and Latin American Cultures area. This pair is currently being offered for the first time.

The purpose of the pair is 1) to broaden student perspectives of human nature by expanding their repertoire of what it means to be human; 2) to confront students with differing world views, including how children develop during the early years of life in several Asian, Latin American, and African societies; 3) to raise questions about how culture

112

and development are related; 4) to involve students in the discussion of what "normal" or "good" child development is; and 5) to evaluate the universality and cross-cultural validity of current theories of human development by applying them to societies outside of mainstream American culture. By specifically comparing the dominant American tradition of child-rearing with the environments, socialization practices, and cultural values in these societies, students will gain a better understanding of both their own and other cultures. (From: Proposal for an AALAC Paired Course Offering, 1988)

Since Child in Other Cultures has typically emphasized development and socialization of children in Middle Eastern, East Asian, and African cultures as well as Latin American and minority U.S. groups, this course required little modification. Advanced Child Psychology, in contrast, follows an introductory child psychology course and has typically focused either on comparison of theories of child development or on specific topics, such as cognitive and social development. According to the Liberal Education guidelines, both courses needed to have an AALAC focus, so the psychology class required extensive modifications, some of which also provided shared experiences for students in the pair.

1. The text for the course needed to be comprehensive, to be aimed at advanced level students (since all students had previously taken an introductory child development course), and to deal with children's development in AALAC cultures. It was relatively easy to find a text that dealt at an advanced level with the topics of social, personality, cognitive, and physical development in the U.S. However, it was impossible to find one that covered those topics in Asian, African, and Latin American cultures as well. After considering several options, it was decided to use a topically-oriented textbook plus six articles that report research in AALAC countries. Four of these were also assigned in Child in Other Cultures.

2. While the articles provided some useful information, they were not sufficient, so other sources were necessary.

a. A reading assignment in professional journals was redesigned to fit the AALAC guidelines by having students read reports of cross-cultural studies of mother-infant attachment, summarize them, and present their findings to the class.

b. Since students could not go to AALAC countries to observe children there, it was necessary to find other ways of giving them some first hand experience. Therefore, field trips were scheduled for both classes to observe two Asian-influenced minority groups in Los Angeles: an Islamic center where both adults and children attended religious services and two Hare Krishna settings, an evening family meeting and a preschool.

c. For further examples of AALAC cultures, films (e.g., "Infant Development in the Kibbutz" and "Pixote") and guest speakers (e.g., a sabra who grew up on a Kibbutz) were used as resources. Again, several of these were shared by both classes.

d. A readily available resource, the instructor of Child in Other Cultures, was also scheduled as a lecturer for the Advanced Child Psychology course. Since she has lived and done research in both Turkey and South India, her slides and lectures added to the Advanced Psychology students' AALAC experiences.

3. Students needed more experience with U.S. child development than their text could provide, so they observed the campus preschool and its parent group. This also provided them with material that could be directly compared with their observations of the Asian-influenced groups.

4. Students in both classes kept journals that covered their reading other learning experiences.

5. The final exam will contain at least one essay that requires students in the pair to integrate material from both courses in their answers.

To date, this new pair seems to be accomplishing its purposes. Class discussions and essays show that students are becoming more aware of the influence of culture on development. While they were quite accepting of the idea that culture would affect the socialization process, its influence on physical and motor development was somewhat harder to accept. Currently students are wrestling with the notion that culture is related to cognitive development and academic learning in very complex ways, in addition to the problems caused by teacher-student language differences.

CONCLUSIONS

On the basis of their experiences with planning and presenting several pairs in different areas and with different instructors, the authors submit some general comments by way of summary and conclusion.

1. It is a fact of life that, as a general rule, for two courses to pair successfully, the instructors have to be compatible, be willing to compromise, and mutually respect each other and what they are each trying to do in their classes. "If you don't fit—don't do the pair—you could do more harm than good!" You have to work together a lot of the time; you have to sit through each other's classes; you have to compromise on things like joint readings, joint papers and projects, and scheduling; you must be supportive of each other. The same pair, covering the same material, using the same assignments, taught in basically the same way—but taught by a different pair of instructors—is a completely different experience for all concerned.

2. It is essential to attend each other's classes as often as humanly possible—optimally, every time. It is only in this way that students can get the full benefit of the interaction of the faculty with each other in the two different contexts, and

it is only in this way that the instructors can fully understand and take advantage of the discussions and interactions going on in both classrooms. Instructors often find themselves helping each other by making on-the-spot connections from their own perspective that only occur to them as they listen and participate. Just knowing the material to be covered, or the approach to be taken, or the point of view of the other instructor is not enough. The students themselves and their concerns, personalities, and past histories are a major factor in the total equation—and these change from semester to semester.

3. "Practice makes perfect" or "You have to teach it at least once (twice?) to get it right!" Regardless of how much preplanning you do, you have to actually participate together in the teaching of the pair once or twice to get it to do what you want it to do.

4. Remember the non-pair students! Be careful that they don't get left out of the discussions and that they (or the pair students) don't feel overloaded with work or discriminated against. They can gain greatly from the other instructor's contributions, too, even if they don't take her/his course.

5. The presence *and participation* of the other instructor in the class also teaches, by example, respect for the teacher and the learning process, how knowledge and understanding are gained and used to solve problems and settle issues, that it is OK not to know but not OK not to try to find out, that in order to learn it is important and necessary to ask questions—whether of a person or of a book, that we are all seeking education all the time—not just the students, that we learn from each other—not just students from teachers. (And the instructors do in fact often gain as much as the students by way of knowledge and understanding in the course of this interaction.)

PAIRED COURSE DESCRIPTIONS

THE EXCEPTIONAL INDIVIDUAL AND SOCIETY (CSI)
Psychology 374 Psychology of Exceptional Individuals
Physical Education and Recreation 384 Therapeutic Recreation
This pair examines the characteristics and needs of atypical individuals in our society today. Psychology of Exceptional Individuals focuses on diagnosis, behavioral expectations, and special educational and community support needs of the atypical person throughout the lifespan. Therapeutic Recreation applies this knowledge to the organization and implementation of therapeutic and recreational programs in various community settings with many different kinds of people. Students who take the pair benefit from this combination of theory and applications as well as from the opportunity to approach the study of atypical people from both psychological and sociological perspectives.

THE INDIVIDUAL IN DISTRESS (CSI)

Psychology 372 Abnormal Psychology

Social Work 344 Coping with Crisis

This pair focuses on the individual who is experiencing distress: the psychology course provides theoretical perspectives on the development and management of deviant, maladaptive behavior, and the social work course examines the subjective responses and experiences of individuals reacting to stress and explores the implications of constructive or maladaptive resolutions to crises for both present and future psychological health. In addition, the social work course introduces students to community resources that provide service to people who are in crisis situations. Both courses reflect contemporary concepts about human beings. Abnormal psychology cannot be fully understood without taking into account contemporary cultural, social, and political influences on mental health. The development of crisis intervention practice in community mental health clinics in the last twenty years reflects changes in individual and societal needs in our post-Industrial Revolution society.

HUMAN BEHAVIOR AND THE SOCIAL ENVIRONMENT (CSI)

Psychology 222 Biological Bases of Behavior

Social Work 274 Child, Family, and Society

People's developmental, problem-solving, and coping capabilities are determined by their biological nature, their environment, and by a complex interplay between heredity and environment. This pair develops this notion by examining the biological aspects as well as the psychological and sociological determinants of behavior. This systems approach to analyzing various theories of development and behavior will enhance the ability of students to see how their development, as well as the development of others, is influenced by the interrelatedness of biological, psychological, and social systems.

AN INTERDISCIPLINARY FINE ARTS COURSE

Floyd W. Martin

University of Arkansas at Little Rock

An interdisciplinary fine arts course was first offered at the University of Arkansas at Little Rock in 1986–1987 as one of four two-semester, six-hour "core" courses for the university's Donaghey Scholars Program. The other core courses concern Rhetoric and Communication, the History of Ideas, and Science and Society. After two years, it is clear that the course "The Individual and the Creative Arts" has been successful in acquainting students with some historical concepts in the arts, and in developing an ability to respond actively to visual and performing arts, primarily through writing short essays on events attended.

The student population for this course has been a selective one, for the Scholars Program accepts approximately twenty-five particularly motivated students each year. Many of the principles used in this course were later examined for inclusion in new general education fine arts courses required of all students at the University of Arkansas at Little Rock.

The course for the Scholars Program was developed by a faculty committee from the departments of Art, Music, and Theatre/Dance. Although the course was to be more "historical" than "studio" oriented, the committee was made up of both historians of the fine arts and practicing artists. The planners easily agreed that the course should give the students in the Scholars Program an appropriate exposure to the fine arts, and equip them with the knowledge and means to appreciate all the arts following the conclusion of the course.

The course was originally to be a junior level one. However, it now can be taken any of the first three years. Most students will take the course in the sophomore year, in part as preparation for a summer in Europe that is offered to all students in the program after two years. In terms of the course content, however, the level was not a major factor, since this was to be an introduction to the arts for students with little or no previous experience.

There was considerable discussion concerning the organization of the course. The two extremes were a course entirely chronological, trying to cover all major issues in the arts, or a course concentrating on a few periods only. This was the breadth versus depth problem. A broad chronological approach, while comprehensive, would require a superficial analysis of works of art. The other approach, limiting the course to a particular period, for example the Renaissance or the Twentieth Century, allowing more in-depth analysis of works of art, would suffer from lack of completeness. In wrestling with the breadth versus depth issue, the committee had to keep in mind that this course would be for most students the only one in the fine arts during their college careers.

The organization agreed upon was somewhere between the two approaches. Ten important groupings of "isms" that are common to the arts were used as the major organizing principle. The ten topics were Catholicism, Secularism, Humanism, Classicism, Romanticism, Realism/Impressionism/Symbolism, Modernism, Primitivism, Expressionism, and Regionalism/Nationalism. It was thought that a student who could leave the course with a basic understanding of these terms could approach the arts with confidence.

This approach does have its problems. For example, Catholicism is a forced term used to encompass the idea of art and religion. Romanticism in the visual arts is a shorter period chronologically than in music. Realism in the theater is not entirely parallel to that in painting. These differences, however, provide the basis for significant discussions within the course.

Also problematic are necessary omissions. The structure leaves out some important things such as Baroque painting, Bach and Handel, and Restoration drama. But it is not the purpose of the course to cover everything, so these omissions need to be considered in that context.

Once the course was underway, it was clear that even this organization was too ambitious for the time available. The "isms" were divided into major ones (ten class periods each) and minor ones (four class periods each). The major movements are Catholicism—or Art and Religion, Humanism, Classicism, Romanticism, Realism/Impressionism/Symbolism, and Modernism. In the second year Classicism was used to begin the course, since novices could digest the content of the ancient world and the eighteenth century more easily than non-western or western medieval material.

The normal procedure in our Scholars Programs core courses is for two faculty from different departments to teach together, and sufficient funding is provided to "borrow" these two people from their departmental responsibilities. The Fine Arts faculty felt strongly that there should be one person each from art, music, and theater, and so this course is taught by a team of three. Such an arrangement offers faculty involved opportunities to discuss concepts and ideas inside and outside the classroom to a degree uncommon in a commuter urban university.

The committee planned three types of experiences. First was traditional lecture/discussions in the classroom, with presentations by faculty or invited guests. Second were discussion sections meeting at various times other than the scheduled time for the course offering more hands-on experiences. These have included simple photography projects, a session on drawing in perspective, observing a music or theater rehearsal, discussing a film after a screening, or attending a workshop on electronic music. Third were performance and exhibition attendance requirements.

This latter requirement, the performance and exhibition requirement, has turned out to be a great success. Each student must attend ten events each semester, and must submit a 2–3 page paper on eight of those events. Of the eight, two must be in visual arts, two in music, and two in theater or dance.

The success of this exercise is two-fold. It forces each student to encounter a number of art forms, and writing about it makes it essential that the student be actively involved in looking or listening. Grades on these papers form the major part of the course grade, and students can re-write any paper for which they desire a higher grade.

Most of the students have had limited exposure to the arts, and this assignment forces them to become involved. Several have remarked during or after the course that if they had not been required to go, they never would have done so, but since they did, they now are interested in attending more events in the future. There is also evidence of a "ripple effect," for students have told us their parents, friends, and siblings have become more interested in art exhibits or performances because of what they were doing for class. Over time this and similar courses will have an effect on the local arts community helping their audiences to grow.

Another aspect of the course that requires an active form of learning is occasional projects during the class. These have included play readings, composition of word-canons, and making collages. Several slides illustrating collages made in the context of the study of classical sculpture and ideal proportions have been collected by program faculty. In one exercise students were asked to use magazines and popular material and create a collage of the Ideal Male and Female of the 1980s.

Yet another successful exercise is the final project. At the conclusion of the first semester each student must individually produce a project. The only instructions given are that it should deal with at least two art forms and, while term papers are not forbidden, students are encouraged to try to do something other than a paper. Efforts have included dramatic readings in costume and sound-slide presentations on Baroque architecture, Aztec sculpture, and other topics.

At the end of the second semester, students are expected to collaborate on a class "final project." This so far has had a theatrical structure, but has included sections that involve music, slides, dance, and video. This project not only provides an opportunity for collaborative learning, something not normally a part of a student's academic career, but also give students some awareness of the creative process. They learn such things as the need for scheduling, planning, publicity, adequate rehearsal, and a healthy respect for such individuals as a stage make-up artist or electrical technician.

The fine arts course must be judged a success if we consider students' responses to it, and faculty involved are very enthusiastic. Many of the areas mentioned above have also been considered in designing a pair of three-hour fine arts courses for all students under a new structure of "core" courses, though logistical problems have made it impossible to simply repeat the Scholars Program Fine Arts Course. Unfortunately, the average class size is thirty-five, meaning it is next to impossible to require eight papers from each student. Nevertheless, our experience has been that writing about required events is one of the best ways to learn an appreciation of the arts, so this concept has been used to the extent possible.

The interdisciplinary approach to the arts through this six-hour course has been rewarding to both faculty and students. Students gain some familiarity with the major art forms, preparing them to be thoughtful audience members in the future. The interdisciplinary approach emphasizes similarities and differences among the various media, and provides a stronger focus on the creative process. Writing about the arts forces each student to think actively about what is seen or heard.

4

GREAT BOOKS: ELITIST OR ESSENTIAL

ELVIS TRIUMPHANT, BOOKWORM PROOFTEXT, LETTERMAN, AND THE FALL OF THE BASTILLE

Leslie Palmer

University of North Texas

I. Little

I grew up with Elvis. Unlike most of my contemporaries, I do not mean this in a metaphorical sense. Nephew to my mother's best friend, Elvis was an usher at a movie theater we went to, and I remember paying a dime to hear him sing at the Humes High talent show.

We did not follow the same path in propagating the ideals of Memphis. No individual had ever achieved so much in the history of that slum. His influence spread around the world. Today there are hundreds, perhaps thousands, of Elvis imitators. When I do mine, my class laughs, and then says, "But Elvis is alive!" So far as I know, I am alone in being Doctor Palmer.

My theory when I first started this paper was that we academics want our students to be like us. Instead of watching *Blue Velvet* or Elvis on black velvet, they should become rediscoveries and recreations of us. We are not candid enough, indeed I am certain we are not gross enough—for if we are generally anything it is devious, manipulative, and subtle—we would never call for clones of ourselves. But the Greeks tell us of Narcissus, and if Elvis was a peacock we sparrows too can love ourselves and in admiration want others to want to be like us.

So my first opinion went, as I moved on this subject between ignorance and opinion looking for truth, quite willing to stay for an answer. As I spent July and August looking for the spiritual legacy held in Western Europe—especially taking July 14 to be in Paris for the bicentennial commemoration, debate, and vulgarization of the French Revolution in all its possibilities, seeing tricolor underwear, hearing claims by the Cambridge Marxist Society that the French Revolution was a celebration of their cause, saying I wish I knew more French history, I began to spiral away from that earlier thought that we like Plato with his philosopher kings wanted in our hubris to rewrite Shelley's *Ozymandias* to say, "Look on my Great Books, ye mighty, and despair." Did we want to be academic kings as Elvis was known as "The King"?

Instead of seeing our concern for Great Books as powerful palace propaganda as the post and lintel system of our world, I began to see that this concern was the Roman arch, a way to move us from a conception with those ancient questions to create a barrel vault, to make possible dramatic interactions with the ideas that our lives again and again make new.

My Great Books and Classic Learning Core students care about the child-custody case of Elizabeth Morgan and her husband, and of Medea and Jason. For some of them, *Medea* opens up spaces of possibility and helps them to see ideas in what had been topical and gossipy. When the problems plaguing them that may seem commonplace to us (but are new to them in their innocence of the Great Books) emerge, they discover that quickening sensation can build entire structures of thought, made possible by the greatness of the issues addressed, as well as by asking, for example, what is unsatisfactory about Aristotle's view of tragedy, or unacceptable, or insufficient, or why do we need a new King of Tragedy? Few of my students intend to build empires, but they care passionately about their freedoms, and Plato with his Republic can speak to them of those freedoms and their passions and send them hurrying to read their political science and history.

Perhaps no fight is more eagerly joined in Literary Criticism than the Battle of the Ancients and Moderns. One need not be John Dryden of *Essay of Dramatic Poetry* fame to see that both can fit beneath the dome, that readers can join all in their reading, whether it be to join the dance on the side of Elvis and rock and roll or the side of the deconstructionist stomp.

II. Less

I was stigmatized at age eight by a grade school teacher—
one of my favorites, by the way. Mrs. Bruce sent an alarming note to my mother, warning her that Leslie "was a bookworm." Nowadays a note saying I was on crack would be less alarming. It was true I read voraciously, most often twelve books a day, eight for teenagers and four for adults, making five or six trips a week to the Cossett library in addition to trips to our community Neighborhood House Library where I had special run of the library's treasures, plus, of course, the few volumes in our school. Moreover, my family bought me books. Speaking of the public library, sad to say, I never saw Elvis there.

I was hooked on reading. More often than spending dimes on music, I spent them on books, pulp magazines, old copies of *Liberty* from World War II, comic books, paperbacks, everything. Because I think my students should be voracious readers, I do not intend to limit their reading to the Great Books the way the Puritans first limited the number of London theaters to two and then, finally, to none. I know few of us would tell poets, painters, and musicians they are no longer necessary, that we have our quota of works of art, need no more works dealing with love and death, justice, equality, social passion, liberty, and the like. We await your greatness.

I am the one who looks at the clock. If I read Great Books from now until my life expectancy is reached, how many books are left? I must read less—less voraciously, less junk, less cereal boxes, and more, more great books, more deeply, more rapidly. Yes, less is more.

My students tell me by their willingness to discuss in our Great Books discussions every Friday that the Great Books are not in their declining years. I have students who are not portraits of me who do demonstrate the glorious excellence of the Great Books tradition. Perhaps none of them will be apt to say "You Ain't Nothin' But a Hound Dog" and "Heartbreak Hotel" are celebrations of all our lives, equivalents in song to a twentieth-century cathedral. Yet.

III. Nothing

Not Necessarily David Letterman's Top 10 List of Reasons Great Books Provide an Excellent Education From Our Home Office in Denton, Texas—

10. You can't get *Classics Comics* and *Cliff's Notes* for that other stuff.
9. You can understand that Euripides/Eumenides joke.
8. No one makes you read *National Enquirer*.
7. So that "Just Say No" is more than an empty slogan.
6. You can decide whether your teachers are Don Quixotes, Don Juans, Fausts, Hamlets, or, most likely, Oedipuses.
5. Because they can pull the plug on you for symptoms of brain death.
4. America doesn't want another Trojan War.
3. You'll know why in the best of all possible worlds you're on *Candide* camera.
2. After kindergarten not everyone likes chocolate milk and cookies.
1. You have to know when to hold 'em & know when to fold 'em; you have to know when to walk away, & know when to run.

Besides, if no one read the Great Books, think what kind of shape the world would be in.

IV. Finally

I remember walking by the Mississippi River. I remember my excitement at thinking about Mark Twain's books, the way my mind took off. It was not the way Twain's Huck went. Instead I "lit out for civilization."

In *The Harvard Guide to Influential Books* (1986, ed. C. Maury Devine, et al.), 113 eminent Harvard professors discuss the books that have shaped their thinking. In September 1989, *Harper's* printed a forum on "Who Needs the Great Works?" Some of the same works were cited, not always with the same appreciation, and unlike the *Harper's* forum, no one mentioned the *Koran*. As I said, there were 113 Harvard professors. Six hundred and seventy-six works or authors were cited, including such items as the *New York Times* and an encyclopedia. One hundred and fifty-seven Great Books authors were cited, if you count 11 references to Shakespeare as 11, 2 to George Eliot's *Middlemarch*, 1 to *Daniel Deronda*, and 1 to *Mill on the Floss* as a total of four, and so on. One hundred and fifty-four of these were to Western authors. One hundred and twenty-three references cited twentieth-century novels or poets. That leaves 386 of the 676 as others, such as modern tomes on urban planning, economics, and even a "good cookbook." That means 57 percent of the works cited as influential were not great. Allowing for posturing, chicanery, and such deception as Harvard professors may be prone to—or inclined to, or willing to stand for—, that sounds about right to me.

My conclusion is that the bookworm was right. Pursue the questions that matter, the questions before you, eat your way through that shelf of volumes, go on—. That pursuit will lead you to books that are great whether anyone tells you they are Great Books or not. That pursuit will ideally lead you to discussion of those with others. With that voraciousness, reading for discovery, there will be awakening, with awakening often comes appetite, appetite leads to commitment to reading, that commitment enables one for the creative use of reading, for the synthesis of that knowledge. I am less certain that one should only have a diet of rich foods than I am that one should be provided such staples. A nineteen-year-old I love says, "I think the schools are quite lenient." In my day as a schoolboy, we had to read Euripides or George Eliot because we would find our own way to Camus or *Clockwork Orange*. I remember a novel class I was enrolled in where we all read *Tom Jones* and *Middlemarch* but where I was the only fool who raised his hand to explain Henry Miller to our naive teacher. That advertising led me to a girlfriend in the class who had discovered D. H. Lawrence all by herself.

It is a lovely elitist attitude to think the Great Books are the property of the rich. If the mob gets hold of the lovely white pages, that creamy vellum and those precious ideas will be ruined, won't they? Those dirty paws will stain forever the fine pages. We'll be like the mobs at the Bastille. Symbolically the contents of those pages and the contents of that old building matter to our lives. I do not believe that it is the property of an elite which we cannot share. As even the subjects of Elvis share in that intellectual property which is endlessly divisible and forever can seem undiminished, I think of a fifteen-year-old I love who when asked if the Great Books provide an excellent education said, "Sure, they do. That's all that needs to be said. It's simple."

GREAT BOOKS AND THE TEACHING OF ETHICS

John Churchill
Hendrix College

I. Great Books Again

Few stories are as widely known as the story of Odysseus, the man who was never at a loss, who returned home after twenty years of war and wandering to find his house filled with obnoxious intruders courting his wife and eating away his substance. Odysseus entered the banqueting hall disguised as a beggar and insinuated himself into the games of the ravenous suitors. He worked his vengeance in the following way, as they gabbled, ignorant of their peril:

> ... He signalled with a nod to Telemachos; and Telemachos slung on his sharp sword, and grasped his spear, and took his stand by the seat, the son armed by his father's side.

> Now Odysseus stript off his rags, and leapt upon the great doorstone, holding the bow and the quiver full of arrows.

> ... Then he let fly straight at Antinoos: he was holding a large golden goblet in both hands, and about to lift it for a drink.

> ... The arrow struck him in the throat, and the point ran through the soft neck. He sank to the other side, and the goblet dropt from his hands. In an instant a thick jet of blood spouted from his nostrils; he pushed the table away with a quick jerk of his feet, spilling all the vittles on the ground—meat and bread in a mess. (242–43)

As Antinoos's blood spread among the spilled feast, Odysseus and Telemachos, father and son united in righteous vengeance, continued the slaughter of the suitors. The scene is magnificent: Odysseus in middle age glowed with the prowess of the seasoned warrior. Telemachos, who weeks before was a reticent adolescent, emerged as his father's mature son—a warrior entering his prime. The suitors were slaughtered in the locked hall, where, defenseless and guilty, they fell like butchered swine. The women of the house were forbidden to witness the battle, but they would be summoned later to clean up the gore, and the servant-girls who collaborated with the suitors would be hanged. This bloody scene of private justice is the penultimate action of *The Odyssey*; only the reunion of Odysseus with faithful Penelope follows.

What could be the point of insisting that students devote their energies to the study of such scenes as this? Why insist that they acquaint themselves with the writings of Homer, Plato, or St. Augustine, or of Dante, Machiavelli, or Montaigne? These questions of justification are current and urgent, because once more the reading of great books has moved to the center of discussions about higher education and the liberal arts. Virtually all recent studies of baccalaureate education urge students' engagement with historically important texts. William Bennett's *To Reclaim a Legacy*, for example, published under the aegis of the NEH, suggests a canon stretching from Homer to Faulkner. The AAC's *Integrity in the College Curriculum* recommends the development of a student's historical consciousness through encounters with primary texts, and explicitly links the study of value with the use of exemplars in history and literature. The University of Chicago—ever a bastion of great books—currently touts its B.A. program called "Fundamentals: Issues and Texts," which combines a traditional emphasis on the close reading of selected important texts with contemporary features such as individual design for each student's program and the organization of studies around thematic, agenda-setting problems, rather than around lists of texts of presumptive universal relevance to be mastered. The Educational Leadership Project of the Christian A. Johnson Endeavor Foundation structures its seminars on academic leadership for presidents and deans around close discussion of *The Republic*, *The Prince*, and similar works of historical importance. In the Wilson Center's *The Teaching of Values in Higher Education*, James Billington writes of the importance of a common tradition of texts. Allan Bloom, in *The Closing of the American Mind*, offers the study of heroic figures in great books as virtually the only positive prescription in a book otherwise barren of proposed solutions to the country's educational and cultural malaise. What lies behind this surge of emphasis on great books? What could justify it, intellectually, pedagogically, and culturally?

The justifications offered by great books advocates invoke a concern for *values*, a concern for the cultivation of the *ethical* dimension of education, and a concern for the conveyance, in higher education, of something regarded as a legacy, a heritage, or a tradition. Though these are distinct concerns, they are closely related, and any assessment of the contemporary resurgence of enthusiasm for great books must both distinguish them and define their interconnection. But the underlying explanation of the renascence of great books in their connection with values, ethics, and tradition, lies in a wide-ranging contemporary intellectual phenomenon—the demise of modernism and the rise of postmodern styles of thought.

What is postmodernism? Michael Messmer has identified three chief dimensions. One dimension is an aesthetic reaction to modernism in art and literature.

It denotes reaction against the styles that germinated near the turn of the twentieth century and grew to dominance in the 1920s and 1930s. Another form of postmodernism is rooted in socio-political thought, and denotes trends of thought shaped by Marxist and Freudian motifs. The third sense construes "modernism" as the designation of the philosophical project launched in the seventeenth century, that grew into the Enlightenment and that set, for the West, a philosophical agenda dominated by epistemology and metaphysics. "Postmodernism," then, in philosophical parlance, denotes the movement of thought which finds that project at an end and seeks a new paradigm for philosophical work. This third, philosophical, sense of "postmodernism" pertains to the renascence of interest in great books. In this essay I proceed from the premise that the eclipse of the Enlightenment and the dimming of its afterglow in the institutions of our culture have necessitated a radical change in our understanding of the nature of values and of ethics, and make room for a new apprehension of the right place of tradition in the maintenance of culture. It is my aim only to illustrate, not to demonstrate or justify that eclipse, but I do aim to show how a postmodern sensibility provides for a coherent understanding of the nature of values, the teaching of ethics, and the critical appropriation of tradition, as well as how, in a postmodern context, those issues converge on the teaching and reading of great primary texts.

II. Postmodernism: The Consideration of Values and the Teaching of Ethics

Despite their differences, the great philosophers of the seventeenth century shared enough interests and projects to justify the claim that, in terms made current by Thomas Kuhn, they worked within a common paradigm. They—Bacon, Descartes, Locke, and others—shared an interest in explicating the nature of human understanding in order to rebuild the edifice of knowledge on grounds cleared by the demolition of Aristotelian concepts, methods, and conclusions. They held out the prospect of the articulation of perfectly explicit methods for the conduct of the understanding. The hallmarks of that paradigm are the scrutiny of concepts through analysis, the testing of beliefs against the canons of reason and the evidence of experience, the establishment of purified, universally applicable rational processes as the sole criteria of credible knowledge, and the cumulative construction of a unified edifice of sound knowledge, based on indubitable certainties and erected through demonstrably valid methods. The great philosophers of the seventeenth century were foundationalists of one sort or another, believing that knowledge must be grounded in the given self-evidence of rational truths or in the evidence of immediate experience. Hence, they placed epistemology at the center of philosophical concerns, and embraced, in their various ways, one form or another of realism—the view that our knowledge corresponds, and can be shown to correspond, to things as they are. They further held—or rather, assumed—that the knowing agent is an individual mind which is essentially distinct from the objects of its knowledge and is only incidentially embodied and acculturated. The individual mind, in the seventeenth-century paradigm, is capable through its own resources of discriminating knowledge from false belief and of orienting itself in the methods that lead to the growth of knowledge. Communities and traditions play only negligible or negative roles in the epistemological project. Finally, the seventeenth-century philosophers held that the proper aim of philosophy was the construction of a perspicuous survey of the whole domain of knowledge in its unity and universality, and in its linkage to the reality made accessible through it to the knowing mind.

If the precise places of value and of ethics are not mapped out explicitly in such a paradigm of knowledge and of philosophy, at least the parameters within which they must be considered are given. They must be derived from, or set alongside, knowledge of objective fact that is (1) founded in purified, universalizable, and explicit methods of reasoning and experiencing; (2) in contact with things as they are; (3) accessible by and justifiable by individual minds; (4) warranted (purportedly) by a sound epistemology. The early chapters of Alasdair MacIntyre's *After Virtue* chronicle the failure, as he sees it, of attempts to accommodate our understanding of value and ethics to the new paradigm. Indeed, he asserts that as a result of those failures, we have inherited only the wreckage of a moral discourse.

In any case, the modern paradigm has come under increasingly effective attack as the twentieth century has worn on. In philosophy, postmodernist sensibilities are exemplified in Richard Rorty's rejection of epistemological projects in favor of a philosophical discourse whose aim is the maintenance of a tradition of edifying conversation. In this project, interpretation replaces epistemology as the characteristic philosophical enterprise, and the aim of the process is the continuity of a certain conversation, not the depiction of reality. Indeed, the displacement of epistemology is the crucial litmus test for identifying postmodern sensibilities in philosophy. Richard Bernstein's aim of displacing the categories that have defined modern epistemology, in his book *Beyond Objectivism and Relativism*, is another clear instance of postmodernism. In theology, George Lindbeck's development of "cultural/linguistic" understandings of religious doctrines, in place of pre-liberal "propositional" and liberal "expressivist" readings, is (in Lindbeck's own description) a "postmodern" or "postliberal" move. Alasdair MacIntyre's account of the unravelling of ethics in the West since the Enlightenment in *After Virtue* is a key ingredient in philosophical postmodernism in the English-speaking world. MacIntyre deploys Aristotelian themes, offers a positive regard for medieval organic community, and delivers sharp criticism of modes of thought rooted in the Enlightenment. The most significant factor in postmodernism in science and philosophy of science is the critique, by Thomas Kuhn and others, of the received modern notion of science as a linear, progressive approach to truth guided by algorithmically defined, exhaustively explicable methods of reason and experimentation. In the social sciences, the broad, rather ill-defined cluster of attitudes known as "cultural relativism" also contributes to the critique of the Enlightenment confidence in discoverably universal norms of thought and action: an essential ingredient in modern liberalism, with its faith in the rationality of human nature.

The roots of the postmodern sensibility lie deep in twentieth century thought, including the later thought of Dewey, Heidegger, and Wittgenstein. Its expressions include the works of many thinkers in addition to these examples. A sketch of a postmodern sensibility will show why a resurgence of interest in great books, classical texts, and even a cultural canon, should be of central interest to anyone for whom that sensibility has replaced modernity as the context of thought, learning, and teaching.

The postmodern sensibility contrasts point-by-point with modernity, as sketched above. This use of the word "sensibility" is intended to suggest that postmodernism consists more in clusters of interlocking attitudes, styles, and procedural tenets than in an articulate propositional credo. There are various ways—not necessarily compatible—of articulating the elements of philosophical postmodernism, but all involve the following: (1) that concepts of rationality and experiential evidence are always inextricably tied to cultures; (2) that, therefore, the project of attempting purified, universal norms of reason and experience is either completely ill-conceived (the radical reading) or susceptible only of partial and provisional success (the moderate reading); (3) that, therefore, all our accounts of "objective fact" are contextually conditioned products of a particular perspective and that we are never in a position to give an account of "things as they are in themselves" to justify our claims to objectivity; (4) that the justifiability of our claims to know (and even to make sense) involve appeals to communities who embody traditions, and that knowledge is therefore—in some sense—social in character; and finally (5) that the project of epistemology is displaced by projects of interpretation; i.e., the production of commentaries relating bodies of knowledge to one another, to the communities that sustain them, and to the interests that motivate and shape their acquisition.

Within this sensibility, the situation of values and ethics is no longer—as modernity had it—one of derivation from or placement alongside, a domain of knowledge of objective fact. It becomes far from obvious that a domain of fact and a domain of values are distinctly separable, or that the processes of developing and justifying accounts of what is true or false and accounts of what is good or bad are radically distinct. Rather, it appears from a postmodern perspective that what the

131

modern sensibility understood as facts and values are mutually implicated in each other's articulation and defense, and that therefore, we need ways of thinking about the human situation that are not premised on the modern fact/value dichotomy. This implies that we should anticipate no major conceptual break between issues about what is praiseworthy and blameworthy, and issues about the nature of the self, its world, and the community it indwells. How, though, does a postmodern sensibility inform issues about values and ethics?

The scene from the *Odyssey* with which this essay began is a useful vignette for the consideration of values. By considering what might be at stake in this scene, we can explore the way in which encounters with rich literature can help us to understand the nature of values. There are instructive problems in attempting even to state the values we find. The list of value-laden issues we might find at stake in these events would include, to name a scant few: homecoming; the vindication of honor and manliness; the repossession and defense of property; the punishment of the wicked; revenge; the mutual devotion of father and son; prowess with weapons; the preservation of marriage and the home; cleverness, deception, and trickery; the hospitality owed to guests; and the greed exemplified in the suitors. Of course, neither Homer nor Odysseus would have generated *this* list of values, a list reflecting the perspective of the Western middle class in the late twentieth century. The recognition of disparities from age to age and from culture to culture in the conceptualization of values—and also of facts—is a primary lesson of acquaintance with great works of other times and places. It is important to assess the meaning of those disparities. What they show is not that we can never understand the values at stake in the *Odyssey*, but that we can appropriate the text only from our own perspective, and can offer accounts of the Homeric values only on terms intelligible to ourselves. To admit that we can say only, in effect, "how it looks from here," is not to condemn ourselves to *mis*understanding, as long as we combine an awareness of the disparity itself with a continuing attempt to indwell the other standpoint. Our perspective will be more adequate if it contains a sympathetic imagination of the perspectives of the characters portrayed and of the narrator. In this case, an imaginative reconstruction of the values as Odysseus would have conceived them, and as Homer's narrator would seem to have conceived them, becomes, as we encounter the text, an ingredient in our own apprehension of it. While we admit the inadequacy of all such reconstructions, to abandon them would be to flatten our own perspective by forfeiting the tension supplied by our awareness of the disparity.

This model of understanding lacks a point of closure, a point at which the process of consideration stops and we claim that we have conclusively understood the values exemplified in Odysseus' slaughter of the suitors. But this lack is not a flaw. The point of considering the values at stake in such scenes is not to attempt the articulation of some final list of values, but to entertain the image of Odysseus as the embodiment of some conception of well-being and fit behavior. Odysseus functions as an exemplar—a model for possible emulation. Internally to the text, he functions in this way for Telemachus, and in the reader's apprehension of the text, he functions doubly as an image of heroic manhood and as an image of the teaching father initiating his son into that station in life. Telemachus, of course, functions too as an exemplar; he is the faithful, learning son, ready to stand and fight at his father's side. These are powerful pictures. To consider them is not the same as to adopt them and to incorporate them into one's own active repertoire of styles. We can distinguish, as perhaps the presocratic Greeks did not, between an appreciative, sympathetic entertainment of an image, and the internalization through which the observer comes to identify himself with it, and to understand himself through the values embodied in it. This distinction raises issues which will appear again and more clearly. The immediate point is that the vignette under discussion presents exemplars, and does so in various interconnected ways. But it does so implicitly, without drawing attention, on the surface of the text, to the fact that this function is in operation. To find a deployment of exemplars that is explicit, and therefore both reflective and argumentative, we can turn to Plato's depiction of the trial of Socrates.

Socrates was tried and condemned by the Athenian assembly. Though he had fought for Athens and had devoted himself to the public good as he saw it, he was politically estranged from the democratic regime in 399 B.C. He conducted himself during his trial with a blend of piety toward Athens and scorn for the malice and stupidity of his accusers. Charged with impiety toward the gods and corrupting the youth of Athens, Socrates explained himself—as Plato portrays him in the *Apology*—in this way:

> Perhaps someone will say: "Are you not ashamed, Socrates, of leading a life which is very likely now to cause your death?" I should answer him with justice, and say: "My friend, if you think that a man of any worth at all ought to reckon the chances of life and death when he acts, or that he ought to think of anything but whether he is acting justly or unjustly, and as a good or a bad man would act, you are mistaken. According to you, the demigods who died at Troy would be foolish, and among them Achilles, who thought nothing of danger when the alternative was disgrace. For when his mother—and she was a goddess—addressed him, when he was resolved to slay Hector, in this fashion, 'My son, if you avenge the death of your comrade Patroclus and slay Hector, you will die yourself, for fate awaits you next after Hector.' When he heard this, he scorned danger and death; he feared much more to live a coward and not

133

to avenge his friend. 'Let me punish the evildoer and afterwards die,' he said, 'that I may not remain here by the beaked ships jeered at, encumbering the earth.' Do you suppose that he thought of danger or of death? (34)

In this speech, Socrates not only appeals to values, but also practices ethics, their reflective study. Ethics, in the Aristotelian sense assumed here, is the inquiry into human well-being and flourishing. Its subject matter is *eudaimonia*, the state of the good and happy soul, the human being who, being neither a beast nor a god, is fitted to live in community, and who, according to an immanent source of natural potential, can develop only in that setting to the highest capacities he or she possesses. Studies of values in the narrower sense pertaining to rules of conduct, where concepts of morality and immorality are generated, is a narrower domain confined wholly within the richer context of ethics. *Eudaimonia*—human flourishing, the possession and exercise of the excellence proper to humanity—is among the noblest objects of inquiry. But how does such inquiry proceed?

Let us notice a troubling passage in Aristotle's *Nicomachean Ethics*. Aristotle notes that discussion of ethics must begin from what is known. So he says,

> ... to be a competent student of what is right and just, ... one must first have received a proper upbringing in moral conduct. The acceptance of a fact as a fact is a starting point. ... A man with this kind of background has or can easily acquire the foundations from which he must start. (7)

It may seem troubling that Aristotle holds that only those who have been well brought up can profit from discussions of ethics, and indeed, even that only those who have been well brought up can *understand* the points at issue. His meaning is that we cannot hope to do ethics theoretically and reflectively (with the capacity for intellectual assessment, comparison, and generalization), until we have been trained into some community of practical ethics whose sources and procedures are quite different from those of the academic philosophy class in theoretical ethics. To see what might be the point of training in a community, let us recall the case of Socrates. He appeals to the heroes of Troy whose actions are familiar to all in his audience and accepted by all as exemplary. Achilles, Patroclus, and Hector compose his list of examples. But we need to be careful about what an example *is*. *Modern* intellectual culture, presupposing the primacy of general, theoretical principles, supposes that examples are *illustrations*. Primarily, modernity supposes, one grasps a principle. Then the example illustrates it, making it vivid and concrete as a secondary step. This notion of the relation between examples and principles is a symptom of the abstracted rationality of the Enlightenment: the philosophers of the seventeenth century strove to purify reason of all particulars. The idealized reason they constructed reduced *cases* to a subsidiary level. But concrete cases provide in fact the only medium in which a theoretical generalization can arise. Cases are not simply illustrations of principles. Principles, at best, summarize cases. To one who lacks familiarity with cases, principles are useless, or worse.

These assertions do *not* entail that it is impossible or wrong to reflect upon and to argue about values abstractly. Consideration of exemplars is not the whole of ethics, but it is the beginning, and it is the sustaining matrix within which alone anything more abstract—e.g., formulation and argumentation of principles—can occur.

This approach reflects a departure from the Enlightment presumption that rationality about values can be, and ought to be, purified of reliance on their instantiation in particular cases. The grounds of that denial have been spelled out by a variety of contemporary philosophers. Alasdair MacIntyre has put it in this way:

> Concepts are first acquired and understood in terms of poetic images, and the movement of thought from the concreteness and particularity of the imaged to the abstractness of the conceptual never completely leaves that concreteness and particularity behind. Concepts of courage and of justice, of authority, sovereignty, and property, of what understanding is and what failure to understand is, all these will continue to be elaborated from exemplars to be found in the socially recognized canonical texts. (Relativism 9)

Others—including Wittgenstein and the ancient sceptic Sextus Empiricus— have made the point more abstractly by demonstrating that any intelligible proceeding, however describable in general rules, rests necessarily on an unarticulated substratum of natural human inclination and trained behavior, and that anything we would recognize as rational action or explanation presupposes some such substratum and can never hope to replace it with theorized prescriptions. As Aristotle says, the study of ethics presupposes that one has been well brought up. As Socrates illustrates, making an ethical case, argumentatively, depends on allusion to recognized exemplars: what Achilles concretely did; how Hector behaved in the particular instance. Harvey Cox has succinctly explained the notion of an exemplar: "the person or persons within a religion or a cultural tradition who exemplifies, embodies, incarnates that which is seen to be virtuous: the good, the noble" (200). Two quick *caveats* are necessary. First, exemplary cases of the base and unworthy are also conveyed by great works. Livy wrote, "We study . . . the past so that the great things men have done can be praised and the wicked things held in eternal contempt" (Agresto). Second, the mere provision of an exemplar, good or bad, in a tradition is a different matter from granting it authoritative standing. In order to see the sort of standing an exemplar may possess, it is necessary to inquire into the nature of the authority of traditions.

III. Great Books and the Authority of Traditions

To the extent that great books function as a cultural memory, they constitute a thesaurus—a treasury of cases, exemplars, models, and paradigms. And to the extent that acquaintance with these provides the starting points mentioned by Aristotle, great books hold the key to being well brought up, culturally, and therefore the key to being capable of understanding more abstract and reflective issues. I have already argued that the unique function of great books is their purveyance of images of human action, of well-being and corruption. These images form the necessary medium for an understanding of moral concepts. It follows that any attempt to teach ethics which fails to involve and engage such images will collapse. So acquaintance with great books or their cultural equivalent is therefore essential to what is often praised as the culmination of liberal education: the development of a sense for values. One does not arrive at this culmination by studying values. Values are not pieces of dry goods available for investigation. We learn to talk sense about values by examining cases such as Odysseus' vengeance upon Antinoos and Socrates' explanations to the Athenians.

But a major problem remains. The possibility of really understanding anything about values rests on training in a community, and the existence of a community rests on the vitality and continuity of a tradition. So being *some*one, being equipped with concepts of right and wrong, ideas about well-being and unhappiness, is an accomplishment achievable only in a community shaped by some tradition. In this connection a central problem arises concerning the nature and extent of the authority of traditions. That problem has the following shape. Recognition of the role of exemplars and the traditions that convey them in making possible our moral discourses tends often to lead to the view that traditions exist to be affirmed, perpetuated, endorsed, and uncritically assimilated. Talk of heritage, legacy, and tradition is often intellectually and ideologically conservative, serving as the academic correlate of cultural and political agendas resistant to, or even hostile toward, change. There is therefore reason to fear that the current opportunity to affirm the importance of great books will be politically coopted. We might hope for a resumption of the role of great books in liberating students from parochialism and in sustaining a culture whose hallmark is an open-textured evolution, generated by disciplined internal criticism. Instead, we may see the reemergence of another familiar role: canonized sets of great books, installed as

136

the touchstones of a dominant, stipulated cultural norm. A fixed canon of texts may be deployed in the defense of an intolerant tradition. Specifically, there is some tendency in the current rhetoric of *reclamation* and *inheritance* to suggest an enlistment of great books in the restoration to cultural hegemony of a partial apprehension of the human experience—a male-dominated, European/American bourgeois tradition. This prospect is heightened by the setting in which students come to great books. Practically every initial acquaintance of students with them is authoritarian in structure. A master, backed with the quasi-coercive clout of an institution, presents to young people who are in his or her power a catalog of ancient and prestigious works. The very setting encourages the master to transmit, and the disciples to absorb, appreciate, and assimilate. Bloom has charged that contemporary students are shaped principally by influences from outside academe, influences which (as Plato charged of the poets) play upon and enlarge the non-rational elements of the soul. Surely the right response, though, is not to attempt simply another appeal to a non-rational agency, i.e., authority, but to attempt to cultivate the powers of reflection and discrimination that will help the student to avoid two extremes: the uncritical absorption of an inherited past, and uncritical adoption of the cultural fashions of the moment.

No one would deny that great books and we who study and teach them have a powerful, rightful role in the perpetuation of culture. James Laney has recently reaffirmed this vital role. But he has also charged that the traditional cultural wisdom has been too exclusive, parochial, and didactic—too prone to function as a mask for injustice and hyprocrisy. The most crucial element in the assessment of liberal education is the question how we bring students into engagement with great books. Unless we can answer that question reflectively and critically, we must, by default, fall into an authoritarian pattern in which a renascence of interest in great books must be merely a restoration of the *status quo ante*, a tradition negligent of every human perspective except that of middle-class, male, European/American culture since 1600. On the other hand, if we succeed in answering this question, I believe, the reactionary vision of reclamation and restoration will prove not true even to the Enlightenment culture which it embraces.

This question about the authority of the traditions conveyed by engagement with great books can best be approached by considering three closely related versions of the issue of openness versus closure. First, must there be a set canon of great books, a closed list of classics constituting the core reading list of "the educated person?" Second, is there a prescribed mode of appropriation of great books, a standard set of values contained in them and conveyable by them, such that the failure to derive this set of values from one's acquaintance with the texts constitutes *mis*understanding? Third, is there an established set of abstract topics, held to be the essence of the culture's commitments, which are instantiated and

137

illustrated in the texts, such that the texts are merely vehicles for their exposition? The answer to each of these questions is "No," and the justification of these answers will constitute a response to the problem about the nature of the authority of traditions.

First, is there a closed list of classics? Throughout this essay I have carefully written of "great books," (lower case) rather than "*the* Great Books." The definite article and capitalization strongly suggest, if they do not assert, the closure of canon. The argument in favor of a closed canon is essentially the following. "If the function of acquaintance with great primary texts is to provide the novices of our culture with concrete cases of action and deliberation as the starting points of moral reflection, and if moral reflection is essentially a community activity, then we shall have to share acquaintance with a more or less unified inventory of concrete cases. Hence, we shall have to read the same set of texts. And if novices are to share with each other and with the rest of us common texts, someone will need to settle on a canon." Allan Bloom apparently embraces this argument when he calls a resort to great books (though he capitalizes the phrase) "the only serious solution to the culture's educational malaise" (344).

But Bloom goes on to catalog the grave drawbacks that attend the attempt to delineate a canon, mentioning, among others, the problem that "there is no way of determining who is to decide what a Great Book is or what the canon is" (344). Bloom here illuminates the fundamental problem in great books canonization. The books themselves are supposedly foundational, yet they stand in need of being *authorized* as foundations. How are foundations—the bedrock upon which justifications rest—themselves justified? This is the insoluble problem generated by foundationalist epistemologies of the Enlightenment, the problem which finally shows the futility of seeking ultimate foundationalist justifications. Every attempt to stipulate a fixed canon necessarily generates the same problem.

Further, the "fixed canon" argument presupposes a fully circumscribed and fully unified culture. The notions of fixity and of determinacy in the canon correspond to the desire for uniformity of the culture. Such cultures are, or *were* at least, possible. It is even probable that the traditional life of humanity consisted in exclusive, isolated immersion in one or another completely distinct and unified culture. But this is hardly the case in the contemporary world, and the vitality of the West has been characterized by openness, by cultural borrowing, and by fusion since the time in which Pericles said of Athens: "We throw open our city to the world" (Thucydides 109). The concept of a culture is not sharply circumscribed, nor free of internal variation, nor free from overlap with or incremental gradation into another culture. We should then expect a culture's literary and humanistic canon to be similarly variable and in the same way vaguely bounded.

The deep significance of the need to stipulate a fixed canon can be disclosed through consideration of the relationship between explicitly framed rules and the cultures within which they are accepted. Wittgenstein showed in *Philosophical Investigations* that the very existence of an explicit rule (and hence the possibility of obeying it) is parasitic on the customs and practices in which the rule is embedded. To suppose that explicit rules are logically primitive, and that cultures are their more loosely defined derivatives, generates a paradoxical infinite regress of interpretations. Wittgenstein's exposition of this fact parallels arguments given by Sextus Empiricus, and shows that, unless we are willing to embrace a radical scepticism, we must grant that every explicit formulation of a rule (law, regulation, recipe, instruction, order, etc.) is dependent for its sense upon some matrix of unarticulated practices engaged in by the community employing the rule. One consequence of this fact is that rules exist and are intelligible only in so far as there exist commonly accepted and agreed upon ways of understanding, applying, and following them. Another consequence is that there are limits to the usefulness of trying to make rules clearer and more comprehensive by providing more and more detailed interpretations. Ultimately, what the rule *means* must be understood without further interpretation. Hence, at some stage in our consideration—in specific cases—we will have to ask where is the line of transition between the domain of the specified rule and the domain of practice and informal custom.

How do these reflections illuminate the perceived need to stipulate a fixed cultural canon? Such a stipulation would be an attempt to articulate and codify a culture's essence. It would be an attempt to capture in *rules* the cultural forms and customs on which all articulate rules must ultimately depend for their sense and application. But, as Wittgenstein and Sextus show, it is precisely the fact that cultural forms and customs are *not* explicit formulations, and hence do not demand for themselves justification and interpretation, that makes them the matrix of practices making rules intelligible and applicable. Codifying custom removes its power to end interpretive disputes, and produces simply more rules which themselves need interpretation and justification. That is why there is no way of providing a conclusive account of who authoritatively sets the canon. One would first have to say who says who possesses that authority, and so on.

This primacy of culture over canon does not mean that no culture could have a fixed, stipulated canon, but that only those cultures recognizing unquestionable authorities could do so. But what is the status of the idea of a canon in a culture marked by pluralisim and an argumentative approach to the status of authorities? As E. D. Hirsch emphasizes in *Cultural Literacy*, the existence of more or less commonly shared cultural information is compatible both with flux over time as to its contents and with the absence of any formally constituted authority determining what is in or out. The absence in the contemporary West of any formally constituted authority means that the determination of the commons is in the hands of a complex, unsystematic, cultural infrastructure of persons, organizations, institutions, customs, traditions, and habits. The cultural commons is marked by the curricula of schools and colleges, by the preferences of publishers and broadcasters, the tastes of critics and reviewers, the inertial habits of the community at large, by the practices of institutions both public and private, by governmental policies, and by a congeries of mutually interacting forces too numerous and too vague for complete listing.

Further, the cultural commons is neither neatly unified nor precisely bounded. Instead of one center, a cultural commons may have many lobes, one or another of which may be emphasized in various conceptions of the commons. Community is not sameness; it is the entertainment and intercourse of differences on common ground. One can imagine different envisagements of contemporary Western culture centering variously, on the Judeo Christian tradition, on the tradition of liberal democracy, on the dominance of science and technology, or on the rise of capitalism and commerce. One can imagine such various versions of the cultural commons overlapping, and in their different emphases exemplifying what Wittgenstein called "family resemblance." To ask which of these is correct might be not only pointless but actually wrongheaded; Alasdair MacIntyre has argued that continuing conflict over its central aims and values is a characteristic feature of any living tradition (*After Virtue* 207). Canonical status, then, is imputed by a culture. Like political authority in liberal democratic theory, it exists and is legitimated through the consent of those who recognize it. And it has all the looseness of the concept of culture itself. To summarize, the canon has internal variety and vague boundaries, and it shifts over time, paralleling, in each of these attributes, the culture itself.

But beyond these considerations, the question about the status of canon also raises the second issue of closure. Is interpretation closed? I have spoken of great books in the essential role of providing exemplars of virtue and vice. Virtue, we hope, echoing the lines from Livy quoted above, will be praised, admired, and imitated, and vice condemned, scorned, and eschewed. But who is to say which exemplars display virtue and which vice? Is there a prescribed mode of appropriation of great books? The relevant concern is this: "If the point of providing the novices of our culture with concrete examples of action and deliberation as the starting points of moral reflection is to provide them with examples of virtue and vice *as* cases of excellence and failure, then some provision will have to be made for enabling the novices to distinguish and recognize the cases for what they are. Either the texts themselves shall have to identify cases of excellence *as* cases of excellence and cases of failures *as* cases of failure, or the novices will have to have received some type of training antecedent to and/or simultaneous with exposure to the texts, which will enable them to recognize [them as such]." At stake here is, among other things, the supposedly culturally conservative character of the study of great books. A set of canonical texts, even if fixed authoritatively, need not be a culturally conservative force, *unless* interpretations are fixed, that is, unless *someone* is authorized to fix the meanings of the exemplars, sorting out virtue and vice. The force of the argument just quoted is to suggest that unless someone does that, the exemplars cannot function. So it looks as if we must choose between fixed interpretations, on the one hand, with culturally conservative consequences; and open interpretation, on the other, with the loss of the exemplars' moral authority.

Jaroslav Pelikan has addressed this issue with lucidity in his essay "*King Lear* or *Uncle Tom's Cabin*." Pelikan contrasts two different styles in which values may be at stake in, and approached through, literature. In one style, to which *King Lear* lends itself, values are *implicit* in the narrative and in the actions of the characters. They are apprehended through *inductive* processes—gathered from the texture of the action. They are handled in an *analytic* way, as objects of investigation and consideration. They are, in Pelikan's words, "caught," not "taught." On the other hand, *Uncle Tom's Cabin* has value structures which are *explicit*, *deductive* (in the sense of being virtually necessitated by the structure of the action), and *didactic*. Literature teaches set lessons. Romantic educators in the tradition of Rousseau would argue that the culture ought simply to stand aside and let the developing novice identify and follow—as he or she surely would—the right exemplars. Neoconservative scholars have held up the unpromising nature of that strategy as a rationale for stipulating interpretations along with the texts. Is there a middle ground which preserves Pelikan's implicit, inductive, analytic apprehension of exemplars, and at the same time provides for their recognition and function *as* exemplars?

The danger in Pelikan's approach, as clearly seen by the neoconservative, is that implicit values might not be recognized, that values left to be gathered might not be, that values brought up for analysis may be rendered impotent, and that, generally, left to themselves, people are liable to spurn virtue and embrace vice. What is necessary, to avoid these problems, is simply that the exemplars, be investigated *as* exemplars, that is, as live options. It is not necessary that interpretations be fixed. The neoconservative reduces the options to this dilemma: there must be fixed interpretations of exemplars, or the forfeiture of any effective consideration of values results. But as soon as we recognize varieties of interpretation, the terrain opens up into a plurality of ways of approaching exemplars *as* exemplars. These will resemble each other more or less. In ways analogous to the complex, unsystematic definition of the cultural commons itself, they will overlap to form a more or less unified—though not uniform—pattern of appropriation. No formally constituted authority is required to achieve effective, reasonably common interpretations of cultural exemplars. Indeed, there is reason to fear that *setting* interpretations—telling the novices how they must appropriate cases—

would be counterproductive. The desire to designate, explicitly, which ones show vice and which ones virtue is yet another instance of the urge to intrude an interpretation between the case and its appropriation. How can we be sure the interpretation won't be taken wrongly? Is another interpretation needed, and would it insure against misunderstanding? What if it didn't? This is, again, the paradoxical regress which Wittgenstein pointed out, a regress which can be scotched only by an appeal to the capacity of the reader to "catch on" and to actively assess and, perhaps, appropriate the exemplar.

At least one recent national report, the NIE's *Involvement in Learning*, lays heavy emphasis on the student's active engagement in the learning process. Certainly students learn more, and more efficiently, when the pedagogy calls on them to act, to respond, and to be involved as more than passive recipients. But there is a grander point. Ultimately, liberal education has to do with *Bildung*—the cultivation of character, the individual's growth into the form of mature humanity. And that process—notoriously—cannot be done in one's behalf by surrogates. Nor is it a process that can be accomplished without *self*-formation. One must wrestle with the content of education, one must appropriate old exemplars and imaginatively adapt them as ingredients in a process of self-formation, or *Bildung*. The self who simply accepts and is shaped by the inherited tradition is on the way toward vanishing, as an individual, into molds supplied by an authoritarian culture. The student who is passive, and who, as the familiar idiom has it, simply regurgitates facts or imitates, woodenly, the proffered models, is not fulfilling the point of the process. Epictetus puts it vividly: "Sheep do not hastily throw up the grass to show the shepherd how much they have eaten, but inwardly digesting their food, they produce it outwardly in wool and milk" (36). We who teach in liberal education do not aim primarily to cram our students with facts which they receive and then cast up again for our inspection. Nor do we wish them merely to learn to behave like Odysseus, or Socrates, or Achilles. Our aims are subtler, and like those of the shepherd, are directed toward certain outward and active capacities which our students may come to command.

Education in ethics through great books is distorted if it asks everyone to use the same exemplars and to use them in the same ways. *Training*, as Aristotle said, gives us starting points; but after that come the higher skills of deliberation. Stuart Hampshire has written (in *Morality and Conflict*) of the inexpungability of moral conflict, and the necessity of painful choice. But this wisdom is made invisible by the teaching that reduces the *right thing to do* to a repetition of an inherited paradigm. MacIntyre (as cited above) tells us that traditions always embody continuities of conflict, and that a lively tradition always is partly constituted by disagreement about the nature of the goods in whose pursuit it develops, and about the choice of strategies for pursuing them (Virtue 206–07). So an acknowledgment of the necessity of exemplars does not require the installation of authoritarian justifications of professorial stature, of pedadogical procedure, or of cultural transmission. Nor does it diminish the role of close, reasoned argument in resolving ethical problems. It is the continuity of argument about exemplars and their significance that sustains a tradition and forestalls deadening closure.

The third dimension of closure pertains to the reduction of the contents of great books to abstract topics. Of course any interesting encounter with a worthwhile text involves the attempt to say what that text is *about*, an attempt that may often, rightly, involve an abstract statement of what the text manifests concretely. But such processes of interpretation differ greatly from the presumption that there exists a set of eternal questions, or a set of issues which inevitably arise anytime anyone begins to reflect. Rorty argues, in *Philosophy and the Mirror of Nature*, against that presumption. The notion that such questions or issues are formulable is part and parcel of the perspective of modernity. Only if we suppose that we command universal forms of rationality independent of our specific cultural and biological circumstances, will we also suppose that there is available to us a transhistorically valid conceptual mapping of the issues at stake in important texts. Modernity is grounded on the supposition that rationality, so conceived, is realizable; postmodernism is premised on its unavailability. Allan Bloom apparently endorses this postmodern stance in his assertion that liberal education "means reading certain generally recognized classic texts, just reading them, letting them dictate what the questions are and the method of approaching them—not forcing them into categories we make up, not treating them as historical products . . ." (344).

This assertion rebuts one of the central props both of conservative and of liberal pedagogical theory. If we possessed an understanding of the eternal issues, we would have confidence in our grasp of the *content* of education sufficient to provide partial grounds for a decision concerning the proper degree of control over the *process* of education. If one supposed that the essential issues are widely manifested, the curriculum and the syllabus would be permissive, full of options and alternatives. If one supposed that they are expressed only in a narrow range of literature, the curriculum and the syllabus would be correspondingly highly prescribed. The liberal's historic emphasis on the evolution and development of the student's latent natural abilities is no less an expression of confidence in our understanding of ahistorical essences than is the conservative's historic insistence on the inculcation of some codified version of the culture's traditions.

The topical approach assumes that we can understand and control the substance of education. But the substance of education, as embodied in great books, eludes packaging because it eludes control. Great works of literature possess a richness of texture which can show us different truths, in different ways,

143

according to our circumstances. To many who read and saw performances of the *Antigone* in the late 1960s, it was clear that the play was about the individual conscience in defiance of authority, a conflict of religious and civil responsibilities. To many in the 1980s, the play may seem to be about the struggle to maintain administrative balance in the face of inflexible demands based on non-negotiable religious commitments. What we take the story of Antigone to be *about* will depend on what our circumstances permit us to see in it. And since our circumstances are always local and peculiar, it is important that we not try to reduce the rich texture of great stories to abstract themes. Great books elude control because they elude final, conclusive definition. We do not *ultimately* understand and control their substance.

Introduction of *topics* as a framework for acquaintance with a tradition introjects an extra layer of hermeneutic density between student and text. The instructor, armed with interpretation, intercedes between them. If the student *knows*, in reading *Antigone*, that it is really about civil disobedience, the text is reduced to an obscure portrayal in the concrete of an abstract clarity. Also, the student is given to believe that the abstractions are real and that the cases (texts) are instances—illustrative examples. This is not only ontologically *wrong*, it is also stultifying. The very clarity of the abstract themes is confining. Such themes are closed and closing. Cases in the concrete, *just because* of their fuzziness and unclarity, are open and opening. Cases give us novelty, new thoughts, fresh ideas. Pedagogy based on texts is open to risk, and involves a certain amount of disorder. It is appropriate that we articulate principles to display ways of understanding texts, but is is important that we not construe our tasks of interpretation as the search for the single exclusively adequate set of abstract themes.

As the repositories of exemplars, great books convey to us no atemporal essences, no eternal verities. They are recognized and employed at particular times and places. Choices of canon are historically conditioned; the subject matter is mixed. The unity of the humanistic enterprise lies neither in method nor in content. It lies in function: great books articulate for use, application, imaginative interpretation, and understanding, a great wealth of exemplary cases of human action, without *some* supply of which we cannot deliberate well about what is good, or just, or noble, or beautiful, or even about what is true. One last citation of Aristotle: "We consider that to be real and true which appears so to a good man. ... And if virtue or excellence and the good man ... are the measure of each thing, then what seem to him to be pleasures *are* pleasures and what he enjoys *is* pleasant" (285). This position is not relativism, but humanism, and to make sense of it we need cases of good persons portrayed for our apprehension. (And of bad ones, too.) Provision of these portrayals, and their analysis, is the task of humanistic education, and this task places the reading of great books squarely at the center of any enterprise we should call *higher* education.

IV. Conclusion

I have argued that the postmodern sensibility, in recognizing the groundedness of all our forms of understanding in the substrata of communities with their traditions and customs, must not be construed as merely a novel articulation of cultural and political conservatism. Such conservatism depends on three forms of closure—closure of the canon, closure of its evaluative interpretation, and closure of its construal into abstract topics. I have argued that each of these forms of closure is incompatible with postmodernism's historicist acknowledgement that the processes of canon formation, evaluative interpretation, and conceptual mapping are necessarily open-ended. That these processes are open-ended means that it is an integral part of cultural maintenance to propose and to argue over lists of great books, to propose and to argue over moral and aesthetic evaluations of their contents, as well as to propose and to argue over ways of construing their contents in conceptual terms. *However*, that these processes are necessarily open-ended means also that it is a mistake to advocate an end to these arguments through an authoritative (or authoritarian) ultimate definition of the canon, its value, and its meaning.

The foundationalist sensibilities of modernism demanded that the validity of our forms of rationality be grounded in something—nature, pure reason, God—that transcends the cultural traditions in which those forms are manifested. Otherwise, in this view, they are without justification. To secure a groundwork, modern philosophers necessarily sought an ontology. Postmodernism seeks, by contrast, genealogies. Alexander Nehamas has argued that Nietzsche—in many ways the *Urvater* of postmodernism—systematically replaces the ontological urge with the project of constructing genealogies. "The unity of each thing," writes Nehamas in explication of this idea, " . . . is to be found in the genealogical account that connects one set of phenomena to another" (104). And, "to ask what the nature of the world is in itself . . . is like asking which family tree depicts the real genealogical connections among everyone in the world" (104). That is, just as many genealogical trees can be constructed, each emphasizing some one lineage in human interrelationships, so there exist, potentially, indefinitely many genealogical accounts of any phenomenon whose explanation we care to undertake. Just beneath the surface of this view lie three connected principles: (1) interpretation: the modern project of justification-by-grounding is replaced by a project of interpreting-by-displaying-connections; (2) historicism: understanding by interpretation requires display of a phenomenon's origins and development—its precursors and parallels; and (3) pluralism: multiple, variant genealogical accounts of any phenomenon are possible and, indeed, desirable—the world is susceptible of different envisionments.

In an intellectual world shaped by this sensibility, there is no point in arguing over a commons of great books and tradition as if our task were to discover given, correct versions of either. Rather, what takes the place of justificatory argumentation is the interpretative task of displaying linkages among the following:

1. exemplars of vice and virtue,
2. the books, plays, stories and so on in which these exemplars are embodied,
3. the explicit ethical teachings that abstract from and explain the exemplars,
4. the accounts of nature and human nature implicated in such explanations,
5. the characters modelled for emulation or eschewal by the exemplars, and
6. the society composed by those who embrace some versions of elements 1 through 5.

Giving accounts of such linkages and thus, genealogically, accounts of the exemplars, books, teachings, worldviews, characters and social forms themselves, amounts to raising a tradition to self-consciousness. There is no doubt that a tradition whose self-understanding centers on the continuity of such open-ended projects of interpretation is sustainable. But it is also clear that such a tradition must forgo the metaphysical comfort of prior assurances of unanimity and closure.

Alasdair MacIntyre, in *After Virtue* and other works, has set as the central question for the postmodern consideration of ethics the opposition, as he sees it, of Nietzsche and Aristotle. Portraying Nietzschean amoralism as the culmination of Enlightenment rationalist individualism, he juxtaposes that nihilism with Aristotelian emphases on a teleologically charged human nature, on moral training (rather than just education in moral concepts), on community and tradition, and on ethics conceived through virtues and exemplars, rather than rules and principles. But several writers have found MacIntyre's *opposition* of Nietzsche and Aristotle mistaken, and have argued for a synthesis in which an Aristotelian perspective is adjusted to the postmodern realities of interpretation, historicism, and pluralism. That project has yet to be worked out in detail, but a synthesis of Nietzschean perspectivism with the main structures of Aristotelianism offers the best hope of making sense of ethics in the postmodern context. It is clear, too, for reasons that stretch both to Nietzsche and to Aristotle, that close engagement with great books will be central in the postmodern understanding of ethics.

Agresto, John. "Doing Justice to the Humanities," in *ACLS Newsletter* (Winter-Spring 1986).

Aristotle. *Nicomachean Ethics.* Indianapolis: Bobbs-Merrill, 1983.

Bennett, William. *To Reclaim a Legacy.* Washington: National Endowment for the Humanities, 1984.

Billington, James, "Afterword," in *The Teaching of Values in Higher Education*, Washington, D.C.: The Woodrow Wilson Center, 1986.

Bernstein, Richard J. *Beyond Objectivism and Relativism.* Philadelphia: University of Pennsylvania Press, 1983.

_____. "Nietzsche or Aristotle: Reflections on Alasdair MacIntyre's *After Virtue.*" *Soundings* (Spring 1984).

Bloom, Allan. *The Closing of the American Mind.* New York: Simon and Schuster, 1987.

Cox, Harvey. "Moral Reasoning and the Humanities." *Liberal Education* (Fall 1985).

Conway, Daniel W. "After MacIntyre: Excerpts from a Philosophical Bestiary." *Soundings* (Fall 1986).

Epictetus. *The Enchiridion.* Thomas W. Higginson, trns. Indianapolis: Bobbs-Merrill, 1955.

Hampshire, Stuart. *Morality and Conflict.* Cambridge: Harvard University Press, 1983.

Havelock, Eric A. *Preface to Plato.* Cambridge: Harvard, The Belknap Press, 1963.

Hirsch, E. D., Jr. *Cultural Literacy.* New York: Harper and Row, 1987.

Homer. *The Odyssey.* W. H. D. Rouse, trans. New York: Mentor, 1937.

Integrity in the College Curriculum: A Report to the Academic Community. The Association of American Colleges. Washington, D.C., 1985.

Involvement in Learning. Washington, D.C.: The National Institute of Education, 1984.

Kuhn, T. S. *The Structure of Scientific Revolutions.* Chicago: University of Chicago Press, 1962.

Laney, James T. "The Education of the Heart." *Harvard Magazine* (Sept.–Oct. 1985).

MacIntyre, Alasdair. *After Virtue.* Notre Dame: Notre Dame University Press, 1981.

_____. "Relativism, Power, and Philosophy." *The Proceedings of the American Philosophical Association*, Vol. 59 No. 1 (Sept. 1985).

Messmer, Michael W. "Making Sense Of/With 'Postmodernism'," *Soundings* (Fall 1985).

Nehamas, Alexander. *Nietzsche: Life as Literature.* Cambridge: Harvard University Press, 1985.

Pelikan, Jaroslav. "*King Lear* or *Uncle Tom's Cabin.*" *The Teaching of Values in Higher Education.* Washington, D.C.: The Woodrow Wilson Center, 1985.

Plato. *Apology.* F. J. Church, trans. Indianapolis: Bobbs-Merrill, 1956.

Rorty, Richard. *Philosophy and the Mirror of Nature.* Princeton: Princeton University Press, 1978.

Thucydides. *The Peloponnesian War.* New York: Modern Library, 1982.

Wittgenstein, Ludwig. *Philosophical Investigations.* New York: Macmillan Co., 1953.

See Eric A. Havelock's *Preface to Plato.* Cambridge: Harvard, The Belknap Press, 1982. I owe appreciation of the force of this argument, and, indeed, this very formulation of it, to Professor Donald C. Reed, Transylvania University. This argument too I owe to Professor Donald C. Reed, in a private communication. See Richard J. Bernstein's "Nietzsche or Aristotle?" and Daniel W. Conway's "After MacIntyre."

CLASSICS, CULTURE, AND CURRICULA

Ronald A. Cordero
University of Wisconsin, Oshkosh

Votaries of the classics would be well advised to pause from time to time to reflect on the reasons which support their allegiance. Doing so could add to their own appreciation of the classics and might in addition equip them to bring others to share that appreciation—an act which, if they are correct about the value of the classics, must surely be one of significant benevolence.

The reasons for valuing the classics which I wish to consider here are only two in number, but each of them relates to particular concerns of our present age, while still involving the timelessness which so agreeably characterizes the classics. The first has to do with the attempt to identify the essential ingredients of the Good Life; the second concerns the attempt to create a society in which those ingredients can be found.

I. Champagne and Shakespeare

What *is* it about the bubbly? Why do so many people devote so much attention to it? The answer can only be that they firmly believe their lives would be less good without it. And they will ordinarily not hesitate to make a similar claim with respect to the lives of others. Those who enjoy Dom Perignon's little discovery tend to think that those who for some reason or other cannot or do not enjoy it are *missing* something. From the point of view of champagne's devotees, it was, for example, an objective misfortune that Shakespeare passed away before it was invented. The Bard definitely missed something, they would say; and if there were only some way to do it, we ought to send him a case.

Now these are views about empirically verifiable matters. The beliefs in question are either factually correct or factually mistaken. Either it would be possible for me to have just as satisfying an existence without champagne or it would not. Either Shakespeare would have been happier if he had had champagne or he would not. And if the beliefs of champagne's advocates are factually correct beliefs, they have consequences of singular importance for anyone trying to lead—or to help someone else lead—an existence as satisfying as may be humanly possible.

I do not intend to try to prove here, of course, that a particular alcoholic beverage is an essential for the Good Life. While I myself will probably go on paying exorbitant prices for imported bubbles, I am not going to argue for champagne as a Good-Life essential. What I do want to maintain here is that our beliefs about the classics are quite analogous to the beliefs many of us have about champagne, and that epistemologically, prudentially, and altruistically, matters are much the same with respect to the two sets of beliefs.

Whether we are speaking of classic works of sculpture, painting, music, or literature, those of us who put a premium on the classics do so because we believe that a life lived without experiencing them would be significantly less satisfying to the person who lived it. We believe that we must have these things in our lives if we are to live as well as possible, and we believe that we must get them into the lives of those whom we would help toward happiness. Life without great literature and great art would not, we feel certain, be the same.

But this sort of belief—like the beliefs about champagne—might be factually in error. It *might* be possible for us—or at least for some people—to have just as satisfying a human existence without any contact with the classics. This is a possibility of which we must be aware and one which we must carefully examine if we are concerned to make an honest case for the classics. We want to be reasonable, and it would hardly be reasonable to urge people to include in their own lives—and for their own good—something without which they could live just as well. If life with mineral water could be every bit as satisfying as life with champagne, we would not want to argue that people ought, for their own good, to have the latter. And if life without great literature or great art could be just as satisfying as life graced by either of the two, then we could not in all conscience recommend that people, for their own good, include one or the other in their lives. If in reality some people could have just as good a life with daytime television dramas as with great literature, we would be wasting both their time and ours by trying to get literary classics into their lives. Our efforts could conceivably produce little more than aggravation for everyone affected.

But how are we to reassure ourselves, or more precisely how are we to *prove*, that the classics are as vital to the Good Life as we ordinarily assume them to be? How are we to establish that life would be worse for want of them? Unfortunately, the way to a satisfactory proof of such a claim is fraught with philosophical difficulties.

There is, for example, the problem of individual differences. Might it not be that individual uniqueness is such that what is a necessary ingredient in the Good Life of one person may not be necessary at all for the Good Life of another? Might it not be the case, for example, that because of the complicated interplay of heredity and environment, some people actually find as much or even more joy through popular music than other people do through classical music? The existence of this possibility should, if nothing else, inspire a modicum of humility in advocates of the classics, who often tend, it must be admitted, to take it for granted that pursuit of the classics is objectively and universally more rewarding than the pursuit of pleasure through more widely popular works of art. But if we are not simply to assume this without argument, how are we to prove it?

The matter is not quite so simple as it might seem. We cannot simply take a wide range of people, expose them to both classics and popular favorites, and tabulate the results. The full appreciation of many works of art requires extensive background and preparation. Surely we cannot expect a painting by Giotto or a play by Shakespeare to have its maximum possible impact on someone lacking the requisite background and understanding. Nor, however, can we prove the superiority of the classics by tabulating people's preferences both before and after they have been given adequate preparation for the classics. There is a chance that the "backgrounding" or preparation which enables someone to fully appreciate classic works of art may actually diminish that person's ability to appreciate more popular art works—that the study and experience which brings someone to full appreciation of Impressionism may simultaneously ruin their ability to appreciate bright paintings on black velvet, or that the coursework which can make me a fan of Shakespeare may ruin me for cowboy novels. Now this effect may not be regrettable from the point of view of the pursuit of the Good Life if we can be sure that once the classic taste is acquired the person's life is indeed more satisfying than it was before. The problem is that we cannot take this to be established simply by a shift in preferences. It may be that after introduction to the classics people are enjoying different things—but enjoying them no more than the things they used to enjoy.

What we will have to do if we really want to establish the superiority of the classics for people in general is to compare the lives of those who appreciate them—either instead of more popular art works or in addition to them—with the lives of those who do not appreciate them. After other differences are factored out—hardly an inconsequential task—the superiority of the classics, if any, should be discernable. If reading classic works of literature like the plays of Shakespeare can really add something valuable to most lives, it should show in the lives of readers. Readers of the classics should *ceteris paribus* find life more satisfying than those who do not read them.

Another major problem confronting the advocate of the classics is the question of just how one is to know which works are—or are deserving of being—classics. How do we tell which works of art are the ones that ought to be a part of our lives? Perhaps we are justified in taking the recommendations of agents and promoters with a grain of salt. If someone stands to make money from our appreciation of a particular work of art, their appraisal of its value for our lives may well be biased. And perhaps we are equally justified in not immediately accepting popular success as a criterion of greatness. When it comes to the question of which art works are greatest, perhaps fifty million French—or a billion Chinese—*can* be mistaken. But are we then to be left with the judgments of experts, who are so notoriously given to disagreement among themselves? Ask the experts, "Which *are* the classic works of art, the best productions of humanity, the ones that we should include in core curricula if we really want our students to be able to achieve the Good Life?" Ask that, and you will not exactly get a unanimous answer.

Fortunately, though, the question is again a factual one, and we can discern at least the general direction in which an answer can be sought. If some works of art are better than others of the same genre when it comes to illuminating our lives, then people with sufficiently broad experience should be able to identify them. Perhaps the best we can do is to consider seriously the counsel of the experts with the widest experience, while remembering that even they—like experts in any factual matter—may be wrong. Their consensus may not be infallible, but it may be the best indication we can get of which works are really the best.

One consequence of this would appear to be a need for experts conversant with more than one culture. Certainly no one human cultural tradition can have a monopoly on the classics. It is extremely unlikely, for example, that our planet's greatest works of literature have all been written in the same language. But then an expert knowledgeable only in the production of one culture could not be relied upon to know which are the greatest literary works of humanity. And that is precisely what we would like to know when we set out to structure curricula.

So clearly we can argue that if one major purpose of education is to enable people to live the fullest, most satisfying lives possible, and if there are certain works of art without experience of which almost anyone's life would be poorer, then education ought to include the preparation and experience that will make the appreciation of those works possible.

With respect to the selection of particular works as classics to be included in curricula, two caveats concerning the universality of greatness are worthy of attention. On the one hand, sad though it may seem, it may be possible for a great work to "slip over the horizon"—to pass beyond the grasp of most people in a given age. While this could not happen, of course, to a truly universal work, it is uncertain how many works are truly universal. If a work demands, for its full appreciation, familiarity with a certain language, profound understanding of a particular historical milieu, belief in a particular metaphysical view of reality, or childhood exposure to certain tonal combinations, for example, then it may not be possible for that work to go on being a classic forever. A time may come when the amount of study required to appreciate it fully becomes so great that the work becomes, for all practical purposes, inaccessible to the great majority of people. Such a work could simply no longer be counted on—after coverage within the limits of the average curriculum—to add something to life that ought not to be missed.

On the other hand, there is also a very real possibility of underestimating the universality of a given work of art. In particular, it could be a serious mistake to discourage students, through the structuring of a curriculum, from encountering a work simply on the grounds that it comes from a different—even a distant—cultural tradition. Although your cultural tradition is X, a work from culture Y may in fact be one which you can come to appreciate fully and without which your life would be significantly poorer. Those who are not of English descent ought not to be discouraged from reading Shakespeare—any more than those without Greek ancestors should be discouraged from reading Plato or those lacking French chromosomes should be told not to bother trying champagne.

II. Alexander and *Cosmo*

What would Alexander the Great have thought of *Cosmopolitan*? That magazine, coming out as it does in a variety of languages in a great many parts of the world, may well be promoting an internationalization of certain cultural elements; and Alexander did have a dream of a universal (cosmos-wide) civilization achieved through the fusion of diverse cultures. Whatever Alexander might have thought of the specific cultural elements being disseminated by the magazine in question, it would appear that defenders of the classics can base a further argument for inclusion of the classics in core curricula on the culturally unifying effect of such classic-laden curricula. Cultural unity can, after all, play a central role in the development and preservation of political unity, and political unity can be a necessary precondition for the Good Life.

If we want our fellow members of society to enjoy the greatest works of human art, we have to maintain in existence the type of society in which those works can be appreciated. When life in a country is seriously disrupted by national or international strife, both time and resources for the Good Life are in short supply. Fortunately, one of the effects of including the study of classics in core curricula would appear to be the promotion of a cultural unity which can significantly decrease the likelihood of political disintegration.

That cultural unity discourages political disunity is a thesis which may not have to be defended here. It is, of course, another factual claim—one which can be evaluated by an examination of the historical record and which could conceivably even be tested through experimentation. What I should like to stress here is the almost magical way in which the teaching of classics from the most diverse cultural traditions can lead toward cultural unity.

There is, of course, nothing new about this at all. It has been going on as long as culturally disparate groups of people have been—as we might be tempted to say nowadays—"interfacing" with each other. When you *really* mix three parts of culture A with four parts of culture B what you get is not an unstable conglomeration, but a unified culture C. A true cultural melting pot, that is, does not work like a centrifuge. (Perhaps the image of a cultural "blender" would be even clearer.) If we insist on a core of classics in our educational system, introducing students to the best human productions we can find, what we start to get is a culturally unified, cosmopolitan population, whose members are less rather than more liable to fall to fighting among themselves.

Such cultural unity, with its attendant decrease in political disunity, can of course be obtained by educating people to share a taste for cultural elements of any sort. Examples are almost too easy to find. Just think, for example, of fashion and music videos. ("Bluejeans and Madonna: International Cultural Unity in the Twentieth Century." The title is tempting, but I don't think I'll write the article.) This trend toward unity in *popular* culture is going to continue with or without the help of those of us in higher education. The motive forces at work—both commercial and hedonistic—are sufficiently strong to ensure that.

What we *can* promote through the wise design of core curricula for higher education is increasing cultural unity based on an appreciation of the classics— the best works of art and literature that humankind has produced. Even if the experts never reach complete agreement as to which works are the best, the very process of debating the relative merits of the top contenders can produce a great deal of shared cultural experience.

If we who love the classics are right, and the classics really do offer something that can raise the Good Life to heights otherwise unattainable, then our students reap double benefits—from the enjoyment of the classics in their own lives, and from the social harmony that the sharing of such enjoyment can promote.

153

WHAT MAKES A GREAT BOOK GREAT?

Mary Troy
Webster University

I approach this topic as a writer, as someone who indulges the notion of writing one of the world's great books, and as a teacher of students who have not read—in some cases, have not heard of—many of the great books our culture has to offer. In answering the question then, I think first of what my students would say, have said: it is the reader, through his involvement and judgment, who makes a book great. I am tempted also to be even more obvious and say it is the author who makes (has made) the book great. But I know the question is asked with an eye toward the canon, toward a consensus, or at least a basis for a consensus, about the core curriculum. So I know, too, that it is the scholars and critics who are responsible. It is they who have pointed to, emphasized, and proselytized a book's greatness. Now though, as discussions on opening the canon flourish in the humanities sections of colleges and universities—as well they should flourish—the canon must be reevaluated periodically; the question needs a more precise answer. What is it that scholars and critics have seen in certain works? What criteria were they using? What have they overlooked? What was, or should have been, their basis?

Even before scholars and critics, though, come publishers and editors. Ever since books have been sold, the publishers have been the first to evaluate a work. Those works that fail the first test are unpublished, are not available for scholars and critics to study. Of course, I recognize this as a simplistic and naive explanation of publishing. What is published is not so much what is great, as what publishing houses believe will sell. Though there are notable exceptions to this now, such as New Directions, what seems saleable will be published. And I believe it was ever thus, ever since books were sold. And if not motivated by profit alone, many publishers selected books of relatives or friends. And even before the printing press made book distribution and sales possible, most authors published and distributed themselves. The point is that we select our great books from an already narrow group, from a certain segment of society, primarily wealthy, white males. Few others had the education, the connections, or the time.

And from this group, some have survived and others have not, again thanks to scholars and critics. But not all books that have survived are great. Some are only examples of a period in history, good examples of a type of writing, of what else existed at the time one of the "great" books was produced. *Everyman*, for example, is among the best of the morality plays, and as such is good and worthy of study. It is not, however, a "great" book. In all cases, a hierarchy has been established. For instance, among those writing during the late sixteenth and early seventeenth century, William Shakespeare is considered by most scholars and critics better than Christopher Marlowe, but Marlowe is placed over Michael Drayton and Robert Southwell.

But I come back to the question. What have these critics looked for? Why have some works come down to us as "great"? The answer to this question is similar to that of another question, "What is Literature?" Or to go further, "What is Art?" An answer to all three questions is Art is that which provides insights on the human condition, that which illuminates or questions our actions, ourselves, and by so doing entertains us. I use entertain here not in its more popular meaning of making us laugh, giving us an escape from our lives, but rather as that which engages us by assisting in the exploration of ourselves and others. A "great" book is about us, and is as full of whatever truth it contains now as it was hundreds or thousands of years ago. *The Canterbury Tales*, Plato's *Republic*, *Madame Bovary*, *Crime and Punishment*, *King Lear* are examples of books whose truths and insights endure. In *King Lear*, we have greed, jealousy, devotion, suspicion, guilt, and honesty coming to the fore through specific situations; we see one action causing many others; we see many human elements highlighted. We see ourselves in action four hundred years before we were born. Emily Dickinson said it thusly:

> The Poets Light But Lamps—
> Themselves—go out —
> The Wicks they stimulate—
> If vital Light
>
> Inhere as do the Suns—
> Each Age a Lens
> Disseminating their
> Circumference—

Charles Dickens' *A Tale of Two Cities* is set just prior to the French Revolution, and is about the French Revolution in the sense that it is about breaking, restructuring, what many people (Edmund Burke, for example) saw as the natural order. The infamous knitter, Madame DeFarge, is victim turned villain. Thus, *A Tale of Two Cities* is about us whether we are French or Ethiopian, revolutionaries or royalists. And to go back even further, Socrates' refusal to save his own life by telling his judges what he knew they wanted him to say, but what he could not say because it was not truth, is about us, too. Many of us, however, do tell the judges what they want to hear, and in fact are encouraged to do so by learning how to take tests, how to interview. Nevertheless, Plato helps us see ourselves through Socrates.

But do not all thinking people have insights, conclusions, questions, ideas about humanity? Yes. But not all insights are equal. To say this in a democracy as self-conscious as ours is to invite argument; nevertheless, Emily Dickinson's lamp does shine brighter than Henry Wadsworth Longfellow's. That is clear. Yet even Henry Wadsworth Longfellow did have some insights, at least one. How could he not have? And insights alone are not enough anyway. How those insights are presented, how clearly, how vividly, how memorably, how movingly distinguish good from great. Alexander Pope in his *Essay on Criticism* says because thoughts and ideas are seldom original, it is the words used that give ideas force. "Words," he says, "are the dressing of thoughts." While great books should contain elements of clarity, we often like the style to be as beautifully complex or as poetically ambiguous as the ideas in the book, as ourselves. At least we are not happy with proverbs, with cliches.

One of the truths that great books, and good ones, too, provide time and again is that no one group is smarter, kinder, more deserving than any other, and this includes the white male majority. The judges of literature, however, are not democratic. They should not be concerned with the sex, race, or creed of the authors of those "great" books; there should be no attempt at a representative canon by mixing and matching the authors' backgrounds and politics, but by mixing and matching the voices and ideas in the works themselves. A criticism Pope makes of critics is that they judge the man, not the work, and this criticism remains valid today. In fact the humanities might be better served if all works were anonymous, allowed to stand on their own.

The white male authors of the past have spoken to us of prejudice and greed and artificial class distinctions and domination and subjugation and equality. Their personal lives and morals notwithstanding, because they really are beside the point, the authors more often than not see the imperfections in the system and through their works, praise or highlight the individual. This is not meant to imply a morality or any code of conduct that should be part of the critic's decisions. In fact, a great book could easily be judged immoral, could *be* immoral. What it has to be is true, about us. Would a woman of Plato's time have had different truths to impart? Certainly. Is it a loss that there was not an educated woman whose ideas were written and passed down? Again, certainly. Does this make Plato less relevant, less true? No. Absolutely not. It is true we have lost many sides of the human experience through not educating certain groups, but we cannot rewrite history to produce, for example, a good black woman writer from the middle-ages. (But I am in favor of searching for any forgotten or overlooked but good or "great" works.)

When I say a great book shows us ourselves, I do not mean that narrowly. I do not think a Native American need be told only what it was like to grow up on a reservation. Actually, I believe all of us could benefit from such a telling. What a great book does is take us out of ourselves; it lets us expand our experiences. I am not like Anna Karenina, nor do I know anyone who is, not exactly. But Anna is real. She is a character in whom I see parts of myself and parts of others and the whole of no one but herself. Though she was created by a man, I believe she is a true woman character, because I do not expect her to be *the* woman character. There is no one woman to whom we—male and female—could refer to and say, "She is it." I also see myself in Levin, and he is a male. I see less of myself in Jane Austin's Emma Woodhouse, but again, seeing myself is not the whole point. I see Emma and accept her reality as a character who misreads all of life's clues. So Tolstoy and Flaubert and Austin and Brontë and Welty and Morrison all can give us women characters, just as they can give us men.

And we should not try to do away with the racial or sexual bias of the canon, because greatness transcends such considerations. We should be willing, though, to re-evaluate, to condense some sections or works, to discard others, to add newly recognized "great" books. Our history is continuous, and as some books gain the status of great and are added to the canon, some others must be dropped. Students in London during the English Renaissance studied the Italian Renaissance, especially Plutarch, studied also the Romans Cicero and Seneca, and through them the Greeks. They did not study Chaucer or themselves, though we now study a few of them. Some American students in the late twentieth century still study Plutarch and Cicero, but few study these as part of the core curriculum, the canon of "great" books.

History, of course, helps to make a book great. A book I write next year, one I have written, should not be considered great now, regardless of advertising hype. As a writer of contemporary fiction, I am not one who bemoans the state of literature today, nor do I find as much sameness in current work as many critics do. In fact, I find most new fiction good. But history in the form of scholars and critics will determine the greatness of any of it.

Why should a contemporary work not be considered great? There are two answers. One is that greatness needs perspective. A part of greatness is the ability to survive, to still be true, as I have said, hundreds and thousands of years later. The second reason has to do with the canon, with the idea that whatever is called great will be (should be) required, will make up a core that unites educated people who understand the same allusions, can make reference to the same works, and have a basic knowledge of a common heritage as humans. The canon will connect us to the human continuum that even though different remains the same. If students finally like the Wife of Bath and the Nun's Priest, it is because they recognize in both people, of whatever race or sex, who could exist today. They may recognize Ophelia, the girl driven mad by a mad lover, as a popular theme of

157

contemporary books or ballads. And though women lawyers no longer have to pretend to be men, students can see in Portia the individual assigned a role according to an accident of birth. Though again, because so much of the greatness is in the telling, in the work itself, to gloss over these works in order to give quick examples, does them an injustice. A work is not good because it is universal, but universal because it is good.

And contemporary books may be read anyway, even if not required. The canon is surely not the only reading an educated person will do. If it is, it becomes solely part of an unimportant exercise, busy work for the academic. Someone who is forced to read *The Pardoners Tale* (and force is the operative word) and does so with understanding will enjoy Graham Greene and J. F. Powers and J. D. Salinger. A student who reads *King Lear* will read Flannery O'Connor, Toni Morrison, and Walker Percy with delight. Salmon Rushdie, Ruth Prawer Jhimbalya, Maya Angelou, Maxine Hong Kingston, and even Mary TallMountain will be read by those who have been exposed to the "great" books, to those who have been given, even against their will, the gift of language and history and thought. That is, they will read more if they are informed about these books and writers through courses in contemporary work, through not wholly commercial bookstores, through reviews, through readings, and through word of mouth.

So yes, open the canon. Re-evaluate what is in it, add that which is better, which shines a brighter lamp, which I add a word illuminates human nature clearer. But do not do so to add contemporary works; do not do so to add a sexual and racial balance; and do not do so in the belief that the canon, the "great" books, will comprise the only reading of an educated person. A great book that illuminates well will only encourage further reading, further thought, and even further writing.

NOT THE CANON, NOT THE CORE, BUT CLOSE ENOUGH: THE MASTERPIECES APPROACH

Laurin A. Wollan, Jr.
Florida State University

Debate over the core and the canon will go on and on. It may quiet down. But in the meantime, the war goes on with skirmishes and sieges. Maybe one day a sort of peace will settle over the battle fields. (To speak of core and canon is to summon up military metaphors and images!) For the time being, however, the combatants might take refuge, or at least bivouac for a time, in an alternative to core and canon that promises much of what everyone seems to be seeking and even a good deal more, though along quite different lines.

This alternative is the "masterpieces" approach now developing at Florida State University, quietly and obscurely, yet with strong support and even some acclaim from administrators, faculty, and students alike. It is not quite a substitute for the core, let alone the canon, but it may relieve some of the win-or-lose pressures that afflict an all-or-nothing argument.

The idea of the masterpieces approach is simple: students experience a variety of masterpieces organized around a common theme. The works which are read or seen or heard or otherwise experienced are either themselves masterpieces or else describe masterpieces of one sort or another. Each has something significant to do with the common theme, revealing it or illustrating it or extending it in some important way. The result: students experience many aspects, or levels, or elements of a theme, a theme significant in and of itself (justice, love, and so forth)—while experiencing a variety of superb works in one or another of the genres, disciplines, fields.

But First, What Is a Masterpiece?

A masterpiece is a work of excellence, or "any supreme accomplishment," as John Opdycke put it in *Mark My Words*. In the literal sense, it is the work, any work, of a master, or more commonly, a master's best work. *What Makes Sammy Run?*, for instance, is Budd Schulberg's best book, his masterpiece. A masterpiece need not be among the "great books" and often is not. It must, however, be excellent among those of which it is one. For purposes of the course described here, the body of works of which it is one—its "cohort," so to speak—consists of the works of "supreme accomplishment" concerned with a certain topic or theme or idea. Thus, Schulberg's *Sammy*, while not one of the "great books" by any means, is nonetheless a masterpiece among those works concerned with ambition, though far out-class(ic)ed there by *Macbeth*.

A masterpiece need not be literary or even *written*, let alone a work of fiction or philosophy, as long as it is a work of excellence. Works on a theme, however, are likely to be written and, if masterpieces, are likely to have literary merit as well. But excellence need not even be *verbal*, let alone written. An event, a strategy, an invention, a relationship, a structure might be an accomplishment of excellence, hence a masterpiece.

The standard by which a work is included in a thematic "cohort," though less demanding than that by which a work is admitted into the canon of the great books, is nevertheless a high standard. It assures that such works will approach, if not always attain, the qualities of the great works themselves. Masterpieces, in short, are not anemic classics but robust works that engage, challenge and inspire the mind, heart, and spirit by their very excellence.

Masterpieces and The Canon

If the canon is the set of books, or works, by which western civilization is defined, then it will include masterpieces. Indeed, it is inconceivable without them: each and every work in the canon is a masterpiece.

Masterpieces generally differ from classics, however, in having a focus on a dominant idea, to the exclusion of much of anything else. In contrast, the classics ordinarily are rich in attention to or otherwise suggestive of many ideas. They can be taught from many points of view. Because a course on masterpieces will deal with a great idea, the student will surely come away from such a course acquainted with some of the great works.

But, as suggested above, not all masterpieces measure up to and thus qualify for *the* canon. But there are canon and there are canon, canon to the right of us, canon to the left of us, canon in front of us. (Volley'd and thunder'd, I suppose one should add!) Greco-Roman civilization has its canon. It includes those master-pieces of *the* canon that come from its portion of *the* canon, and a good many more by several dozen. (By way of footnote to all of this, a number must inevitably be established. The Stanford controversy presupposes a number, else there is no issue of what comes out so something else can go in. That number might as well be 100.)

So there is then the canon of the Judeo-Christian tradition, of another 100 works. That may seem too many, but not when it is divided into 20 centuries A.D. and many more than that B.C., and three separate streams as well, the Jewish, the Catholic, and the Protestant. And this is to say nothing of the non-western canon, the Afro-American canon, the women's canon, the canon of medicine, of law or justice, or engineering, and so forth.

Thus, the term "cohort" may be better at this point than canon, at least for

160

present purposes, because it gets away from the controversy associated with canon and "canon-busting" and it fits better the subdivisions of great works suggested by this exercise.

All of which leads now to those things, or themes, that are constituent parts of western (and perhaps any) civilization: a recurring concern for—and commitment to—justice, liberty, truth, peace, beauty, order, goodness, and the like. These relate to the canon in an important way. While one way to enter the canon as a whole, that is to say *the* canon, is at the beginning, with Homer, other ways, or points of entry, are thematic—at those clusters of works that have to do with such themes—justice, for instance. Several of the works in the canon have something to do with justice. But, there are other works of excellence concerning justice that are indispensable to any study of justice.

Masterpieces and the Core

The questions of core and canon are separate though related. The question of the canon resolves itself into what is essential to the definition or representation— by its works—of western (or any) civilization. The question of the core is instead, what must be taught, studied, learned by students in the liberal education experience. The canon question and the core question will yield different lists, because liberal education might well include less of the canon and more of something else. But a good deal of overlapping would be expected, too, because liberal education is at least in part, a very large part, about western civilization. But not entirely. And into the area of difference—what liberal education, or the core, includes that is not the canon—can go the masterpieces, to deal with themes the canon covers but does not develop fully.

The Rationale of the Masterpieces Approach

The "why" of liberal education has been well put by Mark Van Doren: "The aim of liberal education is one's own excellence, the perfection of one's own intellectual character. Liberal education makes the person competent; not merely to know or do, but also, and indeed chiefly, to be. . . . The prime occupation of liberal education is with the skills of being." Putting it another way, Van Doren says, "Liberal education is learning not to make a living but to make a life." According to Van Doren, a liberal education "consists of the liberal arts, literary and mathematical, because they control thinking whenever thinking is done; and equally it consists of the great works in which meaning has been given to the ideal statement that human life is itself an art."

Masterpieces go far—when aggregated around themes for coherence— towards these ends. But there is more to be said for the approach. First, as indicated above, reading masterpieces on a theme or seeing them or hearing them or

161

otherwise experiencing them will engage the student and lead to an appreciation of works, creators, artists, inventors, adventurers, genres, disciplines, eras not likely otherwise to be encountered in courses typically found in general education or liberal studies programs. Such courses, many of them, do include masterpieces, but not as systematically, not as abundantly, and probably not as variously as in the approach described here.

Second, such works challenge the student with an idea (generally the theme will be an idea, though not always), an idea not likely otherwise to be explored in any depth, or at least not very explicitly or very thoroughly. Masterpieces go beyond information; they are more than merely insightful or illuminating. No textbook, however well it may scope out a subject or tick off its topics, nor the up-to-dating articles of the month or moment, will do as well as masterpieces for an inquiry into matters so basic. Like the great books, masterpieces will have the student concerned with the most fundamental ideas or aspects of their subject, where the best of thinkers and artists have aimed their efforts.

Third, the array of masterpieces will immerse the student in outstanding examples of a variety of genres, many of which are not ordinarily included among *the* canon (which traditionally is one of great books, not paintings, operas, films, speeches, or statues).

Development of One Such Course: Masterpieces of Justice

So far one such course has been developed and offered at Florida State University. This course, Masterpieces of Justice, the prototype of the series, draws on masterpieces of the literature—and other forms and works of art—concerned with justice, in its broadest reaches. Some of them are truly great works, firmly established in the canon—by Plato, Sophocles, Shakespeare—and revolving closely about the idea of justice. In addition, lesser but important works of excellence (though some are not widely known) take up the idea of justice in various dimensions of its institutions, practices, incidents, and so forth. The offerings and their sequence are as follows:

1. Daumier's Lithographs of Lawyers, *Les Gens de Justice*
2. Sophocles' *Antigone*
3. Plato's *Crito* and *Apology*
4. *The Book of Job*
5. Shakespeare's *Measure for Measure*
6. John Rawls' *A Theory of Justice* (selections)
7. Melville's *Billy Budd, Sailor*
8. Gilbert and Sullivan's *Trial by Jury*, *The Mikado*, and *Iolanthe* (selections)

9. A Br'er Rabbit story, an essay by W. E. B. Dubois, an oration by Frederick Douglass
10. Mary Wollstonecraft's *A Vindication of the Rights of Women* (selection), *The Seneca Falls Declaration*, and Simone de Beauvoir's *The Second Sex* (selections)
11. Lon Fuller's *The Case of the Speluncean Explorers*
12. Kafka's *The Trial*
13. Camus' *Reflections on the Guillotine*
14. Ayatollah Khomeini's *Islamic Government* (selections)

Implication For a Series

If such a course has merit, there must be many more that would realize the conception. Each would take up a theme of significance, not necessarily one that has preoccupied the great thinkers who, while tackling "the great ideas," have not dealt at length (or sometimes even very deeply) with many of the lesser yet important ideas. Each would present works of "supreme accomplishment" that deal with such themes. Thus, the student would explore deeply such topics, in the company of the finest thinkers and artists who span the ages, in a variety of forms: poetry (epic, lyric, even haiku); prose (novel, essay, dialogue, play), the fine arts (opera, oratorio, painting, sculpture, dance), and the popular arts as well (cartoons, editorials, movies). All of this would be in the company of instructors who are not only expert in the field and the work but usually enthusiastic exponents of its argument or type.

To illustrate the foregoing, Masterpieces of War could include: Thucydides on the Peloponnesian War, one of the great books, certainly one of the great histories; Clausewitz' *On War*, a great work of military strategy, which few readers, no matter how well educated, are likely to have read; Mahan's *The Influence of Sea Power Upon History*, likewise and much broader; Tolstoy's *War and Peace*; Tschaikowsky's "1812 Overture"; Crane's *The Red Badge of Courage*, not on many lists of the great books, yet a masterpiece of reporting the experience of war, though a work of pure imagination by one who never fought; Ernie Pyle's *Brave Men*, a masterpiece of reporting on that experience journalistically from first-hand observation; much poetry, such as Randall Jarrell's "The Death of the Ball Turret Gunner"; Bill Mauldin's cartoons of Willie and Joe; Heller's *Catch 22*, like Crane's book, less than great but a masterpiece of its kind; the great photography that emerged in wartime—from Alexander Gardner's in the Civil War through *Life*'s in World War II; films such as *All Quiet on the Western Front*, *Twelve O'Clock High*, *Command Decision*, and *M*A*S*H*; the Luger, the B-17, and the jeep as technological masterpieces; Hemingway's *A Farewell to Arms*, perhaps not his masterpiece but certainly one within its cohort.

Masterpieces of Statesmanship could include such topics as the origin of states (from *I Samuel* and Plutarch's *Gracchi* through the American State Papers to Lenin's *The State and Revolution*); forms of the state (classifications by Aristotle and Montesquieu); theories of the state (e.g., the contract theory in Hobbes, Rousseau, and Locke); the "education of princes" (Machiavelli and Henry IV); statecraft (by Lincoln, Bismarck, Wilson, Churchill); and reflections on the city-state (Pericles), the imperial state (Marcus Aurelius and Gibbon), the feudal state (John of Salisbury), and beyond (such as world-state proposals, from Kant onward).

Where Does Such a Series Go?

A masterpiece series could have several locations. To take the Florida State series as prototype, it could remain where it is now beginning, in the Center for Professional Development and Public Service, with various courses in the series recycled for future offerings by Center.

Other locations for such courses could be elsewhere throughout the university curriculum. Some courses could be shifted to niches at various schools or departments or programs (such as Humanities, American Studies, Women's Studies) having some "claim" to a course by reason of affinity for its theme. For example, Masterpieces of Crime and Punishment would find a "home" in Criminology, Masterpieces of Justice in the Law School, Masterpieces of Statesmanship in Political Science, Masterpieces of War in ROTC, each of which has an obvious concern for the course's theme.

Others could become staples of the honors curriculum, at least in an honors program like Florida State's, which allows great leeway to instructors in the selection of subjects for honors seminars. Masterpieces courses which proved to be "hits" could be repeated endlessly as honors seminars.

Another location figuratively would be in the catalog or bulletin, in a "box" somewhere to indicate the existence of the series, its rationale, and where such courses are to be found—scattered throughout the curricula of the various colleges and departments and programs.

Yet another place for the series could be in a certificate program or something otherwise indicating that a student has completed several of the courses, thereby having acquired a certain roundedness of intellectual experience for those who value that.

Finally, another place for the series, an even more figurative place to be sure, is in the sensibilities (suitably sensitized by masterpieces) of those who had experienced such courses and those to whom they, as converts, had spread the gospel, and who would thereby become a "market" for such courses or even a great books series in the fullblown sense preferred by purists, of courses comprised entirely and exclusively of works in *the* canon which are to be read in their entirety.

Masterpieces Not As Writing But Written About

A special characteristic of the masterpieces approach, indicated above, of works that "need not even be *verbal*," may need elaboration. A distinction must be made: between a masterpiece that expresses something about something; and a masterpiece about which something is written. The Jane Addams selections for a course on Masterpieces of Love would illustrate this: the masterpiece is not Addams' lectures; indeed, if a course were offered on Masterpieces of Lecture, hers would not qualify because they are not especially distinguished as lectures go. If a course were offered on Masterpieces of Woman, perhaps they would qualify because Jane Addams was a great woman and these lectures are an important expression of her mind and character and of her concerns and aspirations. If Masterpieces of Social Work were offered, Addams' lectures might qualify because the settlement house is a landmark among social innovations generally and in social work in particular.

What would be important to identify is a writing that describes and rationalizes the settlement house as an expression of communal love. Someone else may do that better than Jane Addams. Her lectures are an authoritative description and rationale of the settlement house by its pioneer, but there may be better renderings of those than Addams'—and that is what is important.

Must the Masterpieces Course be Team-Taught?

One limitation of the approach is the apparent need for a team of instructors to handle the challenging variety of such works. This may be an insurmountable problem when the theme is a mega-concept like justice or truth or beauty, around which major works of great difficulty are aggregated. The need for teams may be just as great, perhaps even greater, for masterpiece courses organized around certain less conventional themes such as dream, or ensemble, or quest, or discovery. One would hope that a university faculty of liberally-educated, well-read, well-rounded scholars of intellectual curiosity, experience, breadth, and depth (every faculty, in other words!), would include any number, indeed a great number, who are at home with Plato, Dante, Milton, Hobbes, Newton, the Brontës, Marx, Tennyson, and on and on. But the number, even at Harvard, is less likely to be "any number" than "zero." Yet one may wistfully imagine a university—someday, somewhere—in which such liberality, such catholicity will be sufficiently valued that a cadre, a corps for the core, as it were, might be identified, cultivated, and rewarded. Short of that, it seems inevitable that teams must be assembled for each such course. However, the teams may not have to be as large as the roster of masterpieces; perhaps each member, of a team of four or five, could adequately handle three or four works.

There is, however, one sort of masterpiece course that might be carried off by one or maybe two or three instructors. If a theme falls within the scope of a field, as statecraft falls within political science or management within business or public administration, or crime and punishment within criminology or criminal justice, the ability of a few in these fields may be sufficient to mount such a course.

Conclusion

Much of what has been described above will of course require hours and hours of preparation. But that is what college teaching always calls for. And this is to say nothing of the difficulties of developing and administering such courses, let alone politicking, proselytizing, and otherwise promoting the establishment of the series and its location here and there within the curriculum. But one does it, all of it, whatever it entails. Even so, and in all of this, perhaps the chief virtue of this approach is the challenge and excitement and satisfaction that it provides to its teachers. And that may be the ultimate justification of such a series, as it may be of higher education itself.

THE CASE AGAINST THE GREAT BOOKS— AND ITS REFUTATION

Martin D. Yaffe

University of North Texas

I think that "Great Books" courses are the worst of all possible educational programs—except perhaps for all the others.

In defending the foregoing proposition, I do not need to document in much detail the shortcomings of alternative curricula. Nowadays students spend little if any time reading, writing, and thinking about the Great Books firsthand. Concomitantly, prospective employers (among others) complain how rarely college graduates can be counted on to read or write (leaving thinking aside, for the moment) with any high degree of competence or assurance. I infer the obvious: that schools which fail to pay adequate attention to the Great Books are likely to fail in their more basic aims of preparing students with adequate reading and writing skills too. My premise is that in reading and writing—as in, say, athletics—good examples foster excellence. The so-called great authors, in my view, are simply the best examples of readers and writers (and perhaps thinkers) to date. The serious question I am raising, then, is not *whether* students and their professors should be encouraged to consider those examples for what they are worth, but rather *how* those examples might afford some modest prospects for success where current curricula fail. Differently stated: How can we do the next best thing to making Marva Collins our university's Vice-President for Academic Affairs?

Upper-division electives taught by specialists or teams of specialists—such as the two-semester, nine-hour team-taught course here at North Texas—will not by themselves solve the problem. Consider only the most obvious objection. It attaches to all attempts to integrate the Great Books into the undergraduate curriculum insofar as that curriculum is viewed as a congeries of specialties. Namely, the Great Books tend to be dysfunctional. I am thinking of the extraordinary burden any one of those books must place on a student's time and attention, precisely if that one book (to say nothing of all the others) were to be read and written about in the manner which it demands, i.e., in its own terms so far as scholarly attentiveness can recover those terms for the patient reader. Might not that book, its charms as well as its demands, easily usurp or monopolize the time thought nowadays more prudently spent on more "technical" subjects? After all, why should a serious pre-medical student be made to suffer, for example, with Shakespeare's Lady Macbeth her psychosomatic insomnia? (I am thinking of the physician's futile house-call in Act V of *Macbeth*, where the lady, who has murdered a king for the sake of her husband's tyrannical ambition, has now grown incurably insane.) Or, moreover, why should a no-nonsense biochemistry or marketing major ingest, with Homer's Odysseus, a drug which is extracted from the ground by the god Hermes, who in turn explains how its "nature" qualifies it as an antidote to the contagious disease of swinishness? (I am thinking of the piggish appearance and behavior induced in Odysseus' men by the bewitching Circe in Book X of the *Odyssey*.) Or, finally, why must a physics major be encouraged to follow, with the author of the Book of Job, God's whirlwind tour of the all-too-unknown universe? (I am thinking about God's unrevealing revelation given in chapter 38ff., by way of non-answer to Job's groaning question about the cause of his undeserved suffering.)

In short, aren't the Great Books a distraction from the vocational necessities of an undergraduate education? Isn't a student's time better spent with more "technical" or scientific subjects? Aren't all other studies, then, in whatever program we choose to present them, by and large dispensable?

Before offering a suggestion for overcoming the foregoing objection, and elaborating briefly the examples I have given for further consideration, I need to invoke a traditional distinction which is in danger of becoming altogether blurred in today's increasingly eclectic, and often narrowly vocational university settings. The distinction I have in mind would restore the study of the Great Books to their proper rank, namely, as the most important matters for reading, writing, and thinking about, which an undergraduate curriculum can offer. That distinction is the basis for the founding of the great universities which date from the late Middle Ages and the Renaissance, and which still stand as visible inspirations for those founded more recently. The distinction is between acquiring vocational skills on the one hand and acquiring non-vocational but nevertheless desirable skills on the other—more exactly, between what were called the "necessary" arts (economically necessary for making a living) and what were called the "liberal" arts ("liberal" in the sense of being appropriate to someone who can afford to be liberal, or free, with his time, i.e., who is free of the most pressing economic worries of the moment). The "necessary" arts are traditionally taught, not by universities, but through hands-on learning, for example in one-on-one, master-pupil apprenticeships. But should a person who does not need to make a living with his hands, it was asked, therefore lack all education? Or what would it be appropriate for him to learn? The old answer is eminently sensible. It boils down to three things: (1) reading (so one can understand another, even if he is not physically present), (2) writing (or communicating with another who may not be physically present), and (3) thinking (or discerning causal relationships among things in general). In other words, the traditional liberal arts curriculum consists of (1) grammar, or how to read, (2) rhetoric, or how to write and speak persuasively, and (3) logic and the mathematical sciences. Whatever else may have been added to university curricula then or since, the assumption is that those three (or actually seven) skills are separate (though in practice often interdependent) and fundamental to all higher learning worthy of the name. That assumption, it seems to me, is in no way invalidated by the plethora of additions and alterations which modern universities have made to the curriculum. On the contrary, does not that assumption remain the *sine qua non* of any university? Without it, would not the university shrink in importance to the size of an umbrella, sheltering a dry miscellany of accredited tradeschools, uniformed technicians-for-hire, bookkeepers of various descriptions, and playground supervisors for the athletically gifted? Under such circumstances, would not each of the foregoing lack a sense of purpose for its togetherness with the others alongside it? Are not the so-called liberal arts, therefore, the permanent basis by which the distinctive function and overall unity of the university must stand or fall? But if so, then with the healthy cultivation of the liberal arts goes the health of the university, and with their stifling or weakening comes its corresponding decline. It follows that the study of the Great Books, which I have called simply the most excellent examples for the cultivation of the liberal arts, is the true index of the health or vitality of any given university.

But so much for the standards to which I appeal. What about the objection that those standards are, in effect, unrealizable nowadays?

In order to show the groundlessness of this objection, I must begin by freely granting the obvious usefulness of scientific and technical subjects. I ask only that we keep in mind the various crises to which science and technology have led nowadays, and the need to confront these crises in a thoughtful way for the sake of our common future. My point is that modern science or technology alone is insufficient to understand those very crises which it continues to foster by virtue of its daily successes. I am thinking now of, for example, the crisis in health care brought on by the prospect of genetic manipulation as used to refashion human physiology for the sake of eliminating the purportedly undesirable tendencies and susceptibilities to disease in human beings—a dangerous prospect in light of the possible arbitrariness of its goals, the evident uncertainty of its methods, and the likely irreversibility of its aftermath. I am thinking also of our current environmental crisis—the eroding of the biosphere as a result of our undisciplined quarrying, gormandizing, and littering of its precious resources. And I am thinking of our late-twentieth-century geopolitical crisis—where nuclear technology applied to nuclear weaponry threatens the survival of us all. Would we seriously cripple the abilities of our future doctors, businessmen, and scientists to think through these crises by confining their learning exclusively to the technical subjects which, left to themselves, simply further the crises in question? Or would we, if we could, point our students to books which, albeit at a respectful distance, help us understand and moderate our technical excesses?

Consider, briefly, Lady Macbeth's doctor, who suggests that the disease affecting her body, which in normal cases he is competent to cure, in this case stems from a disease affecting her soul, which disease is in turn caused by—or rather causes—the diseases of the body politic. The doctor's frustration may be said to point to the need to understand the connection or boundary between the well-being of an individual body and the well-being of the body politic—a question which goes to the heart of Shakespeare's play on the one hand and of the contemporary health-care crisis on the other, since the push nowadays to stamp out diseases affecting individual bodies, even to the extent of genetic manipulation, is, like Lady Macbeth, both borne by the larger community (e.g., in the form of public funding) and potentially dangerous to that community (e.g., as citizens thereby become subject to possibly irreversible debilitating mutations). The full clarification of the Shakespearean issue points us in the direction of the full ramifications of the contemporary issue, and vice versa. Similar observations may be made concerning the connection between the "nature" of the plant which Homer's Hermes reveals and current environmental threats, and between the cosmos which Job's God half-reveals and the current threat of nuclear devastation. But such connections are more visible to students of educational programs which allow and foster their inherent ability to read, write, and think about the pressing issues potentially illuminated by the Great Books, than to students in programs which do not.

In short, the Great Books I have alluded to are not primarily "technical" or scientific in subject-matter or method, though that fact is not a weakness but a strength, insofar as those books seem fully alive to the *implications* of technical or scientific things. They complement the technical. Hence they help us pose the question of the full scope and limits of the technical vis-à-vis human life as a whole. In that way, they are hardly irrelevant to the most pressing needs of an undergraduate education. Read judiciously and discussed thoughtfully, they are the one thing needful.

5

INTERFACES:
LIBERAL ARTS IN A PLURALIST SOCIETY

THE REVIEWERS REVIEWED: E. D. HIRSCH AND HIS CRITICS

Hughie G. Lawson

Murray State University

What is required to become a good reader? Before reading E. D. Hirsch's *Cultural Literacy*, I thought the answer was good reading skills: the ability to decode complicated sentences, to see sentences in relation to each other, to identify controlling ideas in a text, and so on. Like others I distinguished between skills and knowledge. Reading skill was a kind of all purpose machine for processing text of all kinds.

This idea, says E. D. Hirsch, is a half-truth, for literacy is more than decoding text; writing assumes knowledge common to writer and reader. To share in a culture like that possessed by literate Americans, one must have the background knowledge these Americans have, knowledge readily picked up by the children of educated parents. The great tragedy is that true literacy will be a closed book to less fortunate children, unless they learn it in school. This kind of knowledge is what Hirsch calls "cultural literacy," and as everyone here must know the best-known part of his book of that title is the list of terms he presents to specify the knowledge necessary for cultural literacy.[1]

But the public schools, Hirsch asserts, have long been guided by a theory of education that disparages teaching "mere information," that ridicules "just learning facts." The result is that public schools just don't teach children information they need to share in literate American culture. The lucky ones get it at home, or in private schools.[2]

How important is this contextual information? Very, says Hirsch, reviewing studies that—for this reader demonstrate that background knowledge is essential to critical understanding of writing. Let's have an example here. Suppose you read that the "great blood-bath of 1861–65" settled controversial questions in American life. Would you visualize defeated rebels and freed slaves, or would you draw a blank, as do many of our students? Again and again the author pounds home the point: all writing assumes contextual knowledge, even that of the ordinary newspaper and magazine press.[3]

Hardly anyone denies that critical understanding of written material requires background knowledge. Nevertheless the reception of *Cultural Literacy* differs sharply in two different sectors of opinion, the general press and the academic journals. General response has been on balance favorable. But how different has been the reception in academic journals![4] On "The Editor's Page" of *Phi Delta*

Kappan Bruce M. Smith viewed *Cultural Literacy* as if it were a seditious pamphlet under the heading "A Clear and Present Danger." The education journals have formed a phalanx of opinion against Hirsch's book, their reviews being almost uniformly negative.[5]

One response to this might be to shrug it off; after all, Hirsch is an English professor, a representative of the liberal-arts professors who have nurtured among themselves an unfortunate tradition of scorn for teacher educators. Surely among English and history professors we can find strong support for Hirsch; after all he wants school children to learn more about their subjects. Unfortunately for *Cultural Literacy*, nothing could be further from the truth, for journals for English and history teachers have also printed generally unfavorable reviews of *Cultural Literacy*.[6]

For the first time I can remember, liberal-arts academics have been drawing their wagons into the same circle with teacher educators in defense against what both see as a threat, a bestseller by an English professor complaining that school children aren't learning enough and calling for a change. Usually when a conflict exists between the "laity" and the "professionally informed" over a bestselling book, we conclude that somehow the book represents a form of quackery, a simplistic theory persuasive to laymen, a sort of dangerous home remedy. Defense against this kind of thing is just what we have professionals for. And indeed one critic called *Cultural Literacy* "voodoo education."[7]

My view is different. I think the problem is not with Hirsch's book, but with his critics. *Cultural Literacy* raises a very important issue, which ought to be discussed on its merits, but it is receiving not debate but anathema, not nuanced discussion but crude condemnations of oversimplifications of Hirsch's ideas and sometimes of ideas he didn't express at all. What we have here is voodoo criticism.

If we listen to the beat, beat, beat of the critical tom-tom, we hear one phrase endlessly repeated: tri-vi-al-pur-suit. The temptation to compare Hirsch's list to the popular quiz game has been strong. We shouldn't lose our sense of humor here. Most of my teaching load is a required general education course for freshmen on world civilizations, and hardly a semester passes without former students telling me that they are doing much better at Trivial Pursuit after taking the course. The students make the comment in fun, and that's the way I take it. But that's not the way the critics mean it.[8]

The allusions to the game are linked to a more serious, though entirely false, charge: that Hirsch sees the totality of education as nothing more than memorizing unrelated bits of information.[9] It seems incredible, but it's true; most academic critics have failed to grasp Hirsch's intended meaning. This might be excusable for undergraduates toiling through a Faulkner novel, but folk with teaching jobs ought to be able to understand Hirsch's distinction between the intensive part of the school curriculum where mastery and critical understanding are vital goals and an extensive part where fairly superficial knowledge is adequate.[10] To clarify the point, let's reuse the "bloodbath of 1861–65" example. To know that the allusion is to the Civil War is fairly superficial knowledge, but it could be vital to understanding a text in which the allusion appeared.

My students certainly understand the distinction. They never fail to press me on this issue. On specific points they constantly inquire whether I want mastery and critical understanding or recognition knowledge. For example, in one setting the goal might be to remember that in *Marbury v. Madison*, Chief Justice John Marshall set forth the principle of judicial review of the laws of Congress (cultural literacy or extensive curriculum goal); in another, students need to restate Marshall's argument, consider objections to it, and evaluate its significance (intensive goal). Hirsch calls, not for the replacement of the intensive curriculum, but for the recognition that the extensive curriculum has its proper place, and for a clearer statement of just what kind of knowledge is needed in the extensive curriculum.

Hirsch's critics often miss the logical distinction between necessary and sufficient conditions. An example of this, borrowed I think from William James may help. "You can't make an omelet without breaking eggs." Of course you must do more than break eggs, but without the breaking, there will be no omelet. Breaking the eggs is a necessary but not a sufficient condition. Hirsch has made this point himself: "the extensive curriculum is not a sufficient basis for education by itself. It is simply a minimal description of elements that should be included in every child's schooling. . . . The intensive curriculum, though different, is equally essential."[11]

The same critics who overlook his distinction between the intensive and extensive curricula, have also crudely over-simplified his ideas by raising the "scapegoat term" of rote memorization. There is thus a double confusion. First these critics confuse Hirsch's proposal for a part of the curriculum (the extensive curriculum) with a proposal for the whole curriculum, ignoring Hirsch's careful qualifications. Secondly, they accuse Hirsch of favoring the rote memorization of particles of information isolated from meaningful context, when the whole point of *Cultural Literacy* is that information is needed to construct meaningful context. The error is dual, misinterpretation and faulty logic.

Another logical error appears in the critical attack upon the feasibility of Hirsch's list, of which the most impressive appears in a review by Robert Scholes. Scholes writes with such conviction that it's easy to be swept up in his argument, especially when he introduces evidence to show what's wrong with Hirsch. As case in point Scholes prints a list of about seventy-five terms found in the *Washington Post* for 11 July 1987, but not found in Hirsch's list. At first it seems a devastating argument against the idea of a list to find so many items left out. After all, Hirsch intends to provide students the basic knowledge needed to understand the daily paper. Such an immense list from one issue of the *Washington Post* suggests that Hirsch is living in a dream world.[12]

But let's look a little closer. From Scholes' list of omitted terms, let's select for closer examination a sample, the geographical references: Beirut, Punjab, West Bank, Middle East, Port-au-Prince, Gulf of Aqaba, Liberia, Tanzania, Zambia, Long Island, Queens, Amman, and Gaza strip. As you will see, Hirsch's geographical coverage is considerably more impressive than appears from a Scholes' list of omitted terms. This will necessarily be a dry catalog, but I don't know any other way to show how misleading is Scholes' list of omissions.

Beirut is not on the list, but Lebanon is. Punjab is not on the list, but India and Pakistan are. West Bank is not on the list, but Israel, Jordan, Jordan River, Palestine, Arab-Israeli conflict, and PLO are. Middle East is not on the list. It should be, if for no other reason than to complement Far East, which is. Defenders of E. D. Hirsch will be happy to see that Middle East does appear in the *Dictionary of Cultural Literacy*.[13] Port-au-Prince is not on the list, but Haiti is. Amman, and Gaza strip are not on the list, but see West Bank, above. Liberia, Tanzania, and Zambia are not on the list, but Hirsch added them to the *Dictionary*.[14] Long Island and Queens are not on the list; New York, New York is. Gulf of Aqaba is not on the list, but Red Sea and Sinai are.

As you can see, the *Cultural Literacy* list does omit some geographical terms, but what's present is pretty impressive. Despite the specific omissions, Hirsch's related terms qualify one as geographically well-informed as far as the indicated areas are concerned. It would be easy to extend the argument beyond geography by citing more misleading items from Scholes' list of omissions (vandalism is not on the list, but Vandals is, and so on), but the evidence presented is fatal to Scholes' claim that Hirsch's list is too short to be meaningful.[15]

This attack by Scholes on the idea of a list is a more imaginative version of a fallacy employed by other critics for the same purpose: attacking the list by second-guessing it, with this implied suggestion: because terms desirable to know are omitted, the list is a bad idea. Why is Tolstoy in but not Dostoyevsky? Why Spiro Agnew, but not Pascal? Why the dates for World War II, but not the French Revolution? Why Chicken Little, but not the Billy Goats Gruff?[16] Such criticism at first makes the idea of the list seem merely arbitrary, for anyone with special knowledge can imagine desirable additions. (As one who cut his teeth on the Uncle Remus stories, I was saddened that the briar patch, and the Tar Baby didn't get in. But the plucky and resourceful Br'er Rabbit has survived far greater challenges to his self-esteem.)

Now let's examine the logical problem referred to when we began this study of the Scholes list of omitted geographical terms. Sometimes, it's helpful in considering a polemical point to convert it into a syllogism. Here's what the second-guessing approach looks like in syllogism form.

First, the minor premise: desirable material has been omitted from a curriculum proposal.
Next, the conclusion: therefore, the proposal is absurd.

The minor premise and the conclusion are the two parts usually stated. Invariably left unstated is the major premise: a curriculum proposal is absurd if it omits desirable content.

Merely to read it is to see why it is left unstated. One of the basic problems of life is the allocation of scarce resources among competing goods. To get on with teaching we have to have lists to describe content, and we can't wait for unanimous consent; so, we make judgments, dicker with our peers, listen to the public, pretty much the process Hirsch recommends for arriving at a cultural literacy list. We have to leave things out, for there just isn't enough time for all desirable content.

Thus, Robert Scholes' list of omissions, seemingly such a formidable attack on Hirsch is really a fallacy, for it is founded on an unacceptable major premise. That Scholes is the whipping boy here should not be taken to mean that I hold his work in a general contempt; far from it. Because I'd never heard of him before reading his comments on Hirsch, I read his book *Textual Power*, which says many wise things about teaching literature to college students. Scholes observes that "greater cultural information distances us [teachers] from our students. . . . Considered in this light, interpretation [of literature] is not a pure skill but a discipline deeply dependent upon knowledge. It is not so much a matter of generating a meaning out of a text as it is a matter of making connections between a particular verbal text and a larger cultural text. . . ." To me, Scholes' point seems so close to the idea of cultural literacy that it's hard to understand why he was offended by Hirsch's book.[17]

Aside from these errors, as I see them, in critical thought, many attacks on *Cultural Literacy* are political in nature. Patrick Scott in attempting to explain English professors' "deep professional hostility" to *Cultural Literacy* identified as a partial cause Hirsch's "recent political sponsorship."[18] At one level the political attacks reflect the suspicion that *Cultural Literacy* is an intellectual Trojan horse of the neo-conservative political tendency. Along with William Bennett, Lynne V. Cheney, Diane Ravitch, and Chester Finn, Hirsch is attempting—in this view—to harness American educational institutions to a specific cultural-political agenda.

A careful reader of *Cultural Literacy* will have a hard time finding quotations from the book to support this charge. Instead the political critics simply assert that the book is controlled by latent goals. For example, Robert Scholes links Hirsch with Allan Bloom in this way. "Together they set the conservative agenda for

American education." In this view Bloom writes the agenda for the elite, while Hirsch lays out a plan for educating the masses "sufficiently . . . to respect the superior knowledge of their betters."[19] Critics who echo this line see Hirsch as "elitist." It is not easy for a sympathetic reader to find in Hirsch explicit evidence of an elitist purpose. On the contrary, his argument is that present school practices deny lower-class children the knowledge they need to understand what they must understand if they are to take an active part in the mainstream of American civic life.

To make up for the lack of explicitly elitist statements in *Cultural Literacy* the political critics assert that Hirsch is deceptive or confused, or both. What he "really" wants to do is to restore the cultural authority in America that presumably was undone by the upheavals of the 1960s. His list will, in this view, restore WASP cultural hegemony, denying minorities the right to their own definitions of their culture. Memorizing it will "brainwash the young so that they will never question" the established order of things in America.

His cultural literacy proposal is thus an "ideology of bureaucratized assent, disguised by the denial of ideology."[20] It is not clear what Hirsch individually is accused of. Is he the conscious agent of a reactionary purpose? Or, is he the deluded servant of an ideology whose latent functions he does not understand? Or is he an avatar of the American snake-oil peddler derided in the writings of Mark Twain, H. L. Mencken, and Sinclair Lewis? The political attacks label Hirsch, but they give no analysis of his text to support the label. They fail to persuade.

To recapitulate the findings of my survey: the massively negative critiques of Hirsch are riddled with misreadings, elementary logical errors, and unsupported political name-calling. This is a condition that cries out for interpretation. As Hans-Georg Gadamer has suggested, when we find apparent absurdities in texts, we may learn much by asking how a sensible person could have written them.[21] I do have some thoughts on that, but they are not yet mature. In a general way they concern the originality of *Cultural Literacy*, the contours of educational rhetoric, and changes in academia over the last twenty-five years.

NOTES

1. E. D. Hirsch, Jr., *Cultural Literacy: What Every American Needs to Know* (Boston: Houghton Mifflin Company), xiii–xvii, 2–4.

2. Hirsch, *Cultural Literacy*, 24.

3. Hirsch, *Cultural Literacy*, 33–69. Hirsch's views confirm my own memories of reading education textbooks.

4. Paul Gagnon, "Content Counts," *American Educator* 11 (July–December 1987): 40–46. Gagnon made an early identification of still persistent errors in reviews of *Cultural Literacy*. Hirsch has also tried to correct some of the errors of his critics; see these efforts in "The Paradox of Traditional Literacy," *Educational Leadership* 45 (December 1987):

74–75; "Hirsch Responds: The Best Answer to a Caricature is a Practical Program," *Educational Leadership* 46 (September 1988): 18–19; "The Primal Scene of Education," *New York Review of Books*, March 2, 1989: 29–35; a letter in reply to Herbert Kohl, *The New York Review of Books*, April 13, 1989: 50–51; "Comments of *Profession 88*" *Profession 88* (1988): 77–80. See also Charlotte Cox, "Cultural Literacy: A Conversation with E. D. Hirsch," *Curriculum Review* 27 (September/October 1987): 16–20. These writings have helped me by reassuring me that I grasped the intended meaning of *Cultural Literacy*.

5. Bruce M. Smith, "The Editor's Page: A Clear and Present Danger," *Phi Delta Kappan* 69 (December 1987): 250. For other negative reviews of *Cultural Literacy* in education journals, see the following. Wayne Otto, "Puttin' on the Ritz," *Journal of Reading* 31 (April 1988): 675–76; Thomas Estes, Carol J. Gutman, and Elise K. Harrison, "Cultural Literacy: What Every Educator Needs to Know," *Educational Leadership* 46 (September 1987): 15–17; Donna E. Alvermann, Review of *CL, Journal of Reading Behavior* 20, no. 2: 191–94; Stanley Aronowitz and Henry A. Giroux, "Schooling, Culture and Literacy in Age of Broken Dreams," *Harvard Educational Review* 58 (May 1988): 172–94; Hazel Whitman Herzberg, review *CL, Teachers College Record* 90 (Fall 1988): 145–48; Maxine Greene, review of *CL, Teachers College Record* 90 (Fall 1988): 149–55; Deborah Hicks, review of *CL, Journal of Education* 170, no. 1 (1988): 119–25; Peter H. Rohn, review of *CL*, Educational Studies 19 (Fall Winter 1988): 361–66. Jurgen Herbst, essay review of *CL* along with *The Last Intellectuals* by Russell Jacoby and *The Closing of the American Mind* by Allan Bloom, *History of Education Quarterly* 28 (Fall 1988): 425–32 is less stringently negative; the same is true of Donald J. Gray, "What Does Every American Need to Know?" *Phi Delta Kappan* 69, no. 5 (1988): 386–88.

6. Negative reviews in journals for history and English teachers include these. Wayne J. Urban, essay review of *CL*, along with *The Closing of the American Mind* by Allan Bloom, and *What Do Our 17-Year-Olds Know* by Diane Ravitch and Chester E. Finn, Jr., *Journal of American History* 75 (December 1988): 869–74; John Warnock, review of *CL*, *College Composition and Communication* 38 (December 1987): 486–90; Robert Scholes, "Three Views of Education: Nostalgia, History, and Voodoo," *College English* 50 (March 1988): 322–33; Leila Christenbury, "Cultural Literacy: A Terrible Idea Whose Time Has Come," *English Journal* 78 (January 1989): 14–17; Arthur Zilversmit, essay review of *CL* along with *American Memory* by Lynne Cheney and *What Do Our 17-Year-Olds Know* by Ravitch and Finn, *Reviews in American History* 16 (June 1988): 314–20; Robert A. Denham, "From the Editor: Notes on *Cultural Literacy*," *ADE Bulletin* (Association of Departments of English) no. 88 (July–December 1988): 1–8; Fred M. Newmann, "Another View of Cultural Literacy: Go for Depth," *Social Education* October, 1988: 432–36.

7. Scholes, "Three Views of Education," 327.

8. For examples of The Trivial Pursuit comparison, see: John A. Beinecke, "A Conversation with William Van Til," *Social Education* 53 (January 1989): 30; Bruce M. Smith, "The Editor's Page: A Clear and Present Danger," *Phi Delta Kappan* 69 (December 1987): 250; Urban, review, 872; Greene, review, 149; Estes, Gutman, and Harrison, "Cultural Literacy," 15.

9. The charge that Hirsch favors rote memorization of unrelated bits of data appears in the following. Stephen Tchudi, "Slogans Indeed: A Reply to Hirsch," *Educational Leadership* 45 (December 1987): 73; James R. Squire, "Basic Skills Are Not Enough," *Educational Leadership* 45 (December 1987), 75–76; Gretchen Schwartz, "A Good Idea Gone Wrong," *Educational Leadership* 45 (December 1987): 77; Estes, Gutman, and

Harrison, "Cultural Literacy": 16; William G. Wraga, letter, *Social Education* 53 (February 1989): 83; Michael Henry, letter, *Social Education* 53 (February 1989): 83; Scholes, "Three Views of Education," 327; Christenbury, "A Terrible Idea," 14; Walter Feinburg, "Foundationalism and Recent Critiques of Education," *Educational Theory* 39 (Spring 1989): 135; Wayne C. Booth, "Cultural Literacy and Liberal Learning," *Change*, July–August, 1988, 17, 18; Stephen Brookfield, "E. D. Hirsch's *Cultural Literacy*: A Cocktail Party View of Education," *Chronicle of Higher Education*, September 16, 1987, 32; Joe K. Law, "Bloom, Hirsch, and Barthes in the Curriculum: Negotiating Cultural Literacy," *Freshman English News* 17 (Fall 1988): 33; Helen Moglen, "Allan Bloom and E. D. Hirsch: Educational Reform as Tragedy and Farce," *Profession 88* (1988): 60; Deborah Meier and Florence Miller, "The Book of Lists," *Nation*, January 9, 1988: 25–27.

10. Hirsch, Cultural Literacy, 127–28, 125.

11. E. D. Hirsch, Jr., "Hirsch Responds: The Best Answer to a Caricature is a Practical Program," *Educational Leadership* 46 no. 1: 19.

12. Scholes, "Three Views of Education." Here is Scholes' list (328) of omitted terms: methodology, Sikh, Beirut, middle–class, National Security Council, fiscal year, trade barrier, Air Force, West Bank, lieutenant colonel, Zambia, Judiciary Committee, terrorist, Congressional Budget Office, Federal Aviation Administration (FAA), heroin, Punjab, Port–au–Prince, Farsi, day care, amendment, Appeals Court, Metro, World Bank, ayatollah, AWOL, crosswalk, Standard Oil, child–care center, television debates, consulting firm, Long Island, acrostic, Haidu, envoy, Tanzania, Liberia, death squads, vandalism, Marine, cover–up, protectionism, chief counsel, draftees, computer, vendetta, AIDS, real estate, land fill, prosecutor, Queens (NY), illegal alien, Associated Press, Gulf of Aqaba, kibitzing, Barbizon School, rock music, transcendental meditation, Politburo, Super Tuesday, Amman, contusion, hospice, cosmopolitan, Dvorak, virtuoso, solid waste, Gaza Strip, manuscripts, insurgents, cancer, cross fire, lard ax, Middle East.

13. E. D. Hirsch, Jr., *The Dictionary of Cultural Literacy* (Boston: Houghton Mifflin Company, 1988), 358.

14. Hirsch, Dictionary, 355, 369.

15. Scholes, "Three Views of Education," 328.

16. John Gross, review of *CL*, *New York Times*, April 17, 1987, C27; Lewis Coser, review of *CL*, *Science* 236 (May 22, 1987): 973; James Squire, "Basic Skills," 75–76.

17. Robert Scholes, *Textual Power: Literary Theory and the Teaching of English* (New Haven: Yale University Press, 1985): 28, 29, 32, 33. This similarity between Scholes and Hirsch was noticed in a book highly praised by Scholes in the same review in which he blasted Hirsch. See Gerald Graff, *Professing Literature: An Institutional History* (Chicago: University of Chicago Press, 1987), 256.

18. Patrick Scott, review of *CL*, *College English* 50 (March 1988): 336.

19. Scholes, "Three Views of Education": 324. For other political characterizations, see: Tom O'Brien, review of *CL*, *Commonweal* 16 (September 25, 1987): 542–43; Schwartz, "Good Idea Gone Wrong", 77; Aronowitz and Giroux, "Broken Dreams": Hertzberg, review of *CL*; Greene, review of *CL*; Feinberg, "Foundationalism", 133–38; Moglen, "Educational Reform as Tragedy and Farce". Yet more acerbic political attacks appear in two conference papers: Jeffrey Carroll, "The Vulgar Canon and Its Uses in the Classroom," and James Sledd, "Pie in the Sky; or Teaching New Paradigms Old Tricks," both papers presented at the Annual Meeting of the Conference on College Composition and Communication, St. Louis, Missouri, March 17–18, 1988. For two brief but astute

comments on the sources of hostility to *Cultural Literacy*, see George Steiner, review of *CL*, *New Yorker*, June 1, 1987, 108; and Fauneil J. Rinn, review of *CL*, *College Teaching* 36 (Winter 1988): 37.

20. Sledd, "Pie in the Sky." Sledd has also made an unpersuasive attack on Hirsch's scholarly method; see Sledd and James S. Sledd, "Hirsch's Use of His Sources in *Cultural Literacy*: A Critique," *Profession 88*: 33–39. For a analysis of the errors of the leftist political attacks on Hirsch, see Jeffrey Smith, "Cultural Literacy and the Academic 'Left'," *Profession 88* (1988): 25–28.

21. Gadamer quoted in Richard J. Bernstein, *Beyond Objectivism and Relativism: Science, Hermeneutics, and Praxis*, (Philadelphia: University of Pennsylvania Press, 1983), 132.

THE GREAT DIVORCE: LIBERAL ARTS AND THE SCIENCES IN EDUCATION

James E. Nowlin

Eastern Montana College

Perhaps the title of this paper is a bit of a misnomer. It might have been better to refer to the divorce between liberal arts and science not so much as having occurred "in" education, as the title suggests, but rather as having been caused "by" education. Education, as it is referred to here, is not defined in the nominative sense of a product to be obtained. Rather, the use here is more predicative and refers primarily to teacher training programs. In other words, it is the process whereby we attempt to "educate" the citizens of the country. To put it bluntly, the assertion being advanced here is that the educational process currently at work in America must accept its share of the blame for the divorce between liberal arts and science. Obviously, an examination of every educational process is not possible in this particular forum. However, it does seem possible to examine one part of the process. In this case, the part to be examined concerns the teaching of those who would become teachers, our colleges of education.

We arrive at the heart of the matter. Our colleges of education, by the manner in which they conduct their affairs, contribute to the divorce between liberal arts and science. If there is any truth to this, it is a frightening notion indeed. Any ripple must have a center. The manner in which we teach those who will themselves become teachers is the center of the subsequent liberal arts/science divorce ripple. Students completing programs "certifying" them as teachers go on to touch virtually every young person in the country. If these teachers have been trained to perceive a dichotomy between liberal arts and the sciences, we can be relatively sure that most of them will pass along this perceived dichotomy, even if it is false.

Some of these students will continue their education. Some will go into liberal arts, some into science, and some into education. (Sadly, many will go into the schools of business. There seems to be no cure for this, but the problem will have to be dealt with at another time.) The important thing is that they will go their separate ways never realizing that there is any relationship whatsoever between the disciplines.

This is a deplorable state of affairs. Science is quite possibly the most important aspect of modern life, and students should not consider themselves educated without understanding it. It is a prime potential generator of social improvement. Clearly, we should know and use science, but we can only follow it so far, because it does not tell us where to go. Its purposes can be good or evil.

Human beings decide the purposes, and they do not make these decisions based solely on science. Such decisions are philosophical, psychological, social, and historical and belong in the realm of traditional liberal arts inquiry (Hutchins 1943). The two belong together. Yet we continually create an artificial separation. Many of those studying science will become scientists of a sort. Those in the liberal arts will develop some of the intellectual skills of the discipline. Thus we have a general loss of contact between the "educated" but nonscientific sector of the general public and the scientists. This creates the illusion that scientific concepts are largely inaccessible to the "public," just as the broad concepts of liberal arts are considered inaccessible to the scientists. We can no longer communicate with one another (Stent 1988). Unfortunately, those in schools of education will go on to become teachers and continue to perpetuate this same dichotomous myth for yet another generation. The cycle is destined to continue. One way to short-circuit the process is by teaching prospective teachers the falsity of the dichotomy in such a convincing manner that they will in turn enlighten their future students to the necessary relationship between the disciplines.

Sadly, educational history is not on our side. There are many antecedent reasons for present practices in education. We can examine a small sample of these to try to explain current policies that perpetuate the liberal arts/science myths.

In its formative stages, the American public education system adopted the principles of empiricism. These principles were further refined for education by the logical positivists. Finally, the behaviorist movement in psychology was accepted as a theoretical and methodological base for public education. Unfortunately, those charged with the responsibility for educational policy were not empiricists. Neither were they positivists nor behaviorists. They had some knowledge, much of it second hand, of each of these positions, but they had little in-depth comprehension of any of the three. Because of this partial understanding, they borrowed bits and pieces of each position, creating something of a patchwork educational program.

The practical result was an educational philosophy—though it was not called a philosophy—that stressed learning through the physical senses, quantitative measurement, and conditioning. These ideas were appealing to educational experts because they were thought to be based on the scientific approach to education (even though at no stage of their formal application were these ideas themselves subjected to the rigors of scientific method). The result of all this on our present educational process has been divisive and chaotic.

The importance of the scientific approach to education was due, in part, to the rise of industrialism. Mechanization and specialization, the dual heart of the industrial movement, would not have been possible without the advent of imposing new scientific ideas and technologies. From a standpoint of pure output, this new industrial method was a ringing success—so much so that many involved in education felt that these same methods could improve the "output" of the educational system. Since the heart of the industrial system was primarily scientific, it must have seemed axiomatic that to achieve the same success, the heart of the educational enterprise must likewise be scientific. It is a small step indeed from this line of thought to the adoption of an empiricist, positivist, and behavioral base for education.

Although in forming our educational foundations, we borrowed loosely and carelessly from various philosophies, in forming our method we borrowed too specifically from the industrial paradigm. The establishment of educational theory and practice in the past five decades seems to follow closely the ideals of Frederick Winslow Taylor, one of the guiding lights of the modern industrial movement. His strategies consisted of four steps. First, the gathering by management of knowledge that increases production. Any other knowledge is superfluous. The educational equivalent is management (legislators, boards of trustees, and school administrators) knowing the level of productivity of education. It goes without saying that this productivity is measured empirically and concerns itself with enrollment and graduation data, budgets, teaching loads, and other non-qualitative educational knowledge. Many educational decisions follow this industrial, managerial style. One example should suffice. Most public elementary and secondary schools receive public funds on the basis of attendance. The productivity factor here is the monetary recompense for student attendance. Qualitative knowledge, such as what the students are actually doing while in attendance, is rarely considered.

Second, Taylor advocated a separation of planning and execution. Management removes "ownership" from the master craftsman by taking total charge of the planning. Teachers and students are expected to execute this plan. Execution does not include input or critical appraisal of the executors.

The third part of Taylor's industrial program was detailed managerial control of the labor force. Taylor claimed, on the basis of efficiency, that workers would have to give up their own particular way of doing things and get used to the idea of receiving and obeying managerial instructions covering all details, both large and small, that in the past were left to individual initiative and ability. It seems unnecessary, perhaps even redundant, to give an educational example of this dictum.

Finally, Taylor thought productivity could be increased through wage incentives. This is also the promise and lure for our educational system. One does not need a statistical study to be able to say with some assurance that the primary motivating force for most students is the attainment of a job upon completion of the educational process, the quintessential wage incentive (Ewens 1984).

The age of progressivism, despite its noble goals, was also an underlying cause of the dichotomy in question. It seems fair to say that the basic motivation of progressives, including Dewey, was the betterment of society (Hutchins 1953). They, of course, had many specific goals—reduction of poverty, improvement of working conditions—but the agenda as a whole inevitably aimed toward societal improvement. How best to accomplish this noble aspiration? The answer seemed to be science. Science could provide the technology and play a major role in the amelioration of society's graver ills. Dewey even expanded this expectation. He called for a time when science would be applied to all social and moral problems of the world as well as the technological ones. In science he saw the means whereby intelligence could be effective in the world (Butler 1968). Where best to employ this science? In the laboratory, of course, but to ensure a continuation of new discoveries and technologies would require a continuation and increase of such knowledge in succeeding generations. The educational process seemed the logical place. Once more it is only a small step to begin to see the school as the place to guarantee, in a purely practical fashion, the amelioration of society's ills. Examples abound. Sputnik goes up, and we scurry around to catch the Soviets. One prominent attempt in this direction was the legislative attempt (The National Defense Student Loan Act) to provide students with inexpensive government loans to pursue higher education in the sciences so that we might close the space gap. Fifty thousand drivers are killed on our highways each year. For nearly two decades many states attacked the problems by making driver education a mandatory graduation requirement. Even today driver training is an integral part of school curricula. The fact that approximately fifty thousand people continue to be killed on the nation's highways seems to make little difference, and the scientific method of testing hypotheses and dismissing those that are unsuccessful is once more ignored. We have a drug problem; we begin drug education in our schools, and so on and on.

The common ground in these historical antecedents is their emphasis on science. There is, of course, nothing wrong with emphasizing science. It is certainly the best way to "know" our world. But all of these movements emphasized science as if it existed in an educational vacuum. They made it an either/or choice. The emphasis on science was misdirected. This emphasis was centered on scientific utility and not scientific knowledge. Scientific utility can exist and function to a degree and for a brief time without the rest of the liberal arts program. Scientific knowledge most assuredly cannot. Scientific knowledge exists as an integral and inseparable part of the liberal arts. Every advance in scientific knowledge demands a review and/or change in other segments of the liberal family. This message is not getting to the majority of those who teach in teacher training programs and, therefore, not getting to their students.

What is the result in our educational programs of these historical factors? One result is a double message about science. On the one hand, we in education insist that science is important. But it seems that what we really mean is that science is utility. This meaning seems well taken, because while we say that science is important, we require only a minimal number of science courses in our teacher education programs. Surely there must be students out there who question our sincerity on the topic of the importance of science. Many teacher education programs allow students to graduate with teaching certificates after being exposed to two or three science courses. They must wonder how important it is if this is all that is required of them. If we give them little scientific knowledge, we can hardly blame them if they see it as unimportant, and obviously this is how they see it.

On standardized science tests given in seventeen countries by the International Association for the Evaluation of Educational Achievement, United States students ranked near the bottom in almost every category (International Association 1988). One criticism of such cross cultural comparisons is the idea that other countries spend more time on testable factual data while their U.S. counterparts learn scientific principles and concepts. Alas, this seems not to be the case. For instance, Japanese students taking the 1970 International Association for the Evaluation of Educational Achievement test scored better than American students on both rote memory and scientific comprehension (Walberg 1983). This should not come as a surprise, since Japanese students spend roughly twice the instructional time in the sciences as do their American counterparts (National Science Foundation 1987).

This lack of emphasis on scientific knowledge is apparent even on many college entrance exams. The American College Test (ACT) used by many colleges for purposes of entrance consideration requires little substantive scientific knowledge. There is a major section of the test entitled "Natural Science," but this section actually seems to test reading comprehension rather than scientific knowledge.

In addition, many states now use Minimum Competency Tests, ostensibly designed to isolate educational deficiencies early so that they can be corrected. In many cases such tests culminate in a graduation exam. If the student does not pass the exam he/she does not graduate. Many of these minimum competency tests and graduation exams are divided into three sections: Reading, Language, and Math. There are admittedly a few "scientific type" questions in the math section, but these are limited in scope and sophistication.

In light of all this one cannot help but ask, what is the message we are sending to students? If science knowledge is not stressed in our achievement testing programs, if it is not an important part of our competencies, if it is not important for high school graduation, and if it is only important enough to have two or three requirements in college, then honestly, how important can it be? If students did not realize the content of the "importance of science" message given them by our educational system, we might be justified in questioning their general powers of reason. But the message is abundantly clear and clearly received.

Those who hear the message but choose to disregard it are generally more inclined to go into some area of science as an academic pursuit. They specialize in scientific pursuits while their fellow students studiously avoid such pursuits. The end result is an academic class society with students and programs divorced from one another and often unable to communicate with one another because neither side has an inkling of what the other is about.

These dichotomous messages are reinforced by the tools of the profession, especially the textbook. There are of course exceptions, but in general, the textbooks in our public schools can charitably be referred to as less than stimulating. The Council for Basic Education in a study entitled "A Conspiracy of Good Intentions: America's Textbook Fiasco," insisted that for the most part textbooks for secondary and elementary students contain test-oriented trivia, teaching fads, and inconsistent social messages. These books are not written by gifted writers but by writing committees (Textbooks Misleading 1988). The results are what one would generally expect from a committee.

This paper is not a general condemnation. A more specialized condemnation is appropriate here. Textbook publishers seem unaware that any discipline is in any way related to any other discipline. Literature texts ignore historical, social, or psychological influences, except of course for the authors' birth and death dates. Science texts contain technical scientific information and little else. This promulgates the idea that scientific discoveries are the results of exacting measurements undertaken for their own sake and without any theoretical or philosophical commitment (Kuhn 1970). History texts never make reference to the history of science and its influence on history in general. These texts present material to the students as if everything occurs in a vacuum and is unrelated to other areas of learning. If teachers follow the formats of the textbooks, and evidence seems to indicate that this is usually the case, how can anyone expect any other result from the student than a perceived disciplinary dichotomy?

Where did we learn to teach with such dichotomous tools and in such a dichotomous manner? With few exceptions all teachers pass through teacher training programs at some institution of higher learning. It seems highly plausible that such institutions contribute to the problem of disciplinary dichotomy. It may also be that they are in a position to make some real reversals in such trends, but we will get to that momentarily. First the contributing problems.

Methods courses abound! Most people in higher education agree that it would perhaps not be a bad idea to have prospective teachers take a course on pedagogical principles. One course! Courses on learning theory seem more than appropriate for a prospective teacher. History and sociology and philosophy and law would fit well in a teacher training program. After these few courses, it would seem better for the prospective teacher to become well grounded in the disciplinary knowledge of the liberal arts, including the liberal art of scientific knowledge. The skills of teaching are intellectual skills and cannot be developed in pedagogical methods courses (Adler 1982).

Since knowledge seems to show a fairly consistent pattern of interdisciplinary relationships, it seems logical to educate those who would teach others in an interdisciplinary fashion so that they can appreciate these relationships and pass them along to future students. This cannot be done with educational methods courses. A science methods course can do very little for a teacher who does not possess scientific knowledge. The same can be said for any methods course designed for any other liberal arts discipline. It seems certain that if teachers have little scientific knowledge and minimal liberal arts knowledge, they will assuredly not be able to establish a relationship between disciplines. Yet a preponderance of teacher training programs stress methods courses over true disciplinary content.

The reason for this misplaced emphasis is apparent in the terminology. Methods imply technique. If methodology is the focal point, it cannot avoid leading to egregious errors in education. This emphasis violates a cardinal principle. Every discipline exists as a triumvirate (for purposes of this discussion, education will be considered a discipline). There are philosophical assumptions, theory, and technique. Any theory should be formed on the foundational supports of philosophic assumptions. Specific practices should be governed by the theoretical stance adopted by the field of study. All of these elements are important to the health of a discipline. Method without theory is purposeless busywork. Theory without a well-conceived superstructure of philosophy is an intellectual house lacking a foundation.

Each element has a role, and no field of inquiry can reach its full potential if it erroneously overemphasizes one element of the triad to the detriment of the others. This seems especially true when methodology is overemphasized at the expense of philosophy. Philosophic assumptions are the starting point of any inquiry. It seems obvious that if philosophy is given small consideration it will infect all succeeding theory and technique with a certain amount of error (Collingwood 1940). Any methodology constructed in such a manner could easily make the mistake of presenting science and liberals arts as if they were separate and unrelated entities. This is the trap into which colleges of education have fallen.

It seems appropriate for education to rethink its role. Teacher training programs should have a dual focus, an emphasis on disciplinary intellectual attainment, and an almost equal emphasis on interdisciplinary relations. Education should show that even though science progresses by establishing facts about the world, it is a socially embedded discipline that is intertwined with the other liberal arts. In turn, the liberal arts program gains much of its health from the influence of science (Gould 1988). For a liberal arts program to be coherent, the false dichotomy between the sciences and the rest of the liberal arts disciplines must be reduced in the short term and perhaps expelled altogether in the long term. Our educational process has done much to propagate the current dichotomy. It seems only fair for this process to serve as a place to begin an effort to reduce these myths.

One small starting point could be a change in the way education views philosophy. Instead of the one course in educational philosophy usually required of students in a teacher training program, we might require more in the area of philosophic inquiry, since philosophy is the connecting thread between the liberal arts, the sciences, and education. All three are founded on philosophical presuppositions. A closer and a longer examination of the these presuppositions might help future teachers be better able to see the relational factors involved in each field of inquiry. The alternative is a continuation of the same dichotomous myths perpetuated both by historical and current practices in education. Such a policy would be sad indeed, because science without the rest of the liberal arts is blind, and the liberal arts without science is lame. Changes in our educational policies could do much to alleviate both afflictions.

References

Adler, M. J. *The Paideia Proposal: An Educational Manifesto.* New York: Collier, 1982.
Butler, J. D. *Four Philosophies and Their Practice in Education and Religion.* New York: Harper & Row, 1968.
Collingwood, J. D. *An Essay on Metaphysics.* Oxford: Clarendon Press, 1940.
Ewens, W. L. *Becoming Free: The Struggle for Human Development.* Wilmington, Delaware: Scholarly Resources Inc., 1984.
Gould, S. J. "Pretty Pebbles." *Natural History* 97 (1988): 14–26.
Hutchins, R. M. *Education for Freedom.* Baton Rouge: Louisiana State University Press, 1943.
_____. *The Conflict in Education.* New York: Harper & Row, 1953.
International Association for the Evaluation of Educational Achievement. *Science Achievement in Seventeen Countries.* New York: Pergamon Press, 1988.
Kuhn, T. S. *The Structure of Scientific Revolutions.* Chicago: University of Chicago Press, 1970.
National Science Foundations. *Science and Engineering Indicators.* Washington, D.C.: National Science Foundation Publication, 1987.
Stent, G. S. "The Making of Science." *Partisan Review* 55/1 (1988): 33–34.
"Textbooks Misleading, Boring, Group Charges." *Billings Gazette* 13-A, (April 1988).
Walberg, H. J. "Scientific Literacy and Economic Productivity in International Productivity." *Daedalus* 112/2 (1983): 1–28.

COHERENCE OF HUMAN INSTITUTIONS AND CURRICULUM DESIGN

Joseph B. Harris

University of Wisconsin—Stevens Point

Higher education needs to identify itself as an integral thread in the fabric of civilization and as the matrix of major social institutions. Academically, this is its role in fact, but it is not a role with which it has closely identified itself.

Curricular coherence should project an organic theme in human existence. The curriculum should be used as a resource for sustaining and perfecting human civilization. Thus, the spirit of different cultures might be comprehended, international relations facilitated, and college graduates enlightened as to their own role in society.

This paper approaches the curriculum-coherence problem from the perspective of both the interdependency and the integrity of institutions. Perhaps current conditions in education make this a propitious time for introducing changes. American education is deep into a transition. Some signs point to cyclical changes characteristic of American social conditions, the causes of which need long-term study. Other signs are unique and may signal a readiness for significant, long-term redirection. Shifts of education from a predominantly liberal social posture are evidenced in many ways. However, a weakening of university leadership seems new and unique. It suggests shifts in basic control. Claims of curricular deficiencies are not altogether new, but the intensity of the criticism which comes from many sources, implies validity.

Perhaps never before has the demand for character development in the college student been so strong. This demand has come from government and business sources as well as from the university itself. Equally strong demand has asked for curricular coherence in the colleges. Still other criticism has recognized a need for international curriculum dimensions and development of student leadership capabilities.

Both the small-world conditions and education criticism suggest that the core college curriculum could focus on a critical study of the four basic social institutions: economic systems, governments, religions, and science. In this report, science has been added to the three institutions identified by B. F. Skinner and others (Kenneth Boulding, Jacob Neusner). Especially if an undergraduate curriculum provided a critical analysis of these institutions and their impact on civilizations, then education itself might experience a renewal, the integrity of institutions would be improved, and this improvement might result in a new level of peace and order in the world. This paper responds to recent higher education criticism with a curriculum based on the coherent social themes of civilization. There is a special focus on religion, government and science, three of the four institutions classified as disciplines in the liberal arts.

Higher Education Criticism

A shift in strength of public higher education management from the local campus to state governments is taking place. Kerr and Glade (1986) describe the weakening position of university presidents. Thus the public institutions will be reckoning with government decisions to an increasing extent. As distinct entities viewing the same subject from different perspectives, the university and the government agencies have different expectations of the educational system. Academicians see the need for a driving force, the motivation and direction of students, while the legislature sees need for testing, productivity, accountability and practical value. Thus, academic criticism is philosophical and psychological, and government is behavioral and social.

Philosophical and Social. The critical analysis of higher education which is best articulated, broadest, and closest to the academic environment has come from a reform-oriented group of education deans and other academic officers, the Holmes Group. One observation of this group was the recognition of specific qualities which are vital to both the teacher and the profession. These qualities are commitment, passion for the subject, imagination, and engagement. Basic liberal arts education is recognized as critical to the success of the teacher. The current weakness of the undergraduate program is described in *Tomorrow's Teacher* as both a lack of curricular coherence and an avoidance of a core of enduring and fundamental ideas (Holmes Group 1986). The group further specifies that it is the quality of engagement in learning which identifies a liberal education. Allan Bloom would appear to agree; he suggests that it is the contact with the soul of the student which engages the will and results in motivation (Bloom 1987).

Behavioral and Social. Several examinations of higher education policy have suggested shifts in academic focus which would produce improved leadership qualities. Frank Newman's *Higher Education and the American Resurgence*, published by the Carnegie Foundation for the Advancement of Teaching, makes a strong case for international leadership training (Newman 1985). The panel which developed this report included major figures from foundations, education, and corporations. They see the need for a strong entrepreneurial spirit in developing the required citizenship skills. Such skill development is seen as a most critical demand on higher education. These skills should be applied to the needs of the world community, many of which have economic implications. The Newman list includes abilities to integrate growing numbers of minority groups, awareness of arms control problems, and response to many other needs afforded by scientific and technological advances. Thus, the need for political leadership skills would be required.

The Newman study is the third recent major review of educational need to emphasize the need for the development of will, a desire and determination to participate, venture, and take risks. The other such reports were *Disorder in our Schools* (Bauer 1984) and *The Closing of the American Mind* (Bloom 1987).

Many have sought the advancement of morals, ethics, and values in higher education. J. H. Hexter recently asked for the inclusion of moral judgments in history courses (Winkler 1986, 10). He traces the current absence of value judgments in scholarly thinking to René Descartes. Although this approach to research in the natural sciences is necessary to objectivity, Hexter calls it a "Cartesian mistake" when it comes to knowing other disciplines. David Hamburg, President of the Carnegie Corporation, has proposed the development of community values and standards, as found in scientific enterprise, on a broad scale in education (Hamburg 1986). This development would combat the prejudice and ethnocentrism which have plagued our race since ancient times. George Hahn, at Towson State University, claims that ethics and higher education cannot be separated (Hahn 1986). He cites moral lapses by faculty members from a wide range of institutions and the rising level of student cheating over more than four decades.

Increasingly serious student behavioral problems could also be cited. In recognizing the need for passing judgment, Hahn describes an essential element in liberal education as argument and debate, challenge and defense to which no thinking should be exempt—a position supported by Alfred North Whitehead's insistence that breadth of thinking, rightly or wrongly, is a basic freedom within the university. Hahn recognizes moral currents as energizing forces resulting in tempered skepticism, civil courage, and tolerant discrimination.

Frederick Rudolph, formerly of Williams College and the principal writer of "Integrity in the College Curriculum: A Report to the Academic Community," has emphasized that the present course of study serves students and society very poorly (Jacobson 1985). Derek Bok wrote that "There is no reason for universities to feel uncomfortable in taking account of society's needs; in fact, there are clear obligations to do so" (Bok 1982). Donald Kennedy, of Stanford, regards the teaching of moral philosophy as a dimension of higher education which should be formally injected into the curriculum, especially for the professions.

Widespread acceptance that commitment to others, public service, and citizenship should be parts of the curriculum has resulted in the development of a consortium of seventy-five college presidents. This Project for Public and Community Service, based at Brown, is chaired by Howard Swearer and Rev.

Timothy S. Healy and funded by Atlantic Richfield, Ford, and Johnson Foundations.

New Core Curriculum

Consideration of a change in the college curriculum should include grass roots academic designs. These are expressed in general degree requirements which usually reflect university missions or goals as interpreted by faculty, committees, governing bodies, and administration. Requirements ordinarily include reference to human development, to the extension of knowledge, and to service. Required courses include arts, sciences, and humanities and, at least superficially, respond to the mission.

A number of conditions have resulted in higher education's weakly implementing its own mission: 1) a commonly broad statement of mission, 2) a continuing increase in knowledge, numbers of courses, and majors, 3) a lack of accountability for insuring that specific ideas or concepts are learned. The lack of accountability is likely due to growing reliance of university faculties on political methods: response to pressure groups and protection of enrollment levels.

Education does not so much need to rewrite its mission as to develop clear concepts of cultural coherence and human development, the promotion of which are usually accepted as its basic mission. Suggestions for improvement have nearly all sought curriculum coherence, student motivation, commitment, engagement, capability for moral judgment, social responsibility, and related kinds of human resource development. There has been little mention of inadequacies in extending knowledge. Yet clearly the organization rather than the kind and amount of knowledge must be examined. I propose that the curriculum should be organized to explore basic human need as expressed throughout history in basic human institutions: religion, government, economic systems, and science. Such an approach would be international and cross-cultural. It would be practical enough to attract a wide variety of both students and other taxpayers, and it would provide the vision traditionally expected of liberal arts.

Religions

One means for motivating and engaging students is to respond to those questions which have been asked by humanity throughout history. Questions of self, individual worth and value, of God, and the meaning of life have traditionally been questions addressed to religion and philosophy. Such questions are so universal and the answers provided so provincial that, while religions have been on the one hand a wellspring of love and affection, they have on the other been a source of hate and war. They have been intensely motivating in both directions. Thus, there is a need to understand religions and to analyze them critically in order to distinguish the truths they hold from their uses for financial or other personal gain of religious leaders.

With a global trend toward nationalism and conservatism, fundamentalist groups have experienced rapid growth. Some have shown a lack of significant integrity. The popular press has reported many cases of gross leadership, fiscal, ethical, and moral irresponsibility. Critical analysis is needed for both institutional health and protection of the individual.

An American School Administrators report equates the role of religion in human life to that of health, government, and economics, and cites a need for three curricular programs (AASA 1964). One program would describe the role of religion in the humanities and the arts; another, religion's role in establishing and maintaining moral values; a third might describe relationships between government and religion as preparation for citizenship in a multifaithed society. No matter how courses in these three categories were designed, students would perhaps experience both faith and moral development, and could comprehend interinstitutional dynamics. Such development should contribute both to life's meaning and to good citizenship, at least. The administrators' report accepts that appropriate texts might be difficult to find, and, if such courses were taught in public schools, teachers would have to be trained.

Government

Likely, there would be many spinoffs from knowledge of the dynamic relationships between basic institutions. Because religion's strong influence on government is based on a religious fear of gods (Durant 1968), it should provide different bases for allegiance, as psychology and other sciences provide a release from fear. Such dynamics would seem to result in a higher level of integrity for both religion and government. This result would mean a higher level of order and peace in world civilization. According to the Durants, "There is no significant example in history . . . of a society successfully maintaining moral life without the aid of religion" (Ibid).

Since the basic role of government is the establishing of order and since the current conditions of history allow and often promote economic development with greater care than the development of government itself, economic development has often both preceded that of government and been the cause of it.

Science

Because of its explosive growth within the last century, science (pure and applied) has become a major institution in our history. Direct and indirect costs for pure and applied science now consume nearly half of the U.S. federal budget. Science has become the source of hope, an equivalent of money, and a preoccupation of government. Its productive value is such that except for the possibility of self-annihilation, its excesses have not been substantially challenged by religion. Indeed, because of its ability to relieve hunger and suffering, it has been provided almost unlimited moral, if not financial, support by religion.

Summary

Critics of higher education have sought a number of qualities for the student; these include will, motivation, engagement, and commitment; morals, values, and community, along with service to society. Curriculum design is at least one source of characteristics to be developed in students. Wide agreement among scholars suggests that throughout history, religion has sustained faith and imagination for intuitive minds. It has been the source of moral laws which undergird rational action. And though the integrity of government varies, generally, governments have been a source of order, at least as opposed to anarchy and chaos.

Governments provide the conditions wherein the will can be expressed, and motivation rewarded and sustained. Although governments may draw strength from religion, their power comes from science. Through the ages, science has been a major provider of the needs of government—directly through weapons development and indirectly through solutions to health, welfare, and economic problems. Thus, it seems that if the core college curriculum focused on four basic institutions, students would learn both the ultimate source of their survival and the conditions for achievement. They would have knowledge to examine, criticize, and improve the sources and conditions. The practice of examining is a function of both the mode employed by teachers and the designs of educational programs. A practice of critical examination should increase both the interaction between institutions and their integrity. This should keep them healthy.

Curriculum redesign should not be difficult. From current college catalogs it is obvious that the content of liberal arts disciplines focuses on human institutions. The major missing element is that of the role of these institutions and their dynamic interaction. If this interaction is continually improved, then the possibility of human progress should be improved and a favored role of education reestablished.

WORKS CITED

American Association of School Administrators. 1964. "Commission on Religion in Public Schools." New York: Harper and Row.
Bauer, Bary. 1984. *Disorder in Our Schools*. Report of committee from Department of Justice and Education, and White House Office of Public Policy Development.
Bloom, Allan. 1987. *The Closing of the American Mind*. New York: Simon and Schuster.

Bok, Derek. 1982. *Beyond the Ivory Tower: Social Responsibilities of the Modern University*, Santa Monica, CA.: Henessy and Ingalls, Inc.

Durant, Ariel and Will. 1968. *The Lessons of History*. New York: Simon and Schuster.

Hahn, H. George. 1986. Ethics and Higher Education. *Chronicle of Higher Education*. April 9, 47.

Hamburg, David A. 1986. New Kinds of Prejudice, Ethnocentrism and Violence. *Science* 231:553.

Jacobson, Robert L. 1985. Leading Advocates of Reform in Undergraduate Education Find That It's Not Easy to Move From Rhetoric to Reform, *Chronicle of Higher Education*. October 9, 24.

Holmes Group. 1986. *Tomorrow's Teachers: A Report of the Holmes Group*. East Lansing: University of Michigan Press.

Kerr, Clark and Marion Glade. 1986. *The Many Lives of Academic Presidents: Time, Place and Character*. Washington, D.C.: Carnegie Corporation.

Newman, Frank. 1985. *Higher Education and the American Resurgence*. Lawrenceville, N.J.: Princeton University Press.

Winkler, Karen J. 1986. A Historian Criticizes Value-Free Scholarship. *Chronicle of Higher Education*. January 8.

THE ENDURING LESSONS OF THE COMMERCIAL REVOLUTION

Charles P. Carlson, Jr.

University of Denver

As you may have surmised from my title, this paper will concern not a research project but rather an adventure in pedagogy. Beginning last academic year ('88–'89), two colleagues and I have been offering a year-long, team-taught core course at the University of Denver entitled "Commercial Civilization." The course represents an attempt, which we believe to be unique, to integrate a humanities approach with wide ranging introduction to the business and professional environment that many of our students will soon be entering. My paper has been inspired by that experience.

My major responsibility in developing and presenting our course was the historical background. As a medievalist, naturally nothing would do but that I begin with that happiest and most enlightened century, the thirteenth. And, through my teaching interest in the Renaissance, I have long been fascinated by the role of the Italian merchants in developing the earliest techniques and institutions of capitalism. One of the attractions of this course was the opportunity to develop this interest more systematically. But, for the purposes of this course, I knew that a standard economic history survey would not be appropriate. In particular, I saw no reason to expose mostly freshmen students to a detailed discussion of the theoretical debate concerning the vexing problem of the origins of early capitalism. Rather, in keeping with our practical orientation, the pedagogical problem that I set for myself was to determine what lessons in the history of early capitalism are applicable and relevant for today. Or, put another way, are there any constants in the history of capitalism, present from the beginning, that might suggest some reasons for its survival and success as the dominant economic system in Western culture?

In searching the literature, I found two books of particular value. Both examined the problem of early capitalism partly from the perspective of developmental economics, and restated the issue in a manner that was useful for developing a consistent theme on this period; both state the problem not in terms of the origins of capitalism but rather in this form: how is one to explain the fact that Western civilization developed an *affluent* society? One of these books, Douglass C. North and Robert P. Thomas' *The Rise of the Western World* (1973), states the problem as follows:

The affluence of Western man is a new and unique phenomenon. In the past several centuries he has broken loose from the shackles of a world bound by abject poverty and recurring famine and has realized a quality of life which is made possible only by relative abundance. (North and Thomas 1)

The second book was published in 1987 by Nathan Rosenberg and L. E. Birdzell; the title is completely blunt as to its subject—*How the West Grew Rich*. We liked the book so much that we adopted it as a text despite the fact that it is not written at the freshman level.

Both books, of course, reiterate the standard factors found in most treatments of the period—population increase in the thirteenth century, the rise of towns and a bourgeoisie, the creation of a market system, the significance of long-distance trade, the development of distinctive institutions of commerce. It is perhaps useful to mention some of the more distinctive points of interpretation.

North and Thomas, for example, have an interesting discussion of the high Middle Ages as "a frontier movement." They analyze the dynamism which occurred when population increase was combined with expansion into rich virgin lands. Expansion into areas with differing resources resulted in gains in productivity from specialization—that is, the operation of comparative advantage—which also powerfully stimulated trade. (This chapter suggested some interesting comparisons with the colonial period in American history.) They also have interesting observations concerning the relationship of the growth of larger political units, the nation-state, and the growth of larger markets and increased trade. The major thesis in North and Thomas, however, is the central importance of well-defined property rights. They carry this analysis into the early modern period. In their chapter entitled "France and Spain—the Also-rans," their key conclusion is that the absolute monarchies in these countries "failed to create a set of property rights that promoted economic efficiency," whereas the more liberal political institutions in England and the Netherlands ensured the success of those nations. While I do not agree with the authors' contention that this factor was paramount in the West's rise to affluence, one can scarcely doubt that it was a very important one.

The authors of *How the West Grew Rich* also develop a strong central thesis which can be summed up in one word—innovation. However, as they develop it, it is by no means as simplistic as it sounds. Here is a key passage:

The immediate sources of Western growth were innovations in trade, technology and organization, in combination with accumulation of more and more capital, labor, and applied natural resources. Innovation occurred in trading, production, products, services, institutions, and organization. The main characteristics of innovation—uncertainty, search, exploration, financial risk, experiment, and discovery—have so permeated the West's expansion of trade and the West's development of natural resources as to make it virtually an additional factor of production. (Rosenberg and Birdzell 20)

Among the more discrete factors which they isolate is: "the emergence of an autonomous economic sphere and a merchant class"—i.e., rising national governments that pretty much leave the bourgeoisie alone. Most original is their treatment of innovation. They define several forms of innovation: innovation by extension of trade and discovery of new resources; innovation by lowering the cost of production—this, of course, peaks with the Industrial Revolution; and the development of sources of innovative ideas—here they refer to the knowledge structure produced by the scientific revolution and especially to the experimental method. Another interesting concept concerns "overcoming resistance to innovation," which occurs because of "a system of decentralized decision making in capital investment" (Rosenberg and Birdzell 24–34). And the last area of innovation which they highlight is diversity in organization. They conclude with three thematic terms: autonomy, experiment, and diversity.

Both books proved to be suggestive as I tried to solve the pedagogical problem I had set for myself—to collect from these and other sources a summary list of the principal characteristics of the emerging capitalist economy as we can perceive them even as early as the thirteenth century. My next step was to evaluate these characteristics for their relative importance—to consider whether they were unique to capitalism, and also how essential they were to a capitalist economy. My final step has been to ascertain, as the course has developed over the academic year, how the importance of these characteristics might be validated. I performed the first two steps of the exercise in a class brainstorming session, an experiment which I repeated again this year. I began with a standard textbook definition of capitalism as having two distinctive characteristics: private ownership of the principal means of production and a market system as the main mechanism of distribution. The list which the students came up with, with some prompting, was as follows:

—market system—which we carefully qualified to mean a market *system*, not individual markets; it could be regional, national, or even international in scope and was also relatively free, with minimum regulation.
—private property—we defined this broadly to include the means of production.
—free labor—in our times, this is perhaps an academic point, but it is

included for the record. (We use the term in a purely economic sense which has nothing to do with political rights; what is significant is free mobility and freedom to seek employment where a market for labor exists.) It is contrasted, of course, with forms of servile labor associated with feudalism.

—money—"monetization" of the economy is an obvious point, since capitalism is impossible in a barter economy, but an important qualification is that the money supply must be adequate.

—credit and a capital market.

—urbanization—again, an obvious factor.

—a value system—this must be favorable to money-making and enhanced status for the merchant, or, as one student put it, "Wealth is OK."

—individualism and competition—the value system must be tolerant of these two characteristics and permit them to operate positively.

—innovation in technology and business practices because "Change is OK."

—favorable government policy—this means a political environment friendly to business.

This was the list which resulted from my class brainstorming session. Others, of course, could be added. Among these would be:

—a body of merchant law and generally observed standards of morality, including the universal virtues of honesty and integrity.
—a pluralistic political and cultural environment. More on this later.

Now for the next step: to evaluate these characteristics. Which have survived? Which are perennial? Which remain important?

First, the free market system. This remains one of the defining characteristics of capitalism. One of the most important as well as unlikely discoveries in all of human history was the "invisible hand," the self-regulating properties of a free market. Like democracy, the free market defies common sense. Logically, one would suppose that the best economic system is one that is wisely controlled, just as the most logical system of government, as Plato sensibly suggested, is one which leaves it in the hands of an elite class trained in the skills of government. And, as William McNeill has pointed out in his *The Pursuit of Power*, the sovereignty of the market in Western society is almost an aberration, or, in his phrase, "an eccentric departure from the human norm of command behavior." Yet here the testimony of history is overwhelming. Of course, the freedom of the market is always relative. There must be some regulation, and the point in perennial dispute has been the extent and nature of this regulation, but I think it universally true to state that regulation must never stray too far into the realm of control. Initiative and decision-making must remain within the context of the market.

The second point—institutions of private property—is perhaps not quite so absolute as it applies to the means of production. There have been many examples of intermixture of government and private ownership in Western history, and it has often been successful. One example is the financing of the voyages of exploration and commercial sea ventures of early modern times. (We all remember Queen Isabella pawning her jewels to help finance Columbus and Queen Elizabeth's successful investments in what can be most charitably described as a polite form of piracy.) Various forms of mixed economy are characteristic of European nations today. However, with respect to individuals, a near-absolute concept of private property is essential. Here, North and Thomas are correct in their emphasis. While institutions of private property are not unique to post-medieval Western civilization, they are in no other culture so strongly insisted upon. The subsequent history of the West demonstrates the necessity that people in general and merchants in particular be free of the threat of arbitrary seizure of goods and property. Machiavelli sagely observed that a man would sooner forgive a prince for the murder of his father than the seizure of his property, and John Locke made it a central principle of his political philosophy.

The third point is free labor. It would not seem to be a critical element; it is not unique to capitalism, and one can argue that capitalism has tolerated and even temporarily flourished with slavery.

Money is also necessary to capitalism, but is hardly unique to it. But this factor does highlight that a capitalist economy must be adequately monetized, much more so than traditional economies. The revival of mining and an increase in coined money in the thirteenth century was essential to the beginnings of capitalism, and sound monetary policy is always important for a healthy economy. But it was the mistake of the mercantilists to stress this factor too strongly.

However, development of the concept of credit is a much different matter. Credit and credit institutions are unique inventions of Western society and, I believe, the *sine qua non* of capitalism. This, too, is an unlikely development, since the very notion of credit involves a set of values and economic assumptions absolutely antithetical to the traditionalist society of medieval Europe. Those who know the story of how European economic thought was dominated by a combination of Biblical injunctions against usury and Aristotle's bad economics are well aware of the resistance to the new methods of the management of wealth. I would rank the development of credit and credit institutions as the first major instance of the capacity for innovation that has been one of the major factors in the success of capitalism.

Urbanization—a factor often mentioned in textbooks—is as important as money, but again is not unique to capitalist societies. After all, several ancient civilizations were city-state civilizations.

A value system favorable to making money and status for the merchant is perhaps not totally unique to Western capitalism, but much more important than in traditional societies. It again involves a set of values sharply antithetical to medieval society, wherein money-making was disdained from two directions, the aristocracy and the church. Nevertheless, I don't believe it can be reckoned as among the essential factors for the survival and success of capitalism. The bourgeoisie struggled for centuries against a power structure dominated by an aristocracy and still has not totally triumphed, as we learned from one of our lectures, "The Businessman in American Literature." Our dismaying discovery was that there are no businessmen among the heroes of American literature. American literary culture is generally hostile to business, and we suspect that the same is probably true of European literature as well. Our guest lecturer quoted at us those disparaging phrases of Wordsworth concerning the "getting and spending" of money.

(Parenthetically, I note that we plan to put more stress on literature for next year's version of the course. We plan to assign a Horatio Alger story and *The Great Gatsby* as readings, and we will also show film versions of *The Grapes of Wrath* and *Death of a Salesman*.)

Merchant law and standards of morality are also important but not unique. Merchant law goes back at least as far as the Code of Hammurabi, and standards of morality are essential to the operation of any kind of economy. However, we can argue that self-enforced standards of morality are more important in a capitalistic economy because of the relative lack of detailed supervision and the wide freedoms accorded to individual merchants.

The subject of government policy is enormously complicated. Nevertheless, some major generalizations do stand out, none of which are surprising. Certainly, government should not hinder economic development, although the history of the West is replete with examples. And historical experience indicates that, at a minimum, government must fulfill those functions familiar to us from classic conservative thought: maintenance of law and order (obviously needed for the protection of trade) and enforcement of contracts. Beyond this, it is difficult to generalize. Even in the thirteenth century, royal governments found it to their advantage to institute economic policies favorable to enterprise. It is also indisputable that businessmen have uniformly supported government policies that favor their interests; the rhetoric of laissez-faire is heard only in the opposite circumstance. Nevertheless, I believe Rosenberg and Birdzell are correct in pointing out that the mercantile sector of the economy must remain substantially autonomous. And I would reiterate my previous generalization concerning regulation—that the initiative in matters of commerce and economic decision-making must remain within the autonomous sphere of the market.

I would conclude with two critical factors: The first is a capacity for creativity or innovation. Here I admit to accepting much of the thesis of Rosenberg and Birdzell. And I also remain convinced that the explanation for the rise of Western capitalism that I learned from some of the great old names in economic history as a graduate student is still the most convincing one. I still quote from E. P. Cheyney's classic *Dawn of a New Era* in the Langer Rise of Europe series, where Cheyney wrote, "The most fundamental of the changes that marked the passage from medieval to modern times was the increase of wealth, and the principal cause of the increase of wealth was the extension of commerce" (Cheyney 2). However, the critical element was innovation. It was the merchants of the Italian Renaissance who developed the institutions to maximize the efficiency and profits of that long-distance trade, who in effect created the essential institutional structure of capitalism. This is why I argue that credit is the first great innovation in the history of capitalism. I would also assert that innovation is an expression of another Western value, individualism, even that it is the highest expression of individualism in the economic realm. We also found this theme in another of our texts, Peters and Waterman's *In Search of Excellence*, where the authors found that one characteristic of excellence in business organizations is a corporate environment that fosters innovation. A continued capacity for innovation in our business institutions is essential to meet the competitive challenges which face this country in our present global economic environment.

The second factor is pluralism. The pluralistic political environment of early modern Europe is a factor heavily stressed by some recent writers on the origins of capitalism; a plurality of competing political sovereignties produces autonomy and a plurality of competing markets in the economic sector. This is a prominent theme in McNeill's *The Pursuit of Power* and has been most recently expressed in Paul Kennedy's *The Rise and Fall of the Great Powers*, where he uses the term "the European miracle" to describe this development. As he puts it: "It was a combination of economic laissez-faire, political and military pluralism, and intellectual liberty—however rudimentary each factor was compared with later ages—which had been in constant interaction to produce the 'European miracle'" (Kennedy 30). Pluralistic political and economic structures have also resulted in the creation of pluralism as a pervasive value in Western culture. An excellent philosophical treatment of this theme is found in Michael Novak's *The Spirit of Democratic Capitalism*. He argues persuasively that pluralism is one of the most important ways in which democratic values and the folkways of commercial civilization conjoin. This is another mighty theme which I cannot argue here. I would, however, make a more modest observation: I think it can be argued that it is a pluralistic culture which best facilitates the competitive processes which are the major strength of the capitalistic system even as it humanizes those processes. Such a culture also best sustains that capacity for innovation which must be challenged if this country is to meet the competitive challenges of our time.

These have been the principle lessons I have learned from pondering these issues with my students. If not original, I hope they are at least provocative.

REFERENCES

Cheyney, Edward P. *Dawn of a New Era, 1250–1453*. New York: Harper & Brothers, 1936.
Kennedy, Paul. *The Rise and Fall of the Great Powers*. New York: Random House, 1987.
McNeill, William. *The Pursuit of Power: Technology, Armed Force, and Society Since A.D. 1000*. Chicago: University of Chicago Press, 1982.
North, Douglass C. and Robert P. Thomas. *The Rise of the Western World: A New Economic History*. Cambridge: Cambridge University Press, 1973.
Novak, Michael. *The Spirit of Democratic Capitalism*. New York: Simon and Schuster, 1982.
Peters, Thomas J. and Robert H. Waterman, Jr. *In Search of Excellence*. New York: Harper & Row, 1982.
Rosenberg, Nathan and L. E. Birdzell, Jr.. *How the West Grew Rich*. New York: Basic Books, 1986.

LITERATURE AND SCIENCE: A MISALLIANCE

John Idol

Clemson University

Flannery O'Connor once ruefully remarked, "In most English classes the short story has become a kind of literary specimen to be dissected. Every time a story of mine appears in a Freshman anthology, I have a vision of it, with its little organs laid open, like a frog in a bottle."

She might also have had the same vision if she had been a poet or dramatist whose work had been selected for an anthology. As anthologists, critics, and teachers, we do want our readers or students to learn the elements of fiction, poetry, and drama. Like chemists hoping that their charges will learn the periodic table and know what will or will not go with what, we draw up a chart of elements, define them, and show students how to spot and analyze them. Our terms heap high upon one another: plot, theme, character, setting, symbol, irony, rising action, climax, denouement, ballad measure, sestina, epic, romance, romantic epic, oxymoron, iamb, dactyl, naturalism, surrealism, fantasy, and so on and on and on, until we have to call on somebody in our profession, Harmon and Holman, Abrams, Benet, or lesser known guides, to keep track of the elements of literature.

And we try, sometimes with disastrous results, to get our students to identify elements in the works we ask them to read. Helpful as we sometimes think ourselves to be, we even give them study guides alerting them to be on the lookout for certain elements. For all our good intentions, we sometimes get back essays proving that a literary work has been murdered in its dissection. Let me illustrate my point by sharing with you an experience I had nearly two years ago when I read essays by some of the brightest kids in our country, those eager, intelligent, ambitious, and often hardworking golden lads and lasses who, as students in Advanced Placement English courses, wrote an essay on the following poem by Sylvia Plath:

SOW

God knows how our neighbor managed to breed
His great sow:
Whatever his shrewd secret, he kept it hid

In the same way
He kept the sow—impounded from public stare,
Prize ribbon and pig show.

But one dusk our questions commended us to a tour
Through his lantern-lit
Maze of barns to the lintel of the sunk sty door

To gape at it:
This was no rose-and-larkspurred china suckling
With a penny slot

For thrifty children, nor dolt pig ripe for heckling,
About to be
Glorified for prime flesh and golden crackling

In a parsley halo;
Nor even one of the common barnyard sows,
Mire-smirched, blowzy,

Maunching thistle and knotweed on her snout-cruise—
Bloat tun of milk
On the move, hedged by a litter of feat-foot ninnies

Shrilling her hulk
To halt for a swig at the pink teats. No. This vast
Brobdingnag bulk

Of a sow lounged belly-bedded on that black compost,
Fat-rutted eyes
Dream-filled. What a vision of ancient hoghood must

Thus wholly engross
The great grandam!—our marvel blazoned a knight
Helmed, in cuirass,

Unhorsed and shredded in the grove of combat
By a grisly-bristled
Boar, fabulous enough to straddle that sow's heat.

But our farmer whistled,
Then, with a jocular fist thwacked the barrel nape,
And the green-copse-castled

Pig hove, letting legend like dried mud drop,
Slowly, grunt
On grunt, up in the flickering light to shape

A monument
Prodigious in gluttonies as that hog whose want
Made lean Lent

Of kitchen slops and, stomaching no constraint,
Proceeded to swill
The seven troughed seas and every earthquaking continent.

A few students around the country wrote insightfully and well on Plath's presentation of the sow, prompted by the topic assigned: "Consider particularly how the language of the poem reflects both the neighbor's and the narrator's perceptions of the sow and how that language determines the reader's perceptions. Be certain to discuss how the portrayal of the sow is enhanced by such features as diction, devices of sound, images, and allusions." The prompt seems clear enough, something students of whatever level of ability should have been able to handle. However clear the directions, the poem presented problems from the outset for some students: a few thought that the word *sow* was a regionalism for *cow*, many had no gender association with the word and referred to the monstrous swine as "he" or "him," and some had not the slightest notion about the "sow's heat." Words like "swill" and "thwack" and "cuirass" were not part of the working wordhoard of a greater number of them. Few of them seemed to have read *Gulliver's Travels*, though some future Harold Blooms, or better, out there knew about Thor's sea-reducing thirst. Topnotch students read the poem, as it should be, as a splendid evocation of the farmer's pride in his great sow and his good-natured care of her and of the narrator's fancy and whimsy in seeing the sow in many lights, ranging from what she was not right on through to a mythic epitome of hoghood. And they demonstrated how Plath's language and art embodied the presentation of these contrasting views and shaped the response of readers.

But for those students for whom a little learning is a dangerous thing, the poem ended up far worse than a frog in a bottle. When some students had finished with it, it looked as if it had been hit by an atom smasher. The trouble arose, we readers agreed, because students seemed to think that the poem had to be symbolic. That assumption led them to do bizarre things with the poem. When they went symbol hunting, they bagged some surprising catches: some of them put together the farmer's jocular thwack on the sow's barrel nape and man's abuse of women, coming up with the farmer as an archetypal woman-beater and the sow as long-suffering, battered womankind; some of them built a case for the sow as symbolic of Christ, drawing on the words *halo* and *Lent* and a perception of the sow as undergoing a kind of crucifixion when the farmer thwacked her; some of them went outside the text itself, to the copyright information given beneath the poem, to find support for a reading of the sow as a symbol of the atomic bomb. Something had to cause the "earthquaking" mentioned in the poem, and since the poem's copyright date was given as 1957, a date after the Atomic Age began, the sow must therefore stand for all the destruction wrought by unleashing the power of the atom.

Such off-the-wall interpretations of the sow might have been chalked up to the musings of eccentrics and jokesters if they hadn't appeared in scores upon scores of essays, maybe even hundreds and hundreds of essays. Mercifully, after three days of reading essays on the sow, I moved on to the question on George Eliot's views on Old Leisure and New Leisure, where I feel reasonably sure I read sane, penetrating, and persuasively argued essays by students who had tried to tell me that the sow was mauled womankind, crucified Christ, and an atom bomb.

My reflections on the experience of reading these sincerely proposed, stoutly argued, textually supported essays on the sow's alleged symbolic meaning led me to think about how teachers try to prepare students to read literature and about how other teachers work with young scholars to pour the stuff of their disciplines into their heads. These reflections brought some similar instructional methods to light: we define, classify, analyze, compare, contrast, evaluate, speculate, theorize, summarize, divide into constituent parts, and grab at anything we think might work for us. Rather than bounce from one method to another, rather than dwell in chaos, we try to systemize our approach to a subject, whether it be technical, scientific, or literary. For some subjects, a systematic approach works simply and exquisitely, yielding predictable results for either a novice or an expert. Seeing their simplicity and enjoying the ease and comfort of their use in some subjects, we try to apply them to other fields of study.

Time prohibits much by way of examples, but I do want to explore two approaches that work well in science but poorly, in my experience, in literature. As scientists from the Greeks right on down to those wettest behind their ears have known, classification has been, presently is, and no doubt will continue to be absolutely essential in their disciplines, whether aerodynamics or zoology and everything in between. To prepare students to identify flora or fauna, to handle materials in chemistry laboratories, or to sort their clothes before tossing them into washers and dryers, we ask them to learn how to classify things, insisting, correctly enough, that failure to classify accurately could have serious, if not fatal, consequences. We help them to classify by giving precise definitions, clear illustrations, lists of differentia, and where appropriate, laboratory exercises and tests. If our teaching works well, they come away with a method to serve them throughout life. Most of them learn when and where to use classification, but not everyone sees or senses where classification has no proper role. Those using classification properly come most often, I find, from the ranks of scientists; those abusing classification are, for the most part, specialists in literature, those specialists who seem to need pigeonholes for literary artifacts and labels for authors or literary eras. Out of their respect for the elegant simplicity of scientific classification, these literary experts group writers and works under such rubrics as classical, romantic, realistic, naturalistic, impressionistic, expressionistic. After laboring eloquently and long on classicism, for example, as "the temper of writers who, because of inherent disposition or from conviction or custom, have sought to express noble ideas in dignified language and have believed firmly in the power of restraint, the need for decorum, and the value of lucid simplicity" (Hibbard and Frenz 3), a team of anthologists then proceeded to choose Aeschylus' *Agamemnon*, with this unrestrained, passionate cry from Cassandra:

> Ah, horror, horror! What is this I see?
> Is it a snare of Hell?
> Nay, the true net is she who shares his bed,
>   Who shares in working death.
> Ha! let the Band insatiable in hate
> Howl for the race its wild exulting cry
>   O'er sacrifice that calls
>   For death by storm of stones.

Classical drama has episode after episode where human suffering finds utterance in shrill cries of anger and frustration or profound groans of heart-felt grief: Medea defending herself against power-hungry Jason, Clytemnestra taking revenge on Agamemnon, Oedipus ripping out his own eyes, Agave discovering that she has dismembered her own son. All those episodes, and many more like them, are "emotional and passionate," two words regularly appearing when anthologists and critics seek to tell us about Romanticism (Hibbard and Frenz 394).

Who will deny that the following passage about Hell from Dante's *Divine Comedy* (Canto III) has decorum, restraint, and simple lucidity?

"My son," said the courteous Master, "those who die in the wrath of God, all come together here from every land; and they are eager to pass over the stream, for the divine justice spurs them so that fear is turned to desire. A good soul never passes this way; and therefore if Charon fret at thee, well mayest thou now know what his speech signifies."

This ended, the gloomy plain trembled so mightily, that the memory of the terror even now bathes me with sweat. The tearful land gave forth a wind that flashed a crimson light which vanquished all sensation in me, and I fell as a man whom slumber seizes.

In an anthology once widely used in world literature courses, this calm and simply lucid account of Hell falls under the rubric "Romantic." This same anthology puts under that same heading the anti-romantic Cervantes and that arch-romantic, Victor Hugo. Surely something is amiss if the classification system permits such groupings.

Experienced readers of literature know that mature writers call into play whatever mode of expression best serves their needs, whether it be realistic, classical, romantic, surrealistic, or expressionistic. When thoughtful editors and teachers compile anthologies or teach classes, they arrange materials by theme, nationality, or chronology and avoid the problems occasioned by forcing certain writers to wear prescribed labels: classicist, romantic, realist, symbolist, surrealist. Sagely foregoing the elegant simplicity of science, experienced teachers of literature pay homage to the complexity and mysteries of life by confronting and enjoying literature without labels: modern, postmodern, minimalist, or whatever label happens to be in vogue. As experienced teacher and playwright Paul Green says in his wise little book on the art of teaching, *Forever Growing*,

> When we forget our tokens and labels and signs and hierarchy of pigeon-holing and think of the works, the stories and plays and poems, themselves, we find that they are part of the creative process of life and men in life, and as such we can enjoy them, draw from them, be enriched and refreshed through them. Our learned findings of influences and kinds and types only get in the way and are a hindrance. They get between the appreciator and the object of his appreciation—that is, a really *felt* appreciation. (13)

In an age where signs, labels, and logos are increasingly a part of the world we breathe, eat, sleep, work, and breed in, along with our students we sometimes get caught up in pigeonholing: just think of your latest visit to B. Dalton's, Waldenbooks, or practically any modern bookshop. Just think back to the English professor who asked you somewhere along the way to discuss Pope as a classicist or Keats as a romantic. And think how dishonest you felt in building a case for Pope's classicism knowing damn good and well that you'd better gloss over as aberrations such pieces as "Eloise and Abelard" and *The Dunciad*. And think how deeply you sensed that Keats was far closer to the spirit of Homer and Aeschylus than Pope ever was even if he did make a tidy income off his Homeric translations.

210

Then think, if you must, of forcing your students to tell you why writer X is a classicist, romantic, or whatever. If nothing else militates against our asking anyone to tackle the job of classifying anyone as a romantic, we should remember that *romanticism* has well over forty definitions and the count continues spiraling upward. Certainly, the center of no classification is going to hold if we can't agree on the differentia. If mere anarchy is not unleashed, the result is not far from it. Our frogs end up as mere flecks of nerve, muscle, skin, and bone and our labels spread densely over those mere flecks. We often rest content in memorizing the labels and forget that a toad ever hopped freely in our literary garden.

To step away from allusion and metaphor now, I think we have an obligation as teachers to respect the integrity of a literary artifact, its quiddity, wholeness, uniqueness. I think we should remember that not every bird of a feather likes to flock together and consequently should look over every pigeon in our hand before we go seeking out a hole to stuff it in. But here I am back to figurative language again! My unadorned admonishment is: Beware that Idol of the Theatre which tempts you to turn to classification as a means of putting an anthology together, presenting a writer, or evaluating a longish piece of literature. To do so is, too often, to misrepresent authors and place hurdles between our students and their apprehension and comprehension of a literary work, between them and the real toads in literary gardens. All this is but to say that we should come to works of literary art with open minds and hospitable hearts, behaving as Sir Thomas Browne did when he thought of natural philosophers, scientists we now call them, opening their eyes and hearts to nature and putting Aristotle and his grand schemes behind them: "There is no deformity but in Monstrosity; wherein, notwithstanding, there is a kind of Beauty; Nature so ingeniously contriving the irregular parts, as they become sometimes more remarkable than the principal Fabrick. To speak yet more narrowly, there was never any thing ugly or mis-shapen, but the Chaos" (*Religio Medici*). To ensure that full, fresh, heart-and-head encounter with a literary work, we must resist that urge "Still to be neat, still to be dressed" in the guise of classifiers and dividers into constituent parts (Jonson 351).

Division into constituent parts perhaps stands foremost as the Idol of the Theatre literature teachers turn to for help when they introduce the various literary forms to their charges. Something in us cries out for a systematic way to discuss a work or have our students write about it. Our cries and our prayers are answered by the likes of Laurence Perrine, Robert Scholes, Donald Hall, X. J. Kennedy, Brooks and Warren, and a host of others, all giving us and our students learned, and often graceful and insightful, short essays on the elements of fiction, verse, and drama. Standing as they do at the heads of the forms our students are to explore, these introductions, if not handled skillfully by the teacher, will say to students something similar to what a periodic chart says to the chemistry class: just as so many neutrons, electrons, and protons, or quarks, make up elements so do plot, theme, setting, characterization, diction, symbol, and so forth make up certain kinds of literary works. If, in the interest of preparing our students to discuss, for example, a story, novel, or narrative poetry, we give them handouts instructing them to identify features of a work or to answer questions about the elements making up the work we can reinforce the notion that certain elements must be present if a work is to be a genuine piece of literary art. In giving them something in the mode of the literature of knowledge to deal with and to respond to the literature of power, to use DeQuincey's timeless distinction, we willy-nilly create a misalliance between science and literature. That is, if we fail to explain how those introductions to literary forms are to be used or if we fail to point out on our study guides and question sheets that some works need not, for example, have plot or even symbol.

If enough teachers around the nation had said to their bright AP English students, a symbol is part of the quiddity of a literary work, something not forced and strained or over-ingenious, essays on Plath's "Sow" would not have given up AP readers a Brobdingnagian slop eater posing as an abused woman, hanging from the cross as a slaughtered Christ, or exploding in our faces as a porcine atomic bomb.

Lest I dwell too long on those essays and the sad, grimly funny, discoveries those AP students made when they went symbol-hunting, let me ask if you, as I surely have in nearly thirty years of teaching, have not had symbol hunters stalk your classrooms and allegory-detectives preach to you about the hidden meanings of lyrics, stories, plays, and novels? Guns, such as the ones Dick Prosser and the Libya Hill posse use in Wolfe's "The Child by Tiger," become phallic weapons; each gable of *The House of the Seven Gables* represents a deadly sin; the meerschaum pipe in Poe's "The Purloined Letter" is symbolic of an introverted personality. I give only a few I have gleaned just recently; you will have your own favorites, the kind you regale your colleagues with when you grade a batch of essays.

I conclude by inviting you listen to a few more wise words from Paul Green, whose little book *Forever Growing* with its subtitle *Some Notes on a Credo for Teachers* can be read even after over forty-three years of virtual neglect as a heart-felt warning against a misalliance of literature and science:

And these little labels we schoolmasters make and try to paste on the creative process of life are forever peeling off in the turn and twist and scouring of time. They will not stick. How could a label stick on a flowing river, or a stamp on shaking gay green leaves? But our activity continues. As soon as one label wears out or peels off or is blown away in contrary winds of doctrine or passes out of fashion, we have a more scientific one ready for the pasting. And much of the frustration in purposes and hindrances to man's development and joy occurs because of this confusion of labels and names that we are responsible for. They are seals and deceptions stuck not so much perhaps on the body of the process of life and art itself as over the eyes of both the seeker and the seer. (7)

And to these words I add this one bit of wisdom from that great propagandist for science and one of our revered literary men, Francis Bacon:

But the *Idols of the Market-place* are the most troublesome of all: idols which have crept into the understanding through the alliances of words and names.

If we, like Bacon and Paul Green and other great teachers, want to advance the cause of learning, we will know when to call on science for help and when to leave it to its own dream of simple elegance.

REFERENCES

Browne, Sir Thomas. *Religio Medici and Other Writings*. New York: E. P. Dutton and Company, Inc., 1951.
Green, Paul. *Forever Growing: Some Notes on a Credo for Teachers*. Chapel Hill: The University of North Carolina Press, 1945.
Hibbard, Clarence Addison and Horst Frenz. *Writers of the Western World*. Boston: Houghton, Mifflin, 1967.
Jonson, Ben. *Ben Jonson Poems*. Ed. Ian Donaldson. London: Oxford University Press, 1975.
O'Connor, Flannery. *Mystery and Manners*. Ed. Sally and Robert Fitzgerald. New York: Farrar, Straus & Giroux, 1975.
Plath, Sylvia. *The Collected Poems*. Ed. Ted Hughes. New York: Harper & Row, 1981.

CICERO IN THE CLASSIC LEARNING CORE

Anthony Damico

University of North Texas

It is fitting that a conference on the core and the canon take place at the University of North Texas because here the core and the canon are inextricably woven into the twenty-four semester hours of University requirements, twenty hours of College of Arts and Science requirements, six hours of distribution requirements, and six hours of CLC requirements which compose the Classic Learning Core. Students take these required courses in a fixed sequence and professors, as much as possible, use texts from a common booklist. A large portion of this booklist consists of texts usually found in the so-called canon because, when the CLC was being developed, the steering committee agreed that the common reading list should provide a proper framework for a close study of Western culture. Among the authors selected are the usual representatives of Greece and Rome—Homer, Aeschylus, Sophocles, Euripides, Plato, Aristotle, Plutarch, Cicero, Vergil, and Augustine.

One book which may be considered the central text of the core is Plato's *Republic*—admittedly an excellent introduction to almost every important subject in the core except, ironically, political science. At the University of North Texas the required courses in political science involve the study of American and to a lesser degree Texas political institutions, upon the development of which Plato has exercised little influence. Indeed, Thomas Jefferson, composer of the Declaration of Independence, after reading Plato's *Republic*, wrote to John Adams in 1814:

> "While wading thro' the whimsies, the puerilities, and unintelligible jargon of this work, I laid it down often to ask myself how it could have been that the world should have so long consented to give reputation to such nonsense as this." (Cited by Meyer Reinhold, *The Classick Pages*, University Park: Pennsylvania State University Press, 1975, 114)

and Adams heartily agreed. Not only Jefferson and Adams but indeed most of the Founding Fathers, as Reinhold points out, "were repelled by [Plato's] abstract thought and his profound distrust of popular government, 'Plato,' said the Massachusetts statesman Elbridge Gerry, 'was not a Republican'" (Reinhold 114). As a matter of fact, arguably Jefferson's most severe criticism of Cicero, whom he generally admired, was his uncritical praise of Plato (Reinhold 49).

Plato and his political thought, then, contributed little to the foundations of the American republic, long since well and truly laid on principles which, if they were not invented by Cicero, were at least most skillfully synthesized and expounded by him. This at least is one conclusion to be drawn from the scholarship of Reinhold and other American classicists. The English social scientist Neal Wood has also made significant contributions to this inquiry in his latest book, *Cicero's Social and Political Thought* (Berkeley: University of California Press, 1988), which he wrote "out of a conviction that Cicero the social and political thinker deserves far more attention than he has received in recent years ..." (Wood ix). His conviction is especially valid in the context of a classic learning core.

Social and political concepts which Wood finds elucidated in the works of Cicero include:

> the principles of natural law and justice and of universal moral equality; a patriotic and dedicated republicanism; a vigorous advocacy of liberty, impassioned rejection of tyranny, and persuasive justification of tyrannicide; a firm belief in constitutionalism, the rule of law, and the mixed constitution; a strong faith in the sanctity of private property, in the importance of its accumulation, and the opinion that the primary purpose of state and law was the preservation of property and property differentials; a conception of proportionate social and political equality, entailing a hierarchy of differential rights and duties; a vague ideal of rule by a "natural aristocracy"; and a moderate and enlightened religious and epistemological skepticism. (Wood 4)

According to Wood, the works most fruitful for an understanding of Cicero's social and political thought are, in chronological order, *The Defense of Sestius*, the *Republic*, the *Laws*, and *On Duties* (Wood 61). The first of these is a forensic speech for Sestius, who had, during his tribunate in 57, in which he had led the fight for Cicero's recall from exile, surrounded himself with an armed guard to protect himself against the ruffians of Clodius, leader of the popularist opposition. Cicero, turning the actual defense over to his co-counselors, used his time to justify his own political program. In large part this speech—Cicero's best, in my opinion—is an attack on the political quietism of much of the ruling class of his time and a call to duty for young aspirants to public service, whether they be noble or new men like himself.

"The *Republic* and the *Laws*, . . ." as Wood observes, "are essential for an understanding of [Cicero's] conceptions of man, law, and justice; his attitude to the state and politics; his typology of states; his notions of the mixed constitution, of tyranny, of the ideal statesman, and of the social utility of religion." Like his political manifesto in the *Defense of Sestius*, these two books appear to be aimed at "the general reader, particularly a youthful audience," and to be inspired not only by Cicero's belief in "the actual disintegration of Roman civic life" but by the threat presented by the publication of Lucretius' beautiful and effective Epicurean manifesto, *On the Nature of Things*, of subversion of "the Roman civic community and its foundation in the *mos maforum*" (Wood 63).

Although it is true that the *Republic* and the *Laws* are essential for a balanced understanding of Cicero's concepts and would naturally be part of any course on his contributions to modern social and political theory, especially as it influenced the Founding Fathers, they are not by any means unique sources for most of these notions. This is important because these works, which were published just four years before the deaths of Jefferson and Adams and long after the composition of the Declaration of Independence, the Constitution, or the Federalist Papers, were unknown to their authors; therefore, they could not themselves have exerted any influence on them. Many of Cicero's own sources, however, such as Plato's *Republic*, Aristotle's *Politics*, and especially Polybius' *History*, cover much the same political ground, and his own essay, *On Duties*, is the primary source for his social theory. Unlike Cicero's *Republic* and *Laws* these works had never been lost and certainly influenced the Founding Fathers, reinforcing if not inspiring their essentially conservative approach to economics and government. Moreover, the discovery and publication of Cicero's *Letters to Atticus*, his *Letters to His Friends*, and his legal speeches, begun by Petrarch in 1345 and completed by Salutati and Bracciolini, made his thought widely available and influential among the early moderns and made him "For the humanists . . . a venerated teacher of civic virtue, the staunch republican apostle of liberty and relentless foe of tyranny" (Wood 2). He also affected the Founding Fathers indirectly through the works of such thinkers as Machiavelli, Hobbes, and especially Locke, who counted Cicero among the "truly great men" (cited by Wood 3).

On Duties, the last work recommended by Wood,

> is crucial because of its portrait of an ideal gentleman and the attitude expressed toward labor and various vocations. Nowhere are Cicero's positions on private property and its relationship to the state better or more fully explained. Furthermore, it is characterized by a pronounced individualism not only in economic but also in moral and political concerns. . . . Unless *On Duties* is scrutinized the student may miss Cicero's conceptual separation of state from government, his beginning distinction between state and society, and his notions of the trust of government, tyranny, and tyrannicide. (Wood 68)

Whoever doubts this assertion needs only to consult the text of the Declaration of Independence. According to Jefferson, "the Laws of Nature and of Nature's God entitle" a people "to assume among the powers of the earth [a] separate and equal station," i.e., the status of sovereign state. In his *Republic*, III.33. Cicero says that, "True Law is right reason in agreement with nature," and elsewhere, "Since right reason is Law, we must believe that men have Law also in common with the Gods" (*Laws* I.23).

A sovereign state, or *res publica*, is for Cicero the property (*res*) of a people (*populus*, whence *publica*) joined together by justice or right (*ius*) and common interest (*utilitas*). A people, or (*populus*), is "a union of a large number of men in agreement with respect to what is right or just, and associated in the common interest" (*Republic* I.39). This is exactly the sense in which the thirteen colonies could no longer accept their status within the British Empire, since they no longer agreed on what was right or just or were associated in the common interest.

Jefferson maintains that "all men are created equal, that they are endowed by their Creator with certain unalienable rights," and in the same sense Cicero agrees with him:

[O]ut of all the material of the philosophers' discussions, surely there comes nothing more valuable than the full realization that we are born for Justice. and that right is based, not upon men's opinions, but upon Nature. This fact will immediately be plain if you once get a clear conception of man's fellowship and union with his fellow-men. For no single thing is so like another, so exactly its counterpart, as all of us are to one another. (*Laws* I.28–29)

Next Jefferson states that "among these [Rights] are Life, Liberty, and the pursuit of Happiness.—That to secure these rights, Governments are instituted among Men, deriving their just powers from the consent of the governed." Considering that earlier versions of the Declaration read "Life, Liberty, and the pursuit of Property," the compatibility with Cicero's position throughout his works, nowhere better expressed than in *On Duties* II.78—"it is the peculiar function of the state and the city to guarantee to every man the free and undisturbed control of his own particular property"—is obvious. With respect to the consent of the governed, *On Duties* I.124 addresses the expectations of magistrates, who at Rome were popularly elected and required to give an account of their administrations upon leaving office:

It is the proper duty of the magistrate, therefore, to understand that he plays the role of the state and that he ought to uphold its dignity and honor, enforce its laws, dispense its rights, and remember that these responsibilities have been committed to him as a matter of trust.

The Declaration of Independence makes it clear that George III had failed miserably as chief magistrate.

Finally, Jefferson asserts "That whenever any Form of Government becomes destructive of these ends, it is the Right of the People to alter or abolish it." Our Founding Fathers knew nothing about Cicero better than his position on tyranny, best summed up in *On Duties* III.19:

> What more atrocious crime can there be than to kill a fellow man? But if anyone kills a tyrant—be he never so intimate a friend—he has not laden his soul with guilt, has he? The Roman people, in any event, are not of that opinion; for of all glorious deeds they hold such a one to be most noble.

In his severe judgment on tyranny as in much else Cicero emulates Plato and Aristotle, but whereas "They," to quote Wood, "think that the chief goal of the well-ordered *polis* is to encourage human beings to fulfill their rational nature by the achievement of true moral virtue"—a goal which they say few can achieve—and speculate on the one best regime to achieve this end, Cicero, practical Roman that he is, makes it the state's function to protect property rights—something anyone can get behind—and posits a constitution composed of monarchic, aristocratic, and democratic elements which check and balance one another. "For this basic reason," says Wood, "Cicero, instead of Plato or Aristotle, is the significant ancient influence on early modern political thinkers and their idea of the state" (Wood 130). And for this reason he deserves a prominent place in a coordinated program.

SLOUCHING TOWARD BETHLEHEM: THE BOOK OF RUTH IN A SECULAR SOCIETY

Albert Waldinger

Defense Language Institute

In the first place, please let me explain the wording of my title by these lines from Yeats' "The Second Coming":

> The blood-dimmed tide is loosed, and everywhere
> The ceremony of innocence is drowned;
> The best lack all conviction, while the worst
> Are full of passionate intensity.
>
> And what rough-beast, its hour come round at last,
> *Slouches towards Bethlehem* to be born?[1]

Of course, I am not suggesting that Ruth's model of moral order for a disorderly world is sneaky and under the counter, but I am saying that the Book of Ruth must confront the statement made in Joan Didion's 1968 essay about the Haight-Ashbury neighborhood of San Francisco:

> There are only three significant pieces of data in the world today.... The first is ... God died last year and was obited by the press. The second is that 50% of the population is or will be under 25 [a fact which may no longer be true; nevertheless, the cult of youth remains infectious]. The third ... is that they got twenty billion irresponsible dollars to spend. (104)

It is not clear who "they" are, but it is abundantly clear that irresponsibility is rampant. It is also clear that the biblical book, by contrast, stands for the strictest and most all-embracing kind of accountability and that its morality speaks to experience.

Ruth and the Plot of Experience

For this reason, I would like to give you some autobiographical details. You may take them as a kind of non-literary plot parallel to the Book of Ruth.

I was born in danger: in the Vienna of Hitler's annexation of Austria to Germany. The First Movement, then—the first "immigration toward Bethlehem"—

was an escape to the United States—an "emigration," actually, since my family was forced to leave. My mother, in the personal upheaval, maintained a saddened faithfulness, like Naomi or like Ruth who "stood in tears amid the alien corn," as Keats put it.

The Second Movement was to the Holy Land itself: at the age of 33, after I received a Ph.D. in American Literature, my mother, my source of value in "Exile," died, and I "ascended" to Israel with my father. I went with the definite purpose of founding a family there and "raising up the name of the dead."

When I found this impossible, I returned to the United States, anything but "alien corn" for me, and began the Third Movement, which was the continued search for a home and a family, my Bethlehem. By this time, I had been uprooted fairly thoroughly, so I wasn't too surprised when I found that fulfillment involved still further travel: my future wife turned out to be a Filipina and I went to the Philippines to marry her—in the Catholic Church (though not at the expense of denying my own religious identity).

All of these Movements were resumed when I chose to teach the Book of Ruth,[2] King James Version, to young "Servants of the People" in the People's Republic of China, where I was a "foreign expert" in English Composition and American Literature. I chose Ruth—or was chosen by her—for several reasons: in the first place, her story was cast in extremely expressive, historically trailblazing English, so much so that one commentator (Hammond 1987) has even said that the prose of King James set the syntactic patterns of the Modern English I was teaching (657), though to tell the truth I don't believe my students cared much about the formal development of a "Western and Capitalist" language like English. In the second place, the Book of Ruth seemed a true representative of Anglo-American culture, with its emphasis on striving, mobility and productivity (as well as productiveness). At the same time, it was a masterpiece of the art of fiction, capable of generating understanding about the short story (and this was the only kind of "productivity" I was ultimately interested in). And lastly, its morality of service, fidelity and respect for authority dovetailed in large part with Communist Chinese ideals.

Ruth and Fertility

However, there were two major "faults": Ruth's actions are religiously motivated and the policy of the People's Republic of China restricts birth to one child per family and is diametrically opposed to the "Commandment" moving Ruth, which is "increase and multiply" and which prizes children as a blessing ("Happy is the man that hath his quiver full of them" is the way Psalm 127:5 puts it).

Something should be said about the divinity of this drive, which stems from the very first chapter of Genesis (verse 28). There, God not only commands man

220

to fulfill his instincts, seen as holy in normative Judaism; he also orders him to "subdue the earth" or nature (*"pru"*-"increase," *"kivshu"*-"subdue" are both imperatives). This is precisely the voice Ruth hears, her biological clock ticking morally to the rhythm of the Abrahamic Covenant, and it is in perfect tune with the task of Chinese Communists attempting to feed an overpopulated nation, even though these are motivated by nothing deeper than the buzz—and buzzwords—of Marx.

My hope was that my Chinese students would feel the relevance of Ruth's "narrative"—I didn't want to undermine it by calling it a "fictive story" or bureaucratize it by devaluating it as simply another "agenda." I was hoping that the traditional Chinese belief in fertility—over and above "productive development"—would be victorious: after all, one of my students, who "produced" just one child in her own marriage, was herself the "Eldest Sister" of 5, only the last being a much-prized son, born at a time when the Chinese government was still "sexist" enough to encourage people to "keep trying" if they didn't get a boy the previous time around (a situation strongly reminiscent of "Fiddler on the Roof"). Still more important: Ruth seemed to me too strong-backed to buckle under a load of ideological "disabilities." What I ultimately intended was to replace Marxian dialectics with the "dialectical tensions" of the Bible as Alter (1981) describes them:

> . . . a tension between the divine plan and the disorderly character of actual-historical events . . . [as well as the] tension between God's will, His providential guidance, and human freedom, the refractory nature of man. (33)

Such an untamed (and unrefined) quality is the source both of a "drowned ceremony of innocence" and a "blood-dimmed tide."

Ruth and Archetypal Values

I wanted to create the understanding that it was this tension that made the Book of Ruth "canonical" in both literary and religious senses (Alter 1981, 34) and in the traditional acceptation of "recommended" (Kermode 1987, 604). In addition, I wanted my students to be aware that any true archetype of human tension would have to be uncluttered, unlike the cloak and dagger reportage of Kings, for example, or the ornate descriptions of epic. For this reason, it was initially enough for the writer to sketch out a schematic plot: two women, related by marriage, who are shocked into a joint journey to a distant land by the death of their husbands; once there, the daughter-in-law marries the kinsman of her mother-in-law and gives birth to a child, thereby showing how life is renewed after being buried.

This may seem like the pat description of a plot index or a compendium of folktale motifs according to which the story of Ruth would be classified under

221

"Kinship: Levirate." However, it is much more instructive than such a taxonomy because it shows how the storyteller must reduce events to their bare bones in order to fit them into limited space requirements. Such distillation is natural to biblical narrative because, as Alter (1981) points out, it tends to concentrate on "the crucial junctures in the lives of the heroes, from conception and birth to betrothal to deathbed" (51). In other words, the story of Ruth presents only important facts, and young people caught in a round of secular praise to "progress and development"—to much touted triviality—can gain a sense of importance from it.

However, essential events are given prominence only by their attachment to essential values: so the writer of Ruth had to flesh out his skeleton with faithfulness, faith, and the willingness to suffer for a "superior reality"—notice that I didn't say "for a transcendent ideal," because the God of Israel is immanent. In short, he had to infuse his story with love, not romantic love in the movie star sense but completely understood unsentimentality, and near sacrificial devotion. This was love which accepted pain and danger as a part of life.

The characters and the interrelationships in the Book of Ruth were created in order to bring out these values; they *are* the plot as created by a biblical equation of character and fate. Naomi, for example, may well have been born with the root for "pleasant" ($n'm$) in her name (Sasson 1979, 17–18). However, she renames herself according to the root for "bitterness" ($m'r$) (Ruth 1:20) when she arrives in Bethlehem "empty" (Ruth 1:21, *reykam*, alluding to the barrenness of fate as well as to the infertile fields of Exodus 23:15), and she only realizes the positive force of her name when Ruth gives her a grandson and thereby "restores" (and "refreshes") her "life."

Ruth, for her part, understands and embodies the interlocked necessity of bitterness and pleasantness so fully that she becomes more of a vessel of value than a living and breathing widow. Her "cleaving" to Naomi seems abstract and almost didactic—and perhaps this is why it so easily becomes a profession of faith ("Thy people shall be my people, and thy God my God"—Ruth 1:16) which is contrasted to her sister-in-law's unprincipled (though sorrowful) farewell. She is the ideal wife to Boaz and a symbol of whole-hearted giving.

In fact, the source of this whole-heartedness is a mystery. One could even call Ruth an "unplumbed depth" if it were not for the frequency of shallow American parlor portraits of her as a "Rosseauistic peasant, barefoot and poignant amid alien corn," as Popovich (1985) puts it ironically (208). After such "plumbing" by Grant Wood, Ruth does seem worn-out, pawed-over and almost too good to be true. Nevertheless, she remains the very real and serious reminiscence behind Willa Cather's depiction of a Czech farm girl in *My Ántonia* (1918):

All through the wheat season . . ., Ambrosch hired his sister out like a man, and she went from farm to farm, binding sheaves or working with the threshers. The farmers liked her and were kind to her; said they would rather have her for a hand than Ambrosch. (147)

Willa Cather probably intended this image: she saw Antonia as fulfilling a "special mission" (367) in much the same way that she took to herself Ruth's pious words as the drive behind her own exclusive devotion to the secular art of fiction (Woodress 1987, 126). This was a mission which stimulated her to produce archetypes like *Death Comes for the Archbishop* and "Paul's Case" (a secular "case" if there ever was one), "immemorial human attitudes which we recognize by instinct as universal and true," as she said in *My Ántonia* (353).

"Immemorial attitudes" make Ruth into more than just a Moabite "Splendor in the Grass" courtesy of William Inge, Prairie Romantic, and William Wordsworth, British Romantic. She is a genuine "Eternal Feminine"—what Raphael Patai (1967) calls a "Hebrew Goddess" (25)—and her book enshrines traditional patriarchal values in a woman. Of course, Ruth is a matriarch in the line of Rachel and Sara, but as a "natural woman," she was nonetheless fated to be led rather than to lead.

Boaz, on the other hand, was seen as the archetype of heroic masculine maturity by Victor Hugo in "Booz endormi" (Hartley 1950), who contrasted him with the flashy young men who worked in the fields and happened to be *bakhurim* or "marriagable bachelors" (Ruth 3:10). There was a "light" in his eyes (the "light of truth"?) rather than a flickering "flame" (70) meant to attract a good dowry.

This is no negligible nineteenth-century stereotype. Boaz's behavior to Ruth was moved by true kindness, by what in Hebrew is Godlike *khesed* and by Psalm 107:1 is everlasting "mercy": in short, by *Agape* rather than *Eros*. His blessing on the reapers "in the name of the Lord" (Ruth 2:4) echoes the Israelite belief of Psalm 129:8, for example, that any attempt to "bind sheaves" is "afflicted" without such benediction.

Moreover, he rises above the legalistic "redemption" (*geula*) of Levirate (*yibum*), according to which a near kinsman is obligated to release a widow from her straitened circumstances by marrying her and her property unless he renounces this duty by removing his shoe and handing it to the next nearest "kinsman-redeemer" (*goel*) in the ceremony of *khalitsa* (Lamm 1980, 73). Boaz, naturally, works within this tradition; it gives his actions legal and religious credibility. However, out of a deep appreciation for Ruth, he goes the extra mile by affirming the binding nature of the "part of a kinsman to thee, as the Lord liveth" (Ruth 3:14), and this affirmation means that "to redeem" (*ligol*) for him is not simply to let the air out of a stomach bloated by hunger: it means to fill that stomach with his own seed, the seed of David.

Ruth and the Morality of Interpretation

What I am doing here is precisely what I want my students to be able to do: I want them to look at the internal context of a passage as a kind of magnifying glass for its present and future significance. I want them to tap in to an "ancient hermeneutical insight" (Bruns 1987) according to which "the Bible . . . can be read as a self-glossing book" (626), one which refers back to itself. This system of cross-references gives biblical narrative what Alter (1987) calls its "powerfully allusive character" (13) and sets a goal of interpretation as demanding, stimulating, and secular as the Rabbis were exegetical, "eisegetical," and devout.

I want them to see that the story of Tamar and Judah in Genesis 38 (which serves Alter 1981, 5–12 as an object lesson in his criticism of contemporary biblical interpretation) is a thematic foreshadowing of Ruth, dealing as it does with the consequences of an aborted Levirate and providing the background of dishonesty for the realized honesty of the Book of Ruth. Boaz, in this interpretation, is a corrective to Judah. In addition, I want them to see how even a dry genealogical detail in Ruth 4:18, in which "Pharez begat Hezron," can gain significance from Genesis 38:29, in which the same—"Pharez" (Perets) got his name because he "broke forth" (*parats*) from the womb, thereby causing a "breach" into the future.

"Pharez," then, becomes a thematically expressive word and root in the sense of Martin Buber's *Leitwort* which "recurs significantly in a [biblical] text, in a continuum of [such] texts, or in a configuration of texts [by which Buber could mean a variety of devotional juxtapositions . . ." (Quoted by Alter 1981, 93). Buber as quoted again by Alter (1981), even calls such a discovered connection

> dynamic because between combinations of sounds related to one another in this manner a kind of movement takes place: if one imagines the entire text deployed before him, one can sense waves moving back and forth between the words. (93)

Of course, this degree of inspired "discovery" in Orthodox Judaism is strongest in the original Hebrew. Nevertheless, it is amply available to the English reader who can easily make the connection between Ruth's "cleaving" as expressed by "clave," an untypical strong form of the verb in Ruth 1:14, and Psalm 44:25: "For our soul is bowed down to the dust: our belly *cleaveth* unto the earth." In the act, he can flex his exegetical muscles and discovers the *Leitwortstil* (the leading-word style) of the Bible. This is no small accomplishment: there is a very real sense in which the "divine frenzy" motivating the discovery of verbal parallels in a sacred text is also a highly refined secular skill supported by a well-developed morale of exegetical craftsmanship.

I am really only repeating Cynthia Ozick's 1987 description of her grandfather's relationship to Ruth:

> If the woman had not been in the field, [he], three thousand years afterward, would not have been in the study house. She, the Moabite, is why he, when hope is embittered, murmurs The Psalms of David. The track her naked toes make through spice and sweetness, through vetch, rape, and scabious, is the very track his forefinger follows across the letter-speckled sacred page. (364–65)

Consequently, it is philologically accurate, textually learned, and substantively devoted (if not devout) to see an analogy between the comforting of Ruth by Boaz because she seeks the "shelter" of the Lord's "wings" (Ruth 2:12) and Psalm 91:4, recited on the Sabbath, which provides "His wings" as a "refuge." It would even be possible to call the whole Book of Ruth "The Search for Shelter" in place of "The Search for Betrothal," which is how Alter (1981) labels it in his typology (58).

Most important: all solidly internalized and well-grounded interpretations, whether based on a secular or a sacred search for meaning, are justified and can be used to define narrative units in the Bible. My emphasis here is on the "solidity of internalization," by which I mean the strength of support which internal logic lends a given interpretation plus the conviction of the interpreter. I do not necessarily mean the support of tradition, which is religious, institutional, external and beyond the pale for a secular person; but I do include sensitivity to tradition as a part of a solidly internalized and internally logical gloss. According to these criteria, Sasson's 1979 reliance on the folkloristic analysis of Vladimir Propp, which makes "villainy" a defining condition of folk narrative (203), is inappropriate to a biblical text like Ruth, for which evil is existential rather than diabolical and dualistic, a trial rather than a monster or gargoyle.

On the other hand, Alter's 1987 view of the Book of Ruth as a response to the mission of Abraham in Gen. 12:1 has tradition behind it: after all, the first step in Abraham's journey is an important date on the Jewish calendar (the Tora Reading *lekh-lekha*). Accordingly Alter points to the similarity of thematic key words like 'get thee" (*lekh*) to "they went" (*telekhna*, Ruth 1:7). Moreover, he is right in pointing out that

> the destiny of the Covenanted people, for Ruth as for Abraham, means putting behind one the filiations of geography and biology, replacing the old natural bonds with new contractual ones. . . . (14)

This is precisely the meaning behind Victor Hugo's imagination of Boaz's dream as "resting in Ur," Abraham's birthplace (Hartley 1950).

However, in spite of the fact that Alter's parallel emphasizes the spirituality of the Book of Ruth to counter the feeling that her story is "sunk in unmeaning materiality," it remains partial. It must be completed with some such global description as "The Search for Shelter." In addition, it is necessary to take advantage of the Book's open allegory: just as Naomi's naming and renaming creates a plot movement, so do the meanings of Ruth's name create her story.

In English, the verse from "Lycidas" comes to mind—"Look homeward angel now, and melt with *ruth*"— as having just the right measure of compassion for the biblical Ruth's story, as does the modern judgment, "He's ruthless," and such an expression as "You'll *rue* the day."[3] In Hebrew, Campbell (1975) posits "satiation and refreshment" as "semantic primes," but he does so only hesitantly (56). One could rid him of his doubts by pointing to the telling analogy of the fullness of Psalm 23:5—"My cup runneth over" (*kosi revuya/resh-vav-hey*)—to the outcome of the Book of Ruth. In its light, the mystery of Ruth's placid endurance becomes revealed as the power of plenitude.

Ruth and the Cabbalistic Spark
In other words, her name is a "spark," what the Hasidic form of the Kabbala (Tsinberg 1957) calls a *nitsots* (29), much like Buber's exegetical "wave" which sets fire to the edifice of her narrative and makes it into a unified flame. As the cosmic optimism of Adin Steinsaltz (1984) elucidates:

Even where something is primarily evil, no particle or spark of goodness is lost. The sparks, connecting, finally manifest themselves, sometimes after many generations, and in a striking way. (119)

For this reason, the Cabbalistic reading of Ruth has the needed sweep. Steinsaltz concludes:

In a larger context, the story of Ruth is an example of process, a vast ordering of forces and events which extends throughout the Bible. It is a story in which people finally find their rightful place, and in which personal, family, and historical connections finally come to fulfillment. It is not always clear how this happens; but in one way or another, many cycles are completed here. (118)

Theologically, "rightful place" and "goodness" can be subsumed under *khesed* or "grace," the signal of God's—or Boaz's?—providence in Ruth 2:20 (Campbell

1975, 106): "Blessed be he of the Lord, who hath not left off his *kindness* to the living and the dead." However, *khesed* has a secular and aesthetic connotation, that of "fittingness" and "gratitude for a completed circle." It fits the artistic and critical creation of a well-rounded narrative like the Book of Ruth.

Steinsaltz even makes a very "generous" remark about the "hospitality" of Lot's daughters who,

> despite the vileness of their deed, acted as much from the wish to preserve the human species—as it seemed to them—as from passion or lust. It is even possible to detect a veiled similarity between the act of Lot's daughters and Ruth's approach to Boaz many generations later. There was a deep commitment to the continuation of the line, to hold fast to the thread of generations, both in the delicacy of Ruth's hint and in the crudeness of Lot's daughters' act. Yet it is the good intention that persisted through time. (119)

Moab, according to the insights of Cabbalistic tradition based on Genesis (21:37), was the son of Lot and Lot's daughter, so that Ruth, in Steinsaltz's words, is "redeemed by the holy spark" of a profane father (118).

Ruth and the Secular Spark

It is a Hasidic principle enunciated by Tsinberg (1957) that these sparks are "imprisoned" in matter and that a good man's duty was to "release the sparks from their earthly prison" (29). But life is not just a muddy prison—not just loud music from a "noise box"—and divine energy can be found anywhere. For this reason, Hasidism believed in the common man, considering that the mission of holiness was to descend into matter, into the clod, in order to purify it. However, this was not mere stooping. On the contrary: as Buber (1948) describes the doctrine of Jacob Frank, who came after the Baal Shem Tov in the eighteenth century, "ignorance" (being an *am haarets* or "folk person of the land"—or "clod") meant having special converse with God (22), so much so that full contact with the "alien fire" of this "sensual man" was a precondition for divinity (29). Likewise, the Hasidic wordplay in which "I" (*ani*) is converted to "infinite" (*eyn*) (Tsinberg 1957, 27) is a parable for the conversion of self-absorption to altruism which is the main "bibliotherapeutic" task of the Book of Ruth. It was, after all, Ruth's socially-conscious *khesed*, her self-restraint in the interest of a greater good (Sasson 1979), that makes Boaz praise her (84): ". . . thou hast shewed more *kindness* in the latter end than at the beginning" (Ruth 3:10).

In other words, Ruth's story is vital for the teenager who carries a "noise box" over crowded streets because it addresses his world in sweeter and clearer tones—

it makes him "kinder and gentler." However, one can best reach such a deafened sensibility through adaptations—and, to some extent, popularizations. These mean cutting through the noise through equally loud (and sometimes lurid) human interest stories and evocations of love, lust, "filthy lucre," adventure and violence, all of which are present in or suggested by the biblical original. Adaptation means putting on a slouch hat in order to "slouch toward Bethlehem" the quickest way.

It is important that the bareness of the King James Version leaves room for such expansions and interpretations (Hammond 1987, 661), even encourages them by omitting details about such matters as how Ruth and Naomi got to Bethlehem in the first place. In *Ruth: a Novel* (1981), Lois Henderson carries them there with a caravan and introduces scenes of bravery intended to foreshadow Boaz's love more tangibly than in the Bible. In the novel, Ruth protects the caravan from thieves, which wins her the friendship of the Bethlemite caravan leader and smoothes her path in the new society (81). And in *The Song of Ruth: a Love Story from the Old Testament* (1954), Frank Slaughter even invents an entire plot of spying and political machination on the basis of caravan travel from Moab to Judea (122, 130).

Such realistic novelistic techniques are not really novelties: they have a long history of stimulating human appetite to know about basic human plights. In the very time of Jacob Frank (1726–1791), Samuel Richardson, a British printer, wrote *Pamela* (1740), a novel in the form of letters about the seductive ploys of a chambermaid, one of the first literary soap operas in English and European history. The point is clear: the seeking of secular thrills has been extremely widespread and accepted and a bonafide literary form grew out of it. Consequently, promoting the modern understanding of the Bible must involve an understanding of thrill-seeking—without condoning it, of course, and without suggesting that any sensationalistic adaptation could replace the original.

It must be understood that disco-music devotees, Yuppies and all other up-and-coming contemporary types are interested in the relationship of Ruth to the "men in her life," "significant others" like Mahlon and Boaz, and that such interest isn't just curiosity about "unmentionables." They are *not* interested in paragons, but they *are* interested in filling in the emotional information unmentioned in the Book of Ruth. For this reason, Lois Henderson shows us a Ruth under the power of her very average, pottery-making husband, Mahlon, and an attraction to Boaz which is little more than a natural "transference" and expansion of this power to include family, home, name and the preference of the God of Israel over Chemosh, god of Moab.

Frank Slaughter, similarly, shows us an average—and pretty—girl who has somehow received an above-average ritual honor in being named a priestess of Chemosh. But this high position doesn't get in the way of the "Boy Meets Girl" part of the plot—after all, Slaughter wrote his story for the movies first (5): thus,

Mahlon, feeling that it would be wrong to allow himself a gulp-producing eyeful of Ruth's gossamer garment, nevertheless "did not miss her nod of recognition or the smile of encouragement she gave him" (50).

In contrast, Ruth is slightly "turned off" by Boaz, a "strange man of turbulent passions" who simultaneously "repels and attracts her" (74), because she is too timid and conventional for his strong and unambiguous emotions. However, she is forced by a melodramatically contrived power play to take sides: when Boaz becomes the victim of a Moabite plot to conquer Judea, she becomes faithful to Boaz and Israel, thereby approximating the Ruth of the Bible.

The modernity of this outcome is that it shows how power produces morality, "might creating right" instead of the other way round. The task of the Book of Ruth is to reassert the primacy of morality in the order of affairs. It is to fight against the "dying of the light,"[4] as Arnold Rogow entitled his psychoanalytic interpretation of "the death of the superego in contemporary America" (Lascfi 1979, 304). It is to build up the tension of "inner colloquy" (Henry's term 1973), of a secular "inner monologue" sincerely reaching toward dialogue (106). It is an encouragement of Henry's 1973 realization that

the fundamental component in a value system for man in our culture must be protection of the other person [and sensitivity to "The Search for Shelter"] and that such a component is inconceivable without a willingness to suffer pain and deprivation. (118–19)

It is to assert that redemption and *khesed* follows upon hardship as the plot of life.

NOTES

1. These lines were drawn from the introductory page of a book of essays by Joan Didion entitled *Slouching towards Bethlehem* (New York: Delta, 1968).

2. The King James Version used here is *The Bible: Containing the Old and New Testaments and the Apocrypha* (Cambridge: Cambridge University Press, 1982). The Hebrew Old Testament is the *Tanakh* (Tel-Aviv: Sinai, 1966).

3. A sourcebook of English is *The Oxford English Dictionary: PoyRy* (Oxford: Clarendon Press, 1970).

4. Rogow took his title from the last line of Dylan Thomas' "Do Not Go Gentle Into That Good Night," written on the occasion of the death of his father, the poet's personal superego; there, he urges people to "rage, rage against the dying of the light," encouraging outrage at the death of a "guiding light." (Dylan Thomas, *Collected Poems: 1934–1952,* New York: New Directions, 1957, 128).

Alter, Robert (1981). *The Art of Biblical Narrative*. New York: Basic Books.

Alter, Robert (1987). In Robert Alter and Frank Kermode (Eds.), *The Literary Guide to the Bible* (11–35). Cambridge, MA: Harvard University Press.

Bruns, Gerald L. (1987). Midrash and Allegory: the Beginnings of Scriptural Interpretation. In Robert Alter and Frank Kermode (Eds.), *The Literary Guide to the Bible* (625–46). Cambridge, MA: Harvard University Press.

Buber, Martin (1948). *Hasidism*. New York: Philosophical Library.

Campbell, Edward F. (1975). *Ruth: a Commentary*. Garden City, NY: Anchor Bible VII.

Cather, Willa (1954). *My Ántonia*. Boston: Houghton Mifflin Co.

Hammond, Gerald (1987). English Translations of the Bible. In Robert Alter and Frank Kermode (Eds.), *The Literary Guide to the Bible* (648–65). Cambridge, MA: Harvard University Press.

Hartley, Anthony (Ed.) (1950). *The Penguin Book of French Verse: the 19th Century*. Baltimore: Penguin Books.

Henderson, Lois T. (1981). *Ruth: a Novel*. Chappaqua, NY: Christian Herald Books.

Henry, Jules (1973). Values: Guilt, Suffering, and Consequences. In Jules Henry, *On Sham, Vulnerability and Other Forms of Self-Destruction* (106–19) New York: Vintage Books.

Kermode, Frank (1987). The Canon. In Robert Alter and Frank Kermode (Eds.), *The Literary Guide to the Bible* (600–10). Cambridge, MA: Harvard University Press.

Lamm, Maurice (1980). *The Jewish Way in Love and Marriage*. San Francisco: Harper and Row.

Lasch, Christopher (1979). *The Culture of Narcissism: American Life in an Age of Diminishing Expectations*. New York: W. W. Norton.

Ozick, Cynthia (1987). Ruth. In David Rosenberg (Ed.), *Congregation: Contemporary Writers Read the Jewish Bible* (361–83) New York: Harcourt Brace Jovanovich.

Patai, Raphael (1967). *The Hebrew Goddess*. New York: Ktav Publishing Company.

Popovich, Ljubica D. (1985). Popular American Biblical Imagery: Sources and Manifestations. In Allene Stuart Phy (Ed.), *The Bible and Popular American Culture* (193–235). Chico, CA: Scholars Press.

Sasson, Jack M. (1979). *Ruth: a New Translation with a Philological Commentary and a Formalist-Folklorist Interpretation*. Baltimore: John Hopkins University Press.

Slaughter, Frank (1954). *The Song of Ruth: a Love Story from the Old Testament*. New York: Doubleday.

Steinsaltz, Adin (1984). *Biblical Images: Men and Women of the Book*. New York: Basic Books.

Tsinberg, Y. (Ed.) (1957). *"Fun unzer oytser: mayses fun Baal Shem Tov"* ("From our Treasury: Stories of the Master of the Good Name"). New York: Tsiko Farlag.

Woodress, James (1987). *Willa Cather: a Literary Life*. Lincoln, NE: University of Nebraska Press.

FROM PLATO TO ANN PLATO: TOWARD A SYNTHESIS OF THE CORE IN THE HUMANITIES

Jocelyn Chadwick-Joshua

University of North Texas

With such intense scrutiny from within and without, regarding balanced, multicultural core curriculums, particularly in the Humanities, institutions across the country have established self-contained ethnocentrized courses. Designed to attract students who are themselves ethnically and culturally diverse, these courses often attract primarily the cultural or ethnic group identified in the course title. Designed to address multicultural and ethnic diversity *within* the academic canon, the content of these courses often focuses on the ethnic or culture-specific writers, artists, critics, musicians, and historians identified in the course title. Designed to provide students with a broad comprehension of the world ("Goals for a Core Curriculum for the University of North Texas" Preamble, 1), these courses too often act as catalyst, causing students to cloak themselves in ethnic isolation and segregation. It is this last result of many required multicultural courses which concerns me most. As a scholar who is African American and female and a member within the national academic community ardently striving to "do the right thing," I fear that our present motivation for and process of achieving an academic core in the Humanities reflective of multicultural and ethnic diversity will produce results antithetical to those stated above. If we support the current trend in attempting to achieve diversity in the humanities core, I contend that what we will achieve will be ethnic isolation, textual separation, and intellectual alienation. No one wins.

The most effective testament supporting this thesis occurred during spring of 1991 when Professor Nina Gilden Seavey eagerly anticipated teaching an undergraduate course in African American history. Professor Seavey, an African American history scholar, documentary consultant, and presently director for the Center for History in the Media at George Washington University, is more than qualified to teach such a course. In an article entitled "Frozen Out By Race," Professor Seavey recounts the student backlash that occurred when she first met her class. She writes:

> ... I felt the students would be engaged in a level of study that would give them new insights into an important part of America's history.
>
> I was wrong. I walked into a class on the first day that was about 90 percent [B]lack. As I came through the door, many of the students looked

at me and among themselves as if someone were in the wrong room. I assured them that this was, in fact, an intro course in [B]lack history.

Sensing that some of the students were uncomfortable with the color of my skin, I set quickly to work explaining the course syllabus . . . [The students proceeded] to formulate their arguments about why a white woman should not be teaching a course in black studies. I answered that the color of my skin did not govern the quality of one's mind. They were just going to have to get over the fact that my ancestors were Caucasians. (*The Washington Post* 6 Oct. 1991, C7.)

That afternoon Professor Seavey withdrew from the course, "not wanting to become," she says, "a lightning rod for campus racial tensions" (*The Washington Post* 6 Oct. 1991, C7). I referred to Professor Seavey's experience as perfect testimony to my thesis, for she poses a question and reaches a conclusion that far transcends her topic of concern. Seavey states:

The question is: Does a people "own" its history? These students have clearly been taught that they are *entitled* to a haven away from a white man's interpretation of past evidence, that the study of black culture is synonymous with present-day politics and that they are privy to a special kind of understanding of something that happened decades or centuries ago because of the color of their skin. (emphasis my own) (*The Washington Post* 6 Oct. 1991, C7)

Prompted by Seavey's inquiry, I surmised that the "big" question and conclusion are: Does a core curriculum that embraces a multicultural approach qualify as a successful program when it provides self-contained, ethnocentrized courses juxtaposed to traditionally Euro- and androcentric counterparts? The conclusion to this question, I contend, is that many core curriculums with self-contained, ethnocentric multicultural courses create an intellectual milieu antithetical to the type generally desired. If, as E. D. Hirsch asserts, a multicultural component within a core ". . . inculcates tolerance and provides a perspective on our own traditions and values" (*Cultural Literacy: What Every American Needs to Know* 18), then providing students with courses like American history juxtaposed with African American history or world literature juxtaposed with literature of Third World and people of color cannot achieve this goal.

Although proponents of the standard approach would insist on its viability because as many goals for a core curriculum state, this kind of approach insures students' exposure to at least one ethnocentric course, closer examination of this method reveals an ironic development. Whereas a core curriculum with a multicultural emphasis *should* enable students completing such a diverse but coherent program to be able to think critically, to read and write intellectually, and to synthesize information assimilated from a variety of Eurocentric and non-

Eurocentric sources, some of these cores too often create students who are unable to appreciate the full historical, social, and creative significance of an event such as the American Revolution or the Seneca Falls Conference of 1848 because they traditionally study such events in cultural and/or ethnic isolation. Instead of producing the American scholars who themselves represent great repositories of knowledge that is assessed, reassessed, and reassessed again, the core curriculums, as they are now conceived, are producing scholars who resemble Emerson's amputated man—a good hand, a good toe, a good head, but never a whole scholar.

So just how are core curriculums to go about achieving "... greater sensitivity to the issues of America's multicultural and multiethnic communities ..." (9), as stated by my university's "Goals for a Core Curriculum"? How are core curriculums to engender in students an understanding and respect for the "... unity and diversity of cultures, both nationally and internationally" (9)? And how are core curriculums to instill in students ". . . a sense of responsibility for the global problems of poverty, violence, and ecological menace" (9)? These goals link many institutions of higher learning today, including my own.

In this portion of my paper I would like to recommend an alternative. It is not my intent to disparage core curriculums with multicultural studies. Rather, I recommend that traditional, Euro- and androcentric courses such as world literature, American history, state histories, world history, and social science, for example, include appropriate multicultural people, facts, and issues. I stress, here, traditional core courses rather than custom-designed, self-contained multicultural courses because if our goal is to introduce students to universal contributors that shaped their culture, values, and ideas then we *must* maintain the Euro- and androcentric paradigm as a basic construct, or frame. Onto and within this Western paradigm multicultural texts must then be interwoven throughout the academic core so that a complete and historical multicultural canon, replete with the diverse voices that shaped this country, is produced.

The result of such a process would, as the college strand of the 1987 English Coalition Conference surmised, "treat traditional canonical texts *not* as sacred icons to be merely revered, but as human, historical creations that are preserved as long as they serve a changing array of cultural purposes" ("Report of the College Strand" 30). Such an approach would put an end to the need for the all-inclusive, prerequisite multicultural, indoctrination course that is presently enjoying such wide acceptance on many college campuses. These kinds of courses, though experimental, addressing a human cry for equality and equity, do not satiate the real problem of exclusion and marginalization. The intensive, all-encompassing multicultural course, usually a prerequisite for incoming freshmen, in actuality, vitiates the goals of synthesis and inclusion that the core earnestly seeks. Students exit such a course filled with a dizzying array of names, images, and facts, all necessarily taken out of historical context and therefore out of long-term historical significance. Am I advocating the dismantling of the prerequisite indoctrination multicultural course for incoming freshmen? Most definitely. Aside from my personal feelings that freshmen have enough to contend with, I would also assert that institutions of higher learning are not about the business of legislating morals. We are, however, about the business of producing an intellectual atmosphere conducive to dissemination of, exploration into, and critical analysis of the vast wealth of knowledge our institutions contain. Ideally, then, the goals for which most core curriculums strive such as "the understanding of the ideas, ways of thinking, and values that shape the life of an educated individual," "a greater sensitivity to the issues of America's multicultural and multiethnic communities, an appreciation for the unity and diversity of cultures, both nationally and internationally, and a sense of responsibility for the global problems of poverty, violence, and ecological menace" ("Goals for a Core Curriculum" 8, 9) cannot be achieved by one or even three concentrated courses. Rather these goals can only be realistically accomplished when we restructure, or more appropriately, refocus the canon itself into a more synthesized representative quilt that reflects natural, uncontrived multicultural diversity.

And what about the other multicultural courses? The multicultural courses that enhance, or amplify, an undergraduate's awareness of culture and history, courses such as Black history, Asian history, and women in history. These kinds of courses reiterate marginalization and do not significantly create in students a desire to pose questions about "knowing how and knowing why" ("Report of the College Strand" 29). Am I advocating the dismantling of such courses? Yes and no. Multicultural courses that provide students an antidote such as Black or Afro or African American history in lieu of American history should be merged with traditional core courses. Such an inclusion not only provides a diverse student audience with the pertinent facts within the appropriate historical context so that they can intelligently and critically inquire how and why, but it also affords multicultural students the opportunity to see themselves *within* a culturally and ethnically diverse context.

On the other hand, multicultural courses that are specialty courses and electives courses that seek to enhance or round out a student's understanding or appreciation of a particular area, are extremely useful and usually quite provocative. Courses such as Native American folklore, Egyptology, Middle Eastern philosophy, or novels by Third World writers and women of color do indeed broaden a student's knowledge. But significant and substantive appreciation occur only when students can relate, evaluate, and synthesize this information into and against a construct that allows, even demands, that they compare, contrast, evaluate, and formulate opinions. After polling almost two hundred culturally diverse students in world literature on my own campus, for example, I found that most did not associate the nineteenth century in America with women or minorities. And when questioned more carefully, those who possessed some awareness of Elizabeth Cady Stanton, Sojourner Truth, or Nancy Gardner Prince, thought these women were anomalies and in no way were associated with their contemporaries such as Poe, Hawthorne, Irving, Emerson, and Cooper.

When I wrote this paper, I entitled it "From Plato to Ann Plato: Toward a Synthesis of the Core in Humanities." I thought of this title because in reviewing the focus and goals for this conference, I remembered the dialogue between Socrates and Glaucon in Plato's *The Republic*, specifically, their dialectic regarding the difference between and equality of men and women. When confronted with apparent inconsistencies that an opponent might raise in their argument, concerning whether women should receive an education equivalent to that of men, Socrates asserts:

> And if, I said, the male and female sex appear to differ in their fitness for any art or pursuit, we should say that such pursuit or art ought to be assigned to one or the other of them; but if the difference consists only in women bearing and men begetting children, this does not amount to a proof that a woman differs from a man in respect of the sort of education she should receive; and we shall therefore continue to maintain that our guardians and their wives ought to have the same pursuits. (*The Republic*, v. 175)

Realizing, of course, that Plato did not have in mind complete and uncompromised equality, equity, and access by a multicultural audience, I yet view his assertion as foreshadowing where we now stand in relation to the core curriculum and its current and future path, a path of synthesis and the inclusion of diversity. At the same time I also remembered another statement by another Plato written centuries later. In an essay entitled "Education" this Plato stated

> [Education] appears to be the great source from which nations have become civilized, industrious, respectable and happy. A society or people are always considered as advancing, when they are found paying proper respect to education. . . . Too much attention, then, can not be given to it by people, nation, society, or individual. *History* tells us that the first settlers of our country soon made themselves conspicuous by establishing a character for the improvement, and diffusing of knowledge among them. . . .
> We hear of their inquiry, how shall our children be educated? and upon what terms or basis shall it be placed? (31–32)

This Plato, Ann Plato, of Hartford, Connecticut, wrote and published the book of which this quotation is a part, entitled *Essays; Including Biographies and Miscellaneous Pieces in Prose and Poetry*, in 1841. Hers was the only book published by an African American woman between 1841 and 1865, and only the second book to be published by an African American woman (*Afro-American Women Writers* 26).

Ann Plato and her sentiments immediately represented to me the concretization, or metonymy, that Socrates' conclusion foreshadowed. Although ranked as a minor contributor amidst the luminaries of the nineteenth-century American scene, Ann Plato symbolizes the very synthesis that I now recommend for the core curriculum in Humanities. Influenced by Emerson, Whittier, and other Euro- and androcentric individuals as well as by Native Americans and African Americans, Ann Plato represents the synthesis between the disparates within many core curriculums—namely, cultural and racial exclusion by apparent self-contained and required inclusion, on the one hand, and complete, unabashed exclusion by admittedly "soft" and placating courses, on the other.

Those of us who are concerned with the future of the academic core curriculum, then, *should* take a closer look at universities such as Ohio State and even my own university which are striving to accomplish a more balanced representation of the diverse cultures that influenced and shaped this society from *within* the core itself rather than from without. The alternative, according to Dinesh D'Souza in his *Illiberal Education: The Politics of Race and Sex on Campus* and others who concur with his thesis, is either to have an academic core that remains fundamentally Eurocentric and patriarchal with a smattering of contributions by other cultures or to have an academic core that plays to the "minority agenda" and risk losing all of the Western classics (59–93). I shudder to think that either scenario that Professor D'Souza and others are painting will be the one that we as responsible and ethical scholars will elect.

WORKS CITED

D'Souza, Dinesh. "Travels with Rogoberta." *Illiberal Education: The Politics of Race and Sex on Campus*. New York: Free Press, 1991. 59–93.

The English Coalition Conference: Democracy Through Language. "Report of the College Strand." Ed. Richard Lloyd-Jones and Andrea Lunsford. New York: NCTE, 1989. 25–36.

"Goals for a Core Curriculum for the University of North Texas." 13 Sept. 1991: 1–9.

Hirsch, E. D. *Cultural Literacy: What Every American Needs to Know*. Boston: Houghton, 1987.

Plato. *The Republic*. Trans. B. Jowett. New York: Vintage, n.d.

Plato, Ann. "Education." *Afro-American Women Writers: 1746–1933*. Ed. Ann Allen Shockley. New York: Meridian, 1988. 31–32.

Rothenberg, Paula S. *Racism and Sexism: An Integrated Study*. New York: St. Martin's, 1988.

Seavey, Nina Gilden. "Frozen Out by Race." *The Washington Post* 6 Oct. 1991, natl. ed.: C7.

6
INTERFACES:
LIBERAL ARTS IN A PLURALIST CURRICULUM

THE LOGIC AND PEDAGOGY OF APPROACHING THE CANON

James LeRoy Smith

East Carolina University

My approach will be as follows: I will review my colleague's paper, introduce points of question and disagreement, and extend and specify those points in terms of clarifying the logic and pedagogy of approaching "the canon," that is, the *concept* of a canon.

I: My Colleague's Paper:

Professor Marshall has taken the view that making the Western tradition the bedrock of higher education primarily serves to perpetuate the barriers of gender, class, race, and ethnicity. He defends the goal of basing a core curriculum on "some balance or blend of traditions."[1]

In developing his viewpoint, he discusses possible flaws and confusions in recent separate works by Allan Bloom and Sidney Hook. In disagreeing with Bloom, Professor Marshall says it is not a corruption of the Western tradition that has caused the triumph of relativism, but more direct "cultural forces," and insofar as intellectual forces have been relevant at all, they "lie squarely within the Western tradition itself." In disagreeing with Hook, Professor Marshall states that allowing alternatives to the Western tradition does not undermine the habits of rational and objective thought *if* we use the correct methods of teaching. Non-Western works can be just as effective in conveying *human* values and concerns, if they are properly approached.

He then articulates four distinct questions and pursues the fourth ("What is the Western tradition?") by distinguishing its two excluding dimensions, namely that it excludes most of the countries of the world and that it excludes the "folk culture" of even the countries that it includes. Thus, the Western tradition is essentially Euroamerican and elitist.

Next, he focuses on Professor Hook's willingness to loosen the Euroamerican requirement when there is sufficient inherent quality in a non-Euroamerican work. Marshall states that non-traditionality should not imply automatic admissability to a reading list, but yet literary access to totally different life-worlds could be very illuminating, he thinks, for the typical traditional reader.

Professor Marshall then moves to the thesis that the "best" must be admitted from various sources. He avers that standards need not be given up and his favored mandate is to identify the "classics of each genre," much as we would do for poems, plays, novels, and so on. Thus, he begins his move toward a "balance or blend of traditions." In so moving, he is sensitive to the possible charge of "relativism." He asserts two blocks on purported Bloomian reactions. First, Bloom has not come to terms with important changes in American education, apparently good changes as Professor Marshall sees them, changes which have resulted in the pedagogical goal of teaching people to do things, as David Brock has put it.[2] Second, Bloom's alleged "adamancy about universal standards and objective truth lends itself to a closedness of mind comparable to that which relativism encourages."[3]

Professor Marshall continues to see pros and cons: Bloom does not see the importance in contributions from Freud, Marx, and quantum physics. Truth has, after all, been affected by these revolutions, and Plato just does not have the last word, avers Professor Marshall. Yet, Bloom does, Marshall says, have a strong point in characterizing ethical relativism as logically and psychologically incoherent. He takes Bloom to task for making the Western tradition appear monolithic when it is not and for putting too much weight on "intellectual, moral, and political" causes of modernity's apparent ethical relativism. He advises leaning on Aristotelian material-cause analysis to learn that today's relativism is based on "a socio-economic system which belies both the ethical imperatives of social existence and the ontological givens of the human condition."[4]

He then specifies the three major components of our present socio-economic system which contribute to such relativism, viz.: production-consumption according to profit rather than according to need; orientation of the system to consumer wants rather than to social needs; and the heedless use of technology. He identifies texts which encourage such analyses and maintains that such texts should be made part of a core curriculum in the humanities. The presumptions and omissions inherent in these three components, he argues, cry out for humanistic consideration in the curricular lives of our young. In general, this amounts to a proposal that "the record of and reflection on the human encounter with ethical and ontological absolutes" should provide the basis for a core curriculum.

A blend or balance of traditions would be a necessary requisite for such a core. Additionally, he concludes, with Sidney Hook at least on this point, teaching this core should never rely upon inducing acceptance of beliefs by non-rational means or irrational means, nor both.

II. Agreements and Disagreements:

My agreements are many. Surely Professor Marshall's overall position is formulated after considerable time studying diverse source materials, which, he consistently argues, must be made part of any core which is viable. Surely he is right in criticizing any ethical relativism we might find around us. That relativism *is* logically as well as psychologically incoherent. Surely, too, any core of study which has *a priori* exclusionary principles of formation is thereby rendered non-viable, or worse, if we care about democratic institutions and wish to encourage them.

I take our caring about such institutions as a given. My disagreements could be articulated as worries about possible implications of some of his statements and their disposition for bringing about the strengthening of those very institutions. I will list these statements here and proceed in my last part to extend his paper as much as to disagree with it.

Here are those of his statements which I find worrisome, not so much for what they say, as for what they might *allow*:

(1) We must have a "blend or balance. ...." While Professor Marshall makes this suggestion having studied many texts himself, this is not always the case with curriculum makers. His striking emphases on the "ethical imperatives of social existence and ontological givens of the human condition," set wonderfully in the context of his criticism of the components of modernity that have influenced a cultural drift toward relativism, and his assertion that any viable core must include such study, are sure evidence of his credentials. However, to make a satisfactory blend requires sure knowledge of the ingredients. We recall that Bloom's primary indictment is directed toward a system of higher education in which a great many faculty are under-prepared and lack sufficient background in rigorous comparative study. While this is always a problem, sometimes it can be a disaster. Therefore, we must be very careful on this count in the core curriculum kitchen.

(2) *Bloom favors absolutes.* In my study of his text, I find that Allan Bloom is arguing not that Plato is always right, but that we have to study Hesiod to know that Homer is best. His logic is not at all to assert that Plato is unassailable, but that few scholars are actually addressing the force of the Straussian analyses. To think that what the dramatic Socrates said is Plato's view is terrible scholarship, as a study of Bloom's interpretive essay on the *Republic* shows. This is debatable, to be sure, but that debate should be recognized in the core/canon debate, or else we are sent back to my first worry, asserted in (1), above.

(3) *Bloom neglects the accomplishments of Freud, Marx, and the effects of quantum physics research.* This, too, is debatable. The analysis of these accomplishments is a complicated matter. It can be argued, I believe, that problems with historicism, positivism, epistemological incoherence and ethical relativism render non-viable any such asserted accomplishments. That, I believe, is Bloom's view. In any case, we cannot just presume that such accomplishments are themselves unassailable, and Professor Marshall does not establish any case here. Nor can we assume that they are totally wrong, and perhaps that is Professor Marshall's point. In any case, we have, again, a worry referring to (1), above: the

credentials of core-builders.

(4) *We must avoid non-rational and irrational modes of teaching.* Surely this is true, but the point is that there are no value-neutral notions of reasonableness. Thus, we cannot use this criterion as an independent fulcrum from which to approach major questions about a core. That is, just what reasonableness itself consists in is a philosophical, tradition-embedded question that should be visible in any literary, historical, or philosophic core.

With these worries in mind, let us address questions about the logic and pedagogy of approaching the concept of canon.

III. The Logic and Pedagogy of Approaching "The Canon":

I mean for us to focus on the idea of a canon, not, at least not yet, some list of books. I do so, not only with the four concerns above in mind, but also under the guidance of five separate points of notable interest.

First, Allan Bloom and William Bennett, among others, agree on and foster the principle that one has to study Hesiod to know that Homer is best. Generalized, this means one has to study several texts comparatively to generate the *idea of* best in an even barely adequate manner.

Secondly, we should note that those who rail against the Western tradition show the same epistemic, perhaps even ethical, limitations they attribute to their alleged enemies: exclusiveness, parochialism, and, sometimes, even elements of fanaticism, where the latter term might best be defined as hostility toward the young's thinking for themselves with all of the best materials at hand.

Thirdly, as Alexis de Toqueville would have us put it, there exists a dangerous paradox in the history of reasonableness in democratic institutions: while these institutions foster *freedom of action and judgment*, paradoxically they at the same time seem to greatly allow for or even strangely encourage the erosion, even disappearance, of any tradition of, or even the concept of, *reasonable authority*. In that transition, concepts such as community, common good, even shared values, are displaced by individual preference, lifestyles as ultimate goals, and, ultimately, I think, politically debilitating factionalism. As anyone familiar with the Western tradition knows, it itself is an intellectual combat zone of disagreement and hard-won tradition wherein the individual enskilled and empowered with rights *and* duties emerges on the scene as a social goal in the Enlightenment. Today's factionalism seems dangerously empty by comparison, and a sense of the common good seems absent in the cries of the "new" intellectuals espousing "pluralism" and "cultural diversity."[5]

Fourthly, our sense of the implied logic of the concepts we use should convince us that "canon" (as a concept) has to be an open concept, in the Wittgensteinian sense. That is, while we cannot give a list of necessary and sufficient conditions that must be met by a work before it is admissible, we are not without some useful practices regarding admission to lists that might count as canonical. If this is what motivates Professor Marshall's desire for a "blend," then I understand his motive. But, I still counsel caution about the credentials of the blenders.

Lastly, I observe that it is we, we who have been nurtured on some good version of the Western tradition, who are engendering this debate. Where is the opposition at this conference? Without us, it appears to me, there would be no debate. That, in good Wittgensteinian manners, should tell us something.

With these five points in mind, I suggest the following argument for approaching the concept of a canon:

(1) A necessary condition for bringing about a genuinely free community, global or otherwise, imbued with and operated within democratic institutions, is the individual autonomy (with enabled, participative respect for others) of all persons.

(2) A necessary condition for bringing about the individual autonomy (with enabled, participative respect for others) of all persons is the comparative study of methods of inquiry for the sake of reflective equilibrium, a self-dialectic by all, focused on age-old tradition and contemporary convention.

(3) A necessary condition for bringing about such a self-dialectic by all is the establishing of, the implementing of, and the continued cultivation of an open (in the Wittgensteinian sense) canon and a core as a list of readings discussed in chronological and comprehensive concert.

(4) The given is that we want genuinely free global community.

(5) Therefore, we must establish a canon and a core commensurate with the textures and directions of a Wittgensteinian open concept.

I believe this is a challenging logic. I welcome counter-claims.

As for the pedagogy of approaching the concept of a canon, I return to my four concerns, articulated above. If we are not careful to steer around such pitfalls, the above logic, even if sound, will be of no practical avail.

In short, unless curriculum makers accept both the above logic *and* steer clear of those pitfalls, "balances and blends" will be inadequate, attacks on "absolutes" will be misinformed; thinkers such as Marx and Freud and the implications of quantum physics will be sources of presumption and fanaticism, not avenues for thorough, comparative reflection; and, indeed, what is thought to be reasonable will be merely factional (the strained pun intended!).

It's no surprise: logic must drive pedagogy.

1. See Ernest Marshall, "The Western Tradition: Fountainhead of Prejudice or Perennial Wisdom?" The Core and the Canon: A National Debate. Denton: University of North Texas Press, 1993, Chapter 1, essay #2, 10.

2. Cf. Marshall

3. Cf. Marshall

4. Cf. Marshall

5. See Thomas Short's provocative "Diversity" and "Breaking the Disciplines: Two New Assaults on the Curriculum," a paper I found too late to properly treat in my remarks above, and in *Academic Questions*, Volume 1, 1989, published by The National Association of Scholars, Twenty Nassau Street, Suite 244, Princeton, New Jersey 08542, 609/683-7878. Professor Short is Associate Professor of Philosophy at Kenyon College, Gambier, Ohio 43022.

THE CALCULUS-COMPOSITION COLLABORATION

Jeff Zorn

Santa Clara University

By now most of us are familiar with typical patterns of collaborative and interdisciplinary teaching in the liberal arts. The historian lecturing on the Peloponnesian War, for instance, will make reference to Euripides' *Trojan Women* and Aristophanes' *Lysistrata*, or perhaps invite a colleague from the English or Classics Department to fill out the historical portrait. Or perhaps the medieval historian and the medieval literature teacher will offer a joint, team-taught class; or the religious studies teacher and the historian; or even the art teacher, the religious historian, and the literature teacher. None of this surprises.

All of these seem more natural matches than any collaborative work involving a humanist and a mathematician. Even though mathematics and English are the staples of the secondary school and undergraduate curricula, they rarely are presented as related to each other. Key curriculum reports like Harvard's *General Education in a Free Society* and "A Nation at Risk" have said nothing about fruitful collaboration between math and English. Even "writing across the curriculum" literature says little about excursions to the domain of numbers, quantity in the abstract.

For six years, at Santa Clara University, Professor of Mathematics Dave Logothetti and I have offered CCC, the Calculus-Composition Collaboration, to freshmen. We had been an interview team for Phi Beta Kappa on our campus and had concluded that what distinguished most Phi Beta Kappans intellectually was the ability to integrate learning from disparate disciplines. We would see if we could accelerate this process in business, engineering, and science majors taking calculus in their first quarter at college.

The logistics of this collaboration are simple. Dave and I explain our aims in the Course Bulletin and arrange for a common enrollment in his Calculus I section of 44 students and my two Composition and Rhetoric I sections of 22 each. We sit as students in each other's classes, with unlimited interruption rights to make connections between the English work and the math work. He does the reading and writes the papers I assign; I do problem-sets and take his tests. We confer regularly about assignments, teaching strategies, and the progress of individual students.

One aim of CCC has been to articulate for entering freshmen the defining qualities of a successful academic performance, and the successful academic performer. These characteristics fully transcend disciplinary boundaries. Essay writing and math problem-solving both require students to be aware of options for proceeding at every point, sensitive to signals that a line of thought is or is not working, and very careful with details. The excellent composer and expert problem-solver make the most of information and technique available; neither is "thrown" by blockages; both are creative, almost playful, in devising plans and then knowing and purposeful in executing these plans.

To use calculus effectively, students must gain full command of its central concepts. "Limits," "derivatives," "integrals,"—all have application in the further mathematical work students will do. Anticipating these applications, Dave appreciated the value of expository composition in preparing beginners to see the familiar in novel contexts. Writing about difficult concepts *makes* them familiar.

On Dave's midterms and finals (in all his classes now), he sets an essay question. Students know throughout the class that they will be expected to write on topics like this:

Suppose I know L'Hopital's Rule and the basic trigonemetric identities. Write me a clear, detailed essay that culminates in the derivation of the derivative of "y = sin x."

Modeled by Dave's demonstrations, preparation for essay testing induces a less mechanical, more intellectually involved approach to calculus than most students ever have taken in a math class. Students learn to extend the conceptual approach. Jeanne Chua, now a graduate student in economics, recently wrote: "I still find it easier to interpret equations in the English language way. . . . It really helps to explain to myself all the x's, y's, and f(x)'s in words in order to understand the equation better." Jeanne's words underscore the value of a conceptual rather than purely technical approach to math. The more mathematics is presented as technique divorced from concept, aesthetics, and life-as-actually-lived, the more it is isolated from all else students are learning and feeling. The more, too, all concerned are blinded to underlying causes of failure to learn. As I have both observed and experienced in my role of math student, technique with numbers rarely causes difficulty. Reading comprehension is more often the problem, understanding the situation clearly enough to apply elements of mathematical know-how already mastered.

The National Assessment of Educational Progress recently described the results of its 1986 mathematics study as "dismal." One third of the nation's eleventh graders reported that they "usually" do not understand what their math teachers are talking about. Only six percent could solve problems requiring several steps or algebra; the figure was less than one percent among blacks and slightly more than one percent among Hispanics. Chester Finn, Assistant Secretary of Education, called these percentages "appallingly low."

CCC has convinced me that the "English language" approach holds great promise for remediating results like these. Consider an example of the kind of problem that most fully baffles students: "Show that the difference of the squares of any two consecutive odd integers equals four times the integer that stands between them." The truth is, the numbers part of solving this problem is easy, far easier than translating the given information into a form to which numerical technique can be applied. Solving this problem requires understanding of the following concepts: "integer," "squaring," "consecutive," and "oddness/evenness." Many more than six percent of American eleventh graders can understand and work with these concepts. Students also must appreciate what a mathematical "showing" consists of, here a demonstration that an equation holds true regardless of specific numbers chosen to exemplify the quantitative relationships.

The conceptual approach would have students test the equation with what Dave calls a suitably general specific case, say the consecutive odd integers 3 and 5. Does 5-squared minus 3-squared equal 4 times 4? Is 25 minus 9 sixteen? Sure enough. Try another suitably general specific case. Is 9-squared (81) minus 7-squared (49) equal to 4 times 8, or 32? Sure enough. So how to express the general case? Here the mathematical notation for the concept of evenness helps, for even numbers by definition are divisible by 2. The three-number sequence we are asked to imagine, then, is $(2n-1)$, $2n$, and $(2n+1)$, and the equation $(2n+1)^2-(2n-1)^2=4(2n)$. Only here need we apply numerical technique, to multiply $(2n+1)$ by itself, subtract $(2n-1)$ multiplied by itself, to see if the remainder is equal to $8n$, as indeed it is.

This problem is particularly useful in illustrating the tendency of mathematical study to push toward what Robert Maynard Hutchins called "the universal and necessary processes of human thought, not affected by differences in taste, disposition, or prejudice" (*The Higher Learning in America* 84). Working with shape and number *per se* and with heuristics like the suitably general case places in clear perspective the methodologies of every other academic discipline. Here one grasps what Plato suggested in the *Republic* about teaching mathematics "in the spirit of a philosopher and not of a shopkeeper."

For obvious reasons, English teaching cannot be strictly "mathematical," but the benefits to the composition teacher of collaborating with a calculus teacher are many. First is the motivational advantage of exposing business, science, and engineering students to a math teacher who loves to write, and can tutor writing with flair and expertise. Beyond this, one can tap into knowledge and technique required of calculus students and apply it to their written expression. I can teach calculus students about stereotyping, special pleading, and overgeneralizing precisely *for* their knowledge of the suitably general special case. I can improve their grasp of grouping and balancing items in a sentence with reference to the law of distribution, $a(b+c) = ab+ac$. Other such specifics abound.

Calculus students can easily be taught not to overwrite. Freshmen often believe that inflated, heavily nominalized diction sounds impressively collegiate, and so they write horrors like: "The single aspect of the quarter system that gives students the greatest trouble is the quality of speeded-upness that is imparted." Sentences like these can be exposed for what they are in the resemblance to mathematical expressions like this: "$\sin^8 x + 4 \sin^6 x \cos^2 x + 6 \sin^4 x \cos^4 x + 4 \sin^2 x \cos^6 x + \cos^8 x$." This is the expansion of the expression $(\sin^2 x + \cos^2 x)^4$ but since $(\sin^2 x + \cos^2 x)^4$ equals 1, the expression is equivalent to 1^4 or, simply, 1. Students readily see how much more economical and useful "1" is than the trigonometric expansion, and I have actually been able to convince many of them that "Quarters fly by" is very much like that "1."

The most generally valuable technique English teaching can borrow from mathematics is the problem-set. Calculus problem-sets aim to show students exactly what they still need to master, the breaking points of their skill in problem solving. The problems enable students to use further instruction intelligently. A gap the size of Yosemite Valley stretches between these problem-sets and the scattershot drills and exercises students are subjected to in English classes: introductory paragraphs yesterday, metaphor today, *who* vs. *whom* tomorrow.

Without concrete developmental application, the writing instructor's abstract lessons remain mysteries to all but the most able students. We can *tell* our students everything they need to do to improve their written and oral composition in an hour or two. "Omit needless words," we say, following Strunk and White. But how are they to determine which words are needless? English teachers must help them discover that, more purposefully than we presently do. Useful problem-sets for focus, transition, and diction would, in my opinion, contribute more to student learning than any "applied" linguistic or psychological research and any post-structuralist theorizing with which I am familiar. English teaching overall has been disserved, I think, by status-anxious leaders of the profession who have bought into notions of "support" for the classroom teacher wholly inappropriate to the work the teacher is asked to do.

Finally, last year Dave and I collaborated on a new course combining his Mathematical Logic class and my Argumentation and Research Writing class. This was a more natural match than calculus and English 1, with its blend of formal and informal logic, its concern for evidence, and its demands for proper organization of information. More rigorous evaluation of our collaborations now awaits us, as well as further development of the materials we have written for our classes. Our experiences thus far encourage us to push ahead with these efforts.

WORKS CITED

Robert Maynard Hutchins, *The Higher Learning in America*, New Haven: Yale University Press, 1936.

LINKING FRESHMAN ENGLISH TO WESTERN CIVILIZATION

Gene Mueller
Henderson State University

Garry Ross
Northwestern State University

Of the speaker Aristotle wrote

> His head must be filled with knowledge, and the knowledge must be well-ordered so that he may know *where* to look for a particular kind of argument. (*Rhetoric*. trans. Cooper 155)

and of argument he wrote

> Now, first of all, let this be understood: Whatever the subject on which we have to speak or reason—whether the argument concerns public affairs or anything else—we must have some knowledge . . . of the facts. Without it, you would have no materials from which to construct an argument.

He goes on to say

> How, let me ask, could we advise the Athenians whether they should go to war or not, if we did not know their forces, whether these were military or naval or both, the size of these forces, what were the public revenues, and who were the friends and foes of the state, what wars it had waged, and with what success—and so on? (156)

Aristotle's comment about the speaker is not a passive voice sentence. Rather he is using a stative verb. The speaker, in order to be successful, must be knowledgeable. He/she must be in a state of knowing. His/her knowledge guides him/her in two ways: It provides him/her with content for a message, and it provides him/her with a sense of direction in which to go to find the commonplaces or topics for the most effective arguments.

Aristotle is not saying that the speaker needs to be taught; he is saying that one wanting to be a speaker must come to the task with knowledge already in place.

He or she must already "be filled with knowledge," and the task at hand becomes one of preparing for the occasion not one of preparing a knowledge base.

Of course, the speaker does not spring forth, filled with knowledge, waiting for the occasion. Rather, Aristotle is writing for knowledgeable speakers. For him, it would be absurd to assume that anyone would try to speak without knowledge. One could imagine his amazement had anyone suggested to him that a speaker could present well without knowledge.

However, "in this contemporary world of ours today"—to quote an often used phrase in freshman compositions—we are asked to teach writing as if the learner of it needed no content knowledge from which to draw substance as well as arguments. In the defense of creativity, we are encouraged to let the student use his or her own language to relate (and I use the word as the student would) the miseries of losing a first love—usually to a best friend—or to describe, with as many abstractions as possible, the apparently meaningless design of "my bedroom wallpaper." Best friends are lost "in the most painful experience of my life." (Saying it is quite enough. There's no need to ask the reader to experience the pain.) And apparently meaningless designs suddenly become "something real interesting that I've never thought about before. I guess I just never really looked at it just real close."

And, of course, the teacher who understands the logical relationships that punctuation shows or suggests that proofreading skills are important is considered a pedant or, at the very least, one overly concerned with usage and grammar rather than with content. There, then, is the rub, the quarrel over content. One is apt to quote a George Henry Lewes review of a nineteenth-century novel, "The author has nothing to say and says it" and then parody Lewis Carroll, "But he says it so well."

But, alas, the content issue becomes a two-edged sword for the freshman because he or she is asked to do two things that really are pretty hard to do for even the most experienced writer. The freshman is asked to draw content from personal experience; and since his or her experience is often either too shallow to yield valuable content or too personal for the writer to want to make it a source of content, the writing process can never get off the ground. And with the absence of meaningful content comes the absence of meaningful invention. After all, one of the major contributions of content to argument is its source as a guide to the commonplaces or topics where good arguments can be found.

Indeed, for Aristotle, the major purpose of invention was to discover how to present content, not to discover content as so many contemporary theorists suggest to be its purpose. This confusion about invention has led to one of the major problems in the teaching of composition. The student—the often underprepared, under-read, unreflective student—is asked to be the source of content for what he or she chooses to write. I am not arguing that the average freshman is not bright. I'm arguing that the average freshman does not yet know enough to make himself or herself the source for meaningful content in papers.

Linked Courses: Rationale

One of the reasons that freshman composition is not as effective as it should be is that the process school's emphasis on invention has shifted from what was emphasized in the classical tradition. For Aristotle, rhetoric was the available means of persuasion. It was not the discovery of subject matter from which to construct discourse. For him, invention was the discovery of persuasive technique, not so much the discovery of what to say as the discovery of how to say it. He accepted that a discourse was the product of a mind that was familiar with subject matter, a mind that needed help in the discovery of technique not in the discovery of knowledge.

Current rhetoricians and compositionists view invention as primarily the discovery of what to say and secondarily as the discovery of how to say it. The readers that are used in freshman composition are usually a collection of personal experience essays from which the student is to draw parallels in his/her own life and imitate the essay. The focus of the course becomes neither a focus on rhetorical and compositional technique, nor a focus on the acquisition of subject matter knowledge from which to write. Students are asked to write on topics that are either too personal for them to develop any objective distance or are trivial to the student who does not recognize that his/her personal experiences are significant enough to warrant serious consideration in an essay. Invention becomes the pursuit of an illusion for many students because they do not have a clear subject matter base from which to work.

The linking of courses seems to be a workable alternative to both traditional freshman English courses and writing across the curriculum. Traditional courses have the drawbacks outlined above and writing-across-the-curriculum courses have the disadvantage of not having a trained compositionist respond to the writing that is done. By linking introductory history courses (I mention history only as an example) to an introductory writing course, the instruction in writing becomes an instruction in the use of language and technique in which subject matter knowledge is developed in the linked course. The writing instructor no longer has the two-fold purpose of developing a knowledge base in the students as well as developing in them a knowledge of technique. The history instructor no longer has the two-fold chore of teaching history and how to write history. Both courses would benefit from the expertise of two instructors instead of the partial expertise of one.

Implementation

The course will actually be two courses that retain their separate identity for transcripts and transfer of credit. The courses are, Freshman English and Western

Civilization Since 1660. A common set of readings will "link" the courses together.

Each course is a three-credit semester course. Students will register for the linked courses by corresponding section number. Given the nature of the course, with its emphasis on writing, enrollment will be limited. Although the student will earn six credits, students will meet five times weekly (rather than six) to minimize schedule conflict and to allow for special assignments.

The five sessions shall consist of two history lecture sessions, two writing sessions, and one discussion session. History lectures will present Western Civilization in chronological order, with particular focus on those events from which readings have been assigned, e.g., "The Industrial Revolution." Lectures will explain how events selected for deeper coverage are related to the general history being studied.

The writing sessions will focus on the writing process and assist students in "laying out" their writing assignments. We will emphasize the need to engage in re-writing and will evaluate both content of the paper and how well the paper conforms to the conventions of Standard Written English. Students will be asked to use the University's Writing Center so that they can take advantage of the computer word processing package (*Norton Textra-Writer*) and the guidance that the Center's graduate assistants can offer them. The discussion session will involve both English and history faculty. Discussions will focus on the readings as well as how to relate the readings to the written assignment, e.g., "The Industrial Revolution: An Analysis."

There will be two methods of student evaluation: (1) the written assignments, and (2) exams: a mid-term exam and a final exam. The exams will test the students' knowledge of history, as presented in the history course. Twelve written assignments will be given, with a minimum of five hundred words per assignment (a total of six thousand words). All twelve assignments will apply toward the English final grade; ten of the assignments will apply toward the history final grade, along with the two exams previously mentioned.

Wherever possible, students will be asked to read from primary sources. The readings have been selected for their accepted historical importance as well as their pedagogical relationship to the writing task. For example, the readings on World War II provide a unique picture of warfare from the point of view of combatants and those who suffered directly from bombing. The student, consequently, should have ample material from which to write a narrative essay on World War II.

The following section outlines the focus of the course.

READING AND WRITING ASSIGNMENTS FOR LINKED COURSES

I) ABSOLUTISM—Narrative
A) Excerpts from *Pepys Diary*
B) From *Century of Louis XIV*:
    "Louis Reflections on Kingship"
    "Saint-Simon's Description of Louis XIV and His Court"
    "Moreri's Description of France"
    "Louis XIV, Head of State"
    "Planning for the Immortality of Louis XIV"

II) ENLIGHTENMENT AND ITS FOUNDATIONS—Definition
A) Excerpts from the following:
    Montesquieu, *The Spirit of Laws*
    Hume, *An Inquiry Concerning the Principles of Morals*
    Locke, *An Essay Concerning Human Understanding*
    Diderot, *The Encyclopedie*

III) AMERICAN AND FRENCH REVOLUTIONS—Precis
A) Excerpts from the following:
    Paine, *Common Sense*
    Sieyes, *What Is the Third Estate?*
B) *Declaration of Independence*
C) *Bill of Rights*
D) *Declaration of Rights of Man and of Citizen 1789*
E) Wordsworth, *France in 1790*

IV) INDUSTRIAL REVOLUTION—Analysis
A) Excerpts from the following:
    Engels, *The Condition of the Working Class in England*
    Marx, *Labour and Capital*
    Parliamentary Hearings of Factory Conditions
    Statistical Tables

V) NATIONALISM—Descriptive
A) Excerpts from the following:
    Bismarck, *Reflections and Reminiscences* Vol. I
    The Memoirs Vol. II
    Memoirs of Prince Hohenlohe Vol. I
    Autobiography of Giuseppi Garibaldi
    Baffier, *Jottings from a Worker's Notebook*

VI) IMPERIALISM—Persuasive
A) Excerpts from the following:
    Bridges, et al. (eds.), *Nations and Empires*
    Pelissier, *The Awakening of China*
B) Kipling, "White Man's Burden"
    "The Enlightenments of Pagett MP"
C) Beveridge's Speech of April 27, 1898

VII) WORLD WAR I—Cause and Effect
A) Excerpts from the following:
    Versailles Peace Treaty
    Austrian Red Book
    Montgelas, *The Case for the Central Powers*
    British Documents on the Origins of the War 1898–1914
    Kautsky (ed.), *Outbreak of the World War: German Documents*
    Geiss, *July 1914*

VIII) COMMUNISM—Compare and Contrast
A) Excerpts from the following:
    Lenin, *State and Revolution*
    Walsh (ed.), *Readings in Russian History*
    Trotsky, *The History of the Russian Revolution*
    The New Course
    Rigby (ed.), *Stalin*

IX) FASCISM—Definition
A) Excerpts from the following:
    Mussolini, *Autobiography*
    Mosse, *Nazi Culture*
    Speer, *Inside the Third Reich*
    Sturzo, *Italy and Fascism*

X) DEMOCRACY AT RISK—Analytical
A) Excerpts from the following:
    Macmillan, *Winds of Change 1914–1939*
    Werth, *Twilight of France* (1966 ed.)

XI) WORLD WAR II—Narrative (combat)
A) Excerpts from the following:
Newmann, *The Black March*
Keegan, *Face of Battle*
Hershey, *Hiroshima*

XII) THE COLD WAR—Argumentative
A) Excerpts from the following:
Truman, *Memoirs*
Kennan, "Containment" (*American Foreign Affairs*, 1951)
Khruschev Remembers
Fleming, *The Cold War and Its Origins*

A PROBLEM IN RHETORIC:
TEACHING WRITING WITH WESTERN CULTURE

Steven Marx

Cal Poly University, San Luis Obispo

But rather than the large theoretical questions of canon revision that grabbed national headlines last year, I want to talk about a more mundane and limited question that I tried to deal with while teaching at Stanford between 1984 and June 1988. That question addresses one of the practical concerns of this conference on core curriculum: how does one effectively combine a course in English Composition with a course in Western Culture?

It was first presented to me in Spring 1984, when I was hired by the English Department to coordinate and teach in its newly designed "track" of the University's required Western Culture survey. After two years of brainstorming and politicking, the Department had received approval to mount a pilot project that would couple an interdisciplinary lecture-discussion course called "Literature and the Arts in Western Culture" with its own freshman writing requirement. Senior professors would deliver three lectures per week to a large group of all the students registered in the track; small groups would subsequently meet in sections to discuss the readings and lectures with non-tenured Ph.D. section leaders, who would also conduct twice-weekly composition classes that used the works treated in Western Culture as the basis for writing assignments. This arrangement would appeal to incoming students as a good deal which got two requirements out of the way in a single eight-unit course, and it would benefit the English Department—by raising its visibility and its FTE, by attracting new majors, and by providing the benefits of large lectures linked with small, writing-intensive classes. The problem delegated to me was to work out a curriculum that would adapt the topics of English Comp to the readings and lectures—a curriculum for a course called Writing With Western Culture.

Since then, the program has received high student evaluations, has quadrupled in size, and, with numerous beneficial modifications, has survived the canon reforms introduced last year. After eight years, the original writing curriculum is still intact. So I think it's appropriate to describe it here in some detail to those dealing with similar problems.

Let me begin with a brief discussion of the theory behind "Writing with Western Culture" and its connection to the classic tradition of rhetorical education. The central idea of the program is combining. First of all, combining the three aspects of the familiar rhetorical trinity: Reading, Writing, and Thinking. A fine statement of the principle is found on the opening page of *Writing Worth Reading*, a composition textbook by my former Writing Director at Stanford, Nancy Packer:

> Writing is part of the continuum of thinking-reading-writing. The quality of all writing . . . will depend on the quality of the thinking on which it is based. To write effectively, students must first learn to think clearly and critically about significant matters. A giant step toward critical thinking is critical reading. When students engage, even challenge a text, their thinking and their writing will improve. The best writing will come from a scrupulous attention to what one reads and what one thinks. As thinking and reading affect writing, so, too, good writing gives rise to better thinking and reading. (vi)

This principle of Integration was already old when formulated by Renaissance Humanist educators like Erasmus and Roger Ascham as *sapientia et eloquentia*—the pursuit of wisdom *and* eloquence through the study and imitation of the classics. How better to teach the writing skill of paraphrase than to have students produce a precis of Plato's *Allegory of the Cave*? How better to learn the reading skills necessary to follow what Plato says about education than to write a summary of it? A consequence of this approach: the student's effort in one course is directly reinforced in the other. How better to teach patterns of coordination and subordination than have students outline passages of Aristotle's *Poetics*? And how better to comprehend and remember that work's seminal ideas than outlining the text—practically an outline in itself?

Now in their dryness, such assignments may sound like relics of the scholastic *trivium*, but in this respect they are atypical. For in addition to integrating reading, writing, and thinking, most of our work in Writing With Western Culture involves combining two other elements: the students' contemporary personal experience and their imitation of major texts—thereby facilitating a process of Interaction. In practicing the skills of description and narration, for example, students draw upon their own immediate perceptions, but model their accounts upon a passage from an epic. One student, Enrique, writes "The Enreid," a story of his passage through the pandemonium of freshman registration that imitates Vergil's account of the shades jostling their way across the river Styx. Jody—now majoring in Art History—paints a verbal picture of a Greek vase in the Stanford Museum, following Homer's depiction of the shield of Achilles. When we come to the personal essay, students imitate Augustine's Confessions—beginning with a voyage down the corridors of memory, reconstructing the two voices of a past moral conflict, and concluding with a reflection on the understanding of self

257

gained through the passage of time. Thus, the students' engagement with the text, driven by the pressure of writing, infuses the flux of their perceptions with meaning, of their feelings with form.

The two processes of combining—Integration and Interaction—are themselves naturally combined. In their own writing, students experience inspiration, frustration and triumph analogous to those experienced by their classical mentors. They discover that the tradition itself is emergent rather than remote, and that they belong to it. When, several weeks after he writes about Stanford undergraduates crossing the Styx, Enrique encounters fourteenth-century Florentines mobbing the same shores in *The Inferno*, he has a flash of identification with Vergil's pupil and a nice appreciation of Dante's craft in imitating *his* master. Now Enrique begins to understand the process of cultural transmission because he has taken part in it himself. And he grasps that the classics imitate one another not only because the great seek illustrious company, but also because their creators—Vergil, Dante, Shakespeare, Milton, Blake—were schooled by the same two methods of combining: Integration and Interaction. For the poets learned the rudiments of their art in courses not about poetry but about rhetoric—alongside their contemporaries who would become priests, politicians or merchants.

One might even say, as Wesley Trimpi and Joel Altman recently have, that the discipline of rhetoric, the art of effective communication, stood at the heart of the traditional educational curriculum, enlivening and drawing upon all the other arts. And one could, with Aristotle, assert that rhetoric teaches the *practical application* of all the other humanities: logic and philosophy; psychology and politics; ethics and jurisprudence; literature, art and music. These are the assumptions embodied in the syllabus of Writing with Western Culture.

In the course syllabus, each week's Western Culture readings and lectures are listed to the left; the corresponding Composition topics and assignments to their right. First quarter moves from invention to arrangement (or organization) then to revision and argument; second quarter builds on those foundations to develop analogous skills of critical research, style (including grammar, punctuation, diction and voice), and persuasion.

We begin at the beginning, with invention—practicing brainstorming, freewriting, meditation, conversation and questioning techniques, placing strongest emphasis on comparison/contrast as an approach to thinking, reading, and writing. After discussing the relation of creation myths to imaginative creation, students write an in-class essay comparing and contrasting Greek and Hebrew cosmogony stories.

The second ungraded writing assignment is a longer essay written at home, further developing comparison/contrast as a mode of invention and discovery. Students contrast the Greek and Hebraic deities and heroes, and then compare the similarities between heroes and deities in Genesis and *The Iliad*.

By the third week, the emphasis shifts from invention to arrangement, the classes focused on limiting a topic and arriving at a thesis. I clarify the nature of a thesis by defining it as a strong sentence and by defining a sentence as an utterance that can be contradicted. The topic of the paper is a dogmatic assertion of the moral of the ending of one of the two plays just read: *Oedipus* and *Lysistrata*.

Week four focuses on the paragraph and on the purely organizational principles of unity, coherence, and adequate development. The concepts of coordination and subordination are examined in relation to topic sentence and supporting material, in relation to clauses within the sentence, and in relation to Platonic forms and their governance of particulars. The writing assignment is the precis of Plato, which must be presented in clearly structured paragraphs, and the outline of Aristotle's *Poetics*.

Arrangement remains the topic of week five; it's developed in connection with the way parts relate to a whole. Vergil's *Aeneid*, the week's Western Culture reading, provides examples of powerful beginnings, endings, transitions, climactic sequences and ingenious interplay between parts and whole. Students write about how specific passages they select exemplify comprehensive themes and motifs discussed in the literature lecture. Selections from papers of previous year's students demonstrate successful use of introductions, conclusions, transitions, and natural points of emphasis.

Assignment 6 follows upon a presentation of techniques of description and narration—sense awareness, dominant impression, suspense and climax—through in-class writing tasks. It opens with a statement of the doctrine of imitation I mentioned earlier, and then it offers students a wide range of choices on how to apply it. Here is a sample from Enrique's "Enreid":

> The Pavillion was mountainous, huge and impressive. With dark granite columns that spired towards heaven, it commanded awe and fear in the hearts of mortal freshmen. Defended by a large fence and dense shrubbery, it was as much fortress as temple.

> Pushing my way through the pilgrims and common folk that frequented the Pavillion during the Festival of Registration, I swiftly sought the gates of entrance.

> All at once the sky was robbed of light and great darkness encompassed the inner hall. Drawing my sword, I made my way down a damp, cold, concrete stairway into the depths of the Pavillion. There before me a whole seething crowd streamed into many small booths and altars—a whirlpool of vast humanity sprawling aimlessly and without direction. Cautiously I made my way onto the floor of the cavernous interior. Then

suddenly an enormous wave of confusion and despair overcame me: a terrible sense of complete isolation amidst so many strangers. . . . Falling on one knee I appealed to the gods once again, "Oh brave and wise ones above, help me in my plight; I must register!"

I don't have time to also quote the Virgilian model that would show the imitative process in action, but notice the vividness of detail, the focus on dominant descriptive impression, the integral use of metaphor and the building of climax, as well as the selection of a true contemporary rite of passage with its elements of death and rebirth. The gamelike quality of imitation, rather than restraining students' power of expression, liberates a creative playfulness and neutralizes the self-consciousness that often inhibits freshman writers.

The next assignment, entitled "Memory and Reflection," is linked to the reading of the Confessions of St. Augustine. It incorporates the most recent lessons on narration and description into an exercise that recapitulates methods of invention and methods of arrangement. Here are some excerpts from a response by Bill called "Major Rager":

I would have loved to go to the "Major Rager," a wild, loud and completely out-of-control party last April, if only it had been held at someone else's house. I still remember scenes from that night vividly; I can see myself running up and down the stairs as more and more unknown faces came through the wide-open doors. I must have appeared frantic, hands pressed tightly against my face, moaning softly and asking, "Who are these people? How did they know about this? Why are they in my home? All my questions went unanswered as the house filled to the bursting point, people spilling outside onto the streets when the mad crush overcame them. Eventually, of course, the sheriffs arrived, attracted by the blare of numerous stereos and the complaints of neighbors. I can still recall the image of two burly figures, silhouetted against the moonlit sky, hurling keg after keg over the side of the second-story balcony in a frantic effort to avoid detection by the law. Bouncing from stone to stone, they rolled down the steep, woody slope to be greeted with open arms by the small army of partiers strategically deployed throughout the underbrush. . . .

Why does this parental love, so complete and unwavering over so many years, seem to fade into insignificance compared to the fleeting friendships of youth? I think that the reason can be found, ironically, in its very permanence and strength. Most of us become accustomed to a home environment filled with mutual support and encouragement and accept this state as natural and unchanging. It is the human way to take such things for granted, as they are part of the unseen background to our world, ever-present, vitally important, yet virtually unnoticed. Do most people in America ever think about what it means to be hungry and homeless, except when they are reminded by the example of some unfortunate person? In a similar way, I was not really aware of the emotional nourishment my parents gave me every day of my life. It became something I accepted without gratitude, a right to which I was entitled by virtue of my birth, and eventually a relationship which I could use to my own advantage. I imagine that most other people with a happy home life have felt the same way.

Contrast the security in this relationship with the fickle nature of most adolescent friendships. In the high-school social whirl, life is a constant battle to hold on to the friends one has while attracting new ones by whatever means possible. The "bait in the trap," as it were, can be anything from a fancy car or other material possessions to a more subtle approach involving helping with someone's homework or having a large party for one's friends. The latter action is especially effective because it involves an act of rebellion against one's parents. Although this action is clearly an abuse of someone else's property, the sin is an accepted and common one. Even St. Augustine felt pressure to increase his popularity through unsaintly means: "I gave in more and more to vice simply in order not to be despised."

From the modulation of the authorial voice to the ordered presentation of the larger issues growing out of the inner conflict, you can hear the influence of Augustine, both as moralist and as rhetorician. The writer has simply substituted his own parents for God the Father.

From the personal essay, the focus of the course moves to an introduction to argumentation, a division of rhetoric that will continue to occupy students until the end of the course. One of the Western Culture texts for the week is a set of Questions from Aquinas' *Summa Theologica*—a dense, but also an extremely schematic and therefore easily analyzable form of argumentation. The deductive and authority-based nature of the scholastic method gives students a chance to sharpen their purely dialectical skills by learning to argue both sides of the question and to appropriately cite chapter and verse. Here is a sample from Gretchen's essay, "The Dismantling of a Sexist Misconception."

Saint Paul claims that "neither was man created for woman, but woman for man." (I Corinthians 11:9) In order for this to be true, the following three criteria must be satisfied: God must not have created woman as man's equal, the original relationship between men and women must have been one of subordination, and women must serve as only positive influences on men. I will now examine each of these issues in turn.

The first question raised is whether or not God created women inferior to men. Saint Paul believes that He did simply because "man was not made from woman, but woman from man." (I Corinthians 11:8) But, the fact alone that woman was created from the flesh of man does not justify the inference that woman comes into existence as an underling to man, "for as woman was made from man, so man is now born of woman. And all things are from God." (I Corinthians 11:12) Thus, the reasoning that woman was created subservient to man because she was born of his flesh is false, for man is now born from the flesh of woman.

Using Aquinas' tools, Gretchen performs a surgical dissection of Saint Paul's inferences and premises, and builds her own case with the acuity of the Wife of Bath.

The final assignment of the quarter entitled "Appealing the Last Judgment," again demands the cumulative use of skills. Class discussion has focused on argument that is inductive rather than schematic, and has emphasized the detection of unstated assumptions and consequences rather than purely logical fallacies; the paper therefore combines literary with moral criticism. Here are some passages from a paper by Hassan:

Deep inside the Earth, in the ninth bolgia of the eighth circle of hell, Dante places two of the most virtuous men that ever lived. The founder of Islam, the prophet Mohammed, and his first follower, Ali, are sent down among the sowers of schism and scandal. Mohammed has his body split in half from the crotch to the chin. Ali complements this punishment with his head split from the chin to the crown. . . . Besides the physical grotesqueness of the scene, Dante uses obscene language as he passes judgment on the two. To explain Mohammed's wound, he says, "I saw someone ripped open from his chin to where we fart." To describe Mohammed's vital organs being ripped, he says that "his guts spilled out, with the dirty sack that turns to shit whatever the mouth gulps down." These two examples show Dante's disgust for the two men whom he places in the circle of fraud among many other heretics. . . .

Dante was plagued with the misconceptions that were prevalent in his time in Europe. Because Islam was such a political threat to Europe as the Saracens in the West had invaded Spain and most of Southern France, and the Ummayads in the East had destroyed the Byzantine Empire, the Europeans needed a common bond to unite themselves against the enemy. . . .

Mohammed, however, should not be placed in hell at all, for he was a virtuous and holy man. He preached salvation through the will of the omnipotent God. . . . Throughout his life, he tried to live by the will of God, loving his fellow man, giving to the poor, and doing what God demanded of him. He never wanted personal fame nor desired a rise in social class. . . .

My views on this judgment are based partly upon my upbringing as a Muslim. My grandfather, a religious scholar, always told me to follow the example of Mohammed and Ali in obeying God. He always helped me to solve my problems by looking for answers in the Koran. . . . The idea of having Mohammed in hell is absurd and impossible in my set of values, for he is the founder of all that I believe in religiously. Without his dogma, my grandfather's life-time work and belief would be ludicrous. . . . I therefore disagree with Dante's judgment, for it was based on his lack of knowledge about Islam. If he had known the doctrines, he would have at least placed Mohammed and Ali in Limbo among the virtuous pagans if not in Paradise itself, for they still believed in God and led an honest and good life. Although the two religions differ on many points, they both show the way to salvation through God, whether he be called Christ or Allah.

The second quarter opens with a research project and paper—again argumentative in format, and centered around the texts of Machiavelli's *The Prince* and Thomas More's *Utopia*—and also around the critical judgments of commentaries students track down and study. The controversy these works invariably stimulate is heightened in the Western Culture discussion sections, where members of the class debate their positions while in the process of working on their drafts and revisions.

This project lasts for the first four weeks of the quarter. Most composition class time during this period is devoted to grammar, punctuation and mechanics of research and documentation. Those matters lead to the consideration of style— both as tone, diction, figurative language, and as the expression of personal and cultural identity. This topic dovetails with the study of Renaissance poetry and the century of Louis Quatorze in Western Culture. After they produce an original Shakespearean sonnet, students write a stylistic analysis of the diction of Metaphysical poetry which makes use of their research in the OED.

The last part of Writing With Western Culture is devoted to the topic of Persuasion—or rhetoric and power. In connection with their reading of *Paradise Lost* students analyze the manipulative devices that Satan uses to market his apple and compare them with advertisements, political or religious propaganda and seduction poems. In the last assignment of the course students are required to exercise the eloquence they have analyzed and developed over the last twenty weeks in pursuit of some preselected goal—whether it be the change of an academic or political policy, the favors of a friend, the offer of a job, or the granting of a prayer.

I've been calling your attention to discrete examples, but I'd like to emphasize again that this syllabus aspires toward the same kind of coherence we demand of our students' essays. Adhering to the principles of Integration and Interaction, it moves each quarter from the rhetorical topics of invention, through arrangement and style, to revision, and then persuasion. In students, this repeated movement produces a sense of familiarity and review, and also of progress, as the applications become more inclusive and sophisticated.

The coherence of the syllabus is largely wrought by the intrinsic coherence of the subject matter we study in a survey of the Western Cultural heritage. For despite the immense distances between Homer and Joyce or between Exodus and Ellison, despite the radically opposed perspectives of John Milton and Mary Wollstonecraft or between Frederick Douglass and Frederick Nietzsche, nevertheless they are all engaged with one another in the same conversation—a conversation we and our students only need listen to in order to join.

264

THE SEVENTH ART IN LIBERAL ARTS EDUCATION: THE INTEGRATION OF FILM STUDY INTO THE CURRICULUM

Victoria M. Stiles
SUNY Cortland

In 1911, in his "Manifesto of the Seven Arts," Ricciotto Canudo, the first film aesthetician, calls Cinema the "Seventh Art." For him Cinema is the "total fusion of art" and mankind's best chance for spiritual renewal.[1] How horrified he would be with films such as *Rambo*, *Friday the 13th*, *Nightmare on Elm Street*, and the like. Luckily, films with aesthetic, spiritual and intellectual acclaim are still being released here and abroad every year. Thus we have both, the popular and the "serious" branches of film; and the serious films which enrich our lives still allow us to speak of Cinema as the Seventh Art.

According to the venerated American filmmaker D. W. Griffith, film can "make you see." Through different types of films we learn to become more discriminating in our tastes and learn to understand to what extent the visual media in our media-saturated culture shape our perception of the world. Marshall McLuhan's statement that radio, film and television turn our daily lives into "classrooms without walls" contains more truth today than it did in the 60s, for the study of film provides visual instruction which prepares us to cope intelligently and creatively with the demands made on us by life in general. As to Canudo's hope for spiritual renewal through the Seventh Art, I return once again to D. W. Griffith, this first giant among film directors. He was convinced that film was not merely entertainment, but had also "a moral and educational force"; he made this statement in an interview in 1915 and elaborated on it in the following way: "If I had a growing son I should be willing to let him see motion pictures as he liked because I believe they would be an invaluable aid to his education. They would stimulate his imagination, without which no one will go far . . . and they would shape his character along the most rigid plane of human conduct."[2] Serious filmmakers throughout the world shared and still share Griffith's faith in the educational properties of the Seventh Art and in its power to effect behavioral and social change.

Studies show that on the average, a child, by the time it reaches high school, has spent more hours in front of the television set than in the classroom. Therefore one would assume that if Griffith were right, children would be very well educated, but they are not for the simple reason that they don't watch films or any other visual presentation critically. Although children are largely educated and

265

socialized through the visual media, they are not sufficiently guided in making sound value judgments, for even though in school they are taught to read, they are not taught to *see*. The same is true for college students who are indeed practiced viewers in the visual media but in dire need of guidelines to distinguish between mediocrity and excellence. Most of the TV programs they watch are so cliché ridden and predictable that they stultify inquisitiveness and imagination. And when students go to a movie theater, they tend to select films chiefly for entertainment value and emotional diversion; they watch films essentially with an uncritical attitude. There is certainly nothing wrong with selecting and enjoying a film for entertainment or escape value only, but students should also be familiar with films that engage the viewer's intellect. The choice is then up to them.

The fact that people are often visually illiterate is exploited by the manipulators of the visual media in both commercial and political advertising. Nobody will deny that it is through visual means that elections are determined; that through visual means certain products are turned into status symbols without which people think they cannot live. Since our students do not watch critically, it is our job as educators to make students literate, not only in the print media but also in the visual media. This is not only a cultural but also a political responsibility, because without critical viewing of political advertisements, no voter can make an intelligent political decision. Hence we as educators should convince students that the study of good films cultivates and broadens one's mind, expands knowledge and enhances one's imaginative and analytical faculties, all invaluable assets for life.

In assessing the curriculum, we must above all ask ourselves, whether or not we are successful in cultivating students' creative abilities, for on all fronts— civic, industrial and international—we are facing problems that require creative solutions. Yet how well do we cultivate students' creative abilities? Do our classrooms encourage imagination or do they reward the programmed response? We must ask ourselves whether our programs and courses motivate students enough to stimulate and sustain their enthusiastic involvement and creative energies. Wherever we turn, as citizens of a global family or as participants in community issues, the demands are first and foremost on our imaginative capabilities. Our task as educators is a grave one: we are molding responsible citizens.

Since the college years are a student's unique opportunity for acquiring a wide range of knowledge, it is the educator's responsibility to provide a wide range of stimulating learning experiences. As teachers faced with students brought up largely by the visual media, what could be for us a more effective way of teaching than through the familiar moving picture—film, the Seventh Art.

Today as never before, film constitutes a powerful educational tool. If we ignore it as an art and as a communication medium and fail to use its potential in the classroom to extend students' visual literacy, we are not participating fully in the culture of our time. The underlying goal of education in addition to providing knowledge is to develop and deepen students' critical perception so that they will be better equipped in all walks of life to analyze and evaluate intelligently what they see and hear before taking action. Cineliteracy is one way of achieving this.

The study of film has become an established discipline at many universities throughout the world; for decades prospective film and television directors and critics have studied at film schools. The interdisciplinary study of film, on the other hand, is a fairly recent concept, conceived in the 70s, and not yet offered at many universities or colleges. It is the purpose of my paper to advocate Film Study first of all as an interdisciplinary program because of its inherent possibilities for increasing a student's range of knowledge and intellectual versatility. However, film study should not be restricted to cinema courses only but used in other liberal arts courses as well.

At the State University of New York College at Cortland where I teach, we have such great faith in the educational attributes of film that as early as 1973 we added an interdisciplinary Cinema Study program to the Liberal Arts curriculum. Until May 1989, students could only major in this program, but this year a Minor was approved as well (see Appendix I).[3] Let me first explain the *interdisciplinary* nature of our Cinema Study program which was possible because of the enthusiasm of some professors to concentrate on film study in one or two of their courses and because of their willingness to expand their field of specialization: Eight cinephile professors from various disciplines present cinema from the point of view of their areas of expertise. They are offering courses in their specific disciplines, cross-listing them with cinema (see Appendix I). The frequency with which these courses are taught varies from course to course; only History of Cinema is taught every semester. On the average five courses are offered per academic year. The Cinema Study faculty comes from the following disciplines: Art, English, Geography, History, International Communications and Culture, Music, and Political Science. At present we have five majors—one more than the Philosophy and Music departments! Since, on the average, thirty students are enrolled per course, most take a Cinema Study course either as an elective or to satisfy a requirement in their major. We encourage our Cinema Study *majors* to minor in areas such as art, economics, literature, music, political science, and other career-related areas such as acting, advertising, journalism, literary criticism, or social work. The new minor in Cinema Study provides *all* students with an added choice for a minor but should prove of special appeal to students from Communication Studies, English, History, Recreation and Leisure Studies. Our program is not production-oriented but geared to film study from the point of view of criticism and aesthetic appreciation within a cultural, historical, political, and social context. Our Cinema courses teach essential skills: *seeing*, reading, writing, and debating. Short papers and/or term papers are required in almost all Cinema classes; the reading requirements are demanding, and class discussion is at the core of every course. Thus in addition to cineliteracy, reading, writing, and verbal skills are developed. Furthermore, since films mirror historical, political, and social changes in the world, they help to bring about cultural awareness. The foreign films which are used in almost all of our interdisciplinary cinema courses help to educate students for competence to deal with other cultures, because it is vital to think in global rather than in national terms only.

Our Cinema Study program has been coordinated so far through the Department of International Communications and Culture. A cinephile and film scholar, Professor Robert Hammond, a member of that department, started the program at Cortland in 1973 and acted as coordinator until 1984. At that time I became coordinator and have held this position ever since. However, in theory the program could be affiliated with any one of the participating departments, depending on who is elected as coordinator. It is an autonomous program, operated virtually without major funding from the administration. At the present time, a mere $500 per year are allotted to the Cinema Study program (until 1983 it was $700). In order to help finance film rentals we charge a $15 lab fee per student. To cut film rental costs, we purchase films on video cassettes whenever they are available and of good quality. We are thus slowly building a substantial video-cassette film library and rent films only when the film is either not available on cassette or of poor quality. Luckily our college has three lecture halls with rear-view projection equipment and large screens. Unfortunately the image is some-what grainy, and there is a 10 percent loss of the image on all four sides. However, substituting at least half of the films shown per course with video-cassettes was our only recourse, if we wanted to keep the program alive, and even the purists among the Cinema faculty cooperated when it became a question of either bowing to necessity or cancelling the program.

So much for our Cinema Study program at Cortland. It is far from ideal—that would entail a full-time Cinema Study faculty and substantially greater funding than we have at our disposal now—but we have managed to survive for sixteen years and shall continue to do so, providing the program retains the vital threefold support: Of the administration, a dedicated Cinema Study faculty, and interested students. That being the case, we will continue our privileged task of increasing our students' range of knowledge and intellectual versatility through our interdisciplinary program.

In order to assess the educational properties of the Seventh Art in liberal arts education at Cortland College, I conducted a teacher-student survey this semester (Fall 1989) in five courses. I selected on purpose courses taught by professors who are not members of the Cinema Study program but who usually show films in class, so that I could gauge the opinions of those teachers and their students on film as an instructional enhancement (Appendix II, III). Those professors *teaching* interdisciplinary Cinema Study courses and those students *enrolled* in them have already sufficiently demonstrated their confidence in education through focus on film by participating in a Cinema Study course. Unfortunately, out of the eight colleagues I had asked initially, only five finally cooperated; these five professors and a total of 130 students filled out my questionnaire on the function of film in the classroom and made it possible for me to share their opinions with you. The five courses are: "Introduction to Fiction"; "Literature of Sports" (English Department); "The Revolution and French Literature" (International Communication and Culture Department); "The Holocaust" (History Department); "Prejudice, Discrimination and Morality" (Philosophy Department). The film list for these five courses is the following:

"Introduction to Fiction"
Almos' a Man
Barn Burning
Bartleby the Scrivener
Blue Hotel
The Dead

"Literature of Sports"
Fat City
The Natural

"The Revolution and French Literature"
Dangerous Liaisons
Danton
The Marriage of Figaro
Napoleon

"The Holocaust"
Cabaret
Genocide (Thames TV)
The Great Dictator
Image before my Eyes
Jud Suss
Judgment at Nuremberg
Mr. Klein
Night and Fog
Partisans of Vilna
Shoah (excerpt)
Shop on Main Street
Triumph of the Will
Wannsee Conference

"Prejudice, Discimination and Morality"
Ethnic Notions
Killing Us Softly
On Being Gay
Pink Triangles

269

Judging from the survey results, films are indeed an educational enhancement and in the students' opinion the inclusion of film in the courses was 100 percent justified. For an illustration, I will concentrate on two courses and condense the correlation between teacher's intent and teaching results by first quoting the teacher and then ten students per course. The two courses are: "The Holocaust" and "Prejudice, Discrimination and Morality." The teacher of "The Holocaust" has taught his course many times before but is offering it for the first time with a focus on film; hence, this semester he calls his course "The Holocaust and Film." We cross-listed his course with Cinema Study (Appendix I, CIN 251) for the following reasons: The teacher is stressing the visual medium in class by showing a film almost weekly and requiring five film reviews (300–500 words in length) of each student "as a means of communicating an intellectual and emotional understanding of the Holocaust."

Teacher:
I think it is especially important in a course like "The Holocaust" to use visuals to aid in emotional identification with what happened . . . students need to be able to look at film critically since so much of their world comes to them through film. (Also) I want to improve my own visual sensibility.

Students (10 out of 48 opinions selected):
1. I believe that film, when used correctly can be a vital asset to a student's further education.
2. Film is used to reinforce what the teacher has said in class as well as what was said in the reading. People learn easier from things that they can both see and hear.
3. The films have served as a useful insight into the subject. There are many facets to a period in history where reading it is not enough. The visual assistance is truly an asset.
4. To expose learners to the subjects through a different means of communication. Film tends to spark interest and hold attention more than textbooks and lectures do, therefore the students learn more effectively.
5. Used as a visual to help students absorb the information in a way that lectures can not tell. It also gives the students a chance to develop their own opinions.
6. Film involves a student like no other medium. It allows one to observe what he or she cannot experience through reading or lecture. It sharpens criticism skills.
7. A person can talk all they want about a particular subject; but pictures give depth.
8. The eye always predominates over the ear. Visual learning is so much more memorable and gives you pictured examples in your mind that you have with you forever.

9. The function of film in this classroom is to add another, more attention grabbing technique to the subject matter discussed in this course. Extremely effective!

10. Film provides the visual images that words just cannot get across.

"Prejudice, Discrimination and Morality" course:
Teacher:
I use film in order to provide concrete evidence of some of the many theoretical points and issues that I deal with in my course. For example, *Ethnic Notions* deals with the history of stereotypes regarding Blacks in this country. It lends a forceful, concrete content to our discussion of the inflexibility of stereotyping. Film also provides an alternative voice in the classroom and gives added weight or sometimes a different perspective on a problem.

Students
(10 out of 24 opinions selected):

1. Film is an active way of learning . . . it brings real life situations into the lecture and reinforces the learning . . . films can make an issue or point clearer through visual usage.

2. Film serves as a useful tool in creating a visual medium to translate information or summarize an idea.

3. Experiencing visually allows you to gain better understanding than just reading or hearing about ideas.

4. I think that film is very educational. It helps the professor to get his/her point across by illustrating visually what he/she is lecturing about . . . it leaves more of a mark embedded in our brains when we view something visually.

5. The function of film in the classroom is to get across a point which is hard to explain unless it is seen visually. It makes the point more lucid to the student allowing the teacher a chance to build on that point.

6. I believe that films in the classroom are important in that they diversify the learning experience and offer visual stimulation. More often than not they appeal to "real world" situations as opposed to the theoretical classroom experience.

7. Film gives another "dimension" concerning "teaching" and "learning"; it takes you "there." Visuals are still the strongest methods of learning about issues of the past and present!

8. . . . it is a very beneficial way of relating things out of the classroom to what we are talking about inside the classroom. Students can understand concepts, but not until they actually see them will they be internalized. I feel films are a very good way of doing this.

9. The function of film in the classroom is to give concrete support to theories

we discuss. It gives the learner another route to facilitate retention of the subject matter. It also breaks up the boredom.

10. Film provides students with a more in depth view of the subject material that is being discussed. It presents examples and different views of different situations. I feel it is very helpful to a student's understanding of some material. Besides, a picture is worth a 1000 words!

I believe my survey shows that film is an educational enhancement in some liberal arts courses at Cortland College. But how about its function in science courses? According to our Dean of Arts and Sciences, Dr. Hubert Keen who is a professor of Biology, film does play an important role in such areas as earth science and biology. According to him, "some aspects of science . . . rely heavily on observation and in these fields film is a very good substitute for direct observation by students." He also pointed out an important reason "for the use of film in the teaching of science," namely as "a motivational tool." Since film increases motivation for learning, and helps to bring about new insights into a given subject matter, be it in the Humanities or the Sciences, without doubt the Seventh Art has a vital function in the classroom. Judging from students' opinions, films stimulate their imagination and call for emotional as well as intellectual involvement.

You can see why we are struggling to keep an interdisciplinary Cinema Study program alive at Cortland despite the scant financial support: We believe in teaching through film and in the virtue of an interdisciplinary approach to teaching. Its virtue is that experts from a *variety* of disciplines offer courses, thus providing students with a multifaceted perspective. A professor of aesthetics presents film aesthetics in the framework of philosophy; a professor of geography approaches film with emphasis on geography, culture, and sociology; an art history professor presents the visual side of the medium with the eye of the experienced art historian; a professor of history places a particular film in its historical context, and so forth. The result is a comprehensive perspective and an in-depth study of film within a specific field of study, which leaves the student with greater versatility and a broader span of knowledge than conventional instruction in a single discipline could provide. Perhaps such an interdisciplinary approach to teaching with a focus on the Seventh Art in its varied aspects is a first step towards attaining our professional goal as educators: the molding of intellectual decathletes!

1. Ricciotto Canudo, "Manifesto of the Seven Arts" translated by Steven Philip Kramer. See "Documents of Film Theory: Riciotto Canudo's 'Manifesto of the Seven Arts,'" *Literature/Film Quarterly*, vol. 3, 3. Summer 1975, 253.

2. "D. W. Griffith, Producer of the World's Biggest Picture. Interview with D. W. Griffith." In Harry M. Geduld (ed.), *Focus on D. W. Griffith*. Englewood Cliffs, N.J.: Prentice-Hall, 1971, 29.

3. For the appendices to this paper, please correspond with the author.

BUSINESS ETHICS NEED NOT BE OXYMORONIC: APPLYING LIBERAL ARTS TO THE MANAGEMENT CURRICULUM

David A. Fedo
Curry College

I.

The longstanding tension between liberal and professional education—between learning for life and learning to make a living—is one of the major themes of modern education. Here I wish to address a slightly different theme: the underlying tension, some would say contradiction, in the free enterprise system between the right of an individual, whatever the motive, to make money, and the need for that individual, whatever the circumstance, to be socially responsible. It seems to me that without a reconciliation of these tensions, both on our campuses and in American business, the *whole* student cannot be educated, nor can the public at large be adequately served.

Having said this, I immediately acknowledge the difficulty of the task in our current social and intellectual climate. In education, the debate over the fragmentation of the baccalaureate curriculum has been polarized in recent years by, among other things, former Secretary of Education William Bennett and Professor Allan Bloom, who, with much media attention, seem to be calling for a return to the good old days—the halcyon days of the Ivory Tower when everyone knew and understood what the true literary canon was, and when there was a shared set of assumptions and values about the world and about one's place in it. Nothing less than the preservation of our sacred Western Heritage was at stake. The enemy included "professionalized" undergraduate education—the monster of rampant vocationalism. Ernest Boyer summarized this hypervented criticism in his recent book, *College: The Undergraduate Experiencing America*, by reporting that, driven by careerism and overshadowed by graduate and professional education, "many of the nation's colleges and universities are more successful in credentialing than in providing a quality education for their students."[1]

In business, corporate raiders and rapacious Wall Street inside traders have so dominated the contemporary landscape that a new language has emerged to describe the players and their strategies. We have sharks, Pac Men, greenmail, and tin parachutes; the disease of mergermania has required from the media an imagination of the highest order just to give it a taxonomy. In today's business environment, where making money seems to be the only god left in the temple, Ivan Boesky is castigated because he was caught, not because he was corrupt. Are

274

there no limits, we ask, to the ends CEOs and junior executives will go to increase the bottom line? Yet, how different are we, moving into the 1990s, from the economist Milton Freedman, who wrote unapologetically in 1970, "There is one and only one social responsibility of business—to use its resources and engage in activities designed to increase its profits. . . ."[2]

Yet I believe there *is* hope in education and business. That there may be fewer English or Philosophy majors in our colleges is not really the point. More and more faculty, agreeing with Alfred North Whitehead that the goals of liberal and professional education are more in harmony than not, are coming together to develop a baccalaureate curriculum that genuinely integrates the arts and sciences with the disciplines of the professions. For example, in *Unfinished Design*, a recent report published by the Association of American Colleges on undergraduate engineering education, the AAC details the creative integration of the liberal arts into programs of students at such diverse institutions as the University of Florida, Colorado School of Mines, and Stanford. In the health professions— pharmacy and nursing, for example, at the undergraduate level—humanities courses on aging and disease are by now well established, with cluster courses in the social and behavioral sciences also playing a significant role.

"Liberal education is nothing if not practical," wrote Mark Van Doren, critic and longtime Columbia professor of English, some years ago.[3] That is not all of the story, of course; Professor Van Doren, a Shakespeare scholar, well understood the meaning of enrichment—but demonstrating the connections and usefulness of the arts and sciences to the world students *know* is certainly one of the ways the liberal arts can touch lives, whatever the academic major.

II.

Some points of this discussion apply to my own institution, Bentley College, a medium-sized, private, post-secondary school near Boston. At Bentley, ninety-five percent of 3,850 undergraduates are seeking bachelor of science degrees in business—in accounting, management, marketing, finance, and computer information systems. In many ways, this business focus is Bentley's most important strength, and it is a clear link to its past—the College was founded in the Back Bay in 1917 as a proprietary school of accounting and finance. It moved to Waltham in the western suburbs of Boston in 1968. In another way, the focus on business provides a challenge: if the arts and sciences are really to matter at Bentley, they must be made to count in the academic programs of students whose primary interest lies elsewhere.

Perhaps surprisingly, the news from our campus—and from the campuses of many business schools—is encouraging. As in engineering and the health sciences, joint initiatives on the part of arts and sciences and business faculty have begun to deconstruct the curriculum in positive ways. A new Interdisciplinary Studies Program at Bentley has sparked an interest in multidisciplinary team teaching. "Values and Choices," one of the courses designed to demonstrate humanities perspectives on such organizational problems as productivity and leadership, was cited in 1986 for its "innovation" by the American Assembly of Collegiate Schools of Business, the accrediting body for business institutions. A combined BA/MBA degree program, formed just three years ago, is already tapping a new market for Bentley, and has led to promising collaboration on curricula by our undergraduate and graduate schools. In addition, renewed interest among business educators in the international dimension has created a tremendous window of opportunity for our arts and sciences faculty. Enrollments in Modern Languages, to take one example, are up by over two hundred percent in the last four years.

III.

At Bentley, however, the extraordinary development in the field of business ethics best represents the attempt by the College to fully integrate liberal and professional learning. This development began in 1976 when the National Endowment for the Humanities awarded Bentley a planning grant to introduce a series of interdisciplinary business ethics courses into the baccalaureate curriculum. Heading the project was Professor Michael Hoffman, chairperson of the Department of Philosophy, whose background was thoroughly traditional; his first book was on Kant's Theory of Freedom. Yet Professor Hoffman and his colleagues were so encouraged by this new venture, and saw such potential in the application of ethics to the corporate setting, that a year later they founded what was called the Center for Business Ethics, with the ambitious goal of "providing a nonpartisan forum for the exchange of ideas on business ethics in contemporary society."[4] The Center was to be national in scope, and Professor Hoffman sought broad participation from academia, business, government and a variety of public interest groups.

From modest beginnings, this Center, nurtured by members of the Department of Philosophy, and supported by others from within and outside the Bentley community, prospered. The number of business ethics courses at Bentley grew— stand-alone electives on multinationals and corporate social responsibility among them—and business ethics modules in management courses were piloted. The Center collected and disseminated business ethics bibliographies and course syllabi from dozens of institutions, and has supplied consultants to colleges and universities as well as corporations seeking to implement or enhance programs, curricula, and ethical codes of conduct. In addition, Fortune 500 companies are periodically surveyed by the Center regarding their progress toward implementing business ethics models, with the results published widely. Of all the Center's outreach programs, the national conferences, scheduled every year or two on the Bentley campus, have had the most far-reaching impact. These conferences, held on such broad themes as corporate governance, the work ethic, mergers and takeovers, and the management of computer technology, have drawn major speakers from government, higher education, the media, and private industry. Often, the sharply contrasting points of view give sessions a kind of gritty, if not exactly high, drama. The *Proceedings* of each conference have extended the debate and discourse well beyond the Bentley campus.

The success of the Center for Business Ethics, and the success of similar centers in recent years, seem to fly in the face of the numerous corporate ethical failings and Wall Street scandals to which I referred earlier, and which, like war and famine, have become almost commonplace in the daily news. Is guilt now at work even in the corridors of executive power? Are managers, as *Newsweek* put it recently "scrambling to restore a system of values to the workplace?"[5] Or is the skepticism of many—that business ethics is indeed an oxymoron—really true?

Professor Hoffman, in a speech delivered in Milan in June, 1988, at the First Italian Business Ethics Conference, saw an answer in broader terms. He said in part:

> ... [The development of business ethics] can be traced to the philosophical ideas which have dominated our culture. Our present century has been weaned on relativism—the denial of ethical absolutes, on *pragmatism*—equating knowledge with observable experience, and on *behaviorism*—interpreting human actions as totally determinable and predictable. The unifying thread to all this is the reduction of everything . , . to material reality or physical experience. Within this . . . framework science and materialism have flourished, and ethics and values have been relegated to matters of emotion, attitude, and feeling. Such an ideology permits no objective level of significance or reality for the development of the nonmaterial, nonmeasurable dimensions of our lives such as freedom, morality, and divinity. . . . [S]omething about the human spirit . . . resists this sterile picture and cries out for a different ideology which will preserve our humanity and provide our lives with value.
>
> I see business ethics . . . as arising out of the moral crisis created by our inadequate philosophical development. [It] is an attempt . . . to revive the . . . legitimacy of making moral claims in the world of practical affairs. The success of this depends on its philosophical grounding.[6]

What Professor Hoffman was saying is that an understanding of the most enduring values of our culture, and the human quest for something outside of ourselves, can give meaning to our lives, from the spiritual to the most transient

277

or trivial. Ethics—and ethics applied in the business setting—reminds us that we have a responsibility to our neighbors, to our environment, and to the public "good," and that nothing absolves us of that responsibility, even the making of a fortune.

Of course, the *implementation* of business ethics programs into the curricula of colleges is not always easy. Even at Bentley, where the track record has been good, there has been resistance, much of it having to do with who controls the curriculum—the business or the arts and sciences faculty. In the long run, the initiatives in business ethics begun in the Department of Philosophy have been recognized as benefiting our undergraduates; they have enhanced the stature of the Department and won the respect of academic colleagues elsewhere. Enrollments in the Department's traditional courses—in logic, existentialism, and ethics, for example—have been strong, and the scholarly output of the faculty has been solid. The Department's Philosophy and Public Affairs Lecture Series, the longest such colloquium at Bentley, has enhanced the intellectual climate on campus with speakers on such diverse topics as South Africa, surrogate motherhood, and the ethics of immigration. Thus in many ways the Department has become a model arts and sciences department within a professional school, combining the best of learning that is both liberal and applied. This *balance* is the key. In an uncertain time in American higher education, the story of philosophy at Bentley is, for those aware of it, an unambiguously happy one.

NOTES

1. Ernest Boyer, *College: The Undergraduate Experience in America*, New York: Harper Row, 1987, 2.

2. Milton Friedman, "The Social Responsibility of Business is to Increase Its Profits," *New York Times Magazine*, September 13, 1970.

3. Mark Van Doren, quoted in *The Bentley Observer*, Waltham, Massachusetts: Bentley College, Winter, 1982/83.

4. *Center for Business Ethics*, Waltham, Massachusetts: Bentley College, I would like to thank Professor Hoffman and Professor Robert Frederick, assistant director of the Center, for sharing their ideas as I was writing this paper.

5. *Newsweek*, May 1988.

6. W. Michael Hoffman, "Business Ethics in the United States: Its Past Decade and Its Future," paper presented at the First Italian Business Ethics Conference, Milan, June 9, 1988.

COMMON GROUND: THE DEVELOPMENT OF PRACTICAL BUSINESS COMMUNICATION AND HUMAN RELATIONS SKILLS IN THE CREATIVE WRITING WORKSHOP

Fabian Clements Worsham
University of Houston

In most explorations of the benefits students of business and technology can derive from liberal arts courses, scholars focus upon theoretical, philosophical, and impractical benefits such as the opportunity for self expression, refinement of tastes, and the development of humanistic values. Oddly, most writers fail to address the more obvious practical skills which the creative writing workshop can develop—specific skills in oral and written communication and human relations which are essential to success in a variety of business and technical careers.

Creative Writing as Commerce

Just as accounting professors teach their students as though they were going to become accountants, creative writing professors teach their students as though they were going to become writers. Therefore it is necessary for the pre-professional writer (or apprentice) to view his or her work as a marketable product, rather than simply as a hobby or "creative outlet."

In the process of doing this, student writers in workshop learn to abandon defensive postures. Although many students entering beginning-level workshops strongly identify their writing as a part of themselves, most discover very quickly that defensiveness is inappropriate in a group-critique situation.

They learn to separate self from product, and thus they become more open to criticism. Also, once this is accomplished, emotions such as anger and fear no longer block their ability to judge critical statements and incorporate suggested changes. They learn to view their writing as separate from themselves, and become receptive to constructive criticism. This kind of openness is essential to the success of any group-generated or group-refined product.

At the advanced levels students are encouraged to target particular markets. They learn to identify characteristics which appeal to particular publications and to select from their work pieces suitable for a certain journal, or to actually write new work with a particular journal in mind. Although the first drafts of a poem or story are produced independently, the workshop gives members the opportunity to *work together cooperatively* in the final stages to produce a marketable product.

This product is seen as fluid or malleable, not as fixed. Although students may enter the workshop with the view that their poems or stories, once written, are finished, with instruction they learn that the product may go through numerous revisions; some authors continue to improve upon their works even after they are published. Twenty or more drafts of a single poem, for most authors, would be normal. This sort of experience is good for anyone who will later be asked to develop or modify a product of any kind, since openness to new ideas and flexibility are essential in responding to changing markets, environments, or situations. Students learn to weigh the value of criticism and to select from all critical comments the ones which seem most valid. This kind of re-evaluation of one's work often involves consideration of ethical and moral concerns, as well as aesthetic judgments. For example, a student may be urged to consider whether his work makes a statement which is inherently racist, sexist, or ethnocentric. Students are able to see, often for the first time, their own deeply-rooted and often subconscious beliefs and prejudices embodied in their own writing, and are able to confront them in a setting which is less volatile and more supportive than uncontrolled "real world" situations they may find themselves in after graduation.

Misconceptions

Many practical skills are gained from a creative writing class, and even the language that writers use to discuss their writing shows that the "art" of writing is not as mysterious, supernatural, unearthly, intangible, and inspired as romantic lore about writers and the writing process might lead one to believe; it is also solid, tangible, real, down-to-earth, and (mostly) understandable. Writers talk about craftsmanship, "nut and bolts," mechanics, line breaks, concreteness, conciseness, revision, imagery, density, clarity, form, and other not-so-esoteric things. This is especially true in beginning workshops, where discussions of craft are very basic.

Most people who have not been trained to teach creative writing workshops—including many beginning writing students—think of these classes as open forums for "free" expression of whatever sentiment happens to be in the writer's mind, in whatever form (usually "free" verse) that the sentiment (by "inspiration") happens to present itself. This preconception has its roots in the stereotypical image of the poet as a "little god," inspired, tormented, the free channel of divine afflatus. This stereotype was popularized in the late eighteenth and early nineteenth centuries by the Romantic poets—particularly Byron, Keats, and Shelley, and has been consciously cultivated and perpetuated since that time by a few highly visible modern and contemporary romantics such as Walt Whitman, Dylan Thomas, and Allen Ginsberg. Most poets, however, do not fit this description—despite the mystery of the creative process and the awe that their works inspire, most poets are ordinary people who spend a lot of time hunched over a keyboard.

The romantic image of the writer as demonically tormented and suicidal unfortunately runs rampant in high schools, driven by several factors, among them the teenager's natural affinity with this kind of personality (perhaps because of feelings of alienation and need for rebellion against authority). Because they are largely unaware of the poetic tradition (the forms and precedents of poetry), and because they have been exposed to much more bad poetry than good (particularly in the form of greeting cards and "inspirational verse," high school students tend to write doggerel and sentiment. Their teachers are often reluctant to offer firm guidance, either because they are afraid of stifling the students' creativity or because of their own lack of any real training in creative writing.

Often, people who have chosen to pursue business majors in college have no exposure to creative writing beyond the high school literary magazine. They may be offended by the maudlin sentiment, gloomy morbidity and solipsism they found within its pages—and rightly so—or they may simply believe that such feelings are foreign to their natures, and thus label themselves "unpoetic" or "unliterary." I found that several business majors in my creative writing class, who had enrolled "just to write science fiction," were surprised to discover that they liked poetry once they had been introduced to contemporary poetic technique and had discerned the difference between poetry and doggerel verse.

Social Responsibility

As students' sensibilities sharpen, they begin to recognize even very subtle stereotypes and prejudices in the work they critique. They learn to gauge audience reaction, just as a person making a television commercial does: Will certain populations be offended by this work? Do I care if I offend them? Did I intend to offend them? Is it prudent to offend them? What exactly is it about this work that's offensive? Can the offensive language be taken out? Is anything to be gained by it?

As in advertising, one must consider the subtle and often inadvertent messages that a work conveys. For example, one of my students, a young black man, had written a story in which the central character was a black basketball player, and—unfortunately—a stereotypical "dumb jock." I asked the writer why he had depicted the character this way; he answered "Well, this really happened, and this guy was really like that." I asked him, "What kind of image of blacks do you want to convey in your writing?" The student, of course, was free to convey whatever image he chose, but the considerations he was asked to make went far beyond "Did we all enjoy what happened in this story?"

In a creative writing class as in their daily lives, students confront numerous social issues. They learn to recognize racism, sexism, classism, condescension, pompousness, immaturity, and other weaknesses in both the writer's attitudes and in the postures of the characters created, and they learn to dissect the language of a literary work to determine in exactly what words and phrases those attitudes are manifest. The creative writing class brings into sharp focus the unconscious biases embedded in our language.

Students in my creative writing class in the spring semester of 1989 wrote about race relations, alcohol and drug abuse, the homeless, battered women, obesity, friendship, rape, dignity and value of animals, AIDS, teenage suicide, sex, solitude, marital relationships, divorce, and the elderly, as well as other complex, volatile, and pressing social issues. These student writers are not only looking within themselves; they are pressed into an engagement with the world which makes them reach beyond themselves to consider other lives, and they must articulate their ideas and opinions in clear, lucid language.

The Workshop and Group Dynamics

But perhaps the most significant aspect of the creative writing workshop which can be applied to a business career is the understanding one gains of small group dynamics. Workshops are kept small, with an enrollment of eight to twenty students, so that each student's work can be discussed at length. Groups are a part of all large organizations, according to Harold J. Leavitt and Homa Bahrami, who point to the group's ability to provide control and discipline, promote innovation, enhance communication and prevent alienation and anonymity as some advantages of groups within organizations (220).

Phillips and Erickson, in *Interpersonal Dynamics in the Small Group*, distinguish classroom groups from those in business, saying that the small group can "support educational goals," but that "when used in this context, the kind of output expected is different than in problem-solving discussion." Any "solutions" students generate are not "relevant," since the students are not authorities, and their solutions are merely hypothetical. "They do not get a real sense of the pressures involved in small-group decision making since their solution is binding on no one and they can neither gain nor lose as a result" (12–13). This is probably true in more traditional classroom situations, but in creative writing workshop, as in other courses which require students to develop and market a product or service, the solutions are real, not hypothetical. The work created in the workshop is very likely to be marketed. Students are encouraged to submit their writing not only to campus contests and publications, but also to local, regional, and national literary magazines and journals. And in the development of these literary products, success or failure may depend on the group's input.

Robert E. Lefton, in his article "The Eight Barriers to Teamwork," discusses factors which prevent synergism (the improved interaction and problem-solving ability made possible by teamwork). At least five of the eight factors can be addressed through a creative writing workshop. They are (1) breakdown in probing, (2) promotional leadership, (3) intra-team conflict, (4) insufficient alternatives, and (5) lack of candor (18, 20).

Lefton identifies probing as an essential skill, and says that "probing is very rarely taught in our schools and colleges" (18). Lefton does not seem to be familiar with creative writing classrooms, in which the major activity is probing. He lists three ineffective probes: closed-end probes (which provoke a yes or no response) such as "Is this fair?"; leading questions, such as "You don't want to sound corny, do you?"; and brief assertions, such as "Go on." Although these sometimes occur in a creative writing classroom, far more useful (and more often used) are the kinds of probes Lefton labels as productive: open-end probes, such as "How do we know he's being ironic?"; neutral probes, like "Explain why you think so"; pauses; summaries; and reflective statements, such as "You think, then, that she needs to clarify this line" (18). These are the kinds of statements that, in the beginning workshop sessions, the teacher uses, and therefore models for workshop members, who are learning the methods of workshop critique. By midterm most students are fairly proficient in using these kinds of probes, even though probing, as a subject, may never have been mentioned.

Lefton says that "only about 10 percent of managers consistently use these five probes which are essential for getting to the heart of things" (18). However, if those managers had taken a creative writing workshop they would at least have had a great deal of practice in using these essential tools of their profession.

Lefton defines promotional leadership as the tendency for a leader to leak his or her ideas to the other group members before they've had a chance to formulate and express their own. As Lefton says, "Once people know what the boss thinks, the whole discussion is likely to shift in that direction." Whether this is done intentionally or unintentionally, the effect is to choke off discussion and prohibit the generation of what might have been valuable solutions (18).

Promotional leadership is deadening not only to teamwork in a business setting, but also to creative writing workshops. In workshop it may have two sources: the teacher and the author of the student work under discussion. The teacher, by withholding her opinion until after workshop members have expressed theirs, models democratic leadership. The student authors learn to withhold their own input ("what the poem is *supposed* to mean—and as they quickly learn, not necessarily what it *does* mean) until their peers have made their own observations. In this way they learn to avoid promotional leadership both by example and by practice. Usually the teacher's modeling is enough to encourage this behavior, but in some instances student authors are instructed to wait until their peers have spoken, and in some classes they are actually forbidden to defend their work at all. This is an extreme but workable practice which some instructors use in an attempt to totally eliminate defensiveness.

Creative writing workshop is also a good place to learn to deal with intra-team conflict. Lefton emphasizes that effective teams do not play it safe; "they argue, they debate, they say things openly and honestly; they tell it like it is" (20). This is also true in workshop, especially after a couple of weeks have passed and the students feel less threatened by the group situation. Open and direct discussion is fostered by the security which compatible and supportive membership makes possible. It is also true of both groups—in business and in creative writing workshops—that at times individuals may undermine the group's effectiveness by pushing what Lefton refers to as "private agendas" (20). Private agendas in the creative writing workshop may involve intense competitiveness, defensiveness, and egotism, among other things. These attitudes are just as demoralizing and destructive in workshop as in the corporate team, and students in workshop are given the opportunity to learn how to deal with the intense pressures and discomforts that such personalities inflict. For example, one student may wrongly consider his own work above criticism, and yet very sharply, cynically, or superciliously criticize the work of everyone else. Such a student is usually ignored, rebuffed, ostracized or confronted by the students as they attempt to control the situation and regain a productive balance. Most often (especially with effective leadership) the offending student is coerced into appropriate behavior and the group regains its harmony and effectiveness. This kind of experience should be equally as valuable to a student majoring in business as to one majoring in humanities. The opportunity to learn to control conflict among diverse individuals with strongly held opinions is valuable as a human-relations skill which is applicable in countless managerial-level jobs. Lefton also says that groups may fail to synergize because they don't consider enough alternatives. Group members often don't take time to prepare and they don't deliberate long enough (20). The atmosphere and structure of the creative writing workshop, however, promote deliberation, and may serve as a model for this process. This is particularly true with workshop critique of student stories, plays, and parts of novels which are available in advance.

Robert D. Smither, in *The Psychology of Work and Human Performance*, calls the tendency to lock into a solution prematurely "groupthink," and he suggests the Delphi Method as a way of avoiding the psychological disadvantages of group decision making. Through this process group members write their ideas down independently before the group meets; these are photocopied and passed to the other members. Members who differ from the majority are then asked to support their opinions in writing. Their responses are distributed, and the whole group writes again, and so on until a consensus is reached (375–76). Although a consensus isn't necessary in creative writing workshops, instructors often rely on a similar method. Students may be asked not only to read materials in advance, but also to prepare a written critique which is shared in class. In this way, students are required to express their views, and do not succumb to the conforming influence of the group. Students who have taken creative writing workshop will be familiar with the dynamics of "groupthink," and they will have at least one technique to use against it.

In the early weeks of the workshop, students must quickly overcome lack of candor. A primary reason for lack of openness and honesty in workshop, as in the office team, is fear that someone's feelings will be hurt (Lefton 20). It may be true that people drawn to creative writing tend to be sensitive, but the workshop is not (or should not be) a place where such personalities are protected from the realities of day-to-day living. In workshop one learns to armor oneself against the pain of criticism. Students learn how to present negative criticism tactfully, but more importantly, they learn how not to let their feelings be hurt. One must recognize that negative criticism of one's work can be distinguished from an attack against one's self, and that negative criticism often is well-intended, generous, and helpful. Gradually one learns not to slam the doors of one's mind against negative criticisms, and one learns to use them constructively. The rapport which develops within the group enhances this process; all group members have taken considerable risk, and they are equally vulnerable. They begin to detach themselves from the works they have created, and are able to look at them objectively. They learn that even the products of their hearts must stand up against the rigors of the intellect. If students are able to develop these attitudes and skills with regard to their writing, they should be well prepared to assimilate useful criticisms of other, less personal ideas and products that they generate. In this way, the creative writing workshop develops maturity and resilience, and prepares students to meet the criticisms they will face in other parts of their lives.

Communication Skills

Many authors have written of the importance of communication skills in business, but most assume that what is needed to achieve proficiency in these skills is a course in professional or technical writing, in addition to the kind of training in grammar and composition which one receives in freshman composition. These courses are essential in learning to *write* more effectively, but creative writing as an elective could prove equally useful, particularly in learning oral communication skills. Garth A. Hanson, in an article in *CPA Journal*, quotes numerous accountants who attest to the importance of communication skills in the accounting profession, and he provides a list of *oral* communication tasks perceived by accountants to be essential to success (118–22). Although oral communication skills are dealt with secondarily in other kinds of writing classes, in none do they play as large a part as in creative writing workshop. Of the thirty-two skills listed by Hanson, at least fifteen may be addressed in the creative writing class, and by far the largest portion of class time is spent in oral communication. Several items on Hanson's list involve oral communication of deficiencies, bad news, and sensitive information, as well as asking and answering questions and giving instruction. These are daily fare in the workshop. Students regularly read and discuss their own work aloud, and as a result of their participation in creative writing classes, many begin giving formal readings of their work within the community, usually with other students and faculty members, and further develop their skills, presence, and poise.

Tom Stapleton, in the journal *Training*, notes the value of such experience, saying, "especially in today's service economy, employability is judged and advancement based largely on how well thoughts are articulated" (96). He laments the kind of rote learning which is emphasized in what he calls the grade school approach to English grammar, and says that "what's most helpful for most people to know about sentences is how to find or phrase the main idea and what its implications are" (96). An article in *Management Solutions* notes that jargon, pomposity and cliche often interfere with communication at the managerial level. Managers need to learn to "say exactly what they mean in language that can be readily understood" (McArthur and McArthur 20). The same problems are evident in the work of most fledgling poets; they rely on stock expressions, repeat canned sentiment, and often string together words which sound "poetic" without considering (or caring) what they mean. The ability to recognize "empty language" and to replace it with words which are vital, energetic, and meaningful is a skill which can be developed through conscientious analysis and critique of others' work, and through the craft of writing poetry, drama, and fiction. The heightened awareness of language achieved in the creative writing course can easily be applied to the writing of business letters and reports, and to the various kinds of oral communication required in business.

According to M.I.T. Professor Leo Marx, "In many institutions liberal arts subjects are treated as an unrelated, peripheral requirement with little or no relevance to the technical, vocational center of the students' education," and he says that "our real aim should be to achieve a much closer, more dynamic interaction between the two forms of knowledge throughout professional education" (10). Creative writing has been ignored, dismissed, and even ridiculed by specialists in business and technical studies who have not recognized its value in the development of essential and widely applicable utilitarian skills. This is not to say that every business major should take a course in creative writing, but those who express such an interest should not be dissuaded. Advisors to students in business and technical fields should be aware that creative writing is not a waste of time, nor is it totally unrelated to the work these students are preparing for. One

286

of the best writers I have taught was a "returning" student with many years' experience in business and an "A" average in marketing. Her advisor, frustrated by the student's determination to take creative writing, told her "If you really want to take that kind of course, you should change your major." This attitude widens the gulf between the liberal arts and the technical, scientific, and "practical" disciplines, and magnifies the largely illusory differences between us.

Students should not be forced to choose between the "practical" and the "creative" parts of themselves. We are not simply two types of people cut from two patterns, but one group of individuals in which the creative and the practical are variously interwoven, making us the wonderfully diverse creatures we are.

WORKS CITED

* Previously printed in: *Issues in Writing*, vol. 3:1 (Fall/Winter 1990).

Hanson, Garth A. "The Importance of Oral Communication in an Accounting Practice." *CPA Journal* 57 (Dec. 1987): 118–22.

Leavitt, Harold J., and Homa Bahrami. *Managerial Psychology: Managing Behavior in Organizations.* 5th ed. Chicago: University of Chicago Press, 1988.

Lefton, Robert E. "The Eight Barriers to Teamwork." *Personnel Journal* 67 (Jan. 1988): 18+.

Marx, Leo. "A Case for Interdisciplinary Thinking." *National Forum* 69.2 (Spring 1989): 8–11.

McArthur, Jerie, and D. W. McArthur. "The Pitfalls (and Pratfalls) of Corporate Communications." *Management Solutions* 32 (Dec. 1987): 15–20.

Phillips, Gerald M., and Eugene C. Erickson. *Interpersonal Dynamics in the Small Group.* New York: Random House, 1970.

Smither, Robert D. *The Psychology of Work and Human Performance.* New York: Harper and Row, 1988.

Stapleton, Tom. "Thin Gruel?" *Training* 25 (Feb. 1988): 96.

UPDATING MANAGEMENT THEORY TO MATCH THE NEW TECHNOLOGY: A PERSONALITY THEORY RELATING BUSINESS AND THE LIBERAL ARTS

Jerry Baxter and Nancy Kerber Baxter
Northwest Missouri State University

Stage 5: Protean Man and Empowerment

What managers call stage 5 leadership grows out of the sociomoral realm and is defined here as a process of enhancing feelings of self-efficacy among organizational members through the identification and removal of conditions that foster powerlessness by both formal organizational practices and informal techniques of providing efficacy information. The stage 5 leader is a proposed alternative to the "self" as integrated whole, a progression of change. "Protean Man" (Lifton 1970), like his mythological namesake, changes the shape of his self in response to a rapidly changing environment. "The Protean style of self-process, then, is characterized by an interminable series of experiments and explorations, some shallow, some profound, each of which can readily be abandoned in favor of still new, psychological quests" (44). A perpetual state of "identity diffusion" (Erikson 1959) becomes the ultimate life style.

There is an additional concept that is important for understanding Protean Man; one which modifies each of the stages of leadership which have been discussed. Self-evaluation, the degree of well-being or satisfaction experienced at each stage of development, will have important consequences for behavior (Coopersmith 1969). Festinger (1954) postulates a drive for self-evaluation, while Branden (1969) insists that there is actually a "need" for positive self-regard. Piaget (1967) contends that all the successes and failures of the subject's own activity become registered in a kind of permanent scale of values, successes elevating his pretensions and failures, lowering them with regard to his future actions. As a result, the person is gradually led to evaluate himself, a factor which may have great repercussions on his whole development. In particular, certain anxieties result from real, but more often imaginery, failures; White's (1959) "feelings of efficacy" and Erikson's (1963) feelings of autonomy link the interests or activity-related values to the feelings of self-evaluation, imaginary and otherwise.

Stage 5 leaders, then, view empowerment as a motivational construct instead of a relational construct. In the management and social influence literature, power is primarily a relational concept used to describe the perceived power or control that an individual actor or organizational subunit has over others (Bacharach & Lawler 1980; Crozier 1964; Dahl 1957; Hinings, Hickson, Pennings & Schneck 1974; Kotter 1979; Parsons & Smelser 1956; Pfeffer 1981). Taking its emphasis from social exchange theory (Blau 1964; Emerson 1962; Homans 1974; Thibaut & Kelley 1959), this literature interprets power as a function of the dependence and/or interdependence of actors. Power arises when an individual's or a subunit's performance is contingent not simply on their own behavior but on what others do and/or in how others respond (Thibaut & Kelley 1959). The relative power of one actor over another is a product of the net dependence of the one on the other (Pfeffer 1981). Therefore, if Actor A depends more on Actor B than B depends on A, then B has power over A.

When empowerment is used as a motivational construct, power and control are used as motivational and/or expectancy belief-states that are internal to individuals. People are assumed to have a need for power (McClelland 1975) where power connotes an internal urge to influence and control other people. A more inclusive disposition to cope with life events also has been proposed by several psychologists who have dealt with the issues of primary/secondary control (Rothbaum, Weisz, & Snyder 1982), internal/external locus of control (Rotter 1966), and learned helplessness (Abramson, Garber, & Seligman 1980). Individuals' power needs are met when they see that they have power or when they believe they can adequately cope with events, situations, and/or the people they confront, frustrated when they feel powerless or when they believe that they are unable to cope with the physical-social demands of environment.

As with Protean man, power in this motivational sense refers to an intrinsic need for self-determination (Deci 1975; Erikson 1963) or a belief in personal self-efficacy (Bandura 1986; White 1959). Because power has its base within an actor's motivational disposition, any strategy that strengthens the self-determination need or self-efficacy belief will make employees feel more powerful. Thus, in contrast to the definition of empowerment as delegation (of authority-resource sharing), enabling implies motivating through enhancing personal efficacy (McClelland 1975). Thus, empowerment is defined as a process of enhancing feelings of self-efficacy among organizational members, and best realized when related to expectancy (Lawler 1973). The question, then, is how to ensure that effort will result in a desired level of performance and how to ensure that performance will produce desired results.

Suggestions For the Process of Empowerment
Item: Develop Employee Self-Determination

Developing self-determination in employees is the key to transformational leadership—the key to empowerment; it is, in fact, an end value. Self-determination is also linked to other staples of transformational leadership and empowerment: high performance standards and high incentive values. That is, people want to achieve, take responsibility. Therefore, teach reward orientation. Workers want to be rewarded for their efforts with money, recognition, and respect. Thus, help employees to: analyze and learn from life experiences—both one's own and others'; match knowledge of one's own traits and abilities to information about job/career choices; identify and assess the relative importance of one's values, interests, strengths, and weaknesses; develop personal growth goals that are motivating; grow from criticism; persist with a project; generate trust and confidence in others; and accept the consequences of one's actions and build greater resources for self-direction.

Item: Provide the Opportunities for Employee Meaning

Events and situations do not exist until they are experienced and composed privately. Thus, the processes through which people construct meaning out of their experiences should be made accessible to them. Chiefly, these can be the processes of innovation. Creative people are capable of co-leadership. Therefore, help people to: highlight rather than deny novelty; identify quickly and precisely the critical issues when making a decision or solving a problem; identify reasonable criteria for assessing the appropriateness or value of an action by forming problem categories to see how individual problems interrelate; analyze problem links from several perspectives; create a general principle that explains problem patterns; use universal premises to integrate a large number of specific ideas and bits of data from diverse areas of knowledge; use the integration thus achieved to link problem analysis and problem solving reiteratively to create order and harmony in routine thought processes and to assimilate new information for further problem solving; extrapolate essential information and insights from the new material for intuitive thought processes to enhance innovative responsiveness; and create novel insights into innovative responses to enhance the attribute of openness being receptive to many points of view and to the processes of meaning.

Item: Use Goals to Develop Communication Networks

Goals can become the sequential regularities or patterns that permit people to construct meaning and progress from simple to more complex (encompassing) modes of understanding. Communication networks can be the vehicles for new organizing processes to enhance evolving visions of personal and interpersonal worlds. Therefore, help people to: identify their own values; assess their own values in relation to the values held by other people and the organization; analyze a problem's levels of meaning from the personal to the universal; analyze a problem that prevents the operation of an ideal or growth toward it; assess a course

290

of action in terms of its long-range effects on the general human welfare and to make decisions that will maximize both individual and collective good; express one's feelings appropriately and understand the feelings of others; be willing to take the risks of co-leadership and to participate in the setting of job goals or objectives; become responsible for the cycle of activities required to complete the product or service or the rate, quantity and quality of output; and for the interdependence of the person or group on others for completion of a cycle of activities; and become autonomous through self-regulation of work content and structure within the job, self-evaluation of performance, and self-adjustment in response to work system variability.

Concluding Remarks

"Clusters" of workers will be at the core of tomorrow's organizations. Workers will, therefore, need to be empowered so that they are autonomous, responsible, and adaptive; they will need to be co-leaders who can use technology as a lever against the increased complexity and pace of change in their business environments. As top management seizes on its ability to monitor without restricting freedom, employees will have more control over their own work, and there will be fewer rigid policies from a less visible headquarters. Management will be a part-time job as group members share responsibility and rotate leadership while engaging in a series of projects. When projects are completed and new "clusters" are created, work will remain diverse and challenging. Future work, then, calls for the transformational leadership of empowerment. With each passing year our machines, a major product of our culture, assume a greater role in culture's maintenance and continued growth. Part biology, part culture, individuals must, then, develop new traits of mind or march out of step with intelligent machinery. These mind-children must be matched by a culture of self-improvement that promotes adaptive responses to a variable world. As the authoritarian pyramid of industrialism collapses into the organizational pancakes and clusters of the information era, a management theory of transformational leadership that sustains empowerment will become essential to survival.

7

CONTENTS OF THE CORE

NON-DISCRIMINATORY DISCRIMINATION: AN EDUCATIONAL CHALLENGE IN THE POSTMODERN WORLD

Todd Flanders
Northeast Missouri State University

I will never forget the first day of my sophomore class on Plato's *Republic*. I put my first notes down in red for emphasis. "We need not criticism of the past," said the teacher, "but criticism of ourselves. The things which one holds most dearly he should question the most." Could it, I wondered, really be possible to stand at a critical distance from our selves, our episteme, our world view, our culture, our historical moment? The idea ran contrary to everything I had learned in humanities and social science courses my freshman year. And my freshman courses had been "liberating" in what an eighteen-year-old considers the best ways. I had developed what Saul Bellow has called "easy virtue," an attitude that allowed me to do what I pleased with good conscience and at the same time remain uncritical of other lifestyles. God is dead in academe, I found, and all thoughts and beliefs are prejudices, none objectively superior to others. This seemed to me to be the fulfillment of egalitarian democracy, the one value, paradoxically, that had emerged from my freshman courses as a given. Was not what my Plato teacher asked antithetical to the spirit of democratic egalitarianism as I had come to conceive it? After all, criticism of the patriarchal, European past is what had led my freshman profs if not to the truth then at least to a privileged perspective on history. Liberty and equality are our cultural values, I learned from them, meaningful even though eighteenth-century theorists were mistaken when they thought those values to be part of some natural and objective reality. Could it be that, in asking me to question the foundation of my cultural values, my Plato teacher was being, perhaps, un-American?

My sophomoric suspicion of the Plato teacher is representative of the suspicion with which many American college students would greet an argument that knowledge about values might be possible. Since knowledge about values is seen by them to be impossible, tolerance of alternative ways of thinking and living becomes, *de facto*, the most needful and the one rational value. Openness thus understood is what many thoughtful, democratic-minded students perceive to be the goal of liberal education. Courses of gender, race, and non-Western studies are seen by these students best to inculcate this. In a sense, such courses seem to call into question those things that we in the West hold dearest, to put our prejudices to the test. But they do not really do this inasmuch as students are not led to think that criteria exist for *choosing* among alternative value systems. The purpose of such courses is not to make students consider seriously, for instance, advocating the Indian caste system as an alternative social arrangement. The purpose is simply to teach students that such social arrangements exist and that one must appreciate them lest he be seen as ethnocentric. But a university in a pluralistic society need not demand of students an equal estimation of all pursuits and ways of living. Active toleration of numerous "lifestyles" does not mandate theoretical indiscriminateness. Indeed Jefferson supposed that natural elites would not only arise but be provided for in the new republic. A pluralistic society by definition provides room for elites. Although many students would meet with disbelief a teacher's claim that it could be possible rationally to discriminate among better and worse ways of living, in a democratic republic this is precisely what teachers should hope to be able to claim.

(As teachers, we may of course encounter students who believe that they possess knowledge of the absolute and eternal truth. Such students also tend to reject reason as a means for discerning values. Many believe strongly that all things most worth knowing are revealed and that this knowledge comes through faith alone. These students can be more closed to liberal learning than the students I am considering, and raise different questions about the goals of core curricula than the ones I address here.)

The Declaration of Independence, the quintessential exposition of American liberty and equality, presents itself as articulating the self-evident truth about political things. Human equality and unalienable rights are put forth as natural; indeed life, liberty, and the pursuit of happiness can be seen as unalienable only if they are natural. If natural right is rejected, as it is by most today, then positive right is all there is. And positive right is, we know, historically and culturally determined, relative to accidents of time and place. Gender, race, and non-Western studies generally convey only this view, grounded as they tend to be on the assumption that all thought is subordinate to accidental phenomena: one's sex, race, culture, and historical period. Implicit in this assumption is that human beings cannot see beyond horizons determined at birth, that transhistorical, transcultural, and even transsexual discourse is impossible. It is altogether something different to credit liberty and equality to accident than to consider them intrinsic to human nature.

An education for democracy calls for something other than a concentration on issues of gender, race, ethnicity, and class. Every side of the current debate over curricular reform agrees that development of "critical thinking skills" must be a primary educational goal. Yet those on the side that advances the notion that the history of Western culture is a chronicle of racism, sexism, and elitism deprive students of the opportunity to take seriously so-called "classic" texts—texts long credited for the precision with which they define and explore questions of perennial concern. Believing that the teaching of literature means necessarily the espousing of ideology, they would juxtapose literatures promoting ideologies they find more agreeable with classic texts, which they claim have, as customarily interpreted, always and insidiously perpetuated the political and cultural hegemony of white, male elites. But what these teachers see as a remedy against prejudice serves instead to narrow students' intellectual horizons: students are to think critically provided their thoughts prove uncritical of popular revisionist trends.

But this is not critical thinking properly understood, since the students believe themselves unable to achieve a critical distance from their own ideologies. In this scheme, rational distinctions cannot be made among competing value claims; reason can merely "clarify" values within one's ideology. Critical thinking properly understood is *discriminating* thinking, the ability to choose objectively among competing value claims. The word discrimination has fallen into disfavor for the sound reason that in our nation's history many have experienced social and political discrimination on the bases of race and sex. Yet the word, in its salutary sense, must be restored. United States citizens must be able and willing to discriminate between better and worse governments, better and worse economic systems, better and worse cultural practices, etc. Martin Luther King, Jr., knew as much, who did not consider freedom a "value" and who insisted and depended on the verity of American principles.

King's understanding, viewed from popular postmodernist perspectives must be deemed a prejudice like any other. I am reminded of a paper delivered by a Foucaultian from my school at a conference of the Society of Women in Philosophy. In elaborating the significance of Foucault's thought to the feminist cause, she repeated the refrain, "feminism is in danger here today." To which my response is, then why not seek a philosophical rejection of Foucault and his kin rather than embrace and rely on them as champions of the Left? Leftist causes, whether democratic, socialist, communist, or other, have philosophical origins suggesting that the means and ends of social and political life are rationally determinable. Postmodernism holds that truths and even modes of thinking are wedded to history and culture, that they are contingent upon random historical and cultural occurrences, and are thus contingent themselves. The truths of postmodernism are that there are no truths and that reason as such does not exist. Leftist causes are undermined rather than promoted by the irrationalism at the root and in all the branches of postmodernism. Yet paradoxically (as Allan Bloom argues in his book's best chapter, "The Nietzscheanization of the Left or Vice Versa") postmoderns after Heidegger deliberately set out to advance various Leftist agendas. Since postmoderns deny that any philosophy can be disinterested,

I venture that Foucault and Derrida have attained their present stature largely due to their usefulness to the Left. And their usefulness to it in literary criticism, historical method, law, and other fields has proved dazzling.

The post-Heideggerians serve the Left not because the Left can be deemed good. The concept *good* suggests a criterion, the avoidance of which is an acid test for postmoderns. They serve the Left because rival power discourses have been randomly configured so that Leftist ideologies currently prevail. Postmodernism today does not actively support political fascism largely because Germany lost the Second World War. Heidegger himself, whose membership in and commitment to the Nazi party is no longer disputed,[1] proved that postmodernism could as easily serve Nazism as it could a liberal ideology. The point is this: in the absence of *any* standard, the ideology one elects to affirm is arbitrary. In this light, I find it amusing that many postmoderns rush to defend Heidegger's political behavior during the early thirties. They argue that Heidegger's thought should be considered distinct from his politics. This proves particularly difficult when, for example, in the Rectoral Address Heidegger's philosophy and Nazi politics are inextricable. If postmodern philosophy is apolitical, as postmoderns must argue if defending Heidegger, then it makes little sense that the coterie following Derrida, Foucault, et al, are almost invariably Leftists. If, on the other hand, the philosophy is political, as they usually insist all philosophy is, then Heidegger's Nazism and Nietzsche's damaging attack on liberalism need to be reconsidered.

Postmodernism appears on the surface in harmony with liberal values. As various traditions are deconstructed, we find ourselves increasingly liberated from traditional demands. As various claims to political power are shown to be illusory, we can seek empowerment against existing power structures. So long as life requires commitment to values, why should not those values be of our own creation?

Here I repeat the refrain of my Foucaultian colleague: "feminism is in danger here today." Nietzsche's analysis of values creation was in the service of overcoming liberalism, which he saw as dehumanizing. In his hands, irrationalism was a tool for destroying rationalist, egalitarian ideologies. He knew that irrationalism does not foster decency as understood by liberals. A world in which value systems are seen to be fictional and must be created, a world in which commitment to these fictions is arbitrary, a world in which the fictions are necessarily enforced by the willful is not the world of civil rights, gay rights, feminism, free elections, the Communist Manifesto, or the Declaration of Independence. The liberalesque rhetoric of contemporary postmoderns and liberalism are two very different things.

There will be much discussion at this conference about what constitutes a proper college core curriculum in a democracy. Whatever the result of the inquiry, we may assume that a curriculum for democracy should be distinguishable from a curriculum for tyranny. We should, then, take into account essential differences between democracy and tyranny. Hitler was an elected and popular leader, and the Soviet Union experiences a much better voter turnout with its single-candidate elections than does the United States with its two-party system. So, if democracy is worthy of defense, there must exist criteria for democracy that transcend popularity and voter turnout. To this end one should posit good government as a value superior to democracy, for only if democracy proves good would education for democracy be worthwhile.

The United States Constitution establishes a government designed to protect the natural, unalienable rights of human beings. The securing of these rights is the end to which our democratic Constitutional system is the means. In this case the end is deemed superior to the means. The Founders established an independent, non-democratic judiciary because they determined that the public interest, and particularly minority interests, would be better served by this arrangement. In this instance also democracy is of secondary importance. The Founders believed qualified democracy to be superior to the alternatives precisely because human beings are rational and can be expected to participate rationally in the political order.

Time does not allow for elaboration here even of an outline of the Founders' approach to issues of democracy and good government. But they believed strongly that there exist objective criteria for distinguishing good government from bad. Could it not be said that tyranny, slavery, and religious persecution are morbid states of the body politic, much as cancer is a morbid state of the body? Could one not deem, as Harry Jaffa has argued, a polity objectively healthy is one that protects personal liberties to a high degree, that is governed by a constitutional majority peacefully chosen in free elections, where property is secure, where the arts and sciences are cultivated, where there is a steady improvement in public health, and where there is an absence of religious persecution?[2] Could it not be said that these are manifestly rational criteria for preferring one political community to another?

A rationality that enables people to call such a political community good is, I contend, vastly preferable to an irrationality that does not. But saying that something is preferable is different from proving that it is true. Here is where students' inclinations toward discriminating thinking, their propensity to believe that certain things are good at least for themselves, should meet philosophy, history, literature, art, and music. A college education should, to use a Socratic formula, encourage students to begin to philosophize, to ascend from their opinions and prejudices toward knowledge. Students should not be indoctrinated with natural rights theory any more than they should be indoctrinated with anything else. Nor should their theoretical inquiries result in dogmatism of any kind. Yet students cannot be expected to make educated choices between conflicting world views, or between conflicting major programs for that matter, unless they have an educational foundation to make such choices possible. The ability to make educated choices requires knowledge of alternatives of which students are all-too-often ignorant, immersed as they are in present-day American popular culture. For this reason students would benefit most from spending time with works that may initially seem alien to them; works long thought to be significant; works that have endured through the long referendum of history; works that, although they will not answer students' questions definitively, will address and clarify them; works that, as Sidney Hook wrote just prior to his death, "help us best understand our contemporary culture, related as it is in thousands of ways to the cultural achievements of the past."[3] Engaged in such study, students will not become dupes of an antiquated white, male, aristocratic ideology. They will not find in Thomas Paine, Marx, or Dickens apologies for the behavior of ruling classes. They will not find in Jane Austen or Tolstoy an impetus for voting Republican. They would find in such writers, however, the clearest articulations of enormously diverse ideas and sentiments. Reading older writers seriously, trying to understand the arguments as the authors understood them, can free students of the interpretive limitations placed on them by the narrowness of their own experiences.

The postmodern, "new historicist" approach to reading literature provides no remedy for students' narrowness of experience, even if the greatest works are studied. The new historicist Gary Taylor, toward the end of his new book, *Reinventing Shakespeare*, writes, "I have tried to encourage you throughout the foregoing narrative not to trust me."[4] And so I do not; he convinces me completely. Why trust a critic who does not even believe his own criticism? So convinced that an authorial voice in literature is tantamount to tyranny in politics, new historicists insist on the radical contingency of meaning. Under the tutelage of such people, students read literature as though interpretation is a competitive sport, trying to reconfigure interpretations in ever more spectacular ways. In the process, both the texts studied and the students' attempt at interpretation are cheapened. Not teacher, not student, not author can pretend to know anything about a text, and certainly not about any reality that the text might attempt to point toward.

Professor Pickens has spoken, and others will speak, in defense of the Western tradition, so I will not elaborate an argument here.[5] I will suggest, however, that labeling the history of Western thought a "tradition" is, at the very least, imprecise. To claim that Machiavelli writes in the tradition of Aristotle or that Marx writes in the tradition of Augustine is absurd unless one means simply that each attempts to develop coherent arguments. Yet it would be accurate to say that the literary tradition of liberal politics is Western. That most works in this tradition are written by white males may well be due to past folly; but to insist that because of this they are inherently phallo- or ethnocentric is absurd. The rights elaborated in the Declaration of Independence are defended in this tradition, rights that are now, rightly, seen in the United States to belong to all regardless of race or sex. The Declaration of Independence has been invoked in numerous democratic movements, suggesting the broad application of its teachings across cultures. This is not to say that societies predicated on liberal theory have not witnessed grave abuses by the powerful; clearly they have. But dreams of liberty and equality are more likely by far to be realized in these societies than in others.

Liberalism must no longer be seen as the "L word." Students should be led to reflect upon the sobering demands of self-government, always realizing that liberal democracy has certain theoretical underpinnings. They should study seriously alternatives to liberal democracy, not specifically to weaken or strengthen their attachments to it, but to evaluate different theories in the context of their practice. Foremost, students should not take their freedoms for granted: June of 1989 in Beijing stands as a moving testimony to life without freedoms. American students universally condemned the Beijing massacre as a profound offense against human rights. Since they believe so strongly in the practical defense of human rights, they should be offered the intellectual tools to defend those rights in theory.

NOTES

1. The extent of Heidegger's Nazi involvement is persuasively documented by Victor Farias in *Heidegger and Nazism*, a 1989 English translation which has been published by Temple University Press.

2. Jaffa, Harry V. *What is Political Science?* Claremont: The Salvatori Center for the Study of Freedom, 1988, 18–19.

3. Hook, Sidney. "Civilization and its Malcontents." *National Review*, October 13, 1989, 33.

4. Taylor, Gary. *Reinventing Shakespeare: A Cultural History from the Restoration to the Present*, as quoted by David Norbrook in *The New Republic*, October 16, 1989, 50.

5. See Donald Pickens, "Present at the Creation." *The Core and the Canon: A National Debate*, Denton: University of North Texa Press, 1993, Chapter 7, essay #1, 50.

CORE REQUIREMENTS IN THE PROFESSIONAL SCHOOLS: A MODEL FOR DETERMINING CORE CURRICULUM

John P. Eddy
University of North Texas

Pat H. Simpson
Temple Junior College

This article presents a research model for determining curricula in higher education. Teachers need to include the knowledge and skills students have already acquired as they help students progress from one course to the next (Resnick and Resnick 1983; The Carnegie Foundation for the Advancement of Teaching 1987). Proper sequencing of materials is needed in order to address basic problems in curriculum today (Menacker 1975). The model of research proposed here can help to determine which specific knowledge and skills may be sequenced in which specific way. Although the discipline addressed here is microbiology, the model should work for any discipline.

A survey questionnaire using Likert-type scaling with five categories indicating different depths of coverage for topics in microbiology was developed, and instructors were asked to indicate whether they believed that more or less coverage was desirable. Two groups of teachers were surveyed. One consisted of junior/community college teachers. The second consisted of senior college teachers who teach upper level courses requiring beginning microbiology as a prerequisite. Our purpose was to determine how nearly the expectations in introductory courses coincided with those of teachers in more advanced courses. The results of this study were used to make a number of curricular determinations, including the identification of a large number of *common elements* and *core elements*. We define core elements as those curricular items assigned at least moderate coverage by 50 percent or more of the senior college teachers who require beginning microbiology as a prerequisite to some course they teach. We define *core elements* as those curricular items assigned at least moderate coverage by 50 percent or more of *both* populations.

SPECIFIC RESULTS OF THE MODEL

This study helped us to identify *what* knowledge and skills are currently being taught in junior/community colleges in Texas. A questionnaire was sent to the teachers of such courses, and also to senior college teachers who teach courses which *require* beginning microbiology as a prerequisite. The survey of this latter group was to determine what preparation is needed for students progressing to upper level microbiology. Information gathered from the two groups was then compared to determine if differences exist in the depth of coverage assigned by the two groups of teachers.

The survey consisted of 188 items distributed in 14 topics. It was designed with Likert-type scaling, with responses in five categories based upon the varying depths of coverage which the teachers believed appropriate for each item. A test-retest was run to determine the reliability of test items. Chi square was calculated to compare first responses to second responses. This analysis revealed 179 reliable test items on the questionnaire. Chi square was also calculated to determine the homogeneity of responses of the two populations of teachers. Of the 79 items where differences occurred, senior college teachers believed that more depth of coverage should be assigned to 58 of the items. Most items in which senior college teachers indicated more depth was needed were in five topic areas: history of microbiology, chemistry, microbial genetics, microbial activities in nature, and laboratory activities.

Moderate coverage (or more) was assigned to 142 items by 50 percent (or more) of the senior college teachers. These items are the *common elements*. These *common elements* need to be taught in beginning microbiology so that students who progress to upper level microbiology courses will possess the knowledge and skills necessary to the mastery of more complex information. Moderate coverage (or more) was assigned to 94 items by 50 percent (or more) by *both* senior and junior/community college teachers. These items are *core elements*.

Results of such studies can be used for many things. When determining the curriculum for a particular course, teachers can use the results of such a study to know what other teachers of the same course are teaching. The model can help teachers identify what specific skills will be required at the next level of progress. This model can also be used in producing more precisely sequenced textbooks which meet teachers' real expectations.

DESCRIPTION OF RESULTS

The questionnaire was constructed from numerous sources including textbooks, publishers' surveys, course syllabi, and personal knowledge. It was validated by a panel of microbiologists, and reliability of the test items was determined by the test-retest method. Twenty-three teachers out of 42 responded to both the test and retest surveys. Chi square was used to compare first responses with second responses. The hypothesis tested was that there was no difference between first and second responses. A large chi square indicates a large degree of agreement between first and second responses. The larger the chi square is for an item, the smaller the item's critical value. Items with small critical value ($p <$ 0.0500) indicate a low probability of differences between first and second responses on that item. Nine items of the 188 had a low critical value ($p < 0.0500$), indicating that these items were probably not reliable.

The survey questionnaire was sent to microbiology teachers during the spring of 1989. Before the end of the semester, a total of 80 teachers out of 116, or 69 percent, responded—30 out of 42 or 71 percent of the junior/ community college teachers and 50 out of 74, or 68 percent of the senior college teachers. Percentage frequencies of responses to each survey item were determined for the two populations of teachers. Chi square was used to determine the homogeneity of proportions between the two populations for each item. The hypothesis tested was that the two populations of teachers assigned different depths of coverage to each item. The homogeneity of responses between the two populations was indicated by a small chi square and a large critical value ($p > 0.0500$). Items with a small critical value ($p < 0.0500$) indicate a difference in depth of coverage between the two groups of teachers.

DISCUSSION OF FINDINGS

Nine of the 188 items were unreliable. Junior/community college teachers and senior college teachers agreed on the appropriate depth of coverage for only 100 items of the remaining 179, giving homogeneity of proportions on 56 percent of the reliable items. The two populations of teachers disagreed on depth of coverage on 79 items, or on 44 percent of the surveyed items. Of the 79 items where differences occurred, senior college teachers thought more depth of coverage should be given to 58, leaving 21 items in which junior/community college teachers indicated that deeper coverage was needed. Most items in which senior college teachers wanted more depth fell into five of the fourteen topic areas: history of microbiology, chemistry, microbial genetics, microbial activities in nature, and laboratory activities.

Some differences between what junior/community college teachers stress in beginning courses and what senior college teachers *think* should be stressed were expected. However, differences on 44 percent of the items appear to be significant. A number of differences in coverage were expected since junior/community colleges teach a unique population of students. In many cases, microbiology students taught by the junior/community college never plan to attend a senior college and will not need certain information and skills required in higher level courses in microbiology. Many such students are allied health majors, and perhaps the most urgent training for these vocationally oriented students is in the areas of health and disease.

Prerequisites are required for many of the microbiology courses taught in junior/community colleges. Many of the differences in depth of coverage might be due to the junior/community college teacher's recognizing that certain knowledge and skills are taught *before* students take beginning microbiology. This could be true especially in chemistry. Even acknowledging these exceptions, however, we still note large differences in the expectations of the two populations.

One of the goals of this study was to identify some common elements in the different topic areas of beginning microbiology. *Common elements* are particular knowledge and skills which students need to be taught in beginning microbiology if they are to continue into upper level microbiology. These *common elements* are identified in this study as having been assigned at least moderate coverage by 50 percent or more of the senior college teachers who responded to the survey questionnaire. Of the 179 reliable items on this survey, 142 *common elements* were agreed to by senior college professors.

MAJOR FINDINGS

1. Of the 179 reliable items on the survey questionnaire, 142 can be identified as *common elements.*

2. Of the 179 reliable items, junior/community college and senior college teachers disagreed on the appropriate depth of coverage on 79 items.

3. Senior college teachers assigned more depth of coverage to 58 of the 79 items than their counterparts.

4. Most of the 58 items which were assigned more depth of coverage by senior college teachers are found in five topic areas: history of microbiology, chemistry, microbial genetics, microbial activities in nature, and laboratory activities.

5. Most of the 21 items that were assigned more depth of coverage by junior/community college teachers are in areas related to disease, as evidenced by the depth of coverage assigned to items in the topic "microbial diseases according to microbial groups."

CONCLUSIONS

1. Junior/community college teachers teach beginning microbiology in a significantly different way than senior college teachers think they should.

2. Junior/community college teachers emphasize knowledge and skills concerned with disease and the treatment of disease.

3. Senior college teachers prefer students to be taught knowledge and skills which will enable students to understand and use modern research techniques.

IMPLICATIONS AND RECOMMENDATIONS

It is evident from this study that differences exist in the depth of study to which numerous curricular items in beginning microbiology are being assigned by junior/community college teachers on the one hand, and senior college teachers on the other. One might question whether the same is true for virtually any other course taught in junior/community colleges. Beginning microbiology is possibly a special case, since so many vocation al students who do not plan to pursue further educational goals take this course. However, studies similar to this one need to be undertaken if we are to understand the problems of articulation in core courses.

Many of the junior/community college teachers who responded to this survey commented that the knowledge and skills they teach are dictated by the needs of their particular students. They claimed that most, if not all, of their students are allied health majors, thus justifying a curriculum with an emphasis on health and disease. Most of these students will take no further courses in microbiology. Instead, they will use their training to care for the sick and aged. Unless a senior college has courses designed for the same type of student, junior/community college teachers may well be doing a better job serving these students.

Since senior college teachers cover certain items in more depth, junior/community college students who do transfer to senior colleges may lack knowledge and skills expected of them by senior college teachers. Junior/community college teachers should not only provide the proper training for students who are allied health majors, but they should also provide the proper training for students who might continue to upper level microbiology. The junior/community college teachers can now examine a large number of curricular items (142 *common elements*) that senior colleges expect students to have been taught in beginning microbiology. They can now know possible deficiencies their students may suffer when they transfer to senior colleges. Using this research, junior/community college teachers can examine the 58 items assigned in greater depth by senior college teachers and make needed curricular changes. Junior/community college teachers can also examine the 21 items in which senior college teachers gave less depth of coverage. This study provides excellent material that microbiologists can use to determine what other teachers think should be taught in beginning microbiology.

The information gathered in this study could be used to write a textbook and a laboratory manual which would better serve the needs of teachers of beginning microbiology. National and international surveys need to be undertaken using similar instruments for other academic fields. The results could again be used to improve curriculum as well as improving textbooks and laboratory manuals throughout higher education.

Works Cited

For copies of the survey instrument, a relevant bibliography, or more information about the research method described, please contact the authors.

The Carnegie Foundation for the Advancement of Teaching. 1987. *College: the undergraduate experience in America.* New York: Harper and Row.

Menacker, J. 1975. *From School to college: articulation and transfer.* Washington, D.C.: American Council on Education.

Resnick, D. P. and L. B. Resnick. 1983. Improving educational standards in American schools. *Phi Delta Kappan*, 65 (3), 178–80.

THE HUMANITIES AT THE CORE: A MODEST PROPOSAL FOR GETTING OVER THE SIXTIES

Carl Raschke

University of Denver

I

Henry Ford said that "history is bunk." Hegel said that it is the autobiography of the World Spirit. His contemporary Wilhelm Dilthey said that history only becomes intelligible when it is deciphered within the forms of historical knowledge, which he called the "human sciences" and which today we might refer to as the humanities. Neither history nor the humanities are intelligible apart from the dislocations and transitions of the very times that mold them. The humanities, like higher education itself, are in a state of upheaval and transition. It is no mere happenstance of history that, for the first time in American history, education has become a premier issue in presidential campaigns. This development may not be merely an event. It is possibly more than an episode. It may actually be a trend. If we may quote the great nineteenth century novelist Victor Hugo: "Nothing else in the world . . . not all the armies . . . is so powerful as an idea whose time has come."

Is it possible that education generally, and the humanities in particular, represents an idea whose time has come? The controversy over the quality, goals, and maintenance of education, in actuality, mirrors the issue of whether a nation, and a culture, will set its mainmast toward the sunglow of glory, or the lowering hurricane of the cloud of contention. The issue itself is neither peripheral, incidental, nor trivial. It is an issue of endurance. There is something more than a pomp-and-circumstance sort of cliche in H. G. Wells' dictum that "human history becomes more and more a race between education and catastrophe." One should not, either out of piety, duty, or even necessity, equate the humanities with the study of history per se, but it is possible to draw some kind of logical diagram where the pedagogical purposes of "humanistic learning" are crosshatched with the broad domain of historical knowledge—a knowledge that affords us cognitive and moral maps, that rescues us from the burdens of impulsive politics, particularly in a nuclear age, a knowledge that furnishes a well-distilled serum to immunize against the poisons of our own confabulated innocence. We do not or should not, contrary to the fetishistic scribblings that decorate our disciplinary and subdisciplinary grimoires, study art merely for art's sake, philosophy perhaps for its own sake, or English literature in order to render adoration somehow before the blessed virginity of the text. We have in the cloisters of our brains, darkly resident while we recite our guild initiation rituals about the deepmost designs of the discipline, some scraggly notion concerning the integrity and unity of knowledge, which can only be comprehended while it manifests as the immanent opulence of historical knowledge.

The idea of the humanities as the self-revelation of culture and as the *coherence of historical knowledge*, with its peculiar social ramifications or larger existential significance, is not really a new idea. It is an old idea that simply refuses to slink away. If we may invoke the idiom of earlier scholarly generations, it is possible to call it a "universal idea," an abiding notion, an enduring concept, or— God forbid—a transcendental sort of truth. European civilization, from which our own intellectual rudiments are hammered and annealed, has not been suspicious of the priorities assigned to historical knowledge in the manner American culture has. The irony is that the American experience, which valorized and put almost a supernatural construction on the reality of historical change, has not been able yet to find a system of cultural categories for transposing historical experience into historical knowledge. The fault may lie in what the theological and political thinker Reinhold Niebuhr once aptly dubbed the "irony of American history." We have erected artificial barriers and made overly factitious distinctions between theory and practice, research and instruction, public obligation and private morality. Perhaps that is why, as Nietzsche would put it, "we scholars" are cautious, even to the brink of paranoia sometimes, about proposals concerning "core curricula," even while such a pedagogy represents an endeavor to enumerate a usable fund of historical knowledge.

It is no accident that the "search for a core" has been imparted the academic cry of "back to the classroom." The classroom may be envisaged, more than metaphorically, as a simulacrum of the *real* American experience. America itself has been a living classroom where the untutored aspirations of a variegated humankind have been allowed to proliferate and seed themselves, where both esoteric and exoteric discourse has mirrored the giddy self-awareness of social, political, and institutional pluralism. The "melting pot" has always been something more than a stew of immigrants. It has been an allusion to the concrete synthesis of values, symbolic structures, and the most fundamental sorts of belief. The synthesis has not proceeded out of historical necessity, but out of a transcendental charter so-named on American currency itself—the *novus ordo seclorum*. Truly, America is the only nation in the world history that was ever built for the long-term and with visible evidence of success upon an *idea*. The core classroom, therefore, may serve in its own right as a veritable Ellis Island for the processing and certification of the huddled mass of historical knowledge. The classroom is where the core is made, because it is where the dictata of the mandarinate are compelled to yield before the unscrupulous curiosity of those bent on little more than an education. The classroom becomes a kind of *primal scene*, as the psychoanalysts might say, where many of us—tutored and untutored, brahmins and dilettantes, literate and hardscrabble—have been repeatedly forced, sometimes even against our will, to commit *unspeakable acts of articulation.*

The classroom, and by extension the core, betokens a final loss of second innocence, an innocence that many of us are not prepared to lose with dignity. The question of the future of the humanities is a question of whether we will somehow stumble back into the classroom from our self-assigned exile in the confabulated world of what we often assume to be heaven-derived disciplinary mandates and begin to rub elbows with another form of huddled mass that defined the educational mission of higher education within American democracy—something known as "the public."

The fundamental thematic of the humanities is the problem of *representation.* As the philosopher of culture Michel Foucault has shown in certain of his earlier works such as *Order and History* and *The Archaeology of Knowledge*, much of the developmental logic of modern Western thought is the controversy over the measure, reach, and modality of the structures of representation. I am using the term "representation" here in a somewhat technical, semiotic sense—that is, the manner in which language and the various non-discursive instruments of communication function to create coherence within a complex body of individual units of expression. It states not only politically, but metaphysically, the problem of representation does not arise within a culture that devalues non-conformity and singularity. The problem of representation can only manifest when the cultural impulse toward maximum diversity flounders in the teeth of an intransigent anxiety toward the unification of activity and knowledge.

II

I raise the issue of representation because in many respects it has become the prepossessing concern of the humanities since the 1960s. The well-publicized and usually cantankerous debates in the humanities that embellish the pages of the *Chronicle of Higher Education* are extensions of the politicized agendas that dominated scholarly forums in that tempestuous decade, and continue to dominate today. In the wake of the Dan Quayle controversy, *Newsweek* magazine devised a cover story in which it asked in bold lettering: "Will we ever get over the Sixties?" So much of the altercation over the character and mission of the humanities rests on certain subtexts which were created during that era. Those subtexts find their way into a wide variety of specific "texts" of curriculum, such as the preservation of the "canon" vs. what might be called the "Stanford" position

310

concerning the "alterity of unspoken voices." These fracases often sort out in terms of the rhetoric of humanists themselves. Consider what is often identified as the problem of "inclusion." At first the problem had to do chiefly with the inclusion of ethnic studies and attention to the role of women. Women's studies, as a domain of discourse if not a disciplinary specialty, seems to have been generally accepted in the academy. All along the argument over inclusion has been for the most part the same general argument which has been going on in America since its founding and which attained privileged status during the Civil Rights Movement of the sixties. Later the argument became the leitmotif of the radical critique of that decade. The drive for economic inclusivity, for instance, was the nub of Johnson's Great Society program. Even the establishment of the National Endowment for the Humanities, which has been one the great financial patrons of core curriculum development, was premised directly on the value of inclusion. The Johnson administration argued that the humanities should have their own funding agency, comparable to the sciences, mental health, social services, and so forth.

Today the argument over inclusion has wandered from the political arena as a pragmatic push toward fulfillment of the American pluralist passion and fortified itself as a kind of autonomous ideology used, like the deconstructionist attack on the rule of representation in literary theory, to challenge all traditional claims to cultural pre-eminence and sovereignty. The force of such an ideology directly affects the core. What is asserted at Stanford is what was asserted by graduate students at Harvard in 1969—that the "unspoken voices," who were not literate, not male, not European, not "ruling class," had not been represented in the formation of the canon, and therefore should be given equal play with Shakespeare, Cervantes, Aquinas, Keats, and so forth. Such a statement of fact is trivially true, but to assert it as a baseline principle in the orchestration of core humanities curriculum is not as immaterial as it may appear to the partisans of progress. The same sort of problem was not solved during the educational jousts of the late sixties, and it will probably not be settled in the current climate because the principle, which rests on the theory of ideology, is a tenet of Marxist sociology as contrasted with the classical history of ideas model that has overshadowed for centuries the criteriology of the curriculum. The sociological method of interpretation, on which the damnation of the canon is based, posits that all ideas amount to "ideology," which is to say that they are to be examined as nought but as forms of cryptography or camouflage to be "read" entirely in a different way—often the utopian, political predilections of the instructor. Interestingly, however, the view that there is a canon to be criticized and subverted represents in some odd ways an *ideological* commitment. It has only happened in the last few decades, when the broader construct of Western civilization itself came under attack by virtue of

311

the sixties conceit that Western culture was inherently hegemonous, domineering, exclusivistic, and imperialistic, that the suggestion there was such a thing as a "canon" in history, literature, philosophy, art, and so forth became fashionable. The rhetoric of canonization mirrors the fashionable political assumption, which requires its own subtle syntax of "conspiratorial" aims, that identifiable social or institutional interests have somehow consciously collaborated to authorize particular texts and render anathema the more discomforting ones. Such a rhetoric ignores the actual historical dynamic by which a book or an author achieves "classic" recognition, which is often—as in the case of writers such as Dickens and Tolstoy—an immediate outgrowth of popular acclaim. An assault on the "canon" in this regard is actually an assault on the popular will. The question then cannot be dismissed: should what is technically known as the "sociology of knowledge," which belongs within the idiom of intellectual criticism which the philosopher Paul Ricoeur termed "the hermeneutics of suspicion," be advanced as the plumbline for the sorting out of what constitutes humanities per se?

The second issue that urges us forth from here is the alleged "political" makeup of the humanities as well as the judgment that no constellation of the core is possible that does not *a fortiori* reflect the structure of factionalism and dominance within a given institutional setting. It has often been asserted during faculty discussions that all debates within the humanities are inherently and thoroughly "political." In some ways this position is the pale corollary to the hermeneutics of suspicion and is usually alleged as some kind of self-evident rebuttal to the classical view that there is an ideal and "universal" canvas on which to limn the outputs of humanistic work and inquiry. The question, however, presses concerning what precisely is "political." In a very mundane sense so much argument over what should be taught, or not naught, *is* a matter of university politics—the jockeying for position in the budgetary soupline, the genuine or imagined aggrandizement of one department at the expense of another. Proponents of the stance that the principle of selection in the humanities is always "political," surely, do not have this somewhat banal inference in mind whenever they seek to foster disenchantment with the language of ideal curriculum types. They are thinking of something more celestial. Yet the empirical situation surrounding most such arguments testifies to the rather primitive motivations from which such lofty statements emanate. The hermeneutics of suspicion seems to have been a more lethal implement in the hands of faculty committees contending with the retrenchment plans than amid magisterially-minded champions of intellectual criticism in the grand old style.

In an important respect the rhetoric itself falls back upon the politicization of higher education in the sixties, which arose when student groups demanded that universities adopt a public position against the Vietnam War and, later, a whole ledger of social ills and injustices that were purported to exhibit some cause and effect relation to what was occurring in Southeast Asia—for example, racism, poverty, Third World repression. Not to take a position on the Vietnam conflict was in itself regarded as baldly political. The politicization of the academy paralleled the polarization of American society during the period. The same contours of polarization are very much with us today, although the more visceral invocations have long ago retreated back into silence and the erstwhile passions are spent. What was once an ad hoc response to a social explosion has now been institutionalized in the mentality of a generation, from whom so much of the intelligentsia itself is sired. The theory of ideology holds that seemingly straightforward, self-admitting propositions are really misstatements of unconscious social prejudices and predatory material interests. Should we ask if the statement that the humanities are inveterately political is not some kind of ritualized, disingenuous confession for the maintenance of the "we vs. them" *Politik* that emerged two decades ago? George Orwell, the dour prophet of totalism in our midst, once pointed out that if indeed "all issues are political issues," then we are left with the consequences of politicization itself, which he described as "a mass of lies, folly, hatred, and schizophrenia," all of which may point to the fate of the academy if attitudes do not change.

The third problem emerging from the sixties is that of preference for extreme specialization over the coherence of understanding. The movement for the "core" may mirror this desire to overcome the extreme fragmentation of scholarship that has been endemic for over twenty years, but the core itself is not a new thing at all. In fact, the core is a very old thing that harks back to the roseate dawn of what the Greeks called *paidaeia* and we today call learning. The idea of the liberal arts, to which even the most professionalized institutions of higher learning give reverent lip service, was an original vision of the cohesion of knowledge. Saint Augustine talked about *sapientia*, or "wisdom." The classical curriculum made a distinction between the *trivium* and the *quadrivium*. But whether trivial or quadrivial, the assumption was that knowledge not only did hang together in principle, but a lack of cohesion signified in some way the atrophy of learning. As the Medieval curriculum became increasingly rarefied, arcane, and compartmentalized—particularly under the influence of the professional clergy—the notion of "scholasticism," which later European intellectuals identified with "barbarism," took hold. Scholasticism was not some sort of stylistic fungus overspreading and permeating a healthy host. Scholasticism indicated a kind of natural selection process in the evolution of well-endowed and rigidly institutionalized forms of instruction and investigation. To quote an unknown nineteenth century scholar, "when the thinker becomes fat and the mind an overstuffed fowl, reason settles to the level of pettifoggery and pure grammar." Debates become debates about

313

process, rather than product. Discourse becomes entirely self-referential. The end of scholasticism, and the beginning of that intellectual *coup d' etat de main* we call the Renaissance, was founded on a turn from self-reference to significant questioning. It started with something as simple and elegant as the rediscovery of rhetoric, the art of language as conversation and persuasion as opposed to the analysis of inference and predication. The Renaissance ideal and the ideal of the core curriculum are twin modes of the same historical and cultural tendencies.

One should not talk so much about the turn to the core curriculum as innovation, but rather as a restitution. Renaissance is an even more appropriate word. But every Renaissance, or "Reformation" if one prefers an analogue from theological history, also has its irredentist Counter-reformation. The "core" is a somewhat alien conception for the highly politicized academy, particularly in America. To a certain extent it is alien to the pragmatics of American education as a whole. What exactly is the "core?" A lexical definition or two might be in order. The first is the disgruntled undergraduate's definition: "core" as in apple core—the bitter and seedy part you throw away after you've chewed on all the pulp. A second might be the aging sixties radical's definition: "core" as in the core of a nuclear reactor—the hot and dangerous stuff you don't want exposed to the outside, lest there be at best a meltdown and at worst an explosion.

I offer these somewhat facetious illustrations because the notion of the core—particularly the core as characterized within that vast jewelled citadel of abiding inspirations we call the "humanities"—is still more a shibboleth than a standpoint. The danger today is that we will embrace the rhetoric of core while continuing to impose our own idiosyncratic, and sometimes insidious, political, moral, or professional objectives onto the core. The brute fact is that the deliberate effort of today's still politicized—in the sixties we said "radicalized"—professorial contingents to press for academically irrelevant dispensations, despite the overwhelming social outcry for standards and coherence, amount to the intellectual version of pederasty. A quote from Alexander Solzhenitsyn to underscore the importance of the core is in order here: "Humanity's salvation lies exclusively in everyone's making everything their business. . . ." Is that proposition really as outrageous as it seems? The problem of the humanities is the problem of representation. The problem of historical knowledge is the problem of representation. What ideas or, to use trendy language, which "system of signifiers" represents the business of humanity? Artificial distinctions such as canon vs. "unspoken voices" make a special claim for representation, a clash of representations. Or are the humanities, naively and stupidly put, in the business of what is representing what is really human?

To paraphrase a colleague of mine, do we read Confucius because he is an obligatory gesture of inclusion in the direction of Chinese ethnicity? Hardly. Do we read Hannah Arendt—one of the greatest minds of the twentieth century—because she is a woman political philosopher, or because she is Hannah Arendt? We peruse the lives and writings of great women, living and dead, because we are incomparably enhancing the richness of the historical knowledge of humanity—the *humanities*. Women's studies in its struggle with the "canon" is really a demand that the richness of humanity be amplified in ways we have not yet grasped, by acknowledgement of the ascendant tide, that began to rise late last century, of the literacy, creativity, and critical articulations of one half of the human race. The fact that women's "voices" were not resonantly heard in the fourth century B.C. does not somehow confer a categorical imperative to teach undergraduates that Athenian drama was not to be appreciated because of its "phallo-centric" biases. German voices—the mute "barbarians"—were not heard in ancient Athens or Rome. But by the eighteenth century the force of their own cultural hegemony placed them in the canon automatically. It is an argument for the genius of the present, where women have gained the stature and "voices" due to them never before. It is almost a self-certifying truth. But it is an argument for the humanities on the very home turf of the humanities. We do not need to make superficial and tendentious "political" arguments for inclusion. The humanities by their very constitution are inclusive, and we need to remember that. The humanities represent humanity, and we need to ruminate on that simple-minded fact. The ethic of the humanities should be the authentic categorical imperative of the philosopher Immanuel Kant: act in such a way that you treat every human being as a representative of humanity in its entirety.

III

Let me now turn to the urgency of studying the humanities, and the critical role of the humanities "core," not simply as a representation of *humanitas*, but as a matter of national survival. A nation that has shed its memory of the past is bound to succumb to abysmal temptations of the future. A people that pawns its sense of legacy for trite and immediate political satisfactions runs the gravest risk of losing its entire reason for existence. A culture that persists in valuing only the most implausible utopian puffery as a kind of narcotic refusal of the burdens of true greatness is destined for extinction. An opinion-leading and image-creating elite that, while invoking the traditions of conscience and intellectual liberty, is a harbinger of struggle and a foretaste of chaos.

America, however, today is tottering on the historical edge of a second "civil war." The war does not promise to be between flannel-clad armies and armor-plated gunboats scuttling from port to port, but between a half-articulate union of the wealth-generating segments of the American populace and a broad confederacy of educators, so-called "knowledge workers," and the media's symbol-makers who make increasing claims on the produce of the land. The gathering conflict is not a contest among "interests" as much as it is a strife over ideas. The one side claims the Jeffersonian heritage of a free and independent entrepreneurial class unimpeded by government; the other side reflects the still-lingering Puritan desire for a divinely perfected politics in which "economic" freedoms are subordinate to the moral mission of the state. The one considers the maintenance of national prosperity as a secondary task, condemning American "greed," "commercialism," and "materialism" as the triune original sin of Republic. The other looks upon mercantile and industrial civilization not as a bane, but as a blessing and seeks to defend its prerogatives with lobbyists and legislation rather than with appeals to the greater verities concerning the universe and the human predicament.

C. P. Snow's infamous distinction between the "two cultures" of science and the humanities has frequently been cited as the perennial source of schism in the life of letters. In the American context, however, the sense of "two cultures" most transparently refers to the combat between the teaching of the humanities with its ancient, aristocratic heritage and the popular demands of professional and commercial culture. The argument, which runs as far back as the colonial era, has not yet erupted as a manifest social distemper because of the historic insulation between what the philosopher Michael Novak has termed the "moral/cultural" order and the agents of democratic capitalism. In the nineteenth century the guardians of culture and morality were, because of the relative scarcity and prestige of advanced instruction, virtually synonymous with the leadership cadres. The period following the Civil War saw a rapid shift in the constellation of relationships, as the so-called "captains of industry" increasingly rose to the status of cultural heroes.

By the early part of the twentieth century the tension between the values of America's intelligentsia and the world of business became quite clear. The Progressive Era had begun essentially as a literary attack on the new society that was dominated by "predatory" corporate enterprise. The acclaim given to such writers as Thorsten Veblen, and lately Sinclair Lewis, attested to a growing philosophical split between the heirs of Benjamin Franklin and those of Cotton Mather. By the late 1920s the "alienated intellectual," heretofore a species native to Europe rather than to the New World, had become established on the American scene. In the 1930s he was institutionalized. At the same time, the advent of the New Deal and the mobilization of artists, social theorist, and various "brain trusters" on behalf of the new, Keynes-inspired polity of government-tutored capitalism was largely responsible for the permanent separation of America's knowledge and commercial classes. The steady growth in less than half a century of a bureaucratic sector charged with administering the purely *public* funding of

316

what has come to be known as "human services"—e.g., science, mental health, professional training, family relations, education, the arts, and the uncounted quandaries of livelihood and leisure—has decidedly skewed the conventional reading of American memory as well as identity.

America has nurtured what sociologists have imprecisely designated as a "new class," which is in actuality a somewhat insecure constituency of scribes and mandarins at odds with private wealth and dependent on the patronage of the public sector for both its support and its overall delineation of purpose. So long as America's unchallenged economic pre-eminence could be counted upon to underwrite the more global aims of the "two cultures," no fundamental political or ethical issues arose. But the age of government spending retrenchment, even if it is not an age of absolute economic limits as was generally believed in the 1970s, may force a collision of wills, and ultimately a fierce national dissension, concerning the use of government for the promotion of "competitive," commercial goals for the nation versus the caretaking of mandarin interests.

A mandarinate by its very constitution is more concerned with self-maintenance than with the genuine burdens of leadership in society. The conversion of a genuine moral and cultural leadership stratum into a subclass of social functionaries is not a twentieth century innovation for which America can be proud. The deterioration of the standards, symbolism, and guiding beliefs behind what has all along been known as the "idea of America" in the hands of its very own culture-bearers is a tragic event comparable only to the blighting of the nation's inner cities a generation earlier. Just as the decline of America's urban areas after World War II brought about "white flight" and "black rage" resulting in destructive ghetto riots, so the crumbling of the country's academic and cultural resource centers starting during the Vietnam period has fostered an angry and envious reserve of "ghettoized" intellectuals who have little regard even for their own heritage. In principle, America's two culture problems could be addressed through a deliberate and wisely funded revitalization of the very institutions of nurturance and instruction that have been seemingly neglected. Such a sentiment lies behind the different grand plans for reforming education in general and removing a nation from "risk." Yet the pathology goes much deeper than the degree to which money is allocated. Just as Americans quickly learned that welfare grants were not the magic bullet for welfare problems, so they must quickly figure out that open-ended educational and cultural expenditures are not an Alice-in-Wonderland answer to recurrent "crises" in the classroom. Even "merit pay" for competent teachers makes little sense if the very criteria of merit, have vanished from sight.

Ironically, the defection from American culture by sizable segments of the old intelligentsia has been counterpoised by the rapid proliferation of a new group of cultural consumers, whose concerns and tastes frequently fail to match the

317

dictates of the mandarinate. The surge in popularity of art museums, adult education programs, library symposia, summer music festivals, and historical heritage projects across the nation reflects not only a high level of literacy resulting from several generations of mass liberal education, but a somewhat discreet passion for the tokens and blessings of Western civilization. The ceremonial hand-wringing of political conservatives and progressives alike over the apparent "decline of the West" may prove quaintly irrelevant in the long run once these new signals of a late twentieth century *American Renaissance* are actually heeded. In the same way that the impulses of renaissance in the fifteenth century Italian city states could not be ascribed to the clergy, but were felt primarily by the suddenly prosperous bourgeoisie allied with what today we would call "independent scholars," it is the case also today that the drive for American revitalization is ironically coming from the much maligned "yuppies" or professional nouveau riche. The widely documented, and virtually condemned, "narcissism" of the well-educated baby boomers masks this trend. New elites are always narcissistic in certain proportions. The yuppies' alleged "culture of narcissism" may be more a psychological projection of the mandarinate with its weapons of media definition and its rage at the spectacle of entrepreneurial success. The yuppies are, according to the caricature, both hard-working and self-centered, traits which curiously correspond to the "private vices" that Mandeville redescribed as "public benefit" and Adam Smith pronounced as the waving of an "invisible hand" at the dawn of the industrial epoch. Even more significantly, it is the energy of the yuppie self-regard, not the prideful preoccupation with recondite criticism and social malaise characteristic of the mandarinate, that may possibly be abetting the rebirth of culture.

A similar renaissance of American culture and values took place in the last quarter of the nineteenth century. Known as the "Chautauqua" movement after the lake in upstate New York where the first sessions were held in the 1870s, the phenomenon overshadowed the American intellectual scene until the First World War. Chautauqua was not only the forerunner of adult education in the United States, it was also the locomotive of intellectual change during the dispirited and cynical aftermath of the War Between the States. William James, Ulysses S. Grant, William Jennings Bryan, and Theodore Roosevelt all spoke on Chautauqua platforms. As Victoria and Robert Case have written in *We Called It Culture*, an anecdotal history of the Chautauqua era: "By 1912, the name *Chautauqua* had a definite connotation throughout the length and breadth of the nation. The once obscure Indian word conjured up a picture of lake and grove, of banners flying, of happy-faced youths of both sexes studying religious and cultural subjects and engaged in healthful, excellently supervised recreation. It suggested an open pavilion beside a lake or stream, 'under God's great canopy,' where world-famous leaders, lecturers, and the orators spoke to rapt thousands. Its very syllables held the throb and roll of great orchestras." Chautauqua was both secular ballyhoo and Sunday School, serious inculcation in the humanities for everyman and everywoman as well as a strain of weekend circus. It was entertainment and scholarship folded into one. It was commercial, yet packaged for the public weal. Interestingly, the age of Chautauqua was very much like our own. It sprang up a little over a decade after the nation's most prolonged, unpopular, and debilitating war. It rose on the tide of economic expansion and the flowering of literacy. It aggressively affirmed yearned-after ideals, values, and past inscriptions just when the jaded minions of official literacy had declared them obsolete. Social Darwinism and Machian physicalism were for late Victorian esthetes what deconstruction and "textual materialism" are nowadays. Chautauqua took wing in the nineteenth century because the citadels of higher education were immured in a sterile classicism that could not be communicated to a population hungry for learning, enrichment, and what was then called "uplifting." The mandarinate had not yet been conceived. Chautauqua even overleaped the confines of "lake and grove" and by 1900 had become the conceptual nursery of the Progressive Era. Were it not for Chautauqua, the first American revitalization movement that culminated in the Wilsonian crusade for democracy would never have occurred.

The "second civil war" is not inevitable. However, it can only be averted if the conservatorship of culture is wrested from the monopolistic and often self-serving regime of America's mandarinate. The solution, of course, is not to retire professors and replace them with intellectual hucksters. It is neither to silence the media nor to slow the stream of dollars into education. The default of the mandarinate is as much a consequence of the slippage in critical standards throughout the culture on the whole as of the petty aggrandizements of any privileged elite, which always shepherds its own interests first and foremost. The stakes are, without qualification, the long term survival of democracy.

The solution lies in the building of a new non-partisan consensus which recognizes that the power of ideas and the emblems of popular artistic vision are as important to "national security" as defense hardware, that "competitiveness" requires the commitment of every citizen to more profound aims of civilization as well as to the more quotidian objectives of skill development, investment, and productivity. Abysmal temptations and utopian diversions can be put aside if the humanities are restored to their active, robust, and traditional role in the shaping of American culture as it enters the international marketplace not just of goods and services, but of *thoughts* themselves. Whether those thoughts that will lead to a genuine American renaissance and a cultural revitalization are allowed to pass through the tariff walls imposed by both the purveyors of lowest-common-denominator ideology, not to mention the mandarinate, is a matter to be entertained by public policy formulators and private benefactors. The outcome is not at all an incidental thing about which to conjecture.

IV

At the same time, the humanities can become a broader linkage not only within the domain of conventional liberal arts disciplines that bear its name, but a form of general linchpin of both method and knowledge that forces coherence in the professional disciplines as well. At present, there is a growing interest in the study of the humanities as a kind of companion and propaedeutic to business and management theory. Much of the interface so far has been mapped out in the rather ill-defined terrain known as "business ethics," a version of what used to be called applied moral philosophy. But the study of business and economic activity is fundamental to the wider appreciation of civilization with its commercial currents, transformations, and institutions. Weber's thesis concerning the "Protestant ethic" is an earlier effort at theorizing that belongs within such a genre. Today the idea of "culture" is emerging as the heuristic principle for binding together the liberal arts with the professional specialties.

The study of culture as a system of significations has been the province of the social sciences for many generations. However, in recent years the problem of so-called "cultural studies," representing an effort to bring analysis of the material substrata of society to bear on the investigation of symbols and texts, has been raised like a buccaneer's flag in the midst of the humanities. The limitations of what has been called "cultural studies" per se are starred by the penchant of its practitioners for overt, Marxist ideology. Yet the movement, for all its faults, points to a deep-seated distrust toward the classical segregation of the study of literature, history, philosophy, religion, and the arts from the new, broad-ranging "sociological" sensibility that crept into all academic discourse during the 1960s. If we divest cultural studies of its most brittle Marxian axioms and pay attention to its tacit appreciation of historical relationships between general literacy and economic factors, we are bound to imagine a general rapprochement between the heirs of Adam Smith and the bearers of what has been known as "high culture." This rapprochement of texts and other high cultural articles has not yet been established. Linkages, of course, have been made in those special applications of conventional humanities disciplines, such as film criticism or media theory, which take as their primary subject matter the offerings of popular entertainment. However, the drive for a coherent model that enables us to comprehend the range of mass culture is still lacking. Matthew Arnold's Victorian stigmatization of mass culture as "barbarism" remains our canon even to this day. The deep structure of such a view derives, as we may probably surmise, on the preservation even to this day of Medieval clerical traditions in the academy, where priestly and lay forms of "salvation" are, with appropriate orthodox anxiety, carefully distinguished. The notion that there is a "commercial" side to civilization, and that the

320

values and heroisms and conceptual motivations of the historical actors on that slope of the cultural dividing range are equally worthy of intellectual scrutiny, is a challenging one. At the same time, the study of culture not as an end in itself, but, as a kind of prolegomenon to the study of images and icons of the democratic populace, deserves new regard. This new regard is especially compelling in light of the passage of the liberal arts as a code of honor for the gentleman and the permanent succession of professional education as part of the trend toward career learning.

Take advertising as a case in point. The textbooks on advertising as a methodology of communication and persuasion are often couched in the idiom of institutional strategy and the technic of behavioral change. The dominant paradigms of social interaction drawn from the social sciences have not been at all helpful in decoding the psychological cues, symbolic codes, and effervescent messages that can be used to explain, or illumine, the world of advertising. The history of advertising reflects the history of economic change, particularly the movement from a largely mercantile and agricultural society with a dependence on personal, primary group marketing formats to industrial mega-structures with a built-in bias toward impersonal forms of product identification and the necessity of using a kind of hieroglyphic mysticism based on unconscious and fanciful associations with consumer objects to promote mass-produced goods in appropriate high volume. The fact that the shift in advertising methods from product-centered messages to product-related messages with heavy undertones of subliminal manipulation took place in the 1920s about the same time as the rise of psychoanalysis is no simple happenstance. A richer and shrewder understanding of the power of the symbol went hand in glove with the deployment of the new psycho-semantics toward the creation of material desires and the means of satisfying them through consumption. Today the study of what anthropologist Mary Douglas has called "the world of goods" and their various fetishisms has a close affinity with various kinds of structural and "post-structural" forays into the world of art, meaning, and signification. A four-color ad for vodka with the obligatory vamp in the black chemise leering toward her escort, deliberately cast as America's everymale, has its own subtle iconography that should not be scoffed at. The traditional art historian's essay on the book of hours may even provide some perspective not available to the management formalist who dreams the routine dream of precise demographics and quantifiable market share.

In a word, the core of the humanities must manifest itself in the architecture of a humanities core curriculum. But the humanities is "core" to more than curriculum—it is the license to run a civilization. We should ask ourselves if we are really wise stewards.

PLURALISM AND COHERENCE: THE UNIVERSITY OF DAYTON MODEL

John Geiger and Michael Payne
The University of Dayton

There are many models for imparting coherence into the liberal arts curriculum.[1] This paper examines the theoretical foundations of a model used in the CORE program at the University of Dayton. Providing coherence to requirements in general education, this program employs the theme of "pluralism and Human Values" to unify the CORE courses.[2]

The CORE Program ensures coherence by focusing on individual decision-making and by adopting a particular perspective on the nature of decision-making in a pluralistic, democratic society. This paper explicates and defends that perspective. It concludes by outlining how this perspective provides coherence in the CORE Program.

The Concept of a Pluralistic Society

To clarify the notion of pluralism, we rely on Robert Nisbet's conception of the plural society.[3] Nisbet sketches six conceptual elements of a pluralistic community: 1) Plurality—The plural community is a plurality of communities, a *communitas communitatum*, and is therefore culturally plural; 2) Autonomy—Each community in the larger community should have maximum group autonomy; 3) Decentralization—Centralization of social power is a threat to smaller social units and hence to pluralism; 4) Hierarchy—The plural community stratifies of function and responsibility; 5) Tradition; and, 6) Localism.

Taken together these six elements provide adequate criteria for distinguishing between plural and non-plural communities.[4] The argument of this paper rests on the premise that the plural community is culturally pluralistic. If Nisbet's conception of the plural community is acceptable, this premise follows from the elements of pluralism and autonomy. Further, the *plural* community is by definition a community of *many* communities, not of *one* community.[5] A society that did not allow cultural pluralism would be monistic, not pluralistic.

Cultural Pluralism and Democracy

Our society is both culturally pluralistic and democratic. However, as Nicholas Appleton has argued, cultural pluralism appears to conflict with democracy: "If it is true that a diversity of groups enriches a democratic environment and that groups play a major role in the development . . . of individuals, there is also the potential for groups to restrict an individual's opportunities and autonomy" (153). In the democratic conception of the person, Appleton continues, "Each individual personality is unique, is to be held in high regard, and worthy of development" (151).[6] Appleton argues that this tenet of democracy may be denied in a culturally pluralistic society if a cultural group exercising its autonomy denies individual free choice.

Appleton's point is illustrated in *Wisconsin v. Yoder* (406 U.S. 205, 1972), a case in which the Amish argued that a state statute requiring school attendance up to the age of sixteen violated the free exercise clause of the First Amendment. The Amish objected to high school education because the values it teaches conflict with Amish religious values and the Amish way of life. The Supreme Court ruled in favor of the Amish. But in a partial dissent, Justice Douglas raised the question whether Amish children are entitled to have some say in the decision to attend high school, in view of the fact that some Amish children might desire occupations requiring higher education. "If the parents in this case are allowed a religious exemption," Douglas wrote, "the inevitable effect is to impose the parents' notions of religious duty upon their children" (406 U.S. 209). This case exemplifies the tension between individual freedom and cultural pluralism: If the cultural group has the right to make decisions for the individual, then individual choice may be denied. Therefore, a democratic, culturally pluralistic society could contain non-democratic groups—which seems inconsistent.[7]

This apparent inconsistency within a pluralistic democracy creates a significant problem for individual decision-making. Mature persons must themselves decide whether to permit their cultural group to make important decisions for them.[8] What is problematic is that neither democracy nor cultural pluralism provides criteria for deciding whether to choose with or against one's group or which way to choose when groups compete. The apparent inconsistency in a pluralistic democracy arises from the fact that sometimes group and individual can be in conflict: each asserts priority over the other. Ultimately, when group and individual are in conflict, "cultural pluralism" must side with the group, while "democracy" sides with the individual.[9]

Thus in cases of conflict, neither side can provide a middle ground between group and individual. *If* there is a middle ground, it must be supplied independently of the claims of cultural pluralism or democracy.

We submit that a pluralistic democracy like ours posits a balance between the claims of pluralism and democracy as an ideal to be achieved through public dialogue and debate. That is, our society posits a balance, implying at least two sides to an issue, rather than a unilateral, dogmatic assertion of truth. Hence, our pluralistic democracy is anti-dogmatic. Thus, the public dialogue and debate will be continuous and the truth arrived at will be partial, controversial, and revisable.

The Core Program Perspective[10]

The CORE Program's perspective on individual decision-making responds to the problematic nature of decision-making in a pluralistic democracy. Its perspective is shaped by the belief that as responsible members of society students need to understand, appreciate, and examine the competing claims of pluralism and democracy. Hence, the CORE perspective on decision-making is that students need to develop as concerned, reflective decision-makers in the context of these competing claims. Students need to reflect on the ways in which cultural groups and democracy exist in dynamic tension. This view assumes that students need to appreciate this tension and, rather than attempting to reduce it, to understand that it is the condition in which the truly educated person makes free choices.

This does not deny that the history of western thought is largely a search for underlying unity (Nisbet, passim). Albert Camus wrote that "There is not one human being who, above a certain elementary level of consciousness, does not exhaust himself in trying to find formulae . . . which will give his existence the unity it lacks" (231). The CORE Program starts and ends with this search, but insists that the search rather than the discovery is the key to life-long education, and that unity finally means deciding for oneself to live a meaningful life.

The CORE Program accepts the view that a meaningful life is aware that culture constitutes both a constraint on finding meaning and also the vehicle in the search for meaning. The CORE history courses emphasize this theme by examining the role of enculturation and criticism in the development of cultures and historical figures. The program also accents this idea through the concepts the faculty think represent the "best of the cultures." Among these concepts are the traditional disciplines, presented as superordinate concepts which can facilitate understanding in a given area of inquiry, and which can provide ways of experiencing and of making life meaningful.

This notion reinforces the fact that faculty from different disciplines share texts and treat common subject matter from their various perspectives. This sharing reinforces the idea that no concepts are beyond challenge and that there are multiple ways of interpreting and making meaning through human choices.

If students are to participate in democracy and use culture as a vehicle for making decisions, they must stand apart from self and culture to critically reflect. The CORE Program assumes that such critical reflection will not be appropriated by students if it is not infused throughout the curriculum. Consequently, all CORE faculty incorporate into their courses strategies for higher level thinking. Concomitantly, the faculty recognizes that reflection needs to be developed; hence, there is a progression within the program. Students move from defining and applying ideas to analyzing and evaluating them. Thus, the program's capstone courses in Philosophy and Religious Studies employ the highest level of critical

324

reflectivity to examine the central democratic concepts of freedom, equality, and justice vis-à-vis the nature of cultural pluralism.

The CORE Program realizes that the development of critical reflection can result in estrangement from one's culture; thus, it emphasizes community in two ways. First, two social science courses examine types of communities, the nature of the person in community, relationships between culture and community, and the ways in which communities promote dignity or estrangement from the larger world.

But community is primarily emphasized in the program as faculty and students define and experience themselves in a learning community. This community has been maintained and developed in several ways, including: limiting the number of students and faculty participating in the program; summer workshops in which faculty share syllabi and teaching strategies, and plan the program; regular meetings during the term at which faculty discuss common readings; team teaching; attendance by faculty and students at cultural activities, social events, and celebrations of the program's and the students' successes. But the essential element that builds community is the common understanding that teaching and learning have meaning only if they develop in relationship. Hence, dialogue, debate, and cooperative learning are at the heart of the CORE courses.

Coherence

Since individual decision-making is problematic in a pluralistic democracy, students need to develop as reflective decision-makers in the context of the competing claims of pluralism and democracy. But how does acceptance of the problematic nature of decision-making in a pluralistic democracy bring coherence to the CORE Program? Such acceptance cannot provide coherence in the sense of some underlying unity of reality. Rather, the program views coherence as an ongoing process developing in and through the search conducted by students and teachers as a community of life-long learners in pursuit of fundamental human values. The coherence is initially a communal venture developing through cooperative learning. But ultimately coherence comes from the individual student who must finally decide when the teacher is no longer the authority. Then the student must decide how to formulate his or her own conception of how to live and what is to be valued in life.

Notes

1. The models used at Harvard, Columbia, and the University of Chicago are well-known, and recently attention has been given to newer models at Brooklyn College, Alverno College, and St. Joseph's College in Indiana.

2. The CORE Program consists of twelve courses in English, History, Philosophy, Religious Studies, Natural Science, Social Science, and Arts.

3. Nisbet observes that "It has been the fate of pluralism in Western thought to take a rather poor second place to philosophies which make their point of departure the premise of, not the diversity and plurality of things, but, rather, some underlying unity and symmetry, needing only to be uncovered by pure reason to be then deemed the 'real,' the 'true,' and the 'lasting'" (385).

4. The essential elements of a plural community appear to be pluralism, autonomy, decentralization, and localism. The last two may be debatable, but hierarchy and tradition do not seem to be essential elements (necessary conditions for a plural community). Conservative pluralists, such as Hegel and Burke, saw hierarchy and tradition as more central to plural community than did the liberal pluralists, such as Tocqueville, or sociological pluralists, such as Durkheim and Weber. We say "more central" because no doubt conservatives have a different conception of hierarchy and tradition than do liberal and sociological pluralists. In the end, the issue may be terminological.

5. Etymologically, the term "plural" is a variation of the Latin word *plus*, meaning "more," which is the comparative form of *multus*, meaning "much."

6. Appleton's argument rests on John Dewey's conception of democracy, which we adopt. We do not here provide an argument justifying our adoption. Our concern is to point out an inner tension, if not inconsistency, in societies in which there is both cultural pluralism *and* strong individual rights. We think individual rights are central to the American conception of democracy; so we focus on democracy. If this is incorrect, then we will focus on the liberal society, in which individual rights are certainly central.

7. We emphasize that we are not asserting that there *is* an inconsistency, but Justice Douglas was not so sure. We leave open the question whether the inconsistency may be only apparent. Our concern is to emphasize that a plausible, though not necessarily conclusive, argument may be made that there is an internal inconsistency in the idea of a pluralistic democracy.

8. We assume that there are few, if any, exceptions to the claim that individuals are at least in childhood members of at least one cultural group. We also exclude those who are coerced, or who cannot make decisions for themselves.

9. We say "ultimately" to indicate those cases in which cultural pluralism and democracy seem to be in conflict.

10. The University of Dayton CORE Program has been designed, implemented, and evaluated with support from the National Endowment for the Humanities and the Lilly Endowment.

Works Cited

Appleton, Nicholas, "Democracy and Cultural Pluralism: Ideals in Conflict." *Philosophy of Education*, 1982.

Camus, Albert. *The Rebel*, tr. Anthony Bower. New York: Alfred A. Knopf, 1954.

Nisbet, Robert. *The Social Philosophers*. New York: Thomas Y. Crowell, 1973.

Strike, Kenneth. *Liberty and Learning*. New York: St. Martin's Press, 1984.

THE QUADRIVIAL ARTS IN THE LIBERAL ARTS CURRICULUM

John C. Kohl and Theresa Welch Kohl

Trinity Valley School and The College of Saint Thomas More

By "quadrivial arts" in the title of this paper we mean the four mathematical arts: geometry, arithmetic, astronomy and music. Our discussion is, accordingly, devoted to the role of these and kindred disciplines in the general liberal arts curriculum. That such an inquiry was thought necessary arises from two contrary points of view. On the one hand, there is the widespread identification of the liberal arts with the "humanities," a term which variously includes much but definitely excludes mathematics, the sciences of nature, and a variety of human activities scientifically considered (the social sciences). On the other hand, there are various historical reminders that mathematics, astronomy, and related studies were integral parts of the liberal arts curriculum straight on from classical antiquity, through the Middle Ages, the Renaissance, and up to the present.

What role, if any, then, do the mathematical disciplines play in a renovation of a liberal arts curriculum? We have approached this question by focusing on what was taught in the schools during late antiquity, approximately 350 to 600 AD. It was during this epoch, the "twilight," so to speak of the classical age, that the liberal arts were formulated into a "canon," or rule, of seven disciplines: grammar, logic, rhetoric, geometry, arithmetic, astronomy, and music. We will have more to say about the term "canon" later. The last four of these canonical disciplines—geometry, arithmetic, astronomy, and music—had for a very long time (at least since the fourth century BC) been recognized as the mathematical arts and to constitute among themselves a sort of unity. It was to this unity that Boethius in the sixth century AD first gave the name *quadrivium* or "four ways."[1] By examining these arts at this period we have avoided complications introduced by technology and economics. Prior to the fifteenth century of our era, none of the disciplines listed above was pursued primarily or exclusively for the advantages that might accrue, either immediately or indirectly, to human bodily comfort, ease, or material well-being. The term "liberal" in the "liberal arts" refers quite precisely to their pursuit in the absence of compelling circumstances of material necessity. From a contemporary standpoint, therefore, to inquire into the liberal character of the liberal arts might be said to be tantamount to asking about the uselessness of the useful.

In this historically directed study we have focused primarily on the Latin satire of Martianus Capella, a younger north African contemporary of Augustine of Hippo and one of the seven major authorities in late antiquity (the others being Augustine himself, Boethius, Cassiodorus, Isidore of Seville, Macrobius, and Calcidius) responsible for conveying the ancient arts, especially the mathematical arts, to the early Middle Ages.[2] Martianus is thus important. He is also comprehensive, including in his writing the divergent and contradictory opinions of many earlier authorities even to the point of risking rather astonishing inconsistencies. Finally, Martianus was persuasive, achieving for the liberal arts some popularity among the Romans, Goths, their descendants, and others who were not particularly enthusiastic for academic activities. He did this by dressing up his presentation as an allegory entitled *The Marriage of Philology and Mercury*,[3] in which Mercury, a god, marries Philology, a mortal, who is subsequently divinized, and has to get approval for his dowry from a senate composed of the other gods. The dowry consists of seven handmaidens, the seven liberal arts, each of whom must present her art in a speech before the celestial tribunal (and before us).

In general, what do these handmaidens tell us? The presentation begins with the three non-mathematical sisters, Grammar, Logic, and Rhetoric, who became known in the later Middle Ages as the *trivium* or "three ways."[4] There were four parts to the ancient teaching of grammar; two active, reading and writing, and two passive, understanding and criticism. The two passive parts, or what we would now call "literature," dealt primarily with poetry. The emphasis in Martianus' presentation, as in collateral grammatical expositions by authors of the same epoch, is on the two active parts, reading and writing. Considerable importance was attached to reading with correct diction and pronunciation, which reminds us that reading in ancient times was aloud; silent reading, even in solitude, was the exception.[5]

Grammar's order of presentation is to start with the simplest elements first— the letters themselves—and treat of their kinds and pronunciation, and then go on to do the same for letter combinations in syllables, syllabic combinations in words, word combinations in phrases, then clauses, and finally sentences. A complete utterance, a sentence, at bottom consists of a noun and a verb, a subject and a predicate. At this point logic (dialectic) takes over, inquiring into the truth or falsity of complete utterances, which are now spoken of as propositions. A proposition may be an assertion of one of four kinds: All are; Some are; All are not; Some are not." The truth or falsity of a proposition has to be established in the light of other propositions, called premises, whose truth has been previously established. At a minimum, two such premises are required for each conclusion, and the three statements so related are collectively called a syllogism. A familiar example: "All men are mortal. Socrates is a man. Therefore, Socrates is mortal." Various modes of valid syllogisms are established, depending upon the types of assertions and order of their terms.

Men commonly make lengthy arguments composed of chains of syllogisms, called *enthymemes*, in which many of the premises (the more obvious ones) are not stated as such but are to be inferred. The art of speaking well, in particular, of speaking persuasively before public assemblies and in courts of law, is called rhetoric. Logic and the choice of examples and evidence are the two bases of the rhetorician's craft. In addition to these two, the order of arguments, the style of speech (that is, choice of figures of thought or syllogisms and choice of figures of speech), memorization, and delivery are important. The importance of memorization and delivery comes from the fact that in ancient times all speeches, although composed in manuscript beforehand, were intended to be delivered from memory before an audience. The three arts of the trivium thus take a man from infancy, literally that period in life where he is incapable of speech, to the eloquence of mature manhood, where he participates fully in public life and the affairs of state.

With the introduction of the first of the mathematical sisters, Geometry, in Martianus' nuptial pageant, we reach, as it were, a new beginning in the allegory of the liberal arts, complete with an invocation to Minerva and praise of her wisdom. Geometry reminds us that her name means "earth measure," and she spends most of her time describing the natural features of the earth, its peoples, and habitations—what we today would call "geography." Prodded by the gods, who grow bored at this description, she finally turns her attention to mathematical geometry. Geometry is here primarily concerned with the elements of geometry, that is, with the various sorts of geometrical figures, such as plane and solid figures, with definitions of terms, such as the problem and the theorem, and the laying down of postulates and common notions, such as, that parallel lines don't meet and that if equals are added to equals, the sums are equal to each other. It is largely left to her closely related successor, Arithmetic, to discuss mathematical arguments. After dealing with the divine associations of the Monad or One, the unitary source of all numbers, and the first nine numbers following it (the Pythagorean decad), Arithmetic sets forth definitions of the various properties of numbers (oddness, evenness, primeness, compositeness, perfection, imperfection) and proceeds to list various provable assertions concerning them, such as, that the product of any even number is always even, or that the squares of two prime numbers are relatively prime to each other.[6]

When Arithmetic leaves the stage, she is followed by Astronomy, who begins with a general picture of the cosmos as a sphere of fixed stars and their constellations turning daily about the central earth. The equatorial plane of this sphere is cut slantwise at an angle (23.5 degrees) by the plane of the ecliptic circle, and it is upon this oblique, ecliptic plane (or at small angles thereto) that we find the planetary orbits about the central earth: the sun, moon, and five planets, Mercury, Venus, Mars, Saturn, and Jupiter. Astronomy has the task of trying to

329

make the apparent motions of these individual, planetary ("wandering") bodies, as they were observed from the earth, geometrically comprehensible. In terms of Euclidean geometry this meant an account of their motions compounded of regular circular motions: revolution of bodies on circles eccentric to the point of their observation and/or on circles whose centers, in turn, revolved on other circles (epicycles). But Astronomy tells us that the planets are not simply wanderers but confounders, confounding us with their irregular motions, because the sun's rays strike the planets and cause these anomalies.

Finally, the silent vastnesses elicited by Astronomy are punctuated by the songs of Harmony, seventh and last of the liberal arts, whose melodies not only move us men but the gods as well. Indeed, her songs animate the entire world. She was present, Harmony tells us, when the world was designed and created. The element of song is the tone, and tones are arranged both with respect to pitch and with respect to duration.

Mercury himself delivered the four-stringed lyre into the hands of men; it was subsequently developed into the seven-stringed cythera and indeed into harplike instruments of more than seven strings. How were the strings of these instruments tuned? They were tuned according to the divisions of "the harmonic ruler, a single string stretched taut along a measuring stick, marked off in equal units, a *canon*. If the string is depressed in the center so that only half of its length vibrates (1 to 2 ratio), it will sound an octave higher than the original (the *diapason* interval). If two thirds of it vibrates (2 to 3 ratio), we have the dominant or fifth (Do to Sol, the *diapente* interval) and, if three quarters (3 to 4 ratio), the subdominant or fourth (Do to Fa, the *diatessaron* interval).[7] The *diapente* and *diatessaron* together constitute a *diapason* or octave (2/3 x 3/4 = 1/2). Depending on how the fourth and fifth were divided, we have various genera of scales and octave species, or modes, upon which the melodies were played. Legend has it that the Greek mathematician and philosopher, Pythagoras, in the sixth century B.C. discovered that the three consonant musical intervals, that is, tones which were pleasant when sounded together, were expressible by the first three whole number ratios, thus linking up the sensed movements of the soul with movement captured in elementary arithmetical ratios.

If we turn from pitch to the second aspect of music, duration, we find similarly inspired treatments of verse as a canon of metrical feet, that is, periodically recurring measures, as for example, pentameters (five-foot verses), hexameters (sixfoot verses), etc. Consideration is then given to what combinations of metrical units, such as the dactyl, iamb, or spondee, divide the verse in a manner pleasing to the ear.[8] In his treatment of the subject, Augustine of Hippo writes:

God has arranged that even a sinful and sorrowful soul can be moved by rhythm and can rightly perform it, even down to the lowest corruption of the flesh. So degraded, rhythm becomes less and less beautiful, but it must always have some beauty. God is jealous of no beauty due to the soul's damnation, regression, or obstinancy. Number, the base of rhythm, begins from unity. It has a beauty by equality and by similitude, and it has interconnection by order. All nature requires order. It seeks to be like itself, and it possesses its own safety and its own order, in spaces or in times or in bodily form, by methods of balance. We have to admit that in number and rhythm all, without exception and without limit, starting from the single origin of unity, is complete and secure, in a structure of equality and similitude and wealth of goodness, cohering from unity onwards in most intimate affection.[9]

In the study of the quadrivium we are taken, as it were, from the play of lines drawn in the sand and the array of pebbles placed upon the earth to the contemplation of a larger world which encompasses and lies beyond our direct experience. Thus, as the three arts of speech are engaged in raising men to political maturity upon the earth, so the mathematical arts raise men from mundane to extramundane concerns. But there is a further relationship between these arts which must be mentioned.

Music in its ancient setting emerges as the art of moving the soul in its most powerful and pervasive form, a pure rhetoric rooted in the nature of things. In fact, our synopsis of the ancient canon suggests a general parallel between the arts of the trivium, on the one hand, and those of the quadrivium, on the other. It begins with the elements of grammar, on the one hand, and those of mathematics, geometrical figures and numbers, on the other. Out of this emerges the modes of logic, on the one hand, and the demonstrable properties of geometrical figures and numbers, on the other. These modes and demonstrations introduce a sort of movement, a persuasiveness, which is then specified in the disciplines of rhetoric and of astronomy and of music. The quadrivial arts of mathematics hold up a sort of mirror to the trivial arts of speech, and conversely. We suggest that it is indeed out of this mirroring that the activities of human speech are made visible and brought to light as arts—that is, as produced from and built up successively from articulated elements artfully fitted together. The arts of speech, writing, and argument, on the one hand, and those of mathematics and music, on the other hand, arise as such out of this complementary, mirroring relationship. Put in historical context, this suggests that the contemporaneous elaboration and refinement of the political arts and the mathematical arts in classical Greece was not simply a fortuitous occurrence, a mere coincidence.

At this point, however, a problem arises, which must be mentioned, albeit only briefly. That there are only three arts of speech and four in mathematics suggests that the parallel we have been drawing is not an exact one. This inexactitude is indicated in the synoptic treatment of the liberal arts by Cassiodorus, a Roman who lived a century later than Martianus. In Cassiodorus' *Institutes*[10] arithmetic is paired with music and geometry with astronomy. This follows an ancient tradition according to which the pair arithmetic-music treats of discrete magnitudes, namely number and tones, both at rest and in motion, respectively, whereas the pair geometry-astronomy treats of continuous magnitudes such as lines, surfaces, and spaces, in the same two respective states of rest and motion. That the geometrical pair is not directly reducible to the arithmetical pair is epitomized by the discovery of incommensurability, or, if you will, irrational numbers, which legend again attributes to Pythagoras himself. There are simply some magnitudes, such as the diagonal of a square when measured by one of its sides, which cannot be expressed as whole numbers or as the ratio of two whole numbers, however large. Put differently, in the celebrated harmony of the celestial spheres there would seem to be some necessary disharmony. Time does not permit us here a further development of this problem, the attempt at whose resolution, we suggest, opens the way to higher studies, namely, that enterprise known as philosophy.

Over thirty years ago, in May, 1959, the late British novelist and physicist, C. P. Snow, described to an audience at Cambridge University the intellectual life of Western society as increasingly being split into two polar groups, the literary-artistic on the one side and the scientific-technological on the other side.[11] To these two sides Snow gave the term "The Two Cultures," a locution which, to its author's surprise, became a widely circulated and discussed topic on both sides of the Atlantic, both in learned circles as well as in the popular press. Our inquiry into the ancient liberal canon has revealed the roots, we think, of Lord Snow's polarity as a necessary one, necessary to the formation of the liberal arts as arts themselves. But Snow found it necessary to speak of it not as a polarity but as two separate entities, two "cultures," and some thirty years experience and reflection on the situation has not led us to reverse his earlier assessment. We wonder, somewhat sadly, whether the dictum "Two Cultures" does not more properly mean "one culture falling apart."

NOTES

1. Thus Archytas of Tarentum (fourth century BC) in a fragment writes: "Mathematicians seem to me to have excellent discernment, and it is in no way strange that they should think correctly concerning the nature of particular existences. For since they have passed an excellent judgment on the nature of the whole, they were bound to have an

excellent view of separate things. Indeed they have handed on to us a clear judgment on the speed of the constellations and their rising and setting, as well as on (plane) geometry and numbers (arithmetic) and solid geometry, and not least on music; for these mathematical studies appear to be related. For they are concerned with things that are related, namely the two primary forms of Being." (translated by Kathleen Freeman, *Ancilla to the Presocratic Philosophers*, Cambridge: Harvard University Press, 1977, 78)

Boethius' introduction of the term *quadrivium* occurs in the proem (Book I, Chapter 1) to his treatise on arithmetic: "Among all the men of ancient authority who, following the lead of Pythagoras, have flourished in the purer reasoning of the mind, it is clearly obvious that hardly anyone has been able to reach the highest perfection of the disciplines of philosophy unless the nobility of such wisdom was investigated by him in a certain four-part study, the *quadrivium*, which will hardly be hidden from those properly respectful of expertness." (translated by Michael Masi, *Boethian Number Theory: A Translation of the De Institutione Arithmetica with Introduction and Notes*, Amsterdam: Rodopi, 1983, 71)

2. See the article "Scholasticism" in the Eleventh Edition of the *Encyclopedia Brittanica*.

3. A study and English translation of this work appears as *Martianus Capella and the Seven Liberal Arts*, 2 vols., by W. H. Stahl, Richard Johnson, and E. L. Burge, New York: Columbia University Press, 1977.

4. The *trivium* as a collective entity apparently did not emerge until the ninth century AD. See E. R. Curtius, *European Literature and the Latin Middle Ages*, translated by Willard Trask, Princeton: Princeton University Press, 1953, 37.

5. See H. I. Marrou, *A History of Education in Antiquity* (transl. George Lamb) Madison: University of Wisconsin Press, 1982, 154. "The child read aloud, of course. Throughout antiquity, until the late Empire, silent reading was exceptional. People read aloud to themselves, or, if they could, got a slave to read it to them."

6. It is important to note, however, that at no point in Martianus' allegory is there given any proof or *apodexis* in the Euclidean manner of any mathematical proposition or relationship. He confines himself to examples only.

7. The three consonant intervals, octave (1:2), fourth (3:4), and fifth (2:3) and the difference between the last two, which constitutes a whole tone or second (8:9), constituted the basis for music in the West through late antiquity. The theory is summarized in Boethius' *Principles of Music (De Musica)*. In Medieval times the canonical intervals deemed consonant began to be extended. In 1877 the German physicist, Hermann Helmholtz (*On the Sensations of Tone*, translated by A. J. Ellis, New York: Dover Publications, 1954, 187) listed the additional intervals and their string length ratios as follows
Major Third (4:5), Minor Third (5:6),
Subminor Fifth (5:7), Minor Sixth (5:8),
Major Sixth (3:5), Minor Seventh (5:9),
Subminor Seventh (4:7), Supersecond (7:8),
Subminor Third (6:7), Supermajor Third (7:9).

8. Specific attention here must be given to the writings on rhythmics by Aristoxenos, a student of Aristotle, and the much later *Treatise on Music (De Musica)* of Augustine of Hippo.

9. W. F. Jackson Knight. *St. Augustine's De Musica: A Synopsis*. London: The Orthological Institute, nd, 122–23. The quotation reflects *De Musica* vi.17.56. Compare the trans. of Robert Catesby Taliaferro in *The Writings of St. Augustine, vol. 2. The Fathers*

of the Church. New York: Cima Publishing Co., Inc., 1947, 375.

10. Cassiodorus' *Institutes*, Book II, Chapters 4 through 7. The order in Isidore's *Etymologies* (Book III) is still a different order: Arithmetic, Geometry, Music, Astronomy.

On the pairing of the quadrivium, we note Nicomachus of Gerasa (first century AD) in his *Introduction to Arithmetic*, Book I, Chapter III: ". . . it is clear that two scientific methods will lay hold of and deal with the whole investigation of quantity [*poson*]; arithmetic, absolute quantity, and music, relative quantity. And once more, inasmuch as part of 'size' [*pelikon*] is in a state of rest and stability, and another part in motion and revolution, two other sciences in the same way will accurately treat of 'size,' geometry that part that abides and is at rest, astronomy that which moves and revolves." (Martin Luther D'Ooge translation, New York: Macmillan, 1926, 184)

11. The Rede Lecture, Cambridge University, May, 1959. An expanded version appeared as *The Two Cultures: And a Second Look*, New York: New American Library, 1963.

IN FAVOR OF A FINE ARTS PRACTICUM REQUIREMENT

Richard Jones
Cornell College

I would like to begin by presenting two scenaria: one real, the other the product of Madison Avenue. The real one first:

A young actor is the victim of an accident which prevents him from ever again moving faster than a walk. His specialties had been stage combat and dance, so his career as an actor is effectively short-circuited. But there are bills to pay, and his first child is soon to be born. He takes a job as a bank teller. A few years later, he's the trouble shooter his central office sends out to solve problems at the branch office. His undergraduate theatre teacher is incredulous at hearing this: "But you hated math!" she exclaims. "Yeah," he replies, "but it's not about math. I can motivate them and get them to work together. . . . I rarely have to fire anyone because I'm really good at figuring out what jobs they are temperamentally suited for. I mean management is really about improvisation, directing, and casting, isn't it? All that stuff that the MBAs talk about, but haven't a clue of how to do."[1]

The second scenario is a television advertisement for NatWest International Bank. In it, a banking executive, obviously working for one of NatWest's competitors, bewails the loss of an important account because "some other bank" solved in a week the problem that his firm had labored at unsuccessfully for two months. His underling makes the mistake of starting to say "What we need . . . ," only to have his head handed to him by the senior man. "What we NEED," snarls the superior, "is creative problem solvers. WHERE are today's creative problem solvers?" Well, I'd say they're taking theatre courses at a small college in Pennsylvania . . . and music courses in Wyoming, and dance in California.

Probably no one here today doubts the validity of a liberal arts education as preparation for a career in virtually any profession: the dissenters are out there, of course, but they're not likely to be at this conference in great numbers. I'm here, however, to talk specifically about the fine arts—the performing as well as the visual arts—and their centrality to the liberal arts curriculum. Here, I suspect, there is more disagreement, especially when I say that courses which emphasize the analysis or the history of an art form (and I include literature here) are necessary but not sufficient to a liberal education in the arts. Most colleges, whether they have core curricula *per se* or distributive requirements, lump together courses from the fine arts and the humanities under the same requirement. Certainly the two divisions are related—I teach about half of my courses in one, half in the other—but they are anything but identical or interchangeable. So while almost every college has some sort of requirement for the analysis of art, relatively few require the creation of art. This myopia results in an institutionalized emphasis on analysis over creation, on passivity over activity, and on third-hand knowledge over first-hand knowledge. The goal-orientation of most courses outside the arts becomes the norm, with the process-orientation of most arts courses regarded as eccentric if not aberrant or even perverse. Finally, the public nature of arts presentations provides a student not only with a different sort of venue for his/her ideas, but also with experience in the important real-life problem of how to deal with public and/or conflicting criticism. Similarly, the student must learn to cope with different pressures and expectations: a poor term paper in sociology earns a very private D; an underprepared violin recital is quickly public knowledge.

Let us start with my assertion that failing to require arts courses or their practicum equivalents emphasizes analysis over creation. Judging by the way most college catalogues read, a student is heartily encouraged to find out about Shakespeare or Mozart or Rembrandt or Gertrude Stein, but actually to be one of those people is not looked on so highly. Shakespeare is an especially good example for a number of reasons. First of all, here was a man who earned his living as an actor, supplementing his income on occasion by selling a new playscript to his company. Although he was reasonably well-read, he was not a scholar, and he took an artist's license with geography and chronology alike. And the very skills for which we praise him the most highly, the ability to synthesize the universe around him, to encapsulate philosophy or politics or ethics into the form of a dramatic narrative written primarily in verse, to illuminate life through art without ever confusing the two: these are the skills at which we don't require today's undergraduates even to try their hands. We often require analysis of *Hamlet* or *Macbeth* or *King Lear* . . . but where is the next masterwork to come from if today's future playwrights are encouraged only to read, not to write?

Now, this is not to say that the fine arts are the only division of the college in which a creative mind is a positive asset. Indeed, quite the contrary. The physicist or historian who has no imagination will never be more than mediocre; and that is precisely why colleagues in other divisions of the college ought to encourage . . . yes, require, their students to become involved in the division of academe which most emphasizes the creative, the right-brain, the Dionysian. For, just as we must acknowledge the truth that all fields require all forms of thought, so must we acknowledge that different fields prioritize different things: the scientists value logicality, the humanists and social scientists analysis, the artists creativity. The artist who does not live in the world has nothing about which to create art, so the liberal arts are necessary to the arts; but the flip side is also true: the poet, the

336

composer, the sculptor all interpret the world in ways that are no less true than the journalist's . . . and the artist is considerably less likely to make specious claims of objectivity.

Of course, there are many kinds of creativity. The creation of a script by a playwright is a different sort of process from the creation of a character in that play by an actor. The same can be said for a musical composition and the instrumentalist or vocalist who plays or sings it, or for a dance piece involving creative input from choreographer and dancer alike. But creative forms inevitably resemble each other more than they do analytical papers for two fundamental reasons. One is the public nature of the performance (more on this later). The other is that the performance of an artistic work is more than simply a response, more than an interpretation. Indeed, interpretation is only the first step: after that comes the real work of illumination. It is neither surprise or coincidence that the two seminal books by Konstantin Stanislavsky, he of the oft-misinterpreted "method," are *Building a Character* and *Creating a Role*. Acting (like singing and playing an instrument and dancing and painting and sculpting) necessarily involves not only the intellectual but also the emotional: and if we're to discount the possibility of irrational (or, more accurately, non-rational) truth, we might as well abandon any attempt to study religion or ethics or anthropology . . . or astronomy and history, for that matter.

More important, the actual creative process is at the center of most fine arts courses. Few scientists would agree to a science distribution requirement that could be fulfilled exclusively by reading biographies of Newton and Galileo. Many colleges have specific requirements including at least one course in a laboratory science, based on the eminently reasonable propositions that 1) scientific method is the essence of science, and 2) the only way to understand scientific method is to use it in the laboratory. Analogously, the artistic process forms the basis for everything artists, be they sculptors or composers, scene designers or choreographers, do. Curiously, however, the same rationale which requires lab work to fulfill science requirements does not always seem to apply to the necessity of lab work to fulfill an arts requirement. I confess that the more I think about this disparity, the more baffled I become. Granting an "arts" credit to a student who has never tried to sing a harmony line or been covered in ceramic dust or wrestled with a dramatic monologue strikes me as the equivalent of granting drivers licenses to anyone who has passed a written test, without ever requiring them to have sat behind the wheel, or to awarding athletic scholarships purely on the basis of how well a student performs on a test about the arcana of a given sport's rules.

Furthermore, the arts are active by their very nature. We live in a society which increasingly (and unfortunately) demands more and more to be pre-

337

packaged: we get our news from sitting in front of a television set, allowing someone else, often a "talking head," to filter out not only what we ought to believe is important, but what we ought to think about it. Our food is microwaveable, restaurants are specifically designed to discourage lingering over that final cup of coffee, and even the arts are increasingly pre-fab: video rentals surpass box office receipts for most movies, and I defy anyone to tell me the plot of *Starlight Express*. But the actual creation of a work of art is little different now than it was centuries ago: only the techniques have changed. The "passive artist" is an oxymoron: it takes work to transform a blank canvas into a vital statement of an idea, work to realize the potential of a sheaf of sheet music, work to make an audience understand why Hedda Gabler behaves the way she does. And, importantly, this work is intrinsically personal and self-reflective. The arts are active and individual to a greater extent than any of the other divisions of academe. And that is an intrinsic good.

A related issue is the problem of choices. It is all very well for a critic to proclaim that a given passage can mean x *or* y, that a painting can be balanced by mass *or* color or that a movement in a symphony can work equally well at either of two *tempi*. But the artist, whether "creative" or "interpretive" *must* make choices. The critic can speak of ambivalence: Iago may or may not be a racist: but the director and the actor must decide one way or the other, make their choice consistent, motivate it throughout a three-hour long production, and stand behind their choice in the face of public criticism. Similarly, the artist is constantly required by the nature of artistic expression to simplify and clarify: I find myself constantly telling actors, "don't tell me, show me!" and "you can't footnote a line reading." And yet I expect, and my audiences expect, a complexity of character-ization that belies the apparent simplicity of the presentation.

Of course the whole question of audience response leads us to the issue of the public nature of arts activities. I tell students that I'm not sure if theatre requires actors, I know it doesn't require dialogue, but I'm sure that it does require an audience. A painting which is seen only by its creator does not cease to be a painting, but I would argue that it is not yet art: that art pre-supposes communi-cation, and that communication requires both sender and receiver. I am not arguing here that every arts course ought to conclude with some sort of public presentation (both my departmental colleague and I teach arts courses which do not), but that the presentation of work before the members of the class (at least) is absolutely necessary. While the recognition that one's work will be seen by more than one's professor, and that one's artistic work is in some way a reflection of oneself, has often served to catalyze the work ethic, the predictable problems of unfair and often demeaning criticism routinely develop. I need hardly mention that the campus newspaper probably has at least one or two self-professed

338

authorities on things artistic. Occasionally, these people provide a valuable service; more often, they don't. We tell our students that life isn't fair; while that's seldom much consolation, it is, perhaps, one of the most important lessons they will learn at college.

Much of the criticism, of course, is based on the absurd notion that the arts are "easy." Almost without fail, I am forced to remove from my directing class a student who signed up not only without the prerequisite course (Acting) but without any theatre experience at all. Usually, these students have been assured by their advisors that their lack of preparation poses no real problem, and that we in the arts would be happy to accommodate them simply because they choose to be accommodated. This attitude extends to grading, the main source of the "arts are easy" myth. Imagine two students: let's call them Alice and Betty. Both are extremely conscientious. Alice is a brilliant chemist with no acting ability; Betty is an outstanding actor with no aptitude for science. Both enroll in both chemistry and acting courses. I will absolutely guarantee that Alice will get better grades. She will earn her A in chemistry, regardless of how hard (or how little) she actually works for it, and she will get at least a C+ (probably a B) in acting if she does all the work and honestly gives it her best shot. She'll still be an awful actor, but the acting teacher will pay particular attention to how far she's come. On the other hand, Betty might well end up with a B+ in acting, although she's clearly the most "talented" actor in the class, assuming she doesn't work particularly hard and doesn't improve much, and she'll have to claw and scratch for a C- in chemistry, where she will learn a great deal, but not enough to overcome her lack of pre-course preparation.

I'm not arguing here that process-orientation is correct and goal-orientation incorrect: in fact my own theatre history classes are fairly heavily goal-oriented. Rather, I'm suggesting that different disciplines employ different grading policies, leading to the misconception that one discipline is therefore "easier" than another. This distinction is upheld both formally and informally through the academy: the artist is "talented," which is somehow a different (and lesser) thing than being "intelligent." The philosophy student will claim that his lack of musical "talent" ought not to be held against him in a music course, but will argue that the music student's inability to distinguish between Hegel and Husserl is a function of laziness or intellectual inferiority. And so it goes.

Finally, some issues which artists encounter routinely are far broader than the limited world of the art or the campus. For example, I attended the callbacks for a student-directed production I supervised. The young director had chosen Lillian Hellman's *The Little Foxes*, certainly an important work of American drama and an ambitious but not unreasonable choice for an undergraduate directing project. We thought we had things well in hand when the actor we were considering for

339

the role of Cal, indeed the only black man who auditioned, decided that he really didn't have the time to commit to the play. Now, this is a play which has subjected its author to charges of racism (undeservedly so, I think, but such charges must always be taken seriously). And now there's no black man to play the black male character. So—what are the options? Well, we could recruit another black man (one who hadn't auditioned), we could cast a black woman (we had three quite reasonable auditions for the role of the black woman) and either pretend she was male or try to rewrite the character to female, we could cast a white man, we could try to write character out of the play, we could drop the show and do something else. All of these positions have their advantages and their disadvantages. But this young director was forced to choose one, and to make her choice 100 percent public. That she chose differently than I would have is hardly relevant: that she chose, and that she was prepared to accept whatever consequences ensue from her choice is the essence of what we as artists, and as educators, and as adults, do. In no other area of academe is a student so often and so thoroughly confronted with questions of self-cognition and personal perspective. Few other disciplines demand the sort of (dare I say it?) creative problem solving that arts students encounter almost daily.

The arts, then, function at a number of levels to fulfill needs of undergraduate students, needs which are not sufficiently addressed elsewhere. A fine arts practicum requirement would serve not only to develop larger and more informed arts audiences for the future (really a by-product rather than a goal), but would have the immediate advantage of requiring first-hand engagement and self-reflection. The average college graduate won't ever use the material from an introductory level fine arts course directly; neither will he or she use calculus or quote Heidegger or Dickens. But the arts quietly endow a student with real-world skills in problem solving, in group dynamics, in applied ethics. It is important to note here that the reason for an arts requirement is that students ought to be engaged actively in the arts, but there are a host of corollary reasons, just noted, for those who choose to discount the primary rationale.

At Cornell College, where I teach, every BA candidate is required to take one course or the equivalent in the fine arts. Distinctions as to which courses qualify and which do not are made on the basis of course content, not departmental affiliation: arts history courses, music appreciation, dramatic literature courses don't count; writing poetry or fiction do. "Adjunct credits," worth the equivalent of 1/4 of a course (or 1 semester hour), are awarded to students for participation in artistic activities: acting, playing in the orchestra, etc. Four such credits fulfill the requirement. This isn't the only way to go, but it seems to work pretty well for us. No system is perfect: we can no more guarantee that our students will learn to appreciate the arts than that they will learn to admire scientific method or seek out additional reading in Plato. But we do guarantee exposure: and the ancillary benefits of fine arts requirements are manifold.

A system which purports to offer a student the essence of a liberal arts education while bypassing the fine arts is either naive or arrogant, and it is certainly stifling. To require the analysis of art without requiring active engagement in the creation of art is to reaffirm the distancing and disassociation endemic in modern society, to devalue both creation and the creative process, and to discourage original thought by placing a premium on the rehashing of old ideas at the expense of new ones. Our society cannot long survive such a mindset, and it ought not to be reenforced on our college campuses.

NOTES

1. See Iva Jean Saraceni, "Developmental Issues in Setting Theatre Competencies." Presented at the national conference of the Association for Theatre in Higher Education, August 1989. Reprinted in the *Newsletter of Theatre as a Liberal Art*, Fall 1989, n.p.

TEACHING ABOUT ART IN THE LIBERAL ARTS WHAT'S AT STAKE

Carol Hall

Howard University

I question not my Corporeal or Vegetative Eye any more than I would Question a Window concerning a Sight. I look thro' it & not with it. (William Blake, *A Vision of the Last Judgment, 1810*)

In the mind of the artist, art historian, or art critic, a painting is a unique artifact, an object composed of canvas, pigment, brush strokes, color—an object that cannot be reproduced. But that is not the "cultural reality" of the painting. What a person knows about the "Mona Lisa," for example, might be based on photographs, conversation, criticism, engravings, cinema, satirical drawings, television, the labels of espresso coffee tins, or even a song by Nat King Cole.

In E. D. Hirsch's *Dictionary of Cultural Literacy*, under the category "Fine Arts," thirty-six artists are listed and the section is illustrated with seventeen photos of works of art, but there are only six paintings and three pieces of sculpture afforded a separate entry. They are: Paintings—"American Gothic" (Grant Wood), "Birth of Venus" (Botticelli), "Mona Lisa" (Michelangelo), "The Last Supper" (Michelangelo), "The Spirit of '76" (Archibald M. Willard), and "Whistler's Mother." Sculpture—"The Venus De Milo," Michelangelo's "Pieta" and Rodin's "The Thinker." Clearly, these images are seen as special cultural icons. In fact, one would be hard-put to live sixteen years with eyes open and avoid seeing some of them. Their value in Hirsch's primer is not based upon their existence as "works of art," but rather as coded emblems in the game of cultural literacy. These works become images "with symbolic and communal associations" (*Dictionary* 155). "Classic," in Hirsch's definition, means "something that has achieved broad currency" (*Dictionary* 155). If Hirsch's work has some impact on the formation of high school curricula and the composition and content of textbooks, one might expect a culturally literate freshman to come with these images stocked in his visual memory. What harm can come of it? High school, even elementary school, is the place to furnish familiarity with general concepts, short definitions, and flash-card knowledge. It takes no special training or preparation to give these received images to the student. Exposure to a photograph in a book is sufficient. Photos can be neatly tucked in a text so that after four years of high school liminally or subliminally, the thing takes. But such a catalogue of icons has little to do with art. My purpose here is not to find fault with Hirsch's approach but to use it as an example of the prevailing attitude toward visual arts in university core undergraduate courses. All too often, the arts are seen as adjunct decoration and in civilization courses, a sort of cultural "show and tell" in the classroom and in the textbook.

In the recently released report from the National Endowment for the Humanities, "50 Hours: A Core Curriculum for College Students" (*The Chronicle of Higher Education* Oct. 11, 1989), the first semester of the proposed "Western Civilization Course" would include discussion and presumably pictorial reproduction of the Parthenon, Chartres, and the Sistine Chapel. The second semester would include the paintings of Monet and Picasso (Mozart and Beethoven are also included—the possibility of a multi-media slide show presents itself). American civilization brings us Copley, and, with a bow to the women, Cassat, and O'Keefe. Clearly, the visual components stand in service to the written texts that will take the student on his journey towards cultural competence.

One can make the argument that all undergraduate exposure to "art" propaganda—literary, visual, or musical—is a kind of vulgarization. Are teachers of humanities prepared to "teach" works of art from various periods on any other than a superficial level? This is, of course, the charge leveled at the generalists and the "Great Book" surveys in core programs. John Erskine, who was instrumental in formulating the General Honors Program at Columbia after the First World War, countered such objections by stating that "every book had to be read at some time for the first time, that there was a difference between a reading acquaintance with great authors and a scholarly investigation of them" (Graff 134). There has to be, it seems to me, a rationale for introducing works of art in a humanities course of any kind—one that goes beyond the decorative and the illustrative features of enhancing a textbook or presenting a pleasing slide show. It is to be granted that a general humanities course cannot treat the work of art from the technical perspective of studio art. The idea, is after all, to teach "about art" here. Students need to know, however, the difference between a painting and a photograph, what materials go into making a work of art. They need to know, also, that the work of art is not identical with its reproduction or with the cultural baggage it might pick up on its way to receiving wide currency, or, to be more precise, to its vulgarization.

The coming together of "classical" and "popular" images in the photographic media is at the center of talking about art in today's curriculum. High culture is often the designation for the old and the ossified. Those who would keep discussion of contemporary works out of the curriculum and those who fear the dominance of the dreaded "popular culture" run the risk of giving the impression that art is a dead thing in a museum. Perhaps it is the notion of culture that needs reassessing. Today's "high" art was yesterday's disreputable entertainment. One

343

only has to think of the novel, long considered unworthy of serious academic consideration—especially that serialized and popular stuff of hacks such as Dostoyevsky and Dickens, both now in NEH's proposed "Western Civ. II." It is worth noting, as well, that the "classics" of visual art are almost always of necessity presented in the classroom in the subversively popular photographic medium. But Hirsch's high-school senior is likely to run into the "big six" paintings in other places.

Since the fifteenth century, paintings have been reproduced as prints. Works judged important, for whatever reason, were "transmuted by graphic technology into familiar images," and could gradually get onto more intimate emotional terms with the public than they could ever establish from fixed and often unaccessible sites. At first only reproducible in outline suggestive of composition, graphic techniques became more sophisticated in tones and shadings to give a more accurate suggestion of the total work. According to Anne Hollander

> The most important result of the camera's development was a kind of synthesis of high and low art. Through photographic reproduction, great paintings could be instantly transmuted directly into popular imagery *as photographs*. Their real looks, their basic beauties and virtues could be exposed to everyone, in the same medium that exposed the beauties of the cityscape, the half-opened blossoms, or the neighbor's kids—and the same one that entertained and swayed the eager public with all kinds of crude, slick, funny, and sentimental junk. (Hollander 32)

This ability to disseminate reproductions—in black and white, on postcards, posters, in color is "one of the many problems," according to the historian Etienne Gilson, "that arise from the constant interfering of aesthetics with education" (Gilson 64).

It is from a television corn-flake commercial that "American Gothic" came first to many Americans in the sixties. T-shirts brought us the "Thinker," and "The Last Supper" has been printed in atrocious shades of pink and blue on a million Protestant Sunday bulletins. Hardly any image has been as satirized and lampooned in cartoon and comic sketch as much as "Whistler's Mother," a painting that was never called by that name by the artist. On the other hand, television, that evil seen by many to usher in the end of reading among the young, has produced programs that take the viewer through the history of art as could never be done before. When it is done well, as in the case of Bronowski's bravely interdisciplinary approach to "Civilization," it teaches connections and invites viewers to look again and question clichés; when it is done not so well, as in the series being currently aired on public TV, "Art of the Western World," it is simply the talking to death of art in hushed and sanctifying tones. One could argue that all exposure is better than none for the cause of art, and this is probably true. What matters here is how art should be presented to the non-art major in the undergraduate curriculum.

Clearly, all reformers of the curriculum wish to produce students who are able to "think critically" in order to solve the problems of a troubled world. If art has any place in this process at all, should those students also not be challenged to "see critically?" To question and challenge the images that have been set to "define" our culture? If we value art in our society, it is not enough for the educated community to be familiar with the form and composition of the images of works of art that have received for whatever reason the name of greatness. They need to be informed about the aesthetic and political implication of visual images. We need to introduce them to the place of the visual image in society: the requirements and the possibilities of the various visual media, their use and misuse as educational propaganda, their relationship to the written word.

The colleges of fine arts on campuses that house the works of art produced by students and faculty and that oversee the development of practicing artists have become increasingly isolated from the colleges of liberal arts. Courses dealing with film, video, or photography are being assigned to schools of communication or are being challenged as not "academic" subjects. Undergraduate philosophy courses in aesthetics are likely to be surveys of how previous ages wrote about what they saw. The student needs to question what he sees every bit as much as he needs to question what he reads, and like it or not, he sees a lot more than he reads today. Painting did not stop with Picasso and Monet. It is still going on. Students should be aware of the artistic activity on their own campuses and the controversies that inevitably surround artistic expressions.

When Hirsch asserts that "*80 percent of literate culture has been in use for more than a hundred years*" and that "the materials of literate culture that are recent introductions constitute about a fifth of its total" (*Dictionary* xiv), he is suggesting that what is contemporary is not worth considering. Time, indeed seems to "sanitize" the controversial. In like manner, the winds of time have removed the bright decorations on ancient Greek statues and buildings, giving the impression of a serene, white marble stillness, and the smoke of the years has added a dark veil over the frescoes of the Sistine Chapel. Restoration, with all its political and ideological ramifications should be a subject discussed in the classroom. The Sistine Chapel restoration project and the controversy surrounding it would be a meaningful context from which to "teach" the "Sistine Ceiling." The problem with thinking of the artistic production of humanity as static and over is that it does not challenge the student to seek; only to take in passively. The history of art, like that of all disciplines is the story of controversy and not of consensus. "The university," as Gerald Graff has written, "is a curious accretion of historical conflicts that have been systematically forgotten" (Graff 257). "The boundaries that mark literary study off from creative writing, composition, rhetoric, communications, linguistics, and film, or those that divide art history from studio practice, or history from philosophy, literature, and sociology, each bespeak a history of conflict that was critical to creating and defining these disciplines yet has never become a central part of their context of study" (Graff 258).

Citing the controversy and civic outrage engendered recently in the Chicago community by two works of art by students at the Chicago Art Institute, Carol Becker, Chair of the graduate division at the Art Institute, wrote in an "Opinion" piece in *The Chronicle of Higher Education* (June 21, 1989) that art students should be offered "a truly rigorous core curriculum, with courses in art history and in social, cultural, philosophical, and literary history taught *in sequence*." In addition, she suggests that art students take courses that trace the role of the artist in society, to demonstrate that the concept of the artist is not a romantic, eternal construction but rather a historically determined one. Thus, the students would discover that there have been times when artists played a more decisive role than they have within the past decade of American history. Carol Becker's article seems to be suggesting that if artists were better humanists, they would be more respectable artists and could avoid the "seduction of slick vacuity." In other words, artists would not offend the community, artists [read citizens] would behave themselves. One wonders what influence such a course of study would have worked on the art of Paul Gauguin. [The NEH report suggests that in order to answer the questions "Who are we? What is our destiny?" we ought to consider the approaches of Gauguin as well as those of Thoreau and Einstein (*Chronicle* Oct. 11, 1989: A16)]. Becker's argument could be turned around, just as well, to suggest that the liberal arts students who one day may be called upon to express an opinion on unconventional or controversial works of art need to know something about art as a contemporary practice, an on-going inquiry, a search for new ways of expression. Surely, there have been some artists who have been "good" citizens—usually, however, not because they have pursued a core curriculum in a chronological order.

The ideological, religious, political, and economic backgrounds in which a given artist works play a role in the final place his work will take in the culture. Problems of patronage, conservation, restoration, and censorship are largely extra-artistic matters, but they are matters which will become the province of the educated classes in a democracy, which lacking kings and popes, depends on a few very wealthy individuals and the educated community at large to support artistic endeavor.

The recent controversy over the exhibit "Robert Mapplethorpe: the Perfect Moment" at the Corcoran Gallery of Art has brought the question of artistic censorship to the front pages of many newspapers. Robert Brookman, curator of the exhibit, which was very successfully shown under the auspices of the Washington Project for the Arts, sees the fuss about Jesse Helms' defeated amendment to restrict government funding of controversial works as a good thing (Yasul, *The Washington Post* Oct. 23, 1989). Sidney Lawrence, curator of the Hirschhorn Museum and Sculpture Garden says: "I think it's made everyone think about what art is and the purpose of art in our society" (Yasul). Henry Mitchell has pointed out that the cancellation of the exhibit is indicative of the lower value that our society as a whole places on the visual arts:

> Literature is singularly happy that its protection is acknowledged. . . . But the lesser arts, painting, sculpture, photography, and so forth, have not fared so well, mainly because relatively so few people care about them. Pictorial art has not gone through the same fights that literature has, and few care to defend it. . . . The Constitution is silent on pictorial art, as on so many other matters, leaving the problem to be worked out by the citizenry at large. (*The Washington Post* July 28, 1989: B12)

The educated citizen, the one we hope to produce at the end of a liberal arts education, should be aware of the importance of his support of freedom of expression in the pictorial arts as well as in speech and in the written word. This same citizen, after having been equipped with contexts, will also understand the importance of art as an on-going and dynamic force in the world human affairs.

In this presentation I have focused on ways of *teaching about* the creative, visual arts in the curriculum, primarily in humanities courses. Clearly, the problem of how best to insure a degree of visual literacy among liberal arts students is an interdisciplinary one, which must be approached from several points of view. As in all interdisciplinary ventures, careful planning is necessary to avoid chaos and charges of becoming "hobbyhorsical" or presumptuous (Wellek 66). The big question of "who will teach such matters and how" is open to discussion.

The place to start is in a coming together of the disciplines of fine arts and liberal arts—such communion happens at conferences such as this one, but rarely among members of the faculty when they return to the isolation of their respective disciplines.

Becker, Carol. "Art Students Require a Truly Rigorous Core Curriculum, to Help Them Develop Intellectually As Well As Artistically." *The Chronicle of Higher Education.* "Section 2," 21 June 1989: B1–B2.

Cheney, Lynne V. "50 Hours: A Core Curriculum for College Students," excerpted in *The Chronicle of Higher Education.* Volume XXXVI, No. 6, 11 Oct. 1989: A16–A20.

Gilson, Etienne. "Originals and Reproductions," *Painting and Reality.* Bollingen Series XXXV. 4. New York: Pantheon Books, 1957.

Graff, Gerald. *Professing Literature: An Institutional History.* Chicago and London: The University of Chicago Press, 1987.

Graham, John. "Ut pictura poesis," *Dictionary of the History of Ideas.* Vol. IV. New York: Charles Scribner's Sons, 1973, 465–76.

Hirsch, E. D., Jr. *Cultural Literacy: What Every American Needs to Know.* New York: Vintage Books, 1988.

Hirsch, E. D., Jr, Joseph Kett and James Trefil. *The Dictionary of Cultural Literacy: What Every American Needs to Know.* Boston: Houghton Mifflin Company, 1988.

Hollander, Anne. *Moving Pictures.* New York: Alfred A. Knopf, 1989.

Mitchell, Henry. "Art and the Common Man." *The Washington Post.* 28 July 1989: B2.

Wellek, René. "The Parallelism Between Literature and the Arts," *English Institute Manual.* New York: 1942.

Yasul, Todd Allan. "Mapplethorpe's Legacy: 'The Moment' Lingers on in a Move to Hartford." *The Washington Post.* 23 Oct. 1989: B7.

RELIGION STUDIES IN SECULAR EDUCATION: YES AND NO?

J. Daley

The University of Toledo

In his essay, *On Liberty*, J. S. Mill proposes a curriculum for various levels of education. He argues that at the most advanced level individuals should only be required to show that they understand the variety and diversity of opinions or views that are held on controversial subjects or matters of opinion. "Examinations" should be required for "a gradually extending range of subjects, so as to make the universal acquisition and, what is more, retention of a certain minimum of general knowledge virtually compulsory." Thereafter "examinations should be voluntary." But to keep the State from "exercising an improper influence over opinion," "knowledge should even in the higher classes of examinations be confined to facts and positive science exclusively." On matters of opinion, the "examinations on religion, politics, or other disputed topics should not turn on truth and falsehood" but understanding that "such and such an opinion is held, on such grounds, by such authors, or schools, or churches." In the study of philosophy, for example, he argues that "a student of philosophy would be the better for being able to stand an examination both in Locke and in Kant, whichever of the two he takes up with, or even if with neither. . . ." Further, on this view of and approach to higher education Mill points out "that there is no reasonable objection to examining an atheist in the evidences of Christianity, provided he is not required to believe in them." These examinations would, however, have to be "entirely voluntary."

For Mill, the purpose of this argument is that those who are religious would be instructed in their religion. That much the state could reasonably require. "Under this system, the rising generation would be no worse off in regard to all disputed truths than they are at present; they would be brought up either churchmen or dissenters as they now are, the State merely taking care that they should be instructed churchmen, or instructed dissenters." And only, of course, "if their parents chose" to allow the child to be so instructed. Historical considerations bearing on the notion of churchmen and dissenters are undoubtedly of direct concern to Mill. Throughout *On Liberty* he argues that as far as freedom of thought and discussion is concerned, individuals should be free to express their own views on religion or other matters of controversial political, moral, legal, and social importance; they should also be acquainted with and knowledgeable in an empathetic manner with the opinions they oppose. Putting aside for the moment the specific historical basis of Mill's argument, is there anything there that might pertain to "religion studies in secular education" in the United States? Does Mill's argument, if extended to higher education in the United States, have any continuing validity and merit? This overly-general question is meant to point out that the study of religions in secular education is relevant to understanding and dealing with the complexities of a secular society. Various political and social difficulties could be more intelligently understood and handled, perhaps, with an increased awareness and understanding of religion and why others deem it so significant. Religion studies might well be "enlightening" in ways that the other, better known "Enlightenment," has obscured for secular education.

"Truth" or "falsehood" is not, as Mill proposes, the issue, but rather an understanding and "hearing" of the opinions of religion. Whether a person be an atheist, agnostic, theist, or "indifferentist" the study should be considered a serious intellectual matter. A secular education could be judged deficient to the extent that it does not acknowledge religion studies. Further, this deficiency might be judged even more serious in the twentieth century because of the likely explosive influence that religion exerts upon political affairs in many, if not all, parts of the world. For example, in Northern Ireland, the Middle East, the United States religious beliefs are invoked as relevant to the social orders which government attempts to regulate. Consider the attempted abolition of religion as a detrimental historical and social institution in communist or socialistic societies in the Soviet Union or Cuba or even Sweden. And from still another perspective, apartheid in South Africa is bound up with certain, however controversial, beliefs of a particular sect of Christianity. These contemporary conflicts alone suggest that religion studies would not be impractical or irrelevant to understanding and action in the present.

Religion studies—like any study—will not necessarily change anything for the better or the worse in these situations. The political complexities are vast and intricate enough that no one study could accomplish that. They could, however, contribute to understanding these situations and in that way qualify as worthy studies for secular education. Secular education could benefit from religion studies because they would provide those who enter business, law, politics, engineering, medicine, or health professions with a knowledge that should not be ignored as far as world conflicts go, or patient-doctor relations or foreign trade. The intrinsic value of religion studies might be sufficient for many of us. However, there is a side to religion studies in secular education that offers an instrumental or extrinsic value—a practical, applied value. Hence, at present in the United States with the concerns of higher education for "doing," and "practice," religion studies hold out the possibility of contributing to and advancing peace and international understanding. Put differently, religion studies, if they are pursued in an intellectually serious way, could contribute to the understanding of human conflict and in doing so help to improve the approaches to conflict resolution. Certainly in the context of increasing emphasis on the "necessity" for "global" and/or "multicultural" education, religion studies should be accorded a primary role. Religion in the more basic sense of a way or form of life, what individuals believe, rightly or wrongly, they are living for, shared understanding, whether others are religious or not, should be considered indispensable.

Further, there may be a reason for religion studies, in the humanities at least, that has nothing to do with uses or practical concerns. Whatever the religious beliefs in question may be, Christian or Hindu or Islamic or Buddhist, or other, they reflect something about the human condition that is intrinsically worth knowing if we are to understand others and ourselves. That rather grand remark leaves judgments and evaluations, what Mill would call opinions, of and about religion out of the question for the moment. Right now the argument is that countless numbers of human beings and human cultures and civilizations in the past, from their very origins, up to the present and probably into any near or remote future, have found religion to be one, if not *the* only, basis by which their existence takes on some worthwhile purpose, meaning and value. For this reason alone, religion studies should be able to justify a place of value in any secular education. That so enormous a segment of humanity, past, present, and future, will have found what makes life worth living in religion, surely yet arguably, makes religion an important component of the studies of any human being, particular preferences and interests notwithstanding. Many of us would grant that religion is a famous (or infamous?) opiate of the people, mere superstition, an illusion with (or without?) a future, projection, sheer anthropomorphism, indoctrination, an out-moded, unscientific, oppressive, repressive, authoritarian, puritanism (in the bad "sexual" sense?). It is one cause, if not *the*, cause of so much human destruction in the form of war, hysteria, persecution, ignorance, hypocrisy, censorship, plus many more evils that could be listed here. For example, various civil and other wars or violations of human rights and freedoms not only past but around the world at present, cannot be denied or ignored. From this standpoint religions assuredly are not worth being studied. Might religion studies be a manifestation of what Herbert Marcuse dubbed "repressive tolerance"?

Or might it be that the above "litany" shows that the multitudinous dangers and evils of religion are historically complicated? Controversial questions that are not carefully examined and discussed are often taken for granted—"everybody knows that." For example, has the connection of religion with war and persecution, in particular Christian sects, come about through religion? Or has religion often been an expedient means to justify what was precipitated through political, economic, commercial, even educational and institutional purposes in the histories of cultures and civilizations? That argument is not directly the issue here. It is raised primarily to entertain the real possibility, historically and philosophically viewed, that religion may have received increasingly "bad reviews" beginning with and continuing since the Enlightenment. The gradually increasing prominence of science and technology in the more consciously planned development of social orders, especially in the so-called "West," may well have led to an increased misunderstanding of the value of religion as a *study* in secular education.

The above catalogue could, however, be granted without qualification as well. But if it were, then some other catalogues would also in fairness to the historical records of accomplishments, have to be granted. That is, it should also be acknowledged that religion has brought humanity immense blessings and benefits, and has not been merely malevolent, but also benevolent.

What might these benefits be? For a start, there is the argument from intrinsic value already mentioned above. This argument can be used to show the blessing of beliefs; whether true or false (not easy to answer either way), beliefs enable innumerable human beings to find something of value in their lives. They have done so under the most miserable of conditions not only in the past, but also in the present and probably will continue to do so in the future. Those of us who have no need of religion for that purpose or see no value in that "use" of religion may demur, understandably so. In the spirit of *On Liberty* religious views at least furnish ideas and thoughts for discussion; however, those who do find even that purpose and/or use in religion will, also understandably, demur in return. Checkmate, then?

Or as Mill argues, those who see no value in religion and see it historically, both past and present and most likely in the future, as detrimental need not believe in these religions, any of their doctrines or dogmas, but should understand them and study them on the basis of whatever evidences are indicated. Those opposed may hold their opinions that religion is pernicious, but religion studies only require the acknowledgment and understanding of opposed opinions. In a Millian approach to secular education, religion studies would oblige us to look at the blessings as well as the brutalities of religion; to study and understand all sides, however reluctantly or grudgingly, not just the time-honored "two" sides. Further, as some would ask, have any of the brutalities of religion in the past or present yet matched the concentration camps of the Nazis or the Gulag of Stalin's Soviet Union, not to mention the treatment of the Ukraine and other secular horrors?

A final but necessarily brief argument for religion studies in secular education is the influential role of religion in the origin and development of knowledge and secular education. To oversimplify a complex historical process, there is no serious reason to doubt that earlier in Western civilization religion was more closely interwoven with other beliefs about the heavens, the earth as the center of the universe, the nature of the human being, and the place of the human in the rest of nature. These beliefs and the formation and structure of knowledge and understanding at earlier periods in Western history were not so sharply separated or "segregated" as they now tend for the most part to be. And though by the end

352

of the eighteenth century (the Enlightenment), the development of the natural sciences had no relation to religion, it still remains true that religion contributed to their origin and nature. Of course the conflict between religion and science, the notorious Galileo and later the Darwin affairs, among other less well-known conflicts, should not be ignored. Religions also interfere with and retard, although they do not eventually prevent further secular advances and developments. Though that too is historically and conceptually a complex and complicated matter with conflicting interpretations, still the interfering influence of religion, though unsuccessful, should not be dismissed. That side of religion should also be discussed and, if condemned, then at least understood. Again, while this argument does not do away with the "evils" perpetrated upon human beings and society through religions, it does bring out that the study of religions can enable us to understand not only the history of the natural sciences but also their nature. This argument also assumes, however, that an understanding of the history of the natural sciences is worthwhile, an assumption by no means widely shared even in secular education. Granted that view, it follows that religion studies might contribute to an understanding of secular education: what secular means and why the secular is accorded so much (too much?) intellectual and practical prominence in the contemporary world. Despite some critical qualifications, my arguments so far favor religion studies in secular education. Are there not, however, some serious objections?

First, religion is no longer central to the diverse secular structures and institutions of society. Accordingly, the studies that any educated citizenry needs should include computer science, physics, economics, political science, even geography or composition rather than religion. These studies enable individuals to find their way around the rational and technical complexities of contemporary societies. Religion studies would not furnish that kind of practically indispensable knowledge and understanding.

Second, religion has had to, and should continue to, give way to the process of secularization, especially in education. Education in the present must be directed to shared abilities and purposes, dispensing with any particular sectarian or ideological beliefs and convictions. Though the place of religion should be secured and protected as far as freedom to worship or not to worship goes, it should not any longer be considered educationally serious enough to warrant a prominent, much less required, place in secular education.

Third, the question of what any curriculum in secular education should encompass is complicated and controversial as matters stand. Whatever else religion may be, it does primarily speak to the personal dispositions and interests of individuals. It requires at some stage that persons freely decide what their view of religion is. As fundamentally a matter of faith, and faiths that vary so much from one individual and/or society to another, religion studies are important but not

353

educationally that important. Scientific, technical and other secularly valuable studies should be considered indispensable because they concern what we all must, religion or lack of religion aside, face together.

Fourth, even the argument from the intrinsic value of religion, the view according to which religions express a responsive experience to the human condition, something of value and worth in the world and in human beings, is well enough known and, hence, not essential to secular education. Many or most of us know how significant in a superior (and often unquestionable and undiscussable) sense religion is taken to be. Whether we agree or not, that superior significance so readily ascribed to religions does not call for serious study. Even for those who do find religion that significant, it is not a "subject" to be studied so much as an experience to be felt and lived rather than analyzed and understood. Those who seek an education can manage the understanding of the value and worth of religion on their own. Their education in increasingly secular societies does not, however, require religion studies. It makes more sense, and is more valuable for them and for societies, to require and/or encourage studies that they can not master on their own, not grasp without the assistance of a purely secular education.

Replies could be made to these objections or questions. They are intended, however, for the sake of discussion to show some of the arguably serious difficulties in the view that this essay presents, particularly the objection that religion studies in secular education pose a substantial risk that in subtle yet intellectually devious ways they would be used for indoctrination. They may encourage uncritical approaches to religious beliefs that are politically reactionary or the causes of unnecessary conflicts in various regions of the world, especially in those regions of the world that are most desperately in need of scientific and technological knowledge.

And yet is it not possible that the opposite might equally well come about, namely, that religion studies in secular education would facilitate multicultural understanding and the advancement of scientific and technological knowledge? There is no necessary conflict here. With the recognition of the place and value of religion in human history and society, alongside the equally important place and value of the natural sciences and technologies, could not the extrinsic and intrinsic worth of religion studies contribute as much to secular education as scientific and technological studies? In the spirit of *On Liberty*, these critical questions should be impartially considered. What any curriculum should include is a difficult question. But what any curriculum should be careful not to exclude *a priori* may be even more difficult, all the more so if the basis for the exclusion has not been looked at from various perspectives.

REALITY: THE ABSOLUTE CURRICULUM

John Richard Schrock

Emporia State University

What is a "Core" and What is a "Canon"?

It is a hallmark of scientific papers that terms are carefully defined. It is also a frustration of the core curriculum debate that the "core" and the "canon" are so readily confused and used interchangeably.

The "core curriculum" as used here refers to any body of knowledge that a society decides "everyone should have in common." That "core" will be taught formally in schools and informally by other institutions (e.g., churches) and by society's media. The "canon" is the set of readings that may or *may not* be used as common texts for the formal core curriculum.

It is clear that NEH Chair, Lynne Cheney, has proposed a fifty-credit-hour *core curriculum*, but a canon functions to underlie only twenty-four hours, a minority, of that core. Look closely at the majority of that core: the natural sciences and mathematics, communications and performing arts, and foreign language. Learning in these classes means being able to work through puzzles of nature, solve problems accurately, effectively communicate with other people in English and in another language. The test for this learning is performance in the real world. The texts that hold our students against this reality are updated regularly—new biology texts, new language texts—because our understanding of the real world is constantly evolving. Now Mendel and Darwin did some very important basic work in biology, and Euclid was lucid in math, and we could use the *Analects* to study Chinese. But these specific works do not help students be modern biologists or mathematicians or linguists. If you study these works, it is to study the history of science or the philosophical content, not science or Chinese—and that history or philosophy is then part of the twenty-four hours of "civ."

In the minority twenty-four credit hours of civilization and social studies coursework a common "canon" of readings is proposed as the central if not sole content of coursework. It is argued here that the history, the arts, the literatures, are also tethered to a standard of "reality" if they are to be taught with intellectual integrity—as opposed to dogmatic proclamation.

"Reality" in the Non-Sciences

We recognize when the social imagination seriously contradicts reality. It was a vivid image from a decade ago. As the jets streaked over the bombed out

Iranian villages, black-clad Moslem women held their fists to the sky and cursed "American devils." Of course, those were Russian-made MIGs that landed at Iraqi bases, and they had no U.S. support—the mental images had no correspondence with physical reality. The belief was by definition "insane." Tragically, this insanity is the direct consequence of, and only possible through, the imposition of a uniform formal and informal educational base, including a core curriculum. Such an education is intensely administered by nations whenever they go to war. It is more gently diffused in peacetime by mere ethnocentricity and history. As teachers, we are its formal messengers. Without being tethered at every point possible to reality, our history, our literature, our art, any core curriculum and any canon are likewise "insane."

This thesis rests on the following arguments: 1) Science is successful and predictive only because it is reality-based; 2) The images in the arts and humanities are no different in kind from the images in the sciences; they too are reality-based; 3) There is a set "human condition" and perspective that limits the images available to humanity; 4) The real-life experiences of each person illuminate the "meaningfulness" of the abstract words conveyed in a chosen canon; thus a canon is interpreted provincially even when it is uniformly delivered across the world; 5) While language and culture limit our images, the selection of a uniform canon provides narrow and restrictive blinders that prevent people from imaging new arts and sciences in ways that more closely reflect the human condition in the real world; 6) A canon by its very nature is elitist, ignoring what is "not cultured," and this curtails empathy and a valid study of the "vulgar" realities; 7) The biological model of information transfer (genetics) provides a real case, not an analogy, of what degree of balance between narrow cloning and wild diversities is needed for a species to survive over long periods of time; 8) While all canons are in the end authority-based, reality is an absolute curriculum we can ignore only at our own peril.

Each argument is supported by evidence from the real world.

The Reality-base of Science

What makes one idea pedestrian, another one "great?" Many cases indicate it is "conformance with reality." Professor Harold Urey was the author of a long-held theory on the origin of the moon's surface; indeed, this was the version in all the standard textbooks. When the Apollo venture to the moon brought back moon rocks, a sample finally arrived to be dumped on his lab table. It took Dr. Urey but a few minutes' inspection before he looked up and said he'd been wrong all those years. That is greatness.

A younger audience will remember the commission that investigated the explosion of the space shuttle Challenger. After long and inconclusive testimony on the uncertainties of various spacecraft parts working in cold weather, physicist Dick Feynman reached over and dunked a small o-ring in his glass of ice water—and it lost its resiliency. End of argument. That is greatness.

The hype that everything is relative, that all resides in the eye of the beholder . . . is bunk. For a short time, scientists may argue over the interpretations of experiments in so-called "cold-fusion," but in the end it will either lead to plentiful cheap energy or nowhere; there will be no cold-fusion sects and anti-sects thirty years from now. Some scientists are not as willing to yield to reality as Urey, or they are dedicated to an ideology more than they are to science. Lysenko held out for inheritance of acquired characteristics against the reality—and set Russian genetics back twenty years. Others mutilated toads, charred chimpanzee jaw-bones, and fabricated data for promotion. But they were exposed, most quite rapidly. Reality "covers" for no one.

Science Does Not Differ In Kind From the Humanities

Non-scientists may cry foul. The argument usually runs this way. New ideas come either as discoveries, inventions, or creations. You discover something that has always been there for the looking. And if one person doesn't find it, sooner or later another will—similar to Columbus discovering America. An invention requires a little bit more. If Edison hadn't invented the light bulb, someone else would have, but it might look somewhat different. But "real creativity"? That is unique to one individual. Only a Picasso could paint that picture, and if he had not been born, such pictures would never have been painted. Hence, science is somewhat inevitable and plodding, made primarily of discoveries and inventions. The creations of the arts and literature—now those are supposedly unique inspirations.

Both Gunther Stent (1972) and Jacob Bronowski elaborate how this is desperately wrong. Indeed, Bronowski as a fine mathematician, scientist, and Blake scholar, devotes many of his essays, collected in *A Sense of the Future* and *The Visionary Eye*, to detailing how human imagination is involved in the same tasks in both the arts and the sciences. The unique ways in which Mendel "sets the problem" then become our characteristic view as we learn Mendelian genetics. We "think" pea plants and, from later workers, fruit flies and lab mice when we "think" genetics. Genetics would be a different image if it were set to water lilies and cockroaches and kangaroos. Newton's "calculus" has a different flavor from Leibnitz's system, just as art would have a different flavor without Picasso.

So how can we tether the mental images of love and loyalty and beauty to the real world and take their measure, as we would test a physics formula? Consider the human capacity for empathy. It underlies each person's ability to read the symbols written by others not present and even long gone, and to see others in

357

oneself. This property, unique to the human situation, is no less an object of study than reflexes. This is not to say that we will soon be measuring the worth of poems with graphs. What is meant is that greatness in art and literature rests, as in science, in the imaging of the real human condition in a real, natural world. We look at art or read literature, and we place ourselves in the position of the author and say "I know how she/he felt."

This argument unfolds best in a delightful dialogue between proponents of the "two cultures" in Bronowski's "The Abacus and the Rose." The startling conclusion is that great art and literature nowhere develop and flourish unless there is also great science underway. If a civilization is not developing new and more accurate images of the physical world, then it does not develop great art nor literature. They are of the same fabric: the human imagination "playing upon the surface of the real." In science, it is the reality of the physical and living environment. In the humanities, it is the reality of the human condition.

The Human Condition and the Human Perspective

So is there really a "human condition"? Only non-biologists would ask. The unique perspective of the human condition is a distinct, narrow band on the spectrum of diverse life forms. A giant whale "sees" the world in great uniformity as it cruises the oceans. Its huge baleen combs screen out fish and seaweed and krill, and it slurps them down with no gourmet distinctions. At the other end of the spectrum, the microscopic bacterial spore that lands on your moist ketchup-stained tie likewise has a uniform environment—ketchup as far as its bacterial "eye" can see. Of course it can't see as we can, but it does "perceive" insofar as it chemically detects needed nutrients and responds by replicating until the sources are either used up or dried up.

We obviously have a "human condition," and it is well defined by the measurements of sensory biology. When a person is handicapped by a lack of the usual conditions, we have a growing technology that helps "fill in" for missing hearing or eyesight. If we want to feel the viscous flow of air over a bee's wings as it flies, or the magnetic "pull" that may send monarch butterflies to Mexican mountains each fall, we have to settle for analogous experiences available to us as organisms about five to six feet tall and with very limited sensory ranges.

Experience with Reality Underlies All "Meaning"

Although you are limited to the "human condition," the real-life experiences of each student in your classroom underpin the "meaningfulness" of all the abstract words used in your lectures, your reading assignments, your classroom discussions. Rear children in rooms with blank white walls and your canon is meaningless; all the "great works" fall to zero meaning. As students grow up in environments more and more isolated from the natural world, what they will image when they read a passage from a canon will be far less than what the author imaged. "What dagger is this I see before me" will have greater meaning to an older generation that remembers what real butcher knives were used for on the farm. As a teacher, you fight to picture for them the flavor of life when the play was written—why a "meaningless" phrase now was so loaded with emotion then. And yet you know that in the end, it will only be as meaningful as their life is experience-filled. In science, it is becoming ever more critical not only to give students information, but to give them experience. It is no different in the arts and literature.

Provincialism

All students have twenty-four hours of life per day. The problem for students in the Iranian village is that their twenty-four hours is spent learning how their forefathers viewed the world rather than checking the ground truth of what they are told and what they therefore interpret in what they "see." It is this complex and burdensome process of provincialism, this ethnocentrism, that faults the canon. Cheney is provincial. No insult intended. In promoting Western scriptures, she joins William Bennett in exuding this confidence that the great western writers basically said it best.

Most college students discover their high school provincialism during the first vacation home from college. The world was so simple when they grew up. Now that they return and visit with old high school buddies who stayed home to work at the local factory and support a Camaro, it dawns on them for the first time how limited their local view of the world was. This broadening and liberalization will occur again if they visit distant cities or live overseas. Sadly, the "Western Civ" core is often taught with small town mentality, and it is usually heard by local ears with provincial experiences.

If Adam Smith and Karl Marx are taught both in the U.S. and the U.S.S.R., why do their students and ours make such uniformly contrasting judgments? Do American students really recognize that Adam Smith does not champion cut-throat competition and does not endorse the concept that the common good is served by each person working for private gain? Do our students question the obvious problems of capitalism when the stock market crashes . . . again? Do they realize that if you are in the army or police or at a public school or university, you are participating in a socialist institution? I cannot remember being angrier in my life than when I discovered that Karl Marx is as central to the foundations of sociology as Mendel is to biology. The damned American schools hid it from me. They hid it from my teachers. So I had "innocent" teachers. But innocence, like ignorance, is no excuse. We teach a castrated Marx just as the U.S.S.R. teaches a castrated Adam Smith. The intellectual emasculation occurs both in the informal socialization and in the delivery of a formal canon, and until we are willing to assure that capitalists teach Adam Smith in U.S.S.R. classrooms and Marxists teach Marx in U.S. classrooms, we are agents of the same process that sets Iranian women to cursing "American devils."

To me the most unexpected aspect of this debate is the arrogance of Western academics. There is no disputing the role of other canons—*Das Kapital, Mein Kampf*, Kadafy's green book and Mao's little red book—in regimenting the thinking of large numbers of people, not just to see their social problems in one perspective, but also to *not see* them in others. How can academics recognize the role these books had as "canons" in their cultures without recognizing the equally detrimental role of our traditional canons? Obviously the German in 1930s Germany failed to recognize he had a problem with his image of reality. Today Western academics are making the same mistake. It is ironic that Assistant NEH chair Jerry Martin defends Cheney's core curriculum at the same time he laments "false dichotomies" and disclaims having any viewpoint about Marxism. The irony is that Western languages probably evolved much of their black-white, up-down dichotomous nature from Roman and Greek classics that posed the world in such a way—Korzybski even characterizes the problem as "Aristotelian" thinking. And how odd it is that a professor who worked at a public university does not recognize that he has had close working knowledge of a socialist organization. Not only do we not recognize that most of our colleges and universities are socialist institutions, we do not see stock market crashes that wipe out old folks' savings as "problems" of capitalism. To expose this vast sea of cultural blankness, simply ask college students the following questions:

—Have nuclear weapons ever been used in war? (Thankfully, not yet.)
—Who was the first man in space? (Now was it Shepard or Glenn?)
—And the first woman in space? (Wasn't that Sally Ride?)

Of course if students stop to think, some may recognize that the U.S. did end the war with Japan with nuclear weapons and the "firsts" in space were Russians. But they function in day-to-day life with the feeling that we were nuclear innocents and first in space. I selected these because they are common opinions and yet wrong beyond dispute. There are literally thousands of other "factlets" that are likewise wrong, yet have legitimacy in American minds. The first eleven Chinese executed after the "democracy demonstrations" were arsonists who burned a train and killed civilians, not pro-democracy innocents. We are seeing and hearing more what we want to see and hear than what *is*. Teachers and a set core are the instruments of this blindness. Sadly, there is reason to believe that the

360

limitations of our students' experiences and the distortion of the past are just as unyielding in our classrooms as in many "totalitarian" states.

The Canon Prevents the Development of New and Better Images

It is not enough to give "equal time." While culture limits our images, the canon provides further restrictive blinders that prevent people from imaging new arts and sciences that more closely reflect the human condition in the real world. When a new image does surface from those "odd" individuals who can see through or around the current mindset, the new framework is often not recognized or it is dismissed.

Often the most challenging questions come from young students in the lower level classes. Such students are not sufficiently familiar with the standard paradigms and explanations to know not to ask "obviously-answered" questions. And graduate students who "know" the current perspective also accept it and do not look for alternatives. It is from young students who "don't know better" that teachers such as Dick Feynman detected the weak spots in our current fabric of knowledge. Often the greatest advances are made when someone "naive" brings in the techniques of another field against all the wisdom of the resident experts.

Bennett, Cheney, and others seem eager to give credit to the Western canon for all the benefits of Western civilization, but few are willing to acknowledge that it is to blame for any problems, and that it serves to exclude new and more functional images. Here are some concrete examples.

Semantics almost made it into the "core"—so to speak. In the early seventies, phase elective courses were *the* educational innovation (an unusual innovation since phase elective was a change in content rather than pedagogy). For a brief moment, the core curriculum James Conant established for high school students broke wide open and there was a proliferation of courses in the English and language arts curriculum. Along with science fiction and women's literature was a block on semantics. The very effective lessons of Korzybski and Hayakawa and Irving Lee were legitimate for a brief moment. Then the petulant educational establishment dismissed phase electives as frills (without any evidence of ineffectiveness) and lumbered off into the back-to-basics and time-on-task movement.

Some ideas that have the potential to help us in serious social and science dilemmas originate outside the Western tradition. One serious situation is the current need to "professionalize" education. From several assessments it is obvious that we have substantial incompetence in the classroom. Framed within the characteristic western mode of reasoning, efforts have generally focused on a linear analysis: What does an expert teacher of an effective school do—then train preservice teachers to do these things. The result is a drift to an assembly-line technician mentality where teachers follow Madeline Hunter outlines or other

361

prescribed checklists. How else could a Westerner think of professionalizing education?

Yet, in China, this question has been framed differently for the last 2000 years. The Confucian school was a cult of the professional. You trained a perfect gentleman in the sense that he learned general principles of conduct (i.e., when in a situation, treat the other person as you would want to be treated). But each situation is considered unique and to be judged on all its facets. In direct contradiction, the Chinese legalists, represented by Han Fei-Tse, who believed you could never educate a whole population to be such gentlemen and that you must spell out precisely what citizens may and may not do in all situations. When legalists were shown ways to get around the laws, they responded with more laws to close the loopholes. The legalists and the professionals constituted two major schools of thought and for 2000 years, Chinese rulers adopted one or the other.

When this model is applied to the problem of professionalizing American education, we see at once that the current drive to make good teachers through checklists is "legalism," subject to flaws that would be obvious to anyone who grew up in China. This error, also rampant in other professions, is summarized in the statement of one physician who left medicine last year: "Once I could do what was right for a patient. Now I must do what the HMO and Blue Cross checklists require, and add unneeded tests to protect myself from possible litigation." But we lack the Eastern tradition; therefore, the common recourse visible to us is this legalistic checklisting. Preparing competent and wise professionals able to handle each situation on its individual merits seems not to occur to the myriad education-ist boards pondering reform and new certification standards but locked within the Western intellectual traditions.

Elitism

When John Stuart Mill spoke for education of ". . . capable and cultured human beings . . ." he went too far. We need "capable" human beings; this is the interfacing-with-reality factor. The "cultured" phrase adds elitism. Most of history has been written by whom? By the "cultured," of course. Thus we do not find recorded the vulgar attitudes of Roman and Greek common folk, but instead the "proper" perspectives of the privileged few. Today we ignore waves of photocopied cartoons and jokes on President Bush, Jewish American Princesses, and Ethiopians. Why should such realities be hidden from students while Nobel Prizes won by one-billionth of the human population are center stage? Graffiti is part of the lives of many people, and it affects their social lives and their political views. If we are to understand society at large, we must study *all* its aspects.

Although scholars are sheltered from "lower class" realities, you are acutely aware of the shortcomings if you learned a foreign language in formal language classes: all proper words, but no slang. And then when you go overseas or listen to real conversation, you are woefully deficient. Pure elitism. So pervasive is this propriety that Reinhold Aman's heroic efforts with *Maledicta* only expose the tip of the iceberg of academic snobbery.

Propriety and tact likewise hide from us from cases where our current paradigms do not adequately manage the human situation. Educationist trends, more fads than paradigms, linger with us too long because teachers are simply too polite to voice how stupidly ineffective the methodology is. Education professors persist in pushing nice sounding but faulty pedagogy from a fear of being insulting. But any change of substance, any revolution, requires realistic outspoken criticism. How can you know you are wrong if nobody tells you? The most worrisome aspect of the argument used by proponents for a uniform core or canon is that it echoes the terminology used by the Third Reich that instituted the Nuremberg Laws "for the protection of German blood and honor."

A canon by its nature is elitist, ignoring what is not "cultured," and this curtails empathy for the "non-academic" and ignores the valid study of the common "vulgar" realities. If garbage on TV affects the population, then we have no choice but to study it.

The Absolute Curriculum

Mao had his red book. Khadafy has his green book. Robert Maynard Hutchins had his Great Books. John Dewey strove to "select the influence which shall affect the child and to assist him in *properly* (my italics) responding to these influences." Jacques Maritain found ". . . the chief task of education is above all to shape man . . . ." Thorndike would use education to "aid us to use human beings for the world's welfare. . . ." Each of the above asks for allegiance. Each honestly proclaims "My way . . . I have found the truth."

Reality imposes a different standard. Not your view. Not my view. Just reality. "It is, therefore I teach."

Each year I have a class of seniors about to enter biology teaching. They have science preparation as strong as that of any biology teachers in the country. Yet fifteen years of indoctrination in classrooms has convinced them that teacher-generated consequences are real consequences. I confess that I only partially succeed in getting them to see that getting stung when you mess with a beehive is a real consequence different in kind from getting an "F" because you didn't know the quiz about bees. Their task should primarily be to facilitate students' "playing upon the surface of the real." Instead, our schooling systems encourage them to copy their own education models. But only reality, not the teacher, "tests true." Only reality, not the teacher, dictates "real consequences."

This is their most important lesson. To evaluate it, I assign the "American biology teacher in Beirut" trial, a take-home assignment where they are supposedly kidnapped and charged with being a propagandist for Western ideology. I include detailed charges in the scenario, obvious cases where such teachers act as propagandists to perpetuate bias and train the protosoldier. But the captors are "intellectually honest and willing to listen to your arguments. Luckily you are a science teacher. Save your life."

If the preservice teachers have understood the nature of science and are aware of its international foundations, and if they do universal lab and field work (for gravity and the chart of elements are the same everywhere), then they avoid "execution." Otherwise, they receive another lesson on the difference between teacher evaluation and real consequences.

But I have really cheated when I say "luckily you are a science teacher." For any teacher in art or literature should also be able to elaborate how he or she helps students see the universals in human experience. Few non-science teachers would avoid "execution."

Lessons on Information Transfer From Biology

Ironically in the latest discussion of the canon (Hitt et al. 1989), proponents raise what they call a biological metaphor: a canon serves the function of gonads to pass on the inheritance to the next generation. It provides the "chromosomal constants" of our culture. However, a biologist immediately recognizes the problem with this line of reasoning. Constant use of the original canon serves as a template; all of the variation that springs up in future generations is repeatedly lost. In biology, diversity—not uniformity—is the rule. That is why we have sex. That is why we die.

To compare cultural information transfer with genetic information transfer is not really an analogy or a metaphor; it is a comparison of two real systems for accomplishing similar tasks. It is valid to look at the features of one that have evolved to make it successful, and use this look to evaluate equivalent strategies in the other. This line of argument is drawn from a discipline that has determined that there are pleasure centers in the brain, and that eating and sex are pleasurable because they result in behaviors that perpetuate the species. Therefore, if survival (combined with its pleasurable aspects) is the prime criterion for an information transfer system, then we can deduce the following about core curricula.

Rigid replication of information does not provide the variation to survive in a changing world. Organisms that reproduce asexually are able to exploit a uniform environment that matches their abilities. As long as they have access to this environment, they waste no energy on generating variation, and they are superior to sexual critters. Thus some ancient bacteria live in volcanic lakes and probably vary little from their ancestors several billion years ago. The coelacanth is a primitive lobefin fish, a living fossil, that found sanctuary in the monotonous deep seas of Madagascar. The cultural equivalent to this is the rigid canon, where all of a population is cultivated on a monoculture basis. We see this uniformity in the scripture-based subcultures of Iran and in American fundamentalist schools. While they celebrate the fellowship of sharing the same backgrounds, understanding the same subtle nuances, etc., they have little potential for seeing from a perspective outside their group. They must either construct a uniform environment where they can survive with little dissonance, or become isolated coelacanths amidst a sea of change. Wherever we have relied on monocultures we have had disasters—from the 1840s potato blight to the 1970s corn rust.

But uniformity in time and space is the exception, and 99 percent of life forms have found mechanisms for introducing and maintaining variation. Indeed, there is selection for variation itself, and that invention of course is sex, first developed by algae. It is so successful in producing variation that there is virtually no chance of a couple producing identical offspring aside from identical twins, and no chance of replicating either parent at all. But the amount of variation in the environment is not always great and the rate of change is not always fast. Thus, many organisms hedge their bets and, like aphids, can clone themselves while the monoculture is spread before them, and then become sexual when it is time to disperse young to unknown and variable frontiers.

The satisfying aspect of examining biological information transfer is that it does not yield a pure answer; neither exact copying nor wildly variable reproduction has evolutionarily "shaken out" as the all-time best strategy. Organisms simply can't get too radical. When a variation becomes just too extreme, too "unlike" others, it cannot interbreed. It has become reproductively isolated. "Intercourse" no longer occurs. Now this is an interesting choice of terms, and it reveals more than accidental correspondence in the phenomena. When "social intercourse" no longer occurs, we are also intellectually isolated. To illustrate, when you overhear "proletariat" or "comrade," you fold your arms in defense— you adamantly do not view the world in those terms. You were not brought up to think this way. Your canon was different. When the contrast becomes so extreme that you cannot communicate with each other (i.e., have "social intercourse"), you are a different species. In biology it is called the biological species concept and here we can call it the social species concept. The bottom line is that an animal cannot decide to walk away from its hereditary information; it must run the gauntlet of natural selection or go extinct. But at any moment, we can choose to change our information base. We can move to another way of life, if the information variety is there. The formula is simple. We must not institutionalize a monoculture, for in that direction lies certain extinction at our level of complexity and change. But we should not (and probably cannot) generate wild diversity to the extent that the next generation has no historical, literary, or artistic experience and abstractions in common; at that point they would lack sufficient common experience to communicate.

The wisdom is well generalized in Mao's rapidly withdrawn challenge to "let a hundred flowers blossom." Not a thousand, for that is probably far too high a number for society to apply and allow selection to winnow. And not one "flower." The canon promoted by nostalgic classicists Bennett and Cheney is closer to this blueprint for extinction. If we are to advance in new images to problems, I need a much greater mix of students with diverse cultural backgrounds in my class, and they must be willing to interact.

There is one last revelation from biology. All complex organisms die. However, the copies of information, genes, live on in the "germ line" that extends through the series of cells that generate successful sperm and eggs. People are temporary support units that nourish and protect this germ line. The successful evolution of humans as unspecialized organisms that image their environment indicates that the transfer of learned information (culture) has been naturally selected as a maintenance unit for the germ line. What is most unexpected is that aging and ultimately death appear not to be the mere accumulation of errors in cell copying, but are part of a process that was also selected for. The germ line is immortal; the support unit is not. Why would a germ line put a limit on the lifetime of its support unit and periodically rebuild a new one; why "death" and why "birth"? Why not immortality . . . for me?

I believe the answer is obvious. The selection in genetically determined structures is for those who can survive to produce the largest number of offspring, not those who can survive the longest as one support unit. In non-genetic information transfer, this would be not for one happy old-timer, but for many children who can better handle their germ lines' environment. As the environment changes, it appears that it is more efficient to recombine for genetic variety and restart the learning over again, than it is to try to teach an old dog new tricks. My father saw the great wars and learned to drive Model T's and coupes. I grew up in the Civil Rights era and saw the DNA revolution. Could either of us set aside these mindsets and "retool" our personalities to handle the new selective landscape of the 2000s? Biology dictates that task will fall to our children. Unlike genetic information, learned culture may be fabulously malleable. Yet its residence is not.

Mortality has been selected for.

Death is necessary.

The canon must change.

WORKS CITED

Bronowski, Jacob. 1973. *The Ascent of Man.* Boston: Little, Brown and Company.
_____. 1965. *Science and Human Values.* New York: Harper and Row.
_____. 1977. *A Sense of the Future.* Cambridge: MIT Press.
_____. 1978. *The Visionary Eye: Essays in the Arts, Literature and Sciences.* Cambridge: MIT Press.
Cheney, Lynne. 1989. *50 Hours: A Core Curriculum for College Students.* Washington, D.C.: National Endowment for the Humanities.
Korzybski, Alfred. 1933. *Science and Sanity.* Lakeville, CT: Institute of General Semantics.
Hitt, Jack, E. D. Hirsch, Jr., John Lakiski, Jon Pareles, Roger Shattuck, and Geyatri C. Spival, 1989. "Who Needs the Great Works." *Harper's Magazine.* September, 43–52.
Roll, Eric (ed.) 1985. "Jacob Bronowski: A Perspective." *Leonardo: Journal of the International Society for the Arts, Sciences and Technology.* Vol. 18, 215–81.
Stent, Gunther S. 1972. "Prematurity and Uniqueness in Scientific Discovery." *Scientific American* 227: December, 84–93.

LIBERAL EDUCATION—REALISTIC EXPECTATION OR CHIMERA? (THE CASE STUDY OF THE UNIVERSITY OF WEST FLORIDA)

Arthur H. Doerr

University of West Florida

The development and maintenance of a curriculum which contributes to a liberal education is an arduous task which requires the honest efforts of able academicians and the active support of administrators, staff, students, governing boards, university patrons, and the general public. The retention of such a curriculum once developed, and the maintenance of support once acquired, are even more difficult than program initiation and implementation.

It is a given that many factors shape curricula designed to provide a liberating focus to the college or university student, e.g., nature of the student body, time constraints imposed by the focus of the institution, the quality and intellectual activity of the faculty, honest philosophical differences as to the nature and purposes of such a program, and practical matters such as FTE generation. Clearly, pragmatic considerations cannot be eliminated, but the principal focus of any such effort must be upon what is appropriate from an intellectual and educational standpoint. There must be a sense of purpose and mission, and participants must be convinced that the effort is worth the undertaking. Initiatives stemming from any other motivations are doomed to failure.

Above all, curricular requirements to support a liberal education must be, oxymoronic as the suggestion may appear, structured, rational, cogent, and coherent. At its most basic, such a curriculum must teach students to read with comprehension, to write with effect, to speak persuasively, to understand and put into practice basic scientific and mathematical principles, to recognize and value the heritage of the West, to appreciate the social nuances of human beings at work and play, to develop an interest in and concern for the human and humane, and to assess and evaluate the languages and characteristics of other cultures, all within the context of a sound logical, ethical, and moral framework.

Tradition, entrenched interests, and student apathy or militancy have militated against the development and maintenance of such a curriculum at many institutions. Liberal education has fallen upon hard times at many universities notwithstanding almost universal lip service to the concept and a seeming flurry of activity in the past decade.

Five years ago at a young, small university in a remote place we had the opportunity to develop a liberal education curriculum where none had existed before. The University of West Florida was then an upper level and graduate institution which depended upon transfers for all its students, and, as a result, liberal education efforts had largely been in the hands of others. In recognition of some of the weaknesses of such an institutional structure the Board of Regents of the State University System of Florida, after a great deal of lobbying by all the upper level institutions in the State University System and over the strenuous objections of community and junior colleges, permitted the development of a limited lower division. Against that backdrop faculty and administrators worked assiduously—and together—to develop a rigorous curriculum with limited student choice to insure that new freshmen would have at least some exposure to the liberalizing elements in mankind's intellectual heritage.

That curriculum follows:

	Semester Hours
Analysis and Argument	3
Algebra or higher level mathematics	3
Statistics	3
Introduction to Data Processing	3
Science (includes at least two courses with laboratories)	11–12
General Biology and Botany or Zoology	
Chemistry I & II	
Physics I & II	
Kinesiology or Physical Geography	
Foreign Language	8
French I & II; Spanish I & II; German I & II	
World History I & II	6
Social Science*	9
American Political Institutions & Processes	
Advances in Understanding Human Behavior	
Principles of Economics Micro	
Principles of Economics Macro	
Arts and Letters	9
Ethics in Contemporary Society (required)	
Art History	
World Drama	

*In this category, only three semester hours *must* come from these three courses. The remaining six may come from any social science course (anthropology, economics, geography, history, political science, psychology, social work, or sociology).

Music in Western Civilization	
Speaking and Interpersonal Communication	
The Theatre Experience	
Career and Life Planning	2
Electives (from any courses offered by the	6–14
College of Business, Education, and Arts	
and Sciences	
Total	60

Some elements were prosaic; a few were unique; all were designed to expose students to what it means to be Western in the fullest sense of tradition and prospect. It was designed to help those who matriculated to live life more appreciatively, effectively, and productively.

Two or three elements deserve additional commentary. Analysis and Argument was designed to combine logical reasoning with written exposition of ideas. In a sense, it substituted for and expanded upon English composition. The World History class not only utilized the services of several historians but included one or more lectures by scholars from other fields including but not limited to, biologists, chemists, physicists, political scientists, anthropologists, geographers, sociologists, and psychologists. At that time, the President of the University (political scientist) and the Vice President for Academic Affairs (earth scientist) lectured regularly.

Perhaps it was the euphoria of the charter freshman class, maybe faculty members extended themselves to do their very best, and it's possible that newness precipitated a positive Hawthorne effect, but student reviews of the program were outstanding. Pass rates on various institutional and state-wide standardized tests taken by students after they had been exposed to the liberal education curriculum were well above averages of the other state institutions (including the Flagship University). By any rational measure the response to and results of the liberal education curriculum were extraordinarily good. It appeared that students were being educated rather than trained.

I wish I could report that this was the end of the story and that the university and its faculty and students lived happily ever afterward in a kind of mutually reinforced academic embrace. Unfortunately the end is not yet. There are signs of curricular deterioration, and auguries for the future are not as happy as some of the architects of the program had hoped.

The maintenance of the integrity of any kind of rigorous program requires constant vigilance and a kind of academic integrity and intellectual statesmanship which are always in short supply. From the very beginning there were attacks upon the University of West Florida's liberal education program, but they came from outside the university and from a surprising quarter . . . from the foreign language departments in several area high schools. A particularly good Latin program existed in several of those schools, and Latin teachers and their students wanted demonstrated Latin competency to fulfill the modern foreign language requirement.

Please understand that we accepted demonstrated competence in any major modern foreign language as fulfilling the language requirement, and we fully appreciated the good work of the Latin teachers and students, but our focus was on a *modern* foreign language. We wanted to at least establish the foundation for monolingual Americans to be able to develop their language skills to compete in the international marketplace. For that reason, we were unwilling to accept Latin as fulfilling our requirement.

Subsequently, other internal voices began to mount subtle and not so subtle attacks. Faculty members wanted to insure that *their* courses were included, and students sought easier options to existing requirements. I regret to say that more than a few faculty members pandered to that student desire for reduced rigor. After additional committee deliberations a revised curriculum was developed and adopted. It follows:

	Semester Hours
English/Arts and Letters (15 semester hours)	
Writing	3
Writing II	3
Ethics and Contemporary Society	3
6 semester hours from the following:	
Theatre Experience	3
World Drama	3
Art History	3
Speaking & Interpersonal Communication	3
Music in Western Civilization	3
Mathematics/Sciences (13 semester hours)	
College Algebra (or Higher)	3
(Math, Statistics)	3
(Lab Science)	3 (4)
(Science)	3 (4)
Social Science (12 semester hours)	
World History I	3
Political Institutions	3
Social Science Elective	3
Social Science Elective	3
Career and Life Planning	2
(required 1st semester)	

Foreign Language (or equivalent)	8
Electives	10–18
Total	60

In my view the new curriculum is weaker in several substantial particulars, most notably In the sciences and in the expansion of choice. No one would argue that the original curriculum was perfect. Indeed, many would detect flaws.

I am concerned that the unique aspects of Analysis and Argument were sacrificed to a more or less standard English composition class. I regret that the mathematics and science requirements have been reduced and that a student can graduate with only one laboratory science course. He/she might indeed graduate with physical geography and kinesiology as the sole science experience. (I'm concerned about this in spite of the fact that I teach physical geography, and it has proven to be the most rigorous of all lower division science classes.)

The World History requirement has been reduced from two semesters to one, and most (all?) of the lectures outside of history have been eliminated. It is, as a result, less catholic in approach and not as integrative as in the past.

The number of electives has broadened, and the students have become adept in finding the easy marks or the classes which have less rigorous requirements. In short, the coherence, cohesiveness, and rigor of the program have begun to erode.

Our experience demonstrates, again, that any liberal education curriculum needs to guard against what I will call the *smorgasbord factor*, i.e., the tendency to broaden choice to meet all the territorial needs of faculty from virtually every discipline. Indeed, the very success of the smorgasbord factor is principally responsible for the disarray of liberal education in the country generally. Further, efforts must be made to resist the *pandering syndrome*, i.e., responding to student demands for relevancy, ethnic concerns, gender issues, difficulty of subject matter, or faculty demands. The pandering syndrome inevitably leads to diminished quality and a blurring of focus.

These curricular assaults are sure to come from a variety of quarters, and the chances are good that the enemies of cogency, coherence, and rigor will raise even more strident voices in the future. There is, of course, always room for measured and positive change, and universities must avoid the rigidities they're often charged with. What must be resisted is change that responds to concerns which are emotional rather than intellectual, to issues which are fiscally driven rather than academically motivated, and to extramural pressure rather than intramural introspection.

Bloom, Hirsch, and others have pointed to major problems in our educational systems and in our society. There is a drumbeat of criticism of higher education, much of it justified, and educational reform and change are being imposed on many institutions by trustees and state legislators who are responding to real or perceived public concerns. Student performance compared to that in the rest of the industrialized world leaves little doubt as to our educational shortcomings. All parts of our programs should be strengthened, not weakened, and a good place to begin is with liberal education programs. The ability to understand, appreciate, and adapt coupled with basic skills of reading, writing, and ciphering are powerful weapons in an educational- and life- skills environment. It's a significant beginning which may prove to be an effective end. The nation is still at risk.

Ours is not just an educational dilemma but an economic crisis, not just an example of the malaise Jimmy Carter was right to describe, but a test of will to set right those things which are wrong, not just concerns of local dimensions but matters of national concern. Each of us can make positive contributions to the liberation of minds and the appreciation of our heritage. It's time that we went about that business. It may be later than we know. Perhaps now more than ever that age old biblical admonition applies. "Where there is no vision the people perish."

8

PLEASURES OF THE INTELLECT

TEACHING THE HUMANITIES MEANS HUMANIZING THE TEACHER

Joseph Krause

Oregon State University

As we approach the end of the century, educators in the humanities seem to be verging towards passivity, if not anonymity, when faced with the important social and ethical questions of our time. It is not coincidental that, as global pollution, militarization, and poverty increase, obfuscation and specialization have stretched a protective canvas over scholarly inquiry and research. If our environment and natural resources have never been in greater jeopardy, the publish or perish doctrine has never been in better health. It is also not a coincidence that educators are reassessing the intrinsic importance of the humanities core at the very time they are refusing to take a stand—in the name of academic neutrality—on the Strategic Defense Initiative and divestment from South Africa.

A friend who teaches physics in a Midwestern liberal arts college informed me that he had circulated intramurally a petition asking his colleagues in science to pledge that they would not collaborate on Star Wars' contracts. Although he did not receive many signatures, what disappointed him the most was the fact that he was accused of politicizing the academic community and of being ideologically motivated in his opposition to value-free science.

Yet this accusation can be countered if one interprets teaching and research as acts of communication which, like all such acts, seek to legitimize knowledge for political ends.[1] If neutrality is impossible in the teaching world, what could be more conspicuously political and ideological than an academic career that is subservient to federal weapons' contracts? I would concur with Michael Yates, professor of economics at the University of Pittsburgh, that "value free science allows its practitioners to hide within their disciplines, to refuse to take a stand on political issues on the ground that to do so is unscientific."[2]

Conversely, those who insist that scholarship, research, and teaching are inextricably linked to politics—and hence should be value-laden—also embrace the principle of pluralism. This makes it difficult for them to clearly define educational policy. They have a progressive vision of education that cannot be translated into specific secondary or university programs: to exclude the views of their conservative opponents would betray the idea of pluralism that they espouse. The result is seen in many of today's universities: a fragmented liberal education system that seems to be navigating in the dark without a compass. Hence, as one university history teacher has stated, ". . . Harvard has a 'core curriculum' that has no core. My own department does not teach a standard introductory history course because, in large part, we cannot agree on what should go into it. Instead we offer a smorgasbord, perplexing and delightful."3

There is, consequently, a range of questions that can be raised concerning liberal education teaching in our country. Has pseudo-scientific exegesis become the guiding axiom in the humanities today? Are humanities teachers removing themselves from the *meaning* and the *implication* of the very knowledge they endeavor to convey? Are they living in a myth of political neutrality? Has the body of knowledge that we casually label the humanities become so dismembered that it is of no practical educational use? Or has this corpus of knowledge exhausted itself? Will it henceforth remain despondent, incapable of responding to the issues and passions of our day?

Although each of these questions could be approached individually, I would like to propose some general and, hopefully, constructive answers to these problems by discussing their relationship to the present public debate on the humanities core. In doing so, I shall also endorse a position that calls for a rehumanization of the teaching profession.

The ongoing debate on the purpose and scope of a liberal education curriculum is, by and large, predicated on two opposing positions. One side, represented by Allan Bloom and E. D. Hirsch, understands knowledge as a finite corpus, pregnant with social values. This corpus, if transmitted from one generation to the next, ensures cultural identity and cultural literacy. The valuable seeds that it harbors should be preserved and nurtured to grow. The other side, represented for simplicity's sake by Robert Scholes, argues that cultures are diverse and change-able entities: transmitting a quantifiable body of knowledge legitimizes a conser-vative and scientific world view, and is tantamount to stunting pluralism, and hence cultural growth, through paternal domination.4

The recent exchange of ideas on cultural politics has brought humanities teaching fully into the limelight, transforming it into the central cog of America's sputtering education machine. Most educators would probably agree that the debate, far from being either superfluous or faddish, reveals a larger intellectual crisis in Western society.5 In the 1950s, the scope of a liberal education curriculum was defined by cataloging great works. The educational importance of this edifying catalog was self-evident: who, at that time, would have questioned the immortal significance of, say Sophocles or Voltaire? Today, however, there is no impunity granted to those who establish such an inventory of classics. The controversy surrounding Hirsch's *Cultural Literacy* indicates to what extent the notions of relativism and pluralism have permeated American education in the last thirty years. Today the principles of cultural tolerance and cultural diversity are certainly more widespread. Even if these principles have yet to gain real popular support, and hence create the deep systemic changes necessary to tangibly reduce racism and sexism, they do represent the positive side of this debate. The debate also contains a second, less enlightened side, in that the Hirschian controversy reveals a profound malaise, if not crisis, in late twentieth-century thinking. Consumer culture, the changing social role of the individual, information technology, and a declining commitment to urgent social problems are at its source.

Certain salient aspects of the debate explain why this is the case. Many have repeated that the controversy over the canon is really a confrontation between conservatives and liberals, between an elitist and a democratic interpretation of the humanities core. Yet, as Henry Giroux and Harvey Kaye emphasized in *The Chronicle of Higher Education*, the debate should be refocused. It fundamentally should not be concerned with the transmission of knowledge or establishing a specific catalog of literary works. Instead, Giroux and Hayes argue, "the most important question becomes that of reformulating the purpose and meaning of higher education in ways that contribute to the cultivation of an informed, critical citizenry. . . . "[6] This quote also conveys the views of prominent figures like Seymour Sarason and Theodore Sizer who argue that American students are docile and passive because school curricula have traditionally emphasized content rather than acuteness of thought or critical appetite.[7] Although it would be presumptuous to imply that the actual content of the core is a peripheral matter, it certainly does take on a secondary importance when you consider that both conservatives and liberals are exclusively concerned with the absolute or relative merits of a written or literary canon. In privileging literary works the debate excludes cultural expression based on oral tradition. This automatically eliminates Native American culture from the catalog. Both the elasticity and depth afforded in space and time by oral narratives and non-written expression are not projected by an educational system that places a premium on the possession of knowledge; a possession achieved by fixing and delineating our heritage and our imagination on paper.

An imbalance exists in favor of the written word. The West approaches its own culture in the same way that it interprets the remaining stone-age cultures on our planet: in an anthropological, Levi-Straussian manner. Rather than propagate a living culture, it seeks to dehydrate and capture the essence of what is alien or remote in time. Motivated by a nostalgic longing for coherence, the last several decades have transformed liberal education into a social scientific research discipline, instead of allowing it to achieve a productive dialogue with society.[8] Those who believe that the meaning of history is based on discontinuity are transformed into ethnologists of microcosms: they find coherence by identifying the discrepancies buried in cultures or in literary works.[9]

As teachers of the humanities we are still entrenched in the nineteenth-century positivistic dream and, as beneficiaries of state or federal awards, we are more and more dependent on a research grant system that, because it is highly selective, advocates and streamlines a vision of coherence seeking to support that dream. Are we turning into excavators and scrutinizers, running through the fields of history with a magnifying glass and a jar of formaldehyde? How often do liberal arts colleges or humanities' centers invite storytellers, folklorists, or Native American dancers to their campuses, or any of those communicators of culture who stand outside of the literary workshop circuits, who have no publication record, who are not conferred an identity by federal grants for research projects?

In other words, those who defend pluralism are also advocating cultural literacy rather than the manifestation of cultural expression. They are tolerating dissonance in order to ultimately privilege the dream of consonance. The humanities core is resembling Joyce's *Finnegans Wake*: everything imaginable can be found in its pages, but it is only readable to the initiated. As such, the canon is concerned with the valorization of writing to the detriment of a spoken, living, manifestation of culture. And, because writing deals with representation, with mimesis, its primary objective is to reinforce and justify a particular vision of reality. Jacques Derrida, in his hermetic and, therefore, only marginally useful work on the origins of language and political change, returns to both Plato and Rousseau to explore the history of writing as a vehicle for authority and, hence, as a rational means to eradicate the living and lyrical dimensions of language.[10] The literary canon places the reader at the end of a cultural continuum, allegedly to allow that person to achieve a fuller sense of individuality. But the real purpose of the canon is to explain the legitimate evolution of that continuum. Thus the canon—be it conservative or liberal—can be interpreted as a modern mechanism for social stratification rather than for ethnic diversity or individual emancipation.

The postmodern theorists Mas'ud Zavarzadeh and Donald Morton, both in the English Department at Syracuse University, have produced a broad and far-reaching analysis of traditional epistemologies, particularly in their historical relationship to personal identity and to the politics of education. For them ". . . knowledge is ultimately a mode of epistemic behavior situated in society: it is those regimes of truth that, for ideological, economic, and political reasons, have been successful in suppressing other competing discourses of truth and have come to be regarded as 'knowledge' by an interpretive community." Truth, they conclude, "is political as well as epistemological."[11]

Despite the fact that such a Darwinian interpretation of the cognitive process makes policy even more difficult to formulate, liberal education teaching can be substantially ameliorated—in a true pluralistic sense—by de-emphasizing the humanities as an intellectual vault or public archive where the student finds both identity and fulfillment. The identity of the modern psyche is tending more and more towards fragmentization: this is not necessarily an obstacle for progress; it may be the prerequisite for institutionalized tolerance. In addition, prominence should be given to a conception of the humanities that is directed towards our global civilizations at the end of the twentieth century. Such a conception would not abstract the humanitarian nor conceal existing cultural expressions.

In addition, such a conception would expand the parameters of the debate by situating liberal education in a dynamic global context. I believe that many educators have eschewed their responsibility to help build what former Senegalese President Leopold Senghor has called a "culture of the universal." Cast in these terms the humanities become an instrument to articulate and to encourage diversity rather than a canon for the preeminence of a single dominant culture.[12]

Furthermore, this new conception is in urgent need of application. While we, as educators, argue the merits of one subject over another, while we discuss the importance of Plato over Aristotle, of Voltaire over John Stuart Mill, we are indirectly retarding the advance of human and civil rights, because we are analyzing curriculum contents rather than our resolve to turn thinking into substance. We have discretely avoided an evaluation of ourselves as spokespersons for liberal education and, moreover, we are advocating a fragile solution for progress. Simply stated, that solution reads: "If you teach the humanities, and students are pregnant with the Western cultural seed, eventually our social problems will be resolved thanks to our enlightened patriarchal tradition."

This solution presumes that the humanities contain an unlimited potential for the future, an intrinsic alchemy that will produce magical transformations. Yet, it could be the formula for mystification rather than liberation. In extolling the merits of the humanities we should be assessing their impact, or lack thereof, on the structures of authority that regulate our societies. If this assessment is not performed we may get stuck in a more dangerous intellectual crisis, that is, in a continued ideological war, in which no differentiation can be made between freedom of individuals and freedom of markets, between overconsumption and widespread famine, between industrialization and environmental pollution, between deterrence and nuclear brinkmanship.

The report issued by the Carnegie Foundation in 1986 is an example of an unimaginative, highly conservative document that implicitly refuses to assess American education within a larger social and global framework.[13] The report only makes a two-dimensional link between the *integrated core* that it outlines and the priorities of educators. The successful implementation of a humanities core is not merely contingent on the balanced mixture of scholarship and teaching, on research and pedagogy development. The proper equation between sound curriculum and faculty priorities depends far more on our willingness, as teachers and administrators, to define our role beyond the school and the campus.

This concerns post-secondary education in particular: if it continues to stand locked within the narrow confines and interests of the academy, its role will be increasingly defined by the laws of consumerism. Because of the hegemony of market discourse in the information age, university faculty seem to be more and more inclined to commercialize the entire process of learning, in order to replace education with *leadership potential*.

Developing this type of potential in students would consolidate the university's function as a structure for market values and as a grooming station that prepares the bold for economic survivalism. Should this consolidation occur, it would hide students from the instabilities, complexities, and, above all, incoherences that define the social and intellectual landscapes at the end of the twentieth century. This is not to imply that the ideal cities of the Renaissance and of the Enlightenment have disappeared in a puff of smoke. Nor does it mean that dialectical materialism is a thing of the past. However, it does mean that extant scientific methods, educational theories, and political doctrines founded on the underlying coherence of knowledge are partially anachronous with present social realities and with a new type of subjectivism. If Seymour Sarason is correct in claiming that American education is still patterned on the vertical structures of the nineteenth century,[14] it would then be plausible to assume that the substance of educational policies is sorely out of phase with the modern world, and above all, with the modern psyche.

Postmodern theory, in general, and feminist theory, in particular, both seek to break the Platonic and Scholastic molds that have favored idealization, essentialism, universalism and, more recently, individualism. These molds, according to them, have traditionally been ways to explain cognitive activity, and maintain an ordered but masculine view of the world.[15] In their opposition to this view of learning, postmodern critics, who are partially indebted to Freudian psychoanalysis, do not qualify the individual as necessarily a finite entity.[16] Translated into practical terms, this type of interpretation can certainly provide us with a better picture of the psychological currents that are intrinsic components of Western thought today. The movement away from ethnocentrism and sexism has infused the individual with a feeling of fragmentation and discontinuity. However, this need not be perceived as the negative result of social progress. In fact, it should be understood as a constructive opportunity, particularly for educators, to reformulate the psychological framework of the present and of future generations.

This notion is of considerable value if we wish to find some solution to the divisive debate on the humanities canon. If we approach our students as containers for doses of knowledge, the debate can only be articulated in terms of content, fixed for conservatives, flexible for liberals. If, however, we perceive, as our point of departure, knowledge and the identity of individuals to be founded on the social uncertainty and fragmentation that surround us, then we can turn our attention to the constructive business of linking education to real social progress. As Alison

Wylie has stated, "Whether we can ever achieve an overarching unity of understanding is beside the point."[17] In short, the central objective should be to rehumanize liberal education by placing the teacher squarely into the modern context. If cognition and individualism are conceived in these terms, educators would be able to adopt policies that put a premium on expressive or manifest culture rather than on literacy. Such a conception would do much to globalize rather than commercialize education. It would also do much, as Peter Mandler has argued, to ". . . justify the place of women's studies, cultural criticism, social and labor history, and historical sociology. . ." in our educational programs.[18]

In the humanities we have been too fond of tracing our Western genealogy to Scholasticism and then further back to Hellenic thought, usually at the expense of our Moslem and Jewish antecedents. Yet we overlook the fact that Scholastic philosophy was composed of many quite divergent ways of fusing faith to reason. If Thomistic thought eventually emerged as the canon, it is of little doctrinal significance to us today. What does persist, however, is the resolve to encourage possibilities for discourse and to discern the moral obligation that reason implicitly contains.

Regardless of whether the utopias of the modern era have been fraught with contradictions, educators cannot accept the challenge of developing liberal education curricula if they are not participating in that discourse and in that moral obligation as a living journey.

NOTES

The original version of this article, "Liberal Education and Social Commitment: Looking Beyond the Core," appeared in the *Gallatin Review*, vol. 10 (1), (Winter 1990–91), 116–24.

1. The relationship between legitimate knowledge and the political character of information and communication is thoroughly discussed by Jean-Francois Lyotard in his book *La condition postmoderne* (Paris: Editions de Minuit, 1979).

2. Quoted from an article that appeared in *The Chronicle of Higher Education*, May 14, 1986, 84.

3. Taken from Peter Mandler's article "The 'Double Life' in Academia: Political Commitment and/or Objective Scholarship?" in *Dissent*, Winter 1989, 98.

4. Much has been written on the question of cultural literacy and on the cultural politics of education. *Profession 88*, published in 1988 by The Modern Language Association of America, offers an excellent selection of articles that evaluate Hirsch and Bloom's respective positions. The issue ends with a response by Hirsch to the accusations leveled against him, along with a final reply by Andrew and James Sledd, Robert Scholes, Paul Armstrong, and Helen Moglen. The liberal position (advocating pluralism) is well defined by Robert Scholes in his article, "Three Views of Education: Nostalgia, History, and Voodoo," in *College English*, 50 (1988), 323–32.

5. Alain Finkielkraut, in *La défaite de la pensée* (Paris: Gallimard 1987), and Russell Jacoby, in *The Last Intellectuals: American Culture in the Age of Academe* (New York: Basic Books, 1987), argue that educators are both the source and victims of this intellectual demise. Paul Berman presents a cogent analysis of the crisis in his article, "Intellectuals After the Revolution: What's Happened Since the Sixties?" in *Dissent*, Winter 1989, 86–93.

6. Henry A. Giroux and Harvey J. Kaye, "The Liberal Arts Must be Reformed to Serve Democratic Ends," in *The Chronicle of Higher Education*, March 29, 1989, A44.

7. This position is articulated by Seymour Sarason, *Schooling in America: Scapegoat and Salvation* (New York: Free Press/Collier, 1983); and by Theodore Sizer, *Horace's Compromise: The Dilemma of the American High School* (Boston: Houghton Mifflin, 1984). The latter is the first report from a study of high schools, cosponsored by the National Association of Secondary School Principals and the Commission on Educational Issues of the National Association of Independent Schools.

8. Bruce Kimball, in his book *Orators and Philosophers: A History of the Idea of Liberal Education* (New York and London: Teachers College Press, 1986), argues that liberal arts education has, historically, been based on *ratio* and *oratio*, on thinking and expression. It has not been principally directed towards empiricism and the mastery of technical skills.

9. Alain Finkielkraut pursues this argument in *La défaite de la pensée*, op. cit., 73–83.

10. Jacques Derrida, *De la grammatoloqie* (Paris: Editions de Minuit, 1967). The writer states, "For the rationality of [writing] separates it from passion and from song, that is, from the living origin of language." 426.

11. Mas'ud Zavarzadeh and Donald Morton, "Theory Pedagogy Politics: The Crisis of the 'The Subject' in the Humanities," in *Boundary* 2, 15. 1–2 (Fall/Winter 1987), 1–22. Their tenets are developed further in, "The Nostalgia for Law and Order and the Policing of Knowledge: The Politics of Contemporary Literary Theory," in *Syracuse Scholar*, Spring 1987, 25–71.

12. Leopold Sedar Senghor, *Liberte III: Negritude et civilisation de l'universelle* (Paris: Seuil, 1977). In this book Senghor distinguishes between a dominant universal culture and a global culture of the universal.

13. For the complete text of the report, see *The Chronicle of Higher Education*, Nov. 5, 1986.

14. Seymour Sarason, *Schooling in America*, op. cit.

15. The debate between Sandra Harding and Alison Wylie on science and feminism presents the salient features of modern critical theory's understanding of epistemology. See, Alison Wylie, "The Philosophy of Ambivalence: Sandra Harding on The Science Question in Feminism," 59–73; and, Sandra Harding, "Ascetic Intellectual Opportunities: Reply to Alison Wylie," 75–85, both in the *Canadian Journal of Philosophy*, Supplementary Volume 13, 1989.

16. See Zavarzadeh and Morton, "Theory Pedagogy Politics: The Crisis of 'The Subject' in the Humanities," op. cit. 4. Also, Todd Gitlin's "Postmodernism: Roots and Politics. What Are They Talking About?" clearly presents the constitutive elements of postmodernist theory and style. In *Dissent*, Winter 1989.

17. Alison Wylie, op. cit. 72.

18. Peter Mandler, op. cit. 99.

WILLIAM JAMES AND RHETORIC: THE ARGUMENT FOR BELIEF AS BELIEF IN ARGUMENT

Glen McClish

Southwestern University

Today, through brief analyses of "The Dilemma of Determinism" and "Is Life Worth Living?," I wish to set before you William James' "justification of faith" (1) as a kind of justification of argument itself. (For related analyses of "The Will to Believe," see McClish; Walker and McLish 87–90.) In doing so, I will argue—implicitly, at least—for the inclusion of traditional religious texts in the ordinarily secular study of argumentation. Before I begin, I must declare that my passions both for James and for argument motivate my words today. If you reject everything else that I say here, I hope that you would at least reconsider James' work and that you would entertain my belief that, in so many ways, the study of argumentation *is* the study of our civilization.

But enough of the exordium. Let us review James' central arguments and strategies in "The Dilemma of Determinism" and "Is Life Worth Living?," exploring their significance for the teacher of argumentation as we go. In order to reinforce my conclusion that these essays help both to elucidate and justify argument itself, I will close with a brief look at Aristotle's *Rhetoric*.

"The Dilemma of Determinism," James' defense of free will, was originally delivered to Harvard divinity students in 1884. James begins the speech not as a self-righteous dogmatist, but as a pragmatist, stating that he is unable absolutely "to prove to you that freedom of the will is true" (146). Effecting the persona of the gentleman scholar, James claims that if free will is a reality, then "[i]ts truth ought not to be forced willy-nilly down our indifferent throats" (146). He merely desires that his audience act "as if it were true" (146).

Two important lessons about argument—or, to use a more classical term, rhetoric—are presented in James' opening. Most apparent is the sense of goodwill he expresses toward his audience. He approaches these Harvard divinity students with friendliness and respect. Rather than "forcing a conclusion" or "coercing assent," James magnanimously and respectfully sets as his goal "deepening our sense of what the issue between the two parties really is" (145). The second—and closely related—point is James' effort to establish a congruence between the style of his rhetoric and its content. His gracious, nondogmatic approach supports his initial premise that those arguing "the free-will side of the question" should abandon the hope "of a coercive demonstration" (146). This congruence or consistency between form and content suggests that the speaker is endowed with liberal amounts of good sense and trustworthiness. Not surprisingly, the three principal components of character created by James' introduction—goodwill, good sense, and trustworthiness (or the appearance of good moral character)— correspond precisely with Aristotle's basic advice about formulating an effective *ethos* (91).

Before James reaches to the body of his argument, he works fastidiously to establish terminological common ground. He lays out the fundamental opposition between "determinism" and "indeterminism" with considerable care, thus assisting the teacher of rhetoric to demonstrate the crucial importance of precise definitions of terms. The fact that most of our students are unfamiliar with these specific philosophic categories makes the general necessity of effective definitions all the more salient. Perhaps even more impressive, though, is his discussion of "the eulogistic word *freedom*" and "the opprobrious word *chance*" (149), which stands as a wonderful analysis of the potency of "loaded" or "slanted" language.

James' effort to salvage the loaded term "chance" and award it a key role in his argument is noteworthy because of the difficulty of the effort. As implied above, the word had developed a strong dyslogistic character in the age in which James wrote. As he works to rehabilitate chance, James casts the philosophic concept as a common weed, declaring boldly, "I fancy that squeezing the thistle boldly will rob it of its sting" (153). This metaphoric gesture is illustrative because of its concise explanatory power. Devotees of "The Will to Believe" will recall the rhetorical force of the famous boarding-house metaphor with which James suggests that when facing "forced options in our speculative questions" we cannot always "wait with impunity" for the "coercive evidence" to arrive (22).

Beyond the niceties of this elegantly formed trope, though, are the very practical realities of continuity. It would be most instructive to call students' attention to the very next paragraph, which begins "The sting of the word 'chance' seems to lie ..." (153). In effect, James has both the creative genius to invent vivid figurative language and the rhetorical sense to stay with his images long enough to establish necessary continuity. Through short memory and sloppiness, many of us undermine, clutter, or neutralize the very tropes and figures on which we build our writerly vanity. James' steadfast dedication to the "maggots" and "carrion" metaphor later in the argument, although rather unsavory, is similarly exemplary (177–78).

Indeed, it is this very thorny concept of chance that occupies James for the next several pages. By the time he closes this section of the argument, though, he has earned for the term a much more positive connotation:

> ... we now know that the idea of chance is, at bottom, exactly the same thing as the idea of gift,—the one simply being a disparaging, and the

other a eulogistic, name for anything on which we have no effective *claim*. (158–59)

Having now established his *ethos* and set key terms in their strategically proper places, James announces that he has brought us "within sight of our subject" (159). For the student who believes that effective argumentation is a matter of instantly dumping one's thesis upon the audience, then piling up supporting arguments as rapidly as possible, James' methodic, thorough, sophisticated preliminaries are most corrective. Although he refers to this introductory material somewhat modestly as "all our tedious clearing of the way" (159), I am consistently impressed with his skill in surveying the lay of the land.

The essential structural strategy of James' argument is *expeditio* (Brandt 130–31), "enumeration" (Perelman and Olbrechts-Tyteca 234–36), "elimination," or "method of residues" (Fahnestock and Secor 172–74), that rhetorical tactic with which the writer sets forth a number of seemingly reasonable options, then systematically demonstrates that only one—or none—of the options is in fact acceptable to the audience. First, James exposes the dual quagmires confronted by "determinism": an eternal "pessimism" about the moral condition of the universe (161) or—even worse—a morally debilitating rejection of all responsibility for judgment (163).

In order to escape from this initial "dilemma" (164), James moves to a second category of deterministic spiritual options, "*gnosticism*" or "*subjectivism*" (165), in which one regards the world not "as a machine whose final purpose is the making of any outward good, but rather as a contrivance for deepening the theoretic consciousness of what goodness and evil in their intrinsic natures are" (165). As James enters his analysis of the subjectivist solution to the sticky question of moral judgment, he primes the audience for his argument by stressing not the negative aspects of the approach, but its *prima facie* appeal:

> For, after all, is there not something rather absurd in our ordinary notion of external things being good or bad in themselves? Can murders and treacheries, considered as mere outward happenings, or motions of matter, be bad without any one to feel their badness? And could paradise properly be good in the absence of a sentient principle by which the goodness was perceived? Outward goods and evils seem practically indistinguishable except in so far as they result in getting moral judgments made about them. . . . (167)

This instance of *prolepsis* (Brandt 50), or strategic anticipation of the opposition's argument, is characteristic both of James in specific and of effective rhetoric in general. In teaching James, I encourage students to pay particular attention to the moments when he gives his opposition a beautiful rug upon which to stand—a rug that he will eventually remove. Such *prolepsis*, because it compels James to present both sides of the debate, bolsters his trustworthiness, thus enhancing his *ethos*.

Despite the length and vigor of James' initial proleptic support for the subjectivism (at one point he asserts, somewhat playfully, "No one, I hope, will accuse me, after I have said all this, of underrating the reasons in favor of subjectivism" (170)), of course, all three "great branches" of subjectivist thinking—"scientificism, sentimentalism, and sensualism" (165)—are rendered unsatisfactory. When James leaves theoretical discussion and descends to his favorite realm, the "practical order" (170), he finds that the subjectivist instinct inevitably leads to "the corruptest curiosity" and "exhausts itself in every sort of spiritual, moral, and practical license" (171).

Having portrayed the juxtaposition of pessimism and subjectivism as fundamental to "the dilemma of determinism" (166), James finds his "escape" "by the practical way" (173) to a third alternative. This final option, which James freely admits is a special kind of "faith" (176), is based on the importance of personal accountability for conduct regulated by indeterministic free will. The joy James expresses in the movement from the first two (rejected) options of the *expeditio* to the third serves not only to mark and enhance his argument, but to celebrate its form:

> Take, then, the yoke upon our shoulders; bend our neck beneath the heavy legality of its weight; regard something else than our feeling as our limit, our master, and our law; be willing to live and die in its service,— and, at a stroke, we have passed from the subjective into the objective philosophy of things, much as one awakens from some feverish dream, full of bad lights and noises, to find one's self bathed in the sacred coolness and quiet of the air of the night. (174)

Through this grand paradox (i.e., salvation through servitude)—which is reminiscent of the brilliant strategies of another great pluralist and rhetorician, John Donne—James delights in both the free will for which he has *argued* and the rhetorical strategy he has *marshaled*, for indeed one begets the other. For me, James' triumphant *expeditio*, itself a passionate exercise in free will, demonstrates that rhetoric itself is very much a part of his system of belief. Similarly, when James labels "chance" the "salt" that keeps the world "sweet" (179), we can see that he enjoys the rhetorical strategy of paradox as much as the point he is making about free will.

388

It is at this late stage in the argument that James finally confronts the potential tension between belief in free will and belief in Providence. With his brilliant chess analogy (181–82), James melds these potentially contradictory faiths into a coherent philosophical position. In the end, for James, it is the possibility that Providence allows our moral decisions to make a difference in the "*here* and *now*" that "gives the palpitating reality to our moral life and makes it tingle . . . with so strange and elaborate an excitement" (183). Rhetoricians should note James' formidable patience. Saving a crucial term such as "Providence" until so late in the discourse is extremely difficult for our students to understand, yet it is often crucial to developing the argument and drawing the audience along effectively.

As we look back over James' argument—and this analysis of it—we will find metaphors of movement expressed throughout. Our feet were stuck in a "pessimistic bog" (163). Temporary "refuge from the quandary" of this pessimism lay, we were assured, "not far off" (164). Later, James speaks of "the dilemma, the labyrinth, of pessimism and subjectivism, from out of whose toils we have just wound our way" (176). These allusions to motion, which highlight means as well as ends and resonate with Lakoff and Johnson's discussion of argument as metaphorical journey (89–91), once again suggest James loved rhetorical "movement" as well as conclusions—the argumentative path, as much as the final destination, is valued for its own sake.

Most important, perhaps, James' justification of faith in free will—complete with its inclusive introduction and generous proleptic gestures to his opposition—enhances the teaching of argument in a free society because of its thoroughgoing commitment to pluralism and to "a pluralistic, restless universe, in which no single point of view can ever take in the whole scene" (177). James' rhetorical strategies and his philosophical position both depend on free choices and competition among ideas. There is no doubt that James argues to win, and that he believes that some choices and arguments are better than others, but his dedication to his cause necessitates that he recognize the rights and dignity of his opposition.

James' suggestions in the sister essay "The Will to Believe" about the proper environment for scientific and philosophical debate are relevant here: "No one of us ought to issue vetoes to the other, nor should we bandy words of abuse. We ought, on the contrary, delicately and profoundly to respect one another's mental freedom" (30). The "intellectual republic" (30) advocated in "The Will to Believe" meshes effectively with the competitive "market-place" (xi) of beliefs imagined in James' Preface to the essays, in which "the freest competition of the various faiths with one another, and their openest application to life by their several champions" is nurtured (xii). Faiths, he declares, "ought therefore not to lie hid each under its bushel, indulged-in quietly with friends. They ought to live in publicity, vying with each other" (xii). Together, the intellectual republic and the market-place of beliefs exemplify, I believe, the kind of intellectual activity that should transpire in any classroom, and particularly those dedicated to the study of argument itself.

But it is high time to move to the second half of *my* argument. James' faith in free will and his pluralistic approach to rhetoric and philosophy set forth in "The Dilemma of Determinism" form crucial background for the more explicit endorsement of religious belief developed in "Is Life Worth Living?" This piece, first delivered to the Harvard Young Men's Christian Association, begins by demonstrating James' great empathy for the melancholic character. Once again working to build a viable *ethos*, James establishes his wisdom and goodwill toward the audience by laying out the plight of the depressive. The listener or reader who knows what it is to question the value of life should find James' persona trustworthy on this subject.

As a quintessential rhetorician and pragmatist, James establishes a practical, audience-specific frame in which to build his case for the value of life. To do so, he imagines that we are reasoning with someone who is on the verge of committing suicide (38). Having set the stage for the argument, James once again adopts the *expeditio* as his master strategy. The traditional religious injunction against suicide is considered first (38), but deemed utterly ineffective if the lust for life is absent.

The second option, "natural theology" (40), which allows the melancholic to seek meaning in the beauty and grandeur of the natural world, loses its ability to heal and inspire when we realize that both good and evil abound in nature:

> Beauty and hideousness, love and cruelty, life and death keep house together in indissoluble partnership; and there gradually steals over us, instead of the old warm notion of a man-loving Deity, that of an awful power that neither hates nor loves, but rolls all things together meaninglessly to a common doom. (41–42)

"Visible nature" is nothing but "plasticity and indifference," "a moral multiverse" (43), "a harlot" (44). In fact, suggests James, "the initial step towards getting into healthy ultimate relations with the universe is the act of rebellion" (44) against natural religion. And so we feel the tug of the *expeditio* pull us on.

With the natural religion behind our imaginary depressive, we consider the next *raison d'etre*, "vital curiosity" (47) about life. More inspirational, but still mundane, is the innate pugnacity that compels one to fight against evil and bolsters "manliness," "pride," and "honor" (50). James generously dubs this "naturalistic basis" (51) for living "an honest stage" (51) on the road to mental health, but once again the *expeditio* moves us forward toward more spiritual terrain.

Travelling into what James labels "the soul of [his] discourse" (51), James carefully defines "religion"—distinguishing it from the "natural" version in the process—and proleptically considers the scientists' response to his definitions. As in the case of "The Dilemma of Determinism," James' efforts to define his terms and confront his opposition's arguments squarely and fairly are exemplary. Particularly insightful is his effort to demonstrate the fundamental faith that fuels scientific advancement. Here is a taste of the argument: "Without an imperious inner demand on our part for ideal logical and mathematical harmonies, we should never have attained to proving that such harmonies lie hidden between all the chinks and interstices of the crude natural world" (55).

Having established the premises that even science depends on faith for advancement, that much good can come when scientifically-minded people follow their instinctual urges to understand the world, and thus that "our inner interests" *can* have a "real connection with the form that the hidden world may contain" (55), James has cleared the way for a sweeping endorsement of religious belief. For indeed, if "often enough our faith beforehand in an uncertified result *is the only thing that makes the result come true*" (59), then it is possible that acting on instinctual religious belief could reinforce the very supernatural order that has enabled the actor. It is this possibility, James tells his potential suicide, this chance to participate in—even make possible—the divine mysteries of the universe, that makes life most "worth living."

To believe in the spiritual world that encompasses the physical world we know sensually "*may* be the most essential function that our lives in this world have to perform" (58). "God himself," James suggests, "may draw vital strength and increase of very being from our fidelity" (61). Rather than living in a chilling, catatonic world of maybe nots, James dares his suicidal friend to endorse the hopeful, life-affirming maybe and act upon the endorsement. A willingness to assent, rather than to doubt, should be our spiritual—and rhetorical—mindset.

In an extremely compact, eloquent way, James has set forth what, nearly eighty years later, Wayne Booth virtuously struggles with for over two hundred pages in *Modern Dogma and the Rhetoric of Assent*:

Whatever the truth about this moment, I think that popular negation and affirmation (on both the political right and political left) are conducted on assumptions that are no longer tenable. The predominant mode intellectually and spiritually is shifting toward a postmodernism that may have transcended, at last, the shocks of negation that produced the modern temper. For surprising numbers the burden of proof has been reversed; we are now rejecting a form of rationalism that began with doubt and demanded explicit reasons for every belief and every allegiance. We must

391

now learn to live in a world in which we begin with assent and in which the first question will therefore be, "Why not?" The shift will not be easy to live with for most of us, but it need not be finally threatening except to those who fear that there are no good reasons for saying no. (201)

It is time, at last, for the peroration. Over two thousand years ago, Aristotle—responding to Plato's otherworldly attack on public speaking as it was practiced in the courts and deliberative bodies of the ancient world—argued that rhetoric was necessary because society required a mode of discourse to handle issues for which absolute answers are unavailable. Aristotle suggested that in the day-to-day life of the state, important decisions must be made and the consent of the governed must be attained to enact them. "The duty of rhetoric," he claimed, "is to deal with such matters as we deliberate upon without arts or systems to guide us" (27).

In an important sense, James' explicit endorsement of faith and his implicit celebration of rhetoric correspond with Aristotle's defense. Like Aristotle, the ancient pragmatist on civic matters, James, the modern pragmatist in the realm of faith, defends discourse that leads to decisive, practical action. Aristotle defended rhetoric on the grounds that "things that are true and things that are just have a natural tendency to prevail over their opposites" (22). Likewise, James argues for a pluralistic, Darwinian—but gentlemanly—marketplace of ideas in which faiths of various kinds compete, and the best ones gain our assent. Thus, James' faith in his belief becomes a kind of faith in the evolutionary power of argument that mirrors Aristotle's ancient justification of rhetoric.

As an advocate of free will, pluralism, religious belief, and rhetoric, James demonstrates the value that sincere, effectively constructed arguments have for society. James' famous conclusion to "The Will to Believe" concisely expresses his jubilant faith in faith, rhetoric, and willing assent:

We stand on a mountain pass in the midst of whirling snow and blinding mist, through which we get glimpses now and then of paths which may be deceptive. If we stand still we shall be frozen to death. If we take the wrong road we shall be dashed to pieces. We do not certainly know whether there is any right one. What must we do? 'Be strong and of good courage.' Act for the best, hope for the best, and take what comes. . . . If death ends all, we cannot meet death better. (31)

Similarly, his readers—our students—will in their own ways bring down from those mountain passes of our society many a freezing traveler—if, that is, they believe in their right—their obligation—to argue and to risk before all the facts are in. If, in effect, they are willing to embrace the natural uncertainty inherent in real-world argumentation, and if they are steeped in a rhetorical way of thinking that emphasizes free will, pluralism, a fair presentation of opposition, and a faith in their own faith, then their rhetoric could become not merely the expression, but also the cause, of considerable salvation.

WORKS CITED

Aristotle. *Rhetoric and Poetics*. Trans. W. Rhys Roberts and Ingram Bywater. New York: Random, 1954.

Booth, Wayne. *Modern Dogma and the Rhetoric of Assent*. Chicago: University of Chicago Press, 1974.

Brandt, William J. *The Rhetoric of Argumentation*. Indianapolis: Bobbs-Merrill, 1970.

Fahnestock, Jeanne, and Marie Secor. *A Rhetoric of Argument*. New York: Random, 1982.

James, William. *The Will to Believe and Other Essays in Popular Philosophy*. New York: Dover, 1956.

Lakoff, George, and Mark Johnson. *Metaphors We Live By*. Chicago: University of Chicago Press, 1980.

McClish, Glen. "Controversy as a Mode of Invention: The Example of James and Freud." *College English*: 53 (April 1991): 391–402.

Perelman, Chaim, and Lucy Olbrechts-Tyteca. *The New Rhetoric: A Treatise on Argumentation*. Trans. John Wilkinson and Purcell Weaver. Notre Dame: University of Notre Dame Press, 1969.

Walker, Jeffrey, and Glen McClish. *Instructor's Resource Manual, Investigating Arguments: Readings for College Writing*. Boston: Houghton, 1991.

THE HISTORICAL CONDITIONS OF VISUAL LITERACY

Garth Montgomery
University of Texas at Dallas

Since the invention of motion pictures, the term 'visual literacy' has tended to have two distinct connotations in historical pedagogical circles, here and abroad: (1) a symptom of social-cultural dissolution, and (2) a means for overcoming, if not combatting, that dissolution. In the English-speaking world, during the 1920s and 1930s, British and American students of historical pedagogy turned their attention to the study of the effect of film on students, and to attempts to create an 'educational' (as opposed to 'entertainment' or 'propaganda') environment in which to view historical films.

In Germany, in October 1945, former employees of the Nazi-period Education-tion Ministry's 'Office of Film and Photography in Science and Education' (the RWU) contacted U.S. occupation authorities in Munich, about the possible production and exhibition of educational films about Thomas Jefferson and the Declaration of Independence. Their belief that they could do the best possible job of using film to teach the lessons of democracy to German students was based on their over twenty years of using film in historical and political education, and of scientific observation and education of filmgoers. From the 1920s, the goal of their attempts to coordinate media research and historical education had been to create a distinctively 'educational' viewing formation, in which the personality of the viewer of historical 'reality' on film could be manipulated for educational purposes. Well into the Nazi period, German researchers in both historical pedagogy and media science nurtured the hope that the coordination of media education and historical/political education would somehow influence relations between state and society.

I want to suggest that the experiences of historical educators who, during the 1920s and 1930s, attempted to create educational viewing environments are relevant to our thinking about how to promote 'visual literacy' among history students today. Whenever they attempted to encourage 'visual literacy,' academics almost inevitably ran into competition (over the organization of images, viewers, and viewing contexts) from commercial and political institutions which were already engaged in the visual representation of history. For our purposes, examination of that competition offers something of a history lesson in its own right.

In Germany, after the First World War, the popularity of commercially produced 'World War I' films was a matter of concern to history teachers (both liberals and conservatives), who were trying to keep sensationalist historical entertainment and party-political propaganda out of the classroom. Government-sponsored and academically-produced history texts about the war faced stiff competition from treatments of war-time society and culture in popular histories, historical novels, and films. History teachers worried that government-sponsored histories of World War I, as well as popularized versions of those histories, were so narrowly conceived around tactical and strategic questions as to be inaccessible for the bulk of the German population.

Since the 1880s, pedagogical discussion about appropriating feature films for the purpose of historical education was related to the expression, by liberals and conservatives, of the view that changing social and cultural conditions (apparent to teachers, in their most dangerous form, in the threat posed by the German Social Democratic Party) required curricular reform which would foster the education of the 'whole' person. After imposition of the Treaty of Versailles, and a parliamentary democracy, ideas about the educational use of film became an important element in the debate about the introduction of more 'relevant civics' ('lebensnahe Staatsbürgerkunde'). German history teachers expressed an interest, with frequent reference to the educational philosophy of John Dewey, in "American" methods of political education: classroom exercises in creating model communities; class trips to factories, banks, and slums; and the use of mass media (in particular, film).

At the same time, commercial film producers were promoting the formal characteristics of 'realistic' films about the First World War, emphasizing the use of archival footage and official army recreations, the use of various types of written sources (the government's diplomatic records, war diaries, and war novels), or the use of veterans as actors, or actual war heroes reenacting their famous deeds. [Examples of films promoted in this way include *The World War, Part 1* (1927), *Westfront 1918* (1930), *1914: The Last Days Before the World Conflagration* (1931), *Douaumont* (1931), and *Tannenberg* (1932).]

German history teachers' response to the promotion of 'realistic' war films centered around attempts to create an 'educational' viewing formation, distinct from that of either entertainment or propaganda. University-level media scientists provided teachers with advice, couched (for the most part) in strictly utilitarian terms, on how to create such a viewing environment, how to control media stimuli, how to monitor 'reception,' and how to evaluate the sociological factors which influenced viewers' recognition of 'reality' on film. In the process, teachers (appointed, by the republican government, to the review board at the Film Office of the Central Institute of Education and Instruction, or ZEU) became involved in awarding tax-breaks, and 'educational' and 'artistic' ratings, to commercially-produced films which 'realistically' portrayed different aspects of the First World War.

Liberal and conservative history teachers shared the belief that war films could be incorporated into an educational viewing formation; that film and viewer could be coordinated in such a way that the 'realistic' socio-cultural content of the film would resonate in the personality of the viewer, and that this resonance could then be manipulated for educational purposes. Melodramatic and episodic narrative devices, as well as visual distortions and inaccuracies, which were intended to appeal to the mass audience, inhibited the operation of an educational viewing formation. If they could be eliminated, the cinema (powerful agent of social and cultural dissolution) could become a vehicle for popular education about the socio-cultural realities of Germany's war-time history. Teachers in Weimar Germany adhered to the essentially contradictory idea that while commercial pandering to the taste of the mass audience was the source of formal departures from 'realism,' an 'accurate' evocation of the way in which the mass public experienced war-time socio-cultural realities was the prerequisite for an 'educational' film treatment of that historical period.

Besides reflecting monumental obliviousness to the political situation, the October 1945 proposal by former employees of the Nazi-period Education Ministry concerning the production and exhibition of educational films about Thomas Jefferson and the Declaration of Independence also reflected the power and the persistance, after 1933, of ideas about how 'realistic' film could be used for 'educational' purposes.

In 1934, the German Propaganda Ministry enforced a compromise between two organizations which were each committed to their own 'modern' media-educational approach to the use of historical films, the Education Ministry's Office of Film and Photography (the RWU), and the Nazi Party's Propaganda Directorate (or RPL). Regional and municipal film offices affiliated with the Education Ministry (the 'Bildstellen') brought carefully selected 'realistic World War I' films into the history classroom, while the regional film offices of the Party Propaganda Directorate (the 'Gaufilmstellen') had a monopoly on the exhibition, for the purpose of the 'political' education of youth and adults, of the wide range of commercially produced features. University-level investigation of audience response to 'realistic' films continued to provide a media-scientific justification for the distinction between 'educational' viewing and the consumption of 'propaganda' and 'entertainment' film. In contemporary pedagogical sources, the compromise was credited for keeping 'sensationalist' historical entertainment out of the classroom, and for contributing to the distinction between historical and political education.

While the formal properties of historical 'realism' on film remained relatively unchanged, the distinctly 'modern' coordination of media education and historical/political education in Germany, before and after 1933, led to the development of cultural-political strategies (including the formulation and manipulation of different promotional campaigns and reception settings) which were intended to take advantage of the seductive power of moving images, without encouraging the intellectual or spiritual degeneration of the viewer.

More recently, historians in and out of the classroom have taken to discussing how films reflect both popular attitudes and covert cultural values. Since the 1940s, ideas about what constitutes historical 'reality' on film, as well as ideas about the scientific and educational use of film as an historical source, have developed considerably. All the same, I'd like to advance the argument that, when it comes to understanding (and teaching about) the historical conditions of 'visual literacy,' certain ideas about the inherent competition between 'educational,' 'entertainment,' and 'propaganda' viewing formations are still relevant.

Liberal and conservative history teachers in Germany during the 1920s and 1930s shared the view that the history curriculum had to somehow take account of the way in which mass media conditioned the student's view of the world. This problem is also touched upon in the argument put forward by the German literary scholar Hans Robert Jauss that reception theory "does not exclude the standpoint and activity of the subject, but rather includes him as the condition of knowledge . . . ," and that while the subject is every bit as time-bound as any given text (written or filmed), an encounter between the two elements should give rise to an historical dialogue. It might also be suggested that German history teachers' ideas about the 'educational' use of film are echoed in the recognition that, as the film scholars Tony Bennett and Jane Woollacott have argued, "texts are productive of meaning only within particular and determinate reading formations." German history teachers' awareness of the influence of promotional strategies and reception settings led to the formulation of some very contradictory ideas about the possible results of using film in historical education. At the same time, introducing students to historically determinate conditions of visual literacy, to the situation of a time-bound subject in an historically- and culturally-specific viewing formation may enhance their understanding of the value of film as historical evidence.

In a course on American social history, a UT-Dallas colleague uses *The Life and Times of Rosie the Riveter* (Connie Field 1980). In the film oral autobiographies are organized into a narrative history of women's employment (1941–45) which covers a variety of topics, including: 'skilled labor,' 'unionization,' 'racism,' 'children,' 'work in family,' 'casualties in war,' 'communism,' 'celebration of peace,' 'forced retirement of skilled labor,' 'post-war capitalist development,' 'morality and marketing' ('domestic' and 'feminine'), and 'menial labor for women.'

I know that my colleague happens to agree with Sonya Michel, a feminist historian who has argued that "the effect of women's telling their stories goes beyond mere 'talking heads': a sound track full of women's voices not only lets us hear strong women tell about their lives but, even more important, demonstrates that some women have deliberately altered the rules of the game of sexual politics.... [Radical filmmakers, like Connie Field] have been critical of the ways in which mass culture reinforces the hegemony of the dominant class. . . . They devise ways to offset this effect . . . so that they can create films that foster not certainty but a critical consciousness."

This is a tall order, given the fact that the filmmaker has minimal control of the educational viewing formation of the college classroom. The students need ancillary documentation, in order to be able to determine the accuracy of statements in the oral autobiographies; at the same time, the film itself provides a substantial amount of evidence of the media environment in which these women lived.

Through the incorporation of contemporary popular music and entertainment, advertising, political propaganda, and informational media (radio, newsreels, and 'educational' documentaries) *The Life and Times of Rosie the Riveter* presents a record of the contemporary media environment, which reflects a variety of interrelated reading, listening, and viewing formations. My colleague shows the feature film *Rosie the Riveter* (Joseph Santley 1944) in its entirety, and uses *Life and Times* . . . in order to give her students a sense of the historical setting of contemporary 'reading' of the feature film as entertainment, and in order to establish, in the process, some perspective on the status of the women in the film as readers, listeners, and viewers of mass media.

In a course on the treatment of the Nazi period in the German cinema of the last ten years (offered to students who had taken at least a modern European history survey), I ask students to evaluate: (1) the consequences, as represented in the films, of the repression of the history of the Nazi period on relations between the generations, as well as visual forms which are intended to foster dialogue between the generations; (2) representations, in the films, of history as a commodity (as fare for propaganda and entertainment), and evocations of readers, listeners, and viewers who consume history in that form; and (3) a culturally-specific historical media event. One aim of the course is to encourage students to consider how these German films about a history which they had studied are also part of a dialogue (the expression of historical understanding in one culture) in which they are not participants. As in my colleague's course on American social history, visual literacy requires some awareness of the social and cultural forces which create historically-specific relations between films, and between films and viewers.

Joachim Fest's film *Hitler: A Career* (1977) (based on his best-selling and critically-acclaimed biography of Hitler) is comprised almost entirely of film footage from Nazi sources, and contains a narration which makes the case that Hitler's political success was the result of his masterful manipulation of the mass media. Critics of this widely popular film objected to the way in which it appeared to absolve the older generation of responsibility for historical developments, and to objectify the 'Hitler phenomenon' in a way that defeated, rather than encouraged, understanding. In the class, we went on to consider how, in attempting to come to terms with a history that had been repressed, and to encourage a dialogue between the generations, films like *Germany in Autumn* (1978), *The Tin Drum* (1979), and *Germany–Pale Mother* (1979) introduced accessible representational forms—identifiable subjects—into film treatments of modern German history.

In Rainer Werner Fassbinder's *Lili Marleen* (1980), the war-time pop hit 'Lili Marleen' serves as a vehicle for exploring how mass culture serves as both a commodity and a form of communication. The film itself exaggerates the characteristic formal elements of the filmed melodrama of the period, in order to promote the film audience's recognition of the dual, and historically-determinate, nature of both the film and the song, as well as their identification with the historical audience for the song.

In *Our Hitler* (1978), Hans-Jürgen Syberberg also attempts to shift the viewers' attention from the sociological fact of Germany's identification with Hitler, to the mechanisms and consequences of such identification. The film avoids literal representations of Hitler (referred to in the film as 'the medium who hypnotized the masses') in favor of a visualization of the projection of Hitler and the mechanism behind that projection, the contemporary mass audience that regards him. Syberberg uses several formal strategies (including mannequins and rear-screen projections) designed to render transparent the viewer's identification with his or her own projection of Hitler.

The film *Heimat* (1984) represents the experience of everyday life over seventy years in a German village; the emphasis is on the gradual transformation of the village by transportation and communication technology. In the process, the director, Edgar Reitz, attempts to suspend hindsight in order to promote a personal understanding of the pre-Holocaust mentality. *Heimat*'s overwhelming success in Germany, both as a television series and as a commercially-released feature film, was fraught with political implications, and has been the subject of intense speculation about how contemporary German audiences 'read' their history on the screen.

According to the German film scholar Gertrud Koch, "what is being buried in *Heimat* is not the 'simple truth' of the 'little people' that morality does not thrive on an empty stomach, but the precarious consensus that one cannot speak of German history without thinking of Auschwitz.... [The film] reproduces the old gaps, pseudo-experiences and token acknowledgment of history which played a significant part in the post-war period."

All of these films attempt to stimulate contemporary (German) viewer identification with the historical past. That identification is facilitated or hindered by historically- and culturally-specific cues in and around these media products (these commodities which communicate) which influence their 'reading/viewing' as 'education,' 'entertainment,' or 'propaganda.' In their evaluation of the films as evidence of contemporary German attitudes about modern German history, I ask the students to relate their source criticism to a discussion of the battle over the viewing formations.

Historians' interest in films has never been exclusively confined to either the text (with regard to the iconography of cinema, the representation and distortion of reality through focus, camera placement, framing, lens selection, lighting, film emulsion, editing techniques, etc.), or the context (the unmediated illustration— through the use of actuality footage, newsfilm, newsreels, magazine films, documentaries, compilations, or feature films—of historical phenomena). As with any other type of source criticism, the use of film in historical education requires ancillary documentation, about what's represented on screen, and about how it's represented.

It's when we start to compare and contrast films from the same period, in terms of contemporary evaluations of not only their formal similarities and differences, but also their 'educational,' 'entertainment,' or 'propaganda' value, that we begin to see how historically-determinate conditions of visual literacy constitute a form of historical evidence in their own right.

ON READING *THE AENEID* AT AGE FIFTYSOMETHING

G. L. Seligmann

University of North Texas

I must confess, at the very start, that the title is very accurate, even in its inexacitude. I had not read Vergil's great epic until I became involved in teaching in our Classic Learning Core (CLC). I can date when I joined the CLC Faculty but it was sometime later that I purchased the Penguin version of Vergil and sat down to work my way through it.

Having confessed my cultural ignorance, let me also say that I have never written a paper quite like this one. Prior to this my scholarly efforts have been amply documented condensations of primary research on narrowly conceived topics, of interest, generally, only to a specialist. What you are getting today is the working out of an original idea. Well, it may not be original in the sense that no one has ever dealt with it before—it seems so obvious to me that I can't see how others have missed it—but it is original in the sense that I have never read anything like it. Moreover once it began to take shape in my mind, I decided against doing any formal research on the matter, thus ensuring that it would remain unsullied by expert opinion.

In short I put into practice a suggestion uttered long ago by a historian I have worshiped from afar, Walter Prescott Webb of the University of Texas, to the effect that historians should spend more of their time with their feet on their desks thinking. I also fear, however, that in doing this paper I may have run afoul of one of his condemnations—to wit, that of the historian who sits down at his desk with twelve books and when he gets up a week later there are thirteen books. In other words I have created for myself the common scholarly dilemma of a rock and a hard place or in a more fitting figure of speech, Syclla and Charybdis.

Not being a total scholarly klutz I knew something about my text when I dove in. I also had some idea of its importance in the history of literature, that is I knew that Vergil had been Dante's guide. I suspected that to some degree Dante had accepted his guide's views of the ancient world, although I had not contemplated where Dante had placed Ulysses in *The Inferno*. Of course not having contemplated where, I had certainly not looked at why. One of the side themes of this paper will be to look at the why of Dante's decision, and a probable follow-up of this paper will be another paper presenting a defense brief for a Ulysses falsely sentenced.

401

Several things struck me in my first reading of the poem. I was much taken with the image of Aeneas fleeing Troy after the defeat leading his wife and children and carrying his household gods and aged father on his back. It struck me then and still as the almost perfect image of "virtue" as defined in the author's lifetime. Such a depiction was, I believe, a major goal of Vergil's and one reflected throughout the work. This definition of an ideal form of virtue is one of the things that makes the epic such a valuable historical document and certainly indispensable to a program such as the CLC with its triune themes of "Reason, Virtue and Civility."

A second thing that struck me was the very high esteem in which the author held the Trojans. I, looking on them with purely modern eyes, had figured them for a bunch of overly complacent folk who lost because of both their arrogance and the Greeks', especially Ulysses', cunning. I realized, of course, that this high regard for the Trojans was not limited to the ancient world. After all, Phi Kappa Phi, the only scholarly society that saw fit to honor me for my relatively undistinguished undergraduate career, has as an integral part of its initiation ritual a specific and positive reference to the "crennelated walls of Troy." Although I will return to this theme later, it too is not the central theme of this paper.

What I would like to look at, in such depth as a paper of this length will permit, is another theme that struck me as interesting. Simply stated *The Aeneid* resonates with a loathing of the Greeks. On first reading this struck me as odd. Several years later it still strikes me as odd. And why should it not? After all the principal historical source available to Vergil was, of course, Homer, and Homer was Greek. To be sure, Homer treats the Trojans well in his epic. They are honorable warriors and are so characterized.

If there is a villain in *The Iliad* it is clearly Achilles. His treatment of dead Hector violates all accepted norms and Homer makes that very clear. And as for heroes, there are many in *The Iliad*. *The Odyssey* also has its share of heroes and villains, but Ulysses is certainly to be counted among the former. This being true why, by the time of the early Empire, were the Greeks in general and Ulysses in particular so contemptible?

Let me approach this question indirectly, by dealing first with the concept raised above, that of the "honorable enemy." As was mentioned above, Homer did not see the Trojans as anything other than an enemy capable of both honorable and dishonorable acts, and thus judged on an individual basis. Hector is quite honorable, Paris less so. Achilles behaves badly, Patrocles and a host of others behave well. One could explain this in anthropological terms by saying that it is not so strange; after all they were similar societies, they had similar religious practices, etc. For example, look at something as recent as the air war in World War I. As we all should know the British, French, German, and American airmen both killed and respected one another. And why should we be surprised. They shared cultural values. When the enemy behaved properly, proper behavior mandated that such behavior be recognized.

The problem of explaining "honorable behavior," however, appears to be more complex than the shared cultures and values would suggest. Let me suggest one other text where this behavior appears—*The Song of Roland*. In this epic the hero(es) are Christian, the enemy is both Moorish and Muslim, and the basest villain is a Christian.

To refresh your memories let me briefly recount the story. The armies of Charlemagne are withdrawing north out of Spain having defeated the Moors. Roland with a number of France's finest warriors and a relatively small force is left behind to serve as a rear guard not knowing that the French nobleman Ganelon has treacherously informed the Moorish King of the French plans. The Moors attack the outnumbered French and eventually overwhelm and kill all of them. Before that happens Roland finally sounds his great horn to recall the main French army. Ganelon attempts to convince Charlemagne that this recall is not serious, but he is overruled. The French return to the battlefield and their lifeless heroes. After a trial by battle which Ganelon's kinsman Pinabel loses, Ganelon is:

> . . . strongly fettered hand and foot
> To four swift steeds, and then a furious mob
> Drove them with sharpened sticks through a wide field.
> His mortal frame was rent apart, his limbs
> Torn from his wretched body, and his blood
> Crimsoned the grass. So perished Ganelon-ay,
> If any man betray a fellow man,
> It is not right that he should boast thereof.

Treason and betrayal have been made odious.

This brief examination of the "honorable enemy" in an epic greatly separated by time and circumstance from Homer suggests that there is something deeper than shared cultures at work in Homer's attitude of admiration towards the Trojans. Whatever it is it clearly is not present in *The Aeneid*.

When I began investigating this problem in earnest several years ago I thought I had the explanation for Vergil's "Greek hatred." It seemed to me to lie somewhere in what might be called "Greek envy," a malady I believe the Romans suffered from. After all, they knew several things about the ancient world. They knew of the accomplishments of the Greeks, and they knew they had conquered the Greeks and were their masters. I also believe that the Romans remained somewhat in awe of these subjects who were simultaneously subjects and cultural masters. If this did, in fact, happen this way it should not be surprising. The phenomenon apparently also occurred in the barbarian invasions and conquests of ancient China.

For a good while I was quite content with this interpretation. After all an explanation involving this sort of psychological ambivalence, insecurity, if you prefer contemporary psychobabble, is certainly in keeping with modern trends in historical and literary interpretation (if a layman is permitted to say anything about contemporary literary interpretation). Unfortunately this kind of contentment, or is it complacency, does not last long in the scholarly world. This summer, after my piteous appeal to appear on this program had been grudgingly accepted by a rather arrogant program chairman, inspiration struck. I was browsing in the university library and came across a rather interesting book *The Western Way of War: Infantry Battle in Classical Greece* by Victor Davis Hanson.[1] Since I am, in another area of my life, Book Review Editor for a journal entitled *Military History of the Southwest*, I often read in that area.

I found it to be a spectacular little book—in many ways an ideal monograph. It is, as the subtitle suggests, a very tightly focused work. At the same time it is, as the title suggests, concerned with a much broader subject which grows out of its narrow focus.

At the micro level Hanson deals with the nature and ethos of Hoplite warfare, the post-Homeric form of Greek warfare. His account, firmly rooted in copious and wide-ranging research, is detailed, interesting, and, I believe, authoritative. He describes who the Hoplites were, how they fought and what their cultural values were. The picture of warfare that he presents is different from that of *The Iliad*. Hoplite warfare was much more disciplined, less heroic, and more straight-forward than that of Homer's wars. This later form of warfare consisted of short, bloody battles. Opposing phalanaxes clashed head on and fought it out shield to shield until one was pushed back in defeat. The Homeric patterns of warfare with their emphasis on smaller group battles, often individual struggles, occurred occasionally in Hoplite warfare but it tended to be a sidelight to the major struggles locking larger numbers of men in mortal combat in a very confined area. Because of the nature of Hoplite armies, close to the entire male citizenry of the city-state, the wars had to be brought to a swift conclusion. Neither side could afford a prolonged struggle *a la* the siege of Troy.

On the macro level this style of warfare, Hanson argues, had a major influence on the ethos and values of war and of warriors. In this post Homeric and, indeed, post Hoplite value-structure killing was to be done face to face, formation to formation. This set of values has come down to the present. To give but two examples note the British reaction first to the Native American and then the

American colonists' style of warfare in the eighteenth century or to our response to irregular or guerrilla warfare in the twentieth century.

To the best of my knowledge of Roman warfare, the Romans accepted without question the value structure which grew up around Hoplite warfare. Their military ideals were those of their immediate predecessors not those of their Homeric predecessors. In this value context the Greeks won at Troy by dishonorable means, i.e., the subterfuge of the Trojan Horse. Simply stated, this was against the code of the honorable warrior. Had the Greeks fought "fair" they would have met the Trojans face to face, force to force.

Thus the groundwork is laid for the treatment of Ulysses and the Greeks by Vergil. Beyond doubt *The Aeneid* has an agenda beyond the mere telling of the tale. Quite clearly one aspect of that agenda is the articulation of the Roman value structure, specifically what the Romans viewed as civic virtue. One good way of showing what the virtuous life is all about is to give examples of its opposite. What better example could one turn to in the ancient world than the Homeric heroes? They were perhaps the best known characters in the Mediterranean world. If the Greeks had won at Troy by dishonorable means and the Trojans had behaved virtuously who then were the exemplars in an epic extolling the virtuous life? If simultaneously you had some other reason to disparage the victors why not idealize the vanquished? A situation wherein you can disparage a society you have misgivings about and praise a society which represents no threat to you is not a bad situation to find yourself in. And that is what I think Vergil did.

NOTES

1. Victor Davis Hanson, *The Western Way of War: Infantry Battle in Classical Greece*, (New York: Alfred A. Knopf, 1989).

9

CURRICULA AND SOCIAL CHANGE

CHALLENGING THE MEANING OF 'TEXT'—THEREFORE, I (Y)AM DEFINING TEXT AND LOOKING AT THE WESTERN CANON TO SEE THE APPROPRIATENESS OF A NORTH AMERICAN CONTEXT

Nancy Elizabeth Fitch

Lynchburg College

The paucity of African American scholars and the impact of that paucity on the generation of new African American educators, present certain ethical problems that we would like to think would not appear in humanities disciplines. The humanities have traditionally been the most open and inclusive of fields and have been thought to enhance one's understanding of the world, provide certain values and standards and a degree of tolerance to the subjective nature of some humane subjects. But intolerance is systematic even in the humanities, in great part due to the deep differences in cultural perspectives which have been an issue since the 1960s when more women and scholars of color gained access to positions in higher education. It is in higher education that the latest debate on the origins and meaning of American civilization and the influence of western civilization upon it are taking place. As those differences and cultural perspectives were surely there at the founding of the nation when Americans first began talking about "history," "culture," and "civilization," their resurgence is not (as first believed) a passing fancy on matters of style, language or dress, but a reflection of deep philosophical, and cultural differences and choices—as well as some unacknowledged commonalities. These differences and commonalities include the roles played in our evolution by oral tradition, language, literacy, and print. Therefore, without the input also of scholars of color, the humanities may limit themselves. It is *those* scholars who have raised their voices most clearly, seeking the inclusion of legitimate American (and thus African American) influences—including oral and aural influences—in the Western core and canon.

The dichotomies of Western and Eastern thought come through not only in traditional subjects like history—a subject which almost always takes a written form—but even more clearly in jazz and the blues, which I see also as historical *texts*. For example, western music is concerned with the tradition of score notation, including the scoring of both original and arranged music (written improvisation). Here are important differences between the auditory (an aspect of the oral tradition) and recording (the making of those records, tapes, and compact discs that create texts in jazz). Differences also arise between feeling artifacts (the affective) and tactile artifacts (the objective); between subject and object; between analysis and deduction, appreciation and intuition. Differences appear between an end product that is linear and hierarchical (thus "progressive" while at the same time "classic") and that which is circular—having no beginning or end, but a process for the building up of energy, reenforcing and enriching itself: evolutionary like a palimpsest. This circular view of history, which is Eastern and African, is not limited to the East, but is also found in the West—in Vico and James Joyce, for example. The hierarchical can be seen in the caste system of South Asia and thus it is not peculiar to the West. This suggests that these categories are not absolute, though it may take an Eastern perspective to see that.

There's a wonderful image in Tony Hillerman's Native American mysteries—the "Long Thinker." It is the image of an artist, historian, or master of culture who is not constrained by time or space, but who casts a long shadow while performing a natural human function—thinking—and who is revitalized by those stepping not into his or her shoes in replacement, but shaded in the shadow, being an extension of that shadow. That is worth striving for, I think.

The Seventh International Edward Kennedy "Duke" Ellington Conference raised issues on the oral and the written and on objective and subjective forms of historical documents/artifacts that are apropos to this discussion. The audience—95 percent white—was interested in Ellington as a concert artist, composer, and arranger, and in the 200,000 pages of documents which were presented to the Smithsonian Institution by his son, Mercer Ellingon. This gift alone has great impact on scholars in African American history and, specifically, in American music. There is still a paucity of written, primary source material *in the humanities* on blacks, though nonwritten texts go a long way toward fleshing out the field. In American history we continue to look for other nonwritten texts which may be available. The written, however, even in music, as seems always the case in the West, has been given more weight than the improvisational, experimental and unwritten, even though these are the very features of the genre of jazz. One scholar at the Ellington conference observed that in Europe Ellington gave more concerts than performances in cabarets and jazz festivals and did less studio work. On this side of the Atlantic, the ratio was reversed. The orchestra, the traditional forum for "serious" music and that serious music's primary "instrument," was more important. One commentator remarked that what made Ellington a major twentieth-century composer was that he was more than a tunewriter; he was a writer for the orchestra, and in that regard he was as good as Mozart and Beethoven. Such statements are significant, for they give to Ellington a legitimacy from outside the (high) standards of his own milieu. They also lend themselves to the belief that Western civilization is European and not American and syncretic. In an unquestioning, unthinking deference to European origins there are sometimes incompatible values and standards which can not legitimately measure this modern (versus "classical") culture based on the egalitarian and vernacular, rather than the elite and exclusive. The matter is succinctly put by Vartan Gregorian, President of Brown University, when he says "democracy and excellence are not mutually exclusive" (*Mirabella* 1989). Excellence does not have to be "old." Excellence and its traditions and standards in the United States must be based on the values of its founding peoples, the English and the African, who are co-creators of the American civilization that we know to this day. I can not speak of what the future may hold for the constituent parts of American civilization.

By extension, the importance of history-making/recording then must also take into account Ellington's records (the unwritten and auditory) as examples of historical texts. These texts give us the documentation of something that history is not much interested in—the thing of the moment—the improvisational, the unscored yet textual which appears only on recording instruments and really only once—in flashes of genius which are not following text but troping upon it. Improvisation is a challenge to the idea of history as something lying only in the past and old versus something timeless or fleeting, and it presents us with an issue not often discussed—the meaning of time in culture as well as differences in what constitutes history and the cultivated life. Without considered reflection, the present is often devalued, because everyone shares it, and it is "popular" or vernacular. In terms of document/text development, Nelson George is correct when speaking of contemporary music in *The Death of Rhythm and Blues* (Pantheon Books 1988). He writes, "Blacks create and then move on. Whites document and then recycle" (108). This is not a criticism, at least not to me, but an acknowledgment of difference. What is exciting is that the (musical) historical record/text is never the same, but changes in interpretation and style according to any number of variables including performing personnel, audience, even occasion—and what is preserved as history in improvisation is the flux of the text in all of its historical possibilities. If I seem to question the intellectual adventure and capacity to challenge of that which is scored or written down for the purpose of mimicking and preserving "just the way it was," then I am guilty, but no more at fault than those who, on the other hand, are paperbound. It is a different mind-set and one worth considering. In the case of jazz, as with any other thing, the good will be as enduring and in fact, timeless as that which is "old" and identified with one master, rather than with all the masters who create the theme anew every time it is performed. The elements of collectivity and of the involvement of the spectator/audience in the making of history are other aspects of the African mind in particular that create this historical perspective. They are the very aspects of Africism most often misunderstood, devalued and discounted in the Western tradition and those excluded from the canon and core which impact on American civilization.

The process of preservation is informed by a tendency to lean toward an institutionalization which takes things out of the present and away from the vernacular roots which created them. The issue then becomes, whom is culture for, whom or what does it serve, and who are the culture-bearers? European culture is considered in a complimentary way to be serious and highbrow. It is owned (appropriated) by the educated few who are trained to analyze/understand it rather than empathize with it, feel it, or even live with it. "Popular" culture is not considered serious because it is accessible; in fact this discussion of core and canon is really about accessibility. Walter Mignolo, of the University of Michigan, makes the point that the technology of writing—the conceptualization of the book as "object"—has led to the *exclusion* of people, and I extend his thought: it has led to a form of feudalism like that which arose in the Dark Ages, rather than to Enlightenment (though, of course, the American Enlightenment missed the boat on nonwritten texts and that provided a slave class in the American colonies and later the United States). According to Bruce Mannheim, another worker in the vineyards of the idea of "language and conquest" (I would say "literature and conquest"), literacy and language "evolved into tools of exclusion, control and social dominance" (Mannheim 1989). And he missed one; they also evolved into cultural hegemony by the West.

Who decides, and by what criteria, which texts are the most revealing and of what? A project is underway to present a seventy record collection of Ellington's work in a "Masterpiece" series published by the Smithsonian Institution. But who determines what is a "masterpiece"? The project begs the larger question: should any government agency in a country with such racial and ethnic diversity (which is often mainstreamed/compromised or destroyed) think it can or *should* determine matters on the cultural nature of a so-called "sub-group" (which I would contend is not a sub-group but co-creator of American civilization)? On the other hand, if we are fortunate enough to have persons empathetic to the Other traditions out of which some of their culture comes, shouldn't we ask what makes those traditions what they are—in this case a text within a context of orality and spirituality having to do with African heritage and American captivity/slavery and the overcoming of captivity, with dance (physical movement) representing the mind and intellect, and with intuitiveness, improvisation and anger—what Margaret Walker calls "black humanism"?

Another question arises: What is the role of the community of nonscholars? They may be the real interpreters of the text, as they are the people who live in the vernacular with it. The fact that we are dealing with music, which carries with it the burden of the sobriquet "universal language"—does not negate the need for interpretation within cultural, spiritual, and aesthetic contexts. For instance, those aspects of a text designed to mimic the values of another (even dominant) culture, may lead to misinterpretation and/or homogenization. It is important not only to have more scholars who are people of color interested in and trained to work in areas of their own respective heritages, but to include them in defining research agendas. It is also important to involve the community in interpreting and collecting material to be preserved and, in what is increasingly important—oral documentation or oral history (historical spectator/audience "interpretation"). For all groups, oral history has always been a part of collective memory, traditions and myths, but again it is often not considered (any longer) a legitimate form of history-making. Here again, the place of orality and aurality in African American history arises; the argument of Western scholars traditionally amounts to, "if you don't see it, it isn't there; if you can only hear it, it still isn't there." But we do well to listen to the Ashante proverb, "Mate Masie," which means "I have kept what I have heard"; it validates that which is not written and makes it eligible for any core or canon that impacts on American civilization. In the context of African American, we need to look *at* and *for* other "texts" for documentation, and that would include material culture with non-alphabetic writing as well as the latest field in African/American research—African American archaeology.

What constitutes and who decides what is worthy of preservation and what is the role of the community? Historically, elite groups have made those decisions. Albert Murray, author of the "blues idiom" concept, has praised and built up what he and others have called "the vernacular"—that which is everyday, secular, and indigenous versus the sacred; the Little Tradition in juxtaposition to the Great Tradition. At the Ellington conference Murray said that Ellington's work came from the blues idiom (a vernacular history/text) of his antecedents, an idiom whose most important symbol may be the train, symbolizing the movement, if not the momentum, of the evolution of an African American people in the United States. The image is of movement and evolution—not of the stationary; it parallels how these respective groups, African American and European-American, view their work and then *do* it. The image reflects the adaptation of the African-descended to *Western*, but not to American culture. American culture is rather a Western/African culture which African Americans themselves helped to create. In music, this capacity of adaptation is the "improvisational" nature of jazz—the breaking away from the text (as in the blues, Amiri Baraka's "memory of jazz") and in embellishing, troping and experimenting—improving and making better.

From this discussion of cultural issues come some ethical issues. Necessarily, Westerners and Easterners and Africans have different ideas about what is important, about what constitutes a historical record. These questions by themselves beg the question of who makes the choice of what is to be preserved, and for what interpretation, use or adaptation; does the artifact live, or is it officially declared "dead"—"sacred"—"do not touch or it will disintegrate in rarefied museum air"? There is the question of who does the work; the musician is not necessarily the musicologist, and the musicologist may not be interested in the history of music. Does it necessarily follow that the outsider is objective and the nativist scholar so subjective that his or her work cannot be considered? Is the nativist scholar "too involved"? These are questions that plague the humanities, but which can be raised here also in terms of Ellington, particularly on the issues of origins and genesis. Where does this creativity come from—not just his technical expertise, but who is his muse? Is it solely an issue of music? Is it enough to say—is it even beside the point to say, as did Roger Kennedy (Director of The National Museum of American History of the Smithsonian Institution) that Ellington is important "not because he is American, not because he is African American, but because he is good?" I understand the sentiment, but is it enough to be "good"? More important, how can Mr. Kennedy, as a government official, discount the music's Americanisms, strip it of meaning and disassociate it from American historicism which has so much to say to the Western tradition, which, the National Endowment for the Humanities notwithstanding, is not static but still evolving? Had Ellington not been "American" (we don't even have to talk "black") would his music be as significant? His music is not European, but it comes out of the cauldron which is America—meaning Europe and Africa. His genius was so mixed in this culture that no one outside that experience (an experience which includes white Americans) can *know*, in the sense of empathizing rather than understanding.

America historically is tied to race; her history is about race and race relations, and of two races, the British-American and the African, and that is where jazz gets its tonal coloring and where Ellington got his brown to black/blue imagery reflected in "La Plus Belle Africane," and "Black, Brown and Beige," "Black and Tan," "Blue Indigo," and "Symphony in Black." One commentator said that some of Ellington's work reflected "anger"; where would that have come from? We might ask why his sacred orchestral works include dance? Could it be that the spirituality, the sound and the movement coming out of the African mind—having many faces and many colors—are behind art, even in the diaspora? Is this the kind of ephemeral influence W. E. B. DuBois was trying to capture in *Souls of Black Folk*, and Margaret Walker in "black humanism"? If we must take apart and analyze, is it not dangerous on one side and self-serving on the other to ignore these questions?

Duke Ellington's first artistic talent was in the visual arts. He brought that talent with him to sound. Color tones distinguish Russian classical music from German, and Hungarian from French, and color tones come from folk motifs or the vernacular. The great classicism of European music, then, comes from the folk; elite classes only appropriated it. If that be so, Ellington's antecedents in the United States may also come from the blues text with its social concerns about legal and economic injustices, and personal heartbreak; it may come from people who composed and performed the music before it was in the mainstream and accessible—before it was acceptable. Ellington is reported to have said at the first Negro Arts Festival in Dacca that he "had been playing African music for thirty-five years," but it came *through* the American South and the urban North and the spirituals and gospel that were the basis of his sacred works and from the body as musical instrument and source of movement.

There is an overriding aspect of American democratic traditions which Eastern Europeans and third world peoples find important and have found inherent in this music: namely, individualism (e.g., the improvised solo) as well as the democratic consensus of orchestra, nation, or community. It is this which disinclines the world's oppressed, at least, to separate the music's origins from its text.

The distance that some Americans and Europeans need to come to appreciate the role of music in American life and the influence of democratic traditions in its themes as well as the role of blacks in American music in bringing about democratic ideals which extend the Western tradition built upon the Graeco-Roman—was reflected when Mr. Kennedy, introducing Congressman John Conyers (who led the drive to recognize jazz as a national treasure) mentioned that Conyers' current cultural project was to have the United State Congress recognize a national "Tap Dance Day." The audience, unaware that it really should know better, laughed. It was simply unaware of the importance of tap dancing to the American canon. The House Joint Resolution, however, eloquently explained the importance of this African American art form: tap dancing is a "multifaceted art form [and] is a manifestation of the cultural heritage of our nation, reflecting the fusion of African and European cultures into an exemplification of the American spirit. . . . [and it] has had a historic and continuing influence on other genres of American art, including music, vaudeville, Broadway musical theater, and film, as well as other dance forms . . . [and] is a joyful and powerful aesthetic force providing a source of enjoyment and an outlet for creativity and self-expression for Americans on both the professional and amateur level. . . ." In other words, music *is* our history too and is used to write and preserve history aurally. This won't make sense without its oral traditions and the cultural specificity of its muse, and the American civilization core and the canon won't make sense without it.

Paul Robeson said that he "hear[d] his way through the world." Sound and voice are basic instruments in any black person's repertoire. In the linear Western view of things, one moves, however, from the oral to the written, and the oral becomes precursor/forerunner and in the scheme of things, the stepsister of progress. This tilt toward the written is not as objective as it might seem and certainly not benign. The oral and the aural have been discounted, distorted; yet it is that interchange between living performer/speaker/historian and audience that allows for a dynamism that cannot die, but also cannot be static and merely reflection on white paper. Ellington said that his music was the history of his people, and whether he meant African Americans, blacks, or Americans in general is no matter; he saw it was text. In the current acrimonious discussion about Eurocentricism and multicultural diversity, we need to make sure that that which is non-written is very much extant and has a place in defining who we are. The late Barbara Tuchman sets up the dichotomy very nicely, a dichotomy that has characterized the United States since its inception; she said, "Without books, history is silent, literature dumb, thought and speculation at a standstill. . . . Without books the development of civilization would have been impossible. . . . Books are humanity in print." But the oral tradition is the basis of history and community, and community is the basis of human consensus that allows human beings to live and reason together. The oral and the aural are the first basis, dare I say the only basis, of human interaction—print, books and (silent) reading are individual processes. Verbal interactions, the values and traditions we are taught in folklore and folktale, in our music, are the basis upon which civilizations and cultures are made, and they are not silent. They lived until (and after) there was print, and print became accessible to all stations of people (though not to all individuals). They were not dumb; they reached many people unreachable now because of print illiteracy. And of course thought and speculation come from argument and discourse—words describing the oral/aural process.

What we have in discussing the core and the canon by looking at Duke Ellington and this conference is the tension between formal structures and the vernacular. What is important is that the African art tradition is not institutionalized for inclusion in the core/canon to the extent that there is no intimacy and relativity. But that is what Tuchman says only written texts offer. If we are to achieve Tuchman's idea of book as civilizer and culture as "humanity," we must be sure that the text doesn't become institutionalized or made into an object, but that, as Mignolo suggests, it be allowed to remain a concept and idea—rather than a "thing." In that way will even diverse persons with moments of shared heritage come together. That should, in the final analysis be the point of a humane discipline and the focus of what our students take away from a liberal arts education.

NOTES

George, Nelson. *The Death of Rhythm and Blues*, New York: Pantheon Books, 1988.
Gregorian, Vartan, *Mirabella* 1, 1989: 52.
Mannheim, Bruce. *Research News*, The University of Michigan Division of Research and Development and Administration, January-March, 1989: 5

THE CORE AT A HISTORICALLY BLACK COLLEGE: HOW DOES IT DIFFER? SHOULD IT DIFFER?

Benjamin D. Berry, Jr.

Prairie View A&M University

Let me begin with a disclaimer: this is not a research paper, but rather an essay based on some reading, a bit of remembering of my own experience as an undergraduate in a historical black college, and some discussion with colleagues at Prairie View and other institutions around the nation. The question asked in my title has been a problem for what is called the Core Faculty of the Benjamin Banneker Honors College since its inception. When the first five members of that faculty gathered in the summer of 1985, we devoted most of our time to this question. Our conclusion was that, indeed, our core should reflect the African heritage of the majority of our students, but we were not able to reach a consensus on the degree to which that heritage should displace the traditional western orientation that had formed the center of our own education.

In the summer of 1989 an expanded and mostly-new core faculty met to engage in a discussion of the core curriculum of the Honors College and, as expected, devoted the lion's share of our time to the same questions which had plagued the original faculty. Equally not surprising, we reached a similar conclusion and failed also to achieve a consensus on the same point. What I will present today grows out of those discussions, and out of informal discussions that have occurred between those two summer meetings. Obviously, I have not been able to convince my colleagues of the rightness of my position, for we would have settled everything this summer. Perhaps I will have better luck with this audience.

The first of the two questions—How does the core differ at the historically black college or university (HBCU)?—requires some historical background. For the most part, HBCU's have patterned their general education curriculum, or core, on the practice of the predominantly white institutions which have served as their models in other areas as well. At the outset, the faculties of these institutions, the majority of which are located in the South and were founded at the end of the Civil War, were whites from the North who were themselves educated by the colleges and universities which comprise what is now known as the Ivy League. These liberal whites who journeyed south to bring literacy to the ex-slaves, brought their Ivy League understanding of what constituted an educated person.

In the early 20th Century, control of these institutions was passed from white missionaries to home-grown black educators. However, the curriculum did not change radically from that already in place, even in those institutions which emphasized so-called industrial education where, when the liberal arts were taught at all (and they were taught perhaps more than most of us would have thought), the program followed that of the white institutions in both content and pedagogy.

The core curriculum which I encountered over a half century later was closely patterned after that presented at the better white institutions of the time. That is to say, I studied the thought and culture of the western world, I received a thorough grounding in the history of western civilization, the philosophy of the ancient Greeks, the theological traditions of Europe, and the social science of Germany and America.

As I look back on this education and the time frame in which it was received, I must bow to the wisdom of those who shaped that curriculum. The institutions of segregation, dictated by law in the South and by custom in the North, created an isolation of the black community and its youth which had to be overcome, if movement out of the depths of poverty and degradation was ever to be accomplished. It was, therefore, necessary to break through that wall of segregation by instructing the future leaders of the black community in the culture and tradition of the western white world.

It would be the graduates of the HBCUs who would lead the struggle for civil rights in the 1940s, 50s, and 60s. The education provided these young people in the HBCUs was education for leadership in their communities. Both DuBois and Booker T. Washington, those two giants of black education in the late 19th and early 20th Century, recognized the leadership role of the college-trained black, even while they disagreed on the direction that leadership should assume. The traditional core in the liberal arts institutions, and what liberal arts were offered in the so-called industrial training schools, was a liberating force in the hands of the black educators of the past. It provided those black students with the intellectual weapons for the struggle for racial equality and black freedom.

In this regard, the core at the HBCU did not differ in its content from that of the predominantly white institution, but the manner in which it was presented was radically different. Unlike the modern critic who argues that the university needs to return to a Great Books general educational program in order to preserve the standards of the past when the curriculum and politics of the university guaranteed a favored place for white males, the black educators who presented the core curriculum to me as an undergraduate did so in the hope that the ideas gleaned from the Great Books would set me and my peers on the road to freedom and major social reform.

418

While the core curriculum of the HBCU was patterned after that of the PWI's, it made room for the Wisdom of Africa and the African diaspora as it is transmitted in literature and in oral tradition. In this regard, it diverged in a very important way from the core of the white institutions which, at least in my experience, did not allow for such deviation. This is best seen in the contents of *Introduction to Contemporary Civilization in the West*, the source book prepared for the course in Contemporary Civilization at Columbia College (Third Edition, 1961). This book contains no selections drawn from cultures other than European and Euro-American, and it was (and remains in some circles) the standard for the core course of the liberal arts curriculum.

In summation, the answer to the first question is, the core curriculum of the past in the HBCUs was patterned after that of the white institutions, but differed in some very important respects, and it was both necessary and beneficial to the black students that the similarities as well as the differences were there.

However, times change and so do curricula. Changes occurred in the late 1960s and 1970s in response to the demands of some students that the core become more relevant. Changes have occurred in the 1980s in response to a new minority demanding a return to traditional values (e.g., Allan Bloom, and friends). The recent debates at Stanford were the result of the meeting of these conflicting demands and we should recognize that this kind of conflict is possible and probable for any institution seeking to revise its core curriculum in the 1980s, even HBCUs. Indeed, we have been wrestling with this very dilemma at Banneker. Our struggle will serve as the entry to the second question presented in the title: Should the core at a Historically Black institution differ?

The core curriculum of the Banneker Honors College is the direct product of the mission of that institution. Founded in 1984 as a response to the need for more minority students entering and completing graduate and professional schools particularly in science and technical fields, the College opened its doors offering majors in the nine areas exhibiting the most severe underrepresentation of minorities. The founding core faculty, employed after a national search, stated at the outset that rigorous studies in the sciences and technology should be balanced with equally rigorous study in the humanities (something not readily admitted by the technology-oriented adminstration), and we began the process of carving an Honors Core curriculum out of the General Education requirements of the university rather than creating a series of new core courses. It was our objective to allow a student to complete the requirements of the Honors College without the burden of a series of courses in addition to the number required of other graduates of the university while at the same time engaging in true honors study. We were also aware of the bureaucratic labyrinth which must be negotiated in order to add new courses to the university inventory.

419

Honors sections of English composition, Literature, Political Science, History, and Mathematics were created. Two new courses were added: a Freshman Colloquium and a course listed as World History but taught as an interdisciplinary course bringing together philosophy, intellectual history, psychology, world religious and contemporary issues. This course was given the name "Modes of Thought."

"Modes of Thought" has become the centerpiece of the Banneker Core curriculum and warrants further discussion as we explore changes in the core curriculum over the six year history of the Honors College.

The first years of "Modes of Thought" reflected the felt need to emphasize the Afro-centric philosophy of the majority of the original core faculty. The course therefore included some of the traditional writings and thought of western civilization courses, but placed great emphasis on the study of African, African American, and Eastern thought. The reading list of the course during these years included *The Sufi Message of Peace of Hazrad Inayat Khan*, Van Sertima's *African Presence in Early Asia*, *The Kaballon*, Jahn's *Muntu: The New African Culture*, and Rodney's *How Europe Underdeveloped Africa*. While this is not a complete listing of the reading list for an entire year, the sample gives a sense of the orientation of the course.

This same orientation was reflected on the reading lists for Introduction to Literature which, again included some of the traditional selections, but gave emphasis to the African and African American tradition; in Political Science which considered the politics of race and the question of Civil Rights almost to the exclusion of other issues; and in History which selected African-American History as *the* topic for study in depth. The core faculty believed that, as an honors college associated with a historically black university, it was our responsibility to emphasize the African and African American background of the majority of our students. In the conflict between relevance and traditional western values, relevance was the obvious victor.

In 1989 there are but two of the original core faculty remaining, and the faculty has grown to nine members. In our planning this summer the content of the core has been altered to reflect a new orientation. What has changed is not the student body—the freshman class of 1989 is remarkably similar to that of 1985—but the faculty's concept of how best to fulfill its mission of preparing students for graduate and professional school. Recognizing the national trend toward traditionalism, the faculty this year, while continuing to teach the African and African-American tradition, has given more emphasis to the sources seen as important to western civilization. Thus, the reading list of "Modes of Thought" includes more traditional works of Plato, Aristotle, Sophocles, Martin Luther, Thomas Hobbes, John Locke, Rousseau, Marx and Thoreau, along with Martin Luther King, James

Baldwin, Nelson Mandela, and Angela Davis. Similar shifts may be seen in the lists for Political Science, Literature and History. The current core faculty feels that it has come closer to striking a balance between the demands to be relevant to the population of students in the HBCU, while preparing them for entry into situations which demand a knowledge of the traditions of western civilization, i.e., graduate and professional schools.

The black student is no longer a victim of the same segregation and the resulting isolation as was the black student of my generation. However, there are still barriers which the contemporary black student must hurdle before he or she can become a fully equal contributing member of American society, and these barriers are no less forboding than were those of segregation. In addition to the racial roadblocks thrown in the path of young blacks, there is the problem of self-awareness resulting from the fact that a significant percentage of black college students enter the university having been taught for twelve years by white teachers who, while perhaps very good in some areas, failed to provide that student with a sense of self as a black person. Indeed, in all too many instances, they have done all within their power to denigrate the culture and history of their students. Add to this the media definition of black culture as being limited to rap music and drugs, and the self concept of the black freshman in 1989 is not far from the negative self-concept identified by Robert Coles over twenty years ago.

We, as a faculty of an honors college associated with an HBCU, have the responsibility of doing our best to correct that deficiency in our students' education, for a good self-concept is a major requirement for success (even survival) in the world of the dominant culture (white). Thus, the Core curriculum must be sufficiently different from that of the PWI to make this correction, while at the same time preparing the student to move smoothly and comfortably in the white world of business, industry or academe.

I am suggesting that the Core curriculum at the HBCU is the centerpiece in an effort to produce persons who are bi-cultural, that is, who are comfortable in their own ethnic culture and who are able to function well in the dominant culture. These are not marginal men as described earlier by Everett Stonequist (*The Marginal Man*, 1938) for they are not out of place in either culture, as Stonequist said the marginal person was. Rather, they speak the language of the dominant culture, understand its thought patterns, appreciate its music, art, drama, literature, even its cuisine. However, they are also able to talk, walk, dance, sing and eat (within the bounds of health requirements) with their ethnic brothers and sisters.

As I was preparing this, my wife, feminist that she is, pointed out that several highly selective white institutions have begun to do something similar in relation to women's studies. Skidmore College, in revamping its general education curriculum, was careful to be inclusive of the ethnic university of humanity, but emphasis was placed on the role of women in human history and culture. Wellesley College, while maintaining an ethnically diverse student body and a curriculum that is reflective of this diversity, nontheless has historically given a central place to women in its teaching and in faculty research.

One could also point to the Jewish University—Brandeis for example—which is strong in the general curriculum, but does not give its Jewish heritage a back seat. These institutions have recognized the possiblities and potential inherent in developing bi-cultural graduates. Wellesley graduates Dianne Sawyer and Linda Wortheimer are competent in their fields and strong advocates of the rights of women, to use some well-known examples. Martin Luther King, Jr., a HBCU graduate, was not only a strong fighter for the rights of black people, but was also a fairly good theologian, well-versed in the traditional thinkers of western and eastern theology.

As an aside, it would do well for all institutions of higher education to give serious thought to the idea of developing at least bi-cultural, if not multi-cultural, students. The idea of a world dominated by western culture and western societies is an anachronism which we would be ill-advised to perpetuate in our educational institutions. Our students need to be conversant in the languages and cultures of the Far East, Latin America, and the Middle East, and we cannot accomplish this with the myopic vision of reality suggested by Bloomites.

I have thus far presented only sociologial justification for the Core curriculum I am advocating for the HBCUs. There are also sound educational reasons for an inclusive Core. We in the academy are constantly decrying the inability of the American populace to engage in something we like to call critical thinking, or to be what Bloom has termed "discriminating." It is my contention that a core which presents only one view—inhibits that ability more than it promotes it. Those who have been most insightful concerning the sacred cows of western society have been either those who were not a part of that society by virtue of geography, or were its victims. The Core curriculum which engages students' minds with the thoughts of minorities, women, and non-westerners sharpens the critical abilities and promotes a discriminating attitude.

The Core curriculum at the HBCU must be different because the faculties and administrations of predominantly white institutions have not come to the position that multi-cultural facility among its students is necessary, while we are more than aware that at least bi-cultural abilities are critical for the survival of our graduates. In the best of all possible worlds, the curricula of the two types of institutions would not differ, and indeed in some of the better colleges and universities, they do not differ from what I have suggested here. However, the pressure to solidify the one-culture concept is strong—from funding agencies, the academic press, and state legislatures.

The most dangerous of those pressures is from the state legislatures which are rapidly mandating "rising junior tests" of general education which will measure the mastery of the tenets of the Dominant Culture *only*. This will force all institutions or higher education—public and private—minority and dominant group—to teach the same core curriculum—the one dictated, not by the state educational board, put by the framers of the tests, who may or may not be in sync with the wishes of the state board of education, and who are rarely if ever cognizant of the needs of minority groups. While the new core proposed by the Texas Coordinating Board, to use an example close to home, makes some provision for recognition of the cultural diversity of the state and humanity in general, western culture and thought dominate the curriculum, and will dominate the assessment instrument, whatever that may be, which will be used as the gatekeeper between lower division and upper division study.

I have argued elsewhere that the HBCUs have historically prepared their students for those entrance tests which guard the doors to graduate and professional schools—the GRE, LSAT, MCAT, etc.—and have done so while giving their students a sense of self through a multi-culture-oriented core curriculum. The new concept of state-mandated rising junior tests will all but prevent that kind of dual preparation by forcing all schools to use the same core curriculum in the first two years of undergraduate study.

Thus, I am arguing, not only should the core at the HBCU differ, but that difference deserves recognition by the educational establishment which includes the state legislatures, coordinating boards (by whatever name they may go in different states), and NEH and other funding agencies. In a world that is no longer dominated by western thought and culture, we can ill afford the dinosaur of a one-culture education. The HBCUs have led the way, historically, in multi-cultural education—it was necessary for racial survival—and, if the rest of higher education refuses to follow, it should at least not seek to stop us.

THE CURRICULUM AND SOCIAL CHANGE: TWO NINETEENTH-CENTURY VIEWS

Brendan A. Rapple

Boston College

Some light may perhaps be thrown on the problems pervading contemporary American education by considering them vis-à-vis analogous problems in other educational systems of earlier periods. In this paper after recounting the views of two nineteenth-century writers, Matthew Arnold—poet, educationist, literary, religious, and social critic, and William Morris—poet, artist, printer, novelist, and social critic, on the inadequacies of the educational structure in the England of their day, I employ these views as catalysts for my comments on and proposed solutions to twentieth-century American curricular questions. Although this conference has the "Core and the Canon" at the college and university level as its main theme, my remarks are applicable to the elementary and secondary educational stages as well as to the tertiary. However, I make no apology for this as I believe that curricular concerns at the latter level are inextricably blended with those at the earlier levels and that if we wish to improve college and university curricula it is essential that we also introduce improvements, as a sound foundation, to curricular content in schools.

The greatest problem Matthew Arnold saw pervading the English was their lack of "culture," a fault especially evident when contrasted with the openness to new ideas, the understanding of the modern *Zeitgeist*, and the intellectual awareness of such peoples as the Germans and French. For, to the typical Victorian the notion of progress was usually seen in material terms. To his compatriots, declared Arnold, civilization invariably "meant railroads and the penny post."[1] However, he himself preferred to look to the "intellectual deliverance" marking a truly modern age, and which was characterized by "the intellectual maturity of man himself; the tendency to observe facts with a critical spirit; to search for their law, not to wander among them at random; to judge by the rule of reason, not by the impulse of prejudice or caprice."[2] But neither the "Populace" nor the "Barbarians," the working classes and the aristocracy respectively, partook of this "intellectual deliverance," nor, did the middle classes, the "Philistines," increasingly England's rulers. In fact, the nation, Arnold averred, was tending to "anarchy" rather than "culture."[3] Moreover, Arnold, who for thirty-five years, from 1851 until his retirement in 1886, earned his living travelling throughout England and Wales as one of Her Majesty's Inspectors of Elementary Schools, and who consequently knew more about his nation's schools than the vast majority of his compatriots, was assured that the failure to attain an "intellectual deliverance" was very largely due to the abysmal educational provision at all levels. He was adamant that the educational system must be changed.

William Morris' views on the inadequacy of English society were quite different to those of Arnold. For Morris' main censure was directed at the economic system, capitalism, which aimed at gaining ever increasing profits far more than at furthering human ends. He repeatedly contrasted the merits of medieval, pre-capitalist, rural England, a society which enjoyed true wealth, with the horrors of industrial "blackness of night" where Mammon was all and Samuel Smiles' *Self Help* the creed. What was urgently needed was the utter destruction of capitalism and a truly socialist and egalitarian society established. Moreover, Morris blamed the educational system for advancing capitalist interests and for reinforcing the rigid class structure. His floruit coincided with the era of payment by results in elementary schools when the mechanical, fact-grinding, memoriter pedagogy practiced in earlier years by such as Dickens' M'Choakumchild still ruled and which necessarily killed all efforts to truly educate children. The main aim of this educational structure, Morris held, was to produce those who would unthinkingly become cogs in the vast capitalist machine. As we read in his lecture, "Useful Work Versus Useless Toil":

> At present, all education is directed towards the end of fitting people to take their places in the hierarchy of commerce—these as masters, those as workmen. The education of the masters is more ornamental than that of the workmen, but it is commercial still; and even at the ancient universities learning is but little regarded, unless it can in the long run be made to pay.[4]

Existing education was merely a "commercial and political" training of individuals to assume predetermined roles within the "division-of-labour system" to continue "the usurpation of true Society."[5] Moreover, even if a child managed to secure any real education it would avail him little in living under the inegalitarian, inhumane conditions of capitalism. In such a society, Morris declared, pupils "are not educated to become *men* . . . the conditions under which true education can go on are impossible."[6]

If Arnold and Morris were at one that England's education was in drastic need of change, they were by no means in agreement concerning the constitution of such change, and, more specifically, what were the desired curricula. Arnold, despite his regard for the classics, fervently believed that their primacy at the post-elementary levels should cease (this was becoming more and more common on the

Continent), such subjects being no longer sufficient for the increased socially-mixed numbers who were seeking education beyond the basics. Modern languages and natural sciences, as well as the humanities, now had their place in attaining his desired "intellectual deliverance."[7] Even at the elementary level where the curriculum rarely ventured beyond the 3 R's, Arnold advocated that a subject like Germany's *Natur-kunde,* i.e., "knowledge of the facts and laws of nature," should be taught.[8] True to his notion of "culture," he was arguing for a liberating, broad, truly humanizing curriculum, not a narrowly focused, straitening one. What the English needed was "a disinterested endeavour to learn and propagate the best that is known and thought in the world."[9] A student must touch as many points as possible of the "encyclopaedia," the circle of knowledge, and not be content with just one part of its circumference. A true liberal education, by which a man gets "to know himself and the world" required that no one branch of knowledge be stressed to the total exclusion of others. As the Continentals realized, a true education must include science.

Arnold often employed the terms "science," "scientific," "scientific sense" in a broader context than the mere natural sciences.[10] Indeed, when referring to the increasing role of "science" in the modern world, he generally meant the disposition, as he wrote, "towards knowing things as they are."[11] Man's "scientific sense" was "the sense which seeks exact knowledge."[12] Even the humanities could be scientific when studied in the appropriate manner, as was frequently the case in Germany.[13] And it was above all such science which Arnold was convinced England urgently needed if ever she were to rise from her slough relative to some of her neighbours. The inculcation of this quality would be a major step towards ridding the middle classes of their philistinism, the aristocracy of their barbarism, the populace of their incipient anarchy, thereby helping all three to attain an "intellectual deliverance." But at the moment the English, he considered, "hardly even know the use of the word science in its strict sense, and only employ it in a secondary and incorrect sense."[14] In short, not only was natural science slighted in the curriculum, but schools also failed to instill that scientific intellect called by the Germans *Wissenschaft,* that is "science, knowledge systematically pursued and prized in and for itself."[15] And this was particularly lamentable, Arnold held, since it was through the proper education that a nation's modern spirit, its intellectual temper, was best fostered; as he wrote in *Culture and Anarchy:* "education is the road to culture."[16]

Morris also consistently viewed education not as something pertaining just to individuals but as a process and result thoroughly intertwined with the wider society. But where Arnold saw education as a major vehicle for effecting societal changes, Morris maintained that it could do little until after society itself was altered. However, with "Socialism Triumphant"[17] and capitalism vanquished, education would play an essential role in preserving a truly egalitarian, non-competitive, community-oriented society. In fact, real education would be identical with socialist living, not something undertaken in a schoolroom for a few hours a day for a limited number of years, preparing "for a life," as he declared, "of commercial success on the one hand, or of irresponsible labor on the other; and therefore in either case with a definite object, more or less sordid in view." Rather, education would be a lifelong process. As Morris wrote in *Socialism: Its Growth and Outcome*: "no man will ever 'finish' his education while he is alive, and his early training will never lie behind him a piece of mere waste, as it most often does now."[18] "Will education," he asked rhetorically in his utopian novel, *News from Nowhere*, "be a system of cram begun on us when we are four years old, and left off sharply when we are eighteen?"[19] In fact, in this work schools are no more, the very word being only understood in connection with herring or painting.[20]

Arnold, as we have seen, tended to view the curriculum as a means for developing the intellect since it would be by the advancement of communal intellectual culture that a society would be improved. Morris, however, held that intellectual education was only part, and not necessarily the main part, of the curriculum, if education by living deserves such a technical name. To take one's place in a truly socialist society required a very broad education embracing one's artistic, physical, manual, as well as intellectual development. Certainly, reading and writing and also "the art of thinking," which, Morris declared, was "at present not taught in any school or university that I know of" would be habitual in the ideal socialist society. However, as important would be swimming, riding, sailing, carpentry, smithying, sheep shearing, reaping, ploughing, cooking, baking, sewing. There was no one set of skills or subjects to be mastered; all depended on an individual's talents. True liberal or "freeing" education would necessarily depend upon one's abilities. However, though one person's education would necessarily differ from that of another, an essential common denominator of everyone's liberal education would consist in its being exercised for the community. Education must transcend the individual and aim at the good of society.[21]

The educational views of Arnold and Morris count for more than academic interest, for we may still look to them for lessons. America, as the 1990s approach, just as Victorian England, is pervaded by social, political, economic, sexual, and ethnic problems and inequalities. "Anarchy," metaphorical, if not actual, ever looms and it is certainly moot whether Arnoldian "culture" can be effected by the existing educational structure. Also, only a very optimistic individual would suggest that society's manifold inequities could be eliminated by education alone. Still, many today believe that changed curricula at the various levels would be a powerful means for ameliorating the educational and social malaise. Arnold, of course, was in no two minds, arguing that changes in education, and especially revised curricula, would be a most effective way to stop England's decline and reform society. As mentioned, he was very pleased by some Continental institutions' curricula which embraced both the sciences and the humanities. In fact, he was one of his century's most prominent comparative educators and he consistently affirmed that the English could indeed learn much from abroad.[22] We today in this country can also look with benefit at the educational practices of other nations. It seems that every month now some report is published pin-pointing the U.S.'s poor showing in the educational sphere vis-à-vis other countries. And more often than not it is in mathematics and in the sciences, pure and applied, that American students are conspicuously trailing. Though we often pay lip service to the notion of liberal education in our institutions, generally such education pays far too little attention to scientific subjects. Admittedly, it is not easy to provide an education which touches all parts of the circle of knowledge. Arnold's encyclopaedia is only for the few. Still we seem to be depriving far too many of our students of an adequate education in mathematics, chemistry, physics, biology (nor do we always compensate with an excellent dosage of other disciplines). To prepare for later specialization the curriculum must have a broad, truly liberal foundation. And this must include science. Why science is being neglected and how America can emulate foreigners in improving scientific teaching must be intensely studied by comparative and international educators. But, it is my impression that such comparative critics are not too plentiful, are just as likely to be sociologists as educationists, and, in fact, are arguably getting fewer. But it is now high time that more personnel study very carefully the educational practices of other nations. We no longer can remain insular, reluctant to learn from abroad.

But the problem is far wider than that we seem to care little why the Japanese, Koreans, and other nationalities are better at scientific or technological subjects. Americans are just not overly interested in other nationalities, period, and this ethnocentrism is reflected in the typical curriculum. Arnold considered that a major problem with the English was that they were narrow, provincial, insular. He fervently wished that they become more cosmopolitan in outlook and practice; to become imbued with a feeling for international, as opposed to mere domestic currents, particularly in the intellectual field; to display, in short, an increased understanding that England, though important, occupied only part of the world's stage. As he declared in 1864: "By the very nature of things, as England is not all the world, much of the best that is known and thought in the world cannot be of English growth, must be foreign."[23] We might transpose this sentiment to modern times and to this country, for I believe—and this is a generalization to which there are numerous exceptions—that many Americans are every bit as insular and as ethnocentric as Arnold's Victorians. I have no doubt that the typical German, Swede, or Italian knows far more about the U.S. than the typical American does about European nations. Perhaps this is understandable. Nevertheless, American pupils are taught too little about foreign societies, the result being a manifest provinciality which, if allied to smugness, will inevitably contribute to retarding America's progress in what is increasingly a global village. It is now essential that curricula focus more on non-American history, geography, languages, culture in general, so that students gain an increased knowledge of societies other than their own. The resulting enlarged comparative perspective will help Americans attain an "intellectual deliverance" analogous to that desired by Arnold for the nineteenth-century English.

A valid objection to Arnold's curricular views is that they focused too much on intellectual development. In the present debate on the curriculum intellectual content also tends to be stressed, whether the subject be Latin or Gay studies, Greek or Women's studies. William Morris was quite right to maintain that education should be concerned with more than fostering the mere mind. The curriculum must also cater to physical, artistic, manual needs. Still, I also hold that we might profitably bear in mind Arnold's belief in the necessity to inculcate in pupils an appreciation and love of science in its original meaning of exact, systematic knowledge which is valued for itself. While curricular content is naturally of great importance, essential also is how the content is taught and for what ends. Greek might be taught disastrously, as it frequently was in Arnold's day, while peace studies, black studies, women's studies might be studied in a truly scientific manner.

A major problem today is the prevalence of a species of Utilitarianism, a nineteenth-century philosophy despised alike by Arnold and Morris, which makes the interest of the individual paramount. A solipsistic world-view reigns, the concomitant result being that the community's wellbeing is often held to be secondary. I believe that it would behoove us to remember the conviction of these two Victorians that education and the curriculum should invariably be viewed in terms of the wider society rather than of the individual or of small groups. Arnold, as we have seen, held that the proper educational processes would effect that "intellectual deliverance" which would improve all society. Morris, on the other hand, admittedly believed that education could do little to change society; however, after the socio-economic-political bases of the wider world were altered, education would be a potent force in preserving the community's wellbeing. Thus both tended to think of forests rather than trees. Modern educationists must also focus their curricular goals on the "big picture." Curricula must aim at educating students as much as possible for interacting with mankind at large. There must always be an effort to relate subjects to the wider society outside the classroom or lecture hall and the student's own immediate environment. There should not be very different curricula, as was the case in Arnold's and

Morris' day, for different social, economic, ethnic, sexual classes. Educationists should take great care that black studies are not viewed as only for blacks, women's studies as only for women, the Great Books as only for white males of the dominant classes. The curriculum must be a cohesive, not a devisive societal force. In short, true education, as well as transcending the specific disciplines, should transform more than the individual student—it must aim at the common and universal good.

It is probably obvious that I agree with Matthew Arnold's conviction that we should borrow educational ideas from abroad, that we should pay more curricular attention to both notions of science, that we should enlarge our students' *Weltanschauung* by including more non-American content in the curriculum, that educational goals—and this was shared by William Morris—should aim at the wider society's wellbeing rather than individual interest. I conclude by returning briefly to Morris' general educational and curricular views. Again, let us posit the basic premise that our educational system and our society in general require drastic improvement and that a most important motivation behind the present curricular debate is to establish how appropriate subjects might ameliorate more than mere education in the classroom but also affect positively the wider society itself. While I most emphatically consider that education is a very potent force for altering society, I am also realistic enough to believe that it can only do so much. Thus, to a certain extent I agree with Morris. It is, needless to say, essential to debate whether the works of the western intellectual tradition should constitute the core of the curriculum or whether place should now be made for other newer, more minority-oriented subjects. But as a force for effecting far reaching changes in society I have little doubt that education *alone*, no matter what constitutes the curriculum, must remain well-nigh ineffectual unless backed up by other social, political, and, above all, economic action. Morris was right: if we wish, as I presume we do, education to be truly egalitarian and a meaningful vehicle for liberating and humanizing society, there must already exist a reasonable societal infrastructure which is itself egalitarian and liberal and humane. But we still, I fear, have some ways to go before possessing such an infrastructure. Only when we do will the curriculum hope to attain all its goals.

Notes

1. Preface to *Mixed Essays*, in *The Complete Prose Works of Matthew Arnold*, ed. R. H. Super, 11 vols. (Ann Arbor: University of Michigan Press, 1960–1977), 8:370. (Super's text will hereinafter be referred to as *C. P. W.* with the appropriate volume number).
2. "On the Modern Element in Literature," *C. P. W.* 1:24.
3. See *Culture and Anarchy*, *C. P. W.* 5, passim.

4. Quoted in Clamp, Peter. "William Morris: A Claim for Education." *The Journal of Educational Thought* 21, No. 1 (April 1987) :41.

5. Morris, William. "The Society of the Future," and "Thoughts on Education Under Capitalism," in May Morris, *William Morris: Artist, Writer, Socialist*. 2 vols. (Oxford: Blackwell, 1936), 2:462, 500.

6. Morris, William. "Thoughts on Education Under Capitalism." ibid., 2:500.

7. *Schools and Universities on the Continent, C. P. W.* 4:127; see also Letter to K (Jane Martha, his sister), Sunday (January 1866), *Letters of Matthew Arnold, 1848–1888*, ed. by George W. E. Russell. 2 vols. (London: Macmillan, 1896), 1:365; Preface to *Higher Schools and Universities in Germany* (1882), *C. P. W.* 4:31.

8. *Reports on Elementary Schools* (1876) and (1880). See *First Report of Royal Commission, Parliamentary Papers, Education General*. (Shannon, Ireland: Irish University Press, 1970), 34:209–10 (Arnold's evidence before the Cross Commission); also "Common Schools Abroad," *C. P. W.* 11:97–98; also *Special Report on Certain Points Connected with Elementary Education in Germany, Switzerland, and France, C. P. W.*, 11:27.

9. "The Function of Criticism at the Present Time," *C. P. W.* 3:283.

10. See *Friendship's Garland, C. P. W.* 5:44.

11. *On the Study of Celtic Literature, C. P. W.* 3:298.

12. *St. Paul and Protestantism, C. P. W.* 6:9.

13. "Literature and Science," *C. P. W.* 10:57.

14. *Schools and Universities on the Continent, C. P. W.* 4:311. See also Letter to his mother, February 28, 1866, Russell, *Letters* 1:371.

15. *Schools and Universities on the Continent, C. P. W.* 4:263.

16. Conclusion to *Culture and Anarchy*, Cornhill edition (1868) *C. P. W.* 5:527.

17. Morris, William and Bax, E. Belfort. *Socialism: Its Growth and Outcome*. (Chicago: Charles H. Kerr, 1913): 217 et seq.

18. *Ibid.*, 238.

19. Quoted in Lindsay, Jack. *William Morris: His Life and Work*. (London: Constable, 1975) :20.

20. Morris, William. *News From Nowhere in News From Nowhere and Selected Writings and Designs*. ed. by Asa Briggs. (Middlesex: Penguin, 1980) :206.

21. See Clamp, 43–44.

22. See Rapple, Brendan A. "Matthew Arnold and Comparative Education," *British Journal of Educational Studies* XXXVII, No. 1 (Feb. 1989) :54–71.

23. "The Function of Criticism at the Present Time," *C. P. W.* 3:282.

THE HUMANITIES IN THE TWENTY-FIRST CENTURY

William R. Tucker

Lamar University (Retired)

It is likely that a group of humanities specialists meeting toward the close of the last century would have seen the future in terms of the continuation of "progress," of the ever-upward movement of societies everywhere (and certainly in the West) toward new heights of rationality and material comfort. We today have nothing like their confidence as our guide. Rather, we project our existing anxieties on to the coming century. It is my argument here that these anxieties are residues of past circumstances in this century, that it is imperative that we look forward, not backward.

Furthermore, there is every reason to be confident about the coming decade and the next century. Using the methodology of the Futurist writers—that is, using projections of current trends—a general view opens up: the two Superpowers will revert to the more normal status of Great Powers. Five or more Powers in this traditional category will cooperate to solve environmental problems. Terrorism and Third World poverty can be dealt with through Great Power efforts and without the disastrous effects of Superpower rivalries. Power will be increasingly economic rather than military in nature.

By contrast, our current mood of anxiety concerning the future was brought to my attention recently when I casually mentioned to a colleague of long standing the topic for my remarks here. A humanities teacher, an academician who has received honors and recognition, he replied, "The way things are going, there won't be any humanities." I did not ask him to explain. Since our friendship goes back more than two decades and we have had frequent conversations about serious things, I could surmise the cause of his pessimism: it was ideological in nature. His tone was defiant, and his outlook was defeatist.

Since 1914 our century has been marked by ideology. I use the term "ideology" here not in the Marxian sense of a false consciousness, that is, bourgeois consciousness, but in the quite different sense of a road map in the mind that allows us to sort out the myriad facts that confront us continuously, a map that invites us to draw conclusions about things social and political. In this sense, our lives have been dominated by ideological conflicts, crusades, and wars both hot and cold. Inevitably, moral fervor has permeated the statecraft, the politics, and the education and the culture of Americans during most of the twentieth century.

Nor have humanities specialists been standing apart from the fray. We have supported Wilson's "self-determination of peoples" (without always being aware of some possible implications) and his internationalism centered around an organization world-wide in scope. Our teachers, and many of us as well, spent a great deal of moral fervor and not a little self-righteousness on the Progressive Movement, the New Deal, and the defeat of fascism. Reason itself seemed to dictate the pursuance of these causes. But in the late 1940s, when the fruits of progress were visible, other and different circumstances intervened. I am referring to the Cold War. We in the humanities were forced by others to deal with an ideological drama that we had neither expected nor could really understand.

The Cold War spawned in the United States the McCarthy episode, which was if anything proto-fascist (and I use the term cautiously). It had a deadening effect on the humanities and on humanities scholars. It gave us the spectacle of Congressional committees impairing the reputations of citizens in the name of a dubious nationalism founded on fear, exposure, and repression. It fed on anxieties magnified by successive traumas: the Alger Hiss case; the Rosenbergs; the "loss of China;" the Soviet atomic bomb; the subversion of the only democratic country in Eastern Europe, Czechoslovakia; the infamous trio of British agents of the KGB who had access to the highest decisions taken in Washington and London, Kim Philby, Guy Burgess, and Donald McLean; Korea; Sputnik—there seemed to be no end to the blows raining down on American pride and, presumably, American national security as well.

There was a parallel development. In retrospect it is a curious fact that in the decade between 1955 and 1965, we were told repeatedly that domestically the United States had entered a new era called "the end of ideology," that, finally, a broad consensus of all Americans had been achieved. Basic needs had been met, thanks to the post-World War II prosperity, group conflicts were easily compromised, and there was no longer any serious challenge to the American system, social, economic, or political.[1] A new age was at hand, where there would be a concern only with techniques, particularly management techniques.

We are still living with the consequences of this misperception of reality. Behind a façade of consensus there was the increasing American presence in Vietnam; resentments over sexual discrimination were rising; minorities were dissatisfied with segregation, discrimination, and the existing distribution of wealth. There was an energy problem, urban blight, and the outbreak of terrorism. Revolutionary change was in the air.

How did the humanities faculties react? Traumatized by the McCarthy episode, the proliferation of loyalty oaths, and the spectacle of college administrators who had hastened to assure the protofascists that their respective institutions harbored no subversives, humanities scholars could next contemplate the fact that these same administrators had no stomach for standing up to the new militants and revolutionaries who swarmed over the campuses. Indeed, faculty members often sympathized with the ideologues of the New Left, joining with them in exposing the injustices and the hollowness of a system that had humiliated professors, devalued them, scrutinized their teaching and research (and sometimes their reading lists in the library) for evidence of subversion, and had, in general, treated them as if they were potentially disloyal Americans.

While there was undeniably a quest for social justice in the actions and attitudes of many humanities scholars, there was also the fact that they were reacting to past indignities. In this regard I perceive an analogy with the French military in this century, an image of French soldiers in their horizon-blue uniforms exposed to fire from machine-gun nests in 1914, and of troops ensconced in the Maginot Line in 1939 to find safety in an expected war of attrition. As we look to the 1990s and beyond, to what extent are we still chafing from the humiliations of an earlier onslaught and devising our strategies accordingly? To what extent have public attitudes toward humanities scholars been conditioned by the perception that we are recalcitrant and unresponsive to the new configuration of the world today?

To us, our receptiveness to almost anything coming from the "Old" or the New Left makes sense. We remember, or have heard, that self-appointed defenders of Western Civilization had thought of the humanities as weapons in the "battle for men's minds," or for bolstering the nation's morale in a "mortal struggle" against worldwide subversion. Scholars were expected to enlist as troops in the Cold War and to use their subject matter as psychological weapons. But is all this relevant today? Are we still taking shelter in an academic Maginot Line?

As for the Left, we might note that among its leaders there has been some startling evidence of disarray. An especially interesting case is that of Simone de Beauvoir, the feminine half of the "royal couple" and a writer who was the seminal influence in the women's liberation movement with her book *The Second Sex*. She was the epitome of the modern "committed" intellectual who has little interest in knowledge as such and who wishes, instead, to influence conduct. Like Marx, her intent was not to explain the world but to change it. And yet at the conclusion of her autobiographical memoir, *Force of Circumstance*, de Beauvoir made the startling confession, "I was gypped."[2] In the next volume she dispelled any misperceptions about her meaning: she was not fretting about growing old, as some had thought. The phrase was to be interpreted ontologically, revealing a profound disappointment with the fruits of her commitment. After all her hopes and effort, mankind was still unhappy and the absolute that she had hoped for had ended in "existential failure."[3]

Not even the Frankfurt School of critical theorists, surely one of the century's most important intellectual phenomena on the Left, has been immune to disenchantment. Theodore Adorno, after giving us *The Authoritarian Personality*, went back to what had been his major concern all along, music criticism. Marcuse, godfather to the New Left of the universities and mentor to Angela Davis, turned aside from political and social preoccupations during his years of retirement or, more accurately, analyzed these concerns through the prism of aesthetics. Marcuse, who had made a point of his rejection of the elitism and mindless consumerism that characterized "bourgeois societies," drove a Cadillac and was well-tailored and faultlessly manicured.[4] While acknowledging the influence of Marx as well as Hegel and Freud on his outlook, he nevertheless could not stand the sights and sounds of the *hoi polloi* with their transistor radios and their uncouth behavior.[5] The author of *An Essay on Liberation* admitted, finally, to being "very authoritarian," and before his death in his native Germany he confided to friends his grief over the disappointments that had come his way. Where, indeed, is multidimensional man? His last book was on aesthetics.

Another member of the Frankfurt School, Leo Lowenthal, had devoted his scholarship to analyzing the disintegration of the "bourgeois consciousness," and promoting what he termed the "collective of outcasts" as the true face of humanity today.[6] He never denied that there was a "permanent crisis of the individual"[7]; yet in contemplating that crisis he revealed an affinity with such conservative writers as von Baader, Bonald, and de Maistre, with their compassion for the classes that bear the burdens of society.[8] Nor did he hesitate to picture Marx as a bourgeois thinker after all, insofar as Marx saw nature as an object of exploitation for man's benefit.[9] (I might add that the appalling ecological state of the former Soviet Union, of Czechoslovakia, and, indeed, of Eastern Europe generally, would seem to confirm Lowenthal's insight.)

Other examples of impasse on the Left come to mind: I am thinking not so much of the demise of influential New Left personalities or the arthritic performances of certain aging rock groups such as the Rolling Stones, as of countless revolutionaries, now middle-aged, who are addicted to BMWs and Volvos and who seem to have only an occasional recall of an earlier, turbulent era.

While considering the possibility that our outmoded ideological concerns are leading us into a self-imposed isolation, we should also note the impact of hyperpluralistic politics on the community we serve. We have supported the organization of emerging minority groups and various factions into political pressure and action battalions. We have advocated psychological separateness and have, indeed, celebrated this divisive configuration of American society.

Today, however, this pluralistic American polity resembles more and more an arena in which warring factions engage in combat—verbal, litigious, sometimes violent—in the pursuit of self-determined ends. The role of government consists primarily of efforts to satisfy as best it can the demands placed upon it by groups. According to the rules of the game, it is especially important that no group leave the playing field with a sense of utter defeat. In this scheme of things there is no important role for the Executive but the administering of programs benefitting this collectivity of groups; the Legislative Branch is there to listen and provide; and the federal Judiciary increasingly is called upon to deal with controversies so burning in nature that elected officials are only too happy to see them handled by the non-elected. But power abhors a vacuum. Into this vacuum two forces, sometimes called the fourth and fifth branches of government, have settled: the information and entertainment media and the pressure groups.

Humanities scholars run the risk of not being heard, or even considered seriously, in today's confusion of voices, sometimes strident, often demanding, and in the demonstrations and protests aimed at capturing—and holding—the attention of the public. Is it surprising that people in increasing numbers seem to be turning to private pursuits and hedonistic satisfactions?

I suggest that we turn our thoughts toward moderating the sensationalism of the media and the special-pleading of the groups with something that is sorely needed in our polity—our ability to serve impartially, our habit of putting burning issues into broad perspective, and our long tradition of disinterestedness. No one need convince us that we have something important, even vital, to say to the broader community. We are the heirs of the *philosophes* of the Enlightenment, and our contributions to the restoration of a rational civil society can only be called indispensable. We deserve media attention at least as much as the "activists," "advocates," and "spokespersons" whose unharmonious voices we hear from every side.

Further to complicate the world we in the humanities are forced to deal with, the long-standing division of the planet into blocs—East-West, capitalist-socialist—is coming to an end. The level of capital accumulation is supplanting the level of armaments as a primary consideration. Collectivist economic arrangements are almost everywhere being challenged by people who desire the results obtained through individual initiative and the market economy. Even democratic socialists are being forced by the new circumstances to admit that economic freedom and individual freedom are interconnected. This seamless web of freedoms was the product of centuries of development and this historical linkage continues to be valid.

There is at the same time a parallel movement with more somber, even sinister, implications: there are increasing signs of political disintegration. The revival of nationalisms in the Eastern Bloc cannot be taken as victories for the Western security system because the Western nations are in some cases showing similar signs of unrest. In our century great empires have dissolved and everywhere today central governments that once seemed so invincible are demonstrating a weakness that we not long ago thought impossible.

The modern state arose, after all, out of the fratricidal strife of the feudal period and the Wars of Religion. (And in this connection I would ask, parenthetically, how many college students are familiar with the Peace of Westphalia?) In man's natural state as envisioned by Hobbes, there is a latent or actual war of every man against every man, and men's lives are "solitary, poor, nasty, brutish, and short." Only governmental authority can hold in check the passions of factions and civil strife. All this is familiar enough. And yet in a time when injunctions to block this or that governmental action pour from judge's benches like rain in Seattle, it is possible that Americans are chipping away at one of the pillars of stability in a shattered world.

We in the United States have also paid an enormous price for participation in the Cold War. There are cracks and fissures in America too and it does no good to paper them over with slogans or to maintain that they do not exist. To all appearances, never have Americans in peacetime been unhappier than they are today. Fear, suspicion, anger, cynicism—all these emotions grind us down and obscure our national unity and our national purpose. Guidance in these matters might be obtained from Alexis de Tocqueville when he reminded us that Americans' real passion is not for liberty but for equality. If a relentless striving for equality is a Mandate from Heaven—*vox populi, vox dei*—it is never-ending and can never satisfy.

With our focus always on equality, we have come to rely on a horizontal scale where our perceptions and our values are concerned. To say, for example, that the great languages are those that have produced great literatures violates the egalitarian principle and places the subject on an unfamiliar and distasteful vertical scale. To argue that, contrary to Michelet and Marx, the history that has affected us most is political and intellectual, is to leave out of consideration the broad masses of men who tell us that they have labored and sacrificed throughout the ages in order that the few might lead or pursue intellectual concerns. Mount Vernon and Graceland, Lincoln Center and Nashville—who can say that one carries more significance than the other? *Richard III* and *A Nightmare on Elm Street* are both films that have been appreciated and who can say that one is superior or inferior to the other? Indeed, "elitism" in any form is not highly regarded in our society, and the egalitarian principle seems to demand that mass culture and folk culture be given much more than their due.

We are as a nation paying a price for this devaluation of values. President Carter referred to a national malaise but made no attempt to specify its causes. De Tocqueville is helpful here: "The desire of equality always becomes more insatiable in proportion as equality is more complete."[10] Or, again, "Among democratic nations men easily attain a certain equality of conditions: they can never attain the equality they desire. It perpetually retires from before them. . . . To these causes must be attributed that strange melancholy that oftentimes will haunt the inhabitants of democratic countries in the midst of their abundance."[11] Could it be that de Tocqueville's "strange melancholy," and what he calls in another place a "strange unrest"[12] are akin to Jimmy Carter's "malaise?"

Or we might consider José Ortega y Gasset's conceptualization of the common man and the noble man, categories that have nothing to do with birth, station in life, race, or sex for that matter. Ortega's common man is not the same as Eric Hoffer's who dazzles us with his talents and possibilities.[13] Nor is he the common man so beloved by politicians on the campaign trail. Ortega's is a man who is quite satisfied with himself just the way he is, while his "noble man" is one who does not perceive himself to be fully formed in every way, who has a continuing desire to learn and a concern for accomplishment.[14] Is it possible that Ortega's common man is fated to be a permanent part of humanity under whatever climate or regime? Is it possible that some inequalities are self-willed?

We might reread Spengler and Toynbee on the decline of civilizations, however unwelcome their conclusions might be. We might rediscover Michels, Pareto, and Mosca, the "iron law of oligarchy" and the "circulation of elites." What I am suggesting, of course, is this: that some important parts of our Western intellectual heritage are being neglected not through sloth or ignorance but because we prefer not to be disturbed by ideas that do not harmonize with our past and current ideological convictions.

Over sixty years ago, when Germany was still the Weimar Republic, Julien Benda wrote *The Betrayal of the Intellectuals.* According to his view, too many prominent literary personalities were committed to political causes. They did not see, he argued, that intellectuals are actually clerics in the sense that they are called to serve the life of the mind and serve it impartially, that they are members of a priesthood of learning. (The original French title of his book, *La Trahison des clercs,* conveys a clearer meaning).

But with the rise of Nazism and the mobilization of many French (and other) intellectuals against the fascist menace, Benda himself joined the fray. In 1935 he was a member of the French bureau of the Soviet-inspired International Writers Association for the Defense of Culture. In 1936 he joined in an appeal to "the Universal Conscience" on behalf of the Republican forces in the Spanish Civil War. In the following year he publicly declared that "the intellectual is perfectly in character in descending from his ivory tower to defend the rights of justice against barbarians."[15] Given the circumstances of the time, few would fault Benda for his passionate involvement in the war of words and ideas against fascism. And yet, with the outbreak of the Cold War we find Benda being transported by the French Communist Party to still another international conference of intellectuals, this time in Poland, where he pathetically professed to see justice on the side of Stalin's Soviet Union.[16] Times had changed, but Benda had not. We might well ask the question: where does commitment legitimately begin and where does it end?

I have suggested here that we too are confronted by changing times. A new synthesis is before us, combining the traditionalist outlook of the Cold War era, however distorted, with the newer forces claiming the recognition and validation they were once denied. The new synthesis opens the door to a new Renaissance, to a new era of achievement guided by humanistic values. And, I repeat, we have a major role to play in this unfolding dialectic.

Certainly, there are impediments. There are those critics of the Western Tradition who argue that the humanities have been used as tools for the suppression and exploitation of non-Western peoples and their cultures, and that these horrors should be exposed for what they really are. Surely we can all agree that the Western Tradition should not be used in the future for purposes of cultural imperialism or cultural chauvinism, any more than it should serve as a weapon of ideological warfare.

Still, the revival of the Western Tradition—with modifications to be sure—is necessary if we are to help millions of Americans find an anchor in a period of unsettling change. Throughout the humanities men are asked to confront themselves in all their cultural, intellectual, and moral dimensions, to critique as well as to appreciate the Western values that have prevailed in the United States. The new synthesis points to the rediscovery of a sense of community, with individuals of both Western and non-Western origins participating in common endeavors. Rational discourse can at last take precedence over the warfare of groups and over outmoded ideological fixations as well. In this atmosphere the authority of government and its ability to lead can be restored. Those of us concerned with the humanities can resume our vocation as role-models of objectivity, sincerity, and above all, civility both in our dealings with students and with the community at large.

In mentioning service to the community I am referring to some of the most important legislation in the United States in this century, the acts of Congress establishing the National Endowments for the Arts and the Humanities, respectively. Taking the latter into account, we already see some twenty-five million Americans each year participating in thousands of humanities-oriented programs made possible by the NEH and the state councils.[17]

The national and state councils are composed of academicians and persons from non-academic pursuits as well. Humanities scholars serve as advisors in these programs funded through cultural centers, local humanities councils, producers of television programs on humanities-directed subjects, libraries, museums, historical and heritage societies, and theater centers. They are also program participants. Scholars are thus involved in the meaningful presentation of humanities topics and open discussions. The discussion format is especially notable since it allows humanities scholars to enter into direct communication with members of the broader community, with significant benefits to both parties concerned.

Apparently our public and private educational endeavors have been rewarded. Many of those attending these programs have attended college, to be sure, but there are also those who have not. They are in both cases motivated by sincerity and good will and they relish the opportunity to be involved in intellectually satisfying experiences. And there can be no doubt that as jobs become more technical in nature, this desire for contact with matters of the mind and the spirit, with what is always good and valuable, will grow.

As participants in these community-based programs now and in the future, we need to ask ourselves whether we will be willing to recommend tenure and promotions for our peripatetic colleagues who take part in this restoration of a fractured community and a fractured world. Surely, as they sometimes leave the groves of our Academy and wander off into the cities and towns of America, these "applied humanists" deserve academic recognition and rewards.

In the coming years there will be a search for excellence in every facet of American life and we will be major participants in that search. We can redesign a vertical scale of values and stop pretending that the ignorant, the trivial, and the bizarre have intrinsic value. We can discard our sense of isolation and impending defeat that stems from our ideological preoccupations. Having done that, we can once more discover that our role is to simply serve. We can follow our calling as *presenters* of things intellectual and humane to our respective communities. We can experience the pleasures of broader contacts with a public that sincerely would like to know us better and benefit from our insights.

These directions were well-described by James Veninga, Executive Secretary of the Texas Committee for the Humanities. "One finds," he said, "in the authorizing legislation for the National Endowment for the Humanities a vision of America as a learning society. One finds a vision of citizens in touch with history and culture, a vision of citizens understanding the world about them, and a vision of citizens translating this understanding into civic action."[18] In this statement we find a blueprint for the coming century and our place in it.

440

1. Kenneth M. and Patricia Dolbeare, *American Ideologies: The Competing Political Beliefs of the 1970s.* (Chicago: Markham, 1971), 1.

2. Simone de Beauvoir, *Force of Circumstance*, tr. Richard Howard, (New York: G. P. Putnam, 1964), 658.

3. Simone de Beauvoir, *All Said and Done*, tr. Patrick O'Brien, (New York: G. P. Putnam, 1974), 117.

4. Conversation with French writer Jacques Nantet, who was an acquaintance of Marcuse, May 1, 1972.

5. Maurice Cranston, "Herbert Marcuse," *Encounter* (March, 1969), 38–50. Cranston adds, "The idea of mankind appeals to him, real men—most of them—sicken him."

6. Leo Lowenthal, *Critical Theory and Frankfurt Theorists: Lectures, Correspondence, Conversations* (New Brunswick, N.J.: Transaction Publications, 1989), 115.

7. *Ibid.*

8. *Ibid.*, 241.

9. *Ibid.*

10. Alexis de Tocqueville, *Democracy in America*, Tr. Henry Reeve, Ed. Henry Steele Comminger (London: Oxford University Press, 1946), 408.

11. *Ibid.*

12. *Ibid.*, 406.

13. Eric Hoffer, *Reflections on the Human Condition* (N.Y.: Harper and Row, 1973), 57.

14. José Ortega y Gasset, *The Revolt of the Masses* (N.Y.: W. W. Norton, 1932), 69.

15. Quoted in Herbert Lottman, *The Left Bank: Writers, Artists, and Politics from the Popular Front to the Cold War* (Boston: Houghton Mifflin, 1982), 107.

16. *Ibid.*, 271.

17. *The Humanities and the American Promise*, Report of the Colloquium on the Humanities and the American People, Charlottesville, Virginia, October, 1987, 30.

18. "Testimony of James Veninga, Executive Secretary, Texas Committee for the Humanities, on behalf of the State Humanities Program before the Appropriations Subcommittee on the Interior of the U.S. House of Representatives, March 17, 1988, 9.

LIBERAL EDUCATION AND THE RULING CLASS

Linda Seidel

Northeast Missouri State University

"I can't think why anybody should learn Latin," says Tom Tulliver in George Eliot's *The Mill On the Floss*. "It's no good." His schoolmate Philip Wakem tries to explain: "It's part of the education of a gentleman. . . . All gentlemen learn the same things." Unlike John Henry Newman, who argues that the recipient of a liberal education "has common ground with every class" (130), Eliot clearly indicates the class bias of what passed for liberal education in nineteenth-century England.

Several years before, in *The Stones of Venice*, Ruskin had complained about the artificial distinctions between "liberal and illiberal professions" (182) and the destructive specialization that resulted from those distinctions:

> . . . we want one man to be always thinking, and another to be always working, and we call one a gentleman, and the other an operative; whereas the workman ought often to be thinking, and the thinker often to be working, and both should be gentlemen, in the best sense. . . . All professions should be liberal, and there should be less pride felt in peculiarity of employment and more in excellence of achievement . . . (181–182).

Liberal education, then, in nineteenth-century England prepared the gentleman for a "liberal," gentlemanly occupation or for the fitting exercise of his gentlemanly leisure. When it became necessary to train the operatives of whom Ruskin speaks—the artisans, craftsmen, and skilled technicians—separate polytechnic institutions were invented so as not to contaminate the so-called humanistic curricula of the ancient universities. Thus, the sons of aristocrats, while forced to rub shoulders with the sons of the upwardly mobile upper middle class, were largely protected from intrusions into their colleges by out-and-out working class types.

To be fair to the Victorians, who did, after all, ask some of the best questions about the functions of education any society has ever asked—questions we are still struggling to answer—I must say at once that the classist, sexist bias of liberal education was hardly an invention of nineteenth-century England. From its beginnings, liberal education was the province of the gentleman. In ancient Rome, to which Bruce Kimball, in *Orators and Philosophers*, traces the origin of the term "liberal arts" (29), the adjective *"liberalis* denoted 'of or relating to free men'" (13). Thus, liberal education, to begin with was not defined by curriculum, but by the group to whom it was available—free men; women and slaves being, of course, excluded, as were those men made relatively unfree by their poverty and the consequent necessity that their lives be mainly occupied by work.

Today, although many apologists for the liberal arts wish to liberate and empower the enslaved and disenfranchised, liberal education is still the training ground for the ruling classes, the arena where the would-be elite meet and begin to exercise their "leadership skills." But the leadership skills provided by liberal education, according to Caroline Bird, may amount to little more than social polish—the "right accents," the correct tastes in books and art, the "attitudes" that make a man, a gentleman (118). In *The Case Against College*, Bird argues, satirically, that "the liberal arts are a religion, the established religion of the ruling class" (109):

> As with religion, no proof is required, only faith. You don't have to prove the existence of God. You don't have to understand the Virgin Birth. You don't have to prove that Camus is better than Jacqueline Susann. Camus is sacred, so Camus is better and so are the people who dig him. If you don't dig Camus, the trouble is not with Camus, but with you (109).

While not all observers agree with Bird, those who urge that liberal education has now become egalitarian nevertheless glance back at its aristocratic origins— if only to deny them. In *The Closing of the American Mind*, Allan Bloom, who twits his students for preferring Camus to Plato, laments: "There is hardly a Harvard man or a Yale man any more. No longer do universities have the vocation of producing gentlemen as well as scholars" (89). The more democratic Bart Giammatti puts it somewhat differently when, in arguing that liberal education should produce "good citizens" and "civility," he insists that "[c]ivility has nothing at all to do with gentility, any more than citizenship . . . has to do with good breeding or polite manners" (12).

Whether one agrees or disagrees with Bird (that liberal education is lamentably elitist) or with Bloom (that liberal education is lamentably egalitarian), it is true—both would agree—that liberal education is increasingly available to middle class students. Historically, the rise of the middle class in economic power has been accompanied by better education—indeed, ruling class education—and the competition of the middle class with the aristocrats for political power. In America today, where we put little faith in aristocratic birth (if, indeed we acknowledge such a thing), wealth and education may be the chief qualifications for ruling class status. Thus, liberal education has functioned to advance social mobility within the hierarchy at the same time that it has done little to challenge that hierarchy. But if, as Stanley Aronowitz argues, "intellectuals are typically servants of the mighty" (210), then it is not surprising that universities have functioned to perpetuate the established order. Given the aristocratic history of liberal education, and given the aspirations of many of the young people who seek it out today, is it possible that we value liberal education not for what it is or does, but because of who has it? Is it possible that we value liberal education not as a course of study that liberates the mind, but as a commodity that gains us entrance into the correct social circles—while being cheaper and easier to show off than a yacht? In short, is liberal education inescapably elitist, its value dependent upon whom it excludes?

Or, as inhabitants of a democratic country, have we in the United States all become "free men" eligible for the education of a citizen? Can we all become citizens? Can all professions, as Ruskin suggested, become liberal? And if they can, can we cease to see liberal education and vocational education as antithetical to one another?

I have no answers to these questions. Furthermore, I can see that asking these questions raises others, especially matters of definition: What is a citizen? What is a liberal profession? How are liberal and vocational education supposed to be different from one another?

I would like to offer some tentative answers to this second set of questions if only by way of making further discussion possible. Ruskin is some help here. In his complaint about the class-based distinction between thinkers and workers (that is, manual laborers), he urges that all men should both think and work. The liberal profession, then, involves *thinking*. Other passages in *The Stones of Venice* suggest that the liberal profession also involves creativity and enough variety so that the worker may avoid a soul-deadening, narrow focus.

If the liberal profession includes thinking, creativity, and variety, then liberal education ought to prepare one for those things. And just about everyone who has written or spoken about education during the last two centuries would agree that it is supposed to teach the student how to think—to discipline the mind, as Newman (and many others) would put it—whatever that may mean. This mental discipline is not to be confused, Newman says, with "particular studies, or arts, or vocations" (129), but he does allow that liberal education is "practical" in that it "train[s] good members of society" (130).

Newman's definitions, while in large part contradicting those of Ruskin, are completely consistent with the class bias historically built into liberal education, which is supposed to teach people how to think, but not about anything in particular, and prepare them, in some vague way, to be good citizens—presumably by teaching them the stuff that all the other good citizens have learned and which they can quote to one another knowingly at high-toned social gatherings.

444

Newman's distinction between liberal and vocational studies has (unfortunately?) persisted—even if contemporary educators do acknowledge the oversimplification represented by that antithesis.

But Newman may not be our best model here. To return to the tentative definitions offered so far: we have said that liberal education is that which is supposed to teach one to think and prepare one to be a good citizen, but which does not necessarily lead one to any particular profession. My definition of a good citizen, with a glance back at the Greeks, is a person who, feeling a sense of responsibility toward the other members of his or her society, participates in some significant way in decision-making in that society.

Having offered some tentative definitions, I'd like to reformulate some of my questions: Can education give us an understanding of the interconnectedness of all things and all people which we must have if we are to function as citizens of the world in the twenty-first century? If it can, will that education bear any resemblance to what has traditionally been called "liberal"? Can we make that education accessible, at some level, to nearly everyone? Can that education function, not to train for the high-paying jobs they have been told they want, but to help them find a vocation, in the old fashioned sense of a "calling," a vocation that will permit—at its best—self-fulfillment even as it encourages work of social value? And can that education help us create a society in which no one's work is simply slavery?

Obviously I cannot answer all these questions. Instead, I offer you a story, a parable from *Tales of the Dervishes: Teaching-stories of the Sufi Masters Over the Past Thousand Years*:

> One dark night a dervish was passing a dry well when he heard a cry for help from below. 'What is the matter?' he called down.
>
> 'I am a grammarian, and I have unfortunately fallen, due to my ignorance of the path, into this deep well, in which I am now all but immobilized,' responded the other.
>
> 'Hold, friend, and I'll fetch a ladder and rope,' said the dervish.
>
> 'One moment, please!' said the grammarian. 'Your grammar and diction are faulty; be good enough to amend them.'
>
> 'If that is so much more important than the essentials,' shouted the dervish, '*you* had best stay where you are until *I* have learned to speak properly.' And he went his way (Shah 193).

Much like a late twentieth-century educator, the dervish talks about the "essentials" and suggests to his colleague that the latter does not understand what the essentials are.

For the past several years we educators have been arguing about what the essentials might be—and thus, what we should be attempting to teach our students. Some would agree with the grammarian that knowing grammar is more important than being able to get out of a well because one uses grammar every day, and well-climbing abilities are not often in demand; no one climbs out of wells at polite cocktail parties or executive lunches. And one can always hire a lower-class type to pull one out of the well or fill up the holes. Possibly one might even buy the right sort of machine to elevate oneself out of the well. Anyhow, for these people, grammar takes precedence over well-climbing—largely because grammar is a more upper-class thing to know.

But then some would point out that you can make a buck on wells. After all, even a snotty grammarian will pay pretty decently to be gotten out of the well—especially after you've let him stay down there for awhile. With the right kind of training, you could start your own well rescue company or you could operate a well fill-in service—as long as you paid your brother to surreptitiously dig more wells. Pretty soon, your service would be regarded as socially indispensable, and you'd be living a comfortable bourgeois life.

A third group of educators would argue that the best educated person is one who can devise a plan to solve the well problem and can also write an acceptable letter to the grammarian enlisting his support. After this problem solver takes care of the well problem in an efficient, socially useful way, she will use her analytical skill to tackle other problems plaguing her society. She may make a lot of money or a modest amount, depending upon how lucky she is. But she and other problem solvers like her enjoy their work and believe they are contributing to the welfare of the community.

The members of this last group, using the full range of their intellectual powers to make life a little better for themselves and their neighbors are, in my opinion, good citizens whose education has contributed to their good citizenship. They are more knowledgeable than the grammarians—even if they can't quote Shakespeare at appropriate moments—and are more useful than the well-service people, who have a vested interest in never really solving the well problem completely.

Now replace dangerous dry wells with any major problem you'd like to name: AIDS, acid rain, radioactive waste, homelessness, the poverty of our young. Don't these things threaten us all? Whose job is it to think about them and begin to devise solutions?

I would argue that it is the job of the nation's citizens to think about the nation's problems; that it is the job of the world's citizens to think about the problems of the world. I would argue further that the magnitude of the challenges we face suggests that we need to make education for citizenship as broadly accessible as possible. And I would argue that liberal and vocational education need not oppose each other, but complement one another if indeed they do not blend together.

446

Several years ago the former Commissioner of Higher Education in the State of Missouri advised eliminating the nursing and agricultural programs from Northeast Missouri State (now the state liberal arts institution) as if those programs acted as contaminants because they contain obviously useful knowledge; as if students who go on to care for people and for the earth do not need to have the broadest possible perspectives; as if the wisest sort of self-interest did not need to inform those (nearly sacred?) activities.

If education for citizenship means education for problem-solving, what will the curriculum look like? How can we prepare ourselves to work toward the answers we seek? By studying that which is known—or seems to be known—relative to the questions we wish to ask.

Now there are educators like Bloom and Adler who believe that all the student really needs to do in order to be liberally educated is to read and think about the Great Books of the past because the Great Books deal with "perennial human questions"—the questions that never go away. Questions like "What is the meaning of life?" or "What does it really mean to be free?"

While I do think that students and teachers ought to ponder the meaning of life and the nature of freedom, I do not think that sort of pondering can be our only activity. Sometimes learning how to sustain life must precede pondering its meaning. Sometimes the immediate, topical question is more compelling than the eternal one. In the midst of John or Sally's quest for the meaning of life, he or she might want some immediate information on how not to get AIDS. The abstract meaning of freedom might be less urgent than determining how to provide medical insurance for the millions of Americans who do not yet possess it (and I would argue that there is a connection between the two, that having medical insurance *does* have something to do with freedom). The books of the past show us where we have been and how we have arrived at this point; some of them may even give us blueprints for the future. But the rest of the story is ours to tell, and we will need plenty of practical wisdom in order to tell it.

Practical wisdom: what one achieves by thinking and working, reading and doing. Let me adopt that version of Ruskin as my formula for the moment. The knowledge of the past exists to be revised by us just as we revise ourselves. No revision is possible if we have never read the text in the first place; no revision is possible if we believe the book to be sacred. Let us, then, make our revisions and tell our story, for as Ralph Waldo Emerson says in "The American Scholar," "[t]his time, like all times, is a very good one, if we but know what to do with it" (27).

Reprinted with permission by author and Perspectives: the Journal of the Association for General and Liberal Studies, *Columbus, OH: Ohio Dominican College, 19.3 (1989).*

Aronowitz, Stanley. 1989. "The New Conservative Discourse." *Education and the American Dream: Conservatives, Liberals, and Radicals Debate the Future of Education.* Eds. Harvey Holtz, Irwin Marcus, Jim Dougherty, Judy Michaels and Rick Peduzzi. Granby, MA: Bergin and Garvey. 203–15.

Bird, Caroline. 1975. *The Case Against College.* New York: David McKay.

Bloom, Allan. 1987. *The Closing of the American Mind.* New York: Simon and Schuster.

Eliot, George. 1961. *The Mill on the Floss.* Ed. Gordon S. Haight. Boston: Houghton.

Emerson, Ralph Waldo. 1970. "The American Scholar." *'The American Scholar' Today: Emerson's Essay and Some Critical Views.* Ed. C. David Mead. New York: Dodd, Mead.

Giammatti, A. Bartlett. 1988. *A Free and Ordered Space: The Real World of the University.* New York: Norton.

Kimball, Bruce A. 1986. *Orators and Philosophers: A History of the Idea of Liberal Education.* New York: Teachers College Press.

Newman, Cardinal John Henry. 1973. From *The Idea of a University. In Victorian Prose and Poetry.* Eds. Lionel Trilling and Harold Bloom. New York: Oxford.

Ruskin, John. 1853. From *The Stones of Venice.* In *Victorian Prose and Poetry.* 174–89.

Shah, Idries. 1967. *Tales of the Dervishes: Teaching-stories of the Sufi Masters Over the Past Thousand Years.* London: Jonathan Cape.

ELITISM IN THE TEACHING OF LITERATURE

James T. F. Tanner

University of North Texas

My purpose is to examine what I believe to be some insidious forms of elitism (the conscious or unconscious belief in rule by favored or privileged groups) in college-level teaching of literature. Further, I will suggest a few pedagogical strategies by which the effects of innate elitism can be alleviated.

Intellectual elitists believe (consciously or unconsciously) in rule by favored or privileged groups; they attempt (consciously or unconsciously) to further the interests of favored or privileged groups; and they often express conscious or unconscious pride of inclusion in favored or privileged groups. Because we believe that literary education in a democratic society aims to enlighten the community at large (not just a select portion of that community), we must consider elitism an abomination to be cast out, root and branch.

It must be observed at the outset that American educational institutions reflect the culture in which they are embedded. Cardinal Newman's British notion of the university as a "community of scholars" has little to do with the reality of the contemporary American "multiversity." Even students chosen to attend American universities are selected by elitist standards. And American society, though egalitarian in contrast to other cultures, has not by any means eradicated elitist attitudes. Our society continues—like all societies—to experience economic class struggle. We have upper-class, middle-class, and lower-class constituencies in our communities as well as in our classrooms. Nor is racial strife unknown in our cities and in the academy. Religious divisions afflict us. Numerous minorities demand a place of dignity within our democratic experiment. And the most ancient oppression of all—the masculine suppression of the feminine—has in recent decades been brought emphatically to public attention. American universities in recent years have come to be perceived as credential-granting agencies rather than as sanctuaries for intellectual speculation. Richard Sennett and Jonathan Cobb, in *The Hidden Injuries of Class*, observe that "the aristocratic ideal of the cultured individual who develops a refined way of life" has been replaced by the ideal of "the person deemed most productive qualitatively, and within any context, quantitatively," the individual "who makes something of himself." Our students hardly bother to deny their lust for credentials and their distrust of any obstacle (such as a foreign language requirement) that stands in their way. All these forces challenge the persistently dominant ideology of American society as well as that of the American university—an ideology all-too-patently caucasian, Anglo-Saxon, Protestant-Christian, masculine, heterosexual, middle-class, patriarchal, genteel, inhibitory, and complacent. The late Abbie Hoffman once described American universities as "bastions of rest." And American middle-class intellectuals (some Britons consider this an oxymoron), who constitute the faculty in American Academia, inevitably disseminate elitist notions.

Academic intellectuals in America are always suspected—and usually guilty—of elitism. It is not that American intellectuals consciously desire to impose elitist standards; their most intense struggle, on the conscious level, is to avoid the charge of vulgarity. Joseph Epstein several years ago pointed out that "in intellectual and academic life, vulgar is something one calls people with whom one disagrees." Our most austere critics have always found Academia to be elitist. Perhaps it is appropriate at this point to quote Eric Hoffer's definition of intellectuals: "They are people who feel themselves members of the educated minority, with a God-given right to direct and shape events. An intellectual need not be well educated or particularly intelligent. What counts is the feeling of being a member of an educated elite." Hoffer awakened us to intellectualism as a manifestation of the will to power. In more recent times, of course, Foucault has taught us that knowledge *is* power; those without knowledge, or access to it, are—to put it quite simply—the powerless. I would, however, remind my fellow Foucauldians of Will Rogers' deconstruction of the concept of knowledge: "everybody is ignorant, only on different subjects." The ignorance of literary intellectuals, in particular, was pointedly demonstrated several years ago in C. P. Snow's *The Two Cultures*.

Snow's opposing categories—humanist versus scientist—are, in fact, visible today, though the terminology might be slightly different. Nowadays, in the discipline of literary theory, we would refer to these two groups as "spiritual" elitists and "scientific" elitists. The spiritual elite, with its concern to save "mystery" in literary study, fears, more than anything else, systematic (or scientific) approaches to literature. Their own largely implicit and unexamined systems would in such cases come to be contrasted to the more "scientific" systems. The scientific elite seeks, of course, to explain and cast out mystery; all that was Id shall be Ego. Neither elite has been willing to admit any groundings in contemporary American society.

In 1949, Russell Lynes published, in *Harper's Magazine*, an essay entitled "Highbrow, Lowbrow, Middlebrow," a naughty denuding of social hierarchy in American culture. Lynes clearly understood that his categorization (highbrow, middlebrow, lowbrow) was a mere substitution for the much older categorization of upper class, middle class, and lower class, the newer trinity—like the old—grounded in economic class warfare. Highbrow means elite, middlebrow means bourgeoisie, and lowbrow means the unwashed. In brief, the highbrow "has

450

worked hard, read widely, traveled far, and listened attentively in order to satisfy his curiosity and establish his squatters' rights in this little corner of intellectualism, and he does not care who knows it." (It seems clear that most English professors are members of this exalted constituency.) Brander Matthews had somewhat earlier commented that "a highbrow is a person educated beyond his intelligence." The middlebrow, according to Lynes, is hell-bent on improving his mind as well as his fortune. The lowbrow "doesn't give a hang about art *qua* art. He knows what he likes, and he doesn't care why he likes it."

Lynes' categories cohabit well with Philip Rahv's division of American authors (and, by extension, of those professors who champion particular authors) into two classes, "palefaces and redskins," a binary opposition suggesting an eternal struggle between refinement and savagery. But is Henry James really that refined? And is Walt Whitman really that savage? Rahv observes, of course, that the terms "patrician" and "plebeian" would serve quite as well, and that the paleface is a "highbrow" and the redskin a "lowbrow." According to Rahv, "at his highest level the paleface moves in an exquisite moral atmosphere; at his lowest he is genteel, snobbish, and pedantic." The redskin, on the other hand, is at his best "in giving expression to the vitality and to the aspirations of the people . . . but at his worst he is a vulgar anti-intellectual, combining aggression with conformity and reverting to the crudest forms of frontier psychology." Whichever of these two categories a particular thinker prefers, arguments come readily to hand in justification. One is also reminded of George Santayana's depiction of the Puritan versus the Hedonist in *The Last Puritan* (1935) and of his other works dealing with the conflict between idealism and materialism. Paul Fussell's delightful little essay entitled "Notes on Class" which appeared in 1980 is well worth consulting in this connection. Fussell finds nine social classes in America: "Top Out-of-Sight, Upper, Upper Middle, Middle, High-Proletarian, Mid-Proletarian, Low-Proletarian, Destitute, and Bottom Out-of-Sight." Fussell wittily associates all these social orders with their preferences and taboos. All these conflicts— highbrow versus lowbrow, patrician versus plebeian, puritan versus hedonist, paleface versus redskin, upper-class versus lower-class, idealist versus materialist, the haves versus the have-nots, conservative versus liberal, elect versus reprobate, high-tone versus common yahoo—are suggestive of deep-seated antagonisms in our culture. Such binary oppositions have their origin in class struggle, and the rhetoric of antagonism resembles that of sociopolitical ideology. Nor is this rhetoric far removed from the rhetoric we observe within English departments in their vituperative debates over canon formation and canon dissemination.

Class consciousness is rampant in departments of English, affecting almost every facet of academic life. The holder of the Ph.D. degree who insists upon being called "Doctor" and can thereby "put down" the unfortunates without the degree

451

is a clear example needing no further comment. The hierarchy of rank (professor, associate professor, assistant professor, instructor, teaching fellow, teaching assistant) hardly contributes to the "search for truth" that is sometimes said to be the function of a university. The exploitation of lower-level faculty whereby they are relegated to teaching composition instead of literature is another common example; composition has become the menial labor of departments of English, the teaching of literature—especially on the graduate level—having become the privilege of the elite. Heavy workloads and low pay imposed upon non-tenured and "adjunct" faculty need little comment. Dismissal of regional dialects and minority speech patterns is the norm. Traditional grammar is championed. "Standard English," an elitist notion if ever there was one, is recommended on purely expedient grounds; if one wants a good job, one had better damn well speak and write standard button-down English. "Marginal" literary genres, like science fiction and detective novels, are relegated to the trash heap. In curriculum matters, elitist notions constantly reappear. American literature ranks below English literature; Texas literature is seldom mentioned even by citizens of Texas, maybe *especially* by citizens of Texas. Literary specialists are often downright proud of their ignorance of linguistics. Birthright apparently confers special privileges; texts produced in the remote past carry cultural prestige. Even inferior scholarship on the British medieval period is commonly said to be preferable to *any* scholarship dealing with contemporary American literature. Dead languages are, as one would expect, devoutly reverenced. *Beowulf*, for instance, is not respectable unless it is taught in the original Anglo-Saxon tongue, notwithstanding the existence of many excellent translations in the language actually used by twentieth-century students. There is resistance to modernizing Chaucer's *Canterbury Tales* or to disseminating them in modern translation. Purists complain when Shakespeare's plays are staged in modern dress, or when his diction or spelling is modernized. In all connections, elitism affects the academic study of literature.

But if elitism is a fact of life in American education and, in particular, in the teaching of literature, what can we do to alleviate its adverse effects?

First, I would recommend that we make use of popular culture in our teaching of literature. Both Henry James *and* Bugs Bunny have earned a place in our world. I would endorse Robert Pattison's view of rock music as a potential source of pedagogical materials, and one that does not actually threaten conservative institutions. To quote Pattison, "The commentators who see in rock a Dionysian challenge to the church of Christ are exaggerating the case. The rocker is capable of adoring Dionysos in the disco by night and Christ in the cathedral by day. Rock merely continues the American democratic tradition of religious tolerance and diversity."

Second, we must help our students to read literature in context. And the most important context for any literary text happens to be the experience of the individual reader. The old-fashioned historical notion of privileging an original context, the context of first utterance of a literary text, will not do if we are to transmit genuine values to our students. Professors of literature could certainly find a worse motto than "different strokes for different folks."

Third, we can help our students *evaluate* literary works. Lawrence E. Cahoone in an important book, *The Dilemma of Modernity* (1988), has written: "Human beings . . . are always presented with a choice between meaning and non-meaning, between regarding the world and their existence as significant and valuable and feeling them to be meaningless and valueless. This choice is not usually a conscious decision." And is it not precisely in the disciplined study of literature that this choice can be most readily brought to consciousness? Our students *do* evaluate literary texts for what they are worth to themselves. The fact that evaluation must be based on relative standards need not embarrass us; it has always been so.

Fourth, we can avoid exclusion of minorities in our canonical decisions. Carl Sandburg once said that "the word *exclusive* is the ugliest word in the English language." Have we forgotten that the Bible emerged from a despised minority group? If we are teaching literature as the embodiment of the power of language to bring about effects in the real world, we will not do irreparable harm by introducing our students to previously excluded writers. Walt Whitman, in his 1855 Preface to *Leaves of Grass* (a work that ought to be canonized by this conclave), proclaimed that "the attitude of great poets is to cheer up slaves and horrify despots." Might we not, along with Walt Whitman, resolve that no despot of any stripe will take comfort in our practices, and that no slavery (in whatever transformation it appears) will receive our approbation? Perhaps the ultimate goal of democratic education *is*, in many senses, "to cheer up slaves and horrify despots." Worse pedagogical doctrines have been espoused.

Fifth, we can be wary of critical dogmatisms that urge us to study the sign and ignore the referent; that is, we must distrust those theoretical positions that would make literary study an isolated, monkish activity alienated from the everyday world of work, money, love, hate, suffering, and death. Literature is "referential" even if only "problematically referential," as Harold Bloom would have it.

Sixth, we must somehow eradicate the gulf that has arisen between literary study and the study of the techniques of writing. A rhetorical approach of some sort is needed to break down this division. James L. Kinneavy's *Theory of Discourse* has established a good beginning in the restoration of this unity.

The words on the page of a literary text are so much more than words on the page; they refer, however problematically, to a universe of context beyond the page, to a world of objects mysterious in themselves, worthy of our concern. We must somehow relearn and pass on to future generations the lesson that Augustine gleaned from St. Paul: "the letter killeth, but the spirit giveth life" (2 Cor. 3:6).

453

RENAMING THE SPECIES

Melodie Alexander

Institute of Movement Analysis

Why are men less beset by test anxiety than women? Why do women do better on verbal skill tests and men on spatial skill tests? Is there a physiological and anatomical reason for gender differences in classroom participation? Are GREs and SATs biased from a physiological and anatomical viewpoint? And finally, should the curriculum be designed with these anatomical and physiological gender differences in mind? Such questions form the backdrop for the topic of this paper.

Looking at gender differences from a physiological and anatomical viewpoint does not limit the findings to just the increased knowledge in the physiological world, but increases knowledge throughout all disciplines. I hope to provide the reader with sufficient data to recognize that a woman's body is different enough in physiological and anatomical detail to be evaluated and studied completely on its own without generalizing data gathered from studies on male-only subjects or unequal male-to-female subject ratios.

As far back as 1972, Hutt discussed the necessity for examining these differences in all aspects of research when he stated:

> Girls and boys differ from each other in a multitude of ways—physically, psychologically, and behaviorally. . . . It must seem only too evident that such pervasive differences are of biological origin. . . . The literature on human sex differences are of biological origin. . . . The literature on human sex differences was extraordinarily sparse. What little there was dealt mainly with the sociological and cultural aspects of sex differences. (72)

We as teachers and researchers *must* look at not only the individual's test results to determine their intellect, but must also consider their anatomical and physiological makeup, which is also an indicator of their intellectual strengths and weaknesses when we set about curriculum development.

As to when does sexual differentiation begin, Garai and Scheinfeld (1968) first commented, "From the moment of conception males and females exhibit radically different patterns of development" (174). One example was found in a study examining gender differences as the germ cell begins its division. Lander and Lincoln (1988) observed that recombination rates of male and female meiosis differ.

Illustrations of these anatomical and physiological gender differences can be found in such areas as the brain, about which Alpher (1985) wrote an article titled, "Sex differences in brain asymmetry: A critical analysis" that examined the human brain as the source of sex differences in behavior. Alpher (1985) stated, "Differences in cognitive function are related directly by the investigators to differences in brain function and structure" (17). He acknowledges that, because socialization of the sexes begins at the moment of birth, a separation of biological and environmental influences on behavior is impossible. And as well, I am not denying the role an individual's culture, environment, and society influences plays in their brain activity, but at the same time, no one should deny the influence of anatomical and physiological innate differences.

Lansdell (1964) observed a sex difference in the venous drainage in the brain as well as in the two hemispheres of the brain. He noted that the right vein of Trolard is larger than the left in girls and that:

Since this is often the major vein in the hemisphere opposite to that used in speech, is it possible that the differences in venous drainage are related to the superiority of girls over boys in certain verbal skills? (550)

In a later article by Lansdell (1972) where he discussed the asymmetry of function of the human brain in regards to the left side being dominant for speech and the right side for perception he noted that, "The function of each temporal lobe in regard to this trait [verbal ability] appears to be opposite in each sex" (854).

There are a multitude of anatomical and physiological reasons why women do well on verbally emphasized tests and poorly on mathematical and spatially oriented tests. And, tests such as the SAT (Standard Achievement Test), ACT (American College Test), and GRE (Graduate Record Exam) are in fact, specifically designed for a woman to fail. Joseph Alpher (1985) stated this thesis clearly when he remarked:

Many biologists and social scientists have theorized that sex differences in cognitive ability and in behavior are biological in origin and that these differences are responsible for, to give one example, the relatively small number of women in the physical sciences. (7)

As Kail and Siegel (1978) note, "Women's verbal abilities are consistently greater than men's, while men's spatial abilities are consistently greater than women's" (557). Therefore, females are more adept at verbal tasks, males at visuospatial tasks (Martin 1978). Martin explains this difference:

> The left 'verbal' hemisphere may process information in a serial or sequential fashion, an analytic process dependent upon parts and features of stimuli, while the right 'visual' hemisphere may process information wholistically, a parallel process dependent upon whole configurations or gestalt properties of stimuli. (227)

This is of key importance, because it may affect the outcome of test results for women on parts of intelligence tests such as the SAT, ACT, and GRE, where a majority of the questions are in the form of pattern arrangement and mathematical probability. Smith (1964) commented on this subject, "The sex difference in spatial ability may reflect a greater capacity for males to perceive, recognize, and assimilate patterns within the conceptual structure of mathematics (123).

Mathematical ability was defined by Hamley in 1935 as, "A compound of general intelligence, visual imagery, and ability to perceive number and space configurations, and to retain such configurations as mental patterns" (McGee 1979, 897). Today, mathematical ability is still defined as relating to space configurations (*Webster's Ninth New Collegiate Dictionary* 1986, 733).

One researcher went as far as to declare:

> Sex differences in visual spatial process should seem to have practical implications for females in the workforce. Are there certain jobs that are more or less suitable for females? . . . To the extent they exist, sex differences in that dimension will indeed matter whether explicitly recognized by society or not. (McGlone 1980, 246)

Wielson (Springer and Deutsch 1981) has suggested that separate school programs should be designed to suit the innate abilities of each sex (129).

No one uses their brain to its fullest extent, and therefore, both women and men have similar capabilities to do well within each area of expertise, be it verbal or spatial. *Still*, we need to examine these findings and consider them when we design curriculums for both men and women.

One last note, if the quoted material appears dated, it is due to the lack of comparative research using both women and men as well as the scarce research on gender differences in all areas of anatomy and physiology of the human body.

REFERENCES

This paper is from selections from a book by the same title. No part of this paper may be used without the written permission of the author.

Alpher, J. 1985. Sex differences in brain asymmetry: A critical analysis. *Feminist Studies*, 11, 7–37.

Garai, J. E. and A. Scheinfeld. 1968. Sex differences in mental and behavioral traits. *Genetic Psychological Monograms*, 77, 169–299.

Hutt, C. 1972. Neuroendocrinological, behavioral, and intellectual aspects of sexual differentiation in human development. In C. Ounsted & D. C. Taylor (Eds.) *Gender Differences: Their Ontogeny and Significance*. London: Churchill Livingstone.

Kail, R. V. and A. W. Siegel. 1978. Sex and hemispheric differences in the recall of verbal and spatial information. *Cortex*, 14, 557–63.

Lander, E. S. and S. E. Lincoln. 1988. The appropriate threshold for declaring linkage when allowing sex-specific recombination rates. *American Journal of Human Genetics*, 43, 396–400.

Lansdell, H. 1964. Sex differences in hemispheric asymmetries of the human brain. *Nature*, 203, 550.

———— and C. Davie. 1972. Massa Intermedia: Possible relation to intelligence. *Neuropsychologia*, 10, 207–10.

Martin, C. M. 1978. Verbal and spatial encoding of visual stimuli: The effect of sex, hemisphere and yes-no judgements. *Cortex*, 14, 227–33.

McGlone, J. 1978. Sex differences in functional brain asymmetry. *Cortex*, 14, 122–28.

McGee, M. 1980. Inadequate criteria for hypothesis testing in cerebral asymmetry research. *The Behavioral and Brain Sciences*, 3, 243.

Smith, I. M. 1964. *Spatial ability: Its educational and social significance*. London: University of London.

Springer, S. P. and G. Deutsch. 1981. *Left brain, right brain*. San Francisco: W. H. Freeman.

457

10

PEDAGOGY:
WHAT TO TEACH, HOW AND WHEN

TEACHING THE CORE BEFORE COLLEGE: INTRODUCTION

Derek Baker

University of North Texas

The inspiration for the three papers and chairman's opening remarks which follow came during a chance lunch-time encounter and discussion with a faculty member of the College of Education. What began as a light-hearted exchange between the Conference program organiser and the Director of the Child Development Laboratory very quickly led to more weighty discussion of the absurdity of presuming that the Core and the Canon appeared, Athena-like, only as students proceeded to university education. Before the end of the meal it had been agreed that there should be a special session directed to the discussion of 'the Core before College,' and of its teaching, not simply in secondary education, but in elementary and early childhood education.

Clearly, it is easier for those teaching at university level to adjust to the idea that there is, or that there could be, both a core and a canon in the high schools: indeed, many university faculty complaints about the poor quality of high school students could be condensed into the single complaint that in all-too-many schools there is neither core nor canon to the education supplied. It is, however, also very dangerous to make this connection between school and university, and to institutionalise the assumption that high school and university are comparable institutions divided only, and rather arbitrarily, by age. Both the conditions and the requirements within high schools are far-removed from those obtained in the universities: core and canon in the high school will be, and must be, substantially different, and university faculty who are not in the trenches of educational training need to be extremely wary of any facile assumption that their provisions, remedies and requirements can simply be varied to suit a younger age group, or, indeed, that university schemes of education are relevant at all in schools.

If this is true of secondary education it is certainly so of even younger children. Few university faculty would normally expect to base their core and canonical education in the elementary years, but this is precisely what emerged in Conference discussion, and if the emphasis was almost wholly on the need to plan and develop schemes of reading, and to select and promote good elementary school books, full development of the student in his university career was of importance and concern at this age—and even earlier.

Few of those attending the Conference would have been likely to accord any importance in their debates to the years of early childhood, and yet this was the incontrovertible result of the conference section represented in this chapter. What this did was to divert attention from the details of the core and the canon, the substance of almost all debate at the Conference and yet, in this perspective, not primary in importance but secondary, and focus on the qualities which underlie that debate, the qualities out of which any worthwhile education is comprised, whatever the transient details of particular schemes. It was salutary to be faced with this revelation, and university educators concerned with framing educational schemes would do well to start by educating themselves in the objectives of early childhood instructors, in 'educationally appropriate practice,' in following this through into the elementary school which, at its best, builds sensitively upon what has been achieved in the early years, and in achieving a real understanding of the problems and the potentialities of secondary education—perhaps then echoing that 'all I really needed to know I learnt in kindergarten.'

There was one other consequence of the wider perspectives of this session: university students constitute one element in the overall youth population, and they are not in the majority. Pre-college students are the majority, and university educators would do well to relate their minority schemes to the education of that majority as well, and to take into account the substantial social problems which accompany, and not infrequently determine, the education of young Americans. It is not simply university students who, arguably, need a core and a canon, and for life as well as 'education,' narrowly seen. As this session showed, those who attempt to determine the essential components of higher education need to come out of academe and into the real world of education to validate their schemes.

TEACHING THE CORE BEFORE COLLEGE: THE NATIONAL CONTEXT

James Miller

University of North Texas

Faculty in the College of Arts and Sciences at the University of North Texas are to be commended for developing and implementing the Classic Learning Core program. Students as well as faculty have given the program high marks. The program has also been an unqualified success in the eyes of parents of UNT students, as well. A departmental structure built around a specific academic discipline provides an efficient vehicle for scholars to develop knowledge and for the preparation of specialists in that field. However, for several reasons, it is somewhat less effective in teaching the liberal arts core to all university students. The first reason is that each discipline is generally taught in isolation and there is rarely an attempt by instructors to include and/or to integrate knowledge from other disciplines. The second reason is that traditional liberal arts curricula cover so much ground that it is difficult for students to get a sense of coherence and to sort out meaningful generalizations from the information. The third reason is that students sometimes find upper level questions on exams difficult to answer because they lack the background necessary to integrate knowledge and to state testable hypotheses across disciplines.

In a broad sense, the entire elementary and secondary school curriculum is a liberal arts core and is designed to provide the young with a knowledge base that will enable them to make sense out of the world in which they live. The parallel between the last two years of high school and the first two years of college is especially notable. Nevertheless, curriculum revision is an ongoing activity in most public schools as they seek to improve instruction and to teach a heterogeneous population of students with differing abilities and aptitudes.

Curriculum revision in public schools is also, at times, a result of external pressure, usually in response to a lack of student achievement on standardized tests. In the post-Sputnik era of the late 1950s and early 1960s, federal funds as well as foundation support were provided to support curriculum and methodological changes in virtually all K–12 subject areas. The epistemological underpinnings of most of the projects were those of Professor Jerome Bruner who argued that (a) a school boy learning physics will learn more physics if he is acting as a physicist than if he is acting as anything else, (b) teachers should teach the structure of the discipline, and (c) key concepts of academic disciplines can be taught in an intellectually honest way to children of any age. So-called "teacher-proof" materials, prepared by academic specialists and professional educators, emerged from curriculum centers across the nation: BSCS Biology, PSCS Physics, Greater Cleveland Mathematics Program, Carnegie-Mellon History Project, Indiana Government Project, and the Boulder Geography Project, to name a few. The teaching strategies for these projects were referred to variously as reflective teaching, inquiry teaching, socratic, divergent and convergent thinking, but whatever the name, the purpose was to teach the structure of the discipline, utilize a spiral curriculum, and for every student to think like a professional in each academic discipline, i.e., a physicist thinking about a physics problem.

A Rand Corporation study, a decade later, concluded that only vestiges of the projects remained, that public schools were highly resistant to change, and that this resistance increased as one went up the educational ladder. In fairness to public school teachers, it should be pointed out that they could hardly be faulted for failure to implement the new curricula. For one thing, few teachers had sufficient academic preparation to understand the structure of the discipline that they taught, and in some fields, the structure was not that clear even for the best academicians in the field. Secondly, many teachers had experienced only lectures in their preparation programs and therefore had few if any inquiry models to guide them. Thirdly, the ground-covering fetish has a long and well-established tradition in public school education and it is reinforced by standardized tests. Lastly, teachers quickly found that class schedules sometimes didn't fit well with the time necessary to conduct a simulation and other activities offered as course materials.

Teachers in schools today are once again involved in curriculum revision in response to more than two hundred national and state studies suggesting that American students are at-risk, indeed the nation is at-risk, in the international marketplace. Standardized test after standardized test shows that American students don't fare well when compared to their counterparts in the rest of the world.

I would like to point out that higher education needs to discourage, if possible, the use of standardized tests for testing student achievement in the liberal arts core at the university level. I would predict that students who take the Classic Learning Core courses will not fare well, not because the program lacks rigor and not because the students lack an understanding of the courses that they have taken, but because the standardized test will not test what they have learned. I believe that there is a strong relationship between the Classic Learning Core and the inquiry materials used in the public schools in the 1960s.

TEACHING THE CORE BEFORE COLLEGE: THE FIRST CHAPTER

Carol Hagen

University of North Texas

I have chosen to title my part of this session "The First Chapter" in an attempt to encourage the view, certainly not a new one, that this early portion of individual human history is critical to all that happens later. This is where the scene is set, all the values and attitudes are put into place, and the *characteristics*, if not the characters, which will be obvious throughout the rest of each life's story, are developed. "The apple doesn't fall far from the tree," as my brother-in-law often says, meaning we don't move very far from our beginnings. We can hope, as we work with young children that their lives will develop into long and satisfying stories, with a chance for a happy ending, and that they may also add favorably to the knowledge and experience of the whole of human culture and existence.

I will be focusing on an educational arena which has seen profound change in our country in the past decade or so. It is generally accepted in our culture that the college professor will complain about the education that students have received in the secondary school, and the secondary teachers will find fault with the middle and elementary school. But the early primary teacher, who in the past had to be content with placing the blame on parents, can now add the preschool teacher or caregiver to the list. The numbers of young children in center programs continues to climb; nearly half the mothers of babies under one year of age now work outside the home. The question of a core of knowledge, as well as values, attitudes, and skills, has made its way down into the preschool and is as fervently, and sometimes heatedly, discussed among professionals in the field of young children as it is anywhere.

Throughout history, philosophers and educators have concerned themselves with the question of what is appropriate educational method and curriculum content. Only since the seventeenth century have more detailed systems for the education of children under the age of seven or eight been devised. It is not until Froebel (1837) that a clearly-defined and carefully-delineated program with curriculum content and materials, a core, is described—the kindergarten. Since that time, G. Stanley Hall, Arnold Gesell, John Dewey, Maria Montessori, and a host of others up to the present day, have detailed what is absolutely critical to know in the rearing and educating (and these can scarcely be separated) of young children. Many of these theories, or aspects of them, persist today in some part in education systems around the Western world. In every country, they have been tempered with time and adjusted by particular social, economic, cultural, and political happenings. Whatever our particular opinions concerning a core curriculum, we might do well to attempt to assess the individual beliefs, and values (and perhaps political opinions) we hold which lead us to our conclusions.

It has been our habit in the past to take approaches to the education of older children and attempt to "pass them down," usually with very little adaptation, to suit the need of younger children. I would like to suggest to you today that we might do better to look at what we know, based on research, about the most effective ways of teaching an appropriate curriculum, a "core" if you will, to very young children, and consider adapting this information in our educational practices in the elementary and perhaps even to the college classroom.

When I taught my first "real" college class, after a fair number of years in primary and preschool programs, our own Dr. Earp in the College of Education asked me, "Well, Carol, what do you think about this, after all those years with the little ones?" I thought a minute, and said, "There isn't any difference." He laughed and said, "You know, I think you are right about that." We talked about the similarities, the need to relate learning to real life, to model enthusiasm, to exhibit an attitude of caring, and to "nudge and push."

I want to share with you some guidelines, developed by leaders in the early childhood profession and published by the National Association for the Education of Young Children entitled *Developmentally Appropriate Practice—Birth Through Age Eight*. I believe, with very little adaptation, they can be effective in facilitating learning with students of any age.

1) Young children learn by doing. Knowledge is constructed, it is acquired through interaction with the physical and social world. It comes from *within*. *Trying* it out is necessary for assimilation to take place. "The child is not a vessel to be filled," perhaps not "a lamp to be lit," but perhaps more likely, a spring to be tapped.

Young children: Using the senses and moving their bodies are the basic approaches to learning. It begins with infants, finding out about the world by putting things in their mouths.

Older students: They need *something* to do besides sitting. Surprisingly few of "our profound and influential educational moments" occur during formal lessons.

2) Teachers guide and facilitate, seldom tell or lecture. The environment is prepared, the teacher observes and adds challenges to push thinking further.

Young children: Use a centers approach—materials and equipment are ready and the child interacts.

Older students: Lectures and activities are based on material *outside* the text book that the student is reading.

3) Experiences are planned to foster physical, social, emotional, cognitive, and also creative and moral growth.

Young children: The child is seen as a whole, with varying needs and strengths, and the whole is greater than the sum of its parts—needs cannot be isolated.

Older students: Allow for social interaction, group work, cooperation. In some countries, cooperation is fostered rather than competition. Here, when students work together we call it cheating; others may see the same activity as the beginning of social awareness and maturity.

4) Each child is unique. Ability, personality, and learning style are different, as well as physical, emotional/social, and cognitive development.

Young children: There are "ages and stages," but many variations among children. Children are shy, bold, quiet, outspoken, reflective by nature—and sometimes on days.

Older students: We should expect the same, and also expect and respect cultural diversity, "group" identity—students of any age will be diverse, not from a mold. Allow for differences, and build in a variety of ways for students to exhibit the knowledge being acquired.

5) Interactions and activities are designed to develop self-esteem and positive feelings toward learning.

Young children: Materials are challenging, but the child has opportunities to succeed. Extreme care is taken to limit frustration and maintain good feelings about learning—the child has a long way to go, and it is important that learning is seen as an exciting, worthwhile process of involvement with others.

Older students: Some instructors seem to enjoy an adversarial role—"not knowing," at least in the beginning should be acceptable and safe. An attitude of respect toward the learner is supportive of an atmosphere in which learning can take place.

6) Curiosity is expected and encouraged. Discovery learning, exploration, and the making of choices are a planned part of activities.

Young children: The interests of the child are considered in planning. Open-ended questions, with more than one right answer are used.

Older students: True/false, "one right answer" are seldom used, critical thinking is expected, and choices are frequently offered; students should be allowed to go "off on a tangent," into areas of learning which interest them.

7) Children work mostly in small informal groups or individually. Young children: Group formation changes frequently, depending on the activity. Large group times are brief, usually for songs or stories.

Older students: There is opportunity for small group collaboration or work on individual projects.

8) Materials are concrete, and relevant to the child's life experiences.

Young children: Manipulatives, real objects, are used to teach concepts such as float and sink; raisins may be used for counting, as well as books about family life, pets, etc.

Older students: Manipulatives are still useful; and comparisons are made between cultures, across time, with life today. Curriculum is not only a classified corpus of information, but is an exposure to ideas, with discussion of values and attitudes.

9) Positive guidance techniques are used to foster self-control and autonomous behavior. The "locus of control" moves from the adult to the child.

Young children: Teachers use modeling, re-direction, setting of clear (but few) limits, and lots of encouragement. Pro-social behaviors (cooperation, negotiation, helping) are encouraged.

Older students: The very same techniques apply. Students are treated with respect, and while evaluation is necessary, students receive feed-back and encouragement for *approximate* behaviors, with an expectation of some degree of error and movement *toward* the goal.

10) Assessment is an on-going process, which is approached in a variety of ways. "Testing" tells the teacher what other or alternate information needs to be provided. Tests do not always tell us how the learner should change.

Young children: Data is collected in a variety of ways and may seldom involve a formal testing process—check-lists, anecdotal information, and child enthusiasm may all be useful measures.

Older students: Although our huge classes push us in that direction, the Scantron should not be allowed to take over. "Overnight" learning to pass an exam lasts just about that long. Piaget cautions us not to allow learning to be a "varnish," an extrinsic, imposed condition, rather than an internalized change.

Programs for young children all over the country are evaluating themselves according to these guidelines suggested by NAEYC, in an attempt to teach children in more appropriate ways. Additionally, curriculum is being studied, usually in a more generalized view. As educators, we are probably less inclined to worry about whether a young child has come in contact with a particular piece of information, and are more interested in attitudes toward learning. Studies indicate that "success-oriented" behaviors, as related to academic performance in school, can be tied to four factors which are observable in young children.

1) Autonomy: The child is in control and owns his or her self, is able to take initiative, resist domination and use reason to make choices—exactly the traits we would seem to need in a democratic society.

2) Problem-solving: The child can spot uniqueness, explores and tests (sometimes more than we are comfortable with), desires to cope, reasons using symbols, and knows how to learn.

3) Openness: The child tolerates ambiguity, is trusting and empathetic, is self-disclosing and analytical (can say, "Well, I am not mad anymore, but you still should not take my things.")

4) Integrity: There is a wholeness of being, a value-oriented life is already evident, along with an ability to resolve value conflicts. It is amazing to see this in very young children, who are supposed to be totally ego-centric (example: the baby who pulls from his mouth his beloved pacifier to give to a crying older child).

These kinds of attitudes and inclinations seem to us on this end of the teaching spectrum to be more important than core information. We would, however, argue that there is a core if not a canon for young children, comprised of nursery rhymes, songs and stories (and these stories include *family* stories, the beginnings of the concept of history for a young child—a personal history, and his or her own). This core must be based on, and come out of, the culture of the specific child. *Which* stories, songs and finger-plays is less important; the social context and interaction between the adult and child are the critical components.

In closing, I would like to add that while discussion of a core curriculum is important and relevant to those of us in the university setting, our concerns will not begin to touch the reality that vast numbers of American children face. While we argue about what specific books our older students should be reading, huge numbers of young children have never lived in families where reading materials of *any* kind are present. Some of them, in the second generation, have never lived in families where anyone works—now that is *really* core learning. Until we begin to address the problem of the growing numbers of young children in poverty, we have not looked into the face of reality. The few of our students who have read the core are going to be overwhelmed by their illiterate peers. In past decades, there have been fifteen workers for each retired person—in the years ahead, estimates are that there will be two, one of them a minority. If not for moral or democratic reasons, then for pure economic self-interest (which often is more likely to get our attention) we must do a better job of educating *all* our children.

At the risk of sounding simplistic, I would like to read a quotation from Robert Fulghum's recent best seller—certainly not included in the canon, but probably, this year anyway, an item on someone's cultural literacy test:

All I really need to know about how to live and what to do and how to be I learned in kindergarten. Wisdom was not at the top of the graduate-school mountain, but there in the sandpile at Nursery School. These are the things I learned:

Share everything. Play fair. Don't hit people. Put things back where you found them. Clean up your own mess. Don't take things that aren't yours. Say you're sorry when you hurt somebody. Wash your hands before you eat. Flush. Warm cookies and cold milk are good for you. Live a balanced life—learn some and think some and draw and paint and sing and dance and play and work every day some. Take a nap every afternoon. When you go out into the world, watch out for traffic, hold hands, and stick together. Be aware of wonder. Remember the little seed in the Styrofoam cup: The roots go down and the plant goes up and nobody really knows how or why, but we are all like that. Goldfish and hamsters and white mice and even the little seed in the Styrofoam cup—they all die. So do we. And then remember the Dick-and-Jane books and the first word you learned—the biggest word of all—LOOK.

TEACHING THE CORE BEFORE COLLEGE: THE ELEMENTARY YEARS

M. Jean Greenlaw

University of North Texas

There is a need to distinguish clearly between the requirements of education in the elementary years and the demands of early childhood education on the one hand and secondary education on the other. Secondary education, as has been indicated in the introductory remarks to this section, and in Dr. Hardy's paper which follows, shades—and should shade—into the higher and further education of colleges and universities. At this advanced level, both in high schools and colleges, a whole range of initiatives, approaches and resources can be utilized to serve the purposes of a wide-ranging humane, but vocationally-focused education. The full use of these resources has, in most cases, still to be achieved, but a rich variety of opportunities is available to those active in this field—and attention may here be directed to the programs already developed by the University of North Texas, and those in the process of development, which have already expanded into discussion and cooperation with high schools.

Paradoxically, it might seem, a comparable cornucopia of resources, approaches, methods and activities is accessible in the area of early childhood education. As the Director of the UNT Child Development Laboratory makes clear in her paper, early childhood education at its best is fundamentally and essentially heuristic. The limitations in age, maturity, skill and social acclimatization themselves produce opportunities and situations with enormous potential for the individual and collective education of young children through, primarily, their own processes of discovery, inquiry, and experimentation. In a context of positive encouragement and unobtrusive direction everything is grist to the early childhood educator's mill.

Partly because of the youth of elementary school children in contrast to secondary pupils, and the limitations of more formal programs and settings in the elementary school in contrast to those of early childhood education, elementary school educators are more limited in the opportunities open to them than their colleagues on either side—preschool or secondary teachers. This has, however, the effect of focusing attention on the single, most important resource available to educators in the elementary field—books. It is frequently the case, however, the sad case, that this resource, important at every stage in education but particularly so in the elementary years, is underused and misused. All too often the huge variety of excellent reading materials which have a close connection with the familiar scenes and concerns of the contemporary elementary school pupil—space, rockets, computers, the Olympics, Civil Rights, elections, pop music—and which can, and should, be supplemented by visits to museums and exhibitions (the Ramses exhibition, for example), field-trips and visits, are ignored and neglected in favor of traditional, trite, and irrelevant 'readers.' Such neglect derives not simply from a lack of interest on the part of the teacher, nor from a shortage of funds to purchase new books, but, frequently, from fundamental ignorance on the part of teachers not only about modern books available to them, but about the subjects with which these books deal. I am constantly appalled in the course of my own teaching, and in my contacts with schools, by the yawning gaps in the personal resources and knowledge of teachers, and, by implication, of the inadequacy of their training. There is a huge range of books available to the elementary school educator, which makes possible a wide, stimulating, and demanding education for the elementary pupil, but these books will only be fully and properly used when the educators themselves are properly educated and trained to a personal disposition to continue that education throughout their teaching careers. It has been fashionable recently to stress the need for 'cultural literacy' amongst our pupils at all levels. It is not only pupils who need this training but teachers themselves, and the emphasis in that regard should not be, as it has so often been, an idiosyncratic definition of 'literacy,' accompanied by artificial and selective lists of what demonstrates that literacy, but on the culture implicit in 'cultural literacy.' With that emphasis, with that training for educators and would-be educators themselves, then elementary schools will be able to make full use of the most enduringly-valuable of all educational resources—books.

TEACHING THE CORE BEFORE COLLEGE: THE HUMANITIES AND THE SECONDARY SCHOOL

Clifford A. Hardy

University of North Texas

In consideration of the debate in hand, I must say that higher education is indeed fortunate to have the freedom to consider these choices as compared to the constraints of the public schools. I refer of course, to the constraints of
— The Texas Education Agency rules and regulations
— The State imposed essential elements
— State mandated time allocations
— Rigid text book adoption procedures
— The accompanying censorship problems
as well as a long list of other state-imposed sanctions and situations.

The conflict between the classic core approach and a more practical approach is as old as McGuffey's Reader and has become embroiled in educational philosophy in this century via the process/product controversies highlighted by Parker at the University of Chicago lab school, and of course, by the writings of John Dewey. The controversy continues today in the midst of the reform movement of the 1980s. The debate over the place of the humanities has been highlighted in the 1980s by the findings reported in the Federal Report *A Nation at Risk*, and in the Texas reform measure, House Bill 72. In addition certain writings have impinged on the school reform movement in a powerful way. Among the many we might include are *The Paidiea Proposal* (Adler), *Horace's Compromise* (Sizer), and *Cultural Literacy in America* (Hirsch) as being the most popular if not the most significant.

In a practical sense, there seem to be two basic approaches to fusing an interdisciplinary humanities study (with anything approaching a classic reading list) into the secondary curriculum. The most common, but not necessarily the best, is through the gifted student approach. The State of Texas has mandated the adoption of gifted and talented programs in each school district by 1990. In spite of the fact that Adler in the *Paidiea Proposal* is suggesting "One Course of Study For All" as his basic dictum, what seems to be happening is that the humanities are becoming the province of the "Talented and Gifted" groups. An excellent example is the PACE program in the Plano ISD. The PACE program has implemented a two-year humanities sequence for *select* ninth and tenth grades (over and above the honors classes).

A different approach can be illustrated by the essential school movement as outlined by Sizer in *Horace's Compromise*. The essential school movement now embraces some 150 high schools nationwide. A local example can be found at Paschal High School in Fort Worth. Literally a "school within a school" the essential school frees students and teachers in a variety of ways from traditional restraint. The program allows for four teachers well versed in the humanities teaching a total of eighty students. The program includes two daily time blocks and a daily tutorial composed of the following:

Time Block I   Humanities (Literature and The Arts; History and Philosophy; Inquiry and Expression)
Time Block II Science/Math (Science; Math; Inquiry and Expression)
Tutorial

The students in the essential school must demonstrate their learning with products as well as by oral and written examination.

We can summarize by saying the intent in the current reform movement seems to be toward greater and deeper study of the classics in the secondary school. But whether or not the regulatory roadblocks and/or the increasing use of electronic delivery systems in the classroom of the future will facilitate it or not remains to be seen.

DIALOGUE IN THE CLASSROOM: LISTENING AS A TEACHING STRATEGY TO ENCOURAGE CRITICAL THINKING

Allen H. Henderson and Ronald F. Reed

Texas Wesleyan College

INTRODUCTION

Gallagher (1974) in his book *Campus in Crisis* states that the traditional goal of liberal arts studies is that students will learn to be wise, knowledgeable, effective, compassionate practitioners of the art of inquiry. Learning the "art of inquiry" is central to a liberal arts education. Pedagogical strategies designed to develop the critical thinking skills so important to reasoned inquiry are central to any concept of a liberal arts education. Education in this age of exploding information and specialization too often has come to mean the passive process of being informed, while the active process of reasoned inquiry and dialogue has been relegated to a secondary role in the educational process.

Teaching that fosters reasoned inquiry or analytic thinking throughout a liberal arts curriculum is of critical importance. Many educators (e.g., Bloom 1987; Presseisen 1987; Nisbett et al. 1987; Sternberg 1985; Beyer 1984) as well as several popular futurist writers (e.g., Naisbitt 1982; Toffler 1980) suggest that educational institutions must teach reasoning, critical analysis, and problem solving to the citizens of the twenty-first century. Costa (1987) in fact proposes that the ability to think is a prerequisite to the "basics" or the basic of the basics.

Some of our most influential educational philosophers (e.g., Dewey 1966; James 1910) and other well known contemporary educators (Adler 1982; Combs 1981; Bloom 1987; Postman 1979) have argued that education at the least must advance the student's cognitive abilities to adapt to change and solve problems. These educators frequently propose that critical thinking facilities are developed best through the study of the classics and the virtues which are the product of human history.

Cognitive psychologists (e.g., Nisbett et al. 1987; Bradford et al. 1986; Baron and Sternberg 1986) and proponents of educational programs such as the Philosophy for Children program (e.g., Lipman 1985; Reed 1986; Sharp 1987) advocate directly teaching inquiry skills and analytic thinking. If the collective wisdom of these educators is correct, that the thinking skills reform movement with its activist inquiry approach to education is crucial to the education of all students, then it is imperative that those committed to promoting the art of inquiry or the cognitive skills of questioning, reasoning, problem identification, problem solving, logical analysis, synthesis, agreement evaluation, decision making, and other thinking facilities become advocates for educational change.

Mann (1979), presenting a historical perspective on concepts and training of cognitive processes, cautions against training "processes" instead of people. He also advises educator-advocates and program developers against excessive interpretation of flimsy research results and unwarranted extrapolations that foster an air of scientism when in reality they are arguments that rest on metaphorical or metaphysical grounds, rather than on concrete data. Mann concludes that the urgent need is for us to train or remediate students in those skills required for productive living and, when possible, to impart knowledge and wisdom to them that will make their lives more than mere pursuit of reinforcement.

Henderson (1988) identified two critical evaluation issues that must be addressed by educational programs or teaching strategies designed to promote analytic thinking skills. They are 1) how to measure the outcomes of cognitive processing training and 2) how to demonstrate transfer of training. In other words, what evidence can be presented to indicate that reasoning skills programs or teaching strategies have the effects purported by developers and advocates of these programs or methods? Whimbey (1985) suggests that recent research tends to indicate that, when thinking skills become an integral part of the curriculum and instructional practice, test scores in traditional academic areas increase. However, Winocur (1985) concludes that traditional assessment techniques are inadequate because performance on a test is overt, while thinking is a covert process and thus not directly observable and measurable in traditional behavioristic ways.

Sternberg and Bhana (1986), reviewing research on five leading thinking skills programs, conclude that more rigorous evaluation is needed and that more attention be given to outcome measures, transfer, and durability of training. Bransford, Sherwood, and Vye (1986) indicate that thinking abilities are not just add-ons to domain-specific knowledge, but that reasoning skills and competencies in a domain develop together. Evaluators attempting to avoid measurement problems would profit from becoming familiar with sources of invalidity of measures (Chapter 3—Webb, Campbell, Schwartz, Sechrest and Grove 1981; Chapters 6, 9 & 10—Struening & Guttentag 1975). The issues of outcome measures and transfer are critical to the future of the thinking skills educational movement.

Additionally, thinking skills advocates need to become more familiar with the decision-making process within educational institutions and the current role program evaluation research is playing in that process. Political realities and pressure for accountability are compelling administrators to rely on more objective means of program assessment in order to justify the allocation of human and fiscal resources to particular educational programs. Many different evaluation models (Isaac & Michael 1981) have been suggested as frameworks for assessing program effectiveness. The process of instructional program development—implementation, evaluation, and integration—is a complex process (i.e., Tuckman 1985). Program acceptance is influenced by 1) social-political forces involving community, organizational, and individual personality elements; 2) real or perceived needs; 3) similar or related programs already in existence; 4) current or projected resources both human and economic; and 5) evidence of past program effectiveness.

The importance of the "inquiry" conception of education versus merely an "informing" view of education needs to be emphasized in an age of information overload. Many thoughtful people believe that the future of our civilized, democratic way of life and even the world depends upon reasonable people engaging in dialogue in a spirit of community in order to effectively adapt to the challenges of change. Moreover, reasoning and communication abilities also are assumed to be equally important for the life of individuals. If these assertions are correct, it is incumbent on those educators committed to teaching cognitive processes through an inquiry approach, at the minimum, to integrate inquiry into the liberal arts curriculum.

The goals of the Philosophy for Children Program with its inquiry approach to education exemplifies the educational outcomes called for by the futurists, philosophers, educators, and the informed public. Sharp (1987) expressed the goals as follows:

> To stimulate students to think well, to improve their cognitive skills so that they can reason well, and to engage them in a disciplined dialogue so that they can reason well together, to challenge them to think about important ethical and social concepts drawn from the philosophical tradition, and yet to develop their ability to think for themselves so that they may think autonomously when actually confronted with moral problems. (4)

This paper will examine dialogue and the modeling of questioning and listening activities by the teacher as pedagogical strategies for the development of analytic thinking skills. The Philosophy for Children Program will be reviewed as a model inquiry educational program with an eye toward understanding how it uses the notion of "community of inquiry" to encourage students to speak, listen, and think well. Finally, experience with implementing this model in a liberal arts oriented teacher education program and in introductory psychology classes that are part of a liberal arts core curriculum will be explored.

Philosophy for Children Program

Introduction

The following portrayal of the Philosophy for Children Program is excerpted with permission from the three articles in the *1988 Philosophy for Children: Where Are We Now . . . Supplement No. 2* publication produced by the Institute for the Advancement of Philosophy for Children (IAPC) at Montclair State College in Upper Montclair, New Jersey. These articles were authorized by Matthew Lipman, the founder of the Philosophy for Children Program, and Ann Sharp and Tony Johnson, two leading proponents.

The Philosophy for Children Program is a humanistic enrichment and cognitive skills program. Specific objectives of the program are to strengthen students' reasoning skills, particularly those in comprehension, analysis, and problem solving; to do so in an elementary school version of the humanistic discipline of philosophy; to make students more conversant with the ethical components of human experience; and to foster an atmosphere conducive to learning by converting the classroom into a community of inquiry. Thinking and speaking reasonably are essential in the citizenry of a democracy. Therefore, the program also attempts to make students aware of the richness of their intellectual heritage and to strengthen their academic achievement in other subjects.

In recent years, assessment reports, such as National Assessment of Educational Progress, have suggested that students are deficient in comprehension, analysis, and problem solving skills. Many educators assumed that they were teaching these skills when they taught language arts, mathematics, science education, reading, and writing. As it has turned out, however, the inductive and deductive skills required for reading comprehension, plus the concept-formation and concept analysis skills needed for the processing of information, were evidently not being furnished efficiently by traditional education.

During the last several years, developers have begun to strengthen specific skills through drills and practice. There is little evidence of the success of the programs. The need remains for a comprehensive educational approach that will tie together reasoning, reading, writing, and speaking, and will do so under the aegis of the humanities. Students in every discipline require reasoning and concept-formation skills. These skills are important as they prepare themselves for careers, for participation in the institutions of societies, and for the overall course of their personal lives. For example, to be a citizen requires that one be able to deduce that the law that applies to everyone therefore applies specifically to oneself. To be an employee presupposes that one can logically infer the applicability to oneself of the rules and regulations of the place of employment.

The need for these skills is therefore essential rather than superficial. To assume that these skills develop automatically with maturation, and that specific instruction in these areas need not be provided, puts masses of children at risk. Philosophy for Children makes it possible for children to learn to reason better and to transfer such skills to other disciplines. The program design, in contrast to other critical thinking programs, emphasizes the following:

1. A course in formal and informal logic, similar to a college course in the subject.
2. Specifically designed logical materials that are integrated and related to linguistic usage.
3. A wide variety of exercises in applying logical principles.
4. Providing children with readers in the form of novels and with accounts of fictional children modeling the discovery process.
5. The teaching of reasoning and concept-formation through the exploration of philosophical concepts.
6. Attempts to sensitize students to the ethical, aesthetic, epistemological, and metaphysical aspects of the problems to which the reasoning is to be applied.
7. Structuring class time to make explicit the process of inquiry which is then to be internalized by each student.
8. Reasoning which is not taught as an end in itself but as a means for better dealing with real life situations.
9. Classroom dialogue as the best method of strengthening reasoning skills in such a way as to make use of children's natural conversational tendencies.
10. Materials that are intrinsically interesting, yet easy to use and enjoyable to students.
11. Teacher training that emphasizes using the materials.
12. A curriculum which is sequential and cumulative, rather than episodic at each age level.
13. A curriculum which stresses the emotional as well as the cognitive aspects of the child's experience.

Philosophical Foundation

The Philosophy for Children Program is founded in the discipline of philosophy. It is assumed that children should be encouraged to think for themselves, rather than having others think for them. Rather than compelling children to accept uncritically the world as perceived by adults, educators should encourage and assist children in their struggle to discover and make sense out of a wonderful world. While relatively young children possess the ability to reason, it is not assumed that their powers of reason will develop naturally. While children seem inclined to seek understanding, to search for meaning and truth, such inclinations

479

need nurturing if they are to prevail. The Philosophy for Children Program assumes that thinking is natural and can be enhanced. The program aims to improve the child's natural rational powers, to transform thinking into thinking well.

Thinking well requires self-reflection, and self-reflection is encouraged through dialogue among a community of peers seeking solutions to common problems. In order for children to engage in philosophical learning, an atmosphere must be created that fosters interaction between each individual child and the environment. Such an environment includes peers, teachers, and other adults as well as the physical setting. To encourage such interaction, the teacher must genuinely respect each child's opinions. If students sense that their task is to discover the right answers as determined by the teacher, they are not likely to risk an interpretation or offer an explanation that differs from what is expected. If philosophy is to be meaningful, the teacher must join students in seeking more meaningful explanations than they now possess to problems that interest them all. Such a teacher must recognize that knowledge is continually being created and expanded by humans in their quest for greater understanding.

The Community of Inquiry

Establishing a community of inquiry in which significant dialogue takes place is the most important ingredient for fostering good thinking, but it is not enough. Children need something to think about if they are to think well, and unless they have access to literary materials that stimulate interest in philosophical ideas, they are not likely to develop or sustain a genuine community of inquiry.

In order to transform classrooms into communities of inquiry, children need a Socratic model that is appropriate to their level of maturity. They need to read and talk about children who, like themselves, are struggling to figure things out. Children today need philosophical material presented in the form of a story if they are encouraged to be reflective. The philosophy for children novels meet that need. They offer students a model of a community of inquiry in action. Just as Socrates modelled a process of inquiry for his students and just as Plato's dialogue offers such a model for adults, the characters in the novels provide elementary and middle school students with appropriate models of both thinking and thinking well.

Critical or Criterion-Based Thinking

The movement to upgrade the quality of thinking in school and college classrooms is known as the "critical thinking" movement. At first glance, it seems to be a hodgepodge of competing approach. Upon further examination, however, several things stand out:

1) Virtually all of the competing approaches contend that thinking well involves "thinking skills," although there is no agreement on just what these skills are; and

2) There is general agreement that critical thinking enhances the capacity to solve problems or make decisions.

One of the reasons for the lack of agreement as to which skills are distinctively "thinking skills" is that the proponents of these approaches come from different disciplines, and are inclined therefore to identify as thinking skills those that count as such in their own bailiwicks. Those in English count syntactical skills as thinking skills; those in philosophy nominate logical skills; those in social sciences nominate statistical and other research skills, and other scientists emphasize other inquiry skills.

What generally goes unmentioned in these citations of skills (as well as of the skill-orchestration) is that skills are performances subject to judgment, and judgments are criterion-based, with the result that the very notion of skill is dependent upon the operation of those cognitive instruments known as criteria. Little wonder then that there is such a prima facie similarity between the terms "critical" and "criteria," for critical thinking is necessarily criterion-based thinking.

What keeps critical thinking from becoming fanatically rigorous is its sensitivity to application in highly diversified contexts, as well as its constantly taking itself into account along with its subject-matter, so as to be continually self-correcting. Thinking that is insensitive to context is blundering and obtuse; thinking that is not self-correcting easily becomes uncritical and unreasonable.

The community of inquiry pedagogy of the Philosophy for Children Program assures that students will engage in self-corrective thinking insofar as they have internalized the dialogical process of classroom discussion. The curriculum of the program assures that students will learn to apply and appeal to relevant, reliable criteria, and that they will be sensitive to the qualitative uniqueness of particular situations, this being indispensable for the making of appropriate judgments.

Teacher Training

Teachers have to be carefully prepared to use the Philosophy for Children Program. Under ordinary circumstances, they do not find the materials difficult or complex, but they do have to become accustomed to the requirements of leading a discussion in a community of inquiry. In this sense, the program is highly teacher-sensitive. Some teachers are already predisposed to this method of teaching, and others must overcome didactic methods that are incompatible with the Philosophy for Children pedagogy.

481

The Philosophy for Children Program is significantly teacher dependent. If the model of an educated individual offered by the teacher is a person who is all-knowing, students are not likely to engage in or value philosophical inquiry. If students are exposed to teachers who are intellectually open, curious, self-critical, and not afraid to say, "I don't know," the student's natural inclination to wonder is enhanced. The Philosophy for Children Program assumes that commitment to open, honest inquiry, governed only by the rules of reason, should prevail in the classroom.

Dialogue in Psychology Classes

Many college courses are strictly lecture or "informing" courses. This is true of many, if not most, Introduction to Psychology courses offered across the country and was true of the courses I was teaching in 1982. As a result of collaborating with my coauthor, Dr. Reed, on a Philosophy for Children project in a middle school in 1982, I decided to integrate inquiry activities into my beginning level psychology courses.

After trying several different strategies, I settled on two activities that would allow me to include dialogue as a teaching strategy. The first activity is a small group discussion activity, and the second activity is a writing assignment. Both activities are designed to allow the teacher to listen to the students more and to encourage critical thinking, communication, inquiry and dialogue between the students.

The small group discussion consists of setting aside one 45-minute class period a week for student dialogue. This activity differs from traditional general class discussions in that the class is divided up into groups of three to five students. These small groups are instructed to discuss the issues, key concepts, theories, research evidence and conclusions they are studying that week. Each group is asked to identify and present to the class the three ideas or conclusions pertaining to the topic for the week that they collectively judge to be most important. They also are asked to give reasons for their judgments.

The written assignment requires each student to write a one to two page reaction paper to each reading assignment. The purpose of the paper is to allow each student to express his analytic thinking regarding the concepts, theories, research evidence, and conclusions presented in the readings. The exercise gives students practice with critical thinking and communication skills.

Overall, both of these activities have allowed me to listen to students in a way that was not possible when using the traditional lecture-discussion format. The small group activity has significantly increased dialogue among students and helped them raise more quality questions about the topics under study. The reaction papers have increased involvement in the course and permitted me to more effectively communicate with individual students. The two activities have encouraged inquiry and thinking among my students for the last six years.

WORKS CITED

Adler, M. J. *The Padeia Proposal*. New York: Macmillan, 1982.

Baron, J. B. and R. J. Sternberg, eds. *Teaching Thinking Skills: Theory and Practice*. New York: Freeman, 1986.

Beyer, B. K. "Improving Thinking Skills—Defining the Problem." *Phi Delta Kappan* March 1984: 486–90.

Bloom, A. *The Closing of the American Mind*. New York: Simon and Schuster, 1987.

Bransford, J. D. and B. S. Stein. *The Idea Problem Solver: A Guide for Improving Thinking, Learning and Creativity*. San Francisco: Freeman, 1984.

Bransford, J. D., R. Sherwood, and N. Vye. "Teaching Thinking and Problem Solving." *American Psychologist* 41 (1986): 1078–089.

Cheng, P. W. et al. "Pragmatic Versus Syntactic Approaches to Training Deductive Reasoning." *Cognitive Psychology* 18 (1986): 293–328.

Combs, A. "Humanistic Education: Too Tender for a Tough World?" *Phi Delta Kappan* February 1981: 446–49.

Costa, A. L. "Thinking Skills: Neither an Add-on nor a Quick Fix." In M. Heiman and J. Slomianko, eds., *Thinking Skills Instruction: Concepts and Techniques*. Washington, D.C.: National Education Association, 1987.

Derry, S. J. and D. A. Murphy. "Designing Systems that Train Learning Ability: From Theory to Practice." *Review of Educational Research* 56 (1986): 1–39.

Dewey, J. *Democracy and Education*. New York: Free Press, 1966.

Gagne, R. M. *The Conditions of Learning*. (4th ed.) New York: Holt, Rinehart & Winston, 1985.

Gagne, R. M. and W. Dick. "Instructional Psychology." *Annual Review of Psychology* 34 (1983): 261–95.

Gallagher, B. G. *Campus in Crisis*. New York: Harper & Row, 1974.

Glaser, E. M. *Putting Knowledge to Use: Facilitating the Diffusion of Knowledge and the Implementation of Planned Change*. San Francisco: Josey-Bass Publications, 1983.

Glaser, R. "Instructional Psychology: Past, Present, and Future." *American Psychologist* 37 (1982): 292–305.

Halpern, D. F. *Thought and Knowledge: An Introduction to Critical Thinking*. Hillsdale, New Jersey: Erlbaum, 1984.

Henderson, A. H. "Program Evaluation Issues and Analytic Thinking." *Analytic Teaching* 8 (1988): 43–55.

Huxley, A. *Island*. New York: Harper & Row, 1962.

Institute for the Advancement of Philosophy for Children. *Philosophy for Children: Where Are We Now . . . Supplement No. 2*. Upper Montclair, New Jersey: IPAC, Montclair State College, 1988.

James, W. *Talks to Teachers on Psychology and to Students on Some of Life's Ideals*. New York: Henry Holt & Co., 1910.

Klaber, M. "The School as a Social Situation." *Annual Review of Psychology* 36 (1985): 115–40.

Lipman, M. "Philosophical Practice and Educational Reform." *Journal of Thought* 20/4 (1985): 20–36.

Mann, L. *On the Trail of Process: A Historical Perspective on Cognitive Processes and their Training*. New York: Gruen & Strutton, 1979.

Maslow, A. H. "Goals and Implications of Humanistic Education." Chap. 13 in *The Farther Reaches of Human Nature*, 180–95. New York: Viking Press, 1971.

McKeachie, W. J. et al. *Teaching and Learning in the College Classroom: A Review of the Research Literature*. Ann Arbor: National Center for Research to Improve Postsecondary Teaching and Learning, 1986.

Naisbitt, J. *Megatrends*. New York: Warner Books, 1982.

Nisbett, R. E. et al. "Teaching Reasoning." *Science* 238 (1987): 625–31.

Palincsac, A. S. and A. L. Brown. "Reciprocal Teaching of Comprehension-Fostering and Comprehension-Monitoring Activities." *Cognitive and Instruction* 1/2 (1984): 11–175.

Peters, R. *Practical Intelligence*. New York: Harper & Row, 1987.

Pintrich, P. R. et al. "Instructional Psychology." *Annual Review of Psychology* 37 (1986): 611–51.

Presseisen, B. "Thinking and Curriculum: Critical Crossroads for Educational Change." In M. Heiman and J. Slomianko, eds., *Thinking Skills Instruction: Concepts and Techniques*. Washington, D.C.: National Education Association, 1987.

Postman, N. *Teaching as a Conserving Activity*. New York: Dell Publishing, 1979.

Postman, N. and C. Weingartner. *Teaching as a Subversive Activity*. New York: Dell Publishing, 1969.

Reed, R. "Analytic Teaching." *Excellence in Education*, 1986.

Rogers, C. R. *Freedom to Learn*. Columbus, OH: Charles E. Merrill Publishers, 1969.

Rogers, T. F. *Putting Knowledge to Use: A Distillation of the Literature Regarding Knowledge Transfer and Change*. San Francisco: Josey-Bass Publisher, 1976.

Sharp, A. M. "Pedagogical Practice and Philosophy: The Case of Ethical Inquiry." *Analytic Thinking* 7/2 (1987): 4–7.

Showers, C. and N. Cantor. "Social Cognition: A Look at Motivated Strategies." *Annual Review of Psychology* 36 (1985): 275–305.

Sieber, S. D. "Trends in Diffusion Research." In A. R. Jwaideh and B. H. Bhola, eds., *Research in Diffusion of Educational Innovations: A Report with an Agenda*. Bloomington, IN: School of Education, Indiana University, 1974.

Simon, H. A. *The Science of the Artificial*. (2nd ed.) Cambridge: MIT Press, 1981.

Skinner, B. F. "The Shame of American Education." Chap. 8 in *Upon Further Reflections*, 113–30. Englewood Cliffs, NJ: Prentice-Hall, Inc., 1987.

Sternberg, R. J. "Intelligence as Thinking and Learning Skills." *Educational Leadership*, 39 (1981): 18–20.

———. *Beyond I.Q.: A Triochic Theory of Human Intelligence*. New York: Cambridge Press, 1985.

Sternberg, R. J. and K. Bhana. "Synthesis of Research on the Effectiveness of Intellectual Skills Programs: Snake-oil Remedies or Miracle Cures?" *Educational Leadership* October 1986: 60–67.

Struening, E. L. and M. Guttentag. *Handbook of Evaluation Research*. Beverly Hills: Sage Publications, 1975.

Toffler, A. *The Third Wave*. New York: William Morrow, 1980.

Webb, E. I., et al. *Nonreactive Measures in Social Sciences.* Boston: Houghton Mifflin, 1981.

Whimbey, A. "The Consequences of Teaching Thinking." In A. Costa, ed. *Developing Minds: A Resource Book for Teaching Thinking.* Alexandria, VA: Association for Supervision and Curriculum Development, 1985.

Winocur, S. L. "Developing Lesson Plans with Cognitive Objectives." In A. Costa, ed. *Developing Minds: A Resource Book for Teaching Thinking.* Alexandria, VA: Association for Supervision and Curriculum Development, 1985.

Wittrock, M., ed. *The Handbook of Research on Teaching.* (3rd ed.) New York: Macmillan, 1986.

THE COMMUNITY COLLEGE CLASSROOM OF THE 1990s: A SOCIETAL MICROCOSM

Tahita Fulkerson

Tarrant County Junior College

If my English professors from Texas Christian University (circa 1959–1963) were magically whisked into the English classroom where I teach in the 1990s, a classroom at Tarrant County Junior College, Fort Worth, Texas, they would be astonished and, I'm afraid, a bit out of place. I cannot think of one who could immediately make the transfer.

Let me clarify: I do not indict them, for I revered them, and feared at least one; they inspired me and were my role models. Knowledgeable, professorial in the full sense of that word, they upheld high standards, teaching their beloved literature, good manners, and moral values as well.

But the world of higher education has changed so dramatically since then that I have trouble imagining them in the classrooms of the 90s. For one thing, they would be astonished at the way the students look and behave. The students they saw during the earliest 60s were majority students. Not one black student attended T.C.U. when I was there, and I remember not more than a dozen Hispanics, whom we called simply Mexicans. Those of us who studied Spanish learned it from a staff that included only one native speaker. Taught by white Anglo-Saxon professors, we white Anglo-Saxon students came to class predictably dressed by gender: only males could wear trousers, and no one could wear shorts. Females were coiffured, manicured, and girdled. Regardless of gender, though, we listened attentively and transcribed lectures often verbatim, studied alone in library carrells, and worked hours on revisions of our notes and papers. Generally, we overachieved. We were hardworking Innocents. Indeed, the only student demonstration at T.C.U. while I was there was a friendly sit-in by serious honor students who wanted the T.C.U. library to be open on Sundays. In those days the library closed on weekends and on weeknights at 10:00, the curfew hour for freshmen girls.

Of course, we teachers of today—especially teachers in community colleges—are well aware that students like those are facts of the distant past, as is the world they lived in. At least 60 percent of those we presently teach are less regimented as students, as revealed by their casual attendance and often indifferent classroom performance. Known more often as underachievers, they take life easy, and they certainly seem unconcerned about grooming for an appearance in class. Yet at the same time, huge numbers of our students do assume their own financial responsibility, much more than my generation did. Some of mine work thirty hours a week at a job while they are enrolled for twelve hours, and in fairness, some of these hardworking students are highly motivated to succeed. Still, because they view college as a sideline to the real world they live in, they are very different from college students of three decades ago. And more to my point here, students of the 90s may be even more different.

A few regional statistics explain why: the Arlington, Texas public schools enroll students who speak forty-two languages; Dallas public schools are almost 80 percent minority (Johnston). And while the population of the North Texas metroplex has only doubled since the 1960s, college enrollments in the area have grown twenty times (Geisel). Ironically, despite that growth, the number of traditional 18–22-year-old students seems to be declining, verifying earlier predictions that group would decrease by 25 percent in this century (*U.S. News & World Report*). In place of these traditional students will be different, certainly non-traditional students. It has been projected that by the year 2000, and that is just eight years away, "nearly one-third of the U.S. college-age population—and one-half of the children under eighteen—will be minority" (Quehl 35).

One requires time to assimilate such statistics, and to ponder implications. What kind of student will we have? And how will the inevitable changes in our student body affect us and our curricula? Some teachers pronounce these questions moot, because they say that many—no, most—of these new students will not pass university entrance tests. Indeed, many will never graduate from high school, if we can believe current drop-out rates: Geisel reports that in Texas, with its 20 percent illiteracy rate, only one in eight Mexican girls who start first grade graduates from high school, a figure embedded in the equally shocking national statistic that 3600 students in America drop out of school daily (Denton 34). Until such statistics change, life as we college folk have come to know it, say some, likely will not be changed dramatically.

But given the various states' mandates to remediate these students, many will be discovered before they drop out and will be placed into remedial programs where they will learn to read and write and compute. Many will attain the minimum competence for college work and will enroll at our colleges. And unless the remedial programs can also teach critical thinking and analytical skills, a highly unlikely possibility, these students may be little better than what Enzensberger has satirically called "second order illiterates," a "subspecie" with an adaptive talent for getting things done. They will "decipher instructions on appliances and tools . . . and decode pictograms . . . but [will] move within an environment hermetically sealed against anything that might infect [their] consciousness" (13). Enzensberger's description is exaggerated, of course, but based on changes we have seen in the last few years, particularly based on what we in community colleges know about huge numbers of today's college freshmen, we can already see these traits in too many of our present marginally prepared students. Regardless of ethnic background, regardless of color, these students do not read, do not write, and, according to Walter Karp, do not think (27). They learn visually; need models, examples, and guided practice; prefer group work to solitary carrells; allow word processing programs to do their editing; and as the second "you know" generation, refuse to struggle over precision either in writing or in speech. In English classes, we recognize these students by their questions: "how long do you want it," "how much will it count," and "when is it due." If in that way they seem a bit like the eager-to-please students of the early 50s, we know that they differ in the way they resist assignments requiring organization and creativity. They require explicit instruction. We call them unacademic in part because they are so unlike us; honestly, though, they are unacademic because they do not read and because they are undisciplined, like the culture that has shaped them. But that culture has also pushed them to college. And in this era of academic and fiscal accountability, when we now project long-range, state-mandated tracking of students from remedial enrollments to completion of public college work, these are the students whose withdrawals we will have to document, whose failures we will have to explain.

Facing then this future, we could search for minority teachers to fill our faculty vacancies, thinking surely a minority can understand the needs of the increasing numbers of minority students. But as much as we do need minority teachers to serve as role models for the students and to revitalize us as well, Fields reports that prospective teachers from minority populations in Texas fail the pre-professional skills tests at the rate of 67 percent for blacks and 54 percent for Hispanics, compared to 19 percent for whites. Other states have comparable figures (34). So the answer to the question "who will teach the students of the 90s" is "we will."

What will we teach? I hope we will follow the lead of schools which are embracing writing across the curriculum, classic cores, and humanities enrichment programs. I applaud all such developments, but not because they emphasize the Greeks or Western Civilization or more writing. In truth, I applaud any force which weakens the strong compartmentalization and blind educational specialization that have caused us to lose sight of the interrelatedness of all knowledge. When we are specialists in small areas rather than teachers of the world's knowledge, we invariably find no value in cross-disciplinary philosophical exchanges. And without the stimulation such dialogues provide, we become impoverished intellectually. In fact, we become as ignorant in our own way as we lament that the students are in theirs. And when that happens, "We . . . operate information-rich but experience-poor schools" (Coleman 72).

488

If we are going to succeed as teachers of students in the 90s, regardless of our settings, we must be willing to broaden our perspectives. And that does not mean that we have to go searching for "relevance." Indeed, what could be more relevant to our goals of teaching the broad purposes of writing, the patterns of history, and the thinking required for analysis than to show the interrelatedness of fields of knowledge. As English teachers we could show Leonard Bernstein's fine essays about music, or Charles Darwin's extraordinary metaphors, or even Ivan Lendl's tennis journals. What about Freud's remarkable diaries or his often overlooked correspondence with Einstein? If we could discuss Isaac Asimov as a biochemist, or William Carlos Williams as a doctor, and if our colleagues in history or business could point out that Henry Ford and Henry James were contemporaries, our campuses would be enlivened for everyone, teacher and student alike. Understand that I am not proposing that English teachers teach biochemistry or history teachers teach James. But I suggest that unless what we teach connects somehow to what our colleagues teach, and unless it all connects to the world students struggle in, they will leave our classes unchanged, no better than they were when they arrived. And then we can rightly be charged with educational fraud.

As teachers of liberal arts and sciences, traditionally charged with responsibility for literacy, the changes we face in the 90s may seem overwhelming, especially because many of us are accustomed to academic inertia. As historian David Russell has said, "ten—or thirty—years may not be enough to change century old university priorities and classroom practices" (193). Yet given the societal changes we see, we must act; and the actions required are not really revolutionary. All that is needed is for one group on a campus to take the lead. We may have to do things uncharacteristic for us—for instance, we may need to become more vocal about higher salaries for teachers at all levels. Surely we rhetoricians can find a way to make an example of the fact that Japanese teachers, whose students are praised throughout the world, are paid on a scale equivalent to that of Japanese engineers.

But less political tasks must also be done. We can insist that faculty development programs include speakers who are specialists on how people learn. This particular subject connects directly, as we know, to the philosophical foundation for writing as process and writing across the curriculum programs. We can support proposals for smaller classes across the disciplines. We can initiate informal conversations among teachers of all disciplines and co-sponsor outstanding speakers from all disciplines. And if these tasks seem distasteful, we must at least scrutinize our own syllabi to see how much of what we teach is there just because it is what we were taught. We can at least scrutinize our methods to see if we, the teachers for the 90s, are teaching the way we were taught three decades ago. Our students of the 90s will not require diluted or edited courses, but they will require more active courses. Less lecture, more discussion, varied assignments, more connections to the world of experience—this must be the agenda of college teachers of the next decade. This must be our agenda now.

WORKS CITED

Denton, Tommy. "Dropout Problem." *Fort Worth Star-Telegram* 5 May 1989, 34.
"Education in a New Century." *U.S. News & World Report* 9 May 1983, A5.
Enzensberger, Hans Magnus. "In Praise of Illiteracy." *Harper's*, October 1986, 12–14.
Fields, Cheryl M. "Poor Test Scores Bar Many Minority Students from Teacher Training." *The Chronicle of Higher Education*, 2 November 1988, 1, 32.
Geisel, Paul. An unpublished demographic study done through auspices of Department of Urban Studies, University of Texas at Arlington, Texas.
Johnston, Janice. "Moslem Teen Allowed to Miss Class for Prayer." *Fort Worth Star-Telegram*, 2 May 1989, 1.
Karp, Walter. "Why Johnny Can't Think." *Harper's*, June 1986, 27–35.
Quehl, Gary H. *Higher Education and the Public Interest: A Report to the Campus.* Washington, D.C.: Council for Advancement and Support of Education, January 1988.
Russell, D. R. "Writing Across the Curriculum and the Communication Movement: Some Lessons from the Past." *CCC* 38, 184–93.

11

PEDAGOGY:
OPPORTUNITIES IN THE CLASSROOM

CURRICULAR COHERENCE IN ACTION: THE OPPORTUNITIES AFFORDED BY NORMAL CLASSES

Derek Baker

University of North Texas

The four student sessions—the only ones—programmed into the 1989 Conference relate both to its concern with the debate on the Core and the Canon, and to the previous year's discussion of curricular coherence and interdisciplinary development. The intention in setting up these sessions was twofold: first, to inject practical example and evidence directly related to university teaching, and stemming from it, into what was, overall, a body of theoretical and abstract discussion and debate, and secondly, to demonstrate that 'normal courses'—that is, courses which have a strictly departmental and subject character and place—afford ample opportunity for wide-ranging, interdisciplinary work and expression. There need, in fact, be no necessity to construct new courses and structures, with all the consequent delays and problems, if we are prepared fully to use and exploit the opportunities afforded to us by our normal teaching.

The four undergraduate papers all derived from a senior-level course on 'Revolution and Romanticism,' and were presented by each student as their major paper in that class, which was conducted as a seminar, and which additionally required the preparation and presentation by each student of a substantial topic in class each week. These four papers were also presented, in company with two others from the class, at the Third National Undergraduate Research Conference at San Antonio in April 1989. Each paper embodies the personal choice, and personal interests, of the student, who had a free hand, subject to consultation with the course director, in the choice of a subject. In no case did the choice of subject stem from suggestions made by the course director.

It will be plain from the content of the four papers that the subject matter of the course ranged widely beyond the usual bounds of history courses. Literature, thought, ideas, psychology, music are evident in these papers, and other papers not presented here, and the weekly class discussions, touched on the visual arts, architecture, philosophy, socio-economic and political developments, and science and religion. In short, nothing was excluded on principle, by program planning or by subject/discipline delineation: anything germane or of interest could be included. It has been suggested that in this perspective this cannot be called a 'normal' course: it may in fact and practice not be a 'usual' course, but it is wholly normal if advantage of all the possibilities in teaching such a course is taken. Further, it should not be assumed that such an approach is only applicable in history courses, which have the capacity to embrace the consideration of what are frequently distinguished as other disciplines; all courses, in their different areas, and subject to their differing technical requirements, are open to this treatment if those teaching them wish to essay it. Nor is it necessary for a course director to be an expert, confident in his expertise, in all the fields enumerated; not only is that manifestly impossible, it would also probably work against the full exploitation of the opportunities afforded. Shared ignorance or partial ignorance, uncertainty and doubt shared by teacher and taught, provided that they are accompanied by shared interest and developing enthusiasm, and the excitement of shared discovery, are aids not impediments in the teaching of a course—any course—and the objective is to encourage enthusiasm, interest, initiative, and to promote individual thought and expression.

To what extent these objectives were approached can be assessed from the papers here presented—both the undergraduate contributions which have been discussed, and the two graduate papers which derived from a graduate seminar on 'Literature, Culture and Society in the Later Middle Ages': in all material respects the graduate seminar was conducted in exactly the same way as the undergraduate course. Perhaps it would be better if we concerned ourselves less with the 'American Mind,' whether open or closed, with 'cultural literacy,' whether itemised or not, or with Canon and Core, however defined, and more with the riches of normality, waiting to be exploited.

THE LYRICAL AGE

Roslyn Coates

University of North Texas

The French Revolution is held responsible for the bloody birth of the modern political era, and is credited with inventing many now vital political concepts, such as ideologies, propaganda, and mass political mobilization.[1] And yet, for all the attention focused on the revolution, it remains mysterious. Hosts of historians have attempted to unravel the enigma of the revolution, particularly its causes and effects. But the revolution becomes ever more enigmatic as it is buried more deeply under different interpretations, all full of hindsight, and the revolutionary experience is lost.

The three major interpretations are the Marxist, the Tocquevillian, and the revisionist. The Marxist interpretation is perhaps the clearest, since Marxist theologians allow no mystery in their faith. The French Revolution according to Marx was the climax of the class struggle between revolutionary bourgeoisie and aging aristocracy, ending with the triumphant bourgeoisie making France safe for capitalism.[2] The Tocquevillian interpretation, while admitting class tensions as a factor, does not regard class conflict as the primary instigator, and does not recognize any class as emerging victorious from the revolution. Instead, it sees the concentration of power in the hands of the monarchy as the underlying cause, for the monarchy had had to remove many political powers from the nobility to consolidate its own power, and, by doing so, made the nobles' remaining social privileges unbearably odious to the other classes. The revolutionaries may bravely have believed that they were deposing monarchical rule, but they were really creating a modern and more powerful centralized state in the image of the old monarchy.[3] The revisionists heavily attack the Marxists: Alfred Cobban, the principal exponent of the revisionist interpretation, argues that the revolution was not conducted by the bourgeoisie, but by declining *officiers* and professionals. The revolution, says Cobban, helped the landowners and hindered capitalism. The extreme revisionists claim that the revolution was an accident, caused by misunderstandings between the nobles and the bourgeoisie.[4] For example, Richard Cobb, an extremist, says, "The *sans-culotte* then is not a social or economic being; he is a political accident."[5]

Each interpretation is ultimately unsatisfying, because with hindsight, it shrouds the revolution, depriving it of its original lyrical intensity. They are guilty of the charges that Manzoni, the great Italian romantic poet, brought against history: they confine themselves to "events which are only known from the outside. . . ." The tremendous passions of the revolutionaries are "passed over in silence by history"; these passions can be revealed only in "the domain of poetry."[6] For the romanticism of the era, though often assessed separately, was as intertwined with the revolutionary movements as the bones of Victor Hugo's Quasimodo with those of La Esmeralda. Their relationship is expressed well by Wordsworth, who, in the Preface to the *Lyrical Ballads*, defined poetry as "the spontaneous overflow of powerful feelings"; the same can be said of revolution.

The grand patriarch of both revolution and romanticism is Rousseau, author of the *Social Contract* (1762) and the *Confessions* (1781–88). Indeed, his celebrated observation in the *Confessions* that "I am not made like anyone I have seen: I dare believe I am not made like anyone in existence. If I am not better, at least I am different" has been hailed as "the battle cry of the entire Romantic Movement."[7] This statement sums up the romantic fascination with the individual, the subjective experience, and the strange; but at the end of the *Confessions*, Rousseau also observes that "everything is related to politics."[8]

Rousseau was related to politics in a strange way, for though he wrote disapprovingly of revolution, his work was the guiding star of the French revolutionaries; Robespierre said he would be ". . . happy if I can remain faithful to the inspirations I imbibed from your texts."[9] One of the main ideas taken by the revolutionaries from Rousseau was his most mystical; the general will, a concept developed in the *Social Contract*. Rousseau says that ". . . the general will is found by counting the votes," but the vote may be misleading, for it "must be general in its object as well as in its essence."[10] The general will, therefore, is quite different from the "sum of private wills," which can "cause the ruin of the body politic."[11] Essentially, the general will is the mysterious expression of the body politic, which always, by Rousseau's definition, wills what is best for the body politic. References to the general will run rampant throughout the revolutionaries' constitutions and rhetoric, and the desire to implement faithfully the general will led to a longing for political transparency. Like Andre Breton, they dreamed of living in a glass house, with no distinction between the private and the general will. This desire for transparency also helped engender conspiracy paranoia, for a faction was not of the general will, and what was not of the general will was against it, and what was against the general will was against the revolutions, against the *Patrie*. The blood of the Terror was necessary to consecrate the revolutionaries' glass house.

The revolutionaries also believed that their revolution was as original as Rousseau's works; Robespierre declared in a speech to the Convention, "The theory of revolutionary government is as new as the Revolution which created it."[12] Since the whole nation was to be regenerated by the revolution, new forms of symbolic power were created to replace the old. The king's body, the highest symbol of the old monarchical power, was destroyed, and the tricolor cockade, the liberty tree, and the goddess of Liberty rushed in to fill the vacuum.[13] No longer did the people cry *vive le Roi* in homage to the King; they shouted *vive la Nation* as they danced about the liberty tree.

But dance needs song to accompany it; the dance of liberty was new, and required a new form of lyricism. One of the first to recognize this need was Mme de Stael, who observed in *On Literature* (1800), "Nothing in art must be stationary, and art becomes petrified when it ceases to change."[14] She believed that romantic poetry, free from the rubric of classicism and expressing only the poet's own feelings and experiences, should be the poetry of liberty.[15] The old legendary hero, the knight-errant, was soon replaced by the heralds of the new song: the poets-errant.

The most idealistic of the poets-errant was Shelley, who was deeply influenced by his father-in-law, William Godwin, author of the first treatise of modern anarchism, *An Enquiry Concerning Political Justice*. Like Godwin, Shelley believed that a revolution of mind, not of blood, is necessary to free men from the bondage of kings and priests. After such a revolution, men will live together in a spirit of universal benevolence, and government, which will no longer be necessary, will wither away. In his *Defense of Poetry*, Shelley proclaimed that poets and artists should lead men to this blissful anarchy, for "A man, to be greatly good, must imagine intensely and comprehensively. . . . The great instrument of moral good is the imagination, and poetry administers to the effect by acting upon the cause."[16] Poets are, then, "the unacknowledged legislators of the world." Shelley, like a revolutionary, attacked tyranny, declaring in *Queen Mab*,

> Power, like a desolation pestilence,
> Pollutes whate'er it touches; and obedience,
> Bane of all genius, virtue, freedom, truth,
> Makes slaves of men, and, of the human frame,
> A mechanised automaton.[17]

and praised the future society, prophesying in *The Revolt of Islam*:

> Our toil from thought all glorious forms shall cull,
> To make this Earth, our time, more beautiful,
> And Science, and her sister Poesy,
> Shall clothe in light the fields and cities of the free![18]

England, however, was not very interested in Shelley's poetic prophecies, for it had already had its fill of revolutionary upheaval; the duke of Devonshire expressed a widespread sentiment, when, in response to a Frenchwoman's inquiry as to why England was able to implement democratic principles more peacefully than France, he said, "Madame, the reason is quite obvious. We cut off our king's head a hundred and forty-four years before you did yours."[19] Wordsworth and Coleridge, the first generation of English romantics, were much more representative of England's general feeling towards revolution than Shelley was. They were both initially elated by the French Revolution: as Wordsworth wrote in Book VI of *The Prelude*, "Europe at that time was thrilled with joy,/France standing on the top of golden hours,/ And human nature seeming born again."[20] But after France declared war on England, and the Committee of Public Safety set up its revolutionary regime, Wordsworth became disillusioned: "It was a lamentable time for man,/Whether a hope had e'er been his or not;"[21] Coleridge wrote in a letter of April, 1789, "I have snapped my squeaking baby-trumpet of sedition, and the fragments lie scattered in the lumber room of penitence. I wish to be a good man and a Christian, but I am no Whig, no Reformist, no Republican."[22]

In *Don Juan*, Lord Byron ridiculed the Lake Poets for becoming conservative:

> I would not imitate the petty thought,
>   Nor coin my self-love to so base a vice,
> For all the glory your conversion brought,
>   Since gold alone should not have been its price.
> You have your salary: was't for that you wrought?
>   And Wordsworth has his place in the Excise.
> You're shabby fellows—true—but poets still,
>   And duly seated on the immortal hill.[23]

Byron himself was a notorious liberal, who made his first speech to the House of Lords on behalf of workingmen and who died in Missolonghi while trying to rally forces to free Greece from the Turks. But in England, Byron's lyricism of liberty flowed as a "banner, torn, but flying,/Streams like a thunderstorm against the wind,"[24] and in his eyes "the grand *primum mobile* of England is cant;"[25] so, after his treatment of his wife had alienated him from English society, Byron went abroad, for, "When a man hath no freedom to fight for at home,/Let him combat for that of his neighbors."[26] The Byronic myth cast its spell over Europe, as Byron, the *Childe Harold*, wandered the continent.

In Italy, Byron was welcomed by the liberal Italian intellectuals, and became involved in the *carbonari* movement in 1821,[27] which he described as "a grand object—the very poetry of politics."[28] Both his romantic life (and death) and his romantic poetry greatly inspired the Italian liberals. Mazzini, a prominent leader of the Risorgimento, said in an 1830 essay "At Naples, in the Romagna, wherever he saw a spark which might break into flame, he was ready to come to the fore, ready for the fight. . . . Such was Byron's life, furiously tossed between present ills and future hopes."[29] Cavour, another great leader, recorded in one of his notebooks a quotation from *Childe Harold*:

> Hereditary Bondsmen! know ye not
> Who would be free themselves must strike the blow?
> By their right arms the conquest must be wrought?
> Will Gaul or Muscovite redress ye? No!
> True, they may lay your proud despoilers low,
> But not for you will freedom's altar flame.

Close by this quotation, Cavour noted, "What Lord Byron says in defense of the abused Greeks can be said to the justification of all the other nations, who groan in bondage, and are reproached for the vices that their tyrants have given them."[30] Clearly, Byron's romantic life as a poet-errant, as well as his romantic poetry, was inspiration to the Italian liberals.

They did not really need Byron, however, for Italy was abounding with poets-errant. Napoleon's consolidation of Northern Italy into the Italian Republic had fired hopes for Italian independence and unity, and, as the romantic Giovanni Berchet observed in his *Lettera simiseria di Grisostomo* (1811), "a common literary fatherland" would be necessary to form "a common political fatherland."[31] The Italian romantics—Monti, Foscolo, Porta, Pellico, Giusti, Grossi, D'Azeglio, Settembrini, Nievo, Grerrazzi, Aleardi, Praga, and Manzoni—were all highly aware of this link between literary and political independence. The best-known of the Italian poets-errant was Alessandro Manzoni, who, though too religious to take up the sword, did take up the pen with great fervor. In *Marzo, 1812*, he proclaimed:

> Oh foreigners, Italy now lately returns
> To her own heritage, reclaims her soil;
> Oh foreigners, asunder strike your tents
> From a land which is not mother to you.[32]

Manzoni's lyrics, and the poetry of the other Italian romantics, "colored the Risorgimento with idealistic hues of an artistic nature perhaps unmatched in political movements anywhere."[33]

Goethe received Manzoni's ode to Napoleon, *Il cinque maggio*, with great enthusiasm, and quickly translated it into German.[34] For Germany, which was also struggling for liberation and unification, had its share of poets-errant.

Prominent amongst these poets was Heinrich Heine, who was once lauded as the "German Byron" by one of his admirers.[35] He once claimed, "I have never set great store by poetic glory, and whether my songs are praised or blamed matters little to me. But lay a sword on my bier, for I have been a good soldier in the wars of human liberation."[36] Heine's lyrical evocation of these wars, however, assures that he can be remembered as both soldier and poet. In *Enfant perdu*, for example, he sang of the soldier-poet:

> I fought to hold positions that were lost
> In Freedom's war for thirty faithful years.
> Without a hope to win, despite the cost
> I battled on, expecting only tears.
> Those nights, I often battled weariness
> And fear too (only fools are not afraid)—
> I'd chirp, to banish these in my distress,
> The saucy rhymes of mocking songs I made.[37]

In his satires, *Deutschland* and *Atta Troll*, Heine used bitter ridicule as a weapon against his enemies. These poems made his work an integral part of the Young Germany movement that preceded the revolutions of 1848.[38]

Heine was driven from Germany in 1831 for his liberal views, and since he believed that the French were the "chosen people" of the new religion of freedom, he went to Paris.[39] France, the creator and stronghold of neo-classicism, but by the time Heine arrived at Paris, France was full of poets-errant, mixing literary and political careers. Alphonse de Lamartine championed the democratic and nationalist Society of Rumanian Students in Paris, was involved in the February Revolution of 1848, and was a part of the provisional government set up after Louis Philippe abdicated.[40] His political career ended with the rise of Napoleon III, and from 1852 until his death he lived a life of quiet poverty. Victor Hugo served as a representative in the 1848 National Assembly, and though he supported Louis Napoleon then, his increasingly liberal views caused his newspaper, *L'Evénement*, to be confiscated in 1851. Hugo's biting response, *Aprés Auguste, Augustule*, began his career of overt hostility towards Louis Napoleon, which eventually lead to his expulsion in 1852. Hugo settled on the island of Guernsey in 1855, which was so close to France that his voice could still be heard across the Channel.[41] Both Lamartine and Hugo were also among the first romantic French poets: Lamartine's *Les Méditations poétiques* (1820) are regarded "as marking the beginning of French romantic poetry;"[42] Victor Hugo's *Hernani* was so sensational when it was first produced in 1830 that it caused "a battle between the romanticists who applauded and the classicists who hissed."[43]

The two poets' struggle for poetical liberty and political liberty was essentially the same struggle, for, as Hugo observed in his preface to *Hernani*, "there is, or should be, a connection between liberty in literature and liberty in the state."[44] The poets-errant made that connection, with their lyrical lives and poetry.

Nor can revolutions be understood without making that connection. Poets may not be, as Shelley proclaimed, "the unacknowledged legislators of the world," but they are indispensable guides, for revolutions are ultimately ineffable, and cannot be comprehended by a purely rational approach. The dance about the liberty tree is as intoxicating as the blood that flows freely as wine, and intoxication is a mixture of revulsion and ecstasy. History may debate the causes and effects of revolution, but only poetry can unveil the horrifying beauty of the revolutionary experience, for "Poetry is intoxication, and man drinks in order to merge with it. For that reason, revolutions are lyrical and in need of lyricism."[45]

NOTES

The Lyrical Age is the original title of a novel by Milan Kundera, which examines the relationship between the three entities composing the trinity Youth/Revolution/Poetry. He later changed it to *Life is Elsewhere*, though he preferred the first title. I am happy to resurrect the original.

1. Lynn Hunt, *Politics, Culture, and Class in the French Revolution* (Berkeley: University of California Press, 1984), 2–3.

2. *Ibid*, 3–4.

3. *Ibid*. 6–7.

4. *Ibid*, 4–5.

5. *Ibid*, 149.

6. Gian Piero Barricelli, *Alessandro Manzoni* (Boston: Twayne Publishers, 1967), 99.

7. "Romantic Movement," *The Reader's Companion to World Literature*, (1973), 457.

8. Lee Cameron McDonald, *Western Political Theory from its Origins to the Present* (New York: Harcourt, Brace & World, Inc., 1968), 397.

9. Carol Blum, *Rousseau and the Republic of Virtue* (Ithaca, New York: Cornell University Press, 1986), 35.

10. McDonald, 394.

11. *Ibid*, 392, 394.

12. D. I. Wright, ed., *The French Revolution: Introductory Documents* (St. Lucia, Queensland: University of Queensland Press, 1974), 199.

13. Hunt, 55.

14. Renee Winegarten, *Mme de Stael*, (Dover, Hew Hampshire: Berg Publishers Ltd., 1985), 89–90.

15. *Ibid*.

16. R. W. Harris, *Romanticism and the Social Order: 1780–1830* (London: Blandford Press Ltd., 1969), 20.

17. *Ibid*, 288.

18. *Ibid*, 297.

19. R. J. White, *The Horizon Concise History of England*, (New York: American Heritage Publishing Co., 1971), 92.

20. Harris, 70.

21. *Ibid*, 177.

22. *Ibid*, 218–19.

23. George Gordon, Lord Byron, *Don Juan*, in *Writers of the Western World*, (New York: Houghton Mifflin Co., 1942), 696–97.

24. Vivian Pinto, *Byron and Liberty*, (Folcroft, PA: The Folcroft Press, 1969), 18.

25. Harris, 392.

26. *Ibid*, 342

27. Giorgio Melchiori, "Byron and Italy," *Byron's Political and Cultural Influence in Nineteenth–Century Europe*, ed. P.G. Trueblood (Atlantic Highlands, New Jersey: Humanities Press, 1981), 110, 112.

28. Robert Escarpit, "Byron and France," *Byron's Political and Cultural Influence*, ed. Trueblood, 55.

29. Melchiori, 116.

30. *Ibid*, 117–18.

31. Barricelli, 14–15.

32. *Ibid*, 51.

33. *Ibid*, 14–15

34. *Ibid*, 51.

35. Cedric Hentschel, "Byron and Germany," *Byron's Political and Cultural Influence*, ed. Trueblood, 74.

36. "Heine, Heinrich," *The Reader's Companion*, 238.

37. Heinrich Heine, "Enfant Perdu," in *Complete Poems of Heinrich Heine: A Modern English Version*, trans. Hal Draper (Boston: Suhrkamp/Insel Publishers, 1982) 649.

38. Howard M. Jones, *Revolution and Romanticism*, (Cambridge, Mass: Harvard University Press, 1974), 402, 439.

39. "Heine, Heinrich," *The Reader's Companion*, 238.

40. E. Y. Short, "Chronology of Events," *Intellectuals and Revolution*, ed. Eugene Kamenka and F.B. Smith (New York: St. Martin's Press, 1974), 139, 141.

41. Robert T. Denomme, *Nineteenth–Century French Romantic Poets*, (Edwardsville: Southern Illinois University Press, 1969), 101–02.

42. "Lamartine, Alphonse de," *The Reader's Companion*, 291.

43. Jones, 379.

44. *Ibid*, 380.

45. Milan Kundera, *The Art of the Novel* (New York: Harper & Row, 1988), 138.

FABLE, FALLIBILITY, AND HISTORICAL REALITY

Michael Tate

University of North Texas

Revolutions are strange, complex historical events which ebb, flow, and alter in shades chamelion-like according to their locations, atmospheres, and motivations. Even reflected upon in hindsight they retain their mystery. One person who claims an event is an excellent example of revolution will often be vehemently countered by someone who believes with equal conviction the same event was not revolutionary at all. In spite of such contradiction nobody has ever denied their existence. What Thomas Jefferson called "the course of human events" turns the fate of men through progressions and regressions, moving them to begin processes through which they intend to set their "course" right. All nations of all times have experienced revolution of some fashion, whether military, political, or social.

When scholars study revolutions they usually involve themselves with the examples of socio-economic phenomena or comparative case studies. This is good and purposeful research, and in a scientific way is very informative. But rarely has the universality of revolutionary cause been studied; not the mere connective or cause and effect relationships, but rather the influential processes which are similar to all peoples who seek change: the urge to create an improved, more fair and judicious way of life. Beneath all the politics is this uniqueness of experience which moves the Earth's peoples to revolt. By seeking out these types of experiences in two particular locations it may be possible for us to gain a fuller understanding of revolutions and their ultimate results.

Such a uniqueness of experience exists for the Irish and the Italians. These nations have similarities which can be traced back several centuries. Both began as independent nations descended from ancient peoples: the peninsular Italians descended from the ancient Latins, Etruscans, and the settlers of Sicily; the Irish descended from the ancient Celtic people and, much later, were affected by the settlement of the English and Scottish Protestants. By the beginning of the nineteenth century both lands were under the dominion or influence of a foreign empire: the Italians subject to Austrian power in the north and the direct influence of the Bourbons in the south; the Irish actually incorporated into the United Kingdom by the Act of Union of 1800. In the revolutionary spirit which swept the continent in the nineteenth century both lands would attempt to throw off the shackles of foreign domination and assert a homogeneous culture decreed by the intellectuals within the movements, and in both cases, these enterprises would ultimately unravel into epic tragedy of divided, divergent peoples sharing the same land.

Each national movement shared aspects with the other which shed some understanding on the events and destinies of their actions. In the structure of revolutionary bodies, the Irish borrowed the models created by the Italians. When the movement for repeal of the Act of Union died with its leader Daniel O'Connell in 1847, Irish political leadership passed to a group of young, idealistic radicals committed not only to repeal but to outright independence. They founded the organization Young Ireland. They attempted an uprising in 1848, the year of revolutions, but were stopped before they even began, and the leaders were sentenced to the penal colony at Van Dieman's Land.[1] The structure of their group was based on a continental movement begun by the Italian patriot Giuseppe Mazzini. He founded Young Italy in 1832 to educate and train young men for the struggle for a unified Italy, a new nation derived from a historic past by new, young, educated minds. Back in Ireland, after the fall of Young Ireland, there arose another large, powerful nationalist movement known as Fenianism. Its influence was so great it stretched across the Atlantic Ocean and gained many devotees among the Irish immigrants in North America. The Fenian structure was cellular and secretive, the master plan known only to a few. This was borrowed directly from the secret revolutionary brotherhood which nurtured many of the activists in Northern Italy, the Carbonari.

What the Italian experience derived from the Irish was very different. It was not political or structural but rather intellectual, an *ex post facto* application of thought. Through the study and application of works by the Irish nationalist writers it is possible to gain some insight into, and perspective on, the movement which led to peninsular unification and the formation of the Kingdom of Italy, and reveal with artistic clarity some of the contradictions and fallacies within it. Due to the problems of regional divisions and linguistic variations across the peninsula the creation of a single body of representative Italian literature was almost impossible, if only because the people spoke no one common tongue. The Irish were not handicapped by such divisions. With the benefit of a common language and several individuals of exceptional talent the Irish literary movement worked to create for Ireland a chronicle of both past and present, the sum of all their ages. Through the work of great poets and dramatists like William Butler Yeats and John Millington Synge, the struggle which climaxed in creation of the Irish Free State is chronicled in the prolific nuances of their poetry and drama.

In the absence of such a homogeneous body of Italian works the student must turn elsewhere to find revelations and enlightenment on matters which defy the cold and simple historical facts of names, dates, and places to seek the motivations in the hearts of great and lowly men, for a person's body is useless. Such is the case with Italian unification. Through vision and ideology the Kingdom of Italy was formed, Spiritually, both in 1870 and long afterwards, it lacked a unity of mind and spirit, of ethos. Although this lack of a cohesive Italian literature cripples the social historian, it can be overcome, to some extent, by using the honest, artfully-realized Irish nationalist literature, a viable alternative considering the similar revolutionary histories, and the avowed purpose of both the Italians and the Irish to create nations from dubious national legacies.

The unification of Italy, of course, was not the result of one single action or reaction but rather a flux of many factors pushing and pulling simultaneously to achieve a result. These actions and reactions took their form in the two major figures of the movement: the revolutionary Giuseppe Mazzini, and the Piedmontese Prime Minister, Camillo di Cavour. These two men of radically-different ideology, disposition, and delusion managed to unite the peninsula despite each other. Denis Mack Smith characterized Mazzini as singleminded and oversimplified, popularly-successful despite "the obvious faults in some of his facts and theories,"[2] and Cavour as a "professional politician" who had "little patience with theories" and "a fairly elastic conscience."[3] Together, these men are like Christopher Mahon, the divided title-character of John Millington Synge's drama *The Playboy of the Western World.*

Christopher is a man on the run who brags of committing patricide one minute, and runs scared at a knocking on the door the next; boasting and bellowing, defying and cowering with no balance in his personality. In the end he returns home the same way he was before—an addled mixture of anger, resignation, romance, and reality—with his father, not undead but never dead. Christopher Mahon was a hero of impressions, the "champion playboy of the Western World"[4] right up until he had to reckon with the truth, and his characteristics combined to create a realistic, inglorious person.

The result of Italian unification was the same. The nation which arose was part Mazzini and mostly Cavour, a reflection of neither man's goal, but rather an aggregate whose reality was far from the ideal.

Mazzini's interpretation of history was not altogether flawless. He believed in a romanticized vision of a Republican Rome which, "Behind its eagles wings" said Mazzini, "furrowed the known world with the idea of Right, the source of Liberty."[5] He neglected the bold imperialism and internal dissension of the Roman Republic and its similarities with the Austrians whom he wished to run from the peninsula. His subjective interpretations of Right and Liberty would also have lost their peculiar definitions if placed equally upon the Hapsburg Empire. His misuse and misapplication of historical fact are irreconcilable to his situation and thus undermined his assumptions.

Cavour was the man who would wear the laurel of unifier. However, he was not the great Italian patriot of unification. As late as 1859, Cavour was telling Louis Napoleon that unification was "nonsense."[6] Cavour fancied himself a diplomat and enjoyed moving in the circles of the great statesman but had no qualms about capitalizing on the successes or failures of his foes at home. Derek Beales characterized Cavour as a politician who "showed his skill less in forward planning than in brilliant exploitation of changing circumstances."[7] Thus when the situation presented itself Cavour coalesced the peninsula into the realm of the Piedmontese royal family and the Kingdom of Italy was born. In the end, Cavour was not so much an Italian national patriot as Italian royalist.

After looking at the men who achieved unification we turn to look at the people upon whom their actions would fall. The Italian peninsula is a mostly agrarian land and its inhabitants were mostly peasant. They were not unlike most other European peasants, trapped in the hard, regular cycle of debt and taxation. Their lives were hard, mean, and short in comparison to modern standards. They were usually, if not always, illiterate and formally unschooled. As a result they often lacked the intellectual capabilities of the men who ruled them, and of the men who desired to end that rule. In the end, the Italian peasants were caught in the middle of the process, if not completely missed altogether, their loyalties crossed in a literal tug of war, not knowing which side would provide them with the means not merely to live a better life but simply to maintain the ability to stay alive.

The divisions which pulled on the Italian masses were strong and complex, perhaps even more complex than those of other European nations. The Irish, for example, had an agrarian class strongly unified in its mutual agrarian desire for private ownership of their lands. In Eastern Europe the ties that bound were cultural and linguistic among peoples which were not yet nations. The Italians were not unified in any of these ways. Their problems were too ancient and complex to be brushed away by these simpler "unities." They faced the ancient cultural divisions of the peninsula, the differences which made Tuscans and Lombards and Venetians and Sicilians completely different peoples in regard to culture, loyalties, and development. Furthermore, Italian peasantry would be forced to face the intellectual opposition to the Roman Catholic church and the fifty-nine year stand-off between the Kingdom of Italy and the Vatican. There was much more to be overcome than abstract geographical divisions or the temporal authority of the Popes in the struggle to unify.

These differences amongst the peoples of the peninsula, coupled with the illiteracy and lack of education among them, made the voice of the masses virtually inaudible. Italian literature of the period was almost entirely intellectual. Foscolo's poetry was the voice of intellectual romanticism, and Manzoni's *The Betrothed* a carefully constructed and scholarly exercise in the genre of the historical novel, a point underlined by the author's meticulous translation of the novel into the Tuscan dialect as part of the movement to unify and create an Italian language.

The voice of a people in revolt is to be found in the literary careers of the Irish nationalist writers. The most outstanding and successful of these writers is, of course, the poet Yeats, whose ability to record in verse the events of his age take on a universality and timelessness which make his poems of 1913 and 1916 as striking today as they were then. In regard to the Italian unification they can be especially poignant, giving, by extension and implication, to a people without a voice one which reveals the experiences of a mutual effort, a mutual suffering.

The Irish poet and essayist George Russell composed a poem in the early 1920s entitled *The Lost Others*. In this poem a man is talking about having found the woman of his dreams and pondering who she really is, where she came from, what she left behind, and what he should do now that he has her. She is what he desired, but all the lingering questions leave her essentially irreconcilable to the vision in his imagination. The unified Italy fell victim to the same misgivings as the troubled lover. The goal was accomplished and the struggle was over. What next?

Perhaps the grandest failure of the unification was a lack of vision for the future. Cavour had little vision, dubious purpose, and died the year after unification was accomplished. He left behind a nation divided by the temporal domain of the Pope and a lingering disunity between the peoples of North and South. And Mazzini's legacy, the ideological "redemption of Rome,"[8] ultimately found only perverse success in the rise of Mussolini and the Fascist state. In reality there was little more to Italian unity in 1861 than the geographic consolidation of political power. Once together, the country lacked the sense and spirit of a nation, retaining only political power and lacking purpose.

To further complicate matters there was a certain popular lack of support for unification which stretched all the way back to the Treaty of Vienna in 1814. At that time the cause of Italian unification was still the domain of the intellectuals. Mazzini's Young Italy, as well as his Young Europe, were not the vastly-popular organizations he led many to believe, and the accounting of their memberships often suffered from Mazzini's own inflation.[9] The Italian immigrants in North and South America, a significantly smaller group of people at that time than would migrate after unification, were in most cases exiles, driven out by the Austrians, who would never return. Although they always revered their homelands Garibaldi was the only major figure to return vigorously. And even Garibaldi's Red Shirts found the Sicilians willing to fight Bourbon rule but much less favorably-inclined towards the cause of unification.

As Derek Beales points out, there were many forces in Italian life opposed to unification: the Roman Catholic Church and Roman Catholics as a body, the working classes, and those who desired more local and regional autonomy, especially the regionalists in Sicily.[10] And once the great figures were gone—

Cavour in 1861 and Mazzini in 1871—the nation was left to be held together by men to whom posterity has been indifferent. Within forty years the whole would collapse, just as the place in Yeats' universal masterpiece *The Second Coming* does. Italy was a state where "the centre cannot hold" and "the ceremony of innocence" was lost. The Italy of vision was not real, and the reality was no vision. Mazzini and Garibaldi lost their faith as "the best lack all conviction, while the worst are full of passionate intensity."[11] Mussolini would be the sum of the unification, the Italian "second coming," "a shape with lion body and the head of a man."

But it was not until this "second coming" that Italy was reunited with perhaps the single strongest element of her identity: the Roman Catholic Church. By the mid-nineteenth century the Papacy had become a regularly-Italian position, the religion guided around the world by a man of peninsular origins, and within his spiritual authority he was generally the most widely respected leader of the region.[12] During the European restoration after Napoleon's defeat the Pope's temporal authority was restored and, while not necessarily being more liberal, the church was becoming much more rational, placing less importance on the repression of heretical ideologies, and reviving the Jesuit order in 1814. The intellectual nationalists had begun with very intense religious sensibilities. Silvio Pellico and Alessandro Manzoni were both men who subscribed to a strict Catholicism, and Vicenzo Gioberti's *Of the Moral and Civil Primacy of the Italians* proposed an Italian nation under the presidency of the Pope.[13]

The political nationalists were almost unanimously anti-clerical and completely opposed to Papal authority. Mazzini, Cavour, and Garibaldi all boldly opposed the Church at Rome and the influence she wielded. Whatever fertile ground had been laid between the two dried up when Pope Pius IX issued the Allocution of 1848, disavowing any role in the unification effort. His accession in 1846 had begun with some liberal reforms, including an amnesty for political prisoners and some constitutional reform. But with the uprisings of 1848 and the Allocution, the Pope was forced to flee Rome, and he returned only with the assistance of the Austrians. Upon his return Pius IX's exercise in liberalism was over, replaced with a radical conservatism revealed in acts like the Syllabus of Errors, an implication of his opposition to modern civilization, and the proclamation of the still controversial doctrine of Papal infallibility in 1870, the same year Rome finally fell to the Unionists.

Once again, Mazzini's lack of clarity in his historical formation of ideas is revealed in his attitudes toward the Papacy. In his vision of medieval Rome, the "Second Rome," the Popes were her center. Rome "lift[ed] the laws of earth to Heaven, superimposed upon the idea of Right the idea of Duty common to all, and therefore the source of equality."[14] In this same evocation of history Mazzini refers to the Popes as "holy once however abject today," but fails to say when they became abject, why this happened and what caused it, leaving us only to wonder whether this abjection was based on any spiritual or historic basis or was just another result of his single-minded national vision. Either way, he managed to undermine one of the only truly unified features of Italian culture. Cavour and his successors then institutionalized this anti-clericalism across the peninsula when they exported the Piedmontese laws which included a body of statues called the Siccardi Laws, separating Church and State and placing restrictions on monasteries. This collision of Italian unity and Roman Catholicism would drive Pius IX and his successors into a self-imposed imprisonment in The Vatican. Whether any attempt was made to rectify the situation is doubtful, Denis Mack Smith claiming Cavour and his successors made several "covert" attempts at reconciliation[15] while Derek Beales states Cavour made "no attempt at compromise"[16] with the Catholics. Not until Mussolini and the "second coming" of the Italian nation was a concordat with the Roman Catholic Church achieved.

It was an uncomfortable ending to the long struggle for unification that the single most powerful tool was so completely disarmed. Perhaps it was inexplicable. Amongst poets and dramatists the seeker is hard pressed to find a lyrical voice to describe such a messy finish, even among the diverse work of the Irish. Yeats, in his *Representative Irish Tales*, tried to collect stories indicative of Irish character while avoiding the obvious and divisive edges of politics and religion, and failed,[17] not for lack of trying but for the simple reason that it was not possible.

In the end the unification of Italy was a hollow victory. It did not achieve the greatness of vision which Mazzini so longed for, a place "harmonizing earth and Heaven, right and duty."[18] The unified Italy was only a qualified success, possessing the same doubtful questions Yeats would see in Dublin and record in his poem *September 1913*, memorializing the visionaries and questioning their legacies, wondering was it "For this that all this blood was shed"?

The creation of a "national identity" when studied at length, reveals in essence an endeavor of personal purpose, more often than not replete with half truths, fallacies, frauds, and occasionally the embarrassing recovery of long abandoned ideas. This is not to say that national identities are bad: they have a crucial role in everyone's life, offering each person a set of values and ideas to give his life definition, and a way of gauging his impression of the world. They give form to the common singularity of all humanity. But there is a difference between a created identity and a homogeneous one. We may follow recipes for revolution, but a cut-and-paste culture is not culture at all.

Likewise, nationalism cannot be ascribed. It must be subscribed to. Such identities must start with the mass of the people and work their way upward into the stream of intellectual thought, striking a natural balance in the process. If the process is altered, and no such balance works itself out, the result is cultural chaos. And despotism, the rose of fertile chaos, is all too often the common alternative.

It was despotism which made Italians of the Piedmontese, the Sicilians, the Venetians, the Milanese, and the other peoples of the peninsula. Today, when we speak of Italians we speak of those who share a common culture and a common language with several million others. But the follies of a Mazzini or a Cavour are fraught with dangerous possibilities, and the thin line between historical fiction and historical reality must be respected if individuals are to continue living together within the tenuous sensibilities of a nation.

NOTES

1. MacManus, Seamus, *The Story of the Irish Race* (Old Greenwich, Connecticut: The Devin-Adalr Co., 1921), 590–601.

2. Mack Smith, Denis, *The Making of Italy 1796–1870* (New York: Harper and Row, 1968), 12.

3. *Ibid.*, 12.

4. Synge, John Millington, *The Playboy of the Western World*, in *Modern Drama For Analysis,* ed. Paul M. Cubeta, (United States: Holt, Rinehart, and Winston, 1950), 305.

5. Mazzini, Giuseppe, *Selected Writings*, ed. and arr. by Nagendranath Gangulee, (Westport, Connecticut: Greenwood Press, 1974), 57.

6. Beales, Derek, *The Risorgimento and the Unification of Italy*, (New York: Barnes and Noble, Inc.), 82.

7. *Ibid.*, 76.

8. Mazzini, *Writings*, 57.

9. Beales, *Risorgimento*, 56.

10. *Ibid.*, 90–91.

11. Yeats, William Butler, *The Poems of W. B. Yeats*, (New York: Macmillan Publishing Co., 1983), 187.

12. Beales, *Risorgimento*, 48.

13. *Ibid.*, 58–59.

14. Mazzini, *Writings*, 57.

15. Mack Smith, *Making*, 396.

16. Beales, *Risorgimento*, 91.

17. Yeats, William Butler, *Representative Irish Tales*, (Atlantic Highlands, New Jersey: Humanities Press, 1979), 11.

18. Mazzini, *Writings*, 57.

THE PRACTICAL VISIONARY:
MAZZINI AND THE RISORGIMENTO

Vicki Line

University of North Texas

Though the role of the *Philosophes* and socio-political theorists has been much discussed in the occurrence and development of the French Revolution, and though the Europe-wide events of 1848 have been termed "the Revolution of the Intellectuals", in both cases the final judgement has, in general, been that the intellectuals themselves were, almost inevitably, out of touch with the facts of real life, that their theories were eclipsed, and reshaped out of all recognition, by reality, and that they themselves, like Larmartine, did, and could, play little or no decisive and permanent role in these events. It was otherwise with Mazzini, universally regarded not simply as the father of the Risorgimento, but also as the man who shaped and directed it in every practical respect. Yet, of all the revolutionary intellectuals of the age, none was more visionary, more other-worldly than Mazzini. It is this paradox, and the bases of Mazzini's reputation and success, which this paper considers.

Giuseppe Mazzini committed his heart to the Italian unification movement when, at the age of sixteen, he vowed always to wear black, symbolizing mourning for his country. He had been reared under the influence of liberal parents and was hostile to the Savoy monarchy which had absorbed Genoa. As a student, his preferred reading was the Bible, Shakespeare and Byron, Goethe and Schiller, but especially Dante, whom he viewed as a Christian and Italian. Dante and Rienzi, as well as Romanticism, Napoleon, and the French Revolution, influenced his early political ideas.

> Wherein did Mazzini differ from these distinguished predecessors and contemporaries? He set their ideas on fire. Where they were literary, he was political: where they were critical, he was constructive; where they were merely moral, he was passionately religious.[1]

Mazzini gave up literary study and turned to political activity, which led to his early involvement in the Carbonari in 1827. Accused of subversion, he was imprisoned in 1830 and later exiled. He disliked the symbolism enmeshed in the Carbonari and later became disillusioned, writing of it:

Such did the Carbonari appear to me—a huge and powerful body but without a head; an association in which not generous intentions but ideas were wanting; deficient in the science and logic which should have reduced the sentiment of nationality, prevading its ranks, to fruitful action.[2]

Mazzini came out of prison with a design for revolution and the emancipation of Italy. He believed the failure of previous revolutions was faulty leadership, the setting of political aims rather than social, and failure to use the power of the masses. Young Italy, *Giovine Italia*, was conceived to direct the movement of unifying Italy and uplifting the masses.

That youth counts not the cost was a truth he realized and turned to account.[3]

History would prove this true and would call Mazzini the father of Risorgimento. He envisioned Young Italy as "neither sect nor party, but a faith and an apostolate."[4]

Mazzini was the first to give Italians a concrete aim: freedom from Austria and the Catholic Church's temporal power and priests, and unity as a democratic republic. "Mankind will triumph over the ruins of the papacy and the Nation upon the ruins of Austria,"[5] Mazzini wrote.

First, and foremost, Mazzini was anti-Catholic. His greatest desire was to offer the people an alternative to the repression of Catholicism which would allow them to know God with the Nation as their only intermediary.

While deeply religious, he was not a Christian. He believed in God and in human progress as an expression of God's will. In his thinking, religious belief assured the well being of the individual and his willingness to give up self-interest. He staunchly believed that his contemporaries had been manipulated and corrupted in their beliefs by the Catholic hierarchy, saying,

Catholicism is dead; Christianity itself is an individual not a social religion. . . . Spiritualism applied to society, that must be our banner.[6]

Catholicism was the basic foundation of Italian culture. Mazzini proposed a civil religion, which had a somewhat egalitarian message and emphasized man's duties to his fellow countrymen, as the alternative. His political messages were always expressed in theological terms such as redemption, regeneration, and rebirth. In 1834, he wrote that the revolution required a faith in "good works", those being the necessary political and military deeds to achieve liberation and the unification of Italy.

The mystical quality and religious terminology of his messages were important reasons for Mazzini's popular appeal: the language of theology was familiar to the Italian people. This appeal led to criticism from some of his contemporaries who objected to the mystique surrounding him as the messiah of the national revolution. Quadrio, however, turned the mystique to advantage, by depicting Mazzini as Christ-like and his mother as the new Virgin Mary in his *chiesa militante*.

There were three concepts of Mazzini's political philosophy which were incompatible with Christianity. One was the concept of "God and the People". His God was the Creator of all things and present in human affairs, but the relationship between Mazzini's God and the people was not dependent on ceremonial structures or priests. The Mazzinian concept of revelation was that God's will and presence were revealed through the history of the People, each people assigned a particular mission that could be known by studying its historical development. This doctrine challenged the need for intermediaries or temporal powers or ecclesiastical courts, and it challenged clerical control over education. Viewed as revolutionary, it was a threat even outside the Papal states to existing political and social institutions.

People, as defined by Mazzini, are all those sharing a given area, language and historical tradition; they are capable of understanding their particular mission and all have a part to play in its completion. Mazzini argued that the differences of income, status, and education are unimportant before the higher form of equality that is derived from the principle of "association"; the common effort of the people to relate to the past and make a common destiny. This philosophy of association was too vague to be applied to actual social and economic issues, but it was practical in the resistance to the Catholic establishment and the Restoration governments. And it did reveal an egalitarian character.

Mazzini's vision of the Third Rome bore out his anti-Catholic sentiment. He asserted that in understanding the past, the people would realize that the roots of their civilization went back much further than the rise of papal Rome. They would see that the "eternal City" belonged to them, not the pope, and it would become the natural capital of the new Italy. The necessary stimulation to create new cultural institutions, including a free press and uncensored universities, would lay the foundation for a new political order.

Risorgimento was born through Mazzinian theory. Most of the revolutionaries were members of Young Italy or other secret societies influenced by his teachings. The paradox is, that, in essence, Mazzini's teachings formulated the basis of thought on both sides of the debates concerning the establishment of the new political order.

513

... a party was growing up who had imbibed much of Mazzini's teaching, but who from all reasons which hover between prudence and cowardice was inclined to slower and less direct methods than his uncompromising democratic nature would permit. This was the party of the Moderates. . . .[7]

There were two ways of achieving national independence. One was to train revolutionaries through the network of secret societies for insurrections against the existing governments and the Austrian troops. The other way was to depend upon the diplomatic and military leadership of an Italian ruler who would challenge Austria for his own ambitions. This was to be the battleline between Mazzini and Cavour.

The approach of diplomacy was the choice of the moderates and, before 1848, seemed the more realistic. But, Mazzini emerged from the revolutionary experience of 1848 with a respected political reputation and certainty that they would soon lead a full revolution against Austria. The events of 1850, both domestic and international, returned favor to the view of a diplomatic solution. Viewed by many as stubborn and unyielding, Mazzini yet stood ready to abandon his strategy at any critical moment if it would speed the attainment of independence.

Cavour and the moderates proposed a constitutional monarchy with a parliamentarily-elected indirect representation, to which Mazzini would remain staunchly opposed. For him, liberty for the elite was only one step toward the broad goal of popular participation and, eventually, political equality, identifying with the Jacobins of 1790 and the political models of Switzerland and the United States. The philosophical reasons were stated early in the history of Young Italy:

... in order to stir up in the People and enthusiastic commitment to revolution, we must persuade them beyond doubt that we are attempting it for their sake. In order to persuade them of this, we must present the revolution as the path to the full enjoyment of those rights. Hence, we must propose as the goal of our revolution a democratic system, a system that will improve the conditions of the poorest and most numerous classes, a system that will call upon all citizens to use their talents in the conduct of public affairs, a system built upon equality, a system in which the government will be elected by a broadly-based, inexpensive and simple method. This system is a Republican system.[8]

Two assumptions were the foundation of Mazzini's republicanism. First, under monarchical institutions, there was no assurance that liberty would not perish under even the most advanced of constitutions. The second assumption was that monarchical institutions were "inherently incompatible with the principle of equality." Mazzini set his republican principles aside at times before 1860 because the monarchical leadership seemed to offer a shortcut to independence and unity, but each time he regretted the decision. He knew the national revolution would require the Italian masses to make sacrifices, and he pondered how such participation could be solicited and rewarded. The answer was the promise of some type of political participation, but he stopped short of the immediate indiscriminate adoption of democratic institutions such as universal manhood suffrage. He had learned that an unsophisticated electorate could be manipulated as they had been in France, but he also knew that to withhold that right from the masses would cause bitterness to erupt.

Ironically, Mazzini's feelings toward the masses were more paternalistic than egalitarian. He supported literacy tests for prospective voters, on a practical basis, recognizing that a minimum level of education was necessary for responsible government to exist. In effect, a majority of the population was excluded from political exercise. On the other hand, Mazzini opposed restricting political participation to the propertied class, which he saw as a double injustice to every man from the lower classes who had earned the right to participate in determining the political future of Italy by answering the revolutionary appeal, and as an injustice to millions of poor people for just being poor.

Mazzini tried to develop an "organic and coherent" correlation between the aims of the revolution and his theories of social justice. He was committed to the idea of revolution "with the People and for the People." Mazzini outlined the social objectives of the Italian Revolution in this manner:

> The abolition of all privileges other than those derived from the eternal principle of ability applied to good ends; the gradual reduction [in numbers] of men who sell their labor... a gradual rapprochement among social classes, so as to form one People and to promote the maximum development of individual abilities; and the attainment of laws that meet the People's needs.[9]

Many critized his social theory as being too vague and utopian and most realized that his "associationist" philosophy was inadequate to overcome the enmity between social classes.

In 1834, Mazzini tried to mount an insurrection in Savoy, which failed miserably and had fearful repercussions. Many promising young men were lost in futile uprisings in the 1840s; men potentially capable of leading democratic national movement. And Mazzini, the intellectual most clearly devoted to the national movement whatever the cost, grieved. Even worse, democratic republicanism, especially as espoused by Mazzini, came to be identified in the minds of many Italians with violence, bloodshed, and futility. After the Bologna uprising of 1843, Mazzini was blamed for the failure of his supporters to seize the streets on the designated day. He and his followers were also faulted for the lack of coordination between the Bologna revolutionary organizations and the democratic-led groups of the Romagna. Although the democrats had supporters in every social class, they lacked the critical mass of supporters necessary for revolution. Mazzini had failed to guage the apathy of the people and had read his own faith into his countrymen.

By 1845 Mazzini was pleading with his fellow democrats not to take unnecessary risks. His advice was not persuasive for he had advocated armed insurgency as a forerunner of a nationwide guerilla movement since the 1830's. He now realized the extent to which each failed revolutionary attempt drained the precious capital of the democratic groups. However, he had no way to control the various groups which claimed to act upon his principles.

The Risorgimento democrats were reassessing their goals when Pope Pius IX was elected in June 1846. Even Mazzini could not ignore the significance of the pope's new role, although he remained anti-Catholic. "if Pius IX could bring the Italians closer together and hasten their liberation from Austria," he wrote, "he deserved the good wishes and support of every Italian."[10] He was, however, ecstatic at the papal Allocution in April, 1848.

> Pius IX has fled, his flight is tantamount to an abdication; as an elective prince, he leaves behind no dynasty to carry on. Hence you are now a de facto republic, for there is among you no source of authority except the people.[11]

For twenty years, he had conspired to achieve the fall of temporal power and he was confident the Pius IX would never be able to reclaim that power. He felt vindicated that the pope had fled after three failed experiments in constitutional monarchy. For Mazzini and the Risorgimento, the period from April 1848 to August 1849 was marked with dramatic and unexpected rise to authority followed by devasting and traumatic defeat. He had watched the events leading to this period closely and had written prophetically of the coming storm:

> Europe rapidly approaches a tremendous crisis; a supreme contest between peoples and their despots, which no human powers can henceforth hinder, but which the active concurrence of all the brave and good would render shorter and less severe and whose final result will be a new map of Europe.[12]

The year of revolutions had arrived.

The new governments formed across the Italian states represented nearly two decades of debates about the aims of the national revolution and the means to carry out those aims. Mazzini's influence was apparent in the republican attempts made across Italy.

> Although only a few had personal ties with Mazzini, the best-known leaders of Tuscan democracy defined their political goals in terms not very different from his. [13]

The discussions within the national assembly of the Roman Republic revealed the emergence of a consensus concerning the need for an egalitarian, secular, and socially responsive political system for Rome and, eventually, all of Italy. The Roman Republic was the high point of Risorgimento democracy. Its principles, leaders, and institutions were to remain a source of inspiration for republican and democratic experiments well after the national unification.

By the end of April 1849, the defense of Rome had to take precedence over all else. Mazzini was the symbol of national unity and devotion to the revolutionary cause. He represented the national character of the democratic leadership. Mazzini was an idealist, but he proved that he was no coward as he became the strength of the defense of the Republic, determined to leave a great republican example. On July 1st, the Assembly voted to surrender, with Mazzini protesting to the last. He stayed on in Rome for several days, almost inviting his certain assassination. Neither his goal of national unification nor the democratization of political and social structures had been achieved. Mazzini, from exile, continued to claim to speak for the Italian democracy with its capital in Rome. He believed an historic precedent had been set and that soon representatives would again assemble in that capital, expounding equality, secular government, and social justice.

The assassination attempt against Napoleon III in 1858 set the stage for the Plombiéres meeting and a new start—"a start by Napoleon III, but undertaken because of the decisive influence . . . of Mazzini."[14] Mazzini sensed "intuitively, with the clairvoyance of his passionate nature," that the French alliance was the vehicle to transform the Italian national cause into a monarchist and governmental undertaking. His approach was to stay neutral between republic and monarchy, feeling the final decision should be made by a vote of a national constitutional assembly.

> The fact needs to be emphasized . . . that the process by which the Kingdom of Italy was formed—namely, annexations by means of

517

plebescites and Parliament—did not involve a constitution drawn up by the Italian people on the basis of enlightened reflection and freedom of action.[15]

Mazzini remained violently opposed to a constitutional monarchy. In 1834, he had reiterated,

Constitutional monarchy is the most immoral government in the world— an essentially corrupting institution, because the organized struggle that forms the vitality of such a government stirs up all the individual passions to the conquest of honors or of the fortune that alone gives access to honor.[16]

The three most important events in finally achieving unity were the insurrections in central Italy, the expedition to Sicily, and the expedition into the Marches and Umbria.

All three were Mazzinian-inspired examples of 'thought and action', and popular and revolutionary enterprises. The first two were achieved at least in their initial impetus as popular revoultions.[17]

Despite the fact that he knew the result would be contrary to his own republican idea, Mazzini accepted the leading role of the monarchy because his desire for unity predominated over everything else. He realized the political reality and adapted himself to it in the ultimate interest of the nation. It was an ironic compromise for a man considered by many to be a "stubborn sectarian, the opportunist, pure and simple, the idealist with head in the clouds." It is also a paradox that the hostility between Mazzini and the new order "transformed the chief apostle of the unitary state, as soon as unity was achieved, into the conspirator and nonconformist that he remained until his death."[18]

The historical assessment of Mazzini is a contradiction in itself; seen by many as unyielding to any opinion other than his own and, yet, by others, as ready to compromise at any critical point for the ultimate achievement of unity. His personal writings were viewed as stoic mandates but, in practical reality, Mazzini manipulated circumstances to attain his objectives in much the same manner as did Cavour, his greatest rival. Many historians believe that Mazzini stood in the way of unification while others insist that it could never have occurred without his participation.

Garibaldi replaced Mazzini as the symbol of democratic ideology and the hero of democratic initiative. Mazzini was remembered only as the advocate of

Italian unity, independence, and greatness, not as the apostle of democratic and republican government. Even the considerable number of his former disciples in Italy's elite in the 1870's forgot his vision of the republic. His concept of a Third Rome, greater and more powerful than the Caesars and the popes; was often emphasized instead. Mazzini was once again prophetic when he wrote of that paradox:

> Men fight to lose the battle, and the thing they fought for comes about in spite of their defeat, and when it comes it turns out not to be what they meant, and other men have to fight for what they meant under another name.[19]

WORKS CITED

1. Mazzini, Joseph. *The Duties of Man and Other Essays*, (London: J. M. Dent and Sons), 1907, xiii.
2. Clough, Shepard B. and Saladino, Salvatori. *A History of Modern Italy: Documents, Readings and Commentary*, 31.
3. Wicks, Margaret C. W. *The Italian Exiles in London 1836–1848*, (Manchester University Press), 184.
4. Clough & Saladino, 39.
5. Lovett, Clara M. *The Democratic Movement in Italy 1830–1876*, (Cambridge: Harvard University Press), 1982, 13.
6. Lovett, 13.
7. Mazzini, xxv.
8. Lovett, 35.
9. Lovett, 49.
10. Lovett, 101.
11. Lovett, 56.
12. Mazzini, xxvi.
13. Lovett, 125.
14. Delzell, Charles F., ed. *The Unification of Italy, 1859–1861: Cavour, Mazzini, or Garbaldi?*, (Holt, Rinehart and Winston)"Unification Spurred by Mazzinianism," Luigi Salvatorelli, 27.
15. Delzell, "Did Not Prevent Future Reforms," Salvatorelli, 77.
16. Delzell, "Unification Spurred by Mazzinianism," 30.
17. Delzell, 32.
18. Ibid.
19. Mazzini, xxxi.

PIERS PLOWMAN: BEYOND THE TEXT

Elizabeth P. Cain

University of North Texas

Examination of the fourteenth-century world of William Langland reveals a picture as varied, colorful and exciting as a medieval tapestry. The society of *Piers Plowman* was a vibrant, happy, bustling English agrarianism that is reflected in the warm, earthy tones of wall decorations on English country churches and in the alliterative poetry of the Middle English classic, *Piers Plowman*. To students of history the approach to a primary source is often fraught with misconceptions. To examine a "primary source" only in search of its historical relevance and position in Western history is rather like sampling a gourmet meal only to obtain its nutritional benefits. Rather, a primary source should be explored slowly, so that all the cultural, historical, political, and literary elements may gradually unfold themselves. One should absorb the feeling of a work—the essence of what it truly stood for in its day and age.

Such is the case with William Langland's *Piers Plowman*. In reading the various authorities on *Piers* and wandering through the maze of opinions on authorship, A, B, and C versions, and northwestern dialects in alliterative poetry, it seems that some of the joy of experience has been forgotten in William Langland's work. Yet, there seems hardly another Middle English work so full of life, humor, sentiment, common sense, and glimpses of true humanity as Langland's tale of *Piers Plowman*. What a tragedy it would be if students of history ignored the related fields of literature, art, music and the humanities to follow only the historical method. Let me offer a challenge to all to take the time to examine the whole context—to move "beyond the text" as it were—of a primary source and enjoy the experience of truly getting to know a small facet of cultural history.

In moving beyond the text it is necessary to ask who comprised the readership of *Piers Plowman*, and what was meant by "reading" a work in fourteenth-century England as opposed to twentieth-century America? Fourteenth and fifteenth-century literacy had many different ramifications. "Literacy" often stood for a familiarity with great works, and ability to quote great authors, but not necessarily to read these great works or authors. Margaret Aston in *Lollards and Reformers: Images and Literacy in Late Medieval Religion* cites this as the first and most common level of literacy (Aston 25). Often these people were able to learn quickly by rote and memorize easily. A very good example of this may be observed by reading *The Book of Margery Kempe*. Many times in her book, Margery Kempe bewails the fact that she is unable to read or write and must depend upon a priest to write down her memoirs. Yet this same "illiterate" woman quotes scripture and church authorities at great length and seems to have a remarkable capacity to recall conversations and sermons.

Related to this tendency to learn quickly by rote is the ability of some to compose literature, but not to write it down. Certainly Margery Kempe would fall into this category, and also the authors of the popular Robin Hood legends, and other fables handed down through oral tradition. Although not considered literate by twentieth-century standards, these people were regarded as well-read in their own societies.

Of course, there were groups of people in Langland's time who could read the written work. These readers, so to term them, were important members of their society, for reading was a very social and very vital skill. J. A. Burrow, in his book *Medieval Writers and their Work*, compares these readers to musical performers. The books were seen as scores—to be performed for an audience (Burrow 24–55). When viewed from this perspective, it becomes clear why many passages in Langland and even Chaucer seem redundant to the silent reader. For one listening repetition is needed; whereas to the reader, thoughts and ideas are more quickly absorbed. Indeed, this concept can be traced back to the *Song of Roland* and even further to antiquity in the works of Homer. It is interesting that, when read out loud, many passages in works such as Langland, Homer, and Chaucer are clearer when vocal perfomance of direct address and characterization are used. These and other indicators point to the medieval authors' realization that their works were being read, or performed, out loud.

From these observations it may be seen that the majority of "readers" of fourteenth-century books were probably not readers at all, but were listeners. As Aston points out, only a small minority of the population would fit into the upper levels of literacy: those who could read and write, and those who were so learned as to read silently.

> A well-known passage in the *Confessions* of St. Augustine describes the reading habits of St. Ambrose. 'As he read, his eyes glanced over the pages and his heart searched out the sense, but his voice and tongue were silent.' (Aston 32)

This silent reading must have been unusual enough for St. Augustine to have to account for it. Yet, one must not draw the premature conclusion that vast throngs of English people of the fourteenth century were illiterate, for that would be imposing a modern standard on a medieval world—an anachronism at best and a gross misjudgment at worst. As Burrow points out, from 1100 onwards there was a dramatic explosion of demand for reading material. This may be seen by the availability and survival of texts of Geoffrey of Monmouth's *History of the Kings of Britain*. It would seem that the world was leaving the more cloistered monastic phase and heading into the more open, expressive scholastic phase. More and more people from 1100–1500 were literate—not necessarily as readers and writers—but most definitely dependent on those skills, which gave rise to a society dependent on the written word.

This framework of the growing literacy of the fourteenth century helps explain why a work such as *Piers Plowman* would even come to be written. Books, and especially one with such a wide general appeal as *Piers Plowman*, were eagerly read, enjoyed, and discussed by people of a wider general population than the members of courts and nobility who patronized chivalric romances, courtly love poetry and chansons. Many of Langland's manuscripts came to be in the possession of London burghers and middle-class citizens. This group, and later the Lollards and religious reformers who would use *Piers Plowman* as a rallying point, formed a wider readership to which fourteenth-century authors might write and find an audience for their craft (Hudson 19).

While discussing the literacy of fourteenth–century English citizens, it is well also to consider the actual language used at this time. Throughout the thirteenth and fourteenth centuries there seems to have been a gradual shift from the use of French exclusively at administrative and social levels of society to the use of English. This is evidenced by the following records. In 1327 Andrew Horn, Chamberlain of London, expounded the city's new charter in English at a mass meeting at the Guildhall. The earliest petition that survives in English is dated 1344. And in 1362 Parliament agreed that pleadings in the King's courts should be made in English (Chadwick 25). This shift could be explained by the earlier loss of English holdings in France and therefore the loss of the need for a bilingual court. During the twelfth century it was quite common to see a great amount of traffic between Norman holdings in England and in France. Even the Cistercian abbots of monasteries in England made an annual visit back to the mother house of Cîteaux. Certainly, land holders and knights had business that would carry them between the two countries and require them to be fluent in French as the language of government and society. By the fourteenth century, however, the English language seems to be established as a national language, as can be easily proven by Chaucer's use of English in his great poems. This transition from French to English may have been due more to the growth of towns and cities, the development of London merchant guilds, and the blossoming of the bourgeois who would not have been trained in, nor have need for, courtly French (Chadwick 39).

Indeed, these middle-class men and women may have been some of William Langland's first patrons. Janet Coleman in *Medieval Reders and Writers 1350–1400* states that the extent of corruption of the text in surviving manuscripts of *Piers Plowman* suggests that Langland was favored with a devout middle class patronage which preserved and copied his text in over fifty manuscripts. These devout burghers and rural landowners were literate and enjoyed English texts, passing down treasured books in their wills and collecting their own libraries of English texts (Coleman 125–32).

This love for books, and pride in the English language certainly led to a significant institutional development of the fourteenth century: the establishment of grammar schools for the poorer members of society. The foundation of these schools was recognition of the fact that the ability to read and write was important for one's social and economic well being. Nicholas Orme, author of *English Schools in the Middle Ages*, defines public schools as those open to all who could afford to attend. The public school system encompassed four levels of education: song schools, primary schools for boys ages seven to about ten, which taught prayers, the alphabet and the vernacular language; grammar schools which taught older boys the rudiments of Latin; business schools, chiefly at Oxford, which gave instruction in accountancy, French, common law and dictamen; and the higher schools, which were the established universities of the schoolmen. Motivations to obtain an education were varied by the fourteenth century. Religion was a great motivator, with many people wanting to learn to read their own scriptures and devotional books. merchants felt a great need to learn to read for business, social and leisure purposes. Villeins were generally unschooled because an ability to read would presuppose the pursuit of another career, which was definitely not in the landowner's best interests. Occasionally a landowner would grant permission for a villein's son to go to a grammar school, but this was often a special circumstance (Orme 60–75).

In 1320, according to Ranulf Higden, a monk of Chester who wrote his *History of the World*, or *Polychronicon*, French was the only vernacular language allowed in the English schools. By 1349, however, English had displaced French as the studied vernacular, although some resisted this change and demanded that only Latin and French be used in schools (Orme 69).

So, against this background of growing literacy and language consciousness comes an unusual, quirky book—sublime and brash at the same time. For those who have read *Piers Plowman* and puzzled over its construction and its conception, it is best to consider the state of England itself in the fourteenth century. In eleventh and twelfth century Europe we see a sudden blossoming of thought, of art, of the individual ... almost a European transformation. Suddenly Europe had become politically stable; trade and agriculture increased; the population grew and with it the towns and cities; there emerged a new bourgeois class and a new knightly class; Gothic style replaced sturdy Romanesque in architecture; music developed toward polyphony; romance replaced heroic narratives; universities blossomed; and the arts flourished. Even religion seems to have gained a new sensibility with the founding of the Cistercian order which turned man's attention away from the structure of the church and toward the personal motivation and sanctity of the individual. This twelfth-century Renaissance seems to awaken the whole world.

The opening of the fourteenth century finds this idea of individuality well established, but with the century come other problems. In 1348 a new strain of Black Death appeared at Dorset that ravaged the country. In 1361 and 1462 less vicious attacks occurred, and again in 1369 England experienced the plague. The total death rate of the plague during the fourteenth century had been estimated between thirty to fifty percent of the population. Besides this calamity, we find that England experiences social unrest when laborers and serfs revolt in 1381 over the problems of fixed wages and lack of freedoms. Prior to 1381 minor disturbances occurred, such as men missing haymaking or destroying the landowner's crops, but after the poll tax was passed, a general revolt against the ineptitude of the government swept the country and outlasted all efforts to suppress it. And also, it must not be forgotten that the fourteenth century saw the beginning of the Hundred Years War. Although this conflict was a slow and intermittent war, it nonetheless took its toll on the people of both France and England (McKisack).

And now England in the days of *Piers Plowman* has become a slightly more cynical place. Men have discovered themselves, have gloried in their discoveries, have tasted the bitterness of great tragedies and have turned their energies to reforms of a sort. Once again we must be careful not to define reform in twentieth-century, or even sixteenth-century vocabulary. Fourteenth-century reform was very much within the context of established society. Men felt the freedom to complain and rail against abuses, but, as of yet, the action taken should not be compared to sixteenth-century reforms or eighteenth-century revolutions. Both the church and the secular government had become organized bureaucratic institutions with many levels of civil servants who sometimes did and sometimes did not do their jobs. Langland's most frequent complaint against these various monks, friars, priests, clerks, esslesiastical lawyers, lords and public officials seems to be that they are looking for their own gain, not performing their responsibilities. Langland never advocates an overthrow or dramatic change of society, simply an individual examination of motives and an individual return to doing what is right in one's own office or station. As Langland says in Book X,

The nobles should have more sense than to transfer property from their heirs to Religious Orders; for the monks are quite unmoved though the rain falls on their altars! Even where they have parishes to care for they live at ease, with no pity for the poor—such is their boasted charity! (Langland)

The general English society of William Langland's day was fairly well-established and ordered as Nora Chadwick outlines in *Social Life in the Days of Piers Plowman*. Chadwick divides society into five categories—clergy, secular government, law and chivalry, country life, and town life—and notes that Lnagland has criticism for each and every group. The most highly-structured group of this period would be the clergy, whose many offices ranged from pope, cardinal, archbishop, and bishop on down to priest, clerk, student and regular. The regulars, including friars, monks and cloistered brethren, seem to come in for a great deal of Langland's abuse (Chadwick 21–30).

The secular government of this time was the court of Edward III, and later his grandson Richard II. Although Langland seems to be a little more careful in his criticism of the king, he does use the cat and mice fable thinly to disguise his criticism of Richard II's ineptness. In Chadwick's words: ". . . the sufferings caused by an individual ruler's caprices were only less terrible than rebellion" (Chadwick 41). Of the Lords and Commons Langland has little to say, other than criticizing the Lords for their greed, but it is clear that the Commons as a representative group were beginning to have some voice in the government. Of course the citizens, as opposed to laborers, were a minority of the actual population, but it was representation nonetheless (Chadwick 31–43).

The fourteenth century saw a dramatic change in warfare and the status of knight. At this time the term knight came to stand for a man of lineage who paid others to fulfill his feudal obligations. A knight became more of a country squire, administering his fief, paying mercenaries to do most of the fighting (Chadwick 46).

Country, or rural life, in this century was oriented to the change of season and was most representative of the lower classes. There were only three classes of society in rural England: priest, knight, and laborer. The priest was assigned to a parish by the church administration, but his animals, grain and necessities came from the tithes of the locals. The knight was usually a wealthy landowner who lived a relatively rich lifestyle. This lord, his lady, his many servants, minstrels, clergy, family, soldiery and hangers on would move from one manor house to another in the various centers of his fief. When the resources and food of one were exhausted, the lord would move on again—probably to the chagrin of the country folk at the next stop (Chadwick 52–60).

Town life was quickly becoming privileged for the English fourteenth-century people. Traders, artisans, and merchants became prosperous and congregated in towns for safety and commerce. The freemen, or franklins, served as town officers, and they were generally responsible to the king as the "royal deputies." Their duties included collection of taxes and use of monies for the benefit of the town, which usually meant the establishment of a school (Chadwick 61).

People in towns had more access to entertainment than the rural folk, and story-telling was a popular pastime. Dramatic shows, outdoor games such as the "somer game of souterers," tavern games like "New Fair" and musical events were some of the pleasurable diversions townsfolk enjoyed (Chadwick 62).

Society, whether in town or city, village or farm, seems to be well ordered and harmonious. Men are free to complain about their church and government, and that, of course, has become an integral part of western society.

One very interesting aspect of fourteenth-century life which has particular relevance to the study of *Piers Plowman* is the prevalence of preaching, sermons and sermon literature available to the people of Langland's time. G. R. Owst in his *Literature and the Pulpit in Medieval England* explores the relationship between the composition of *Piers Plowman* and medieval sermons quite thoroughly. Tracts on the formal art of preaching were widely circulated by the second half of the thirteenth century. These tracts usually consisted of a liberal mix of quotations, themes, sermon notes and actual texts for any itinerant preacher to use as a reference (Owst 548–49). Once again, the modern concept of plagiarism must not be applied here, for it would falsely describe the literary practices of Langland's time. Indeed, in an age where identification of authorship and the writing down of works of literature were new concepts, and where the copying and distribution of manuscripts often involved a "rewriting" of the text, it was hardly appropriate to quibble about identifying one's sources or worry about "borrowing" material. A prime example of this is Langland's own borrowing of the cat and mice fable.

In addition to these tracts that were available to clerks and other men of letters, sermons themselves could be heard quite often. Itinerant preaching seems to have been a very popular pastime, and it seems very likely that Langland probably heard hundreds, if not thousands, of sermons in his time. These sermons, like the great personal letters of the eleventh and twelfth centuries, had a very particular structure and form to be followed. A. C. Spearing gives two categories of sermons: the "ancient", which was based on a homily or involved a verse by verse exposition; and the "modern" or "university" which was based on a theme and became very elaborate in structure. These university sermons, rather like polyphonic music or even a fugue, would begin with a *thema*, which was followed by the *divisio*, in which a repetitious layering of different aspects of the *thema* would expand and expound the speakers original point. This elaborate structure, which often involved many subdivisions with their own *divisiones* and was always brought to a close by a *declaratio* and *confirmatio*, served a dual purpose to its audience. Those of the audience who were more educated found the form of the sermon intellectually and aesthetically pleasing. And for the less educated in the audience, the constant repetitions of the *thema* served to drive home the point of the preacher (Spearing, *Criticism*).

After considering the structure and style of medieval sermons and after making some assumptions about Langland's exposure to this literary form, it becomes natural to compare the structure of *Piers Plowman* to a fourteenth-century sermon. A. C. Spearing cites that the difficulty in this poem is not necessarily in its content, but its organization. "The poem sounds like the most confused phantasmagoria conceivable—a nightmare rather than a dream." If the

526

ideas of social reform, individual morality, and Christ as both man and God are taken as the *thema* of this long sermon-poem, then the digressions, repetitiveness and sometimes confused state of the work becomes a little more clear. Could *Piers Plowman* be a long sermon—or, more probably, a collection of sermons? (Spearing, *Readings*) Even more interesting is Siegfried Wenzel's observation that during Langland's time the Biblical concordance as a literary tool was becoming available, as well as a larger variety of Biblical commentaries (Wenzel 111–15). One can almost picture William Langland traveling from abbey to monastery to court library, much like graduate history students do today, cross-referencing verses, picking out a Latin quotation to spice up his text, and perhaps borrowing a good anecdote or morality story from a sermon tract to really make his point. When one considers the types of sources Langland must have used and how he probably used them, controversy over the authorship of *Piers Plowman* seems irrelevant.

The picture of William Langland as a harried graduate student, scurrying around from source to source, somehow endears him and makes him seem much more human. But, after all, the study of history is the study of humans, and the fourteenth century seems to have been an epoch bursting with the warmth and energies of humans, and, more importantly, rather ordinary humans. Although the previous centuries saw a beginning of the growth of individualistic efforts as opposed to organizational efforts, most of these individuals whose voices have been carried down through the centuries belong to just the upper echelons of society. It is suddenly refreshing to begin reading, in the fourteenth century, works by and about rather ordinary people. Not only in literature, but in art also are the beginnings of a move away from just glorification of Church or state and toward representation of everyday life in England. Examination of the Luttrell Psalter, the Queen Mary's Psalter and the Psalter of St. Omer will show some very detailed and interesting marginal decorations of peasants at work. There are women cutting hay, men pulling a hay wagon, peasants plowing a field, courtly love scenes, and even a rabbit playing a portative organ. These manuscript illustrations are not only charming, but show how the themes of peasant life and common people were becoming, if not popular, at least more prevalent. Artists themselves, in a curious twist, began during the thirteenth century to portray themselves either at work in their craft, or in a signature-type portrait within the art work itself. The increase of this type of portrayal is significant in that it demonstrates a shift in attitude from art being created or inspired mysteriously in a divine flash of light, to the pride and craftsmanship of individual artists pleased with their own accomplishments (Egbert).

Some of the most interesting art work of this century that deals directly with *Piers* is the decoration of the walls of country churches. These walls were usually decorated with an oil-base paint, and the scenes were generally of Biblical characters and, particularly for the fourteenth century, the Virgin Mary. Wall paintings in these small churches were the equivalent of stained glass in the larger and richer cathedrals and served the dual purposes of beautification and illumination of the sermons. At Ampney St. Mary's Church near Cirencester and at Stedham in Sussex can be seen wall paintings done by local workshops of Piers the Plowman as Christ and of Christ the Craftsman. E. W. Tristram notes in his article "*Piers Plowman* in English Wall Painting" that the workmanship of these particular paintings is rather unskilled and were clearly objects of reverence for the poor, not the rich. The dating of the art is right around the first years of the fifteenth century, so it is possible that Langland himself might even have seen the paintings (Tristam 135–40). Not only does this show the beginnings of identification of the common man with Christ and an increased awareness of the value of all men, but it raises some interesting questions about Piers the Plowman himself.

Was the figure of Piers invented by Langland, or was the plowman a stock literary character? Who or what does the Plowman represent in Langland's work, and why does he become so popular so quickly? There are, of course, no straightforward, clear cut answers to these questions, and much guess work must be employed. But from the different topics that have been examined thus far, and from the ideas we have of Langland's world, it is interesting to draw some conclusions.

It is known for certain that Langland's popularity increased after his death, and, especially among the Lollards, other tales and poems of Piers the Plowman, or just the Plowman, appeared. There is *The Plowman's Tale*, a sixteenth-century addition to the *Canterbury Tales* which was adapted from a Lollard poem of the fifteenth century, and there is also the fifteenth century Lollard text, *Piers Plowman's Creed* (Aston 78). Spearing also cites other "Langland followers" who, although they do not adopt the character of Piers, definitely follow Langland's style and themes. *Mum and the Sothsegger* is one example of a satire with social commentaries that uses the Langland-like dream techniques (Spearing *Medieval*). *Piers Plowman's Creed* is a more concise poem than Langland's, and it is concerned with the question of authority, belief and action. It presents its solution by contrasting the hypocrisy and pettiness of the friars with the humble, passionate sincerity of Piers. The speeches, or sermons, comprise the action of the plot, and Piers' rhetorical pattern becomes a sermon, then a creed which David Lampe, in his article, concludes put Piers in the apostolic succession in the eyes of the Lollards (Lampe 56).

The post-Langland evidence for Piers Plowman as a literary character is strong. Piers seems to have been a fourteenth-century cowboy: a symbol of goodness, humanity, strength, and Christ at the same time. If the character of Piers seems a bit confused at times in Langland's text, it is probably because once again we are reading through modern eyes. The medieval mind identified with symbols, many times with more than one symbol at a time. Piers is, to the medieval mind, a symbol of the human race—its divergence from laborer to leader; from human to God. Piers can symbolize Christ because of the humanity of Christ. To a rapidly-developing, individualistic world that was putting more emphasis on the value of every man, whether king, freeman or villein, identifying Christ with a plowman—a member of the freeman, laborer class—was a literary device both expedient and appropriate for the times. The honesty of labor, the purity of nature, the straightness of the plowed furrow—all these combine to make Piers a multi-facted symbol for the humanity of Christ (Troyer 42–59).

Did Langland himself invent this popular medieval character? Can we credit William Langland with the ingenuity to devise an appealing figure for the laborer and middle classes to identify with? I do not believe we can go as far as to say that Piers was a creation of Langland. In many ways *Piers Plowman* itself was not a creation but a conglomeration. It is possible that the figure of a plowman was borrowed by Langland from another preacher or text. The character Piers, although probably named by Langland, developed into a meaningful symbol through decades of readers, artists, copiers, and poets adapting him to their needs in their own changing world.

The identity of Piers and, in a larger sense, the meaning of William Langland's work is probably best related not to Piers, but to the plow. The plow, increasingly depicted in manuscripts, calendar decorations, wall paintings, and tiles, becomes a fourteenth-century symbol of the laborer. The glorification of the plow, through the poem *Piers Plowman* and through the eyes and hands of artists, signifies a growing appreciation of the plowman, the laborer, the common man. It is as if a sudden recognition of each man's value has dawned upon Langland's genera-tion—a new societal consciousness of the importance of all and the rights of all. Perhaps with these ideas in mind and with these impressions of *Piers Plowman* and its context, historical and cultural, one can begin to grasp a more complete picture of William Langland, England, and the fourteenth century. History becomes quickly intertwined with art, music, literature, psychology, anthropol-ogy and religion when one can look beyond the narrow confines of just the primary source. But, after all, history is humanity, and humanity encompasses all these things.

One last impression of the world of Langland—the bustling, common-man's England of the fourteenth century. In rural villages of England, like the village of Gerneham which is gloriously portrayed in the Luttrell Psalter, villagers cel-ebrated their Yuletide with twelve days of dancing, drinking, music and hearty merry-making. The first Sunday after Twelfth Night the plow was taken to the village priest who blessed it, and the next morning village boys would drag the plow round all the houses to drive away evil spirits (Sancha). This was Plough Monday, and it was as central to the villager's calendar and life as the plow was to their farming. Plough Monday was Greenwich time, point zero, New Year's Day. Plough Monday was the measure of a laborer's life, for Plough Monday began, again, the common man's work year—his life cycle.

BIBLIOGRAPHY

Aston, Margaret. *Lollards and Reformers*. London: Hambledon Press, 1984.

Baldwin, Anna P. "Historical Context." *A Companion to Piers Plowman*. Ed. John A. Alford. Berkeley: University of California Press, 1988.

Burrow, J. A. *Medieval Writers and Their Work: Middle English Literature and its Background 1100–1500*. Oxford: Oxford University Press, 1982.

Chadwick, Nora. *Social Life in the Days of Piers Plowman*. Cambridge: Cambridge University Press, 1922.

Coleman, Janet. *Medieval Readers and Writers 1350–1400*. New York: Columbia University Press, 1981.

Egbert, Virginia Wylie. *The Medieval Artist at Work*. Princeton: Princeton University Press, 1967.

Hudson, Anne. *The Premature Reformation: Wycliffite Texts and Lollard History*. Oxford: Oxford University Press, 1988.

Lampe, David. "The Satiric Strategy of *Piers Plowman's Crede*." *The Alliterative Tradition in the 14th Century*. Ed. Barnard S. Levy and Paul E. Szarmach. Kent: Kent State University Press, 1981.

McKisack, May. *The Fourteenth Century 1307–1399*. Oxford: Oxford University Press, 1959.

Orme, Nicholas. *English Schools in the Middle Ages*. London: Methuen and Co., 1973.

Owst, G. R. *Literature and the Pulpit in Medieval England*. Cambridge: Cambridge University Press, 1933.

Pearsall, David and Elizabeth Salter. *Landscapes and Seasons of the Medieval World*. Toronto and Buffalo: University of Toronto Press, 1973.

Sancha, Sheila. *The Luttrell Village*. Glasgow: William Collins and Sons Co. Ltd, 1982.

Spearing, A. C. *Criticism and Medieval Poetry*. New York: Barnes and Noble, Inc., 1972.

_____. *Medieval Dream Poetry*. Cambridge: Cambridge University Press, 1976.

_____. *Readings in Medieval Poetry*. Cambridge: Cambridge University Press, 1987.

Tristram, E. W. "*Piers Plowman* in English Wall Painting." *Proceedings of the Suffolk Institute of Archaeology*. Vol. V, 1886.

Troyer, Howard William. "Who is Piers Plowman?" *Style and Symbolism in Piers Plowman: A Modern Critical Anthology*. Ed. Robert J. Blanch. Knoxville: University of Tennessee Press, 1969.

Wenzel, Siegfried. "Medieval Sermons." *A Companion to Piers Plowman*. Ed. John A. Alford. Berkeley: University of California Press, 1988.

_____. *Preachers, Poets and the Early English Lyric*. Princeton: Princeton University Press, 1986.

LITERATURE, PROTEST, AND ALLEGORY IN THEIR SOCIAL CONTEXT

Carol Hammond Field

University of North Texas

William Langland's *The Vision of Piers the Plowman* gives us a glimpse of fourteenth-century England, a world which Vincent Ward's recent film *The Navigator* visualizes as an allegory of our own times, a world which May McKisack called "drowned, mysterious, irrecoverable" (McKisack 527). Although we cannot recover that world entirely, with Langland's help we can envisage it more clearly. *Piers the Plowman* is a dream allegory (as is *The Navigator*), set in alliterative verse, written in the vernacular language that we classify as Middle English. Langland combined medieval allegory with ancient Anglo-Saxon alliteration to such effect that he is not simply recognized as a great social critic and commentator; he enjoys a place among the great English literary figures. And just as the allegory that medieval minds employed so well can be interpreted on several levels, just as *The Navigator* reveals various planes of meaning for twentieth-century minds, so Langland's poem discloses a multi-layered world. On one hand, it paints a vivid picture of everyday life in the late Middle Ages; on another it catalogues the prominent complaints and conflicts of an age renowned for controversy; on a third level, *Piers the Plowman* reveals the religious perceptions of medieval Englishmen ever on a journey—physical and spiritual—for salvation. Finally, aspects of the poem other than context hint at significant changes stirring in English society.

The vision of fourteenth-century England afforded by *Piers the Plowman* should certainly not end simply with Langland. It is only necessary to mention that grand social commentary, *The Canterbury Tales*; the great contribution to the Arthurian romance, *Sir Gawain and the Green Knight*; the haunting elegy, or allegory, of *Pearl*. It was the era of the great English mystics, among them Richard Rolle and Julian of Norwich. The fourteenth century also produced a wealth of sermon or pulpit literature, cycles of drama in the form of miracle plays, and the first "English translation of the whole Bible" (McKisack 523). Among these achievements we cannot ignore that of Margery Kempe, who was the first English autobiographer, if not one of her country's great literary or religious figures. If we are to appreciate what Langland and his contemporaries can tell us about their world, at whatever level, we must first place them in their historical and social contexts, and then attempt to understand the medieval use and expression of allegory.

The outstanding socio-historical events of fourteenth-century England can be briefly identified: the Hundred Years War, the Black Death, the Peasants' Revolt, and the Lollard heresy. England's centuries-old conflict with France was reignited in 1337 when King Edward III claimed the French throne. The war itself was intermittent, and fought in France; its significance to our study is the effect it had on what McKisack termed the "national psychology" (150). The victories of Edward III inflamed national pride. McKisack also noted that the "knightly classes" had to acknowledge the part played by the common men "who wielded the longbows" in these victories (150). The reverse side of that national pride was the Francophobia which the war engendered, and which dominated English foreign policy for centuries. We see it reflected in Langland's depiction of the Devil as a French knight, "'a proud pryker of Fraunce'" (151).

The greatest destroyer was not war but pestilence, the Black Death, that struck England in 1348 and recurred throughout the remainder of the century. The population of England just before the plague has been estimated at 3,700,000; three decades later it was 2,200,000 (Ackerman 27). In thirty years, the Black Death had reduced England's population by one-third. Other estimates put the loss at one-half of the population by the end of the century (McKisack 332). A devastating statistic by any account, this staggering loss of population led to labor shortages and wage increases that alarmed employers and landlords and that resulted in suppressive legislation designed to force laborers to work for set wages and, significantly, for their own lords. This attempt to hold the villein populace in bondage met with widespread resistance from people who were beginning to grasp their opportunity for freedom.

The social unrest that began to express itself in the wake of the Black Death was fueled by resentment against a series of poll taxes, and exploded in the Peasants' Revolt of 1381. The peasants marched to meet King Richard II and demanded the abolition of serfdom and of the poll taxes, and the substitution of rent for services (Hay 37). The king, very coolly for his fifteen years of age, agreed to the demands, and the rebels left. The king's promises were revoked, and the Revolt died out within a few months, not having accomplished any of its aims.

The immediate cause of the Peasants' Revolt might have been taxes, but there was another significant factor. That was the rise of anti-clerical preachers, clearly to be seen in the person of John Ball, a leader of the Revolt, who Denys Hay states "claimed to be a priest, [but] expressed anticlerical and egalitarian sentiments" (Hay 37). This anti-clerical feeling evolved in some quarters into the heresy of Lollardy.

The Lollards were inspired by, although never actually led by, an Oxford scholar named John Wycliffe. Wycliffe challenged the pope's position as head of the Church, and exalted secular over clerical authority.

The secular powers in England did not have much objection to these ideas, but Wycliffe's position against transubstantiation, coupled with the Peasants' Revolt, finally forced his censure. Wycliffe and the Lollards argued against the transubstantiation of bread and wine at the Eucharist into the actual body and blood of Christ, and thus threatened the very foundations of the power and authority of the priesthood. Only an ordained priest could perform this mystic sacrament; if there were no transubstantiation, then the priest's role was not vital. Another Wycliffite and Lollard stand that threatened the Church's position was the belief that the Bible should be accessible to Englishmen in their own language. Although Wycliffe probably did not actually produce the English vernacular Bibles that appeared before the close of the fourteenth century, he certainly inspired them (McKisack 523).

Important as these developments were, neither the Peasants' Revolt nor Lollardy resulted in massive upheaval during the fourteenth or even the fifteenth century, nor were they universally endorsed; Langland, in fact, criticized both in his poem. The Peasants' Revolt did not develop into political or social revolution, and their rise in status would be slow; Lollardy did not lead promptly to fundamental religious change, and Reformation would not occur for more than another century. Even though the undercurrents of change are clearly to be discerned, this was a society just beginning to recognize itself as a nation, a society unaware of its political potential, a society whose members, for all their complaining, still sought salvation within the arms of Mother Church: in all these respects, what people did *not* do was as significant as what they actually undertook. It is this England of continuity and change which is evident in the literature and culture of the time, and nowhere more so than in *Piers the Plowman*. English society in the age of Langland was every bit as complex as his poem implies.

There were roughly four social classes; the nobility included probably only one percent of the total population, the religious class made up about two percent. The other classes—freemen and villeins—accounted for approximately 97 percent of the population of England (Ackerman 27). More than 90 percent of the English people, moreover, resided in rural areas, in "tiny villages . . . located on manors" (Ackerman 29). Just before the plague, about half of the populace lived in some form of servitude (Ackerman 28); by the end of the century, however, a "wholesale exodus from villeinage" was taking place (Ackerman 30). The rising class of freemen was moving to the towns (Ackerman 28).

The role of the Church in this society cannot be overemphasized. Lollards aside, the great mass of people belonged to and believed in the universal Church, which controlled their lives to a degree not easily comprehended in our society. In the West, education was virtually a clerical monopoly at every level. The great universities which had emerged in the early thirteenth century were dedicated not only to the production of scholars, but also to the more mundane education of the army of officials, bureaucrats and administrators, who served government in both Church and State. In the countryside, where 90 percent of the population, freemen or villein, dwelled, "the sole source of enlightenment" (Ackerman 52), religious or intellectual, was the local priest, who, as the complaints of bishops and archdeacons indicate, was in many cases barely more educated than those to whom he ministered.

Unlike the Lollards, most contemporary complainants, Langland among them, did not attack clerical authority. When Puttenham wrote that "He that wrote the satyr of Piers Ploughman Bent himselfe wholy to taxe the disorders of that age" (Skeat vi), he put it well. What concerned Langland, in company with others, was the hypocrisy of the friars, the selling of indulgences, and the general corruption of Church and society by wealth and self-interest.

For England, like all of western Europe, was undergoing an economic change that was challenging social and religious stability: the change to a money economy. The transformation of feudalism—the emergence of bastard feudalism—reflects this; the demand by the rebels of 1381 for rent instead of service payments is another sign. The effect on the Church was also profound. Christianity had from its beginnings displayed an aversion to, a distrust of, wealth and money, but to little effect. Successive movements of reform within the Church had attempted to excise this corruption; the tenth-century attack on simony, the asceticism of the new orders, the appearance of the mendicants, all reflect a persistent tendency for the best minds and the best spiritual examples to rail against the wealth of the Church.

The hypocrisy of a wealthy clergy and the glory of a life of Christian poverty are common themes in fourteenth-century literature, as well as in religious movements such as that of the early Franciscans; these themes were pursued by people who were caught between a religion that shunned money and a society growing more and more dependent upon it. When Langland extolls the virtues of poverty against the vices of wealth, he is in the company of Francis of Assisi, but Langland's preaching is not expressed by ascetic example; it is revealed in the richness of his alliterative allegory, and nowhere better than in his account of the marriage of Lady Meed (reward or recompense) to Sir Falsehood.

"Who is this woman so worthily drest?"
"'Tis Meed the maid, who hath injured me oft,
Who hath Loyalty slandered, my lief one and dear,
And lied to all lords who have laws to observe.
In the palace of the pope she's as prime as myself,
Though justice would ban her, for her bastard birth . . ."

534

. . . .
"Wit ye and witness ye, who wander on earth,
That Meed here is married much more for her goods
Than for virtue or fairness, or freedom by birth.
For sake of her riches, Sir False is so fond,
And Flattery, with fickle speech, enfeoffs them by charter
To be princes in pride, and the poor to despise,
To backbite and boast, and bear false witness,
To scorn and to scold, and slanders to utter,
To be braggart, and boldly to break the commandments. . . ."
(Skeat 26–29)

What we have here is an earthy mastery of social detail which is much more than just good, bawdy fun: the marriage of Lady Meed is rich in allegory. In *Visions From Piers Plowman*, Nevill Coghill beautifully explains the place that allegory occupied for medieval minds:

> Medieval allegory . . . was . . . a whole way of looking at experience. It was based in the belief that the Universe was all of a piece, that the greater was reflected in the less, that one thing could be understood through another, that God could be known through His works. Man . . . was made in His image. Thus what is true on one plane of meaning must reveal some truth on another. All experience, therefore, is packed with meanings at various levels, and one of the functions of a poet . . . is allegorical, to interpret or present the unknown through the known. (Coghill 137)

There were four levels of interpretation in religious allegory. First, there was the simple narrative of the story, the *sensus litteralis*. The second level was the "transferred meaning, its parable sense, from which the reader could infer his own situation . . . or a contemporary social or political event," as described by Coghill (Coghill 137). This was *sensus allegoricus*. The third level gave the moral meaning, and was termed *sensus moralis*. The first three levels are found in secular allegory, such as Chaucer's, as well as in religious allegory. The modern reader has more difficulty with the fourth level of interpretation, *sensus anagogicus*. About the anagogical plane of allegory, Coghill says, "In its intensest form it was a transference of the meaning seen on the human plane to 'the life in eternal glory'" (138). Coghill believes that this mode of interpretation evolved from the Biblical studies of the early Church Fathers. He explains: "To them the Bible was a repository of information, divinely revealed, (a) about the history of the creation

535

and what followed from it, (b) about their own personal human predicaments, (c) about moral truth, and (d) about the life of God" (138).

The Prologue of *The Vision of Piers the Plowman*, can be interpreted on all four levels. The "fair field full of folk" that the narrator describes can be taken literally. It can be perceived allegorically as England. The moral sense lies in the concern of the folk for their worldly business rather than for God. The anagogic sense can be seen in the tower, in which dwells Truth, or God, and in the dungeon, which houses the Devil.

Coghill ends his discussion of allegory by advising that it "is not meant to be *explained* but rather *perceived imaginatively*" (138); thus, while we can attempt an explanation of some of the allegory in *Piers the Plowman*, it is much more rewarding for the reader to employ his own imagination. Scholars are far from agreement concerning the place and meaning of allegory in medieval literature; perhaps we would do better to look for individual illumination rather than for consensus in this matter. Still, a familiarity with the four levels of interpretation makes the reading that much more enriching.

Piers the Plowman is a good place to start any investigation of fourteenth-century English literature, but it is certainly not the only worthwhile reading from the age. Two other alliterative verse masterpieces are among those credited to an unknown poet who also wrote in the latter half of the century. He is called the *Pearl* or *Gawain* poet, in honor of his two greatest works.

Sir Gawain and the Green Knight is England's greatest contribution to the Arthurian romance (with all due respect to Sir Thomas Malory and his successors). In this tale of chivalry and adventure, Sir Gawain of King Arthur's Round Table confronts the terrifying Green Knight. Here is how the poet describes the Green Knight as he enters Camelot:

> From his throat to his thighs so thick were his sinews,
> His loins and his limbs so large and so long,
> That I hold him half-giant, the hugest of men,
> And the handsomest, too, in his height, upon horseback.
> Though stalwart in breast and in back was his body,
> His waist and his belly were worthily small;
> Fashioned fairly he was in his form, and in features
>
> > Cut clean.
> > Men wondered at the hue
> > That in his face was seen.
> > A splendid man to view
> > He came, entirely green.
>
> > (Zesmer 138–49)

536

At this, Arthur's knights understandably "sat stone-still . . . in swooning silence" (Zesmer 159).

This outstanding poet's other masterpiece is a much more sober piece, known simply as *Pearl*. It is a dream vision, and the rampant debate among modern scholars concerning its various meanings does not lessen its impact upon the reader. Is *Pearl* an elegy to the poet's lost two-year-old daughter? Is it a religious allegory dealing with innocence lost and regained?

Perhaps we should follow Coghill's advice and simply allow ourselves to perceive it with our imaginations. . . .

Once, to that spot of which I rime,
I entered, in the arbour green,
In August, the high summer-time,
When corn is cut with sickles keen;
Upon the mound where my pearl fell,
Tall, shadowing herbs grew bright and sheen,
Gilliflower, ginger and gromwell,
With peonies powdered all between.
As it was lovely to be seen,
So sweet the fragrance there, I wot,
Worthy her dwelling who hath been
My own pearl, precious, without spot.

(Zesmer 37–48)

The scope of this paper cannot allow discussion of all of the types of great literature produced in fourteenth-century England. The intention has been to introduce several writers within the context of their society, rather than to examine fully their literary merits. I will conclude with one writer, however, who for me sums up better than any other the social context of her age. She did not set out to be a literary artist—she could not read or write, in fact—but she did leave a written legacy in her book, *The Book of Margery Kempe*.

Margery Kempe was born in Lynn (now King's Lynn), Norfolk, around the year 1373, the daughter of a fairly prominent citizen. When in her early twenties, following the birth of her first child, Margery temporarily lost her mind. It was her firm conviction that she was restored to sanity by a vision of Christ. Years later, after several unsuccessful business ventures, she decided to pursue a spiritual life. She convinced her husband to take a vow of chastity (this after they had had fourteen children), and spent much of her life thereafter on a series of religious pilgrimages. Margery was the recipient of many visions and visitations from Christ, and spent a great amount of time in involuntary weeping and wailing, much

537

to her fellow travelers' chagrin. She was ridiculed for her behavior, even charged with Lollardy, but evidently was nevertheless admired for the sincerity of her religious beliefs. Her book is at times frustrating, and Margery is often annoying (even five hundred years later), but her autobiography makes entertaining and enlightening reading.

Here is an excerpt from Margery's account of her interview with Henry Bowet, Archbishop of York:

> . . . the Archbishop took his seat, and his clerics too . . . And during the time that people were gathering together and the Archbishop was taking his seat, the said creature [this is how Margery repeatedly refers to herself] stood at the back, saying her prayers for help and succour against her enemies with high devotion, and for so long that she melted into tears. And at last she cried out loudly, so that the Archbishop, and his clerics, and many people, were all astonished at her, for they had not heard such crying before.

> When her crying was passed, she came before the Archbishop and fell down on her knees, the Archbishop saying very roughly to her, 'Why do you weep so, woman?'

> She answering said, 'Sir, you shall wish some day that you had wept as sorely as I.'

> And then, after the Archbishop had put to her the Articles of our Faith—to which God gave her grace to answer well, truly and readily, without much having to stop and think, so that he could not criticize her—he said to the clerics, 'She knows her faith well enough. What shall I do with her?'

> The clerics said, 'We know very well that she knows the Articles of the Faith, but we will not allow her to dwell among us, because the people have great faith in her talk, and perhaps she might lead some of them astray.' Then the Archbishop said to her: 'I am told very bad things about you. I hear it said that you are a very wicked woman.'

> And she replied, 'Sir, I also hear it said that you are a wicked man. And if you are as wicked as people say, you will never get to heaven, unless you amend while you are here.'

> Then he said very roughly, 'Why you! . . . What do people say about me?'

> She answered, 'Other people, sir, can tell you well enough.'
>
> (Windeatt 163)

The Book of Margery Kempe has certain things in common with the allegories of Langland and the *Gawain* poet, in that they all reflect aspects of a society experiencing the early tremors of great change. As I have indicated, fourteenth-century English men and women still held to traditional values and to Mother Church, and Margery Kempe, William Langland, and the *Gawain* poet are no exception. They were not Lollards, but they had characteristics in common with them—in particular, their sense of the unifying and strengthening potential of the vernacular English which they used. It is noteworthy that the first English autobiography was written so soon after the appearance of the Lollard Bible. It is significant that the great English mystics, in search, as Margery was, of a personal experience of God, wrote in English. It is important that *Piers the Plowman* and *Pearl* were written in the vernacular. For the rise of English as a literary language accompanied its appearance as the language of Parliament, of the courts of law, and of the royal court. It signalled and certainly promoted the nationalism that emerged from the Hundred Years War. It had not a little to do rith the appearance of Lollard-leaning preachers who helped stir up the Peasants' Revolt. At the same time that common men were beginning to strain under the yoke of the Church and to seek to wield, however feebly, their individual political power, they were beginning to express themselves, and perceive themselves, as members of an English nation. These were disturbing times for English men and women, and their literary creations reflect and portray their uncertainties and concerns. It would never, and could never, have occurred to Margery Kempe that in its way her book was as significant and as ominous as the Lollard Bible. They both herald the beginnings of an evolution that would lead to an ultimate Reformation of a peculiarly English character. That Englishness was their creation, and the creation of the *Gawain* poet, of Chaucer (who usually gets most of the credit), and particularly of Langland. It is an Englishness recognizable still in the verse and prose of Langland's literary descendants; one of those in fact, A. E. Housman, hailed from those same mystical Malvern Hills in which Long Will Langland slept and dreamed.

BIBLIOGRAPHY

Ackerman, Robert W. *Backgrounds to Medieval English Literature*. (New York: Random House, 1966).

Coghill, Nevill. *Visions From Piers Plowman: Taken from the Poem of William Langland*. (London: Phoenix House, 1949, 1964).

Goodridge, J. F., translator. *Piers the Ploughman*. (London: Penguin Books Ltd., 1959, 1987).

Hay, Denys. *Europe in the Fourteenth and Fifteenth Centuries*. (New York: Cooper Square Publishers, Inc., 1966).

McKisack, May. *The Fourteenth Century, 1307–1399*. (London: Oxford University Press, 1959).

Skeat, W. W., translator. *The Vision of Piers the Plowman*. (New York: Cooper Square publishers, Inc., 1966).

Windeatt, B. A., translator. *The Book of Margery Kempe*. (London: Penguin Books, 1985, 1989).

Zesmer, David M. *Guide to English Literature: from Beowulf through Chaucer and Medieval Drama*. (New York: Barnes & Noble, Inc., 1961, 1972).